Latino/a Thought

Latino/a Thought

Culture, Politics, and Society

Second Edition

Francisco H. Vázquez

ROWMAN & LITTLEFIELD PUBLISHERS, INC.
Lanham • Boulder • New York • Toronto • Plymouth, UK

ROWMAN & LITTLEFIELD PUBLISHERS, INC.

Published in the United States of America
by Rowman & Littlefield Publishers, Inc.
A wholly owned subsidiary of The Rowman & Littlefield Publishing Group, Inc.
4501 Forbes Boulevard, Suite 200, Lanham, Maryland 20706
www.rowmanlittlefield.com

Estover Road
Plymouth PL6 7PY
United Kingdom

British Library Cataloguing in Publication Information Available

Library of Congress Cataloging-in-Publication Data:

Library of Congress Cataloging-in-Publication Data

Vázquez, Francisco H. (Francisco Hernández), 1949-
  Latino/a thought : culture, politics, and society / Francisco H. Vázquez.—2nd ed.
    p. cm.
  Includes bibliographical references and index.
  ISBN-13: 978-0-7425-6354-4 (cloth : alk. paper)
  ISBN-10: 0-7425-6354-5 (cloth : alk. paper)
  ISBN-13: 978-0-7425-6355-1 (pbk. : alk. paper)
  ISBN-10: 0-7425-6355-3 (pbk. : alk. paper)
  ISBN-13: 978-0-7425-6888-4 (electronic)
  ISBN-10: 0-7425-6888-1 (electronic)
  1. Hispanic Americans—Intellectual life. 2. Hispanic Americans—Politics and
government. 3. Hispanic Americans—Social conditions. 4. United States—Ethnic
relations. 5. United States—Ethnic relations—Political aspects. 6. Ethnicity—Political
aspects—United States. I. Title. II. Title: Latino thought. III. Title: Latina thought.
  E184.S75V38 2009
  973'.0468—dc22
                                                                        2008027779

Printed in the United States of America

♾™ The paper used in this publication meets the minimum requirements of
American National Standard for Information Sciences—Permanence of Paper
for Printed Library Materials, ANSI/NISO Z39.48-1992.

This book is dedicated to my daughters Sofía Eréndira and Vanessa Xochitl, my son Joaquín Tizóc, and to all Latino/a youth engaged in the struggle for respect and for belonging.

~

Contents

Part V: History of the Present

~

Acknowledgments

I want to express my deepest gratitude to the following people who have been supportive in the production of this second edition. Alan McClare, Executive Editor of Rowman & Littlefield Publishers, for asking me to do a second edition of the book and for patiently entertaining my attempts to turn it into an art book. Terri Boddorff, from the permissions department, for her acumen in finding the necessary information. Doug English and Claudia Gravier Frigo for their assistance in the editing process. Even though he was unable to collaborate in this second edition, I want to thank my *camarada* Rudy Torres for getting me involved in this worthwhile enterprise in the first place, for his continued support, and for his friendship. Artist Patricia Speier-Torres for the attractive and striking covers for both editions. The students in my course *Quest for Democracy,* for their comments and critiques. The unknown reviewers who took the time to send their comments, especially one blind review that offered many useful suggestions for changes in the formatting. My friend Rebeca Treviño for the many hours she spent on the computer proofreading the manuscript and on the phone helping me to clarify and obscure passages. Teresa Córdova for her critical comments on Chicanology and her original contribution to this second edition. Professor William I. Robinson for his prompt replies to my queries. Sonoma State University and the Hutchins School of Liberal Studies, for making the necessary resources available. My fellow Hutchins faculty members especially Director Eric McGuckin the LIBS102 cadre for accommodating my work schedule in the fall of 2007. Special thanks to my "*compañero de armas*" Mutombo M'Panya, who has been a source of wisdom and strength, and to Sue Foley for her tireless and consistent efforts for creating a wonderful working environment during the last decade. My colleague Elizabeth C. Martínez, Chair of Chicano/Latino Studies, a prolific writer and inspiring "organic intellectual." Last but not least, I want to thank my wife Rosa María, my daughters Sofía Eréndira and Vanessa Xochitl, and my son Joaquín Tizoc with all my heart for their moral support and especially for their understanding of a work schedule that kept me from spending more time with them.

~

Preface

There are two main reasons for a second edition of *Latino/a Thought: Culture, Politics, and Society*. One is the geopolitical and social change affecting the status of Latinas and Latinos in the United States with particular intensity the last few years. It also seems timely and appropriate to implement a number of comments and suggestions that student and colleagues have made on how to improve the first edition. When this book was first written and assembled in 2001–2002, the Latino/a population in the United States was poised to become the largest cultural group in the United States. In just a few short years, Latinos and Latinas have achieved that status. They have become the center of national attention, however, primarily because of immigration issues and, allegedly, how these issues impact the economy and the war against terrorism.

This situation is illustrated by the controversial *Foreign Policy* article by retired Harvard professor Samuel P. Huntington, "The Hispanic Challenge" (March/April 2004) based on his book *Who Are We: Challenges to America's National Identity*. Huntington sees the challenge coming primarily from Mexicans, who he considers to be fundamentally different from U.S. Americans. He warns that unless Mexican immigration is limited, there may be hostilities between U.S. Americans and Mexicans similar to the hostilities between Palestinians and Israelis. Obviously, these are critical times not only for U.S. Mexicans, but also for all those who care for the preservation of a democratic society and the development of a sustainable economic democracy that includes *all* Americans who inhabit this continent. The second edition addresses these new developments by including a new piece by William I. Robinson, "*Aquí estamos y no nos vamos!*": Global Capital and Immigrant Rights. Huntington's arguments, which are representative of a deep-rooted anti-Mexican sentiment, are confronted at various points in this book, but primarily in Vázquez's newly written framing pieces: two revised articles from the first edition, A Continental American Quest for Democracy (formerly Americas Patriots Then and Now) and the concluding chapter Latino U.S.A.: The Canary in the Mine of Continental Democracy (formerly Reflection on Latino/as and Public Citizenship) and a new piece Chicanology: Law, Class Struggle, and Power/Knowledge.

In response to students and colleagues' suggestions, this second edition has undergone several major changes. Both introductions have been rewritten and updated with the latest information and statistics when appropriate, and the language has been streamlined to make it more accessible to students. Part I: Origins and Theories has been redesigned so the focus is clearly on the historical and philosophical context, and on the three main methods that are applied to the understanding of Latino and Latina political thought: liberalism, Marxism and power/knowledge or discursive analysis. Maps and tables that were in the appendix are now integrated into the pertinent readings. Thus, the poem *I Am Joaquin* by Rodolfo "Corky" Gonzalez is presented in an interactive format with the Chart of Latinos/as in World Events. Additionally, Vázquez's A Continental American Quest for Democracy now contains the Chart of World Social Movements. This allows the readers to have immediate access to graphics that help understand the text.

Another significant change is that instead of a chronological format, each one of the three main groups now has its own section or in the book. This makes the text less fragmented and readers can focus on one group at a time. The sections are arranged according to a chronology of sorts: Mexicans come first because they were incorporated in 1848 through a war of conquest. Cubans are next because by mid-nineteenth century, waves of Cuban political incorporated themselves into the fabric of U.S. society as they sought refuge from, and planned the revolution against the Spanish colonial government. Toward the end of the nineteenth century, as a result of the Spanish-American War, a military government was imposed on Puerto Rico in 1898, thus constructing an ambiguous colonial relationship that remains an issue to this day. This change called for the relocating, rewriting, and updating all the framing pieces. Thus the pieces having to do with U.S. Mexicans are now in Part II and all the pieces having to do with Cubans are in Part III. Part IV includes some of the same texts on Puerto Ricans from the first edition, whereas other texts have been replaced by a chapter by Juan Antonio

Corretjer on Albizu Campos and the Ponce Massacre. This text, which is now out of print, provides not only the *independentista* perspective on an important historical event but also a clear political and economic context for it. Also new are excerpts from the Foraker Act, the Jones Act, and Public Law 600, which are three congressional laws that have shaped the political status of Puerto Rico.

In Part V, the last section, all these issues that confront Latinos and Latinas are put into a global, transnational context. A context, furthermore, in which the struggle is not only for social justice, but also for a sustainable world. In an effort to bring into clear focus the role of women in this quest for economic democracy, an article commissioned from Teresa Córdova replaces some of pieces on women issues in the first edition. This part also includes the already mentioned article by Robinson on globalization on immigrant rights.

This second edition represents a great effort to integrate the valuable comments and suggestions received from students, colleagues, and blind reviews. My expectation is that this second edition will be a useful tool for the understanding the increasing critical role of Latinas and Latinos in the United States and throughout the American continent.

Francisco H. Vázquez, Ph.D.
January 21, 2008

INTRODUCTION

~

Who Are These People, and What Do They Want?

If Latinos and Latinas were fairly invisible in what is known as "the American Century," they are poised to play a crucial role in the United States of the twenty-first century. Currently this group is 46 million strong (not including 3.9 million residents of Puerto Rico); they make up about 15 percent of the U.S. population and are projected to grow to 25 percent by 2050[1] (about 102.6 million), and those who are immigrants are applying for U.S. **citizenship** at an unprecedented rate. There is an emergent, socially oriented middle class with economic clout that has spawned a cohesive national Latina and Latino lobby, and they are considered to be a political third force.[2] Furthermore, massive protests in 2006 and 2007, in favor of humane immigration legislation, have sparked not only a new civil rights movement but also an anti-immigrant backlash. Speaking of invisibility, before we continue this discussion, it is imperative to address the issue of language. To acknowledge the presence and contributions of women, we use both Latino and Latina and alternate the order. At times, we resort to using the slash and give words an "o/a" ending. This is, admittedly, awkward and cumbersome but it is necessary to remain conscious of the participation of women in historical and political events.

The national elections in the United States in 2000 were so controversial that they masked the fact that a political revolution of another sort was taking place. With 7 percent of the one million voters in the 2000 elections, Latinos/as were the deciding factor in many critical political races, including the contested presidential election. It is said that Mexicans gave the presidency to

Gore in California and that Cubans took it away from him in Florida.³ Latinos and Latinas can also be a swing vote in the 2008 elections. Though at 9 percent they make up only a relatively small share of the nationwide electorate, Hispanics comprise a larger share of voters in four of the six "swing states" that President Bush carried by margins of 5 or fewer percentage points in 2004—New Mexico, Florida, Nevada and Colorado.⁴

Indeed, we can now say that Latinos/as are no longer *becoming*, they *are* a major political, economic, and cultural force in the United States. This is a status that carries much potential in terms of their contribution and also in terms of the danger of a backlash against Latinos/as who, arguably, are the canary in the mine of democracy. Now here is a sad situation: Latinas and Latinos work hard, participate as much as they can in civic affairs, and shed their blood in the many U.S. wars for democracy. And yet, surveys consistently show that U.S. Latinos and Latinas in the United States do not feel included, accepted, and most importantly, treated with respect by their fellow citizens. History, too, demonstrates ample military, cultural, and sociopolitical reasons why this is so. This feeling has been worsened by the recent anti-illegal immigration attitudes, ordinances, and legislation.⁵ These anti-Latino and Latina feelings have also penetrated into scholarly discourse, as illustrated by retired Harvard professor Samuel P. Huntington's "The Hispanic Challenge" in which he claims that Mexican immigrants are fundamentally different from U.S. Americans and raises the specter of race and ethnic wars.⁶ These are frightening notions, given the fact that the flow of bodies is both ways; most U.S. Americans who live outside the United States, live in Mexico.

Consequently, one of the objectives of *Latino/a Thought* is to facilitate an understanding of this paradoxical and potentially dangerous situation. This book is also an important device to counteract the mantle of invisibility that seems to envelope the Latina and Latino population. Informed people of the United States and abroad will find this book useful for the study of the history of Latinos and Latinas, their quest for both an economic and a political democracy, and the possible directions this struggle may take in the future. One challenge to this quest for social justice is the increasing difficulty in sustaining these memories of past struggles. Young people especially are subjected to a fragmentation of consciousness by cell phones, sidekicks, handheld and laptop computers, etc. On the other hand, unlike previous generations, young people are more open to interacting with people from other cultures, nationalities, and ethnic groups. Consequently, the tone of the framing pieces in this book is directed especially to young people; this is evident by the special introduction for students. Latina and Latino youth, in particular, are in dire need of a historical and political context in which to locate their changing identities, the *mestizaje* that characterizes their culture. They also need this context to make sense of and become active in the social, political, and economic realities of their communities and society in general. Most are not taught their own history, and, if they are taught their own history, it is often biased, or one dimensional, or restricted to one particular group. Through the framing pieces, students are encouraged to read the texts with critical minds, suspend judgment, and not take statements as given truths, but as truths in a complex game of truths. In short, students are encouraged to do what no one power, divine or mortal, can do for them: think for themselves. For each reader, however, the objective is to promote understanding by raising the level of discourse of, by, and for Latinos and Latinas in the United States.

Thus far, the topic has been Latinos and Latinas but the focus of this book will be is on Puerto Ricans, Cubans, and Mexicans. With regard to the first edition, the question has been asked: "Why not include other Latinos and Latinas?" Although the original concept was to address U.S. Latino and Latina thought in general, as a result of logistical reasons (size of the publication and the diversity of national and ethnic groups), the final decision was to focus on Mexicans, Puerto Ricans and Cubans. The criterion for this decision is that these three groups were incorporated into the United States through a declaration of war (against Mexico in 1848 and against Spain in 1898). The treaties that ended these wars in effect "delivered" not only territory but also these human bodies to the United States. Symbolically, therefore, these treaties represent a sort of birth certificate of these U.S. Latinos. More concretely, they also established a legal foundation that has ramifications to this day; two obvious ones are Puerto Rico's political status and the U.S. claim over Guantanamo Bay in Cuba. No doubt, an argument can be made that U.S. military and economic intervention has provoked the deliverance of human bodies from other Latin American countries to the United States. Perhaps the Monroe Doctrine through which the United States made it clear to the world that the American continent is off-limits to everyone except the United States serves as a cultural "birth certificate" for Latin Americans. To some extent, these arguments miss the salient points. First, there is definitely a need for a more inclusive book on Latino and Latina thought; this could not be it. More critically, with or without official treaties, this is ultimately a question of justice and human rights not nationalities or historical origins. The fact is that the global economy is forcing people all over the world to migrate, legally or illegally, to countries where there is a concentration of production and wealth, and these immigrants are claiming equal rights with the citizens of the host nations (see Robinson in Part V).

Unfortunately, although most people welcome world trade, they do not want to extend rights to the immigrants that this trade produces.[7]

Defining Latinos and Latinas in the United States

The reasons why Latinas and Latinos have taken the center stage in the politics of the United States vary from the issue of illegal and legal immigration to the increasing globalization of the economy and its effects on the working class in the United States and promoting illegal immigration and the massive protest marches in 2006 and 2007 to questions of homeland security and even threats to the identity of the United States. Historically, these people (especially Mexicans) have proven to be the most useful (and thus the favorite) tool for politicians and demagogues. Although this is exactly what is going on today, the difference from before is the demographic presence, the sheer numbers, and the exponential growth of the Latina and Latino population and their increasingly ubiquitous presence throughout the country.

To round off the numbers, cited previously, including the U.S. citizens of Puerto Rico there are almost 50 million Latinos and Latinas, and they are projected to grow to 102.6 million by 2050. This means the United States has the third largest Hispanic-origin population in the world (after Mexico and Colombia).[8] In the United States, the breakdown by national origin is as follows: 64% Mexican, 9% Puerto Rican, 3.5% Cuban, 3% Salvadoran, and 2.7% Dominican. The remainder is from Central America, South America, or other Hispanic or Latino origin. Although almost half of them live in the Southwest of the United States (48% live in California (13.1 million) or Texas (8.4 million), Latinos and Latinas are spread out throughout the country. For example, there are fifteen states with at least half a million Latinos and Latinas (Arizona, California, Colorado, Florida, Georgia, Illinois, Massachusetts, Nevada, New Jersey, New Mexico, New York, North Carolina, Pennsylvania, Texas, and Washington). In the same vein, there are twenty-two states in which they are the larges minority group (Arizona, California, Colorado, Connecticut, Florida, Idaho, Iowa, Kansas, Maine, Massachusetts, Nebraska, Nevada, New Hampshire, New Jersey, New Mexico, Oregon, Rhode Island, Texas, Utah, Vermont, Washington, and Wyoming). In Los Angeles County, this population is the largest of any county in the nation (4.7 million).

A population of this size also has a big economic impact. The revenue generated by Hispanic-owned businesses in 2002 was $222 billion, up 19 percent from 1997. Mexicans, Mexican Americans, and Chicanos own almost half (45 percent) of all Hispanic-owned firms. In this, too, there is a wide geographical diversity. The states with the fastest rates of growth for Hispanic-owned firms between 1997 and 2002 included New York (57 percent), Georgia and Rhode Island (56 percent each), and Nevada and South Carolina (48 percent each).

It is often said that the Latino and Latina culture is family oriented. In effect, the statistics do support the notion that Latinos and Latinas have stable families: 67 percent of these family households consist of married couples. And 66 percent of these children live with two married parents. It is crucial, however, to understand that this is not because of some intrinsic Latina or Latino cultural essence. Simply put, family orientation depends on material conditions that support a *traditional* culture, one that is characterized by a hierarchy that tends to be patriarchal and authoritarian. But this is *true of any traditional culture anywhere in the world* (including the Amish and Mormons in the United States). Modern cultures, on the other hand, are characterized by the freedom of individuals to make their own decisions, and they, too, can be found anywhere in the world. Research shows that, as some members of the second generation adapt to the *modern* aspects of U.S. culture, they break away from hierarchical and authoritarian structures, and thus acquire the same social characteristics of the general population. This is not always to their benefit but that is another story.

The one statistic that is a source of both hope and alarm, depending on your political orientation, is that in 2006 the median age of the Latino and Latina population is 27.4 years, compared to 36.4 for the population as a whole. When projected toward the rest of the twenty-first century, many questions arise regarding the role of this young population in the economy and the culture of the United States. A similar contentious issue is the Spanish language. There are 32.2 million U.S. household residents ages 5 and older, who speak Spanish at home; that is nearly one in eight U.S. household residents. What is often left out of the debate, however, is that, among all those who speak Spanish at home, more than one-half say the speak English well.

What are the social conditions of these human bodies as of 2005? Their median income is $35,967; the poverty rate is 21.8 percent; and 32.7 percent lack health insurance. All these statistics are the same as the previous year. This situation is, of course, connected to educational levels. Focusing on the Latina and Latino population that is 25 years and older in 2006, 59 percent of them had at least a high school education, whereas 12 percent had a bachelor degree or higher. There is a difference between Cubans and other Latino and Latina groups that, again, should be attributed to material conditions and not some intrinsic cultural essence. Among the same age group (25 and older), 73 percent of Cuban Americans were at least high school graduates, and 24 percent had a bachelor's degree or higher (almost doubled). Educational levels naturally impact the employment statistics. Note for example that although 68 percent of Latinos and Latinas 16 and older are part of the civilian labor force, only 17 percent of the same age population work in management, professional, and related occupations. The remaining 83 percent tend toward the lower level jobs: 24 percent in service occupations; 22 percent in sales and office occupations; 2 percent in farming, fishing, and forestry occupations; 16 percent in construction, extraction, maintenance and repair occupations; and 19 percent in production, transportation, and material moving occupations.

Civic engagement through voting was discussed previously, but another form of contribution to one's society is through military service. As of 2005, there are 1.1 million Latinas and Latinos in the U.S. armed forces. The distinguished record of their participation is often ignored, not only in the debates about the role of Latinos and Latinas in the United States, but it is also often left out of war documentaries and films (such as the recent brouhaha over the exclusion of Latino and Latina veterans from Ken Burns film's on World War II). Although an estimated 250,000 to 500,000 American Latinos fought in World War II, their contribution is virtually unknown to the U.S. public. Thus, it needs to be emphasized here: During World War II, in proportion to their percentage of the population, more Mexican Americans served in combat divisions than any other ethnic group; in the Allied invasion of the European mainland, they died in battle at a rate out of proportion to their numbers.[9] Mario Barrera's documentary, *Latino Stories of World War II* is the first to tell the stories, in their own words, of four veterans who served in the Air Force, the Army, and the Marines. The 1960 movie *Hell to Eternity* describes the exploits of one of them, Guy Gabaldon, although the movie did not mention he was a Latino.[10] The same commitment is evident today: From 1992 to 2001, although the overall strength of the military dropped by 23 percent from 1,775,000 to 1,369,000, the number of Hispanics in uniform grew by a staggering 30 percent from 90,600 to 118,000.[11]

Clearly, Latinos and Latinas have paid their dues. Why do they feel as if they do not belong? Probably because their bodies continue to be abused: Parents of undocumented soldiers killed in Iraq are deported[12]; families are being separated by immigration raids (with children being especially impacted).[13] Even candidates for the U.S. 2008 presidential election do not show respect for Latinas and Latinos.[14]

From the Melting Pot to the Cosmic Race

What is in a name? One often hears the remark, "I just don't know whether to call them Hispanics or Latinos or Chicanos. How can I make sure what is the correct word?" It could even be argued that the mantle of invisibility covering Latinas and Latinos could be attributed to their sheer diversity of nationalities, races, ethnic groups, and religions. This reality has to do more with the nature of power relations. In other words, people who struggle to carve a place in U.S. society necessarily adopt a variety of tactics and strategies to win their rightful place. Moreover, this variety brings along a plethora of names. Once they have arrived, then the names stabilized. Thus, when we consider the U.S. Italian, Irish, and German populations, for example, each of these groups, have in due time become accepted as "real" Americans. They do not need their own ethnic studies at the university. For some people, however, the struggle continues, and the names keep on changing along with their tactics and strategies. Often the names overlap. Thus, there is a Negro College Fund, the National Association for the Advancement of Colored People, Black Panthers, Black, and now African American studies. Similarly, there is the League of United Latin American Citizens, *Movimiento Estudiantil Chicano de Aztlán*, the Hispanic Chamber of Commerce, the National Council for *La Raza*, and the Mexican American Legal and Educational Fund. There is also a variety of names for specific groups of individuals: Hispanics, Latinos and Latinas, La Raza, Cuban Americans, Puerto Ricans and Nuyoricans, Mexicans, Mexican Americans, Spanish Americans, Chicana, Indio, Tex Mex, manita, cholo, pocha, etc. Each name represents an assertion of dignity, of human worth, and a struggle for respect.

Within each group, there are also names that refer to how dark the skin may be (*güero/a, trigueño/a, moreno/a, prieto/a, negro/a*) or to hair texture (*pelo liso* or *pelo quebrado*—straight or wavy hair).[15] There are two sides to these names. On the one hand, they are part of what is here called **pigmentocracy**, meaning a hierarchy based on the color of skin, with light skin being superior and which is apparent in Latin American popular and folk customs, and mass media and among Latinos and Latinas in the United States. In short, this is a form of unspoken, latent racism. On the other hand, as Octavio Romano has pointed out, Latinos and Latinas are the only group in the United States that proclaims its mestizaje (its mixture of races, its hibridity). Indeed, Latinos and Latinas can be from any race or ethnic group. This complexity was evident in the 2000 census, in which Latinos were asked to claim a particular racial origin. "Some of the nation's 35 million Latinos scribbled in the margins that they were Aztec or Mayan. A fraction said they were Indian. Nearly 48% described themselves as white, and 2% as black. Fully 42% said they were 'some other race.'"[16]

Latin America and the Caribbean have in some ways realized the U.S. American dream of a melting pot; although the Mexican philosopher José

Vasconcelos used a different metaphor for it, he called it *La Raza Cósmica* (The Cosmic Race). This means, incidentally, that La raza is, by definition, an inclusive, not an exclusionary term. The term *mestizaje* is increasingly gaining a great deal of currency. In Part II of this book, for example, Valle and Torres, analyze an emerging political and cultural mestizaje in Los Angeles, which is the practice, among the working class Latinos and Latinas to reach out across rigid cultural and political boundaries and form coalitions with other ethnic groups in a common quest for economic democracy. In his public talks, the writer Richard Rodriguez often makes reference to Anglo teenagers dating Mexicans and how most children in California do not look like their grandparents. The latest comprehensive salvo, however, comes from the book *Mongrels, Bastards, Orphans and Vagabonds: Mexican Immigration and the Future of Race in America* in which the author Gregory Rodriguez (no relation to Richard) argues that,

> Mexican Americans are forcing the United States to reinterpret the concept of a melting pot to include racial as well as ethnic mixing . . . Just as the emergence of the *mestizos* undermined the Spanish racial system in colonial Mexico, Mexicans Americans, who have always confounded the Anglo American racial system, will ultimately destroy it too.[17]

Clearly, in addition to all the contributions Latinos and Latinas have made to the United States, there is still much for them to do in the area of racial understanding.

So, what do I call you? What do you consider yourself?

This line of questioning brings to mind the book *Around the Day in Eighty Worlds* by Julio Cortázar, so one possible answer is, "It depends on what time it is." To indicate that this is not a joke, one can then state that just like in Einstein's theory of relativity "up" or "down" can only be defined *in relation to* something else. In the same way, each one of the terms applied to Latinos and Latinas needs to be defined *in reference to* a specific social class, ethnic group, region, political consciousness, or level of acculturation. The point is that we need to be clear what serves as the referent. Thus, if one belongs to several organizations like the ones previously mentioned, one can literally assume, or be perceived as having, like Cortázar, several identities in one day.

Let us now extend this idea of "relation to referent" to one of the most common complaints about Mexicans in the United States, namely that they do not learn the language and that they do not become Americans *like other immigrants*. People who say or believe this are suffering from an optical illusion. In other words, as a result of the geographical fact that Mexico is right next to the United States, and people constantly migrate, it is natural that it takes them a while to learn the language and become acculturated. During that particular time, it is indeed true that they do not speak English and do not know "the American ways." Eventually, though, they do become part of the mainstream. But when they do, and here is the clincher: *They are no longer perceived as being "Mexican."* In fact, some Mexicans over time lose their Spanish language and become so thoroughly assimilated that they do not even think of themselves as Mexican. The problem is that the term *Mexican* does not have as a referent all the Mexicans who have come (or were already here) and have joined mainstream society. The referent is restricted to the recent arrivals. In other words, in the public and the media's eye, the Mexicans are always and only those who just arrived. The important point is that identities, and the terms we use to designate them, are mere social constructions. They are not essences imbedded in the genes or tattooed on the flesh.

To conclude this discussion of identity, for those who wonder if it is possible to know in advance what to call a particular Latina or Latino. The short answer is: "No, it is not possible. You have to get to know them first." It *is* possible, however, to learn what some of the most used terms mean and to what they refer. Many of the following terms are used in the readings, and the definitions not covered below are provided by the context of the texts or the framing pieces.

Let us begin with the term *American* or *americano*. Depending on the time period, or the location it is applied both to Latin Americans and to Anglo Americans. Granted, it is part of the official name of the United States of America. Technically, of course, there is only one American continent and everyone who is born there is an American. The terms South, Central, and North American are figments of a political imagination; for example, Mexico *is* in North America but this term is also applied only to the United States. In view of these inconsistencies, in this book we refer to the population of the United States in general by the term *U.S. American*. When it is necessary to be more specific, we use the term *Anglo American* or *white*. Similarly, we use the term *U.S. Mexican* to refer to the Mexicans who reside in the United States and thus come under the jurisdiction of the U.S. government. When the context requires more specificity, we may use the terms *Mexican American* or *Chicana/Chicano*.

The term *Hispanic* refers to Spain and the Spanish language and is preferred by the U.S. government and the conservative, light-skinned upper and upper-middle classes. This, however, would be like calling all English speakers (e.g., Indian and Australian) *Brittanics* and considering them a homogeneous group. More to the point, there are many indigenous people who do not even speak Spanish and associate Spain with the genocidal invasion of their lands. *Latino* and *Latina* has its own historical problems (its origin dates back to the French intervention in Mexico), but it is a term in the Spanish language, and it has Latin America, not Spain as a referent; it tends to cut across class levels but is more prevalent among liberal groups. *Mexican American* and *Spanish American* (especially in New Mexico, Colorado, and Arizona) are names used by people who have been well established in the United States for several generations and want to differentiate themselves from the recently arrived, poor Mexicans. The latter used to be called *Chicanos*, but this pejorative term became a badge of honor for the militant student movement of the late sixties and seventies. The meaning of Chicano includes a struggle for social change and pride in a heritage that includes indigenous, working class, and immigrant people. In U.S. popular culture and among scholars like Juan Gómez-Quiñonez and Rodolfo Acuña, the term *Mexican* is applied to Mexicans in the United States. In this book, *U.S. Mexican* is used to distinguish the latter from Mexicans from Mexico (the same goes for U.S. Latinos and Latinas to distinguish them from people from Latin America). *Raza* also encompasses all Latino/as, as in Raza Studies at San Francisco State University in California. The term has two sources: It is used colloquially to designate "lower" classes, "the rabble," but, as noted previously, it is also derived from the philosophical concept of a cosmic (hybrid) race: *La Raza Cósmica* of José Vasconcelos. *Cholo* or *chola* is the modern term for *pachuco* or gang member, whereas *pocho* or *pocha* is a pejorative for a Mexican American who has supposedly "lost" her or his culture.

A Synopsis of the Latino/Latina Story: What Do They Want or What Do We Want?

In the eighteenth and nineteenth centuries the fight was between liberalism and the monarchies (such as the U.S. founding fathers and mothers against the British King, Latin American liberators against the Spanish King). The United States was the first nation to promote democracy in the New World (with its Declaration of Independence and the U.S. Constitution). People in Latin America also yearned for democracy and looked to the U.S. Revolution (and the French Revolution) as models. A century later, with the notion that it was God's will (Manifest Destiny) the United States promoted capitalism and imperialism. Through military intervention, it expanded first into northern Mexico and half a century later into Puerto Rico and Cuba. Nationalist Mexicans, Cubans, and Puerto Ricans fought against the United

States in a variety of ways to defend their homeland and keep their sovereignty. The results: Mexicans lost half of their country in 1848; Puerto Ricans became a colony (a possession, also called Commonwealth) of the United States in 1898; and Cubans were allowed to keep their independence (as long as they allowed U.S. intervention) until Fidel Castro took over the government in 1959 and got rid of the U.S. presence.

In the twentieth century, the struggle took the form of social revolutions (such as the Mexican in 1910 and the Russian in 1917). On one side, the struggle for civil and human rights for African-descent, indigenous, and Latino peoples and women, gays, and other marginalized peoples continued in each country in the world. On the other side, the fight that took center stage was the one between capitalist democracy and communist and socialist democracies. This war of ideologies also affected how Mexicans, Puerto Ricans, and Cubans saw themselves in relation to the United States. Whereas some supported capitalism, others supported socialism. This struggle took place not only among countries (such as Russia and allies against United States and allies), but also within countries (such as the McCarthy era in the United States, or between allies of each camp in Korea, China, Cuba, Viet Nam, Nicaragua, Chile, etc.).

At the beginning of the twenty-first century, there has been another shift. There is an increasing expansion of capitalism into the entire world and into most aspects of life to maximize profits and open new markets. Just as the whole planet becomes either a commodity or a labor market, and capital has gone transnational to look for cheap labor (outsourcing jobs), so are many workers forced to migrate to where the jobs are. Immigration, both legal and illegal, has become a world issue because workers look for the best opportunities and wages. Because many citizens of the industrialized countries have to compete with workers all over the world or have lost their jobs, now many of them have grown resentful of immigrants.

The terrorist attacks on the United States and the resulting "War on Terror" has led to security measures that are, arguably, even in violation of the U.S. Constitution. The rights of the state are now becoming more important than the rights of the people. Consequently, although it does take that form in some historical periods, the struggle is not so much for a national or ethnic brand of Mexican American or Puerto Rican democracy as it is an all out war for the idea of democracy itself. In other words, it is not so much the clashes of Mexican Americans and Puerto Rican or Cuban independentistas against the United States government, as it is the struggle of all the people for an economic democracy based on human rights.

Structure of The Reader

Clearly, we live in critical times and Latinos and Latinas are caught in a paradoxical and dangerous situation as a growing yet vulnerable minority in the United States. Consequently, it is critical to promote understanding by raising the level of discourse of, by, and for Latinos and Latinas in the United States. This book is a contribution to that goal. It presents one perspective on Latina and Latino thought and grounds it on a variety of texts by distinguished scholars. These texts are drawn from books representing a variety of academic disciplines combined with pieces from scholarly journals and pamphlets. An effort has been made to represent diverse voices and differences in political tone and orientation, or at least to point to the existence of opposing views and to include important pieces that are now out of print.

Through its distinctive user-friendly design, this book goes beyond the usual anthology that collects a number of related articles and frames them with an introduction and conclusion. Think of it as a small book with chapter-long footnotes, as it were. Here, for example, to provide a historical or political context for the readers, each section and each chapter has an initial introduction with endnotes that serve as reference for further research. Secondly, after each chapter there is a set of essay-type questions that challenge the reader to go beyond the text, to reflect on the topic, and also to elaborate on a particular line of thought, or to think of alternatives that may contradict the author (or the reader!). Furthermore, the main ideas, concepts, theories, and events are cross-referenced through the framing pieces to indicate interconnections among Mexicans, Cubans, and Puerto Ricans or the various historical events. They are also highlighted in boldface and explained in a glossary. Finally, there is a guide for instructors with exercises for classroom use based on Why we love power but hate politics: An Introduction for Students and additional pedagogical suggestions for seminar discussions.

In terms of chronology, the readings covers from the period of the wars of independence from Britain, France, and Spain in the eighteenth and nineteenth centuries to the present, and one of them includes a chart illustrates the major national (Mexico, Cuba, Puerto Rico, United States) and world events going to the conquest of the New World. In terms of theory and methodology, there are texts on liberalism and Marxism as examples of methods to deal with the question of power and a critique of these two from the perspective of discursive or power/knowledge analysis.

Among the questions addressed by the reader regarding Puerto Ricans, Mexicans, and Cuban in the United States are: (1) What political philosophies serve as a model for or are considered the origins of, contemporary

Mexican, Puerto Rican, and Cuban political thought? (2) What is the nature of power, and why is it so difficulty to achieve justice for all? (3) What differentiates Puerto Ricans, Mexicans, and Cubans in the United States from each other? (4) Do Mexicans, Puerto Ricans, and U.S. Cubans see themselves as part of the United States political framework or do they support a separatist position? (5) What are the most important issues for Mexican, Puerto Rican, and U.S. Cubans? (6) What are their visions and strategies political action in the twenty-first-century United States? and (7) How do these three groups address current issues such as racism, the globalization of the economy, immigration, gender, class relations, and relations with other ethnic groups?

Notes and Suggestions for Further Research

1. Paul Taylor and Richard Fry, *Hispanics and the 2008 Election: A Swing Vote?* (Washington, DC: Pew Hispanic Center, December, 2007).

2. Juan Gonzalez, *Harvest of Empire* (New York: Viking, 2000), 168.

3. As part of the *voto castigo* or punishment vote for the affair regarding the little boy Elian Gonzalez who was sent back to Cuba to his father.

4. Taylor and Fry, *Hispanics and the 2008 Election*. According to this survey of Latino registered voters, the gains that the Republican Party had been making since this last election in partisan affiliation among Latinos have dissipated in the past year. The Democratic-over-Republican partisan affiliation edge (identifiers and leaners included), which had been 33 percentage points in 1999, then fell to 21 percentage points by 2006, is now back up to 34 percentage points. Though their electoral clout continues to be undercut by the fact that many are ineligible to vote, either because they are not citizens or not yet 18 years old, Latinos will comprise about 9 percent of the eligible electorate nationwide in 2008. If past turnout trends persist, they will make up only about 6.5 percent of those who actually turn out to vote in November.

5. The latest report on this is by the Pew Hispanic Center 2007 National Survey of Latinos, "As Illegal Immigration Issue Heats Up, Hispanics Feel A Chill," (Washington, DC, December 2007). There is also William V. Flores and Rina Benmayor, eds., *Latino Cultural Citizenship: Claiming Identity, Space and Rights* (Boston: Beacon, 1997). However, as Raymund Paredes has shown in "The Origins of Anti-Mexican Sentiment in the United States" (in eds. R. Romo and R. Paredes, *New Directions in Chicano Scholarship*, Chicano Studies Monograph Series [San Diego: University of California, 1978]), Latino and Anglo American relations are part of an epic discourse going back at least four centuries to the "Black Legend," or the defeat of the invisible Armada. In 1900, José Enrique Rodó, referring to Shakespeare's "The Tempest," claimed that whereas Latinos/as are imbued with the aesthetic sensibilities characteristic of the spirit of Ariel, U.S. Anglo Saxons covet materialism because they are possessed by the spirit of Calibán (Rodó, *Ariel*, trans. Margaret Sayers Peden [Austin: University of Texas Press, 1988]). For a

critical perspective, see Roberto Fernández Retamar, *Caliban and Other Essays,* trans. Edward Baker (Minneapolis: University of Minnesota Press, 1989). *Arielismo* became a literary and political movement that is said to have spawned revolutionaries such as Victor Raul Haya de la Torre, and through his American Revolutionary Popular Alliance, Fidel Castro (Martin Staab, *In Quest of Identity* [Chapel Hill: University of North Carolina Press, 1967]). Nobel Prize winner Octavio Paz says these two peoples, Latinos and Anglos, are the product of two different civilizations and are so essentially different that even economic equality cannot bridge their dissimilarities (*The Labyrinth of Solitude and the Other Mexico, Return to the Labyrinth of Solitude, Mexico and the United States, The Philanthropic Ogre* [New York: Grove Press, 1985]). Within the United States, some complain that Latinos crossed the border illegally; others retort that the border crossed them. Social scientists observe that Latinos/as will eventually become assimilated like all other ethnic groups have in the past, whereas politicians argue that Latinos/as threaten to become another Quebec and complain about a "chromosomatic invasion."

6. Samuel P. Huntington, "The Hispanic Challenge," *Foreign Policy* (March/April 2004): 30–45.

7. Pew Research Center, *World Publics Welcome Global Trade—But Not Immigration* (October 4, 2007) available at www.pewglobal.org.

8. Unless otherwise indicated, these statistics are from the U.S. Census Bureau News Facts for Features: Hispanic Heritage Month 2007: Sept. 15–Oct. 15. Accessed on January 19, 2008. www.census.gov/PressRelease/www/releases/archives/facts_for_features_special_editions/010327.html

9. Gregory Rodriguez, *Mongrels, Bastards, Orphans and Vagabonds: Mexican Immigration and the Future of Race in America* (New York: Pantheon Books, 2007), 182.

10. Available at www.odysseyproductions.info/.

11. Hispanic Center Fact Sheet, "Hispanics in the Military," (Washington D.C.: March 27, 2003),available at www.pewhispanic.org.

12. Domenico Maceri, *New America Media,* Commentary, Posted: September 4, 2007. Available at http://news.newamericamedia.org/news/view_article.html?article_id=d44dad7d12128d8af634c39e814ca402.

13. Randy Capps and others, *Paying the Price: The Impact of Immigration Raids on America's Children, Urban Institute Report* (Washington: National Council for La Raza, 2007).

14. Ruben Navarrette, "Where's the respect?" posted November 13, 2007, at www.postwritersgroup.com/navarrette.htm (accessed November 14, 2007).

15. Roberto P. Rodriguez-Morazzani, "Beyond the Rainbow: Mapping the Discourse on Puerto Ricans and Race," *Centro* VIII, nos. 1 and 2 (1996): 128–49.

16. Quoted from Darryl Fears, "People of Color Who Never Felt They Were Black: Racial Labels Surprises Many Latino Immigrants," *Washington Post,* December 26, 2002, A1, in Antonia Darder and Rodolfo D. Torres, "Reflexiones Pedagógicas, Mapping Latino Studies: Critical Reflections On Class And Social Theory," *Latino Studies* 1, (2003): 308.

17. Rodriguez, *Mongrels, Bastards, Orphans and Vagabonds,* xvii.

~

Why We Love Power but Hate Politics: An Introduction for Students

This book functions at several levels. The readings focus on Mexicans, Cubans, and Puerto Ricans in the United States. The lessons derived from the readings, however, apply to the struggles of all ethnic groups and genders within the United States and all over the world. This is because a theme that is weaved throughout the readings is the relationship between power and knowledge and how this relation affects the quest for democracy and social justice. Furthermore, this book is written primarily for students, and consequently, it attempts to correlate the academic and the personal levels. The purpose of this introduction is to familiarize students with the main concepts that guide the discussions in the framing or introductory pieces or the texts, and secondly, to increase the students' awareness of the relationship between the subject of Latino/a thought and their own personal interests. Thus, it is written in a question/answer format that explores the personal dimension of politics, learning, and power in relation to language and knowledge.

Basic Assumptions

First of all, like all teachers, this text makes the assumption that you, the reader, the student, is interested in the subject of Latinos and Latinas in the United States. That you are curious about politics, the concept of power and how they relate to your education, and that you are willing to delve into the readings, wrestle with sometimes difficult and obscure language and force it to yield the hidden meanings, codes, and secrets of power.

Student Challenges

In reality, however, when a student is confronted with a reader on Latino/a political thought, there is a set of frequently asked questions that the students may not raise in class but may think to themselves or share with their class-mates: I hate politics! What will I learn? How true is this? Whose side of the story is this? Is this one of those books on how Latinos/as have been victim-ized by the dominant group? These are legitimate questions that need to be addressed, first briefly and then more extensively.

"Why Should I Care? I Hate Politics!"

According to a famous phrase by Aristotle, humans are political animals. This means there is a political dimension to almost everything we do, col-lectively or individually, whether we mean it as political or not. Another way of putting it is that every action is subject to interpretation and every inter-pretation has political implications and consequences

"What Will I Learn?"

In this text, you learn about the political history of Latinos/as in the United States and their struggles for respect and for justice. At the same time, how-ever, you learn about the quest for democracy in general. This is important because the political economic system you choose to live in affects not only your future career but your well-being in general and that of your loved ones. Consequently, in this introduction (and expectedly, throughout the text), you may discover ways to understand yourself in terms of the relationship be-tween power and knowledge, to increase your understanding of the politics of education, and to increase your critical thinking and learning strategies. In short, we invite you to play games of truth and power that shape your own identity and to make a map to navigate your own political reality.

"How 'True' Is This Representation of Latino/a Political Thought?"

What "truth" is and how it is involved with politics is one of the main con-cerns of this reader. Although we try to present a variety of ways to look at truth, it is left up to you to decide on your own what truth is based on the ev-idence presented in this reader and elsewhere.

"Whose Side of the Story Is This? Is This Another Book on How Latinos/as Have Been Victimized by the Dominant Group?"

The text contains a variety of positions and voices. However, the quest for democracy, for social justice, inevitably includes victims and victimizers and social systems that oppress and liberate. Who is the hero and who is the fool may change over time and ultimately depends, again, on your own perspective and your own interpretation of what truth is. That does not mean there is no truth with a capital *T*, but it does mean that the way to see it is through our own individual perspectives or truths with a small *t*. The closest that we can probably get to an ultimate, objective truth is by looking at the impact on the human body and the ecology that supports it. To be sure, this is not an argument for moral relativism, meaning that there is no one truth. It means that you have to make your own decisions based on evidence that supports solid arguments. (The nature of truth and power is discussed more thoroughly in chapter 4.)

"What Is Politics, Anyway?"

When I was in elementary school in Mexico, my mother would admonish me: "*No te metas a la política. No andes juzgando, criticando ni alegando.*" (Don't get involved in politics. Don't go around judging, criticizing, or arguing.) I knew what she meant; she wanted to protect me from a particular kind of politics. Student politics in Mexico, as in many countries, can be deadly. When I visited Guadalajara after many years in the United States, I was sad to find that some of my childhood friends had been killed in junior high school and high school during political confrontations. Through my living and schooling experiences in the United States, however, I soon realized that everyone is political in one way or another; to be alive and even to die is to be political. I learned, furthermore, that judgment, criticism, and argument are *the* necessary tools for successful political involvement.

Politics can be defined in many ways. Let us dig deep to find the kind of politics that affects us in a personal way. When you look up *politics* in a dictionary or encyclopedia, it is likely that you will find the following definitions:

1. The art or science of government or governing, especially the governing of a political entity, such as a nation, and the administration and control of its internal and external affairs.

Here *politics means the knowledge* that would help you govern the United States, Aztlán, Puerto Rico, or Cuba, if ever you were to find yourself in that situation. If you were to study and teach politics, the academic discipline is called *political science*.

2. Within a country, what a government (federal, state, local), a politician, or a political party does is also *politics*.

3. An individual can also be "into politics" in the sense that she or he dedicates her or his life or makes a career out of politics.

4. Intrigue or maneuvering within a political unit or a group to gain control or power.

This could be as passionate as office politics or student government, as fervent as Republican or Democratic or ethnic politics, or as zealous and dangerous as fighting to the death to defend your territory, your family, and your dignity. Control of a street gang or high school cliques like the in-crowd or the so-called "populars" in high school also fits into this definition of politics.

5. and 6. The last of the definitions refers to the hidden sort of politics that most of us take for granted: "political attitudes and positions" and "the often internally conflicting interrelationships among people in a society."[1]

Indeed, the psychologist R. D. Laing has written books on the *Politics of the Family* and the *Politics of Experience*. In Spanish, there are terms like *tío político* (literally a political uncle who is not related by blood but by marriage, corresponding to the English usage of in-law). The point is that even if you hate politics, you are involved in them. The obvious implication is that whether you are conscious of it or not, you have a political attitude and you take political positions. Even refusing to take a position is a political position! Within the **political spectrum** you may be in the **center** (a **centrist**), on the **right** (conservative), or **left** or **leftist** (liberal, socialist, or anarchist) and not even know it! In this context, it is pertinent to note that during the 1960s, to the extent that Chicano and Puerto Rican youth became "politicized" by joining the Brown Berets or the Young Lords, gang membership dropped.

We need to question why the personal dimension of politics is the last one in the list of definitions. This dimension reflects the attitude that leads people to say they hate politics. This is a disempowering notion. It is part of the illusion that politics is just something that politicians do, not what we the people do. This gives a sort of invisibility to the politics in our everyday life and to our role as political animals. And yet at the same time, we profess that we have "a government of the people, by the people, and for the people."

"What Is the Difference between Politics and Policies?"

There is one incident that brought politics to its most fundamental level for me. I was once in a hotel in Mexico where the manager told me they had a *política* on cashing checks. It struck me as odd: what does cashing checks have to do with politics? To my surprise, I found that in Spanish *política* means both *politics* and *policy*. Indeed, policy is such a close relative of *politics* that is first defined by dictionaries as "a plan or course of action, as of a government, political party, or business, intended to influence and determine decisions, actions, and other matters," such as "U.S. foreign policy in Mexico" or "the company's personnel policy." As with *politics, it is defined secondarily at the personal level* as "a course of action, guiding principle, or procedure considered expedient, prudent, or advantageous." Examples are in comments we hear in everyday conversation: "my policy is not to borrow money from friends" or "my personal policy is not to date my friend's girl/boy friend." So the policy in your university for paying tuition and the clothing store policy for returns are, at some level, politics. When you do not like these policies and you want to change them, you are involved in political action. So, you go talk to the head of the department or manager and tell him you want such and such policy changed—but is that all it takes? How do we use language to change our political realities?

To become acquainted with your political self, you may want to reflect on the following questions: What are the key events of your "political" life as previously discussed? What are your political views? How have your parents, family, or ancestors influenced them?

It is critical then to envision politics as building from the bottom up, from the political relationship you have with yourself (how you govern your identity, your persona), with your parents, with relatives, with friends, with lovers, and with institutions like school, business, the courts, and the police. Then, at higher levels, there are political relations among individuals, and among groups and the relations between the people and the state. By "state" we do not mean California or another state in the United States, we mean one of the most complex political machines humans have ever built, next to corporations, and in another time, the church. In short, politics is the way we manage the relationship between power and language and power and knowledge at the many levels of economic, social, and cultural existence. Such awareness is important not only for you to understand Latino/a political thought, but also for you to make sense of the world around you and for your own personal development.[2]

"What Is the Relationship between Language and Power?"

There is a Mexican saying: *a las palabras se las lleva el viento* (words are carried away by the wind). An equivalent in English might be "actions speak louder than words"; the implication is that words are just words, meaning that they do not carry any weight. In addition to confronting the possibility that you may be political without even knowing it, we invite you to explore the possibility that language is something solid that resists your attempts to shape it they way you want. Here we discuss the nature of language, the intimate relationship between language and power, between what is said and the economic or political institutional that governs our lives. (This is explored in depth in chapter 4.)

The Nature of Language

A main misunderstanding of the relationship between language and power seems to arise because we tend to think of language and words as *transparent things*, as objects that obey our commands, as entities that carry our intentions and our thoughts without distorting them. We become frustrated when words do not do the job we tell them to do. That is because words have their own baggage, their own meanings. They are material, solid things, like mountains and oceans and deserts. We would not claim to be able to move a mountain with our bare hands, and yet we firmly believe that we can say anything we want. We believe words come from us, when in fact we were born into them. Often when I go over an essay with a student I point out that her or his paper says X, and the student responds, "That's not what I meant!" So who speaks? Language apparently distorts what my students meant to say in their papers. Similarly, when you read texts, some of them are fluid like water and you can "breeze" through them, others are like thick mud and you can barely make your way through them. This "materiality" turns words, statements, discourse, into **commodities** of exchange, within a sort of political economy of language. Think of market of statements that have different values and that can be bought and sold.

Even more drastically, discourse can be like a minefield. Words can explode into contradictory meanings with potentially disastrous results. For example, you might have heard the statement: "if only people knew about it, something would be done and things would change." To illustrate the problem with this assumption, let us briefly refer here to a dramatic story that is discussed at length in chapter 4. On April 13, 1972, Ricardo Chávez Ortiz, a Mexican national, hijacked a Frontier Airlines 737 jet from Albuquerque, New Mexico, with an unloaded gun. The plane landed in Los Angeles, where he asked not for money but for radio time to talk about the unjust treatment of Mexicans, hoping that spreading such knowledge would bring about social change. He got the airtime but, as you might imagine, no major change occurred in the life of Mexicans in the United States. He paid with federal prison time for the right to speak to power.[3] This is a big price to pay for misunderstanding the nature of language!

This misconception about the way language is, unfortunately, rather wide-spread and it affects our everyday lives, our notions of reality, of history, and of our own sense of identity. Language hides things at the same time that it reveals them. Yet, we take the inherent power of language for granted when we should be establishing a vigilant, careful relationship with it. Thus, you need to do more than just read a text, you need to "decode" a text. To do that you need to think vertically, in depth, and to dig for the relations that tend to remain invisible under the horizontal surface of language.

Why Are Some Voices Heard and Not Others?

Let us explore in more detail how the relationship between power and language works. Imagine the voices of the people in any given community, in any social group. Some of these voices are just that, voices that are "carried away by the wind." Other voices do have an impact on desire, politics, or economics, and that is because they intersect with power relations. How do we know they have an impact? Because of the reaction these voices provoke. At a personal level there are voices you hear, remember, and repeat in your mind over and over again. What is it about some things that are said that affect you so much while others you forget almost immediately? At a social level, depending on the status, the position of who speaks, the voice(s) may be categorized as political, scientific, artistic, funny, or worth repeating, or they may be considered stupid, unworthy, or "fighting words." Social class, culture, gender, skin color, and an almost infinite number of other factors come into play to define the position of the speaker. This is another example of how words acquire (or not) specific values within a system of exchange, just like other commodities.

Why are some voices heard and not others? Although Chávez Ortiz was not really heard, even by hijacking a plane, other voices become solidified; they acquire a high value, a certain materiality; they seem to be carved in stone. Laws and policies, for example, represent one of the most concrete and powerful realities that impact our everyday lives. They are made up of words that, if necessary, are enforced by economic and military force.

On the one hand, although the ideal is that no one is above the law and that "all humans are created equal," the reality is that there are individuals whose voices have immediate access to the White House or the U.S. Congress or the Supreme Court and can manipulate laws and policies almost at will. Or as the popular Mexican song "El Rey" (The King) puts it: mi palabra es la ley (my word is the law).

On the other hand, other voices are silenced. There are bodies and events that are rendered invisible because they do not fit into any of the socially

xxxviii   ⌒   Why We Love Power but Hate Politics

accepted categories of what can be said (the dominant political, economic, and desire discourses). Sure we know the poor and the homeless are invisible in some ways. But even when people have lots of knowledge, some of them find it difficult to translate that knowledge into power. Undocumented college students for example, are in fact invisible.[4]

Opening Up Spaces for Your Voice and the Voices of the Other

All the aforementioned leads to the notion that the quest for democracy, the struggle for social justice and for dignity, is also the constant fight to open up spaces for voices to be heard and bodies to be seen. In May of 2006 and 2007, for example, through massive demonstrations, millions of legal and illegal immigrants in the United States tried to implant their own needs and desires into positions of authority, policies, and institutional procedures until the desired social changes take place.

It is not, again, just a matter of speaking up, it is a *question* of investing our words with power. The key point is that this is not a battle on behalf of truth but a struggle about the status of truth and the political and economic roles it plays. Each interest at play in society tries to make their own truth appear as the Truth, regardless of what the actual facts may be. Clearly, these games of truth are not just an issue for Latinos/as, but for everyone who cares about a democracy that is based on the will of the people.

In other words, we are always caught in a relationship with a body of knowledge that surrounds our intention (and sometimes imposes its own intention). Thus, we need to be aware of the potential impact of the following factors: (1) what we say, read, and write, (2) our status or identity (our gender, ethnicity, skin color, political views, social, educational and economic position), and (3) what the dominant institutions or the mass media say. In the final analysis, what does all this knowledge and learning mean for our own well-being and the good of society?

"If 'Knowledge Is Power,' Does that Mean that 'Power Is Knowledge?'"

Thus far we have addressed two misunderstandings: that we hate politics and can do without it and that language is there for us to use anyway we want. A third misconception is about the relation between power and knowledge. It is common to hear people say that getting an education is important because knowledge is power. If this were true, presumably, every high school and college graduate would be powerful. Why is it that people rarely say the opposite, that "power is knowledge?" Just like we saw in the language and power relations, the relation between power and knowledge take many forms (discussed in detail in chapter 4). Let us focus here on how these relations between power and knowledge and how they are reflected by institutions of learning, pedagogy (the science or art of teaching) and how these theories and practices affect you as a lifelong learner and active citizen.

The Theory: Education for Domination or for Liberation

The educational system *categorizes* students into established social categories like class, gender, and skin color. More than just *categorize*, we might say the educational system *subjects* (i.e., ties down) individuals to these particular identities. This is what is known as a process of *subjectification*, and as usual, there are economic, and political factors involved in it. For example, the socioeconomic level of a school district determines the curriculum and the academic performance of students. There is also a correlation between a low-income area and a high percentage of school dropouts. As we shift from an industrial to a postindustrial global economy, most U.S. Americans no longer work in big factories. Most of the factories move to parts of the world where cheap labor is abundant. This means U.S. Americans have to compete with workers all over the world.[5] Consequently, instead of working primarily in manufacturing, they do two main things: process information and provide services for other people.

So your place in the economy and thus in the class structure determines, to a large extent, what kind of education you get and what position you will occupy in society. In addition to social class, race and gender enter into this process of subjectification. Of course, this does not mean that everyone's destiny is determined by socioeconomic or racial factors. There is also individual determination or agency. This means that you are ultimately responsible for your own actions, and there are methods individuals use to struggle against this form of domination. Nevertheless, the answer to the question posed here seems to be that in these games of truth we all must play, *knowledge is necessary but it is not sufficient for power.*

The process of subjectification was addressed by the distinguished pedagogue Paulo Freire in his book *Pedagogy of the Oppressed*. He notes that education can be for domination or for liberation.[6] Education for domination operates on the basis of what he calls "the banking concept of education," and it works this way: sit in the classroom and absorb everything the teacher "deposits" in you via the lecture format; faithfully repeat it in a test to get good grades. Clearly, through this method you will have the ability to regurgitate what you have been taught. It does not necessarily mean you will *learn* about your relationship with the world (and the power/knowledge relations we are discussing here). The key question is about teaching and learning in a way that fosters a close relationship between the individual student and the socioeconomic context of the world in which she or he lives. Are you just learning to pass the test or do you take yourself seriously as a learner? That is, are you just going through the motions pretending you are learning? Or are you aware of the relationship between what you learn (knowledge) and the issues that affect your personal and socioeconomic realities (power)? Incidentally, in this complex and paradoxical struggle for respect and justice, some students "fight back" against the domination they feel coming from schools by dropping out.

Education for liberation or critical pedagogy, by contrast, is based on the transformation that occurs when learning takes place as a dialogue between the teacher and the student, and it leads to a transformation in both of their social outlooks. Or better yet, learning becomes a dialogue between the teacher *and* the student *with* the social world. This kind of learning you carry with you as part of yourself. The learning is not limited to schools but it is continued through your interactions in your everyday life such as during conversations with friends, family, and relatives, from your own experiences, or from movies and television. Critical pedagogy, like critical thinking leads you to *care* about your education because you understand how it can make a difference not only in your life but also in the world around you.

One has to wonder about a democracy that depends on the expression of the will of the people, yet has an educational system that does not teach most of the people to feel validated, to express their own beliefs and opinions, and to practice critical thinking. A system that does teach these things would seem a requirement for any active citizen, especially one on a quest for democracy.

The Practice: Discussion Groups and "Knowing Thyself"

Because education based on the "banking concept" teaches to rely on instructors, on experts, on those "with authority" to define the truth or what is important, there is little if any room for students to articulate their own ideas and opinions. This leads to three consequences among many college students: a lack of self-validation and the inability to encourage members of the discussion group to express their opinions; a lack of trust in the notion that they can learn from their peers; and an inability to listen carefully to what others have to say. Consequently, one way to approach education as liberation is through a student-centered method of teaching, such as the seminar or discussion group (see appendix).

Another important component of education as liberation is critical thinking skills that are based on determining what your "voice" is. This means to know who you are, separate from the identities to which you are subjected (that have been assigned to or forced on you). Now, let us say that you are participating in a seminar to discuss this reader or other readings that have been selected by the group. How do you distinguish between what is important, and what is not important? How do you decide to take a position? How do you play this particular game of truth? When do you use **inductive or deductive reasoning**? Many students are swayed by the arguments in favor and then change their minds when they hear the argument against. But how do you begin to think critically? This is not the place to address this question in depth; there are many sources on this subject.[7] Antonio Gramsci, however, provides a personal perspective:

> The starting-point of critical elaboration is the consciousness of what one really is, and is "knowing thyself" as a product of the historical process to date, which has deposited in you an infinity of traces, without leaving an inventory; therefore it is imperative at the outset to compile such an inventory.[8]

This means that to think critically you need to know who you are. In effect, from our experience, students who do not know themselves as "a product of the historical process to date" usually agree with everything and have a difficult time making up their minds about a particular issue. This difficulty also appears in their writing and in their participation in discussions.

So, if it is crucial to know thyself,[9] how do you begin to compile an inventory of the historical fragments that define who you are? Obviously for Latino/a students, especially of Cuban, Mexican, and Puerto Rican heritage, this reader is one place to start. For all students, however, the reader begins by providing charts and discussion from which you can begin to compile a historical inventory of who you are as a member of human society that has a quest for democracy.

You may want to think of the ten key events, or stepping-stones, of your "educational life." Or you may also write a dialogue with society (e.g., with your school principal or teacher). You may want to write a reflective essay on your educational experiences using Paulo Freire's concepts of education: Have you been educated for domination or for liberation?

Becoming Politically Involved

Once you take responsibility for your own education and you know thyself, you can bring a special awareness and attention to the games of truth all of us must play. As you go through your everyday life you detect the workings of knowledge and power, the rules for the manipulation of discourse and the effect of power on human bodies and the ecology. You can recognize, assess, compare, analyze, and synthesize power relations. In short, you want to become politically involved. But there are so many issues and everything is so complex! How do you get started sorting things out? Here is a tip: When you buy a car you begin to notice, out of the millions of cars in the world, other cars that look like yours. Similarly, when you "buy" a particular pet issue, idea or theory, you also recognize its reflection in books, newspapers, television, movies, conversations, etc. This means that the first step, if you do not already have one, is to pick one issue, or area of interest. When you follow it, it will lead you to a body of knowledge and perhaps power that may be related to a particular profession. It may also enable you to earn a living doing something you enjoy doing. In a way, this brings us back to Aristotle's observation that "we are political animals."

Think about the ideas of politics, language, knowledge/power, and education as they affect your everyday life. What does your political world look like and what role do you play in it? In an essay or drawing (in a poster-sized paper) you may want to illustrate your political realities; in other words, the many forces that affect you, and the ways you can affect them in return.

"What Is the Best Way to Read the Articles in This Reader?"
Continuing with the analogy of having a new car, as you read the articles it helps to know what you are looking for. You may have your own "pet idea or theory," if not, the introductions to the sections and the articles will provide questions to keep in mind as you read them. Remember that language is as material as water and rocks and air, therefore, some of the articles are easier to read than others. So you may breeze through a poem like *I Am Joaquín*, but feel like you are stuck in mud when reading treaties or theoretical articles. Do not be discouraged. It is in the nature of power to hide behind language.

The readings also differ in political tone and orientation. Read with a suspicious mind, suspend judgment, and do not take statements as given truths but as truths in a complex game of truths. An effort has been made to include different political perspectives or at least to point to the existence of opposing views. There is only one thing that you and only you can do (not even God has that power), and that is to think for yourself. Consequently, you must make up your mind about what you want to believe.

Notes and Suggestions for Further Research

1. *The American Heritage Dictionary of the English Language*, 3rd ed., electronic version (Houghton Mifflin Company, 1992).

2. See for example Carol Hardy-Fanta, "Political Consciousness: Being Political, Becoming Political," in her *Latina Politics/Latino Politics: Gender, Culture and Political Participation in Boston* (Philadelphia: Temple University Press, 1993).

3. David F. Gomez, *Somos Chicanos: Strangers in Our Own Land* (Boston: Beacon Press, 1973), 177–87, passim.

4. Douglas McGray, "The Invisibles," *West Magazine*, April 23, 2006, 18–21, 40–42.

5. Thomas L. Friedman, *The World is Flat* (New York: Farrar, Straus and Giroux, 2005).

6. Paulo Freire, *Pedagogy of the Oppressed* (Continuum, New York, 1970). See also, Ira Shor and Paulo Freire, *A Pedagogy for Liberation: Dialogues on Transforming Education* (New York: Bergin & Garvey, 1987), 12–13, and Henry A Giroux, *Teachers as Intellectuals: Toward a Critical Pedagogy of Learning* (Massachusetts: Bergin & Garvey, 1988)

7. See for example, The Critical Thinking Community at www.criticalthinking .org/.

8. Quoted in Edward Said, *Orientalism* (New York: Pantheon, 1978), 25. As Said notes, the English translation inexplicably leaves out the second part of the sentence. Quintin Hoare and Geoffrey Nowell Smith, *The Prison Notebooks: Selections* (New York: International, 1971), 324.

9. Among the Greeks, the story goes that the Oracle of Delphi, who was like the voice of the gods, said that Socrates was the smartest man in Athens. Socrates did not believe it, so he went around trying to prove that there were others who knew more than he did. After a while Socrates realized that although there were others who knew more than he did, he knew the limits of his own knowledge and this made him smarter than anyone else! Over the entrance to the Oracle of Delphi's abode were the words "Know thyself."

PART I

ORIGINS AND THEORIES

~

A Dream of Justice:
Contexts, Methods, and
Practices in Latino/a Thought
Francisco Hernández Vázquez

Latino/a thought may be approached from diverse philosophical, historical, and political perspectives. As presented here, Latino/a political thought emerges out a struggle against absolute power. First, it was the American continental struggle against the monarchies, which was started by the English Americans, followed by the Haitians and then the rest of Spanish Americans. After the overthrow of the European crowns, there has been a continental quest for democracy, an effort to establish democratic societies that are governed by the people. Similarly, within the United States, Mexicans, Puerto Ricans, and Cubans have struggled in their own particular quest for equity and social justice along with other ethnic minorities. An important point driving this discussion is that despite current arguments to the contrary, this is what *all people* in the American continent have in common. The American Dream *is* a continental *Americano* Dream, not the exclusive dream of the Anglo Saxon Protestant, as retired Harvard professor Samuel P. Huntington claims (see chapters 4 and part V.B). Arguably, this is a human dream but that is another discussion.

From the Nationalization of Philosophy
to the Ethnicization of Social Science

When the subject of Latina or Latino political thought comes up, many people, even in academia, tend to wonder if there is a unique Latino/a thought that is part of a Latino/a philosophy. Is there a Latin American philosophy with its own philosophers and specific philosophies?[1] Because one of the themes of this reader is the notion of invisibility that is created by power relations, it is not only pertinent but also necessary to make it perfectly clear: There is, in fact, a history of Latin American philosophy, a collection of the reflections on the same philosophical questions that have challenged philosophers throughout human history and across cultures and countries, namely, the meaning of life (ethics), identity and purpose (social philosophy), the nature of knowledge (epistemology), and reality (ontology).

In effect, approximately from 1880 to 1960 there was a deliberate effort in Latin America (and in other non-European countries), to create a national philosophy, as part of the struggle against European and U.S. imperialism. For example, Gaos argues that, just like the Germans, French, British, and Americans have Idealism, Rationalism, Empiricism, and Pragmatism philosophies, respectively, the Spanish-speaking people have *Emotivismo* (Emotionism or a philosophy based on emotion).[2] The name comes from the preference for the intuitive and for the aesthetic form to express its philosophical thought, such as the poem, the letter, the essay. Spanish-speaking philosophers have shown no inclination for developing grand, systematic political philosophies. Their focus has been on the immediate issues that impact their societies. In Mexico, Antonio Caso, Samuel Ramos, José Vasconcelos, and Octavio Paz, among others, are associated with *la filosofía de lo mexicano* (the philosophy of that which is Mexican). Not coincidentally, about the time that this project of nationalization of philosophy was abandoned, a similar project emerged in the United States with the ethnicization of the social sciences (Chicano sociology, anthropology, political science, etc.; see chapter 4 for a discussion of power and knowledge relations and the social sciences).

Within Latin American political thought, one finds a wide historical and **political spectrum**. It ranges from scholasticism to **Enlightenment**. On the one hand, there are liberal democratic ideas such as those that led to Mexican *independencia* in 1821 and the Mexican Constitutions of 1854 and 1917 and the constitutions of Cuba in 1900 and Puerto Rico in 1950. On the other hand, one finds the conservative and racist ideas of the positivists, known as *los científicos*, in the nineteenth century and that is associated with U.S.-backed militarist, reactionary, and elitist politics of the twentieth century. Marxism and Socialism continue to be predominant in Latin America. Liberation theology is a unique Latin American philosophy, a combination of Catholicism and Marxism. As for Latinos/as in the United States, three major Latin American philosophers, who have influenced Cuban Americans, Puerto Ricans, and U.S. Mexicans are José Martí, Eugenio Maria de Hostos, and Ricardo Flores Magón, respectively.[3]

The National Question: Nationalism and Transnationalism

Words like *nationalization, ethnicization, imperialism,* and others that will appear in various texts as *nation, nationality, nationalism,* and *colonial* are essential for the understanding of Latino/a thought (and political thought in general) and thus require clarification from the outset.

Imagine ancient history when the world was populated by hundreds of "nations," that is, groups of people, clans, tribes, who share common customs, origins, histories, and languages. The word *nation* comes from the Latin *natio,* which means birth or race; from nasci, *to be born;* literally, "where you are born," your home turf. In the Greek language, the word for nation is *ethnos.* Therefore, nations are equal to ethnic groups, equal to tribes, such as the Anglos, the Saxons (yes, they used to be two different tribes), the Franks, the Navajo, and the Maya. There is an implication here of blood ties, of one big family, like with the concept found in discussions of cultural nationalism: Puerto Ricans claim an ethno-nation and the rainbow *familia;* Chicanos claim *carnalismo* (literally flesh of my flesh); and there the ever present *cubanidad).* For white supremacists, like the Nazis and the Ku Klux Klan (KKK), it is the notion of the purity of the blood line. Whether real or imagined, blood ties among a people, lead to notions of justice and vengeance: such as avenging those who have shed the blood of a family member. The nation and the blood ties of its members are a central factor in present day conflicts all over the world, such as in the Middle East and in rural feuds and among urban gang members.

When some nations reach a particular level of economic and technological development, they conquer and possess other nations to create a city-state or *polis* (as in political system) as the Greeks called it. The Maya kingdom and the Roman and British empires are other examples. When this happens, the nations that are conquered become colonies and they are said to have lost their **sovereignty,** that is, the right to self-determination, the right to make their own decisions; or they may become integrated into the dominant nation, the metro-polis (literally, the huge city-state). By the eighteenth century, the word *nation* started to be used in the sense of *country* or *nation-state,* that is, a state that contains other nations. England, for example, turned so many independent nations, into colonies, it was said that the sun never set on the British Empire. One positive aspect of empires is that they allowed for linguistic and cultural differences among their subjects (as long as they paid tribute). The United States, has also "incorporated" Northern Mexico, Puerto Rico (as a Commonwealth), and Guam, the Marianas, Samoa, and many Indian nations, such as the Navajo and the Apache and at one time, the Philippines and Cuba. "The national question" is precisely the relation of domination exercised by one nation over another.[4]

Now, that the term *state* has been added to nation, let us define it. Think of the state as the invention of a political machine, a form of government that not only replaced the empires and monarchies in the seventeenth century, but also tends to homogenize and normalize populations through the imposition of one language and one culture. Another important characteristic is that the nation-state *grants* individual human bodies legal status through citizenship, it *gives* them a nationality. Thus, newspapers identify individuals as Mexican or Canadian nationals, which is another way of saying that they *belong* to those two particular nation-states.

There is a crucial difference between *nationality* and *nationalism*, and it must be addressed to avoid confusion. *Nationalism* describes the feeling of patriotism, or extreme, perhaps even fanatical loyalty to a particular *nation* or *nation-state*. Thus, an indigenous person in the Americas may feel her or his first loyalty is to their nation-tribe, not to the Mexican or U.S. nation-state. There are examples all over the world in which particular nations are not happy being owned by nation-states, and they want to be independent from them. It is in this sense that we may speak of black, Chicano, Puerto Rican, and Cuban nationalism. There is, however, another kind of nationalism, like the one that arises in the United States in times of economic distress and leads many U.S. Americans (including blacks, Puerto Ricans, and Mexican Americans) to turn against those who fit the label of "foreigners," or "immigrants" that is, those that do not belong to "the Nation."

This, too, is the horizon where the "national question" comes into focus. Thus, one is always a national (of one country) but one chooses to be a nationalist (that is, the degree of critical commitment or patriotic devotion).

The national question may also involve issues of class. Do all U.S. Cubans, Puerto Ricans, and Mexicans feel attached to a political nationalism in the same way? Or, on the contrary, are there different nationalisms among the wealthy, the middle, and the working classes? Is nationalism just a tool to get political concessions, part of a quest for economic democracy? Who really wants to stay and who wants to go? Or is it a matter of changing the U.S. society? Finally, as noted by Jorge Duany and Cherríe Moraga, the national question may also involve issues of race and gender.[5]

In the United States, there is a situation in which Mexicans, Puerto Ricans, and Cubans were originally incorporated into the United States through military conquest, and now these populations have been augmented by migration so they are the largest cultural minority in the Unites States. Presently it seems, however, that they are not being integrated into the political life of the country, and they feel they are being exploited because of their national origin. This situation leads some U.S. Americans to wonder, which country these Latinos/as consider to be their *patria*, their fatherland, in other words, to which nation are they loyal? Are U.S. Mexicans plotting to take back the land the U.S. took from Mexico? Indeed, Chicano militants like the Brown Berets (see chapter 10) allude to this possibility as does El Plan of Aztlán. And Puerto Rican *independentistas*, continue to advocate for a free Puerto Rico. Would they be better off breaking away from the United States? Ultimately, though, as the articles in this book indicate most Latinos/as do not agree with these political positions. Ultimately, these questions are raised by politicians to get votes or by hate-mongers on both sides of the political spectrum to use Latinos/as as political pawns.

Nationalism emerges as an antidote to colonialism. Previously we said that empires extend their dominion over other free nations. Once those nations lose their sovereignty, the right to make their own decisions, they become colonies of the empire. When the feelings of nationalism in a colony reach a particular level of intensity, they may lead to a war of independence. Keep in mind that, theoretically, only *genuine nations* can achieve independence; this means that there must be a set of historical, territorial, and economic conditions to sustain the struggle. This is what happened when the United States (and later India and many other former colonies) broke away from England, and Latin American countries severed their ties with Spain. It is in this context that some Puerto Ricans want independence from the United States and that Fidel Castro broke relations with the United States. Basques in Spain and France and Kurds in Iraq and Turkey, are examples of nationalist movements. They are also examples of what some Puerto Rican scholars call ethno-nation, that is, people who are dispersed among two or more nations.[6] The same goes for the Cuban people.

Cuba and Puerto Rico are islands off the coast of the United States, and so they fit the picture of colonial possessions overseas. But what about American Indians, African Africans, and Mexican Americans? Are they also colonial subjects in colonies that are *inside* the United States? Is this a new kind of *internal colonialism* or neocolonialism, as Flores and Bailey argue?[7] Do these involuntary territorial and cultural citizens have a sense of nationality, that is, just a "cultural nationalist" identification with their country of origin (with its food, music, dance, fiestas, and other traditions)? Or do they have a sense of nationalism, that is, a stronger political loyalty "with their people" than with the "people of the United States"? And if it is the latter, have they reached the point defined in the Declaration of Independence when "it becomes necessary for one people to dissolve the political bands which have connected them with another"? This is, in effect, the claim made in the Brown Beret National Policies (see chapter 10) and by retired Harvard professor Samuel P. Huntington. The jury is still out, however. In the 1970s Federico A. Cervantes, made some critical observations regarding the status of a Chicano nation *as a genuine nation* and questions the existence of a widespread Chicano nationalism. Most recently, however, Ramón A. Gutierrez argues that the theory of internal colonialism played an important role in radicalizing Chicano students and challenging the social injustices committed against the Mexican Americans as colonial subjects.[8] The same point and counterpoint regarding Puerto Ricans is provided by the "Young Lords Party 13-Point Program and Platform" and the piece by Ramón Grosfoguel in this reader.[9]

Thus, in the twenty-first century the national question as a vehicle for the pursuit of social justice, remains on the table. Now, however, the global economic system challenges the authority of the nation-states not only through the control of capital but also turning citizens into consumers and by forcing many people to migrate; this, incidentally, not unlike early capitalism that forced people off the land and into the cities (see chapters 26 and part V.B). One result of these new developments is the creation of transnational, political, and cultural identities (see chapter 25).

History, Remembering, and Justice

We can look at history as moving in a straight line and try to trace influences from the past to the present. Or we can look at history as eternal recurrence, as a constant struggle that takes different forms in different time periods, with different vocabulary, and different actors. Incidentally, the film *Groundhog Day*, exemplifies this in the life of an individual who wakes up every day to experience the same events as the previous day with minor variations. The purpose in this case is his personal improvement. Not all historians or philosophers, however, see history as teleological, as having a *telos*, a specific end or purpose. If we look at history as a linear development, how far back do you go in tracing the roots of Latino thought? Do we include the Aztecs, Taínos, Arawaks, or Siboneys (the indigenous people of Mexico, Puerto Rico, and Cuba)? Some do.[10] Does this mean that when Latinas/os have to take political action, they consider their pre-Colombian, colonial, or other legacies or do they react pragmatically, according to a given situation? If we take the case of the Chicano movement of the 1960s, we see heavy use of pre-Columbian, particularly Aztec, symbolism. Yet some Chicano scholars and activists apparently did not see their immediate predecessors from the 1900's. As José Limón's points out (chapter 7) some scholars and activists were convinced that the Chicano movement was a brand-new political radical, feminist, militant, quasi-separatist movement. It seems, then that history does not necessarily move in a straight line and that there are gaps of political consciousness. The important point here is that aware or not, consciously or unconsciously, the struggle for democracy continues in one form or another.

This leads to the notion that history repeats itself. One explanation of this remembering of injustices comes from Greek mythology (see Part V.B). The **Furies** are three Goddesses that are in charge of the home and the body, blood relatives, the clan, and the tribe. They are the keepers of the memory of past injustices and revenge (an eye for an eye). After much bloodshed, they agree with the God Apollo to follow the rules of the government (he represents the city-state and the law, which also favors amnesia of past wrongs). As a precedent of the social contract, the Furies' message can be paraphrased as: "We will give up our rights to seek justice by our own hand and follow the law of the state, as long as there is justice. If there is no justice, we will come out to avenge those that have been wronged."[11] This appears to be the case with ethnic movements, uprisings, and riots directed against the state. This is similar to the U.S. Declaration of Independence; when is one justified in breaking the bond? One could say that Al Quaida is the latest manifestation of the Furies. This implies that it is not a haphazard repetition of history but of memories of past injustices that, like the Greek Furies, erupt with such force that they write their politics with blood. No justice, no peace.

Latino/a thought, therefore, may be located within a rich philosophical and historical context that can be defined as a quest for democracy. Ultimately, though, the key questions remain: Why are things the way they are and who has the power to change them? The answers and explanations cover a wide range. Some say, "God wants it that way." For others the answer lies on to the enforcement of the social contract and human rights. Some value private enterprise (anyone can succeed if they want to) as the key to prosperity, whereas others see it as leading to global capitalism with its appropriation of labor, and thus the equivalent of the exploitation of people. Along the same lines, what some see as the exercise of freedom and free will, others see as the manipulation of values and language as a means to extract more value from people to increase the accumulation of wealth and capital (see chapter 4). Specifically directed to Latinos/as (and other ethnic minorities in other countries), the same questions have led to explanations that include notions of "cultural deficiency" (there is something wrong with their culture), "internal colony" (our human and territorial resources are being exploited *within* the United States) and "class struggle" (we are being exploited because we are workers not because we are Latinos/as).

Although acknowledging this rich historical and philosophical legacy, this reader considers Latino political thought as the result of the actions by Latinos/as as they relate to the U.S. government and the dominant U.S. culture; actions, furthermore, that are based on their corresponding material conditions, and with the goal of achieving social equity and justice. Examples of these manifold actions range from uprisings in the nineteenth century, to membership in political organizations, to voting, proposing and opposing laws, protest demonstrations, boycotts, and the production of representations, images, writings (philosophy, poetry, plans, strategies), and other actions that ultimately impact the human body. Most recently the status of Latinos/as in the United States has been affected by the anti-immigrant sentiment and laws designed to restrict the rights of undocumented people, especially Mexicans to rent or shop. Century-old questions continue to linger, such as the political status of Puerto Rico. Another perennial question surrounds the conflicts regarding the status of U.S.-Cuba diplomatic relations and especially of Guantanamo Bay.

These issues, questions, and policies affect Latino/a human bodies both in the United States and also in their countries of origin. Latino/a thought then, deals with a quest for democracy and justice; justice in terms of the respect for the established law, justice in terms of the abuses based on light-skin supremacy, justice based on an equitable distribution of wealth, and justice in terms of respect for the individual as moral and physical entity with cultural and gender differences. But this is not only about Latinos/as in the United States, it is about all continental Americans and, more generally, about human rights. We are living at a time of interrelated crises: There is a war against terrorism and the consequent assault on civil liberties; there is a growing inequality of income and wealth; and there is increasing fragmentation of civil society into separate identities. Therefore, it is especially urgent that we reflect on what we know and that we focus on reducing the gap between our knowledge and our actions.

Human Rights and Economic Democracy

When we speak of human rights we are speaking of human rights within a legal structure, within a nation-state, this is the liberal democratic definition of human rights. Thus, the human rights we talk about are based on the liberal democratic nation-state that is based on a political democracy. But there is another definition of human rights based on the right of self-preservation. It is the Furies. That is when you take justice into your own hands, when you take an eye for an eye.

The right of self-preservation, depends on an economic democracy, on the well-being of the human body and the health of the ecology that sustains it. It is no coincidence that democracy has flourished among "the people of plenty."[12] It is precisely the economic wealth of the United States and not some sort of divine right or Manifest Destiny that has led to the establishment of a political democracy.

The concept of right rests on the notion of an authority that will enforce these rights. Within a country, there is a legal authority that oversees equality and justice. When that fails, the human body itself becomes the ultimate authority. Patrick Henry: "Give me liberty or give me death!" Or the protesters: "No justice, no peace." More pointedly, the difference between the ballot box and a suicide bomber is the difference between these two kinds of human rights.

If this analysis is correct, then the preservation of the liberal democratic notion of human rights has depended thus far on the authority provided by political democracy. To the extent that the authority of political democracy is threatened by the growing influence of a corporate global economy, so are legal human rights. This is evident in the breakdown of civil society, that is the notion of we the people into gang, ethnic, national, or religious rivalries leading up to terrorism and genocide. One way or another, through legal or personal means, human bodies do claim justice. The problem is not necessarily the corporations or the global economy, but their production ultimately depends on the cheapest labor, turns citizens into consumers, and the economic inequality they create in turn distorts the functioning of our political **institutions**.

One possible solution to the preservation of human rights is to reach the next step of democratic evolution that is economic democracy. As a people, in a democratic fashion, we the people need to set a bottom income and a ceiling to the wealth that can be acquired. That is an economic democracy. Failing that, in view of the diminishing resources that sustain our current way of life, Nature itself will do it for us. Then we will have "the world without us" as Alan Wiseman tells us in his bestseller book, *The World Without Us*.[13]

Clearly, there is a political bias in the framing and the contents of this reader and the question of political balance needs to be addressed. There are, of course, other political explanations for the difficulty in establishing working democracies and how to achieve social justice and readers are encouraged to explore them. Most of these explanations, however, are readily available in public discourse and mass media. It is precisely the point of this reader to revisit knowledge, theories, and explanations that are not part of the mainstream.

Additional caveats are in order. What we are attempting to do here is like an archaeological dig, a reconstruction of a discourse of Latino/a political thought. There is no attempt at completeness; depending on the individual reader, there may be missing pieces of information, necessary authorities, explanations, and theories. As for moral relativism (the philosophy that truth is in the eye of the beholder) in the approach taken in this reader, there is an attempt to make a distinction between the ideals of truth, honor, love, equality, and democracy and the appropriation of these ideals for political purposes, for self-interest, or what we call "games of truth." In this scenario, moreover, there are no pure identities for victims or victimizers, there are no ethnic or racial, class, or gender essences.

To facilitate the understanding of Latino/a thought, Part I includes an interactive exploration of a general historical context through the poem *I Am Joaquin* (chapter 1). Though the historical record clearly shows a strong dose of anti-Latino/a sentiment among U.S. Americans, there is no room for anyone to take the moral high ground. We all conspire for justice and for our own subjection. The point of studying political thought is not to feel guilty about what happened in the past, but to feel responsible for what may happen in the future, and to develop strategies for action. There are three major methods of analyses of power: liberalism, Marxism, and power/knowledge analysis (chapters 2, 3, 4). The first two include charts to help clarify the text. Liberalism is critically important in a time of increasing divisions and tensions among ethnic and cultural groups in the United States and particularly the hostility against Latinos/as. It points out that Spanish Americans and English Americans have a common political birth based on their struggle against absolute power and for social justice (despite arguments to the contrary by retired Harvard professor Samuel P. Huntington). Marxism argues that this commonality, this quest for democracy, has been obscured by a lack of economic democracy and other forms of discrimination based on gender and race. Based on class analysis, Apodaca's piece (chapter 3) presents a detailed description and explanation for this situation. In "Chicanology," Vázquez expands the liberal democratic and the class struggle explanation to include an analysis of power/knowledge relations. Here and throughout the reader, we focus our gaze not only on what has been said but also on the illegitimate knowledges that are hidden behind the horizon of a dominant United States and now a global political-economic culture.

Going beyond philosophy and theory, Part I concludes with a brief examination of the birth of U.S. Latinos, specifically Mexican Americans, Cuban Americans, and Puerto Ricans as (in)voluntary, territorial, and cultural U.S. citizens. This choice is guided by the fact that similar to African Americans and American Indians, they were incorporated into the United States through the use of force or military intervention. The permutation and transformation of the relations of each one of these groups with the U.S. government and the dominant society are detailed by the various texts in the rest of the reader.

*   *   *

Notes and Suggestions for Further Research

1. On a personal note, in 1972 I searched unsuccessfully for a graduate doctoral program in Latin American philosophy in the United States. The most common response to my inquiry was that Latino Americans do not have a philosophy. I decided to put together my own program at the Claremont Graduate University first in philosophy and then in an interdisciplinary program in history (European intellectual history) and wrote my dissertation "European Ideas in Mexico: An Analysis of the Mexican Philosophical Discourse" in 1978. From it came "Philosophy in Mexico: The Opium of the Intellectuals or a Prophetic Insight?" *Canadian Journal of Political and Social Theory* (4, no. 3 [1981]). It is also interesting to note that the *Oxford Encyclopedia of Latinos and Latinas in the United States* (Oxford University Press, 2005) does not include an entry on the topic of Latinos/as philosophy. Recently, however, several publications on Latin American philosophy have become available including: Jorge J. E. Gracia, *Hispanic/Latino Identity: A Philosophical Perspective* (Malden, MA: Blackwell Publishers, 2000); Jorge J. E. Gracia and Elizabeth Millán-Zaibert, eds., *Latin American Philosophy for the 21st Century: The Human Condition, Values, and the Search for Identity* (Amherst, MA: Prometheus Books, 2004); Susanna Nuccetelli, *Latin American Thought: Philosophical Problems and Arguments* (Cambridge: Westview Press, 2002); Susana Nuccetelli and Gary Seay, eds., *Latin American Philosophy: An Introduction with Readings* (Upper Saddle River, NJ: Prentice Hall, 2003); Eduardo Mendieta, ed., *Latin American Philosophy: Currents, Issues, Debates* (Bloomington: Indiana University Press, 2003); Arleen L. F. Salles and Elizabeth Millán-Zaibert, discuss the justification and rationalization of a Latin American Philosophy in *The Role of History in Latin American Philosophy: Contemporary Perspectives* (Albany: State University of New York Press, 2006).

2. José Gaos, *Pensamiento de Lengua Española*. México: Editorial Stylo, 1945.

3. Martin S. Staab, *In Quest of Identity: Patterns in the Spanish American Essay of Ideas, 1890–1960*, (Chapel Hill: University of North Carolina, 1967); Mario de la Cueva and others, *Major Trends in Mexican Philosophy*, trans. R. A. Caponigri (Notre Dame, IN: University of Notre Dame Press, 1966); Harold Eugene Davis, *Latin American Social Thought* (Washington, DC: University Press of Washington, D.C., 1966); Juan Gómez-Quiñonez, *Sembradores Ricardo Flores Magón y el Partido Liberal Mexicano: A Eulogy and Critique* (Los Angeles: Aztlán Publications, University of California, Los Angeles, 1973).

4. Juan Gómez-Quiñonez, "Critique on the National Question, Self-Determination and Nationalism," *Latin American Perspectives* 9, no. 2 (Spring 1982): 62–83.

5. See also Lillian Manzor-Coats, "Performative Identities: Scenes between Two Cubas," in *Bridges to Cuba/Puentes a Cuba*, ed. Ruth Behar (Ann Arbor: University of Michigan Press, 1995), 253–66.

6. Andres Torres and Victor Rodriguez offer a different perspective on what constitutes a "genuine nation" because, in the case of Puerto Ricans (and Cubans), the people are dispersed between two countries (a colony and a nation-state). See, Andres Torres, "Political Radicalism in the Diaspora: The Puerto Rican Experience," in *Despierta Boricua: Voices from the Puerto Rican Movement*, ed. Andres Torres and J. E. Velazquez (Philadelphia: Temple University Press, 1999); Victor M. Rodriguez, "Boricuas, African Americans, and Chicanos in the 'Far West': Notes on the Puerto Rican Pro-Independence Movements in California, 1960s–80s," in *Latino Social Movements: Historical and Theoretical Perspectives*, eds. Rodolfo D. Torres and George Katsiaficas (New York: Routledge, 1999), 79–109.

7. G. Flores and R. Bailey, "Internal Colonialism and Racial Minorities in the United States: An Overview," in *Structures of Dependency*, eds. F. Bonilla and R. Girling (Stanford: privately published, 1973), 149–58.

8. Federico A. Cervantes, "Chicanos as a Post-Colonial Minority: Some Questions Regarding the Adequacy of the Paradigm of Internal Colonialism," *Perspectives in Chicano Studies*, Vol. 1, ed. R. Flores Macias (National Association for Chicana and Chicano Studies, 1977), 123–35. See also, Ramón A. Gutiérrez, "Internal Colonialism: An American Theory of Race," *Du Bois Review: Social Science Research on Race* 1, no. 2 (2004), 281–95.

9. For a range of leftist theories attempting to explain why Latinos/as in the United States are not on an equal socioeconomic level with other U.S. citizens and what reformist or revolutionary strategies and tactics are proposed to achieve a satisfactory level of equality, see the pamphlet by Antonio Rios-Bustamante, *Mexicans in the United States and the National Question: Current Polemics and Organizational Positions* (Santa Barbara, CA: Editorial La Causa, 1978).

10. Susanna Nuccetelli, *Latin American Thought: Philosophical Problems and Arguments* (Cambridge: Westview Press, 2002). She goes back to indigenous roots and establishes justification for their inclusion in Latin American philosophy.

11. Aeschylus, *Oresteia: Agamemnon, The Libation Bearers, The Eumenides*, trans. Richmond Lattimore (University of Chicago Press, 1953).

12. David M. Potter, *People of Plenty: Economic Abundance and the American Character* (The University of Chicano Press, 1954).

13. (New York: St. Martin Press, 2007).

CHAPTER ONE

~

I Am Joaquín: An Epic Poem (1967)
Rodolfo "Corky" Gonzales

This poem poetically connects the gaps and continuities between the past and the present. This literary and historical discourse *re-members* the hybridity of peoples and cultures that began with the conquest, proceeded during three hundred years of monarchy and colonization, a quest for democracy, and continues in the increasingly borderless world of global capitalism. Read the poem for its own sake first and then, as you read the subsequent discussion that connects it to the chart Comparative Chronology of Major Historical Events, you may want to go back to the pertinent passages.

> *Yo soy Joaquín,*
> *perdido en un mundo de confusión:*
> I am Joaquín, lost in a world of confusion,
> caught up in the whirl of a gringo society,
> confused by the rules, scorned by attitudes,
> suppressed by manipulation, and destroyed by modern society.
> My fathers have lost the economic battle
> and won the struggle of cultural survival.
> And now! I must choose between the paradox of
> victory of the spirit, despite physical hunger,
> or to exist in the grasp of American social neurosis,
> sterilization of the soul and a full stomach.
> Yes, I have come a long way to nowhere,
> unwillingly dragged by that monstrous, technical,
> industrial giant called Progress and Anglo success. . . .

I look at myself.
I watch my brothers.
I shed tears of sorrow. I sow seeds of hate.
I withdraw to the safety within the circle of life—
MY OWN PEOPLE
I am Cuauhtémoc, proud and noble,
leader of men, king of an empire civilized
beyond the dreams of the *gachupín* Cortés,
who also is the blood, the image of myself.
I am the Maya prince.
I am Nezahualcóyotl, great leader of the Chichimecas.
I am the sword and flame of Cortés the despot
And I am the eagle and serpent of the Aztec civilization.
I owned the land as far as the eye
could see under the Crown of Spain,
and I toiled on my Earth and gave my Indian sweat and blood
for the Spanish master who ruled with tyranny over man and
beast and all that he could trample
But . . . THE GROUND WAS MINE.
I was both tyrant and slave.
As the Christian church took its place in God's name,
to take and use my virgin strength and trusting faith,
the priests, both good and bad, took—
but gave a lasting truth that Spaniard Indian Mestizo
were all God's children.
And from these words grew men who prayed and fought
for their own worth as human beings, for that
GOLDEN MOMENT of FREEDOM.
I was part in blood and spirit of that courageous village priest
Hidalgo who in the year eighteen hundred and ten
rang the bell of independence and gave out that lasting cry—
El Grito de Dolores
"Que mueran los gachupines y que viva la Virgen de Guadalupe. . . ."
I sentenced him who was me I excommunicated him, my blood.
I drove him from the pulpit to lead a bloody revolution for him and me. . . .
I killed him.
His head, which is mine and of all those
who have come this way,
I placed on that fortress wall
to wait for independence. Morelos! Matamoros! Guerrero!
all *compañeros* in the act, STOOD AGAINST THAT WALL OF INFAMY
to feel the hot gouge of lead which my hands made.
I died with them . . . I lived with them . . . I lived to see our country free.

Free from Spanish rule in eighteen-hundred-twenty-one.
Mexico was free??
The crown was gone but all its parasites remained,
and ruled, and taught, with gun and flame and mystic power.
I worked, I sweated, I bled, I prayed,
and waited silently for life to begin again.
I fought and died for Don Benito Juárez, guardian of the Constitution.
I was he on dusty roads on barren land as he protected his archives
as Moses did his sacraments.
He held his Mexico in his hand on
the most desolate and remote ground which was his country.
And this giant little Zapotec gave not one palm's breadth
of his country's land to kings or monarchs or presidents of foreign powers.
I am Joaquín.
I rode with Pancho Villa,
crude and warm, a tornado at full strength,
nourished and inspired by the passion and the fire of all his earthy people.
I am Emiliano Zapata.
"This land, this earth is OURS."
The villages, the mountains, the streams
belong to Zapatistas.
Our life or yours is the only trade for soft brown earth and maize.
All of which is our reward,
a creed that formed a constitution
for all who dare live free!
"This land is ours . . .
Father, I give it back to you.
Mexico must be free. . . ."
I ride with revolutionists
against myself.
I am the Rurales,
coarse and brutal,
I am the mountain Indian,
superior over all.
The thundering hoof beats are my horses. The chattering machine guns
are death to all of me:
Yaqui
Tarahumara
Chamala
Zapotec
Mestizo
Español.
I have been the bloody revolution,

The victor,
The vanquished.
I have killed
And been killed.
I am the despots Díaz
And Huerta
And the apostle of democracy,
Francisco Madero.
I am
The black-shawled
Faithfulwomen
Who die with me
Or live
Depending on the time and place.
I am faithful, humble Juan Diego,
The Virgin of Guadalupe,
Tonantzín, Aztec goddess, too.
I rode the mountains of San Joaquín.
I rode east and north
As far as the Rocky Mountains,
And
All men feared the guns of
Joaquín Murrieta.
I killed those men who dared
To steal my mine,
Who raped and killed my love
My wife.
Then I killed to stay alive.
I was Elfego Baca,
living my nine lives fully.
I was the Espinoza brothers
of the Valle de San Luis.
All were added to the number of heads that in the name of civilization
were placed on the wall of independence, heads of brave men
who died for cause or principle, good or bad.
Hidalgo! Zapata!
Murrieta! Espinozas!
Are but a few.
They dared to face
The force of tyranny
Of men who rule by deception and hypocrisy.
I stand here looking back,

And now I see the present,
And still I am a *campesino*,
I am the fat political coyote—
I,
Of the same name,
Joaquín,
In a country that has wiped out
All my history,
Stifled all my pride,
In a country that has placed a
Different weight of indignity upon my age-old burdened back.
Inferiority is the new load . . .
The Indian has endured and still
Emerged the winner,
The Mestizo must yet overcome,
And the gachupín will just ignore.
I look at myself
And see part of me
Who rejects my father and my mother
And dissolves into the melting pot
To disappear in shame.
I sometimes
Sell my brother out
And reclaim him
For my own when society gives me
Token leadership
In society's own name.
I am Joaquín,
Who bleeds in many ways.
The altars of Moctezuma
I stained a bloody red.
My back of Indian slavery
Was stripped crimson
From the whips of masters
Who would lose their blood so pure
When revolution made them pay,
Standing against the walls of retribution.
Blood has flowed from me on every battlefield between
campesino, hacendado,
slave and master and revolution.
I jumped from the tower of Chapultepec
into the sea of fame—

my country's flag
my burial shroud—
with *Los Niños*,
whose pride and courage
could not surrender
with indignity
their country's flag
to strangers . . . in their land.
Now I bleed in some smelly cell from club or gun or tyranny.
I bleed as the vicious gloves of hunger
Cut my face and eyes,
As I fight my way from stinking barrios
To the glamour of the ring
And lights of fame
Or mutilated sorrow.
My blood runs pure on the ice-caked
Hills of the Alaskan isles,
On the corpse-strewn beach of Normandy,
The foreign land of Korea
And now Vietnam.
Here I stand
Before the court of justice,
Guilty
For all the glory of my *Raza*
To be sentenced to despair.
Here I stand,
Poor in money,
Arrogant with pride,
Bold with *machismo*,
Rich in courage
And
Wealthy in spirit and faith.
My knees are caked with mud.
My hands calloused from the hoe. I have made the Anglo rich,
Yet
Equality is but a word—
The Treaty of Hidalgo has been broken
And is but another treacherous promise.
My land is lost
And stolen,
My culture has been raped.
I lengthen the line at the welfare door
And fill the jails with crime.

These then are the rewards
This society has
For sons of chiefs
And kings
And bloody revolutionists,
Who gave a foreign people
All their skills and ingenuity
To pave the way with brains and blood
For those hordes of gold-starved strangers,
Who
Changed our language
And plagiarized our deeds
As feats of valor
Of their own.
They frowned upon our way of life
and took what they could use.
Our art, our literature, our music, they ignored—
so they left the real things of value
and grabbed at their own destruction
by their greed and avarice.
They overlooked that cleansing fountain of
nature and brotherhood
which is Joaquín.
The art of our great *señores*,
Diego Rivera,
Siqueiros,
Orozco, is but another act of revolution for
the salvation of mankind.
Mariachi music, the heart and soul
of the people of the earth,
the life of the child,
and the happiness of love.
The *corridos* tell the tales
of life and death,
of tradition,
legends old and new, of joy
of passion and sorrow
of the people—who I am.
I am in the eyes of woman,
sheltered beneath
her shawl of black,
deep and sorrowful eyes
that bear the pain of sons long buried or dying,

dead on the battlefield or on the barbed wire of social strife.
Her rosary she prays and fingers endlessly
like the family working down a row of beets
to turn around and work and work.
There is no end.
Her eyes a mirror of all the warmth
and all the love for me,
and I am her
and she is me.
We face life together in sorrow,
anger, joy, faith and wishful
thoughts.
I shed the tears of anguish
as I see my children disappear
behind the shroud of mediocrity,
never to look back to remember me.
I am Joaquín.
I must fight
and win this struggle
for my sons, and they
must know from me
who I am.
Part of the blood that runs deep in me
could not be vanquished by the Moors.
I defeated them after five hundred years,
and I have endured.
Part of the blood that is mine
has labored endlessly four hundred
years under the heel of lustful
Europeans.
I am still here!

I have endured in the rugged mountains
Of our country
I have survived the toils and slavery of the fields.
I have existed
In the barrios of the city
In the suburbs of bigotry
In the mines of social snobbery
In the prisons of dejection
In the muck of exploitation
And
In the fierce heat of racial hatred.

And now the trumpet sounds,
The music of the people stirs the
Revolution.
Like a sleeping giant it slowly
Rears its head
To the sound of
Tramping feet
Clamoring voices
Mariachi strains
Fiery tequila explosions
The smell of *chile verde* and
Soft brown eyes of expectation for a
Better life.
And in all the fertile farmlands,
the barren plains,
the mountain villages,
smoke-smeared cities,
we start to MOVE.
La raza!
Méjicano!
Español!
Latino!
Chicano!
Or whatever I call myself,
I look the same
I feel the same
I cry
And
Sing the same.
I am the masses of my people and
I refuse to be absorbed.
I am Joaquín.
The odds are great
But my spirit is strong,
My faith unbreakable,
My blood is pure.
I am Aztec prince and Christian Christ.
I SHALL ENDURE!
I WILL ENDURE!

The following discussion of the poem, with its references to the accompanying Chart of Comparative Chronology of Major Historical Events provides a historical context to help students locate most of the major world events especially those covered in this reader. The chart is divided into fifty-year-year periods from the fifteenth century to the present and also into four major political-economic systems: monarchy, liberalism, Marxism and global economy and corporate rule.

Joaquín, the character in this poem is, confronted by a "monstrous, technical, industrial giant called Progress" (1850s in chart). Note that throughout the poem there is an ambiguity between progress being the enemy of all humans, "all God's children," and "Anglo success" or "American social neurosis" as being the enemy of Joaquín or the Chicano people. The editor favors the first explanation but this ambiguity appears in other pieces in the reader and in Latino/a thought in general. Joaquín's multiple identities date back to pre-Conquest times, and thus the chart begin in the fifteenth century, at the time of the encounter between the indigenous peoples of the now-called American continent. Cuauhtémoc was the last emperor of the Aztecs defeated by the "gachupín" (a pejorative term for Spaniards) Hernán Cortés. Netzahualcoyotl was the poet-king-philosopher of Texcoco a neighbor city-state of the Aztecs. Toward the end of the poem, to make the point of the endurance and survival of the multicultural, multihistorical Joaquín, Gonzales comes back to this same period of time: "Part of the blood that runs deep in me could not be vanquished by the Moors." The Moors controlled parts of Spain from the eighth to the fifteenth centuries (almost eight hundred years). In 1492, he same year that Columbus accidentally ran into the unknown continent, the Moors, along with the Jews, were expelled from Spain. Gonzales is tracing a direct line from the times of the Moors to the "muck of exploitation" in the fields, the barrios, and the prisons in the United States.

For the next three hundred years, the monarchies of England and Spain consolidate their power in the American continent (and the rest of the world) until another series of key events (1750–1900) changed the course of history. The struggle for the rights of man (against the divine right of the monarch) was based on the notion that all humans "were all God's children." This is the argument used by "Hidalgo who in the year eighteen hundred and ten rang the bell of independence" In effect, in the 1800s Miguel Hidalgo y Costilla and Simón Bolivar followed the example of their earlier (1750–1800) French, Haitian, and U.S. American (founding fathers) revolutionaries, in the long process of overthrowing the French, Spanish, and English Kings and the attempt to establish a constitutional democracy.

Though out of historical sequence in the poem (before he "rode with Pancho Villa"), Joaquín's struggle continues in the United States because not long after Mexico won its independence (1821), it lost Texas (1826) and the northern half of its territory to the United States (1848). "Equality is but a word./The Treaty of Hidalgo has been broken/ And is but another treacherous promise./My land is lost/And stolen,/My culture has been raped." As a reaction to this, in California he becomes "Joaquín Murrieta./I killed those men who dared/To steal my mine,/Who raped and killed my love/My wife. As Mexicans in the United States lose political and economic power, they engage in what is known as "social banditry." This phenomenon appeared throughout the conquered Mexican territory now known as the Southwest.

Continuing the thread of the poem, the second half of the nineteenth century (1850s), Joaquín "fought and died for Don Benito Juárez guardian of the Constitution. A Mixtec Zapotec Indian, Juárez was president of Mexico for five terms, 1858–1872. Like the U.S. founding fathers and the Mexican Liberals, he was also a mason. As the chart indicates, in this same period of time (1850s) the United States went through a Civil War and later the Spanish-American War through which it acquired Puerto Rico and Cuba among other territories. And this is also when the first social revolution of the twentieth century exploded in Mexico and when Joaquín "rode with Pancho Villa" and also becomes Emiliano Zapata, two of the main figures of the Mexican Revolution of 1910, which established the political structure that still governs Mexico. And yet, Joaquín is also the "fat political coyote" the shadow of the many heroes and heroines. Apparently, Joaquín is also a woman because the poem does say "and I am her/and she is me" but women are definitely not active agents in this historical poem. The historical presence of women, from a feminist perspective, is presented in the reader by Apodaca and other authors. For a feminist literary counterpart to "I am Joaquín," there is Castillo's opening essay in *Massacre of the Dreamers*, "Chapter One: A Countryless Woman," and Anzaldua's chapters 1 and 7 from *Borderlands/La Frontera*.

As we move into the twentieth century two key issues in Latino/a thought emerge: "In a country that has wiped out/All my history/ . . . placed a/Different weight of indignity upon my age-old burdened back." So that now, "Inferiority is the new load . . ." In addition to economics, Joaquín is also dealing with psychological issues: "I look at myself/And see part of me/Who rejects my father and my mother/And dissolves into the melting pot/To disappear in shame." Latinos/as become invisible and this invisibility has a violent impact on their psyche. Yet, Joaquín is a good U.S. American, he fights for the freedoms that are often denied to him: "My blood runs pure on the ice-caked/Hills of the Alaskan isles,/On the corpse-strewn beach of Normandy,/The foreign land of Korea/And now Vietnam." And now, in the twenty-first century, we must add the wars in Iraq and Afghanistan. The key issues of invisibility as a manifestation of power relations and the paradox of belonging to a country that does needs you and uses you but does not respect you will be discussed in detail in the content of this book. These issues become more critical when viewed from the perspective of a surge of nativism and xenophobia against immigrants. A movement, furthermore, fueled by the illegal immigration and the income inequality provoked by the global economy, and by increasing violation of civil rights under the guise of the war against terrorism.

* * *

Table 1.1. Comparative Chronologies of Major Historical Events

Dates	Cuba	Mexico/Mexicans	Puerto Rico	United States	World	
1450s	Arawaks rule over the island	Aztecs rule over tribes in Mesoamerica except the P'urhepecha of Michoacán	Taínos rule Borinquen, Columbus finds island in second trip	Indigenous tribes rule their own regions	Age of "Discoveries" Spain is born as a nation after Jews and Moors kicked out	M O N A R C H Y → →
1500s	Conquest of Cuba, founding of Santiago and Havana	Spanish conquest: 95 percent indigenous killed by European disease	Founding of Caparra, San Juan becomes capital	Formation of Powhantan's Confederacy	Luther launches Protestant Reformation	
1550s	Hapsburg's policies stifle economic and political growth in all Spanish colonies	Spanish explorations and claims of what is now the U.S. southwest	British pirates attack Dutch fleet attacks, building of El Morro Fortress	Formation of League of the Iroquois	Britain defeats Spain's Armada	→
1600s				Pilgrims land at Plymouth, Slaves arrive at Virginia, White-Indian wars	Russian fur traders in Pacific Coast, English Civil War	→
1650s	Hapsburg's policies stifle economic growth		City of Ponce founded on south coast	Founding of New York and New Jersey	England's Glorious Revolution	→
1700s	Bourbons bring more open policies	Bourbons restructure New Spain	Mayaguez is founded on west coast	English and French move into Ohio valley	British attempt to increase colonial revenues	→

Table 1.1. (continued)

Dates	Cuba	Mexico/Mexicans	Puerto Rico	United States	World	
1750s	British attack and occupy	California missions	British attack	Stamp Act riots Boston Tea Party	French Revolution	L I B E R
1800s	Loyal to Spain during War, U.S. investment and offer to buy for $100 million	Independence from Spain Loss of Texas, War with United States	Remained loyal to Spain during Revolutionary Wars	War with England, settlers move into Texas and Oregon, War with Mexico	Congress of Vienna tries to bring stability to Europe, Social uprisings	A L I S M ↔
1850s	U.S. offer to buy for $130 million Spain grants Autonomy, Spanish-American War, The Treaty of Paris	In the United States, Mexicans lose economic and political power. In Mexico, Juárez separates church and state, fights French Intervention Porfirio Díaz Dictatorship	Grito de Lares, Slavery abolished, Spain grants autonomy, Spanish-American War, The Treaty of Paris	Civil War, forges the identity of the United States as one country, Spanish-America War forges the identity of the United States as an imperial democracy	Tremendous growth of scientific thought and applications to industry, agriculture and other technologies, Prussian War as a prelude to WWI	& M A R X I S M →
1900s	Protectorate of the United States, open for political and economic intervention for its own good	Plan de San Diego, Mexican Revolution, LULAC, Repatriation, Bracero Program	Colony of the United States Foraker Act Jones Act Ponce Massacre. Allowed to elect own governor	Philippines fight U.S. rule. World War I, Great Depression, World War II, Cold War, Economic Expansion	First social revolutions in Mexico and Russia, Spanish Civil War	→

				GLOBAL ECONOMY & CORPORATE RULE
1950s	Batista's dictatorship backed United States, Castro's regime, exile community in the United States	Operation Wetback, Bracero Program ends, Chicano Power, Farmworkers Union	Free Associated State of the United States Nationalists attack House of Representatives	Korean War, Cold War. Missile Crisis, man on the moon, Viet Nam War, Civil Rights and Counterculture movements	Fall of Soviet Union, AIDS epidemic, Internet, genocides in Africa and Eastern Europe
2000s	Cubans try to build bridges despite Elian's incident Fidel Castro hands over power to his brother Raul Castro but remains candidate Diplomatic efforts to end the economic embargo against Cuba continue with hope the next U.S. president might do it	First president in seventy years from a party other than *Partido Revolucionario Institucional* (PRI). Contentious election between Manuel Lopez Obrador and Felipe Calderón, who won with less than a 1 percent lead to his closest competitor. Increasing friction over border clashes between Border Patrol and people trying to cross into the United States or living across from the fence	Sila Calderon, first woman governor elected. Votes for remaining a commonwealth as measured by 2004 election for governor show an almost even split with those who want statehood: 48.4 percent versus 48.2 percent	Contentious presidential election, government split evenly among parties. Attack on the United States by Al Quaida 9/11/01 leads to war against Afghanistan, then Iraq and violation of civil liberties and Constitutional Rights. Congress fails to enact comprehensive immigration policy. Fence along the border approved by Bush. 2008 presidential candidates include an African American and a woman for the first time	The global market controls all aspects of life on the planet; global warming, terrorism and income inequality make evident the need for sustainability. Global warming is finally recognized as a major issue. Economy in turmoil, because of housing crisis and high oil prices, fears of recession

Questions

1. Are there any images in this poem that represent a particular stereo-type, or political position?
2. In what sense is it possible to "lose" the economic battle and "win" the struggle for cultural survival? Can economy be separated from culture?
3. In what sense can religion be good as in "a lasting truth that/Spaniard/Indian/Mestizo/were all God's children/And/from these words grew men/who prayed and fought/for/their own worth as human beings." And, at the same time, democracies are based on the separation between church and state?
4. After reviewing the history of Mexican human bodies, Joaquín concludes that in the present he has "a different weight of indignity" upon his age-old-burdened back. What different interpretations can be deduced from this statement? In the final analysis, is Joaquín a victim or a victor?
5. According to Joaquín, the social problems experienced by Chicanos also threaten "the salvation of mankind." What might these threats be and does the poem provide an adequate connection between a concern for a specific group of people and all humans?

CHAPTER TWO

~

A Continental American Quest for Democracy

Francisco Hernández Vázquez

In this text, Vázquez uses a comparative framework to explore the political evolution of English Americans and Spanish Americans. Both peoples share a common history of struggle, against the British and Spanish crowns, respectively. Both peoples used concepts like nation, class, **sovereignty**, natural law, will of the people, constitution, and revolution (as in their declarations of independence) and political and economic institutions to construct their respective national identities. As Americans and as *Americanos*, they both fought for freedom and the right for self-determination, but unfortunately their quest did not include justice for all. Today, almost three centuries later, the struggle for social justice continues. It is precisely against this common background that one needs to address recent racist and exclusionary claims that the United States is based on a creed that is fundamentally different from Hispanic culture such as those from Harvard professor Samuel Huntington.[1] And it is against this common background that one can best appreciate the important political role played by Puerto Ricans, Mexican Americans, Cuban Americans, and other ethnic minorities in the development of democracy in the American continent.

*   *   *

We hold these truths to be self-evident, that all men are created equal, that they are endowed by their Creator with certain unalienable Rights, that among these are Life, Liberty and the pursuit of Happiness.—That to secure these rights, Governments are instituted among Men, deriving their just powers from the consent of the governed,—That whenever any Form of Government becomes destructive of these ends, it is the Right of the People to alter or to abolish it, and to institute new Government, laying its foundation on such principles and organizing its powers in such form, as to them shall seem most likely to effect their Safety and Happiness.

U.S. Declaration of Independence

Public discussion regarding Latinos in the United States quickly shifts to discussions of illegal "aliens" and cultural differences that threaten the integrity and the safety of the United States. At the academic level, the latest incarnation of this argument is the aforementioned professor Huntington. It seems that there is no room in the discussion for the notions of created equal, unalienable Rights, or consent of the governed. Indeed, civil society is increasingly fragmented into cultural, national, ethnic, and race categories. For example, in public discourse, the media, and in private conversations, the status of Latinos in the United States falls within a range that goes from being an undesirable group of people who threaten the identity of the United States, to being victims of U.S. imperialism through the colonization of Northern Mexico, Puerto Rico, and Cuba. From the ravings of hot radio and Internet postings to the halls of academia, Latinos are seen as a threat to the identity of the United States. As the argument goes this is especially true about Mexicans because they are apparently fundamentally different than other immigrants and therefore than other Americans. On the other hand, many Latino/a scholars refer to the relation between the colonizer (the United States) and the colonized (Mexicans, Puerto Ricans, Cubans, and others) as a starting point. Many Latinos/as in fact, see themselves exploited as an internal colony or oppressed as member of the working class despite their long history of allegiance to the United States.

There is another way, however, to look at Latinos/as in the United States and that is that they, along with all peoples in the American continent, share a common political legacy, that Spanish and English along with all other continental Americans, are part of a historical struggle for social justice, a quest for democracy. This quest is, of course, full of contradictions, for as Blake said, "The road to hell is paved with good intentions." This quest for democracy is illustrated in the following chart.

To explore this common political birth, it is useful to consider how human bodies in the American continent changed their status from subjects of kings to members (not all necessarily citizens) of nation-states during an important

Table 2.1. Historical Quest for Democracy: World Historical Social Movements against the Exercise of Absolute Power

	1776 1789 1810–1825	1848	1905	1910	1917	1968	2000
The people in action: mass/ social movements	French, U.S. and Spanish-American Revolutions	Street demonstrations in Europe	Massive strikes all over the world (Industrial Workers of the World in the United States)	First social revolution of twentieth century: Mexican Revolution	Russian Revolution, overthrow of the czar	Cultural or information revolution	Terrorist attacks on United States Anti-immigrant actions
Revolutionary classes struggling for power	Bourgeoisie	Urban workers	Rural workers	Urban and rural working class	Urban and rural working class	New working class	Identity-based groups
Organizations they used to acquire power	Representative assemblies	Insurrectionary parliaments and political parties	Councils/Soviets	Revolutionary party	Communist party	Action committees/ collectives	Militias, terrorist cells, Internet organizations

(continued)

Table 2.1. *(continued)*

	1776 1789 1810–1825	1848	1905	1910	1917	1968	2000
Visions/ aspirations Goals/ objectives	Formal democracy; liberty, equality, fraternity	Economic democracy; trade unions; democratic constitutions	Universal voting rights, unions; freedom from empires	Government for the benefit of the people: *tierra y libertad*	Socialism as the "Dictatorship of the Workers", land, bread and peace	Self-management all Power to the people/ imagination	Preservation of democracy, group identity, global sustainability
Tactics	Revolutionary war, *guerras de independencia*	Popular insurrections	General strike	Organized seizure of power	Organized seizure of power	Struggle for public space/ freedom in everyday life	Insurrection, terrorism, harassment, organized protest

half century of wars of independence (1775–1825). In other words, how did indigenous people, (sub-Saharan) African slaves, Europeans born in the Americas (or in Europe), and Asians come to share identities as either Americans or *Americanos* (in the United States and in Spanish America, respectively)? And how does this process shed light on the understanding of the political experience of Puerto Ricans, Cuban Americans, and Chicanos/as? Are the militant members of these ethnic groups or the people marching for immigration rights modern-day patriots and *insurgentes* who follow the words of the U.S. Declaration of Independence?

> But when a long train of abuses and usurpations, pursuing invariably the same Object, evinces a design to reduce them under absolute Despotism, it is their right, it is their duty, to throw off such Government, and to provide new Guards for their future security.

Or are they rabble-rousers who misjudge, "When in the Course of human events, it becomes necessary for one people to dissolve the political bands which have connected them with another"? After all, Cuba broke away from the United States, but Cuban Americans seem content to be American citizens. And who exactly are "one people," or better yet, who are "We the people" mentioned in the preamble to the U.S. Constitution? Let us now turn to the article on a Continental Quest for Democracy.

*   *   *

From Oppressed Subjects to Free Citizens

Once upon a time (in the latter part of the eighteenth century) Spanish Americans and English Americans actually shared the same political status. They were subjects of their respective monarchs, Fernando VII from Spain and George III from England. And based on their own political traditions and experiences, both peoples applied the ideas of the Enlightenment to "shed light" on the tyranny of church and monarchies. Among these ideas are that law and rights can be derived from a rational observation of nature and that our knowledge is not necessarily limited to revelations from God. This belief in natural law led to concepts such as rights of man and all men are created equal (these are the self-evident truths and unalienable rights in the U.S. Declaration of Independence). It also led to the idea of freedom: of political institutions, religion, and trade, the belief in which was then known as liberalism. These concepts were developed over hundreds of years to oppose the notion that God had given the kings or queens the Divine Right to rule over their subjects and do with them (or to them) as they desired.[2]

A key point of liberalism was that sovereignty (the power to control a country, a people, and everything in it) resides in "the will of the people." But if will is not something you can see or touch, how do you embody this will? As noted in table 2.1, this is where political organizations and representative assemblies come in; they are "political bodies" that speak for the people. As you will see in the readings, Mexican Americans, Cubans, and Puerto Ricans also make use of this process of representing the will of the people through political bodies to assert their own self-determination or to question the sovereignty of the United States. The problem is one of representation: If sovereignty resides in the people but only one class of people (say property owners) makes up the congress or assembly, then who speaks for the propertyless? If only men, who speaks for women? In some cases, the upper or middle classes have to convince the lower classes to fight for the interests of the "ruling" class. Who, then, speaks for the lower classes? And if anyone does, how is this voice categorized as legitimate or illegitimate? Thus, the definition of the will of the people remains a major problem to this day. As we enter the twenty-first century, for example, the key issue in presidential elections in the United States, Mexico, Bolivia, Venezuela, and others, is which candidate represents the interests of the people as opposed to the interests of the corporations.

Not surprisingly, the political thought of the ruling classes is based on practical matters. And here, too, we find similarities among those who assumed the voice of the people in the Spanish American and English American colonies. At first, they were loyal to their kings: They both wanted to remain part of their respective empires; they just wanted to be treated as equals with other provinces and peoples within their respective empires. Secondly, what they wanted was to protect their own class interests: They both opposed the increase in taxation and the protection of the American Indians by the British or Spanish kings.[3]

However, in a fifty-year period, roughly from 1775 to 1825, these two peoples changed their political status from colonial subjects to sovereign, independent nations with their own qualifications for citizenship.

To compare the paths that Spanish American and English American revolutionaries took, we will view three key ingredients in nation making: national identity, economic and political institutions, and procedures. As you discover while reading the newspaper, these are at play not only in Latino or U.S. American political thought, but in politics all over the world (including your neighborhood). More specifically, throughout this reader, we will see them playing a role in the making of Chicano, Cuban, and Puerto Rican identities and in discussions of nationalism.

From English Subjects to "We the People"

If we could transport ourselves to the English colonies in 1665 we would find that there are five separate "sorts" of men: (1) the "better sort" (large land-holders, crown officials, merchants, and allied lawyers and professionals); (2) the "middling sort" (small landholders, independent artisans, shopkeepers, petty officials, and professional men of lesser pretensions); (3) the "meaner sort" (a category of free but depressed men who were laborers, servants, dependent artisans, sailors, nonprosperous farmers, and nondescript drifters); (4) the bonded white servants, an even meaner sort who served some master under an indenture limited in time; and (5) the lowest elements in society, the freed (sub-Saharan) Africans. Only the first two took part in the process of self-government because of the belief that only people with property possessed the independence necessary to participate in political life. The best estimate that can be made of the different nationalities living in the colonies in 1765 are English, 65 percent to 70 percent; Scots and Scotch-Irish, 12 percent to 15 percent; Germans, 6 percent to 9 percent; and all others, 3 percent to 5 percent. Out of a total population of 1.45 million, four hundred thousand (21 percent) were so-called Negroes or mulattoes.[4] The demographics of a nation, the number and "kinds" of people, are important not only because they show the relations of power between the rich and the masses (the class structure), but also because they show the contradictions between the ideal that all men are created equal and the reality of women and men who are left with only the quest for equality and justice, that is, for democracy.

There were several categories of human bodies that did not fit the definition of "people" at that time: brown or "red" bodies (a.k.a., "Indians" [unlike the French and the Spanish, the English were not interested in "converting" Indians to Christianity or entering into mixed marriages]); black bodies (African slaves were not included because they were defined as property and because their race was considered inferior); bodies without a penis (women were also considered inferior and therefore not entitled to the same rights as males). A fourth group of male bodies that could be of any color but were defined as "ethnics" was also excluded. The term *ethnic* initially arose in Puritan writings to signify traits or individuals diverging from the Christian narrative, or for heathens (including not only American Indians but also Dutch and Germans).[5] There was only one people: the Puritans. And though it was made up of diverse groups like the Separatists, the Presbyterians, and the Congregationalists, they shared the nearly fanatical belief that God had determined the outcome of history and that they were the soldiers of Christ, the chosen people destined to build a society that would serve as an example to the rest of the world. Echoes of this notion can be heard in the justification for the war in Iraq.

The year 1775, the beginning of the Revolutionary War, finds the English American colonists enjoying an economic boom and already envisioning their expansion throughout the continent in the coming century as their "manifest destiny." At that time the financial difference between the poorest and richest English/European American was probably the smallest such difference of any in the world. It was easy to move from one class to the next and especially from both directions into the middle. Furthermore, European Americans were beginning to assert the value of individuality over the demands of group identity.[6]

As we will see repeatedly, class structure is important because it indicates the degree of cohesion and stability of the population in a given nation. In effect, the English American colonists were able to successfully fight a war of independence against England for several reasons. Among these is that the American-born Europeans in the British colonies were the majority of the population. They also did not have to worry about an American Indian uprising (the American Indians were divided by intertribal hostilities), or with few exceptions, a slave rebellion (slaves were 20 percent of the population, 90 percent of whom lived in the South; whites outnumbered blacks in all the colonies except South Carolina, which was next to Spanish Florida, a haven for runaway slaves). The unique class stratification in the English American colonies helps to explain why the concept of class struggle is fairly absent from U.S. political discourse. This does not mean the colonists did not have class conflict.

Political institutions and processes are the third key ingredient in nation making. For the English Americans, a tradition of self-governance and the practice of political opposition provided a continuation from the British tradition of representative government. English Americans built on these political technologies through strong political participation in colonial government. Although, as we already noted, this participation was limited to those humans who fit the definition of "better" or "middling" sort, that is, those with property, there is an important lesson here about how people become political. John Adams noted in 1766 that, "The people, even to the lowest ranks, have become more attentive to their liberties, more inquisitive about them, and more determined to defend them, than they were ever before known or had occasion to be."[7] Adams attributed this awakened political consciousness among the poor to the English Parliament's Stamp Act, the first direct tax imposed by Britain on its American colonies to help cover the cost of maintaining troops in the colonies. Because the English colonists did not have representation in Parliament, they argued that this was taxation without representation. There are parallels here with Puerto Ricans, who have no voting representation in the U.S. Congress (and thus pay no federal taxes) and U.S. Mexicans in California, who "became more attentive to their liberties" by becoming U.S. citizens after the passing of Proposition 187, which denied benefits to the undocumented.

It is ironic that, after independence, the English Americans still lacked a sense of nationhood. Because of their emphasis on local government, they still thought of themselves as members of thirteen different states, not as "Americans."[8] Instead of developing national institutions, the founding fathers went back to their respective colonies or states. These served as laboratories for political experiments in the form of new political technologies that we now take for granted, like writing down and publishing the contract between the people and the government, that is, the constitution for each state. Here again we see that outside events forced on them a national political identity. Among these were difficult relations with Spain, discontent among the colonies, and the 1786 Daniel Shays Rebellion (in which two thousand farmers organized an illegal convention and rebelled against the government of Massachusetts—so there was class struggle!).

Although the Declaration of Independence refers to *these* United States, the U.S. Constitution begins with the well-known phrase, "We the People of the United States." Here we have the sense of nationhood, if not nationalism, represented by the U.S. Constitution. But more than a symbol, the Constitution embodies the political institutions, the frameworks that will allow for future power struggles regarding the definition and interpretation of key concepts like "people," "men," "equality," and from the preamble, "justice," "general Welfare," and "Blessings of Liberty," among others. In other words, the Constitution is an institutionalization of the quest for democracy as defined by changing political realities, by games of truth. Indeed, to understand political thought, Latino/a or not, you would do well to keep your eye on the making of political institutions. Such institutions were the stepping-stones that led English American revolutionaries to change their status from subjects to citizens and to consolidate their **nation-state** as the United States of America between 1789 and 1830.

From Spanish Subjects to Mestizaje or The Cosmic Race

With reference to the same three key ingredients in nation making (national identity, economic and political institutions, and procedures), let us briefly compare the English American political economic evolution with that of the Spanish colonies in the Americas. Unlike the homogeneous, cultural, and racial identity that the English American colonists developed through a policy of exclusion during one and a half centuries, the inhabitants of the Spanish colonies had evolved for three hundred years into a multicultural, multiracial society, a "Cosmic Race" according to the Mexican philosopher José Vasconcelos. Human bodies in New Spain (after independence, Mexico or formally, the United States of Mexico) were categorized into different groups. *Peninsulares* (born in the Iberian Peninsula or Spain) occupied the top governmental positions in the Spanish colonies. *Criollos* were Spaniards born in the Americas; they considered themselves Hispano-Americanos and they resented having to take second place to the peninsulares (they were the closest counterpart to the English-Americans in the thirteen colonies). There were also indigenous people from over one hundred tribes, and there were also the *castas* the result of mixed marriages among Spaniards, criollos, indigenous, and Asians and Africans (such as mestizos, mulattoes, etc.). In 1793, Mexico, close to the time of the war for independence, there were 3,799,561 inhabitants, of which 61 percent were indigenous, 11 percent mestizos, less than 1 percent blacks, 10 percent mulattoes, less than 1 percent Spanish, and 18 percent criollos (no figures are available for Asian Mexicans).[9] Unlike the English colonies, here only 20 percent were Europeans. And even the criollo category is open to question because many mestizos obtained *Cédulas de Gracias al Sacar*; these were the equivalent of "certificates of whiteness" that were for sale. In the rest of Latin America and the Caribbean, the proportion of blacks was much greater than in the United States (half of the Brazilian population and about one-third of Cuba, compared with 12 percent for the United States).[10]

What do demographics have to do with politics? Unlike their English American counterparts (who simply excluded American Indians and blacks) the Spanish American revolutionaries had to take into account class, race, and gender in their struggle for independence. (The relationship between demographics and politics also played a major role in the 1820s, when Anglo Americans became the majority in east and central Texas [see chapter 5], and in the year 2008, when Latinos become political players as a result of their population growth.)

In Mexico, in terms of social categories comparable to the English colonies, there were (1) the royal officials (the governing class, considered a foreign elite); (2) the great magnates (the largest merchants and owners of mines, *haciendas*, and textiles with primary interest in the colony); (3) the secondary elite (well-educated professionals; they also engaged in enterprises like food processing, bakeries, *pulque* processing plants, cattle raising, and markets); (4) the small bourgeoisie (owners of small ranchos, mule trains, inns, stores; they considered themselves middle class, or *gente decente*); (5) the artisan class (who identified with their social superiors and tended to own little property other than their tools); (6) the workers (the most numerous, who generally owned no property and relied entirely on their earnings); and (7) the *léperos*, meaning "the destitute and indecent," the homeless and unemployed (a floating criminal class or a marginal labor force, depending on your point of view). Keep in mind that all ethnic groups (with the exception of blacks and the royal officials) could be found in each of these social classes.[11] Thus, at this point in history, it appears that the Spanish Americans were more open to diversity than their English American counterparts. But there is more to the story.

For the purpose of political administration, the Spanish American colonies were divided into four viceroyalties: New Spain (what is now the Southwest of the United States, Mexico, Central America, Cuba, Puerto Rico, and the rest of the Caribbean), New Granada (what is now Colombia and Panama), Peru, and La Plata (what is now Argentina, Bolivia, Paraguay, and Uruguay). This social and economic diversity and the enormous territory it encompassed (from the tip of South America to what is now the U.S. Southwest) led to three different revolutions. In Mexico, the criollos started the movement toward revolution but did not have economic power or political institutions to maintain it, so they had to appeal to the common people for support.[12] Consequently, the revolution included the demand for the liberation of the indigenous people and the slaves and for agrarian reform, but because of the circumstances, it later had to compromise with the landowning criollos, the military, and the church on its demands for social justice. In Greater Colombia, the revolution began as a movement of the upper class criollos. But they had to deal with the mulattoes' demands for social equality and include them in the war for independence to win the war. (A similar situation took place in the Cuban revolution almost one hundred years later.) In Chile and Argentina, there was no social content of importance in the revolution, which was carried out by the upper classes. They were able to get the support of the masses without making many concessions.[13]

What about Cuba and Puerto Rico? The great South American revolutionary Simón Bolívar had plans to extend the Spanish American wars of independence to them until the U.S. government made clear their opposition to the independence of these countries from Spain.[14] As a result, they continued to be colonies of Spain until 1900, when the United States took over them as a result of the Spanish-American War. Arguably, Cuba got its freedom from the United States with the revolution of Fidel Castro; Puerto Rico remains, in the year 2008, the oldest colony in the world.

The movements for liberation started toward the end of the eighteenth century, when the Spanish King, like the King of England before him, increased taxes to pay for the wars among the European monarchies. This had the same impact on the Spanish colonies as the Stamp Act on the English colonies. To be sure, there was significant economic growth and the king wanted part of it, but there was also a tremendous population growth that created a huge gap between the rich and the poor. This created a dislocation among the castes—the laboring classes—making them more politically conscious and aware of their oppression and at the same time established their identity as Americanos. Under these circumstances, the game of truth for the criollos was to have a revolution that would give them political equality with the peninsulares. But they were afraid that Indians, blacks, and primarily, the mestizos, who were a growing majority, would push the revolution beyond its political goals toward social and economic changes that would negatively impact their own privilege. But there is more to this fear than concerns over class struggles.

Unlike that of their English American counterparts, the criollo Spanish-American revolutionary enthusiasm was tempered by reaction to the excesses of the French Revolution known as the Reign of Terror (1793–1794), when French mobs executed thousands of people for political reasons. Closer to home, in 1804 Haiti, led by Francois Dominique Toussaint L'Overture, became the first Latin American colony to gain its independence, when African slaves overthrew the French. This created a fear of black uprisings throughout Latin America, depending on blacks' proportion to the total population. This fear continued to play an important role in the development of national identity in Cuba, where by 1846 the population was 44 percent white and 56 percent black.[15]

Once again we are faced with the question of "who are the people?" as illustrated by the following incident. Criollos and mestizos in New Spain, who identified themselves as Mexicans, distinguished themselves as historians, scientists, and philosophers who were full participants in the modern age. Politically, they delved into the Spanish legal tradition regarding the consent of the governed (established at the time of the conquest) and notions of natural law and right, liberty, common good, and general welfare.[16] Their objective was to prove that because the Spanish King had been deposed by Napoleon, sovereignty (the supreme power to rule) reverted to the people. In an assembly called by the Viceroy to discuss this issue, judge Aguirre, a peninsular loyal to the King, and who was against the notion of "power to the people," asked the presenter, lawyer Verdad, what he meant by "people." Verdad hesitated and then answered, "the constituted authorities." Then Aguirre, "replying, in turn, that those authorities were not the people, called the attention of the Viceroy and of the junta to the original people to whom, upon the principles advanced by the official, the sovereignty ought to revert; but he went no further in clarifying this concept . . . because the governors of the Indian settlements were present, among them a descendant of the emperor Moctezuma."[17] The implication, of course, was that technically, the power would revert to the indigenous peoples.

This incident illustrates the politics of definitions and interpretations that in this reader we call games of truths. El Grito de Independencia (the Call for Independence) of September 15, 1810, however, added a new dimension to the question of who are the people. On that day, the Indians, workers, léperos, and small bourgeoisie took up arms against the Spanish monarchy, and the leader of the uprising, the priest Miguel Hidalgo y Costilla, issued proclamations to free slaves and return the land to the Indians. Thus, unlike the U.S. Revolutionary War, this initial period of the War for Independence included goals that would benefit all of the people, including Indians, Blacks, and mixed-race people. But these goals were not reached. Though independence from Spain brought fundamental change to the Americanos, the criollos used the military, church, and landownership institutions to maintain their privileges.

It was noted previously that the process of building a nation-state requires political institutions and experience in self-governance, which is, obviously, usually gained from participation in government affairs. It was also noted previously that, for the English Americans, property was what allowed individuals the independence to participate in politics. In the Spanish American colonies, this was not the case because chief administrative posts were restricted to human bodies born in Spain, peninsulares. There was a religious-political hierarchy extending from the King of Spain down to the Viceroy, the local government, with the exception of the cabildo (city council). Office holding had elements of being a royal gift given to favored individuals. So, for the Spanish American criollos, wealth and social status were based on landownership but not on self-government. Because the Spaniard recognized the rights of the natural leaders of the American Indians, and supposedly for their own protection, society was divided into a Republic of the Indians and a Republic of the *Españoles*. The American Indian leaders were part of the nobility of Spanish America, but within their own republics they still followed a traditional political system based on paying tribute. In this kind of exclusionary political system, a great deal of politics was conducted outside political office at the personal and informal level, through negotiations or through protests. Petitions could be brought to the viceroy by the Indians or others and he would intercede in their favor. The point is that most people had no access to and therefore no experience in the overall governance of the colonies.

The only political practice in self-government available to criollos was the cabildos. Of all the institutions of the Spanish colony, the cabildo was considered to have a special legitimacy coming from the will of the people, a tradition coming from the Spanish municipalities. However, their function was so rigidly defined by Spanish legislation that the post of *regidor* (councilman) was regarded as largely honorific and by 1556 these positions were sold to the highest bidder. Thus Spanish Americans had no "political training school" to prepare them for democracy after independence. With the expulsion of the Spaniards after the wars of independence, the Spanish Americas had few trained leaders experienced in running national institutions. At the end of the devastating Wars of Independence, each of the four viceroyalties fragmented into several nation-states influenced by the U.S. Constitution but lacking a clearly defined national identity. Soon after independence, for example, the Central American countries broke away from Mexico, as did the Texas territory a dozen years later. A lesson to be learned is that identity alone is not enough to sustain a nation-state; it must have a political and economic system to sustain the national identity.

Unlike the continuity of political thought and practice between England and the English American colonies, the dominant political thought in Mexico led to a rejection of the Spanish colonial legacy and the mestizo-centered, multicultural society, and with this rejection came the introduction of a politics of identity. Lucas Alamán and other conservatives maintained that the true national character was to be found within a traditional Spanish heritage. (This is similar to the positions of some conservatives in Puerto Rico and Cuba one hundred years later.) A few nationalists, like Carlos Maria Bustamante, attempted to circumvent the colonial experience by identifying Mexican nationality with the preconquest Aztec state (a position that appears in the discourse of Chicano political thought, [i.e., the notion of Aztlán]). Others, like José María Luis Mora, asserted that the nation's character must be sought in the "white" race (the Spanish, not the Anglo). This was part of a widespread discourse of racism that saw the nonwhite population as a sickness to be cured through ethnic cleansing.[18]

Although conservatives longed for an imaginary Spanish past, liberals looked toward foreign political models.[19] As noted before, this included not only the U.S. Constitution, the need for immigrants, capital, and technology, but also European, primarily British investments. Later in the nineteenth century, Cuba also rejected the Spanish legacy and reached out to the United States as a model (see Part III).

In the Mexican constitutional assembly of 1823, the principal debate was between the centralists and the federalists (similar to the debate held by English Americans at their constitutional convention). Should power be concentrated in Mexico City or distributed among the nineteen states and four territories? With respect to the English thirteen colonies, Fray Servando Teresa de Mier argued:

> They were already separate and independent one from another. They federalized themselves in union against the oppression of England; to federalize ourselves, now united, is to divide ourselves and to bring upon us the very evils they sought to remedy with their federation. They had already lived under a constitution that, when the name of the king was scratched out, brought forth a republic. We buckled for three hundred years under the weight of an absolute monarch, scarcely moving a step toward the study of freedom.[20]

The liberals won and the Constitution of 1824 organized the *Estados Unidos Mexicanos* along the lines of the U.S. Constitution. But the conservatives won special privileges for the Catholic Church and for the president in times of emergency. The struggle between the liberals (those for freedom, democracy, and federalism) and the conservatives (those for the traditional class and religious privileges) continued for several decades. And it was here that the political economic interests of the English and Latino Americans intersected.

Northern Mexicans in Texas, Nuevo Mexico, and California had been integrally involved in the colonial government, the debates over independence, and the wars for independence, and they now were participants in the centralist/federalist debate.[21] This debate was of particular importance for them because most of them wanted to have a system that would allow them self-government. It was in this political context that U.S. Americans' economic and cultural penetration of Mexico took place. In fact the economic penetration of all of Spanish America by English and U.S. business interests was possible for two reasons: Unlike the English-American Revolutionary War, the Spanish American Wars of Independence devastated the economies of the Spanish colonies and after independence free trade policies opened the borders to foreign economic interests.[22]

What are the implications of this comparative political economic history of the English American and Spanish American for the current debates regarding the presence and status of Latinos/as in the United States, the increasing anti-immigrant and anti-Mexican sentiment in the United States, and the quest for democracy in Continental America?

1. All Americans in the entire continent share the same political roots. People in the entire American continent share the same historical quest for democracy and social justice. This quest solidified during the Enlightenment, which in turn was propelled by the European encounter with the New World indigenous civilizations. Thus, contrary to the assertions of people like Professor Samuel Huntington, there is no purely Anglo American dream. *It is indeed a continental Americano multilingual and multicultural dream.* The European Union is a successful model for the blend of democratic values and multicultural, multilingual societies. Why can the U.S. Americans not look beyond purely economic interests (i.e., North American Free Trade Agreement [NAFTA], Central American Free Trade Agreement [CAFTA], etc.) and parochial cultural notions (e.g., Huntington's "Anglo-Saxon creed") and develop a continental American democratic society that our founding fathers and mothers dreamed of?

2. Different economic development leading to similar social development. English America started off with a healthy economic base and as an exclusionary, Anglo-Saxon Protestant, homogeneous society that has eventually moved towards the notion of a melting pot. Spanish America started off with a devastated economy and a multicultural society based on miscegenation and class struggle. These differences, of course, affected their respective political development. Today, despite the higher economic capacity of the United States, it is precisely their common quest for democracy and social justice that continues to serve as a basis to demand the inclusion of "different" people into U.S. and into Latin American and Canadian societies. After nearly three centuries, at a continental level, societies are becoming increasingly similar in terms of having to address issues of social justice for their diverse populations. Examples are the Civil Rights Movement in the United States, the Zapatistas in Mexico, and the indigenous movements in Bolivia. There is an increasing call for and subsequent development of a body of literature on cultural or transnational citizenship. The work of

Will Kymlicka[23] in Canada, for example, expands on the work by Maria de los Angeles Torres in this reader and the work on Latino Cultural Citizenship by William B. Flores and Rina Benmayor[24] by making specific policy recommendations.

3. Because all light casts a shadow, there is also an unfortunate similarity in the sociopolitical evolution of English America and Spanish America. First a common American or Americano identity was used as a convenient weapon to motivate people to fight against English and Spanish rulers; after independence, a nationalist identity was used as a tool to attempt to control ideas, language, social classes, American Indian nations, and ethnic groups. All the while the absolutist power once held by kings has been reconfigured within democracies led by a global economy that challenges the role of the state as social arbiter. This process has led to the establishment of a system based on class, gender, race (in the United States) or pigmentocracy (in Spanish America, a social hierarchy based on skin color). This system originally benefited primarily the dominant, white, male, European, wealthy, landowning class (whether of Spanish, English, or other European descent). Presently, although still primarily white and or European descent, it also includes an increasingly multiracial and multicultural privileged elite in English and Spanish America, indeed in the whole American continent.

In the final analysis, the problems of justice and equal opportunity for people of all social classes, which figured so prominently among English and Spanish American patriots in the eighteenth and nineteenth centuries, remain unsolved today. And, of utmost concern, the civil society that supported political and economic democracies is becoming increasingly fragmented into identity groups that claim their right for cultural and multicultural citizenship, or on the contrary, hate groups who insist on the preservation of a United States for white, English-only speakers. This apparently is being driven by the increasing proliferation of the global economy.

*   *   *

Notes and Suggestions for Further Research

1. Samuel P. Huntington, "The Hispanic Challenge," *Foreign Policy*, (March/April 2004). See also his *Who Are We? The Challenges to America's National Identity* (New York: Simon & Schuster, 2004). For a critique see Alan Wolfe, "Native Son: Samuel

Huntington Defends the Homeland" (*Foreign Affairs*, May/June 2004) and a debate between the two of them in "Credal Passions" (*Foreign Affairs*, September/October 2004).

2. That these ideas were powerful we can tell because they were considered "illegitimate" and therefore dangerous by the king's authorities; the books containing these ideas were banned and periodically burned in France, Rome, and Spain and of course in their colonies.

3. Harold Eugene Davis, "Ideas in the Independence Movements of Mexico and the United States," *Proceedings of the Pacific Coast Council on Latin American Studies* 6 (1977–1979): 7, 9.

4. Clinton Rossiter, *The First American Revolution* (New York: Harcourt, Brace & World, 1956), 18, 139, 148. As Rossiter indicates, it is impossible to fix the precise proportions of each nationality, which is why these figures do not add up to 100 percent.

5. Wilson Neate, "Alienism Unashamed," *Latino Studies Journal* 8, no. 2 (Spring 1997): 68–91.

6. Rossiter, *First American Revolution*, 179.

7. Rossiter, *First American Revolution*, 237.

8. This is an example of the relation between violence (war in this case) and political consciousness. It was the institution of the army that provided the first traces of an "American consciousness." Similarly, as Mario T. Garcia points out in his discussion of the League of United Latin American Citizens (LULAC), U.S. Mexicans developed a political consciousness as "Americans" through their participation in World War I (*Mexican Americans: Leadership, Ideology, & Identity, 1930–1960* [New Haven: Yale University Press, 1989]).

9. Colin M. MacLachlan and Jaime E. Rodriguez O., *The Forging of the Cosmic Race: A Reinterpretation of Colonial Mexico* (Berkeley: University of California Press, 1990), 197. I converted the figures into percentages.

10. Helen Safa, "Introduction," *Latin American Perspectives* 25, no. 3 (May 1998): 9.

11. Safa, "Introduction," 223–28.

12. For a detailed discussion of the role that different classes played in the wars of independence, see Enrique Semo, *Historia Mexicana: Economía y Lucha de Clases* (Mexico City: Ediciones Era, 1982), 161–99.

13. Charles C. Griffin, "Further Reflections," in *History of Latin American Civilization*, ed. Lewis Hanke (Boston: Little, Brown, 1967), 48–49.

14. José Trias Monge, *Puerto Rico: The Trials of the Oldest Colony in the World* (New Haven, CT: Yale University Press, 1997), 22.

15. Lourdes Martínez-Echazábal, "Mestizaje and the Discourse of National/Cultural Identity," *Latin American Perspectives* 25, no. 3 (May 1998): 40.

16. Luis Villoro, "The Ideological Currents of the Epoch of Independence," in *Major Trends in Mexican Philosophy*, ed. Mario de la Cueva and others, trans. A. Robert Caponigri (Notre Dame, IN.: University of Notre Dame Press, 1966), 185–219.

17. Villoro, "Ideological Currents," 195.

18. Martínez-Echazábal, "Mestizaje and the Discourse of National/Cultural Identity" and Martin, "The Sick Continent and Its Diagnosticians" in Martin Stabb, *In Quest of Identity* (Chapel Hill: University of North Carolina Press, 1967), 12–33.

19. For thirty years the Porfirio Díaz dictatorship (1876–1880, 1884–1911) attempted to make Mexico into a nation-state similar to France culturally and the United States politically and economically. The Mexican Revolution of 1910 returned the country to its mestizo past. Though as Mexican mass media clearly illustrate, a pigmentocracy still dominates the Mexican cultural horizon. See for example Mireya Navarro, "Spanish-Language TV Burgeoning," *Press Democrat*, August 25, 2000, C3. According to this article, television "stars are so blond . . . they seem to hail from Eastern Europe rather than Hispanic countries."

20. *Antologia del pensamiento social y político de América Latina* (Washington, D.C., 1964), 242–43, quoted in Michael C. Meyer and William L. Sherman, *The Course of Mexican History*, 3rd ed. (New York: Oxford University Press, 1987), 314.

21. Juan Gómez-Quiñonez, *Roots of Chicano Politics, 1600–1940* (Albuquerque: University of New Mexico Press, 1994).

22. Eduardo Galeano, *Open Veins of Latin America* (New York: Monthly Review, 1997). Some argue that this was just a new form of colonization (neocolonialism) that deformed the economies of the newborn nations and set the stage for their historical uneven development. Whatever the arguments or theories, the social problems that led to revolution continue to hurt most people to this day.

23. Will Kymlicka, *Multicultural Citizenship: A Liberal Theory of Minority Rights* (Clarendon Press: Oxford, 1995).

24. William V. Flores and Rina Benmayor, eds. *Latino Cultural Citizenship: Claiming Identity, Space and Rights* (Boston: Beacon, 1997).

*   *   *

Questions

1. Which claim is more persuasive to you: (a) that laws can be derived from our observation of nature, (b) that laws are arbitrary social constructions (we just invent them) or (c) that laws are established by God or religion?
2. Besides voting, how is the will of the people expressed in the United States?
3. The article observes that Spanish Americans, unlike their English American counterparts, had no "training schools" to prepare them for democracy after independence. What activities or institutions in which you participate do you consider training schools for democracy? How do you express your political will? Your political voice?

4. To be sure, English Americans were against the "sins" of privilege they clearly saw among the English aristocracy, but their objective was to level off the top, not to raise the bottom, of society. In regard to their own privilege over women, indentured servants, or poor whites, slaves, and American Indians, were they blind to it or was it invisible? This is a question of agency, of intention: Is it that they *could not* see it or that they *did not want* to see it?

5. Note also that if the American Revolutionary War started because it was a matter of Englishmen wanting to treat other Englishmen as inferiors, "to reduce them under absolute Despotism," does not this then raise the same question of liberty for Americans who treat other Americans as inferiors? In other words, to what extent are Chicano, Puerto Rican, and African American militants two hundred years later in the same position the American patriots were in? Do white Americans treat nonwhite Americans as if they were part of an internal colony to be exploited? Is the key question here one of abuse of power? Of justice?

CHAPTER THREE

~

The Chicana Woman:
A Historical Materialist Perspective
Maria Linda Apodaca

Historical or dialectical materialism, more commonly known as Marxism, is a political-economic analysis of society that is familiar in most of the world. In the United States, however, Marxism is associated with "godless communism," and most people reject it offhand. And yet, Marx's analysis of capitalism is a major cornerstone of political science; it is the basis of many social movements today; and it appears in some of the pieces in this reader. For these reasons, it is important to become familiar with the concepts and terms of Marxist analysis. At the same time, it must be noted that there are also pieces in this reader that, implicitly or explicitly, consider Marxism a *necessary but not sufficient analysis* for the understanding of Latino/a political realities.

Before reading Apodaca's piece, it is helpful to review some basic concepts and vocabulary. The term *materialism* refers to the primary importance of the physical, material, economic world as opposed to *idealism* or the world of ideas associated with the German philosopher Hegel. Both Hegel and Marx, however, agreed that history moves through a dialectic, which means the conflict between two forces, followed by a resolution. Then, the resolution conflicts with another force, and the cycle of conflict repeats itself. For Hegel history was the struggle of good versus evil that would end in the absolute glory of God; for Marx it is the historical struggle between social classes, between the "haves" and the "have-nots" and most recently between the capitalists and workers. Marx's materialism differs from older definitions of materialism that saw human beings as passive. For Marx, it is a matter of the dialectical relationship between humans and the material world. The dialectical method stresses the following elements: (1) All things are in constant change. (2) The ultimate source of change is within the thing or process itself. (3) This source is the struggle of opposites, the contradiction within each thing. (4) This struggle, at key points, brings about qualitative changes or leaps so that the thing is transformed into something else. (5) Practical-critical activity resolves the contradictions.

The following chart shows the structure of the ability of society, at any given time or level, to produce the material goods necessary to sustain itself.

Table 3.1. Historical Materialism

The base, or *economic structure*, has a complex relationship with what is known as the *superstructure* and it includes what is generally known as "culture"	SUPERSTRUCTURE People's artistic (painting, music, literature), intellectual, religious, political, and legal systems supported by a given economic structure	It is important to note that language is considered to be part of neither the base nor the superstructure, but as serving all classes at all times.
⇑ The combination of the *productive forces* and the *social relations of production* form *the base, or economic structure* ECONOMIC	The productive forces below determine the *SOCIAL RELATIONS OF PRODUCTION OR THE CLASS STRUCTURE IN SOCIETY* These relations include (1) how people make a living (such as hunting and gathering, farming, working in industry, programming computers, banking) and (2) how people relate to one another in producing and exchanging the means of life (lord/serf, master/slave, capitalist/worker, global economy/consumer).	Language is believed to be like a tool for communication but not exactly, because unlike any other "tool" known to humans, language tends to stay the same even after a particular base or superstructure disappears.
⇑ BASE OR STRUCTURE OF A GIVEN SOCIETY	In the first place are the *PRODUCTIVE FORCES* or the *MATERIAL FORCES OF PRODUCTION*: knowledge and skills, technology (draft animals, tools, machines, computers) and the natural environment. All that is necessary to produce the necessities of life such as food and shelter.	Therein lies the nature of language as a material entity and its importance for the analysis of power

It illustrates the three major components of the productive ability of society, starting at the bottom and moving to the top (though in reality the relationship between them is not much more complex). Each part of the theory is briefly explained next.

The Productive Forces

The productive forces are (1) the material means of production that people use to gain a livelihood from nature; (2) the machines, tools, raw materials, and natural resources available; and (3) the human beings, their knowledge, talents, aspirations, and needs. The development of productive forces occurs through work, labor, activity, and the growth of needs and abilities. As change takes place, people develop further capabilities and desires. This means that people make a living and make themselves at the same time.

People differ from animals in that they engage in purposeful productive activity, that is, they produce their means of subsistence consciously, not instinctively. This is done within a certain mode of production or economic structure. Human nature is determined by the mode of production under which people work to maintain human life—as the mode of production changes, so does human nature.

For example, men and women living under a feudal (medieval) mode of production have values, aspirations, abilities, and needs that differ from those living under a capitalist mode of production. As feudal men and women designed better tools and altered and controlled the environment, they changed themselves. Thus capitalism succeeded feudalism, not only because of technological changes, but also because, in the process of technological change, people changed their values and skills and their outlook on what was important and so on. Development, then, is not imposed from the outside—we do not adapt passively to social changes—humankind makes itself through purposeful activity.

Social Relations of Production

The social relations of production form the class structure of a society, which is revealed in the work process. The productive forces determine the social relations of production and exchange through (1) institutions and practices closely associated with the way goods are produced, exchanged, and distributed; (2) property relations; (3) the way work or labor is recruited, organized, and compensated; (4) the markets or other means for exchanging the products of labor; and (5) the methods used by the ruling class to capture and dispose of surplus product.

Eventually the developing productive forces come into conflict with the prevailing class structure (or social relations of production). New ways of making a living become incompatible with the old ways. For example, commercial activity in the sixteenth century became incompatible with feudal relations in the countryside and with the guilds in the towns (organizations that regulated the production of crafts). This is also exemplified by the imposition of the U.S. economic system on northern Mexico's economy. This growing contradiction takes the form of a class struggle between the rising class associated with the new means of production and the old ruling class. Class struggle, under appropriate conditions, intensifies the contradictions between the means of production and the class structure until, as a result of revolution, new relations of production (compatible with the superior forces) are established. (See table 3.1, the social revolutions are tied to the industrial revolution and subsequent technological developments).

A key related concept discussed throughout the reader, is "the state," defined as a product of society at a certain stage of development. From this perspective it is defined as an institution that protects the property and privileges of the ruling class by preserving order among the oppressed and exploited classes. As such, it is an instrument of class rule. But in some cases the power involved in a class struggle may be evenly divided, so that the state acquires some independence from both the capitalist and the working class.

Superstructure

The economic structure molds the superstructure of social, political, and intellectual life, including sentiments, morality, illusions, and modes of thought, principles, and views of life. The superstructure contains the ideas and systems of authority (political, legal, and military) that support the class structure, that is, the dominant position of the ruling class. Thus, transformation of the economic structure of society eventually changes the character of the superstructure.

Interactions between superstructure and structure are inevitable, numerous, and complex; the way people make a living affects their ideas; ideas, in turn, affect the way people make a living; modes of thought, however, are shaped and limited in the first place by the mode of production. Ideas that become influential in society reflect only the narrow range of the material activities and interests of the dominant class. Many ideas do not gain prestige because they conflict with the real position of the dominant class (e.g.,, current ideas calling for no or even limited growth appear incompatible with capitalist aspirations).

Life is not determined by consciousness, but consciousness is determined by life. Revolutionary ideas can exist side by side with conventional ones, but they cannot by themselves overthrow the prevailing class structure that gave rise to the ruling ideas.

The superstructure contains not only ideas, but also institutions and activities that support the class structure of society, such as the state, legal institutions, family structure, art forms, and spiritual processes. For example, prehistoric paintings indicate the need of hunters to depict their prey accurately and naturally. Later, geometric pottery designs reflected the more abstract, mysterious forces that determined whether crops live or die. The change from gathering and hunting to agriculture also altered family structures, religions, rules and laws, government bodies, games played, and military organizations.

The religious world is a reflection of the real world, a consolation for the degraded human condition. Friedrich Engels linked some changes in religious views to changes in material life over a period of two thousand years, but he carefully noted that once an ideology (religion) develops, it acquires a certain independence of economic structures.[1]

We are now ready to plunge Apodaca's text. Students who have a difficult time studying history may take comfort in her approach: "The development of history must be based on something more tangible than ideas, dates, and individuals. The production and reproduction of immediate life is, in the last analysis, the basis for historical development." Thus, in the following text she uses this analysis to explain the status of Chicanas in the United States and by implication, the conditions of all women and all workers. She traces the conditions of women from Aztec and Spanish/Mexican feudal societies, to contemporary capitalism and ends with a biographical sketch of a woman who lives in the border between feudalism and imperialism.

Note and Suggestions for Further Research

The source for this discussion is Robert C. Tucker, ed. *The Marx-Engels Reader* (New York: Norton, 1972). For a readable, brief, updated discussion of Marxism see Phil Gasper, ed. *The Communist Manifesto Karl Marx and Fredric Engels: A Road Map to History's Most Important Political Document* (Chicago: Haymarket Books, 2005).

*   *   *

Chicana Historiography: Theoretical Questions

The turbulence of the sixties and early seventies once again brought into question the inequalities that exist in the United States. Workers, students, women and other groups began questioning these conditions and attempted to understand the causes of inequality. National minorities began to demand equal rights, better education, jobs, and wages. Among these was the Chicano or Mexican American.[1]

In the universities and colleges Chicano historians and social scientists wrote papers and books to show that Chicanos were not inferior but a people with culture and history. These Chicano scholars often became integral elements in the Chicano people's demand for better education, jobs, and wages.

The history of the Chicano experience, as told by Chicano historians and Chicano social scientists, many times was clouded with sentiment and emotion resulting only in affirmations of the contributions made to so-called Anglo culture (e.g. Campa, 1973; Acuña, 1972). Many of these historiographies lacked historical analysis; some became limited to analyses of racial or cultural conflict. While the contributions made by the Spanish and Mexicans to the development of the Southwest cannot be slighted, since in many ways they paved the way for the entrance of U.S. pioneers into the Southwest, nevertheless, several facts must be clarified about the history of the Southwest.

It must first be understood that the society of Spanish colonialism in Mexico (including the territory which is now the U.S. Southwest) was not the idyllic portrait of benevolence and cooperation. In Mexico and in the Southwest countless Native Americans were enslaved to work the Spanish mines, herd cattle and sheep, and work the agricultural fields. As a result many were consumed by overwork and disease.[2] Secondly, it must be made clear that the early productive developments made by the Spanish and later the Mexicans were feudal in nature (Chevalier, 1972:49). Finally, if we objectively study the productive forces in the Southwest, we will find that it was not until the United States took over the Southwest that large investments of capital released these areas of production from their feudal bonds and allowed for their fuller development (Taylor, 1971:68; McWilliams, 1971). The majority of Chicano historiographers do not deal with these historical facts.

The development of history must be based on something more tangible than ideas, dates, and individuals. The production and reproduction of immediate life is, in the last analysis, the basis for historical development. Production has a twofold character: on the one hand, the production of the means of existence, of food, clothing and shelter, and the tools necessary for that production; on the other hand, the propagation of human beings themselves, the reproduction of the species. The social organization of a particular epoch and area are determined by both kinds of development: "by the stage of development of labor and of the family" (Engels, 1973:71). Analysis reveals that the historical development of Mexico after 1520 until approximately 1850 was based on feudal production and had a corresponding social organization. In the United States the case was different. Its historical development after 1800 until the present has been that of growing capitalist production and a corresponding bourgeois culture. Again Chicano historiographers rarely base their analysis on the productive and reproductive process in the Southwest.

Chicano historiographers have also tended to ignore the role and situation of Mexican and Chicana women in immigration, social production (i.e. agriculture, textile industry, etc.), and working-class struggle.[3] There are some studies (e.g., Green, 1971; Allen, 1931), but rarely are these incorporated into the general histories of the Chicano. In place of histories that show Chicanas as workers, we have been offered pictures of passivity, naiveness, weakness, in a word "*femininity*," the typical Mexican conception of what a woman's role should be. Yet the history of Mexico and the United States show us that the only women who could enjoy femininity, gentleness, and little or no work, were the women of the property-owning class. For the women of the laboring classes, including the majority of Chicanas and Mexicanas, their class situation has meant working in the fields, in factories, as well as at cooking, washing, and sewing. For working-class women and for Chicanas, work was not a choice but a necessity.

Any attempt to enter into an analysis of the historical and political situation of the Chicana has usually been frowned upon in the Chicano movement and by some Chicano historians. The reasons often given are that this type of discussion violates Chicano culture and divides the movement. The underlying reasons are much more fundamental. For a long time the Chicano movement was concerned only with the discrimination that had cut us off from our "historical," and more importantly, from our "cultural" past. The tendency developed to glorify all the cultural traits of the past. To bring up the question of Chicana oppression was to question the family, more specifically to question male dominance, in a word, to question *machismo*. In trying to understand the cause for the subjugation of women, and in particular the Chicana, the question many times led to an analysis of classes. Questions arose as to the difference between the women of the patron class and the peon class in Mexico, and to the difference between the women of the capitalist class and the wage-earning class. But these questions encountered resistance. Socially and historically two obstacles exist to hinder the development of an analysis of women's oppressed condition and although taken by some as *two* distinct phenomena, in practice they are mutually interdependent. The two basic factors discouraging analysis of the Chicana are (1) a class society based on private property with the need for inheritance and (2) male chauvinism. Interestingly enough, these two aspects not only discourage analysis, but in the real world are the material and ideological basis for the subjugation of women and other working-class people.

The development of private property in the means of production necessitated the development of certain forms of social relations. The socio-economic subjugation of women was one of those relations. Along with other rationales (i.e. magic, theology, human nature) used to explain the supremacy of one class over another, male superiority and its counterpart, female passivity, became an explanation and justification for the inferior position of women in society. Explanations of male superiority became embodied in the ideology of male chauvinism. Chicanos, including the historians, being products of two class cultures, feudal and bourgeois, have manifested the ideologies of these class societies. What we need to understand is that chauvinism, from either a Chicano worker or intellectual, or from a bourgeois intellectual, justifies private property, class oppression, and the subjugation of women.

Contrary to most Chicano historians, I believe that we must have histories that can be the basis for future social action, rather than mere academic interpretations. In this sense the need for a class analysis of the Chicana exists. Focusing on the development of the productive forces and the corresponding relations of production, it becomes possible to understand the purpose of forced sterilization, unequal pay, lack of education, etc. Finally, it is only by understanding the relation between the development of private productive property in the Southwest, the subsequent requirement for labor power, and the nature of the subjugation of women under feudalism and capitalism, that the role of the Chicana in historical development becomes clear. Furthermore, class analysis makes it possible to understand how politically and culturally the working class was forced to accept, at least temporarily, its conditions of exploitation. For women of various historical working classes as well as for the Chicana, class analysis allows one to understand:

1. the expropriation of their labor power and that of their families;
2. man's supremacy in the home and in society;
3. society's denial of their importance in social production.

Why has the role of the Chicana in society been hidden? Why has she been described as passive and fragile? How are these two questions related to social production and to domestic production? The answers can only be found in understanding how social production has changed in class society, specifically under monopoly capitalism. We can begin to answer these questions by simply saying that with the early development of private property and classes in ancient society, mother-right was replaced by father-right, and monogamy was imposed on women. Thereafter, it became necessary to veil the role of women in ideals of sacrifice and motherhood. But the answers to the questions are much more fundamental, much more tied to the overall historical development of society. This development is the movement of production and classes. Because as production changes, so does the group or class which controls the society. The overthrow of mother-right was a partial answer. The development of private property and classes, the corresponding need to trace one's property (i.e., inheritance), and the final separation of domestic production from social production is the full answer.

> History teaches us that the class or social group which plays the principal role in social production and performs the main functions in production must, in the course of time, inevitably take control of that production. There was a time, under the matriarchate, when women were regarded as the controllers of production. Why was this? Because under the kind of production then prevailing, primitive agriculture, women played the principal role in production, they performed the main functions, while the men roamed the forests in quest of game. Then came the time, under the patriarchate, when the predominant position in production passed to men. Why did this change take place? Because under the kind of production prevailing at that time, stockbreeding, in which the principal instruments of production were the spear, the lasso, and the bow and arrow, the principal role was played by men. (Marx et al., 1969, emphasis mine)

This is not to say that women were the first class to be subjugated, as some would like us to believe. No, the subjugation of women is integrally related to the subjugation of propertyless women *and* men. The particular subjugation of women must be understood in terms of class contradictions. By classes is meant the relation men and women have to the means of production: on the one hand are the property owners who reap the benefits of production, on the other are the laboring classes who are more or less propertyless and live on the meagre offerings of the propertied class.

The aspect of inheritance is something only propertied classes enjoyed. But in order to give inheritance validity, it had to become a universal cultural aspect; thus the institution of monogamy in all levels of society came into being. The aspect of women's historical position of inferiority results from the inability of any class society to give real economic and political equality. This inability necessitates the creation of explanations for positions of inferiority.

For women this explanation became tied to her biological function and to the caring of newborn children.

The subjugation of women cannot be separated from the overall development of society. In studying this development we must focus on the movement of the productive forces in each mode of production and understand how this affected social relations.[4] In analyzing, we must not confuse social production with socialized [domestic (ed. Note)] production. Social production is the production for society's needs, including food, clothing, technology, and reproduction and maintenance of new members (i.e., labor power) (Marx and Engels, 1972:48). The definition of what a society is, thus what social production is, has changed with each new mode of production. For example, a society of hunters and gatherers rarely constituted more than a clan, a group of people of about ten to twenty related by blood. In this case there is no distinction between social and domestic production; social production is production for the clan only. With further developments in production (i.e., domestication of plants and animals), in division of labor (i.e., pastoral and agricultural, handicraft and agricultural, etc.), and especially the development of private property, there begins to be a differentiation between social production and domestic production. Domestic production became the area where labor power was reproduced and maintained.[5] Production of food, shelter, and technology was being taken more and more away from the domestic area. In a slave society, as in ancient Greece, Rome, and Aztec society, this division may not have been as developed. Under a feudal society, as in Spain and colonial Mexico, this division was to become more apparent. Capitalism, the mode of production that greatly accelerated production, made the division between social and domestic production complete. In a capitalist society production of food, clothing, tools, etc., was removed from the domestic area. Women were given the responsibility of the domestic area, although often participating in social production. Many times they were not allowed to express any authority; they were the property of the man in the house—be it father or husband.

In societies characterized by private property and classes, the condition of women is not the same. On the one hand, the women of the property-owning classes are generally excluded from having any real economic and political power. Many of these women only organize the household affairs, and even this is often taken care of by servants. On the other hand, while the women of the propertyless class are denied political and social power, economically they are important. Their economic importance is one of the aspects of Chicana history that will be presented in a later segment of this paper. For now let me clarify the preceding discussion with the following:

The "savage" warrior and hunter had been content to take second place in the house, after the woman; the "gentler" shepherd, in the arrogance of his wealth, pushed himself forward into the first place and the woman down into the second. . . . The division of labor within the family had regulated the division of property between the man and the woman. *That division of labor had remained the same; and yet it now turned the previous domestic relation upside down simply because the division of labor outside the family had changed.* . . . The domestic labor of the woman no longer counted beside the acquisition of the necessities of life by the man; the latter was everything, the former an unimportant extra. (Engels, 1973:221, emphasis mine)

In each succeeding mode of production we found two requirements: (1) production for social needs (i.e., food, shelter, clothing, technology), and (2) reproduction and maintenance of labor power. In each new mode of production the relation between these two areas of production changed according to the level of development of the means of production and according to the manner by which property was distributed. As society developed, as more was being produced, as distinctions between property owner and worker developed, the division between social production and domestic work widened. In more developed modes of production (i.e., feudalism and capitalism), the separation of social production from domestic production continued until under capitalism this separation was made complete.

Historical Roots: Ancient Aztec Society and Spanish Feudalism

In 1520 the Spanish invaders to Mexico found a society that was highly developed. There were sophisticated systems of irrigation, extensive trade routes, developed sciences of astronomy and medicine, highly developed arts, complex systems of religious hierarchy, and a centralized government. This society called Tenotchtitlan granted to political and religious leaders the right to own various tracts of land and to exact tribute from the surrounding population. Private property existed amidst some communal control of land.

The development of what we now call Aztec civilization is predicated upon a long history of development (Soustelle, 1975). Anthropologists and archeologists have shown that the central valley area prior to Aztec domination underwent tremendous cultural changes. The earliest peoples are characterized as hunters and gatherers. They exhibited many of the cultural items that would place them in that stage of development Morgan and Engels termed "*savagery*" (Engels, 1973), and Marx termed *primitive communalism* (Marx, 1970:19). The situation of the women in these early societies was conditioned by the fact that the campsite (the domestic area) was the main area of production. Because there was no distinction between social and domestic production and because of the low level of technological development, the work of the women was equally important to that of men. In fact we can venture to say that because of the social need to care for the children, the subsequent division of labor made women the gatherers of seeds, plants, and small rodents, whereas men became the hunters, sometimes absent for long periods of time. The food provided by the women was much more important because it was more stable.

This overview of primitive communalism in Meso-America is brief. There remains a tremendous amount of work to be done by historians and anthropologists in this area. Research should be undertaken to examine the role of women in the transformation from primitive communalism to the Aztec stage of civilization. One further comment needs to be made before discussing feudalism and capitalism. Aztec society, contrary to the illusions some may have, was a class society. The whole religious and political organization exempted those at the top from work and gave them the right to extract tribute and mandatory work from those over whom they were given responsibility. Aztec society was based on the labor of masses of peasants who were required to produce corn, beans, and squash; to weave fine cloth; to mine precious stones for Aztec jewelry; and to build monuments for the Aztec ruling class. The condition of women at this time was greatly altered from the primitive communal stage. Further analysis of this time period I leave, hopefully, to other Chicana historians and anthropologists.

The Spanish conquest greatly altered the society that existed prior to 1520, but the essence of social relations remained based on private property. This is why some historians could state that for the peasant in the outlying Indian villages nothing had changed; the peasant still had to give involuntarily of his produce and labor, only now to the new Spanish landlord.

The society that Spain imposed on Meso-America was a particular organization of private property, namely feudalism. Feudalism as a mode of production has as its basis the relationship between a landlord and a peasant. The landlord owns the land and the peasant works the land. In return for use of the land, the peasant gives up a certain portion of his product. This rent many times took the form of personal service, such as working the land of the landlord, serving in the home of the landlord, and going to war for the landlord. Except for nominal protection, the peasant, therefore, received nothing from the landlord. In fact, in a feudal society the producer gives up a portion of his product to the landlord in return for the privilege of using the owner's land. The remainder of the product produced by the peasant is directly consumed by himself and his family.

The political organization of a feudal society is characterized by decentralization. With different landlords fighting to gain control of land and peasants, territory is broken up into warring fiefdoms. Each landlord conducts expeditions and wars at his own expense, taxing the peasantry with ever greater demands for rent and tribute.[6]

In Mexico, the Spanish imposed this social system on the Indian population by granting *encomiendas* and *repartimientos* to the *conquistadores*.[7] Along with the various types of land grants conferred upon the conquistadores, the repartimientos and encomiendas guaranteed the conquerers a source of labor. The Spanish, not satisfied with taking the land and enslaving the Indian, allocated to themselves the right to extract tribute from the various Indians living upon the land.

The Spanish, needing to reinforce their economic and political dominance, systematically destroyed the Native Americans' social, economic, political and cultural systems. They imposed a religion that pacified the Indians into accepting their condition of servitude. They reorganized the political system, giving all powers to the Spanish Crown, its viceroys, and its vassals (i.e., Cortez, Onate, and others). The former Indian rulers were converted into mere puppets. The economy of Meso-America, once a flourishing economy of trade and handicraft production based on a developed system of agriculture, came to a virtual standstill by the middle of the seventeenth century (Chevalier, 1972).

Spain, itself a nation dying under the feudal yoke, gave to Mexico its feudal structure and decaying feudal economy. Needing to maintain its armies and protect its hegemony in the world, the Spanish Crown invoked higher and higher taxes on its colonies. Silver production in New Spain was a source of wealth that the Crown and its conquistadores relished much more than the Mexican land. The mercury used for mining silver could only be bought from Spain, but higher taxes on mercury imposed by the Crown, made silver-mining very expensive. The Spanish in New Spain sent less and less silver to Spain, and those that did send silver and other commodities faced the possibility of British and Dutch raids. Spanish and Mexican trade became increasingly difficult (Cumberland, 1969:91).

The curtailing of silver production was only one of the changes that affected the Meso-American economy. In the early years of Spanish colonization, Catholic missionaries attempted to establish new industries, such as winemaking, silk and other textile production, which would encourage the development of the Mexican economy. The Spanish Crown, wanting to maintain a monopoly over trade and fearing the development of Mexican industries, passed laws against the development of any new small-commodity production (Cumberland, 1969:98).

Other factors which reinforced feudalism and slowed the development of the Mexican economy were the successful introduction of cattle breeding and the enormous decrease in the native population. The tremendous growth of cattle resulted in the destruction of many agricultural lands (Fernández, forthcoming:19). Farms, villages, and sometimes whole valleys were abandoned to cattle haciendas. The decline in the Indian population also added to the abandonment of agriculture and villages. As a result of forced labor, miserable working conditions, and the diseases brought by the Spanish, the native population decreased from approximately twenty million in 1520 to slightly more than a million in 1650 (Cumberland, 1969:49). With the Spanish Crown wanting more precious metals and the creoles and peninsulares in New Spain unwilling to work, further subjugation and exploitation of the remaining Indian population resulted (Chevalier, 1972:54).

Feudal relations of production were reinforced by the tendency of the Spanish Crown to encourage colonization under the domination of rich men. These conditions and the failing economy encouraged the development of a strong *hacendado*, or landlord, to control the area. Chevalier explains the process in this manner:

> Finally, each region and even each locality tended to become isolated and self-sufficient and to huddle under the authority of the large landowners or local leaders, who frequently took over the expenses required for maintaining a police force or waging war on the nomads. (Chevalier, 1972:49)

What was created, then, were feudal fiefdoms with the landlord having total authority over the people and the land under his control.

For the Mexican Indian woman, Spanish colonialism had particular effects. To analyze the condition of women in any mode of production, an understanding of the relationship between social production and domestic production is required. This relationship in a feudal society undergoes various changes as compared to the primitive communal society where social production is basically within the sphere of the domestic area. There was already in the Aztec empire a division between social production and domestic production which was predicated upon the development of large-scale agriculture and the existence of a privileged class that lived at the expense of the masses of peasants and artisans. This division was manifested in various ways. First, production had developed beyond the immediate needs of the clan. The product of the *calpulli* [8] was involuntarily given up either to tribute or taxes or to the empire's "privileged" priests and warriors. In addition, the product of the calpulli was traded for the wares of the *pochtecas*.[9] Corn, beans, and local handicrafts were exchanged for agricultural and handicraft items from different areas. Social production had expanded to maintain the "idle" ruling class and for purposes of trade and barter.

Social production had changed, but domestic work remained the same. This development must be understood in reference to the development of classes, for the condition of women in the property-owning class is entirely different from the condition of women in the working class. The women of the Aztec ruling class were virtually ostracized from producing their immediate subsistence. Their role in domestic work, the maintenance and reproduction of the species, was also minimal. Except for reproduction, the majority of the work in a ruling-class home was done by servants or slaves. Men and women slaves would be brought in to maintain the home (Soustelle, 1975:74).

The condition of the women in the peasant class during the Aztec empire was quite different. Because of their class position peasant women were denied any legal and political status. Economically, however, these women were very important. Based on the requirements for social production, the labor power of the woman of the calpulli was an important item. The product from her labor in weaving, spinning, basketry, and pottery-making would very likely be included in the items for tribute, taxes, and trade. In order to insure a good crop, women's and children's labor power was also needed in agricultural production. Although women shared in the productive process, they were still given the added responsibility of cooking, washing, and sewing for the whole family. The family organization was still that of the extended family, consisting of parents, aunts and uncles, grandparents, and cousins. Many times the lineage was based on patrilineal descent—father-right. The domestic work of the family, then, was not the sole responsibility of one woman.

The Spanish conquerers built upon this already stratified society. Except for the "legal" abolishment of slavery and a more developed division of labor, the relationship of social and domestic production in colonial Mexico remained the same. In feudal New Spain and later Mexico, women were denied any real political and social voice. Catholicism reinforced the feudal patriarchal society with its hierarchy of authority—God, Christ, Pope, King, landlord, father or husband—and its doctrine of obedience and salvation. The peasant man and woman was totally subjected to the authority of the priest and hacendado. For example, it was common for peasants to ask permission in order to marry, and then have to submit to the hacendado's first night rights. If peasants withheld crops, cheated, or in any way misbehaved, their only judge and jury was the hacendado. The woman, in Catholic doctrine, was to be a good mother, self-sacrificing, and especially obedient. The woman of the peasant class was completely subjected to the authority of men—the hacendado, the priest, the husband, and at times to the eldest son.

Again the relationship of social production to domestic production in colonial Mexico was essentially the same as in the Aztec empire. The essential difference was that the Aztec empire was a centralized, urban state, whereas, colonial Mexico was decentralized with much of the authority coming from the rural areas, from the haciendas.

The encomienda and repartimiento system of conscripting labor from the Indian population of New Spain usually required the labor of men (Cumberland, 1969:65). The resultant decrease in village populations combined with a decline due to disease, placed more of the agricultural and handicraft production in the hands of the women. Peasant women in agriculture and handicrafts were not something new; they had always been involved in social production. Because the means of production (i.e., plow, *milpas*, simple tools) belonged to the man and were located in the peasant's home *(solar)*, the woman was able to participate in both social and domestic production (NACLA, 1975). Women from wealthier peasant families many times inherited property from their fathers, but once married this property came under the jurisdiction of the husband. Women of the peasant class were important in many areas of handicraft production. They wove cloth, spun yarn, made soap and candles; some were midwives and *curanderas*, they worked in carpentry and in shoemaking. As stated earlier, the labor of women was very important in agricultural production; they helped in planting, harvesting, and processing the crops; and they went to the various local markets to sell agricultural products and handicrafts. The gains from these activities were used to provide the rent for land and other taxes that were imposed. The remainder was used to maintain the peasant family. Women in a feudal society, therefore, were important in maintaining the society and the family. But because of the need to reinforce class distinctions and the subjugation of women, the work of peasant women was not recognized by the society, and later historians and social scientists sustained this omission.

This situation remained the same throughout New Spain until 1821; after this date changes began occurring in Mexico and the northern provinces of California and Texas. In 1821 Mexico gained its independence from Spain. In Texas growing trade with the United States developed, and American citizens received permission to colonize the state, finally culminating with Texas' independence in 1836. In California the church lands were taken over by private individuals, allowing for some improvement in productive output. However, for the Church Indians of California until 1848, and for the peasant man and woman in Chiapas and Morelia, the situation remained the same. It would not be until the regime of Porfirio Diaz and the introduction of foreign investment that there would begin to occur radical change in the mode of production of Mexico.

Contemporary Roots: Capitalism and Imperialism

After 1848 the situation north of the Rio Grande developed in a completely different manner than in Mexico. Southwest United States was characterized by the development of extensive transportation lines, a development in cattle and shepherding, mining, fishing and world trade in California harbors, and the development of an industry that in the last half of the twentieth century would rival nations for power, namely agribusiness. The development of the major parts of the Southwest can be characterized as capitalist development, more contemporarily as monopoly capitalism.

Capitalism is a distinct mode of production. It changed the whole social development and the condition under which labor power was to be utilized and maintained. However, it is not the purpose of this paper to develop an exposé of the capitalist system and its development in the Southwest. For those who wish to know more about capital, I suggest they read Marx's *Capital*.

However, there are several characteristics of capitalism which are related to the question under discussion. The first is the general tendency of capitalism to concentrate private productive property in the hands of fewer and fewer people, leaving millions of expropriated petty producers in its wake. As the merchant, manufacturer, and the capitalist farmer accumulated wealth, peasants and artisans were left propertyless. On the one hand was created the new class that would dominate society, the bourgeoisie; on the other was created, from the expropriated peasants and artisans, the modern working class, the proletariat. The act of expropriating small property owners continues to this day with the collapse of small businesses and small farmers. Even more imporant, however, is the expropriation of the commodities produced by the proletariat, the appropriation of surplus value by the capitalist.

Dispossessed peasants and artisans, men, women, and children were forced to give up their labor power in exchange for a wage. Labor power became a commodity that could be purchased when needed, and the barest minimum paid for a subsistence existence. The wage given to the worker is never equal to the actual amount of value produced, and it is thus that surplus value is extracted. Thus another important characteristic of capital is developed, namely profit. Contrary to a feudal society where production is for use, production in a capitalist society is for profit. Profit is produced to reinvest in property to create more profit. These essential characteristics, production for profit, expropriation of small producers, and the expropriation of surplus value by the capitalist have manifested themselves in the various periods of capitalist development (i.e., pre-industrial capitalism, industrial capitalism, and finally monopoly capitalism). The main form of capitalism that has affected the lives of Mexicans and Chicanos has been monopoly capitalism (i.e., imperialism).

Imperialism is more than a preferred foreign policy, it is primarily characterized by the concentration of production and capital to such a high degree that monopolies are created which play a decisive role in economic life. *This is its fundamental attribute*. Other attributes are: (a) merging of industrial and bank capital to form a financial oligarchy; (b) the export of capital in the form of loans, and investment to get "cheaper wages and raw materials"; (c) division of the world among capitalist associations; (d) creation of colonies or sphere of influence; (3) state intervention in production (i.e., state capitalism); (f) migratory movements (i.e., immigration) (Lenin, 1965). There are other general characteristics, but these are the main ones that have affected the lives of Chicano men and women.

Capitalism separates the producer from the means of production and leaves the worker propertyless. Capitalism takes production entirely away from the peasant's farm, the artisan's cottage, and puts production into the factories. Whereas production under feudalism was individual, meaning each producer completed a particular commodity (i.e., shoes, wheat, etc.), under capitalism the production of commodities becomes socialized in that many persons are organized in one area producing one commodity. The worker under capitalism gives up to the capitalist all the commodities (value) produced. In return the laborer is paid a wage seemingly amounting to all the time spent at the workplace but in effect covering only part of the total value produced by the expansion of her/his labor power during that time. This separation of the producer from the means of production is the basis for the complete separation of social and domestic production.[10]

It is under capitalist production that the division between social production and domestic production is finally and completely made. Throughout class society women have been given the responsibility in the domestic area for the maintenance and reproduction of labor, but under capitalism this responsibility is separated from its relation to production. Under capitalism women are ideologically conditioned into believing that domestic work is the only area of work for which they are fitted, yet because of the requirements of the different modes of production, women have been and continue to be integral parts of production. Throughout the history of capitalism, women and children have been included as potential and actual sources of surplus value (Marx, 1973; Chicano Communication Center, 1976; Women's History Group, 1972; González, 1976). Under capitalist production, the maintenance and reproduction of labor is crucial; without it profit cannot be created, yet it remains individual and outside the sphere of social production. "The maintenance and reproduction of the working class is, and must *ever be,* a necessary condition to the reproduction of capital" (Marx, 1973:57).

If the reproduction and maintenance of the laboring class is such a necessary condition for capitalism, why then is this area of work not considered important? And furthermore, why has the role of women in social production been denied?

The answer to the first question is that private domestic consumption by the worker and his or her family is unproductive in that it does not create wages for the laborer, the family, nor wealth for the capitalist.[11] This is true for two reasons: first, because capitalists control society and because their mode of production thrives on profit, it follows that the only work which is important for the capitalist system is that which creates profit. The capitalists' only concern is that the worker appear for the time he or she is needed. The second reason has two aspects. Because the working class is deprived of the means of production, each person is responsible for his/her survival. This objective condition is reinforced by the ideology of individualism which stresses "doing your own thing," and "you can make it if you try." Therefore how workers use the wage given them is not the concern of the capitalist as long as wages do not eat a large share of profit.

> All the capitalist cares for is to reduce the laborer's individual consumption as far as possible to what is strictly necessary . . . What the laborer consumes beyond his or her maintenance is unproductive consumption. (Marx, 1973:573)[12]

On the one hand because domestic production does not create wealth for the producers it is unimportant. On the other hand, while it is a prime requirement for the capitalist, its importance is covered up with the wage given to the laborer, and by the ideology of individualism.

The answer to the second question, the hiding of women's role in social production is part of the general tendency to deny to the working class its role in the building of society. Another aspect to this question is the need to explain why women are pulled out of work during periods of recession, after conclusion of wars (i.e., end of the Second World War, the Vietnam War, etc.), and why women tend to fill domestic related jobs, (i.e., waitress, nurse, elementary school teacher). Lastly, by perpetuating this ideology women will accept their responsibility in domestic work, and become members of that ready pool of cheap labor from which capitalism can draw in times of increased production.

The Border between Feudalism and Imperialism: A Concrete Illustration

The preceding has been a theoretical explanation of how the various modes of production have affected the role of women in social development. However, the test of theory is in history. Many search and research history in the confines of libraries and museums, but historical data can become available to us by tracing the lives of those persons who have lived through history. The following is an essay written by José Lona. José Lona was a student in a course I taught at California State University Los Angeles called "Chicana Women in History and Society." As part of the required course work, students were asked to do an oral history of a woman in their lives. José's paper was chosen because the life of the woman clearly shows how women's role was conditioned by feudalism and imperialism.

The essay is included in this section of the paper because it concretely captures the condition of peasant women and also of women who were forced to immigrate with family and husband. Following it will be a brief analysis of the essay, and a brief historical analysis of imperialism in Mexico and the United States and how Chicanas are affected by this mode of production.

Biographical Sketch of the Life of an Immigrant Woman

How many sunrises and sunsets has a person seen in seventy-eight years of life? How many times has one laughed? Cried? Hurt? How many miles has one traveled? How many meals has a woman prepared in a lifetime of being a housewife? How many tortillas can be made in seventy-eight years? How many? How many? How many?

No one knows I guess, because no one has ever really counted what to some are trivial things. But to a person that has lived such a life, these things/events are not trivial. Especially not when your worth is measured by how well you can "keep house," cook, and bear children.

Surely the female child born on July 1, 1898, on the hacienda of Peñuelas, state of Aguascalientes, Mexico, never thought about her life from that perspective. All she knew was that she was God's gift to her parents and that as such, she was indebted to them and had to obey them and, of course, her elder brother also. She didn't have to obey her younger brothers or sister because of the simple fact that she herself from a very young age had had to fill the role of surrogate mother due to their mother's recurrent spells of illness. Little did it matter that her mother was a respected and known midwife, for her own illness often rendered her helpless. Picture thus, a child that since the age of seven or eight was already helping to cook, to sew, to spin, to help her mother in all the household chores and her father in the field. Indeed, one of the most cherished memories of this person is when, as a child, she and her father had to seek shelter from a brief shower by sitting under the belly of an ox until the storm blew over! This event is cherished because of the love felt for her father; of his warmth and closeness while seated under the ox. It didn't matter then, or now, that this family along with thousands of others, were being exploited. It didn't matter because the significance and impact were not understood!

It was simply accepted as part of one's life as a peon that your daily wages from the hacendado were to be twenty centavos and a dry liter of maize! The fact of the matter was that this particular family considered themselves lucky because the father was allowed to raise a little garden for the family's use. No, this family didn't consider themselves really bad off for they were existing . . . weren't they? The important thing was: that one preserve one's honor, and remain a cohesive family. And under the circumstances, this was best done by meeting head-on those challenges you could not avoid, and ignore those that you could—always humble, yet proud. To work was the best index of one's character if you were a man. If you were a woman, the abilities to run a home, to care for children, and to be docile and obedient were most cherished. Thus, for example, a girl learned not to cry in public; especially if such an action brought embarrassment to her father or to her husband! Thus when this child's father moved the family to another hacienda because of a promise that he could "share-crop," and then the ENTIRE crop was appropriated by the hacendado—leaving them hungry and even more destitute; even then she could not vent her hurt, her sorrow!

Perhaps tears and sorrow do erode one's will and resolve, and what begins as a trickle becomes a torrent that leads to collapse. I don't know. What I do know is that this particular child, woman, senior citizen, has shown strength when others were weak; resolve and determination in the worst of crises! Lest you misunderstand me, however, yes, she has, can, and does cry!

She didn't cry, however, when one fine day Zapata's revolutionaries suddenly appeared in the doorway of their hut asking for a bite to eat—"una tortilla con frijoles."

Nor did she cry when her father took her and the other young girls of the hacienda into the mountains to hide them and save them from possibly being raped and/or kidnapped. It is fitting to note, however, that to her recollection not a single girl or woman was raped or otherwise molested on her hacienda. The Revolution destroyed the hacienda and thus the peones lost their "jobs" and what little security they had. Employment was offered by the Mexican railroad to the peones and was taken—the beginning of an era of wandering from one *estación* or encampment to another; raising derailed trains and/or laying or repairing tracks in the process. This child, now a young woman, was still wandering between Aguascalientes and Zacatecas in 1914; however, she was now married. By the end of 1914, however, her husband and she, now swollen with child, had joined the rest of her family in Chihuahua, Chihuahua—still seeking roots, a better existence. In this case, however, existence coincided with bare survival! Chihuahua at this time was a city of refugees, of uprooted persons; all of them destitute, all of them hungry. Needless to say, the best memories are not the stuff of circumstances such as these. But nonetheless, memories there are . . . and plenty! Of father, husband, and older brother working all day at the railroad, coming home to a plate of beans, and leaving immediately again—each with an axe in hope of finding a pack-train with firewood that needed chopping. This dismal ritual was repeated day after incessant day, of waiting, pregnant, in long lines for HOURS in order to cash in a "ticket" for TWO French rolls and some flour . . . often reaching the door only to be told that the foodstuffs had run out, come back tomorrow!

What can one do to ease the crying, the ceaseless crying of children when they are hungry today . . . and hungrier tomorrow?

Under these circumstances, not a damn thing, except rock them and give them water; rock them when your own belly is swollen and bursting with a hungry life within! And when this life, a boy, enters this world demanding to be fed and you cannot feed it because your own body has been so decimated by hunger that you have no milk . . . what do you do? How do you explain to this mewling little creature that you, his mother, have had nothing to eat for three days since his birth, existing solely on tea made from orange-tree leaves! Yes, how much hurt can one person endure in a lifetime? How many tears can one shed? Especially when you realize that you entered the world crying and that sixteen years later, you are still in tears; in fact you are surrounded and engulfed by them!

Little wonder then that this woman-child eagerly followed her husband from Chihuahua to Texas and then to California. Again in hopes of a better life, again working for the railroad—this time however, in the United States. It must be rather disheartening, however, to suddenly find yourself with food and *nothing* to cook it in; with a home but with nothing to sleep on. Left in the middle of the desert in a country where you know neither the language nor the customs; where you know no one! Secundina adapted quickly however, and soon had food cooking . . . in clean empty coffee cans she had gathered along the tracks, along with firewood. Bedding was soon provided by another Mexican woman that was seemingly well-off, comparatively speaking. This woman soon made an offer that Secundina could not refuse—she offered her a job washing the railroad workers' clothes . . . by hand, naturally. This offer was accepted and Secundina worked daily at this chore until she developed an allergy to the strong, caustic detergent she had to use.

She declined the offer of her employer, however, to buy her son since in the opinion of her employer, she was too young and naive to care for him properly! And besides, they could use the money . . . couldn't they? Secundina and her husband soon moved to San Bernardino where another son was born and where they remained until 1918—another turning point in her life.

1918 brought with it both life and death. Life in that Secundina was again pregnant, and death in that the pandemic of flu claimed her husband.

Thus in the space of four years she became bride, mother, and widow! She returned to her family in Chihuahua where a third son was born; and vowed never to return to the United States. After the birth of her son she washed clothes in a boarding house for one Mexican peso a day—against the express wishes of her father who, however, was in no financial condition to help her nor stop her. Because of the terrible wages and the terrible hardships in Mexico, she was forced to return to the home of her *compadres* in San Bernardino in 1919, paying two cents for the crossing of the border. The second phase of Secundina's life began in 1921, when she married for the second time to a man that was to remain her husband until his death in 1969.

With this man she was to have an additional eight children. All eleven children were destined to graduate from high school, one from college. I consider this a remarkable feat, given the fact that this woman never attended school formally but instead was taught to read and write by her mother while home as a child. Who taught her mother is open to question.

Her second husband, José, was born in Guanajuato, Mexico, and emigrated to the United States with his family at a young age. He attended school to the eighth grade, at which time he had to enter the labor market . . . working for the railroad full-time in order to support his now widowed mother and four younger brothers and sisters. When he married Secundina in 1921, he was thus forced to support nine persons, not counting himself. He eventually moved his family to Watts, California, where they lived in a tent on a plot of ground that he slowly purchased. He became a naturalized American citizen and was a steady and consistent voter until shortly before his death in 1969. This man was my father, José Romolo Lona.

Secundina Macias Lona is my mother. Her formal work-history is only that which is mentioned herein. Her reason for being in the United States is the same for her as for thousands of other Mexicans that have left their native land and can be summed up in one short word . . . necessity. This is her country; the country that has seen the blood of her sons flow in war. No, she would never leave, and we would *never* let her be taken against her will.

Summary

It is open to conjecture as to whether male chauvinism or class oppression was most responsible for the subjugation of the person I interviewed, namely, my mother. This is because historically, the two have been linked much as Siamese twins and are thus inseparable. Yes, it is true that her family's original condition was caused by a class society, a semi-feudal system. And it is also true that this system was created by men to be perpetrated on other men . . . and women! As to her personal position vis-à-vis that of men it is also true that, to a point, she was also subjugated.

Given the circumstances of the family, "the times," and thus the constant struggle for survival, this subjugation was subtly shrouded in tradition and custom. And again it is open to conjecture as to whether this differentiation of the sexes did not serve a function—namely that of survival for the self, and for the family as we know it.

Perhaps now that the Chicana is more aware, more educated, more politically and socially attuned, and thus less dependent, she will assume her rightful place alongside her man—rather than below or behind him.

José Santos Lona

Secundina's life begins in the period of Porifirio Díaz. Although under Díaz many changes occurred in economic development, Mexico still manifested feudal relations of production. Her early life in Peñuelas is characteristic of many women who lived on haciendas as peasants, or lived in *ejidos*. At an early age the young women learn to do the household chores and work in the fields. At this time Secundina and her family were already becoming the kind of labor needed for capitalist production, namely propertyless wage labor. After 1910, Secundina and her family joined the countless immigrants coming into the United States. They were like the Chinese peasant of the 1850s and the European immigrant of the East—*PEASANTS WITHOUT LAND AND PROLETARIANS WITHOUT JOBS!*

José's analysis of the relation of male chauvinism and class oppression is accurately described by his statement, ". . . historically, the two have been linked much as Siamese twins and are thus, INSEPARABLE." As stated earlier, class society necessitates the explanation of the subjugation of women vis-à-vis male chauvinism. In understanding the basic relations of production, José has also exposed some of the myths surrounding domestic work and ties it to the question of survival:

> Given the circumstances of the family, "the times," and thus the constant struggle for survival, this subjugation was subtlely shrouded in tradition and custom. And again it is open to conjecture as to whether this differentiation of the sexes did not serve a function—namely that of survival for the self, and for the family as we know it.

The condition that forced Secundina's family to migrate was not due to the natural economic development of Mexico. Porifirio Díaz was the consolidator of the Mexican nation as well as the instigator of economic programs which were to leave Mexico underdeveloped. Under the Díaz regime, mines were opened up, roads and railroads were built, and agricultural production began to grow. However, this seemingly progressive development occurred because of foreign investment. Foreign investment in many ways was the major reason why the migration of thousands of Mexican workers began to occur, and also the reason why Mexico today is characterized as "underdeveloped."

Foreign capital in the late 1800s greatly affected conditions in Mexico. On the one hand industrial development began to occur, but it was a development that favored the foreign investors. The profit produced from this development would go to the owners of foreign investment and loans. Foreign penetration into the Mexican economy left thousands of peasants landless, and hundreds of proletarians jobless. This situation was further aggravated in 1883 when the first land-survey laws were passed. When the last of these infamous laws were passed, approximately one-fifth of Mexico's land was in the hands of foreign interests. The interests that were favored were primarily the railroad and mining concessions. For example, in 1880 Mexico could boast of 700 miles of railroad tracks (in comparison, the United States in 1860 had over 30,000 miles of tracks), yet four short years later 3,600 miles of track existed in Mexico. This tremendous development was financed by foreign loans and investment. By 1910 there were over 12,000 miles of track in Mexico. The majority of railroads and roads were not built to develop the internal economy of Mexico, rather they were built by the United States, Britain, and other nations to facilitate their ventures in mining and their establishment of markets (Cumberland, 1969:216).

By 1910 the United States had become the main foreign investor in Mexico. United States capitalism claimed 82 percent of goods produced in Mexico, owned approximately three quarters of mineral holdings, and investments amounted to $2 billion (Cumberland, 1969:228). Foreign capital may have been beneficial to a certain sector in Mexico, but in the early 1900s, as in 1976, the majority of the people were left in a desperate situation. The people of Mexico had to face what some call "creeping" inflation. Between the years 1876 and 1910, the price of corn rose 108 percent; the price of beans rose 163 percent; the price of chili rose 147 percent; wages increased only 60 percent (in Acuña, 1972:126). These conditions culminated in the revolution of 1910. This disruption of the Mexican society gave the impetus to dislodging the Mexican peasant from the land. Thousands fled the tragedy of war and others were left landless. The Mexican people had two alternatives, either stay in Mexico and die, or leave and join the railroad lines in the United States and hope to live.

Thus began what some have called the greatest migration of a people. McWilliams (1968) gives us a hint as to its magnitude. Between 1900 and 1930 Arizona's Mexican immigrant population increased by approximately 100,000; California's by 360,000; New Mexico's by 53,000; and Texas' by 612,000. These figures are approximations and do not actually give us the total number of people who immigrated. The majority came not as property owners, but as workers. Workers who, because of their condition of being propertyless and also because of the conditions in their country, would go to work in any area that offered the hopes of a meal.

In the 1900s the conditions in Mexico were extremely aggravated by the presence of foreign investment. The Mexican state under Díaz and other Mexican presidents allowed not only for the penetration of foreign capital, but for the direct ownership of land and raw materials by the foreign nations. This economic development did not favor the Mexican nation, thus Mexico is characterized by a semi-capitalist, semi-feudal economy. This condition made Mexico a prime source of cheap labor, cheap raw materials, and a source of profit from loans and foreign aid. Mexico under these conditions also became the most reliable source of "cheap" labor for the growing "factories in the fields," and railroads in the U.S. Southwest. The U.S. government under pressure from agribusiness interests did not patrol the U.S.-Mexican border, thus allowing farmers associations, mining interests, and railroad companies to actively recruit and contract Mexican labor (Galarza, 1964:29).

Mexican labor was considered "reliable" not only because it was cheap, but because it was easily deportable in time of economic crisis. Time and time again the U.S. government has acted as an agent in recruiting and deporting Mexican workers. The U.S. government has also made the climate ripe for U.S. corporations by setting up such programs as the infamous "Bracero Program," and since 1965, the Border Industrial Program. These programs are just two examples of how the U.S. government not only serves the interest of the monopoly capitalist, but is their main tool to maintain economic dominance.

The state has invariably been used to stop striking men, women, and children in the mines of New Mexico, in the fields of the Imperial Valley in 1973, in the school blowouts of Los Angeles in 1968, and in August of 1970, during the Chicano moratorium. The list continues and will continue until the state no longer serves the interest of the property owners.

Unlike the immigration of the Chinese in the 1850s and later the Japanese, the early Mexican migrants in the 1900s came as families. The long miles of common boundaries made it easy for whole families to migrate from Mexico to the United States. Railroad work would provide the way for families to migrate. Other families came as the result of being contracted by agribusiness. Other Mexican families would join the railroad crews, finally making their way to the United States by living in boxcars (McWilliams, 1968:167).

The women and children, in this journey of work, would many times take on jobs in or near the railroad. Chicana women would many times be hired to wash the workers' clothes, or would be hired to cook for the crew. The children would help with whatever had to be done. At other times the women would go to the fields and work, or go to the homes of the wealthy and work as maids, cooks, and wet nurses.

In Texas and California, Chicanas went to work in the huge agricultural combines. They joined other migrant laborers who went from farm to farm to pick the fruit of the season. At other times, Chicanas would go to the packing houses and canneries to prepare the produce they had just picked. As the early immigrants began to settle in towns, barrios, and cities, many of the women went to the textile and garment factories to seek employment. As more time went on and as the Chicana became more stable, some changes began to occur. Instead of wandering endlessly, workers found homes in the old railroad campsite, for example, in Watts and Roseville, California, and El Paso, Texas. Some of the new generation began getting an education. For a small minority of Chicanas and Chicanos, education was a benefit. For the majority, education meant tracking into working-class jobs. For most Chicanas life meant continual work in the home, seasonal employment in factories and stores, or unemployment and welfare.

In coming to the United States, Mexican immigrants underwent culture change. The majority of Chicanos were forced to accept the values and behavior not of "Anglos" but of the bourgeoisie, and were molded by their work place and the educational system into proletarians. Those values of Mexican feudal culture stressing male dominance and obedience were reinforced to make Mexicans into the kind of proletarians needed by the U.S. bourgeoisie (González, 1976). However, because of their condition as proletarians, Chicanos and Chicanas began to develop those cultural values and behavior peculiar to proletarians (i.e., organization, planning, discipline). Under these conditions, and because Chicanas were in the labor force, they too changed their behavior. Chicanas, as *women and proletarians*, began to participate in struggles for equality and justice.

The Chicana as part of the U.S. working class has not always been at home praying, waiting for tomorrow to come. Politically the Chicana has been involved in many historical struggles which have been aimed at advancing the interests of the poor and propertyless. With the inception of the

1910 Mexican Revolution, the Mexicana fought alongside the peasant man. While providing food and other necessities, she many times had to take a gun and fight to protect home and family.

In the fields of California and Texas, in the factories of Los Angeles and El Paso, and even in the mines of New Mexico, the Chicana has fought many a battle for better wages and better working conditions. In the communities, the Chicana has fought for decent housing and medical care, and for better education.

History is filled with the activities of the Chicana. Our task as Chicanas and as historians is to present the history of the Chicana and the Chicano in light of the capitalist development that permeated the United States and the world. To present a different history will mask the already hidden histories, and perpetuate the existence of exploitation and subjugation.

Notes

I would like to express my appreciation to Rosalinda González and Gilbert González for their help in clarifying and organizing the main points in this paper. I also want to thank Getachew Alemu and Felicitas Apodaca for their consistent encouragement.

1. The international border created by the Treaty de Guadalupe Hidalgo is highly important and cannot be taken lightly. On the northern side the strongest capitalist nation would develop, rendering to its inhabitants a distinct social, cultural, and economic system. While on the southern side a nation would develop that would be plagued by imperialist penetration. In this sense I use the term *Chicano* and *Mexican American* to refer to those people born and living in the United States of Mexican parentage, and *Mexicano* to those born and living in Mexico. These categories are not finite, involved is the immigrant Mexican in the United States. For purposes of historical clarification these people are placed with Chicanos because of their objective condition as members of the working class in the United States. For more clarification on the differences between the United States and Mexico see Fernández and Ocampo (1974).

2. For further clarification on this point see Bailey (1966) and Forbes (1960).

3. For recent exceptions to this tendency see Arroyo (1974), Farah Strike Support Committee (1974), and González (1976).

4. Mode of production refers to a particular way in which society produces and reproduces itself. More concretely it refers to the forces of production, including raw materials, labor power, level of development of technology and silence. The second aspect of the mode of production is the relations of production, or the way society comes together to produce and exchange. Involved in this second aspect are class relations.

5. Reproduction and maintenance of labor power refers to the actual feeding, clothing, housing, and procreation of male and female labor.

6. For further information on feudal society see Bloch (1961), Dobb (1973), and Rowbotham (1974).

7. *Encomiendas* and *repartimientos* were the two main historical forms of land grants by which the Spanish landlord received tribute and labor services from the native population.

8. The *calpulli* was the town district occupied and used by a single clan possessing *use* but not property rights.

9. *Pochtecas* were the merchants during the time of the Aztec empire.

10. Social production begins to become distinguished from domestic production when there begins to be produced a surplus in commodities. This development is reinforced by further divisions of labor, primarily by the division between property owners and the propertyless. Capitalism is the mode of production that thoroughly separates social production from domestic production; this is because capitalism leaves the working class with no private productive property, and because capitalism has the highest development of private property (i.e., monopoly capitalism).

11. Laborers engage in two types of consumption. One type is the consumption of the means of production. In other words, consuming the raw materials and machinery that go into the commodities which produce profit. The second type involves the consumption by which the individual provides for himself and the family. "The result of the first is, that the capitalist lives; of the other, that the laborer lives" (Marx, 1973:571).

12. In reading "Simple Reproduction" of *Capital,* it is interesting to note that while Marx reached his own conclusion on productive and unproductive consumption, Marx's footnotes indicate that the economist Ricardo and Malthus had advocated the necessity of limiting laborer's personal consumption (see Marx, 1973:573, footnote 3 and 4).

References

Acuña, Rodolfo. 1972. Occupied America: The Chicano's Struggle toward Liberation. San Francisco: Canfield Press.

Allen, Ruth. 1931. "Mexican Peon Women in Texas," *Sociology and Social Research* 16 (November–December): 131–42.

Arroyo, Laura E. 1974. "Industrial and Occupational Distribution of Chicana Workers," *Aztlán* IV(2): 243–382.

Bailey, L. R. 1966. *Indian Slave Trade in the Southwest.* Los Angeles: Western Lore Press.

Bloch, Marc. 1961. *Feudal Society.* Chicago: University of Chicago Press.

Campa. 1973. "The Mexican-American in Historical Perspective," in Renato Rosaldo and others, *Chicano: The Evolution of a People.* Minneapolis: Winston Press.

Chevalier, François. 1972. *Land and Society in Colonial Mexico, The Great Hacienda.* Berkeley: University of California Press.

Chicano Communications Center. 1976. *450 Years of Chicano History*. Albuquerque: Chicano Communication Center.

Cumberland, Charles C. 1968. *Mexico, the Struggle for Modernity*. New York: Oxford University Press.

Dobb, Maurice. 1973. *Studies in the Development of Capitalism*. New York: International Publishers.

Engels, Frederick. 1973. *The Origin of the Family, Private Property and the State*. New York: International Publishers.

Farah Strike Support Committee. 1974. *Chicanos Strike at Farah*. San Francisco: United Front Press.

Fernández, Raúl, and José Ocampo. 1974. "The Latin American Revolution: A Theory of Imperialism, Not Dependence," *Latin American Perspectives* I (Spring): 30–61.

Forbes, J. D. 1960 *Apache, Navajo and Spaniard*. Norman: University of Oklahoma Press.

Galarza, Ernesto. 1964. *Merchants of Labor*. Santa Barbara, CA: McNally & Loftin Publishers.

González, Rosalinda M. 1976. "A Review of the Literature on Mexican and Mexican American Women Workers in the United States Southwest, 1900–1975," Unpublished, University of California at Irvine, Program in Comparative Culture.

Green, George N. 1971. "ILGWU in Texas, 1930–1970," *The Journal of Mexican American History* (Spring): 144–69.

Lenin, V. I. 1965. *Imperialism, The Highest Stage of Capitalism*. Peking: Foreign Languages Press.

Marx, Karl. 1970. *A Contribution to the Critique of Political Economy*. New York: International Publishers.

———. 1973. *Capital*, vol. I. New York: International Publishers.

Marx, Karl, and Frederick Engels. 1972. *The German Ideology*. New York: International Publishers.

Marx, Karl and others. 1969. *The Woman Question*. New York: International Publishers.

McWilliams, Carey. 1968. *North from Mexico*. New York: Greenwood Press.

———. 1971. *Factories in the Field*. Santa Barbara, CA: Peregrine Publishers.

NACLA. 1975. "Women's Labor," *Latin America and Empire Report*, IX (September).

Rowbotham, Sheila. 1974. *Hidden from History*. New York: Pantheon Books.

Soustelle, Jacques. 1975. *Daily Life of the Aztecs*. Stanford: Stanford University Press.

Taylor, Paul S. 1971. *An American-Mexican Frontier*. New York: Russell and Russell.

*   *   *

Questions

1. Why "must" the development of history be based on something more tangible than ideas, dates, and individuals? What are the "tangible" foundations Apodaca suggests and why should we not accept other explanations as convincing?

2. Apodaca mentions magic, theology, human nature, and male superiority as explanations that have been used to justify the supremacy of one class over another. What is your own explanation why there are social inequalities, why a few people are extremely rich and most are poor?

3. Why is the relation between domestic and social production so important for understanding the status of women, whether in Aztec society, colonial Mexico, or the Southwest of the United States in the nineteenth century? Does it have any importance in the twenty-first-century global economy? Generally speaking, in what sort of domestic production are women involved today?

4. To what extent is Secundina's life "conditioned" by feudalism and imperialism (material or objective conditions) as opposed to the choices she and her family made (subjective conditions)?

5. Apodaca implies that rather than an Anglo culture there is a bourgeoisie culture and that rather than a Mexican or Chicano culture there is a "proletariat" (working-class) culture. How does this definition of culture differ from other definitions in this reader or elsewhere?

CHAPTER FOUR

Chicanology II: Law, Class Struggle, and Power/Knowledge

Francisco Hernández Vázquez

In this text, Vázquez explores with another way of looking at power other than the methods previously discussed, the liberal-democratic (split power into three branches) or the Marxist way (it is a class struggle for control of the means of production). [1] It proposes that the reason we have such a hard time addressing and solving social problems is that power flows in ways that are difficult to understand using these conventional categories. It proposes some guidelines and then provides an example by applying these guidelines to the Mexican population in the United States

*   *   *

[There] is no power relation without the correlative constitution of a field of knowledge, nor any knowledge that does not presuppose and constitute at the same time power relations.

Michel Foucault, *Discipline and Punish*

Taking this quote as a point of departure, it follows that the study of Latino/a thought requires the study of the nature of power. Presently, to understand Latino/a thought and the social and environmental issues that Latinos/as in the United States have to face, there are two predominant methods. One is liberalism, which was designed to deal with absolute power through the establishment of a Constitution that splits power into three branches. The other one is Marxism, which deals with the oppressive exercise of power by focusing on the economic structure of society and the struggle that arises between social classes (depending on their position within the economic structure). The preceding two chapters by Vázquez and Apodaca provide ample examples of these methods. Here we want to address an obvious question that points to the gap between the methods to deal with power and the actual results: "Why, despite worldwide, centuries-long efforts to establish a just society through either constitutions or revolution, 'we, the people,' have not solved critical social problems? Why is it that in many cases we seem to be making the situation even worse?" Closer to home, in the United States, the war in Iraq, the denial of climate changes, the attempts to reverse the social gains from the New Deal and the Civil Rights movement, are but a few examples of the continuing exercise of power beyond the established legal and traditional, ethical structures. Abuses of power are also found throughout Latin America (despite the recent gains in terms of giving representation to the voiceless indigenous and other oppressed populations).

Here we look at an additional, arguably complementary method to study power. More specifically, how power/knowledge relations tend to hide the exercise of political and economic power in such a way that it goes beyond the law and beyond class struggle. This exercise of power is manifested through *discourse*, meaning when language and power combine in such a way that, for better or for worse, they impact human bodies, institutions, and even how we generally perceive reality. Though there are important differences, discourse is sometimes called master narrative, a political economy of knowledge, a **paradigm,** and in this reader, games of truth. As applied to Latinos and Latinas we call this power/knowledge discourse *Chicanology*. Recent examples of this kind of discourse are the debates, attitudes, legislation, and ordinances regarding immigration. Because of his prominence and influence in and outside of academia, a main figure in this discourse is Harvard professor Samuel P. Huntington. He warns that Mexicans are fundamentally different from other U.S. Americans and that they present a threat to the identity and the security of the United States.[2]

A few caveats are in order from the start: This discussion does not mean to imply that the exercise of power can be harnessed once and for all and then we can all live happily ever after. Nor does the author mean that this method is superior to Marxist or conventional political analyses. A realistic perspective, however, can also be based on the realization that constant struggle is part of life and that we must remain vigilant and move along the transformations of power relations to first uncover and then address abuses of power. *Uncover* is the key word here because hegemonic power is more effective to the extent that it remains invisible, unrecognized, denied, or ignored. Consequently, to detect the exercise of power we need to look not at the institutions that clearly and visibly tend to oppress Latinos/as. We need to look, rather, at the reactions to the impact that power has on the most vulnerable human bodies. From this perspective, an illegal act may be interpreted as a reaction to a specific yet almost invisible discourse that tends to define the power relations between Latinos/as and the dominant culture of the United States.

Therefore, we begin with an account of an airplane hijacking for the specific purpose of revealing to the world the oppressive conditions that confront Mexicans in the United States. Something that, apparently, was not known and that needed to be said to force people to change this situation. This account also provides the elements to define the boundaries of Chicanology, a specific discourse that tends to define the power relations between Latinos/as and the dominant culture of the United States.

Secondly, because we are dealing here with the question of why it is so difficult to create an equitable society, we will briefly examine two predominant theories of power (liberalism and Marxism), their history, their differences, and their common assumption that power is always repressive and always located in the group, institution, or person who holds the power. As an alternative (or complementary) explanation of the nature of power, we examine the *parallel* historical development of our legal procedures (law as a way to harness absolute power) along with the development of the scientific study of humans (social science disciplines like anthropology, psychology, sociology, economics, etc.). The key point is that laws that were designed to determine the legitimacy of power have combined with scientific truths, norms, rules, and laws of human behavior to create a disciplinary discourse that tends to hide (and at the same time make more effective) the actual exercise of power.

In other words, we say knowledge is power but we do not consider that power is also knowledge. Therefore, what is proposed is that a disciplinary power is at work here; it overlaps and confuses the scientific "truth" of social disciplines with the legal truth of our legal institutions and procedures. Similar to what Paulo Freire describes in *Pedagogy of the Oppressed*, on the one hand this disciplinary power increases the knowledge and ability of the individual, and on the other hand it limits the behavior of the individual. This is also similar to Antonio Gramsci's notion of subtle almost invisible control that he termed **hegemony.** In other words, if the exercise of power is not contained by our constitutional laws or our rights, then perhaps these games of truth ("truthiness" according to Stephen Colbert) may be at the heart of why we cannot adequately address social problems.

The third part of this essay briefly illustrates one particular discourse that transformed the term *Chicano* from a pejorative term to a social movement.

Paradoxically, this was done through the acquisition of social science knowledge and the establishment of an academic interdisciplinary power that also included the arts. This is an anti-hegemonic, liberation movement, a struggle against domination, but who exactly is the enemy here? What is the master narrative, the dominant discourse? Using a similar analysis of power, the African scholar V.Y. Mudimbe calls it the "Western episteme [knowledge]," whereas the Palestinian-American scholar Edward Said names it "Orientalism." Here the author refers to this discourse as Chicanology (a combination of the word *Chicano*—which started of as a pejorative term and a source marginalized, illegitimate knowledge and became a powerful term to designate a social renaissance—and *logos*, a Greek word meaning "what is said" or "the logic of."

In the fourth and final section of this chapter I come back to the original story of the hijack and use it as a base to provide examples of some of the procedures through which Chicanology discourse works to exercise its power over the voices of the Latino/a people.

If Only People Knew:
Mapping the Geography of Latino/a Discourse

In a poem titled "World" the late Ricardo Sánchez, a Chicano poet that went from prison to obtain a Ph.D. in literature, addresses the issue of law and power:

> World/i assail you/and/question seriously/all you espouse/in/the way/of civil rights/and/other power projections/. . . for/i know that the people/will never know/what it is/that they must know . . .

He also notes the key question that concerns us here: "and i know/that you shall ever/fear/to extend the knowledge/that shall free us . . ."[3]

Perhaps this is why, on April 13, 1972, Ricardo Chávez Ortiz, a Mexican national, hijacked a Frontier Airlines 737 Jet from Albuquerque, New Mexico, with an unloaded gun. The hijacker ordered the plane flown to Los Angeles, California. According to the *Los Angeles Times*, his request was not for money or to be flown somewhere or to release prisoners. He requested "live broadcast time in which to voice the frustrations of a man who feared the world would not listen to his problems, and those of his people, under any other circumstances."

Thus, in terms of the analysis here discussed, this event shows power at its extremes. It involves an illegal act, the threat of violence, and potentially, an international incident. It also involves issues that were being discussed at the academic level. Ironically, while Chicano faculty and students were trying *to prove* the truth of their statements based on their research, Chávez Ortiz *appropriated the means* to attempt to give the status of truth to his statements.

Addressing himself to Anglo Americans, Chávez Ortiz made the following statements:

> I have felt an obligation to do this bad deed but not only for the situation of my family but . . . it is much more delicate and dangerous for the new generation than you can imagine . . . I (told) myself: ask for what you need and make them realize that we are also the children of god . . . I wanted to attract the attention of everyone in this nation and to say to everyone once and for all, what type of human beings we are . . . What I need to say to you and that you need to pay very close attention to (is that) on the path we are following, there are going to come very disastrous and terrible days . . . All you do is let the days go by and maybe tomorrow, maybe the next day, there will be a chance, there will be a new governor or a new president, yakkity, yakkity . . .
>
> Don't always think about your good clothes and having enough to eat and your good friends . . . The Americans (Anglos) go and send rockets to the moon. Yes, go ahead and do whatever you want to do while we become rebellious . . .
>
> All I want is for Mexicans to know that this is Mexican land and always will be . . . This land that we are working on was a divine gift . . . I would not admit to any son of a bitch that my nation is for sale or in servitude . . .
>
> I was held in captivity for two years and all I had was the right to search through garbage cans for something to eat. I also worked for two years without being paid one single cent . . . Where was justice at this time? Where were the authorities? . . . I have a great fear of going out into the street because I am afraid that at any moment a policeman will take his pistol and shoot me . . .[4]

Thus, in thirty-five minutes of airtime, bought with the violation of a federal law, Chávez Ortiz revealed to the world the harshness that surrounds Latino/a discourse. His statements include the following key points: (1) an assertion of the basic humanity of the Latino/a with reference to God, (2) Anglo indifference to social justice and emphasis on materialistic values, (3) empty political promises, (4) the land grab, (5) Latino/a nationalism, (6) the imposition of a colonial labor system, and (7) police brutality.

This collection of observations and accusations, however, is not only the "frustrations of a man" or an example of individual alienation. It is that and much more: leaving aside the question of how "aware" he was of the significance of his act, the statements he made are equivalent to a microcosm of Latino/a discourse, a holographic fragment of the Latino/a historical experience.

Chávez Ortiz's statements, furthermore, point to a series of what we might call "governing" statements that continuously emerge, to some extent or another, as key issues in Latino/a history. These are: (1) racial theories, (2) the land grab, (3) the establishment of a colonial labor system, (4) the system of justice, (5) nationalistic attitude, (6) education, (7) internal divisions, and (8) the right of self preservation. In other words, these statements give Latino/a discourse, a sort of *regularity* that has been in operation since the United States invaded Northern México. These governing statements appear on a regular basis but also at different levels and times, more delicately articulated, more clearly delimited and localized, depending on the appearance of new notions, discoveries, technical improvements and conceptual transformations.

For example, one could take trace these metamorphoses from, say, the guerrilla tactics of Juan N. Cortina or Las Gorras Blancas, the social banditry of Tiburcio Vásquez or Joaquín Murrieta, the increasing sophistication in organizing from the *mutualistas* (mutual aid societies), *Magonistas*, and other union efforts to the G. I. Forum, League of United Latin American Citizens (LULAC), the Viva Kennedy Clubs and *La Raza Unida* Party, etc.

The journey might also take us to a different level of power/knowledge with the emergence of a particular discourse: the Chicano and its student movement, artistic renaissance, and studies/discipline. Today we witness the appearance of a new object of political, economic, and epistemological attention: the Hispanic and the Latino/a. Despite the variation, that is, no matter the level of specificity of the statements, they constitute a Latino/a discursive regularity (a repetition of the same issues) because of the implicit or explicit threat, or actual practice of violence. In other words, we keep saying the same thing, making the same statements, pointing out the same injustices, and struggling against them the same way. Although there are some victories along the way, with subtle and important variations, history keeps repeating itself. The power is there, pulsing along, but invisible when it comes to social change. Before we illustrate Chicano discourse more specifically, it is necessary to consider explanations of the nature and the exercise of power.

The Nature of Power and Social Justice

What is it about power that makes social problems difficult to solve? To address this we need to explore, in general terms, two dominant theories of power. Let us begin by noting differences and similarities. Liberalism attempts to manage the exercise of power through the establishment of a social contract, whereas Marxism does so through revolution. What they both have in common is that they see power as repression and thus, as something negative.

In chapter 2, we looked at how the absolute power of the monarch was split into three branches governed by a constitution and subjected to the rule of law and of rights. This approach is based on the conception of power as an original right that is given up in the establishment of sovereignty, as if it were a commodity; the contract then becomes the broker of political power. A power so constituted becomes oppressive whenever it goes beyond the contract. Combined with an emphasis on free, private enterprise, this leads to what may be called democratic capitalism. When combined with an emphasis on the good of the entire society this leads to what may be called democratic socialism.

On the Marxist side, we have an approach that analyzes political power in accordance with war or repression. In this view, oppression is not just a violation of the contract, but also the continuation of a relation of dominations *despite* the contract. From this perspective, for example, the liberal democratic division of power (the Constitution with its distribution of law and rights) itself only masks the realities of the struggle between "the haves" and the "have-nots." This implies that although the wealth of a nation is created from everyone's labor, only a few are able to accumulate wealth. Consequently, revolution becomes necessary: Power must be wrestled away from those who control the economy. To create a more equitable society, Marxist governments tend to establish a controlled economy, although, as a result of the dismal record of many of these efforts, in Cuba, China and Viet Nam, some sort of free enterprise is being allowed.

What these two attempts at harnessing power have in common is that they establish a fundamental right: either the rights and laws established by society through a constitution or the right to establish a classless society. In other words, power is conceived as being centered on one entity, one place, either the constitution or class struggle), just as it used to be thought of being centered on the monarch during medieval times.[5] What if, however, the exercise of power goes beyond the constraints imposed by law and rights (as the Democrats would have it), and what if it also goes beyond the class struggle (as the Marxists insist)?

Some argue that power resides in the nation-state, which worldwide claims absolute power (sovereignty, law, rights), and humans are not considered legal entities unless they are citizens of a nation-state. This argument implies that power is repressive, especially now with the war against terrorism, the curtailment of civil rights, and the justice system functioning as a punitive instrument. But the relations of power necessarily extend beyond the limits of the state. This is so for two reasons: First, because the state for all the might of its mechanisms (bureaucracies, agencies, departments, etc.) is far from being able to occupy the whole field of actual power relations. For example, prisons can only be run with the cooperation of the prisoners, even though technically they do not "have the right" to do so. Secondly, this is so because the state can only operate on the basis of other already existing social relations (political, social, cultural, entertainment, religious and economic, ethnic, historical, etc.). As Manuel Castells points out, in the 1990s, between "global networks and cultural identities, the institutions of society and particularly the nations-state, were shaken in their foundations and challenged in their legitimacy."[6]

Perhaps power has yet to be harnessed, and we need to look at other ways to understand the way power is actually exercised. What are the alternatives to the liberal and democratic or Marxist and socialist concepts of power?

Let us engage for a moment into a theoretical discussion. One way is to look at the relations that are created between power and knowledge. Historically, there has been a parallel evolution between the establishment of the rule of law and rights on the one hand, and the development of the social sciences on the other. These social sciences are applied as norms and almost invisibly these norms become disciplinary mechanisms. In this manner, a gray area is created in which the power that is exercised is not just legal power but disciplinary power.

During the last three hundred years there has been a shift on how power is exercised. Under feudalism, the monarch's power was dependent on agricultural production, on the wealth and commodities that had to be paid as tribute in addition to other levies and legal obligations, and the monarch had absolute power to do or undo and it was usually put to use in full capacity. Sovereignty, the ultimate authority, was invested in the monarch. The only limit to the monarch became, little by little, the rule of law. After the industrial, and the consequent French and U.S. American revolutions, the exercise of power underwent a significant change. Power became dependent on human bodies and what they do, on their time and labor, and continuous surveillance. Also, power was used in small amounts with the expectation of maximum return. The ultimate authority was placed on the sovereignty of the people. Along with this development, however, there is also a parallel development of the social or human sciences (anthropology, sociology, psychology, political science, and economics), which are concerned with rules and norms of behavior. However, when social sciences speak of a rule they do not mean a *legal* rule. At the same time, norms do imply a process of normalization.

Thus, procedures of normalization increasingly take over procedures of law.[7] In other words, scientific truth somehow becomes part of a legal power to dictate to people what is correct or incorrect behavior.

Disciplines, as bodies of knowledge, truth, and power, as a scientific discourse, tend to increase the forces of the human body (by making them more productive) and diminish these same forces (by making them more politically obedient). They separate power from the human body: On one side discipline forms it into an "aptitude," a "capacity," which it seeks to increase, and on the other side, it reverses the course of the energy, the power that might result from it, and turns it into a relation of strict subjection.[8] As noted before, this is precisely what Freire in his book *Pedagogy of the Oppressed* calls *education for domination* as opposed to *education for liberation.*[9]

In other words, if economic exploitation separates the force and the product of labor (according to Marxist theory), a discourse of disciplinary coercion establishes in the individual the constricting link between an increased aptitude and an increased domination. To be sure, scientific and normative and legal procedures have intersected in a variety of ways. Some are positive such as the Brandeis brief (the first brief in the United States that relied on analysis of factual sociological data rather than pure legal theory to argue a case, and similarly, later on the *Brown v. the Board of Education* [1964] decision that desegregated schools).

Others are negative such as the sociological and anthropological "findings" that defined the U.S. Mexican as belonging to an unchanging traditional culture.[10] Raymund Paredes points out how anti-Mexican sentiment got a big boost the influential *History of America* by William Robertson: "[H]e essentially took old [negative] images and couched them in a variety of 18th century scientism."[11] A recent and most dramatic example of the relationships among social science, public policy, and punitive disciplinary mechanisms is the linking of race with crime and its impact on the black population. At a time when crime rates are dropping, the United States with 5 percent of the population, houses 25 percent of the world's inmates and they are predominantly black and brown. This has led to imprisonment rates that are the greatest racial disparity of any other social arena in U.S. life: At eight-to-one, the black-to-white ratio of incarceration rates dwarfs the two-to-one unemployment ratio. Arguably, this was a strategy to reverse the gains of the black civil rights movement.[12] The problem, of course, is not the social sciences or other disciplines per se, but the insidious ways in which power establishes particular relationships with knowledge that lead to social injustice.[13] This helps to understand why the struggle for social justice is everlasting.

A discourse of disciplinary normalization, then, seems to be coming into increasing conflict with the juridical systems of sovereignty. Thus, to save us from terrorists we need to go beyond the U.S. Constitution. But the critical problem is that against the transgression of disciplinary mechanisms, against the ascent of a power tied to scientific knowledge, we find that there is no solid recourse available to us today, except that which lies in the return to a theory of law and rights organized around sovereignty. In other words, every time we have a problem the only solution is to make more laws. This is the predicament in which we find ourselves today.

Let us reflect on how far we have come in our theoretical discussion of power/knowledge. We hear the saying that "knowledge is power" but not the reverse. Yet, "power is knowledge" or, rather power *produces* knowledge because it never ceases its interrogation, inquisition, or registration of truth. It institutionalizes, professionalizes, and rewards its pursuit. *The key point is that, as a material entity, discourse is like a political economy of truth and knowledge*, a master narrative, a paradigm and in this book, games of truth, and it can be characterized as having the following important traits:

1. Truth is centered on scientific discourse and the institutions that produce it.
2. It is subject to constant economic and political manipulation (for economic production and for political power).
3. It is the object of immense diffusion and consumption (circulating through systems of education and information).
4. It is produced and transmitted under the control, dominant if not exclusive, of a few great political and economic systems (university, media, military, or writing).
5. Lastly, it is the issue of political debate and social confrontation (ideological struggle such as between liberals and conservatives, Democrats and Republicans, etc.).[14]

So, in the final analysis we must produce truth as we must produce wealth. Indeed, we must produce truth to produce wealth in the first place. We are also subjected to truth in the sense that it is truth that makes the laws, that produces the true discourse, which, at least partially, decides the effects of power. In the end, we are judged, condemned, classified, and destined to a certain mode of living or dying, as a function of the true discourses, which are the bearers of the specific effects of power.[15]

Note, however, that knowledge is not so much true or false as it is legitimate or illegitimate for a particular set of power relations. In other words, it is not a battle "on behalf" of truth but a struggle "about the status of truth" and the political and economic roles it plays. This does not necessarily mean truth is relative. Its impact on the human body and the ecology that supports is probably the closest that we can get to an "ultimate" truth.

To summarize this theoretical discussion, we have come full circle in the examination of the liberal and the Marxist theories of power and their limitations. We discussed the historical reasons for their common grounding in the analysis of power in terms of repression and sovereignty and presented a power/knowledge analysis that reverses the trajectory followed by these two theories of power.

This analysis has led us to the discovery of an exercise of power that simultaneously increases the forces of domination, and improves the force and efficacy of its techniques of domination. This is made possible by disciplinary discourses, such as the social sciences, which, behind a constant pursuit of scientific truth, mask their inherent domination and begin to invade the domain of the law and rights.

In analyzing power, then, there are certain guidelines to keep in mind:

1. Where there is power there is resistance. One should try to locate power at the extreme points of its exercise, where it is less legal in character (e.g., issues such as Latino/a gangs, delinquency, deviancy, school drop/push outs, imprisonment, immigrant status, etc.).

2. The analysis of power should not concern itself with power at the level of conscious intention or decision. The analysis is on the everyday life, on how things work at the level of ongoing subjugation, those continuous processes, which target the labor of our human bodies, dictate our behaviors, and even attempt to govern our gestures. For example, to produce a gang member you can expose a child to poverty, negative images about his ethnic identity, treat him or her with disrespect, interact only when some sort of rule has been broken.

3. Power is not to be taken as a phenomenon of one individual's domination over others or that of one group or class over others. Power must be analyzed as something, which circulates, as a process, as a continuous chain, a rhizome. It is never localized here and there, never in anybody's hands, never appropriated as a commodity or piece of wealth.

4. Power comes from below. The important point is not to attempt some kind of deduction of power starting at the top but rather conduct an ascending analysis of power, starting from its micro mechanisms and then see how these mechanisms of power have been colonized, invested, transformed, and extended.

94 ⌇ Part I: Origins and Theories

5. Power "happens" in the moment of the interaction, it is not something separate from it. Relations of power are not in some kind of external, superstructural relationship with respect to other types of relationships such as economic processes, knowledge relationships, sexual relations, etc.[16]

Power/Knowledge Analysis of Chicano/a Discourse

Keeping these guidelines in mind, let us do a brief analysis of the discourse of the Chicano movement in the form of a story or resistance. We may begin by asking the following questions: In such a specific discourse what are the most immediate, the most local power relations at work? How did they make possible this type of discourse? Conversely, how are these discourses used to support power relations? How is the action of these power relations modified by their exercise? Finally, how are such power relations linked to one another according to the logic of a great strategy?

The word Chicano appears wherever there are Mexican people. It is a poetic derivation of Mexicano with the x pronounced with the original Nahuatl sound sh. As part of Mexican American folklore, it appears not only along the U.S. Mexican border but also in Mexican American communities in the Midwest and in states like Colorado. Until it emerged in print, however, it lacked materiality, or as the Mexican saying goes, it was a word that "was carried away by the wind." In technical terms, it was not an object supported by the dominant discourse and consequently it was invisible to most of U.S. society. In the 1940s Mario Suárez took the word, and for the first time, infused it with the status of printed literature by using it in his short stories. As power relations shifted twenty years later, the word Chicano/a was born as a statement, and it became powerful enough to spawn other terms, such as Brown Power and La Nueva Raza. Another, more recent shift led to a decline of the visibility of Chicano/a. Now, for example, we have Chicano/Latino or Raza Studies.

We say that Chicano/a discourse was born in the 1960s, when it was constructed as an object of discourse. At that time there was a particular set of power relations that opened up subjective positions (these are positions of power that individuals who are at the right place at the right time may occupy). Leaders such as César E. Chávez, José Angel Gutierrez, Corky Gonzales, and Reies Tijerina and a critical mass of individuals (mostly university and high school students) occupied these positions and gave their voices the status of truth.

There were also Chicano/a concepts (such as Chicano power, internal colonialism, Marxism, cultural nationalism, the nation of Aztlán, Brown Berets, hijas de Cuauhtémoc, Chicana feminism, and school walkouts) that fit into the *conceptual scheme* of the dominant society of the 1960s (Black Power, Black Panthers, civil rights, feminism, the Viet Nam War, the counterculture, revolution). Finally, Chicano/a discourse depended on the support or opposition of numerous political and economic *institutions* (high schools, universities, political organizations such as MECha–*Movimiento Estudiantil Chicano de Aztlán*, Raza Unida Party, foundations, federal, state and local governments, barrios, and the military, the police and many others).

When the prophetic Suárez first used the word *Chicano* it was just that, a word; later it was infused with power relations and became a social movement with its own labor unions, political party, academic departments in universities, national association, journals, scholarships, and doctoral programs.

We must, however, face the hard question: Did Chicano discourse have an impact on the lives of the Chicano people? Are they and American society in general better off because of it? Chicano/a discourse became a Chicano/a renaissance in areas such as visual art, music, poetry, theater, film, prose, and academic journals. But that is not all. There were also politics by other means: mass demonstrations, violence, and, unfortunately, deaths. The ultimate impact of the power of discourse is on the human body. In other words, power/knowledge becomes bio-power, where and when it impacts life.

Thus, Chicano discourse was in reality just another version of a struggle of resistance against social injustices that are illustrated in this reader. Whether it is against institutional racism, anti-Mexican sentiment, the quest for democracy continues. The moral of the story, up to this point, is that when language combines with diverse power relations to form statements and discourses, and there is a confluence of material conditions and historical circumstances, social change is likely to occur. The trick is, of course, to be able to read historical events to know when power relations will assume a propitious form. This is such a complex task because there is a principle of uncertainty involved; it is no wonder social change is so difficult to achieve, whether by peaceful or violent means.

How do these examples, theories and guidelines help us understand the status of marginalized people? What is their status within the political economy of knowledge and truth we have just defined?

Chicanology, African, and Oriental Discourses

Before dealing with Latino/a thought, let us briefly look at how power/knowledge analyses has been applied to the realities of marginalized people in Africa and the part of the world known as the Orient. In *The Invention of Africa*, Mudimbe is "directly concerned with the processes of transformation of types of knowledge."[17] Using the power/knowledge analysis, he contrasts the knowledge and the everyday realities of the African people with the knowledge of a Western dominant discourse *about* African people. He finds that attempts to address, to articulate, the actual social realities of the African people are subjected to "a silent dependence on a Western episteme [dominant discourse]. In the same vein, Said states, in his analysis of scholarly and other studies that deal with the Orient:

> Orientalism can be discussed and analyzed as the corporate institution for dealing with the Orient—dealing with it by making statements about it, authorizing views of it, describing it, by teaching it, settling it, ruling over it: in short, Orientalism as a Western style for dominating, restructuring, and having authority over the Orient . . .
>
> My contention is that without examining Orientalism as a discourse one cannot possibly understand the enormously systematic discipline by which European culture was able to manage—and even produce—the Orient politically, sociologically, militarily, ideologically, scientifically, and imaginatively during the post-Enlightenment period.
>
> Moreover, so authoritative a position did Orientalism have that I believe no one writing, thinking or acting on the Orient could do so without taking into account the limitations on thought and action imposed by Orientalism.
>
> In brief, because of Orientalism the Orient was not (and is not) a free subject of thought or action. This is not to say that Orientalism unilaterally determines what can be said about the Orient, but that it is the whole network of interests inevitably brought to bear on (an therefore always involved in) any occasion when that peculiar entity "the Orient" is in question.[18]

What Mudimbe and Said are stating here are discourses that take a position against a dominant body of knowledge defined as a discourse of the West that claims to represent but really fabricates a stereotyped version of Africans and "Orientals". But what is that Anglo body of knowledge that "invents" Chicanos, what is the Latino/a counterpart to Orientalism? What exactly are the power relations that Chicanos/as are resisting? Who, what is the enemy?

To be sure, there are stereotyped images of the Latino/a present almost everywhere. Carlos E. Cortés for example, has conceptualized the societal curriculum: "that massive, ongoing informal curriculum of family, peer groups, neighborhoods, mass media, and other socializing factors which 'educate' us throughout our entire lives."[19] Much longer than one lifetime, however, there is also a "historical curriculum" known as "the Black Legend" which can be traced to the sixteenth century.[20] Raymund A. Paredes finds a combination of anti-Catholic, anti-Hispanic, and eventually, anti-Mexican attitudes imbedded in American literature starting with what was available to the English colonists first in the form of popular almanacs, later magazines "took up the fight" and the Dudleian lecture series was established at Harvard in 1750. Part of this series was dedicated to "the detecting and convicting and exposing of the idolatry of the Romish church . . ."[21]

In the early twentieth century, we find the academic disciplines of sociology and anthropology, which played a similar role. They, too, defined Chicanos in terms of a traditional culture, as a people who were not free subjects of thought or action.[22] Similarly, Américo Paredes in his search for the folklore of the Anglo Texan finds what he calls "the Texas Legend," which he attempts to categorize as either folklore, fact or "something else"[23] Echoing the discourse that has been functioning since the sixteenth century, the Texas Legend basically states that "the Mexican is cruel by nature . . . cowardly and treacherous . . . as degenerate a specimen of humanity as found anywhere . . . he descends from the Spaniards, a second rate type of European, and from the equally substandard Indian of México . . . and the Mexican has always recognized the Texan as his superior."[24]

Paredes is puzzled to find this legend *not* in the cowboy ballads, the play-party songs, or the folktales of the common people of Texas, but from another ilk of people all together. From a power/knowledge perspective, however, it is not surprising that he traces the legend to "the written works of the literary and the educated" (where power knowledge is exercised) and "among a class of rootless adventurers who have used the legend for their own purposes (where raw, physical power is exercised). Paredes concludes that this legend is pseudo-folklore that, "disguised as fact," still plays a major role in Texas (we might say Latino/a) history.[25] In effect, as noted before, the most recent manifestation of anti-Mexican sentiment and the connection between the literati and "rootless adventurers" is Harvard's professor Huntington's inflammatory argument that Mexicans pose a threat to the identity of the United States because they are fundamentally different than any other U.S. American or immigrant and the border vigilantes.[26] Yet the fact of racism against Mexicans in the United States is denied by most politicians and scholars. This illustrates the contention that power is tolerable only on the condition that it masks a substantial part of itself. Its success is proportional to its ability to conceal itself.

Stereotypes, academic disciplines, and legends or pseudo-folklore disguised as fact, however, do not quite fit the role of a "corporate institution that manages or produces Chicanos politically, sociologically and imaginatively" that Said finds in Orientalism. Yet, we know such a discourse exists as a hegemonic power because we live under it, struggle against it, analyze it, and write about it. How can a discourse like that have so much influence on our everyday life and yet continue to be not so much unidentified or unrecognized but unnamed? This is no mystery: This situation illustrates the power relations between Chicanos and Anglos. For example, the subject of this discourse, namely, the Latino/a, is identified as "a forgotten people," "a minority nobody knows," and "the invisible minority." Or, once "discovered" or "awakened" Chicanos are defined as Hispanics, Latinos, Mexican Americans, Spanish Americans, and so many other names that no single definition is possible. This highly diffused discourse that appears as stereotypes, social science, legends, or pseudo-folklore disguised as fact is, in effect, a politicized science of Chicanos. This logos gives statements about Chicanos the status of truth, thus it is a Chicanology that serves as a fundamental tool of domination. Paraphrasing Said, we can say that Chicanology is the whole network of interests inevitably brought to bear on any occasion under that peculiar entity "the Latino/a," is in question. No one writing, thinking or acting on the Latino/a can do so without taking into account the limitations on thought and action imposed by Chicanology.

It is precisely the expression of power intrinsic to Chicanology that engenders a Latino/a discourse. More specifically, this is a knowledge that is denied the status of truth. Without the status of truth, Latino/a discourse cannot invest its statements on institutions and their practices, that is on public policy; it is a subjugated or rather oppositional knowledge. Such knowledge is defined as the historical contents that have been buried and disguised in a functionalist coherence or formal system (such as the social sciences). Secondly, it is the whole body of knowledge that has been disqualified as inadequate or insufficiently elaborated. It is popular knowledge, though not common sense. It is a particular, local, regional knowledge, a heterogeneous knowledge incapable of unanimity and owes its force only to the harshness with which it is opposed by everything surrounding it.[27]

Consequently, subjugated and oppositional knowledge are concerned with a historical knowledge of struggles. Whether it is in specialized areas of erudition (such as doctoral dissertations, or books) or in the disqualified popular knowledge (such as *corridos* [ballads], rap songs, jokes) we find the memory of hostile encounters. Films like *Seguín*, *The Ballad of Gregorio Cortez*, and *Zoot Suit*, are examples of these memories; but in the context of availability to the dominant culture, these are, even up to this day, confined to the margins of knowledge. (And they were intended for the general public!)

In the context of power relations between Chicanology as a discourse of dominance and Chicano/Latino/a discourse as a subjugated (and thus oppositional) knowledge we can see the conditions for the appearance of Chicano/Latino studies at the university level. Chicano/Latino studies, then, is a specific form of struggle, a particular practice within Latino/a discourse that stands in a counterhegemonic, resistance, position with respect to Chicanology. In effect, the claim that Chicano studies is an academic discipline (that it is based on a logical, empirical structure and, therefore, its propositions are the outcomes of verifiable procedures) is really the attempt to invest itself with the effects of power which have been attributed to science Medieval times.[28] The important point is that this is not a battle "on behalf" of truth but a struggle "about the status of truth" and the economic and political role it plays. Until this is clearly understood, there is the possibility that Chicano/Latino studies may be appropriated by Chicanology. In other words, it could end up serving as a disciplinary, not a liberatory, a freeing, knowledge.

In terms of the struggle for social justice we now have several definitions: Chicanology is an elusive yet systematic hegemonic discourse that expresses and actualizes domination over Chicanos-Latinos/as. Chicano/Latino discourse is a diffuse, subjugated, oppositional knowledge resulting from the resistance first against Anglo domination and increasingly against a multiethnic privileged class. The academic discipline of Chicano/Latino studies is a specific discursive practice within Chicano/Latino discourse that attempts to acquire power by claiming scientific validity.

As we saw, at the start of this conversation, hijacking an airplane is also a form of resistance to Chicanology. We need to get back to that story and find out how it ends and consider further implications.

Now You See It, Now You Do Not: Procedures for the Control of Latino/a Discourse

Additional statements made by Chávez Ortiz refer to key points of struggle between Chicanology and Latino/a discourse.

> I could very easily force this plane to go to México and I could have demanded three or four million dollars . . . and I assure you that I would have been able to avoid capture there . . . I am a pretty smart person. And I know how to use my intelligence so I can get along well with my family.
>
> You are the ones that make the laws and elect the governments. Well what are you doing, what kind of governments are you electing? What kind of society are you making? . . . I want . . . a clean society not a filthy traitorous society like the one we are presently living in . . . If that is what the laws are like, then the laws are for the protection of the capitalists or, in other words, to protect the government.
>
> There is a Mrs. Bañuelos [U.S. Treasurer 1971 to 1974] . . . She has trampled on a lot of people and because of this she is a son of a bitch[29] . . . only very

capable people and good hearted with good intentions . . . have the right to
obtain positions like these . . .

The children that I have . . . attended school for many years and they know
absolutely nothing. . .[30]

These reoccurring key points of struggle are: (1) the question of intelligence, (2) the ambiguous nature of the law as applied to Chicanos, (3) the
status given to speakers of Latino/a discourse, and (4) educational institutions and processes. As I will discuss, through these points of struggle, Chicanology selects, organizes, and redistributes Latino/a discourse to deflect its
power and to neutralize its impact on public and social policy.[31]

But let us first finish the story of the hijacking. The event ended with the
conviction of Chávez Ortiz on charges of air piracy. He was given a life sentence but released in 1978. To the chagrin of his supporters, his only logical
defense was based on "diminished capacity," not being "mentally competent
and criminally responsible.[32]

This may indeed seem ironic; but from a Chicanological perspective, this
is a technique to invalidate this tactical (as opposed to strategic) articulation
of Latino/a issues.[33] This is a point that needs to be made clear. Humans find
many ways of resisting oppression.[34] In democratic capitalism people are free
to struggle and get what they want, working through interest groups and the
political system. However, when people do not have the economic or political base to create grand strategies, then they resort to small acts of resistance
and tactics to maintain their sense of integrity and the economic means of
survival. This is the line between the legitimate and the illegitimate. The
point of power/knowledge or discourse analysis is that these forms of resistance are not always done as a class of workers against the capitalists, as the
Marxists have expected. Nor they necessarily make sense in the conventional sense of political reform or revolutionary action.

The procedures for the control of Latino/a discourse are illustrated by the
following examples which include the points raised by Chávez Ortiz and others taken from Chicano-Latino/a history:

Prohibition: "Cannot Say That!"

This is perhaps the most obvious procedure and many examples of it are
found in Latino/a history. There was the prohibition to speak Spanish under
penalty of bodily punishment or suspension from school (occasionally, this
still happens). In the late nineteenth century the singing of corridos about
Mexican *bandidos* was illegal and in early twentieth century the practice of
red-baiting (accusing someone of being a communist) stopped people from

speaking up for better wages and working conditions. This led to the demise of unions, such as the Cannery and Agricultural Workers Industrial Union (CAWUI), and organizations like *Congreso de Habla Española* during the 1930s. Certainly Ricardo Flores Magón experienced the effects of prohibition around the turn of the twentieth century. He was incarcerated in Mexico nine times for speaking or writing radical political doctrines against the dictator Porfirio Díaz; in the United States he became a union organizer for the Industrial Workers of the World (IWW) and died in prison in Leavenworth, Kansas.

Reason versus Insanity: "*Estás loco en la cabeza!*"
There is a more subtle technique of intervention in the control of discourse that is based on the contrast between reason (usually on the side of the dominant power) and insanity (usually on the side of those who are subjugated). Thus, Chávez Ortiz had to plead insanity for hijacking a plane as a means to protest the oppression of the Mexicano in the United States. Furthermore, Latinos/as have not only been overrepresented in mentally retarded classes, but their cultural characteristics have been categorized as deviancy. A revealing example of this practice is the statement made by the Texas historian Walter Prescott Webb in reference to the Plan de San Diego of 1915. He did not believe Mexicans wrote the plan because "the disturbances had behind them a purpose, an intelligence greater than that of the bandit leader or of his ignorant followers." Instead, he attributes it to an ambitious Texan or Germans. And although it is not clear who was the author of this plan, it is known that Aniceto Pizaña and Luis de la Rosa, Mexicans native to Texas, led military actions at that time.[35]

Similarly, Commodore John D. Sloat, who took over Monterey Port in 1846, could not understand why Mexican people were planning to rise against him.

> Truly this procedure is more that of insane people than of persons in their right minds, because if they had commons sense they would understand that I am too strong to allow myself to be forced to give up what I have acquired.[36]

This statement echoes the U.S. assessment of the insurgents in Iraq: They must be insane taking on the U.S. Army and Marines. At a different level, in U.S. fiction, there are numerous Mexican characters who suddenly and inexplicably, go temporarily crazy. One thinks for example of Spanish Johnny in Willa Cather's *The Song of the Lark* and Danny in John Steinbeck's *Tortilla Flat*.[37]

It is in this educational, historical, military, and literary context, in this particular discursive regularity, that we can appreciate the force behind Chávez Ortiz's insistence on the validation of his intelligence.

True and Legal or False and Illegal?: "Do You Swear to Tell the Truth . . . ?"

An even more insidious technique to deny the validity of what is said is the assignment of the status of truth or legal to certain events or statements. In other words, the regime of truth appropriates the right to decide the distinction between true and false, legal and illegal statements, the correct method to acquire knowledge, and who is qualified to speak the truth.[38] As noted before (and without denying the existence of some real truth or Truth in itself), in power relations it is not a matter of what is true or false, but of what can be made to appear as true. To find examples of this technique one only needs to open any Chicano history book: the violation of the Treaty of Guadalupe Hidalgo, the blurring of what is justice and injustice in the second half of the nineteenth century, the exclusion of Chicanos from labor unions and schools, the manipulation of immigration laws, repatriation and deportations, the zoot suit riots, and charges of "reverse discrimination." From the perspective of Latino/a discourse and Chicano studies, every one of these instances represents a struggle to establish what really happened or what is legal as opposed to what has been given the status of truth or the status of legal.

Academic Disciplines: "As a Historian, I Believe That . . ."

Even in academic disciplines we find procedures of control in the production of truth.[39] Disciplines allow us to build a discourse but within a narrow framework. They are defined by groups of objects of study, methods, a body of propositions considered to be true (the literature), and the interplay of rules definitions, techniques, and tools. To speak the truth within a discipline, one must obey the rules of some discursive policy that takes the form of a permanent reactivation of a set of rules.

It is precisely the resistance to these rules and regulations that gives rise to a Chicano studies discipline. The first generation of Chicanos who entered higher education found that history, political science, sociology, and other academic disciplines required them to restrict their search for methods to alleviate the social problems in the barrio according to the dictates of their academic discipline.

Through the establishment of Chicano studies, as an interdisciplinary field of study, these scholars hoped to validate their discourse. But this validation has been thwarted by restrictions in terms of material support. Many

Latino/a professors have been denied tenure, Chicano studies courses are often not required for graduation, programs are funded with "soft" monies, publishers often refuse or do not publish articles or books by Chicanos, and many that are published, are not reprinted after they go out of print. There are, of course, exceptions. The rule is, however, that the knowledge provided by hundreds of dissertations, studies and research projects did not have the effect on institutional practices that was intended by the Plan de Santa Barbara or others that assumed a direct relationship between power/knowledge and social justice.

**Status of Intellectual: "Who Has the Authority to Speak
on This Subject?"**

There are various methods to limit the number of individuals who are given the charge of speaking the truth. One of these methods is to create positions from where individuals can speak with power. These positions are created according to five criteria: (1) competence–this can be defined in many ways; (2) a hierarchy or other systems to differentiate the individual from other individuals or groups with the same status; (3) the function of the assigned status in relation to society in general and the Latino/a community in particular; (4) the institutional sites that lend legitimacy to their statements; and (5) the various positions occupied by the speaking individual in information networks. This allocation of individuals to predefined positions of power is determined by a politics of truth, a Chicanology. Consequently, we find ourselves in an uncomfortable position when we realize that our demand for more Latino/a in positions of authority has not been realized in terms of the acquisition of power. Rodolfo Acuña refers to this development as the rise of the Latino/a bureaucrats, power brokers who function as agents of social control.[40]

And this is precisely what Chávez Ortiz denounced in harsh terms in his reference to Mrs. Bañuelos. To be sure, this is not a matter of labeling successful individual as *vendidos* (sell-outs) but a description of the workings of power that go beyond intentionality (we know what we do, we know why we do what we do, but we do not know what our doing *does*). In effect, this situation may be getting worse:

> Certainly relative gains are visible in the modest improvements for the middle class—for the most part, college educated professionals and small businesspersons—and the increment in wealth for the wealthy entrepreneurs. . . . However, because of political self-protection, the advantaged move in step with the reigning conservatism and the distance that separates them from the working poor of their own community potentially could increase.[41]

In effect, in the decade since these words were stated, the gap between the rich and the poor has widened.[42]

Fellowships of Discourse: A Fancy Name for the Good Ol' Boys Network

More restricted than academic disciplines is the control of discourse performed by what Foucault calls "fellowships of discourse." They are similar to a clique or a secret society in that only a few people share information and knowledge. Their function is to preserve, reproduce, or circulate discourse according to strict regulations and within a closed community. This is, for example, the Anglo Texans in 1832 and 1835, borrowing a technique from their revolutionary forefathers, who formed municipal committees of safety and correspondence. These committees, which brought citizens together outside of legal channels, became an important vehicle for bringing on the declaration of independence of Texas.[43]

But power relations flow in many directions. Mexican American organizations such as mutualistas and groups such as the *Penitentes* (a religious group that turned guerrilla and then a political party)[44] also circulated knowledge and information within their own members and excluded everyone else. Latino/a youth in the barrios have their own fellowship of discourse that is restricted by the use of *caló* (a dialect that is specific to a barrio or youth club—sometimes called "gangs"). More commonplace are technical, scientific, medical, economic, teaching discourses, and others that follow different schemes of exclusivity and disclosure; that means using a highly specialized language that by its nature restricts information only to particular groups and only members of that group can understand the language.

Doctrine: "You Are Either with Us or against Us."

On the one hand, doctrine (not only religious, but also political, philosophical) seems to be the reverse of a fellowship of discourse (in which the number of people who are allowed to be part of the conversation is limited). Doctrine, on the other hand, tends towards dissemination. It is the holding in common of a discourse on which as many individuals as possible, can define their reciprocal allegiance and loyalty. In appearance, the only requisite is the recognition of the same truths and the acceptance of a rule of conformity with these truths, which are usually known as a "creed."

Now, if it were a question of just doctrines, it would not be different from scientific or academic disciplines as previously defined. The control of discourse would bear only on the form or the content of what was said or what was believed: Is your loyalty to Jesus or to history? *But doctrines involve both the speaker and the spoken*. Doctrines involve the statements of speakers in the sense that they are, permanently, the instruments and the manifestations of an adherence, a loyalty to a social or ethnic class, a nationality, a struggle, or a revolt. *In short, doctrine links individuals to a certain type of statement while consequently barring them from all others.* Doctrine brings about a dual subjection: From one direction, it subjects individuals to a particular discourse, and from the other, it subjects a particular discourse to a group of individuals. This is obvious in religious doctrine, but the point is that it happens in other settings as well, precisely where religion and politics is blurred, such as among hate groups and terrorists. In academic terms, the restriction imposed by doctrine is illustrated by José Antonio Villareal R. The author of the novel *Pocho*, comments on the effects of the Chicano movement "doctrine" on Chicano literature:

> What resulted then is that an unwritten set of standards began to take form. Codes for Chicano literature were explicit. First and foremost was the fact that we could never criticize ourselves as long as we followed this developing pattern.[45]

Education: So What Did You Learn in School Today?

On a much broader scale, there is education as a social appropriation of discourse. This means that the forms of control of discourse discussed previously are linked together. They create a sort of *corporation* that distributes individuals among the different types of discourse. Looking at it from the opposite direction, an educational system, with all its pedagogical (teaching) powers, distributes discourse to a specific number of individuals; those who "graduate" become part of a sort of diffused doctrinal group with special rights and privileges. In short, every educational system is a political means of maintaining or of modifying the appropriation of discourse, with the knowledge and powers that it carries with it. Of course, it can also be argued that education is the means by which every individual can gain access to any kind of discourse (information, knowledge, and power). In reality, the way education is distributed—who is allowed and who is denied its full benefits—follows the well-trodden battle lines of social conflict. Thus, to a large extent what kind of education you get depends on how much social, cultural, and financial capital you have.

Education as a mechanism for the control of Latino/a discourse combines all the procedures discussed previously, and it manifests itself in the curricula of all grades; it is in effect an extension of the societal curriculum discussed by Carlos E. Cortés. This is because "there is no power relation without the correlative constitution of a field of knowledge, nor any knowledge that does not presuppose and constitute at the same time power relations."[46]

And this is why Chávez Ortiz's children and the vast majority of Latino/a children "have attended school for many years and they know absolutely nothing." There are, indeed, tragic results from the educational system: low academic performance among Latino/a children, and high drop-out/push-out rates, which lead to other battle fronts, such as gangs in the cities and in the prisons. Here, as in other areas, power is effective to the extent that it is invisible, thus the difficulty in finding solutions to the problem of school failure, gangs, and juvenile delinquency: Is it culture? Is it language? Is it a cast-like status?[47]

These then are the methods by which relations between power and knowledge tend to hide the exercise of power that goes beyond the law and beyond class struggle and impacts human bodies, institutions, and even how we generally perceive reality.

Summary and Directions for Future Research

We have seen how power/knowledge relations tend to hide the exercise of power that goes beyond law and beyond class struggle. We used an account of an airplane hijack, as a portal to access not only the key issues in Latino/a history but also to illustrate a dominant body of knowledge. Then we examined the parallel development of the rule of law and the rise of social sciences so that legal power gets confused with disciplinary power. We also saw how the Chicano movement struggles against this body of knowledge titled Chicanology. And finally I looked at the specific procedures by which Chicanology tends to control the discourse of Latino/as in the United States.

We can now respond to the poet Ricardo Sánchez: There are many reasons why "people [do not know] what it is they must know in order not only to survive but to live." It is because the power/knowledge of Latino/as, their discourse, and its inherent power is subjected to many forms of control. It is either forbidden outright, considered insane or irrational, declared a falsehood or illegal, or restricted by academic disciplines, lack of sociopolitical status, secret societies, doctrines, or more generally, the educational process. Of course, Latinos and Latinas are not helpless victims; they continuously struggle to invest discourse (our voices, ideas, desires, etc.) into the decisions that govern the lives (institutional practices, public and social policy).

The focus of this kind of analysis is on the insurrection of knowledge, the voices that are not being heard, that are marginalized, and that are opposed primarily to the effects of centralizing powers that are linked to scientific discourse.[48] Such analysis seriously considers the claims of local, discontinuous, disqualified, illegitimate knowledge against the claims of social science disciplines; which filter and orders them in the name of "true knowledge" and a politicized idea of science. The point is not to claim a special status for these marginalized knowledge. What is being proposed here is an analysis of discourse that may include both academic knowledge and people's memories of struggles. The objective is to uncover the voice of the voiceless and thus establish a historical knowledge of struggles and make use of this knowledge tactically today.

It is critical to add three caveats. As noted repeatedly, power functions in terms of manifold relationships that are determined by specific conditions. Therefore, it is important to note that the struggle between Chicanology and Latino/a discourse has been presented in terms a dialectical relationship for the sake of analysis. It is not, however, as if all Anglos or non-Latinos/as speak an oppressive Chicanology discourse and all Latinos/as speak a liberation Chicano-Latino/a discourse. Secondly this analysis is not specific to Chicanos-Latinos/as. As noted previously, it has been applied not only to African, Eastern, and Middle Eastern peoples but also to women's struggles.[49] A third caveat is that discursive analysis is not intended as a "better" analysis than conventional political science or Marxist analysis. Given the difficulty in achieving social justice, all three are necessary but still not sufficient. The essential political problem is not ideological content or error of a particular knowledge or the psychology of an alienated consciousness. The problem is the political, economic institutional regime of the production of truth. Thus, what we need is to ascertain the possibility of constituting a new politics of truth.[50]

That, of course, requires an extensive discussion that cannot be included here. Such a discussion would include the following items:

1. What exactly is the nature of language? According to Marxist theory language is not part of the base nor of the superstructure.[51] Like the common conceptions of language, this assumes that, as far as its role in production, language is a transparent entity. Arguably, though, language can be said to have a material existence (in oral tradition and in written form) with its own weight, history, and transformations and with which humans establish a dialectical relationship. Some consider it the basis for the "public thing" the civil commons, that which exists outside of market forces (at least so far).[52]

2. If language is, in fact a sort of commodity in the political economy and thus subject to market forces, then this might explain the creation of the global market as an ethical system that guarantees freedom at the cost of destroying all kinds of life forms and ecological systems. This would mean we are faced with a new form of power based on the Nietzsche/Foucault notion of oppression through the appropriation and distortion of

values and discourse. And it just might be this enervating, micro-physics of power that makes class struggle increasingly difficult.

3. This possibility has led to the **postmodern** condition, the questioning of everything that is, was or has ever been considered a Truth. And this is where the confusion arises regarding postmodernism and its usefulness as a political strategy. To be anti-essences, to be against Truths that exclude human beings from exercising their freedom by categorizing them as others (disabled, ethnics, minorities, illegals, gays, feminists, colored, etc.) does not necessarily mean to be against essences that are inclusive such as the notion of human beings as moral entities, justice, or the oppression of classes.[53]

4. Finally, despite the postmodern questioning of the existence of the self. The notion of the sacredness of all life, of humans as moral entities is found throughout the history of mankind. It is in the nature of language and perhaps of humanity, however, that as old as this knowledge is, it is never fully practiced, never fully implemented. It is part of the unsaid and the invisible, those regions from which come What Is Said and What Is Visible. It is from there that we draw our creativity. Or, as the Tao Te Ching (which dates back to the third century BCE) puts it:

> Tao that can be spoken of,
> Is not the Everlasting Tao.
> Name that can be named,
> Is not the Everlasting name.[54]

*   *   *

Notes and Suggested Further Readings

1. This piece expands significantly on my previous article, "Chicanology: A Postmodern Analysis of Meshicano Discourse," *Perspectives in Mexican American Studies* 3 (1992), 117–47.

2. Samuel P. Huntington, *Who Are We? The Challenges to America's National Identity* (New York: Simon & Schuster, 2004) from which he published "The Hispanic Challenge," *Foreign Policy* (March/April 2004), 30–45. See critique of the latter by Alan Wolfe, "Native Son: Samuel Huntington Defends the Homeland" (*Foreign Affairs*, May/June 2004) and debate in "Credal Passions" (*Foreign Affairs*, September/October 2004). One previous critique I raised regarding Huntington's supposedly prophetic "The Clash of Civilizations," *Foreign Affairs* 72, no. 3 (1993), is that he does not take into consideration the role of economic inequality in social uprisings; see "The Political Economy of Culture and The Birth of A Civil Society after NAFTA," *Latino Studies Journal* 8, no. 1 (1997).

3. Ricardo Sánchez, *Hechizospells* (Los Angeles: Chicano Studies Center Publications, 1976), 91.

4. David F. Gómez, *Somos Chicanos: Strangers in Our Own Land* (Boston: Beacon Press, 1973), 177–87, passim.

5. For a more detailed explanation of the historical reasons for this conception of power see my "Chicanology: A Postmodern Analysis of Meshicano Discourse," *Perspectives in Mexican American Studies* 3 (1992).

6. Manuel Castells, *The Power of Identity*, 2nd ed., vol. 2, *The Information Age: Economy, Society, and Culture* (Massachusetts: Blackwell, 2004), xv.

7. Michel Foucault "Two Lectures," in *Power/Knowledge: Selected Interviews and Other Writings, 1972–1977*, ed. Colin Gordon (New York: Pantheon Books, 1980), 106–107. For an intimate discussion of Foucault's writings see Gilles Deleuze, *Foucault* (Minneapolis: University of Minnesota Press, 1988). For an informative discussion of his work, a complete bibliography and biography and his last interview (five months before he died), see James Bernauer and David Rasmussen, *The Final Foucault* (Cambridge: The MIT Press, 1988).

8. Michel Foucault, *The History of Sexuality*, vol. I, trans. Robert Hurley (New York: Pantheon Books, 1978), 141.

9. Paulo Freire, *Pedagogy of the Oppressed* (Continuum, New York, 1970); Ira Shor and Paulo Freire, *A Pedagogy for Liberation: Dialogues on Transforming Education* (New York: Bergin & Garvey, 1987), 12–13. See also Henry A Giroux, *Teachers as Intellectuals: Toward a Critical Pedagogy of Learning* (Massachusetts: Bergin & Garvey, 1988), 114–16.

10. Octavio Romano-V. developed a critique of this view through his journal *El Grito*. See for example "The Anthropology and Sociology of the Mexican American: The distortion of Mexican American History," *El Grito* 1, no. 2 (Fall 1968).

11. Raymund A. Paredes, "The Origins of Anti-Mexican Sentiment in the United States," *New Directions in Chicano Scholarship*, eds. Ricardo Romo and Raymund Paredes (San Diego: University of California, 1978), 157.

12. Glenn C. Loury, "America Incarcerated: Crime, Punishment and the Question of Race," *Boston Review* (July/August 2007).

13. There are many observations of the relationship between social science and disciplinary mechanisms. One specific example is Alexander Liazos, "The Poverty of the Sociology of Deviance: Nuts, Sluts, and 'Preverts,'" in Stuart H. Traub and Craig B. Little, *Theories of Deviance*, 3rd ed., (Itasca: F.E. Peacock Publishers, Inc., 1985). More extensive and recent examples are: James Clifford, *The Predicament of Culture: Twentieth-Century Ethnography, Literature, and Art* (Cambridge: Harvard University Press, 1989) and Renato Rosaldo, *Truth and Culture: The Remaking of Social Analysis* (Boston: Beacon Press, 1989). The most specific discussion of this topic, however, is Michel Foucault's *Discipline and Punish: The Birth of the Prison* (New York: Vintage Books, 1979).

14. Michel Foucault, "Truth and Power," *Power/Knowledge: Selected Interviews and Other Writings, 1972–1977*, ed. Colin Gordon (New York: Pantheon Books, 1980), 131.

15. Foucault, "Two Lectures," 93–94.

16. These methodological guidelines have been compiled from two sources: "Two Lectures", 96–102 and *The History of Sexuality*, 94–95.

17. V.Y. Mudimbe, *The Invention of Africa: Gnosis, Philosophy, and the Order of Knowledge* (Bloomington: Indiana University Press, 1988), x.

18. Edward W. Said, *Orientalism* (New York: Pantheon Books, 1978), 3.

19. Carlos E. Cortés, "The Societal Curriculum and the School Curriculum," Educational Leadership, XXXVI, 7 (April, 1979), 475–79. He extended this conception in "The Education of Language Minority Students: A Contextual Interaction Model," in *Beyond Language: Social and Cultural Factors in Schooling Language Minority Students*, ed. Bilingual Education Office, California State Department of Education (Los Angeles: Evaluation, Dissemination and Assessment Center, California State University, Los Angeles, 1986), 3–33.

20. Paredes, "The Origins of Anti-Mexican Sentiment," 139–65.

21. Paredes, "The Origins of Anti-Mexican Sentiment," 143.

22. Romano-V. "The Anthropology and Sociology of the Mexican American."

23. Américo Paredes, *With His Pistol in His Hand* (Austin: University of Texas Press, 1978), 18.

24. Paredes, *With His Pistol*, 16.

25. Paredes, *With His Pistol*, 23.

26. Huntington, *Who Are We?* from which he published "The Hispanic Challenge," 30–45; see note 2.

27. Foucault, "Two Lectures," 81.

28. Foucault, "Two Lectures," 85.

29. "(Nominated) by President Richard Nixon and subsequently confirmed by the Senate as Treasurer of the United States. During the Senate investigation into her qualifications, it was discovered she was hiring "illegal aliens" from Mexico . . . In the barrio it is common knowledge that she has made her fortune in the Mexican food business exploiting cheap labor from Mexico." Gómez, *Somos Chicanos*, 183.

30. Gómez, *Somos Chicanos*, 177–87, passim.

31. Michel Foucault, "The Discourse on Language," *The Archaeology of Knowledge*, trans. Alan Sheridan (New York: Pantheon Books, 1972), 215–37. This piece contains a more detailed discussion of the various forms of exclusion of discourse.

32. Gómez, *Somos Chicanos*, 186.

33. For a discussion of "tactic" as an act of resistance against a "strategic" force, see Michel de Certeau, *The Practice of Everyday Life* (Berkeley: University of California Press, 1984), xvii–xx.

34. See for example, Stephanie M.H. Camp, *Closer to Freedom: Enslaved Women and Everyday Resistance in the Plantation South* (Chapel Hill: The University of North Carolina Press, 2004), and David G. Sweet and Gary B. Nash, eds., *Struggle and Survival in Colonial America* (Berkley, University of California Press, 1981).

35. Juan Gómez-Quiñonez, "Plan de San Diego Revisited," *Aztlán* (Spring, 1970), 124–32.

Chicanology II ⌢ 111

36. David J. Weber, *Foreigners in Their Native Land* (Albuquerque: University of New Mexico Press, 1973), 129–30.

37. Paredes, "The Origins of Anti-Mexican Sentiment," 165.

38. Foucault, "The Discourse," 217–20.

39. Foucault, "The Discourse," 222–24.

40. Rodolfo Acuña, *Occupied America: A History of Chicanos*, 3rd ed., (New York: Harper and Row, 1988), 377–86.

41. Juan Gómez-Quiñonez, *Chicano Politics: Reality and Promise, 1940* (Albuquerque: University of New Mexico Press, 1990), 195.

42. According to the Federal Reserve, in 1990 the richest 1 percent of America owned 40 percent of its wealth—the greatest level of inequality among all rich nations, and the worst in U.S. history since the Roaring Twenties. Furthermore, the richest 20 percent owned 80 percent of America—meaning, of course, that the bottom four fifths of all Americans owned only one-fifth of its wealth (www.huppi.com/kangaroo/4Inequality.htm, accessed November 19, 2007). For California where most Latinos reside, see *A Generation of Widening Inequality: The State of Working California, 1979 to 2006* (California Budget Project, August 2007) and Nari Rhee and Dan Acland, *The Limits of Prosperity: Growth, Inequality, and Poverty in the North Bay* (Santa Rosa, California: New Economy, Working Solutions, March 2005).

43. Weber, *Foreigners*, 105.

44. Robert J. Rosenbaum, *Mexicano Resistance in the Southwest* (Austin: University of Texas Press, 1981), 145–46.

45. Antonio Villareal R. "Chicano Literature: Art and Politics from the Perspective of The Artist," in *The Identification and Analysis of Chicano Literature* ed. Francisco Jimenez (New York: Bilingual Press, 1979), 163.

46. Michel Foucault, *Discipline and Punish: The Birth of the Prison*, trans. Alan Sheridan (New York: Vintage Books, 1979), 27.

47. See John Ogbu and Maria Eugenia Matute-Bianchi, "Understanding Sociocultural Factors: Knowledge, Identity, and School Adjustment," *Beyond Language: Social and Cultural Factors in Schooling Language Minority Student*, ed. Bilingual Education Office, California State Department of Education (Los Angeles: Evaluation, Dissemination and Assessment Center, California State University, Los Angeles, 1986). A critique and attempt to improve this assessment is provided by Douglas E. Foley, "Reconsidering Anthropological Explanations of Ethnic School Failure," *Anthropology and Education Quarterly* 22 (1991). The latter publication includes a critical commentary of both perspectives by Henry T. Trueba.

48. Foucault, "Two Lectures," 83.

49. Aurelia Armstrong, "Foucault and Feminism," The Internet Encyclopedia of Philosophy, 2006 at www.iep.utm.edu/f/foucfem.htm (accessed November 22, 2007).

50. Foucault, "Truth and Power," 133.

51. J. V. Stalin, *Marxism and Problems of Linguistics* (Peking: Foreign Language Press, 1972); V.N. Volosinov, *Marsism and the Philosophy of language*, trans. Ladislav Matejka and I. R. Titunik (Cambridge: Harvard University Press, 2000)

52. John McMurtry, *Unequal Freedoms: The Global Market as an Ethical System* (West Hartford, CT: Kumarian Press, 1998), 26.

53. Charles Spinosa and Hubert L. Dreyfus, "Two Kinds of Antiessentialism and Their Consequences," *Critical Inquiry* 22 (Summer 1996).

54. Ellen M. Chen, *The Tao Te Ching* (New York: Paragon House, 1989).

*   *   *

Questions

1. How is power in its various forms (political, economic, cultural, etc.) manifested in your everyday life?
2. This article addressed the difficulties in achieving social justice. In terms of your own personal goals how would you describe the reasons why you cannot achieve some of the goals you set for yourself?
3. To what extent are you aware of a master narrative, a discourse, that envelopes and in many ways shapes your actions?
4. To what extent do you feel that your own discourse is subjected to the rules for the control of discourse discussed herein?
5. After considering the three methods to study social change, liberalism, Marxism, and power relations or discursive analysis, to what extent do they increase your own understanding? In other words, based on these explanations, what is you own personal explanation?

〜

Seduction and Aggression: The Birth of Territorial, Involuntary, and Cultural U.S. Citizens
Francisco Hernández Vázquez

Mexicans, Puerto Ricans, and Cubans came directly under the authority of the U.S. government and indirectly under the influence and hegemony of the U.S. American dominant culture through a complex process of political, cultural, and economic, seduction combined with military aggression. Thus, there are some similarities in the way these three groups were subjugated, colonized by, and incorporated into the United States.

The seduction: Spanish-American revolutionaries (and others like the French Lafayette and the Italian Garibaldi) were fascinated by the political invention of a U.S. constitutional democracy because it held the promise of equality and social justice. Furthermore, it served as an ideological weapon against the European monarchies that controlled Latin America (see chapter 2). The Constitution of the United States of Mexico of 1824, for example, had a president, vice-president, a congress with a senate and a house of deputies, and a supreme court. In their quest for independence from Spain as they rebelled against Spanish traditional culture, Cubans created an identity that included *cubanismo* and a U.S. modern, technologically advanced culture (see part III). Economically, the productive capacity of the United States posed deadly temptations to members of the elite, especially in northern Mexico, who had been starved for manufactured goods under the Spanish monarchy (see II.B). Also, in each of the cases under consideration, the countries were politically and economically devastated as a result of wars of independence against Spain. Under these circumstances, there were increased economic exchanges and collaboration between the native elite and the newcomer elite that ultimately favored the United States. Politically, culturally, and economically, the United States was like the proverbial siren's song. It should be noted that people who did not belong to the elite (peons, artisans, and indigenous) did not succumb to this seduction as readily and often revolted against the U.S. invasion.

The aggression: After a more-or-less subtle courting, came the imposition by force of a new order that divested the native population of their land and subjected their labor to the needs of the dominant government and economy. In the case of Mexico, U.S. troops invaded Mexico City, and for a while, the U.S. government considered keeping the entire country. U.S. Senator John C. Calhoun from South Carolina, however, successfully argued in Congress that U.S. Democracy is only for white people, and that "colored races" are incapable of democratic government, and that Mexicans would make inferior citizens.[1] Thus, the United States kept only the northern part of Mexico. (Incidentally, 156 years later, Harvard professor Samuel Huntington echoes a similar argument about the unsuitability of Mexicans for a U.S. democracy.[2]) In Cuba and Puerto Rico, U.S. troops were sent ostensibly to support the movement for independence from Spain. Troops withdrew once the required documents mentioned below were signed or otherwise approved.

The birth in symbolic terms, Mexicans, Puerto Ricans, and Cubans were "born" as U.S. "cultural citizen" when their respective representatives signed their "birth certificates." These birth certificates were, for the Mexicans, The Treaty of Guadalupe-Hidalgo (1848) and for the Puerto Ricans and Cubans, The Treaty of Paris (1899). Subsequent to these peace treaties, Puerto Ricans were further defined by: The Foraker Act (1900), The Jones Act (1917), Public Law 600 (1950), and relations with Cuba were defined by The Platt Amendment (1901). These documents established a legal relationship that affected the individuals living at the time, but they also established a historical and cultural relationship with these countries and their populations. As presented in this reader, throughout the ensuing years and up to the present day, this relationship has been subjected to many controversial transformations.

Although there is no room to include all these documents in this reader, we encourage you to study them. They contain the power to take over half of Mexico, to annex Puerto Rico, and to declare the U.S. right to intervene in Cuba. They also represent much bloodshed, wealth, labor, and land. But who reads legal documents? The language of treaties and acts is difficult to understand. Is it not paradoxical that legalese is so complicated? Yet legal documents represent one of the most concrete and durable realities since the invention of the written word. There are federal, states, and city laws and school policies on how to behave and how to dress. These are examples of legal documents that exercise power over us on a daily basis. They are backed by military, police, school, or parental authority and violation may lead to penalties, even a death sentence. These are realities that populate not only Latino/a thought but also all political thought.

All births are painful, and reality is much too fluid to be contained by discourse. Who negotiated and signed the treaties, the acts and the amendments? Who opposed them? Once signed, can these documents be challenged? As we see in this reader, there were many who immediately challenged the **juridical** (legal) reality represented by these documents with a violent response against U.S. encroachment. At different times and with varying intensity, tactics, and strategies, they opposed their change of status from "nationals" (members of their own nation) to "ethnics" (subordinate members of the United States). And the fight continues today. Some Puerto Ricans are still struggling for independence; some Mexicans feel that the Treaty of Guadalupe Hidalgo violated international law. Julio Chavezmontes argues in *Heridas que no cierran*[3] that there is a basis in international law to argue that the takeover of the Mexican North (now the U.S. Southwest) and the resulting Treaty of Guadalupe Hidalgo are illegal and that the Mexican president should demand compensation. There was also the takeover of Catalina Island in southern California by the Brown Berets, who raised a Mexican flag and denounced the violation of the Treaty of Guadalupe Hidalgo agreements by the United States.[4] In addition of course, the Cuban government challenges U.S. claim to Guantanamo Bay, which was established in 1903 under the threat of force. Guantanamo is used as a military base for the prisoners of war defined as "enemy combatants."

This is the stuff that makes history and politics. One key question raised by this Reader (and left for you to answer) is whether this Latino/a struggle for justice and self-determination is indeed an instance of separatism (as Huntington argues) or a quest for democracy. The next story, about how some Mexicans struggled for democracy in Texas first as part of Mexico, then as part of the United States, provides a dramatic illustration of this point.

Notes and Suggested Further Readings

1. U.S. Senator John C. Calhoun, 1848, quoted in David J. Weber, ed., *Foreigners in their Native Land* (Albuquerque: University of New Mexico Press, 1973), 135.

2. Samuel P. Huntington, *Who Are We? The Challenges to America's National Identity* (New York: Simon & Schuster, 2004).

3. Julio Chavezmontes, *Heridas que no cierran* (México: Editorial Grijalbo, 1988).

4. David Sánchez, *Expedition through Aztlán* (La Puente, CA: Perspectiva, 1978).

PART II

MEXICANS AND AMERICANS

PART II A

~

First Encounters between Anglo Americans and Mexican Americans
Francisco Hernández Vázquez

With the Louisiana Purchase from France in 1803, the United States came into conflict with the interests of Spain. At that time, *Tejas* (the original spelling of Texas) was part of New Spain (Mexico's name as a Spanish colony), and *Tejanos* were considered a buffer between the ever-expanding U.S. Americans and the rich mines of New Spain in Zacatecas. In reality, Tejanos were caught between the Manifest Destiny, the expansionist ambition of the United States on the north, and the vast wealth of the Spanish colony to the south. This situation functioned like a magnet, attracting opportunists from all over the world. Unfortunately, this initial contact between Tejanos and U.S. Americans also happened at a time when negative portrayals of Mexicans were prevalent in the media of the time.

Soon after, between 1810 and 1821, inspired by the French and American Revolution, Mexicans fought a war of independence from Spain that left their country economically devastated. Consequently, the Mexican government immediately established economic relations with the United States and opened its northern border (Tejas, New Mexico, and California) to commerce and Anglo American immigrants from the United States. This well intentioned but naïve policy was designed not only to populate the area with other "civilized" (read: economically developed, light-skinned) bodies who could assist in the economic recovery, but also to help with the struggle against the "hostile" American Indian nations.

Erasmo Seguín, was charged with negotiating an agreement that legally admitted the first three hundred Anglo American colonists under the leadership of Stephen F. Austin. The history of the Seguín family, incidentally, includes involvement by its members in the 1740s Spanish establishment of the Tejas territory, the Mexican War of Independence, the Texas secession, the Mexican American War, as well as the Wars of Reform and the French Intervention in Mexico.

We all seem to "remember the Alamo" but not necessarily the events that led to it. One of these events was the increasing number of Anglo Americans that continued to migrate into Mexico, even as illegal aliens, after Mexican authorities closed the border. Another event echoed the recent struggles against the absolute power of the King: General Antonio López de Santa Anna, President of Mexico, in violation of the Mexican Constitution of 1824, abolished the federal republic and established a central government. This meant that the territory of Tejas would not qualify as a state of the Mexican Republic. This led some Mexican Tejanos like Juan N. Seguín and Anglo Americans who called themselves "Texians" to declare independence from Mexico. Santa Anna won the battle of the Alamo but lost the war in San Jacinto, and Texas became the Republic of Texas for the next decade, until the United States declared war on Mexico in 1846.

In the meantime, the power relations between Tejanos and Texans led to a cruel irony. This irony hinges on what was visible and what was invisible to, and about, each group. As noted before, the Mexican elite welcomed U.S. Americans to Tejas because they perceived them as equals in a struggle to civilize what they considered a wilderness populated with hostile Americans Indians. Soon, however, U.S. Americans came to perceive the elite Mexican Tejanos as uncivilized and therefore not equals, and in fact, eventually treated them like the American Indians they were supposed to fight together. Yet, as told in his memoirs, Seguín's story itself does a certain violence to women and the underclass by rendering *them* invisible. For example, the only piece of information available about Juan's wife (according to the editor Jesús de la Teja) is that she was fat and illiterate. And there is also mention of a Mexican boy "in Mexican garb, looking more like an Indian than anything else," who joins Seguín's troops.

What *is* visible is the struggle of the Tejano people to achieve self-determination in the midst of centralist versus federalist conflicts, legal and illegal immigrants and refugees, and a separatist Anglo American movement within the newly born Mexican nation-state. Born October 27, 1806, Juan grew up with dreams of a free and independent Tejas where a multicultural society would thrive, and this leads him to fight against the Mexican government for Texas independence. He served as senator in the Texas Republic in 1837. As vividly evoked by the tone of the preface, his dream turned into a nightmare as anti-Mexican sentiment threatened his life and he became, as he put it, "a foreigner in my native land" and was forced to flee to Mexico, where he was "[t]hrown in prison in a foreign country." As a condition for his release he had to fight against the United States in the Mexican American War. This is one of the most tragic illustrations of the Chicano condition: Though they commit to the democratic ideals of both Mexico and the United States (or Texas), they are rejected by *both* societies.

As for identity politics, it is important to note that, as a Texas senator, Seguín did not consider himself an "ethnic" politician (and neither did Henry B. Gonzalez, another major player in Texas politics one hundred years later). This has implication for a notion that appears throughout this reader, namely that the quest for democracy is not constrained by national borders nor is it limited by ethnic identities. In other words, they saw themselves as legitimate members of the nation-state, not as representatives of their own ethnic group.

~

CHAPTER FIVE

The Making of a Tejano: The Personal Memoirs of John N. Seguín

Jesús de la Teja

For the sake of telling a brief yet comprehensive story, this chapter is a combination of the narrative by Jesús de la la Teja, who edited Seguín's memoirs, with excerpts from Seguín's own writings. Francisco Hernández Vázquez adds comments in brackets and italics to guide, clarify, and provide additional context. A visual enhancement of these texts is provided by 1979 film, *Seguín*, directed by Jesús S. Treviño. Unfortunately, this film is only available from copies that individuals might have made from television when PBS broadcasted it in 1979.

Seguín's Preface to His Memoirs

[This is a brief summary of his life story in his own words.]

A native of the city of San Antonio de Béxar, I embraced the cause of Texas at the sound of the first cannon which foretold her liberty, filled an honorable role within the ranks of the conquerors of San Jacinto, and was a member of the legislative body of the Republic. In the very land which in other times bestowed on me such bright and repeated evidences of trust and esteem, I now find myself exposed to the attacks of scribblers and personal enemies who, to serve *political purposes* and engender strife, falsify historical fact with which they are but imperfectly acquainted. I owe it to myself, my children and friends to answer them with a short but true exposition of my acts, from the beginning of my public career up to the time of the return of

General Woll from the Rio Grande with the Mexican forces, among which I was then serving.

I address myself to the American people, to that people impetuous as the whirlwind when aroused by the hypocritical clamors of designing men but just, impartial, and composed whenever men and facts are submitted to their judgment.

I have been the object of the hatred and passionate attacks of a few troublemakers who, for a time, ruled as masters over the poor and oppressed population of San Antonio. Harpy-like, ready to pounce on everything that attracted the notice of their rapacious avarice, I was an obstacle to the execution of their vile designs. They therefore leagued together to exasperate and ruin me, spread malignant calumnies against me, and made use of odious machinations to sully my honor and tarnish my well earned reputation.

A victim to the wickedness of a few men whose false pretenses were favored because of their origin and recent domination over the country, a foreigner in my native land, could I stoically be expected to endure their outrages and insults? Crushed by sorrow, convinced that only my death would satisfy my enemies, I sought shelter among those against whom I had fought. I separated from my country, parents, family, relatives and friends and, what was more, from the institutions on behalf of which I had drawn my sword with an earnest wish to see Texas free and happy. In that involuntary exile my only ambition was to devote my time, far from the tumult of war, to the support of my family who shared in my sad condition.

Fate, however, had not exhausted its cup of bitterness. Thrown into a prison in a foreign country, I had no alternatives left but to linger in a loathsome confinement or to accept military service.

On one hand, my wife and children, reduced to beggary and separated from me; on the other hand, to turn my arms against my own country. The alternatives were sad, the struggle of feelings violent. At last the father triumphed over the citizen; I seized a sword that pained my hand. (Who among my readers will not understand my situation?) I served Mexico; I served her loyally and faithfully. I was compelled to fight my own countrymen, but I was never guilty of the barbarous and unworthy deeds of which I am accused by my enemies.

Ere the tomb closes over me and my contemporaries, I wish to publicize this stormy period of my life. I do it for my friends as well as for my enemies. I challenge the latter to contest with facts the statements I am about to make, and I confidently leave the decision to those who witnessed the events.

The Making of Tejano

[Jesús de la Teja's description of the world into which Seguín was born.]

Don Erasmo's son, Juan Nepomuceno Seguín, had been born [October 27, 1806] in a sparsely settled land during very unsettled times. The political and social changes sweeping Mexico and the United States made Texas a cross-roads of revolution and an object of desire. The Louisiana Purchase in 1803 brought the United States and Spain together along the Texas border, which the United States now claimed to be the Rio Grande. In Madrid, Paris and Washington, Texas took on a political importance it had not had for almost a century. In its new role as buffer between the ever-expanding Anglo Americans and the rich mines of New Spain, Texas became the destination of royalist troops intent on protecting the frontier, of Spanish and French refugees from Anglo-American Louisiana, and of filibusters from the United States.

. . . .

Even as an adolescent Juan must have appreciated the importance his father and other prominent *Bexareños* [people from San Antonio de Bexar, Texas] attached to Stephen Austin and his colonists. The significance of his father's hosting James E. B. Austin, Stephen's brother, for over a year could not have been lost on Juan. The young Tejano also witnessed the growing frustration of Bexareños as they saw the Anglo-American colonies prosper while San Antonio remained stagnant, caught between the political power of Monclova and Saltillo and the economic power of San Felipe, Nacogdoches and the other Anglo-American settlements.

. . . .

Juan's economic and social development brought about quick political maturity. Despite being just twenty-two years old at the time, Juan was elected as one of two San Antonio *regidores* [city councilmen] for 1829, on occasion serving as *alcalde* [mayor] during the absences of the incumbent, Gaspar Flores. Regarding the young office holder's political skills, the political chief, Ramón Músquiz, confided in Stephen Austin "Don Juan Nepomuceno Segin [Seguín] is very talented for his age, but he needs practice in order to be a good administrator of justice." During his tenure Juan was asked to perform what could only be considered thankless tasks. His efforts to collect the voluntary contribution for the local primary school proved a failure because of the lack of money in the town. Juan had to suggest to the political chief that the collection be suspended until such time as some hard cash came into town. Only a few days later he found out that he had to enforce a new state law requiring each citizen to contribute the proceeds from three days' labor to the local school. Only slightly less demanding was the compilation of the municipality's annual statistical report, for which he and the other *regidor* were responsible. On occasion he served as judge in minor civil and criminal cases.[2]

His success in handling his first elective office made Juan a prime candidate for future political activities. In the complicated world of post-independence Mexican politics, elections beyond the local level were indirect; the eligible citizens voted for electors who in turn voted for representatives to state and national offices. In 1833 he won twenty-six of thirty-three votes for secretary of the electoral assembly, and was subsequently elected as one of twenty-one electors. The following year he served as president of the electoral assembly.[3]

*   *   *

[Breaking away from Mexico]
[Focus on 1) his military contributions to Texas and his political participation and his defense of the legal and educational rights of Tejanos; 2) the process and conditions that led him and other Tejanos to become "foreigners in their own land," and "suspicious individuals;" 3) how these events foreshadow the relations between Anglo Americans and Mexican Americans in 2007, 171 years later.]

Juan's comment in the memoirs that, "we had agreed that the movement [toward Texas independence] should begin in the center of Texas," makes it clear that the Tejanos were not about to expose themselves to Santa Anna's wrath on their own. They were aware of Zacatecas's fate for resisting the new centralist government: a large force composed of local militias had been routed by Santa Anna's army, which sacked the city before withdrawing. Juan and other Tejano leaders also knew that, despite the existence of a "War Party," the commonly held sentiment among the Anglo Americans was against an uprising so long as their own rights were not violated.

The violation, whether orchestrated by war party members or not, came by way of General Martín Perfecto de Cos, who asked that William B. Travis, the leader of a group of settlers who had ousted the customs officer at Anahuac, be delivered to him. Cos also issued arrest orders for a large group of federalists including Samuel Williams, Mosley Baker, Lorenzo de Zavala, and José María Carbajal. At the same time he issued a proclamation advising the settlers that they had nothing to fear from the new government, but made it clear they must accept the changes without recourse. Not only did the Texans refuse to comply with Cos's orders, they violently resisted the army's effort to collect a cannon that had been lent to the town of Gonzales for Indian defense.

This action at Gonzales, which took place on October 2, mobilized the Anglo Texans and the Tejanos. Juan, commissioned "captain of the Federal

Army of Texas," raised a company of thirty-seven men. His brother-in-law, Salvador Flores, and Manuel Leal organized another company from the San Antonio ranches. The Mexican settlers from the Victoria area organized themselves into a company of twenty-eight under Placido Benavides's command. Desertions from the San Antonio and Goliad garrisons brought additional Tejanos into the ranks of the Texas Army.[4]

The roles assigned to the Tejanos—foraging, spying, harassments, and raids—clearly aimed at taking advantage of their knowledge of the countryside and their horsemanship. This is not to say that the Tejanos did not take part in the major engagement of the early struggle. There is considerable evidence that at least part of Juan's company, probably including himself, took part in the storming of San Antonio, which began on December 5. Immediately after General Cos's withdrawal from San Antonio, Seguín's company joined Travis's in raiding the Mexican army's horse herd.[5]

By January 1836 the Mexican army had been driven from Texas and Juan's company of mounted volunteers had disbanded. Juan himself had been chosen judge of San Antonio, a position he held until returning to military service in February, when Santa Anna advanced on Texas. Also in January, the government commissioned Juan a captain in the cavalry corps, although there apparently was some confusion regarding the appointment. In any case, Juan was busy acting as intermediary between the Tejanos, the Anglo Texans, and the revolutionary government, as well as attending to town business. Among these activities was a run-in with James Bowie over the latter's unauthorized release of a prisoner. As judge, Juan also was responsible for conducting the election that sent Francisco Ruiz and José Antonio Navarro as the only native-born Texans to the convention that declared Texas independence.[6]

Once Santa Anna arrived in Béxar, Juan withdrew into the Alamo along with an unspecified number of Tejanos. There are a number of reports which suggest that between Santa Anna's arrival on February 23 and March 3, some individuals had an opportunity to withdraw; more probably however, they withdrew between the time Santa Anna was spotted and the time he entered Béxar. Among those who chose not to remain were a number of Tejanos who probably felt it was useless to remain in the fort when Houston was organizing an army in the interior.[7]

Juan left the Alamo as a messenger, probably on the night of February 28. Apparently his knowledge of the area and his Spanish made him the logical choice in an attempt to get through the Mexican lines. He never made it to Goliad, his original destination, for on the road he met one of Colonel James Fannin's officers, who informed him that the Goliad garrison was on its way.

Soon, however, Seguín was informed by another of Fannin's men that the colonel had decided to return to Goliad. Juan now headed for Gonzales where, upon his arrival, he found many of the Tejanos who had been in San Antonio until Santa Anna's approach. There he reorganized his company, part of which was ordered by Sam Houston to help protect the evacuation of the San Antonio River valley ranches. Juan specifically sent three men from his unit to help his family leave the area while he and the rest of the company made up the rear-guard of the main body of Houston's army. Before taking up the march, Juan took the time to inform the Bexareño [San Antonio] delegates at Washington-on-the-Brazos, Francisco Ruiz and José Antonio Navarro, about the fall of the Alamo.[8]

. . . .

Juan and his men earned Sam Houston's respect at San Jacinto. Writing a letter of introduction for Juan to the governor of Louisiana, Houston stated: "The Colonel commanded the only Mexican company who fought in the cause of Texas at the Battle of San Jacinto. His chivalrous and estimable conduct in the battle won for him my warmest regard and esteem."[9] Writing to Juan's father some years later, Houston extended his compliments to the company in general, citing Juan's conduct and that of "his brave company in the army of 1836, and his brave and gallant bearing in the battle of San Jacinto, with that of his men."[10]

But Juan earned another kind of notoriety during the war; he was one of the few Tejanos to be singled out by the Mexicans for his participation in the war. For instance, José Enrique de la Peña, a participant in Santa Anna's expedition, published a diary of the campaign in 1836. In it he attacked the ingratitude of the Anglo-American settlers and the credulousness of many Tejanos. But for Juan and two others he reserved the harshest judgment:

> The cry of independence darkened the magic of liberty that had misled some of the less careful thinkers . . . there remaining with the colonists only Don Lorenzo de Zavala and Béjar natives, Don Antonio Navarro and Don Juan N. Seguín, the only intelligent men who incurred the name of traitor, a label both ugly and deserved.[11]

. . . .

Juan's command turned out to be full of controversy and turmoil. Felix Huston, who became commander of the army in October, after Sam Houston's election to the presidency and Thomas Rusk's appointment as secretary of war, was opposed to Seguín's holding the command. One of the "American straggling adventurers" of whom Juan complains in his memoirs, Huston had arrived in Texas well after San Jacinto with ambitious plans for invading

Mexico. *The general obviously had little respect for Juan, complaining in letters to Houston in November 1836 that Seguín was unfit for command because "he cannot speak our language" and was calling for the abandonment of Béxar.*[12] *[Emphasis added]*

When General Huston tried to carry out the evacuation and destruction of San Antonio at the beginning of 1837, Juan successfully appealed the order to President Houston. Although Juan's appeal has not surfaced, the tenor of Houston's reply suggests the Tejano was deeply insulted by the order. After discussing the steps taken to undo Huston's orders, the president concluded: "You will, I confidently hope, be satisfied that no intention has been entertained to wound your feelings, or to compromise your honor! You will therefore retain your command, and command of the post of Bexar." Juan was satisfied, but he apparently made an enemy of Huston and his associates, who may have been involved in a scheme to buy up land in San Antonio cheaply as a result of the abandonment.[13]

. . . .

[Seguín's participation in Texas government and his defense of Tejano Rights]
The withdrawal from San Antonio proved propitious, however, for in April Juan claimed to be in a position both to mount those yet on foot and to return to the vicinity of Béxar. It would seem, however, that Juan was growing increasingly eager to take care of personal interests. Confident that the Mexicans would not soon attack and that his command was on a stable footing, he asked for a month-long furlough. By the fall of 1837 he was again away from his command, on his way to New Orleans where he remained until early 1838. When he returned to Béxar in March he discovered that he had been elected Béxar's senator to the Texas Congress. Traveling to Houston, then the capital of the young republic, he resigned his commission on May 14, 1838, and four days later obtained his pay in bounty land—1,280 acres. He also acquired a donation grant of 640 acres of land for his service at San Jacinto.[14] Having made significant military contributions to the young republic, Juan now turned his talents to the political field, where his efforts were directed at making the coexistence of Tejano and Texan a reality.

Juan again found himself breaking ground, this time as the only Tejano senator to serve during the republic. He could not have had much time to formulate an agenda for himself, however, given the suddenness of the news of his election and the fact that the Second Congress was nearing the end. But even during the remaining nine days Juan proved to be a man of action. He introduced a bill for the relief of the widows and orphans of those who died at the Alamo, and even joined in the debate, though he did so in Spanish. Despite his need for a translator, Juan served during the Third and

Fourth Congresses as chair of the Committee on Military Affairs, and had a seat on the Committee of Claims and Accounts.[15]

As the only Tejano in the senate it was clearly up to Juan to represent the interests not only of Bexareños but of all Tejanos. Juan clearly was concerned both that Tejanos understood the new system of government by which they were quickly being overwhelmed and that their interests were properly represented in congress. His only surviving speech, made during the Fourth Congress, came as result of a Treasury report stating that $15,000 had been appropriated for the translation and publication of laws into Spanish. Perhaps Juan noted a growing disregard for the interests of Tejanos, a sense of their increasing isolation within a now overwhelmingly Anglo-American Texas. If so, his comments ring eloquently for the rights of his minority:

> Mr. President, the dearest rights of my constituents as Mexico-Texians are guaranteed by the Constitution and the Laws of the Republic of Texas; and at the formation of the social compact between the Mexicans and the Texians, they had rights guaranteed to them; they also contracted certain legal obligations—of all of which they are ignorant. . . . The Mexico-Texians were among the first who sacrificed their all in our glorious Revolution, and the disasters of war weighed heavy upon them, to achieve those blessings which, it appears, [they] are destined to be the last to enjoy.

Juan's interest in instruction extended beyond expanding his constituency's understanding of the law. Given his own educational concerns, it is not surprising that he and José Antonio Navarro (the only Tejano serving in the house of representatives during the Third Congress) attempted to use their offices to obtain academic institutions for San Antonio. As Catholics, they found in Father John Timon, appointed by the bishop of New Orleans in 1838 to assess the Church's state of affairs in Texas, an opportunity to provide Béxar with a preparatory school and college of liberal arts and sciences while at the same time bringing needed reform to the spiritual life of Tejanos. Although Seguín and Navarro offered to endow a Catholic college with four leagues (17,714 acres) of land from the Republic,[16] conditions were not yet right and the plan fell through. Juan was able to influence the religious situation in San Antonio, however. After discussing the improprieties of the San Antonio and Goliad clergy with Father Timon, he provided an affidavit on the subject in January 1839 which contributed to their removal the following year.[17]

[How a hero can be turned into a traitor]

Despite Juan's apparent pursuit of his own programs, it was impossible for him not to become embroiled in both local and national political factionalism.

Moreover, the emerging schism between Texans and Tejanos was bound, sooner or later, to have an impact on Juan's relationships with San Antonio's growing Anglo population. In the summer of 1838 Launcelot Smithers, an English doctor who settled in San Antonio shortly after independence, declared erroneously: "there is not any 'danger' of Seguín being elected another term to Congress. His conduct has ruined him with the Mexicans: they supported him before thro' fear of his strength and of his resentment."[18] Adjutant General Hugh McLeod was even more blunt about Juan: "Seguine [sic] is my enemy, independent of his Houston allegiance, at least so I think, and yet the fellow smiles and smiles, but the Navarro family can neutralize him, & I may count upon the Beramendi's."[19] Speaking of a failed 1839 campaign by companies of Anglos and Tejanos against the Comanche, in which Seguín led the Tejanos, Mary Maverick suggested a less than courageous character on Juan's part: "They had been away from San Antonio ten days, when Captain Seguín returned reporting the woods full of Indians and predicting that our men would surely be killed."[20]

The return to San Antonio proved disappointing in another respect, for in January 1841 the first skirmish in Mexico's renewed campaign against Texas took place and Juan was one of its first victims. During a raid on the San Antonio River ranches by a company belonging to the Mexican general Rafael Vázquez's command, Juan lost a number of head of cattle. It was a loss he could not afford at the time, not only because his investment in the Canales Expedition [this refers to General Antonio Canales who asked Texas support to fight General Santa Anna and support federalism] was in jeopardy but because the size of his herd was still small. Juan now set out with Major George T. Howard on a fruitless pursuit of the Mexicans.[21]

Before he left, Juan received a small token of the aldermen's continuing appreciation for him as the mayor of San Antonio, a position which proved a heavy burden, particularly as it brought him into increasingly hostile contact with a growing body of Anglo-American vagrants and adventurers. As early as May of that year the town council found it necessary to formally voice their support for Juan:

> RESOLVED BY THIS BOARD OF ALDERMEN, that the Mayor of this City in their opinion is fully authorised [sic] and empowered by the Act of incorporating said city to execute and carry into effect all laws passed by this body and they hereby vest him with full Executive Powers to that effect.[22]

Juan's efforts to contain the vagrant problem was seconded by none other than Launcelot Smithers, now a member of the board of aldermen, and a strong critic of Seguín three years before. At the September 9, 1841, meeting of the city council he proposed that all individuals in the city who were not residents of the Republic should register with the mayor, and that anyone harboring a suspicious individual should be fined by the mayor.[23] *Considering his previously stated attitude, it is quite possible that Smithers meant "Mexicans" when he referred to suspicious individuals and not the Anglo Americans against whom Seguín directed his efforts. [Emphasis added]*

Juan also faced financial difficulties at this time. Having borrowed over $3,000 to equip the companies he took to Mexico in answer to General Canales's call and having failed to collect on either his investment or his men's salaries, Juan was in need of raising the money by some means. He found an opportunity in the summer of 1841 when Rafael Uribe came to Texas on behalf of General Mariano Arista to discuss cooperating on measures against the Indians who were making assaults on both sides of the border. On his return to Mexico, Juan decided, as he says in the memoirs, to enter "with him into a smuggling operation." Juan mortgaged a sizeable amount of property to Duncan C. Ogden and George T. Howard in order to obtain the goods he took to Mexico: his residence, a house and lot fronting on Flores Street in San Antonio; a house and lot fronting on Main Street on the main plaza; and a league of land adjoining his father's ranch, Casa Blanca.[24]

This trip, though of a strictly private nature for Juan, proved no more successful than his military project of the previous year. Mistaken by General Arista for one of the delegates from the Texas government, Seguín was ordered to leave the country. Juan was now the victim of his previous efforts in support of federalism. In the face of reports that he was recruiting volunteers for a possible revolt by the general against the centralist government in Mexico City, Arista could not afford to have Seguín around. Hoping to make the best of the situation, Juan left his goods behind, only to discover later that his money and remaining goods had been confiscated.

On his return to San Antonio Juan resumed his duties as mayor under a cloud of suspicion, for a rumor arose that he had betrayed the Santa Fe Expedition to the Mexicans. Since President Lamar's ill-advised effort to conquer New Mexico had left only a day before Uribe arrived in Austin, it is clear that Uribe had ample opportunity to learn about the expedition and report to his government. Uribe hurried back to Mexico, and soon after his return "Governor Francisco G. Conde of the Department of Chihuahua published the news of the Texan expedition toward Nuevo México and warned his people against being led astray by the flattering talk of the Texans."[25]

The rumor of Juan's betrayal, in its most eloquent form, is found in the memoirs of Mary Maverick:

It was strongly believed by many that Juan Nepomicino [sic] Seguín, who had held the honorable position of Mayor of San Antonio, and Representative to Congress, from Bexar, and being a man of great pride and ambition, had found himself surpassed by Americans, and somewhat overlooked in official places, had become dissatisfied with the Americans, and had opened communications with the officials of Mexico, exposing the entire plan from its inception as "invading Mexican soil." . . . From this time Seguín was suspected and Padre Garza, a rich and influential priest, was known to carry on traitorous correspondence with the Mexican authorities. Positive proof, however, was not obtained until Padre Garza escaped. Seguín indignantly denied the charge and many suspended judgement.[26]

Judgment was indeed suspended, for Juan not only resumed his duties as mayor, he was reelected at the end of the year.

After reelection Juan had to face the continuing problem of squatters on city property. As early as 1838, Mayor pro-tem Antonio Menchaca wrote to the commissioner of the General Land Office that a number of individuals, including Cornelius Van Ness, John W. Smith, and William Daingerfield among others, were attempting to take possession of land within the corporate boundaries of San Antonio. James Goodman, the single most visible offender at the time Seguín was mayor, was ousted from the property he claimed by Seguín, acting at the direction of the Board of Aldermen. Dr. Cupples, who settled in San Antonio in 1844, remembered Goodman in an interview he gave William Corner in 1890:

> I knew the man Goodman, you speak of; I remember him well, and the years of trouble he gave the city before he was finally ousted from the property on the Plaza, just opposite where Kalteyer's drug store is now was the location of the property he claimed. I remember he once came near to killing Ed Dwyer over that and other matters.[27]

Despite Juan's best efforts, the squatters problem escaped a solution. All Seguín managed was to make an enemy of Goodman.

The Goodman episode turned out to be one of Seguín's last actions as mayor of San Antonio. In the memoirs, Juan maintains that his efforts to repay the loan of $3,000 for which he had mortgaged his property led him to ask General Rafael Vázquez for a pass so that he might conduct some business. Juan, suspecting an invasion, shared Vázquez's letter of reply with the city council and the citizenry, and wrote President Houston for help on January 30, 1842. The response, which came from Secretary of War George Hockley, proved a disappointment: "I regret exceedingly that [the] impoverished condition of our country renders it almost helpless, and that we must depend upon the patrio[tism] of those who are willing to defend it."

Understanding that he and San Antonio could expect no help from the government, Seguín counseled a withdrawal from San Antonio. Many of the Mexican families began leaving and Juan retired to his ranch. The Anglo-Americans, in the meantime, decided to stay and organize a defense. The effort proved useless, however, and when Vázquez arrived in March, the defenders quickly withdrew to the town of Seguin. Although the Mexican forces remained in San Antonio for only two days, from March 5 to 7, they sowed enough suspicion and animosity against Seguín that it became impossible for him to recover.

Despite his joining Captain Jack Hays' company in pursuit of Vázquez, Juan returned to find that he had been branded a traitor. Even enjoying General Edward Burleson's favor—the general refused to hear any charges against Juan but instead ordered him to forage for the army among the ranches of the San Antonio River—Seguín could find no peace. Judging it impossible to remain in the city, Seguín went to the ranches but was constantly harassed. On April 18, 1842, citing "the turbulent state in which this unfortunate county finds itself," he resigned as mayor of San Antonio. By May Juan was on his way to Mexico, "a victim to the wickedness of a few men whose imposture was favored by their origin and recent domination over the country," as he states in the preface to his memoirs. In far-away Nacogdoches Adolphus Sterne wrote in his diary for May 27: "Col. Seguín has joined them, and as is usually the case, when our warm Friends turn against us, they become the most inveterate foes, I am satisfied, that it will be so in this case."[28]

Even aside from the pain of being labeled a traitor, being hounded by the men against whom he had acted as mayor, and being forced to abandon his native land, Juan must have been extremely confused. With the advantage of hindsight, we can sort things out. Vázquez, perhaps hoping to force a break that would bring the Tejanos over to the Mexican side, probably did attempt to discredit Juan and thus further confuse Texans about the loyalty of the Tejano population. Goodman, and the other Anglo-American latecomers with whom Juan had dealt harshly, thus had an opportunity to take their revenge and gain the upper hand over the Bexareños.

An Excerpt from the Memoirs

[In Seguín's own words, he narrates his being forced to move to Mexico and his eventual necessary participation in the Mexican-American War.]
On the 30th of April, [1842] a friend from San Antonio sent me word that Captain James W. Scott and his company were coming down by the river, burning the ranchos on their way. The inhabitants of the lower ranchos

called on us for aid against Scott. With those in my house, and others to the number of about one hundred, I started to lend them aid. I proceeded, observing Scott's movements from the junction of the Medina to Pajaritos. At that place we dispersed and I returned to my wretched life. In those days I could not go to San Antonio without peril for my life.

Matters being in this state, I saw that it was necessary to take some step which would place me in security and save my family from constant wretchedness. I had to leave Texas, abandon all for which I had fought and spent my fortune, to become a wanderer. The ingratitude of those who had assumed onto themselves the right of convicting me, their credulity in declaring me a traitor on the basis of mere rumors, the necessity to defend myself for the loyal patriotism with which I had always served Texas, wounded me deeply.

But before leaving my country, perhaps forever, I determined to consult with all those interested in my welfare. I held a family council. All were in favor of my removing for some time to the interior of Texas. But to accomplish this there were some unavoidable obstacles. I could not take one step from my rancho towards the Brazos without being exposed to the rifle of the first person who might meet me for, throughout the whole country, credit had been given to the rumors against me. To emigrate with my family was impossible as I was a ruined man after the invasion of Santa Anna and our flight to Nacogdoches. Furthermore the country of the Brazos was unhealthier than that of Nacogdoches. What might we not expect to suffer from disease in a new country, without friends or means?

Seeing that all these plans were impracticable, I resolved to seek a refuge among my enemies, braving all dangers. But before taking this step, I sent in my resignation as mayor of the city to the municipality of San Antonio, stating to them that, unable any longer to suffer the persecutions of some ungrateful Americans who strove to murder me, I had determined to free my family and friends from their continual misery on my account, and go and live peaceably in Mexico. That for these reasons I resigned my office, with all my privileges and honors as a Texan.

I left Béxar with no obligation to Texas, my services repaid with persecutions. Exiled and deprived of my privileges as a Texan citizen, I was outside the pale of society in Texas. If Texas could not protect the rights of her citizens, they were privileged to seek protection elsewhere. I had been tried by a rabble, condemned without a hearing, and consequently was at liberty to provide for my own safety.

When I arrived at Laredo the military commander of that place put me in prison, stating that he could not do otherwise until he had consulted with

General Arista, whom he advised of my arrest. Arista ordered that I be sent to Monterrey. When I arrived in that city, I earnestly prayed the general to allow me to retire to Saltillo, where I had several relatives who could aid me. General Arista answered that, as he had informed Santa Anna of my imprisonment, he could not comply with my request. Santa Anna directed that I be sent to the City of Mexico but Arista, sympathetic to my unfortunate position, interceded with him in my behalf to have the order revoked. The latter complied, but on condition that I should return to Texas with a company of explorers to attack its citizens and, by spilling my blood, vindicate myself.

Under the orders of General Arista, I proceeded to the Rio Grande to join General Woll, who told me that Santa Anna, at his request, had allowed me to go to Texas with Woll's expedition, but that I should receive no command until my services proved that I was worthy.

I set out with the expedition of General Woll. In the vicinity of San Antonio, on the 10th of September, I received an order to take a company of cavalry and block the exits from the city. By this order the city was blockaded and, consequently, it was difficult for any person to escape. When I returned from complying with this order, at dawn of day, the general determined to enter the city with the infantry and artillery. I was sent to the vanguard with orders to take possession of the Military Square despite all obstacles. I entered the square without opposition and, shortly afterwards, the firing commenced on the Main Square. John Hernández came out of Goodman's shop with a message from him to the effect that if I would pardon him for what he had done against me he would leave his place of concealment and deliver himself up. I sent him word that I had no rancor against him. He delivered himself up, and I placed him under the special charge of Captain Manuel Leal. Those who had made some show of resistance in the Main Square surrendered, and the whole city was in General Woll's possession.

The next day I was ordered, with two hundred men, to take the Gonzales road and approach that town. On the Cibolo I divided my forces, sending one detachment up the creek, another down the creek, and with the main body proceeded on the Gonzales road. The following day, these parties joined the main body. Lieutenant Manuel Carvajal, who commanded one of the parties, reported that he had killed three Texans who would not surrender in the Azufrosa [Sulphur Springs].

I returned to San Antonio. A party of Texans appeared by the Garita road and the troops were taken under arms. The general took one hundred infantry, the cavalry under Cayetano Montero, and one piece of artillery and proceeded towards the Salado. The general ordered one hundred *presidiales* [former garrison soldiers from Texas] to attack. The commander of those forces sent word that the enemy was in an advantageous position and that he required reinforcements. The answer of the general was to send me with orders "to attack at all costs." I obeyed. On the first charge I lost three killed and eight wounded, on the second seven killed and fifteen wounded. I was preparing for a third charge when Colonel José María Carrasco came to relieve me from my command. I returned to the side of the general and made my report, whereupon he ordered the firing to cease.

A new attack was in preparation when the attention of the general was called to some troops on our rear guard. The aides reported them to be enemies and near at hand. Colonel Montero was ordered to attack them with his cavalry. He called on them to surrender to the Mexican Government; they answered with scoffing and bantering. Montero formed his dragoons; the Texans commenced firing, killing two soldiers. Montero dismounted his troops, also began firing, and sent for more ammunition. The general angrily sent him a message asking whether his dragoons had no sabres or lances. Before Montero received this answer he had charged, sabre in hand, ending the engagement in a few minutes. Only some ten or fifteen Texans survived. During this time, I remained by the side of General Woll and was there when Montero made his report and brought in the prisoners. At dusk the troops received orders to return to San Antonio.

In accordance with his orders not to remain over a month on this side of the Rio Grande, General Woll began his retreat by the road he came. The Mexican families who left San Antonio were put under my charge and, consequently, I was not in the affair of "Arroyo Hondo."

Remarks

After General Woll's expedition I did not return to Texas until the treaty of Guadalupe Hidalgo. During my absence nothing occurred that could stamp me as a traitor. My enemies had accomplished their object; they had killed me politically in Texas, and the less they spoke of me, the less risk they incurred of exposing the infamous means they had used to accomplish my ruin.

As to my reputed treason with Vásquez, when we consider that Don Antonio Navarro and I were the only Mexicans of note in western Texas who had taken a prominent part in the war, the interest the Mexican general had in causing us to be distrusted will be seen. Mr. Navarro was then a prisoner. I alone remained, and if they were able to make the Texans distrust me, they gained a point. This is proved by the fact that, after I withdrew from the service, no other regiment of Mexican-Texans was ever seen. The rumor that I was a traitor was seized avidly by my enemies in San Antonio. Some envied my military position, as held by a *Mexican*; others found in me an obstacle to the accomplishment of their villainous plans. The number of land suits which still encumbers the docket of Bexar [San Antonio] County would indicate the nature of these plans, and anyone who has listened to the evidence elicited in cases such as this will readily discover the base means adopted to deprive rightful owners of their property.

But, returning again to the charge of treason. If I had sold myself to Mexico, the bargain would, of course, have been with the government. It would have been in the interest of Mexico to keep the bargain a secret, and not allow inferior officers to know it. So long as I enjoyed the confidence of the Texans, I might have been useful in imparting secrets, *etc.*, but as soon as my fellow citizens distrusted me, I was absolutely useless. And is it not strange that the Mexican officers should have been so anxious to inform the Texans of my treason? General Vásquez took out a paper from his pocket and claimed to Chevallie that it was from me, but when the latter desired to see the letter, Vásquez refused to show it to him.

But I take the expedition of Vásquez to be my best defense. What did Vásquez accomplish in that expedition? The coming into and going out of San Antonio without taking any further steps. Undoubtedly, if I had been allied with him, I would have tried to make his expedition something more than a mere military promenade. Far from doing this, however, I presented the letter that I received from Vásquez to the municipality of San Antonio; I predicted the expedition and counseled such steps as I thought should be taken.

And why, if my treason were so clear, did the patriotic and brave Burleson refuse to subject me to a court of inquiry? Undoubtedly he knew it to be his duty to put me on trial if the slightest suspicion existed as to my character. He refused, and this proved that Burleson and the superior officers were convinced of the shallowness of the charges against me.

During the electoral campaign of August 1855, I was frequently attacked in newspapers and was styled in some "the murderer of the Salado." For some time I had proposed to publish my memoirs, so I thought it useless to enter into a newspaper war, more particularly as the attacks against me were anonymous and were directed with a venom which made me conclude that I owed them to the malevolence of a personal enemy.

I have related my participation in Woll's expedition and have only to say that neither I nor any of my posterity will ever have reason to blush for it. During my military career, I can proudly assert that I never deviated from the line of duty, that I never shed, or caused to be shed, human blood unnecessarily, that I never insulted a prisoner by word or deed, and that, in the fulfillment of my duty, I always drew a distinction between my obligations as a soldier on the battlefield and as a civilized man after the battle.

I have finished my memoirs; I have neither the capacity nor the desire to adorn my acts with literary phrases. I have attempted a short and clear narrative of my public life in relation to Texas. I publish it without omitting or suppressing anything that I thought of the least interest, and confidently I submit to the public verdict.

Several of those who witnessed the facts I have related are still alive and among us. They can state whether I have falsified the record in any way.

After the War

[At this point we return to the story as told by Jesús de la Teja.]
The war took its toll on Juan. At forty-three he had little to show for an adult life spent mostly fighting in the saddle. Near the end of the war, he showed up at Presidio Río Grande and made contact with the Texans there. In February 1848 John A. Veatch, captain in the regiment of Texas Mounted Volunteers, informed Mirabeau B. Lamar that "our *Texian-Mexican* Seguín, presented himself a few days since desiring permission to bring his family—which he thinks is in Saltillo—to this place. He says he will return to Texas and risk consiquences [*sic*]. He looks careworn & *thread-bare*."[29] Finding his family in Saltillo, Juan determined to return to Texas and wrote in April to Sam Houston, asking for the Texan's "weighty and important recommendation to my former fellow citizens, as also a protection from the President of your Republic." Seguín did not enter into explanations: "You are I think acquainted with the causes which obliged me to leave my country, and as the explanation of them would be long, I defer it till I have the gratification of seeing you." By the end of the year he was back in San Antonio, where he and his family settled down with Erasmo at Casa Blanca.[30]

As public a man as Juan had been throughout his adult life, it proved impossible for him to remain quietly on the ranch for long. In his April 1848 letter to Houston he already hinted at his interest in returning to local politics in San Antonio. In 1852 his interest became reality and Juan won election as Bexar [*San Antonio*] County justice of the peace; he was reelected two years later. He also served as president of his election precinct, which included the ranches along the San Antonio River near his home.[31]

The last important event in Juan's public career was his participation in the establishment of the Democratic Party in Bexar [*San Antonio*] County. The move to found a local Democratic Party stemmed from efforts to offset the growing popularity of the anti-Catholic, anti-masonic, anti-immigration, and anti-naturalization Know-Nothing Party. Although some Tejanos favored the Know-Nothings, many, including Seguín, saw in it the seeds of even worse discrimination against Tejanos. It is a testament to Juan's talents that, despite the presence of other prominent Tejanos in the community who had never been accused of disloyalty, particularly José Antonio Navarro, it was Seguín who became the featured Tejano in the Democratic Party, and Samuel Maverick, the local party president, named Juan to the platform writing committee. Juan also became a member of the Democratic committee of the "Mexican Texan citizens of Bexar [San Antonio] County."[32]

His acceptance by Tejanos and Anglo Texans gave Seguín a new sense of responsibility. It did not come without a price, however. His political activities brought renewed personal attacks from which he had to defend himself. Juan looked upon the memoirs, which he wrote in 1858, not only as a defense against "the barbarous and unworthy deeds" of which he was accused but as a means of keeping alive the possibility of future public service.

His belief that he could once again act as intermediary between Texas and Mexico surfaced that same year when, perhaps fearing designs floating about Texas and Washington, D.C., regarding an American annexation of Mexico, Juan offered his services to Governor Santiago Vidaurri of Nuevo León. Sam Houston, then a member of the United States Senate, offered a bill calling for the United States to establish a protectorate over Mexico and Central America.[33] Juan, who traveled to Monterrey with his wife in the fall of 1858, returned to Texas with a special commission from Governor Vidaurri; he wrote Texas governor Hardin R. Runnels in January 1859 that Vidaurri wished to enter into a treaty with Texas "for the extradition of fugitive slaves, peons, robbers, murderers and incendiaries."[34] Governor Vidaurri thus thought to defuse the Texans' hostility by offering to eliminate their more important grievances against Mexico.

At this point, it becomes necessary to discuss what for historians has been the most confusing aspect of Juan's life. According to some students of Seguín, he participated in the 1850s and 1860s wars of the Reform and French Intervention and later on in Porfirio Díaz's 1871 revolt against Benito Juarez.[35] There is evidence, however, indicating that the Seguín who participated in these wars was not Juan but Juan Jr. For instance, at the very time Seguín and his wife made their trip to Monterrey in 1858, Santiago Vidaurri received word that a Juan N. Seguín and his cousin Miguel Zaragoza (General Ignacio Zaragoza's brother) were on their way to San Antonio with a mule train.[36] A biography of General Zaragoza makes the following claim in a genealogical note regarding the Seguín-Zaragoza family: "Juan N. Seguín, born in 1833, who was the one who accompanied Zaragoza during the War of the Reform with the rank of colonel and who was his third cousin." Moreover, Seguín would have been sixty-five years old in 1871, the year Díaz rebelled against Juárez.

. . . .

Texas did not entirely forget Juan, nor did Texans view him in an unfavorable light during the last years of his life. During his return to Texas in 1874 to apply for his pension, Edward Miles, secretary of the Texas Veterans Association, asked Juan to write some reminiscences for a "Log Cabin History of Texas," a work that was never published. In 1882 the San Antonio *Light* reported that the Seguín family, "one of the oldest and most respected of San Antonio" was visiting from Mexico. Five years later the Clarksville *Northern Standard* published a premature and quite odd obituary of him: "Capt. juan n. seguin, of Laredo, the last surviving captain of the battle of San Jacinto, died in London, England, a few days since. The flag over the capitol building in Austin was run down to half mast on the 9th in his honor." In the last eighteen months of his life Juan also answered requests for information from Texans regarding his activities during the War of Independence.[37]

What is remarkable about these late communications is that there is no sense of hostility, bitterness or regret in Juan's words. His 1887 interview with a reporter from the Laredo *Times,* which was reprinted in other Texas newspapers, evidences a man at peace with himself and with the world around him. Even allowing for some literary license, Juan's questions regarding his former compatriots and their descendants, naming John J. and Edward Linn, John S. Menefee, Thomas O'Connor, and others, suggests that he had many fond memories. This was especially true of Houston: "The old veteran recalled with evidences of pride and pleasure the fact of Houston's friendship, and even partiality, for him, saying that 'Old Sam' was wont to call him his son."

Death came for Juan on August 27, 1890, at age eighty-three. This time there were no obituaries, no ceremonies, no notice of his passing. His memoirs have long remained his only epitaph, yet his achievements and travails have not permitted Texas to forget him. As Tejanos rediscover their contributions to Texas history, as they overcome the barriers that separate Texan and Tejano, Juan Seguín has again returned to serve as intermediary between the two.

*　　*　　*

Notes

1. Músquiz to Austin, January 22, 1829, AP, II: 9.
2. Election returns, December 21, 1828, BA; *Cuaderno borrador* of Gaspar Flores and Juan N. Seguín, June 5, 1829, ibid.; Juan to Jefe Político, June 7 and 20, 1829, ibid.; *Resumen general,* August 10, 1829, ibid.

3. Election of electoral assembly officers, February 13, 1832, BA; Minutes of the electoral assembly, March 1, 1833, ibid.; Minutes of the electoral assembly, February 9, 1834, ibid.

4. Paul Lack, "Los Tejanos: Texas Mexicans in the Revolution," MSS chapter in forthcoming book on Texas War of Independence, 451–52.

5. Lack, "Los Tejanos," 453–54; Antonio Cruz, Audited Military Claims, TSL; Juan Rodríguez, Republic Pension Applications, ibid.

6. Nicolás Flores to Juan, January 23, 1836, BA; [San Antonio Meeting], January 26, 1836; Jenkins, *Papers of the Revolution*, 4:153–55; J. J. Baugh to Henry Smith, February 13, 1836, ibid.; Harbert Davenport, "Captain Jesus Cuellar, Texas Cavalry, Otherwise Comanche," *Southwestern Historical Quarterly* 30 (July 1926): 58; Antonio Menchaca, *Memoirs* (San Antonio: Yanaguana Press, 1937), 23.

7. "Alamo's Only Survivor," San Antonio *Express*, May 12, 1907; Menchaca, *Memoirs*, 23; José María Rodríguez, *Rodriguez Memoirs of Early Texas* (reprint, San Antonio: Standard Printing Company, 1961); Lack, "Los Tejanos," 478.

8. Juan Rodríguez, Republic Pension Applications, TSL; Lack, "Los Tejanos," 479–80; William F. Gray, *From Virginia to Texas* (Houston: Gray, Dillaye & Company, 1909), 131.

9. Houston to E. D. White, October 31, 1837, James Grizzard Collection, TSL.

10. Houston to Erasmo, July 6, 1842, *The Writings of Sam Houston, 1813–1863*, ed. Amelia W. Williams and Eugene C. Barker 10 vols. (Austin: University of Texas Press, 1938–1943), 4:125.

11. José Enrique de la Peña, *With Santa Anna in Texas: A Personal Narrative of the Revolution* (College Station: Texas A&M University Press, 1975), 4.

12. Felix Huston to Sam Houston, November 14, 1836, Houston Collection, Catholic Archives of Texas.

13. Jack C. Butterfield, "Juan N. Seguín: A Vindication" (MSS, DRT, n.d.), 12–14.

14. Refugio B-5 and Fannin B-440, Original Land Grant Collection, GLO; Juan N. Seguín, Audited Civil Service Claims, Comptroller's Records, TSL.

15. *Telegraph and Texas Register*, May 19, 1838; Ida Vernon, "Activities of the Seguíns in Early Texas History" (West Texas Historical Association Year Book 25, 1949), 28; Joseph M. Nance, *After San Jacinto: The Texas Mexican Frontier, 1836–1841* (Austin: University of Texas Press, 1963), 281.

16. Unable to afford the expenses of public colleges, Congress promoted the establishment of private institutions through grants of public land.

17. Charles E. Castañeda, *Our Catholic Heritage in Texas, 1519–1936* (New York: Arno, 1976), 7:25–27.

18. Smithers to John P. Borden, July 13, 1838, Early Letters Received, GLO (microfilm).

19. McLeod to Lamar, August 24, 1840, Lamar Papers, TSL.

20. *Memoirs of Mary A. Maverick*, 29.

21. Benjamin Gillam to Hugh McLeod, January 10, 1841, Army Papers, Adjutant General's Records, TSL; White, *The 1840 Census of the Republic of Texas*, 16; Nance, *After San Jacinto*, 409.

22. Journal A, Records of the City of San Antonio from 1837 to 1849, Material from Various Sources, BHC, vol. 815:79.

23. Journal A, Records of the City of San Antonio, vol. 815: 87, 89, BHC; Vernon, "Activities of the Seguíns," 31–32.

24. Journal A, Records of the City of San Antonio, BHC, vol. 815: 82; Juan and Gertrudis Seguín to Howard and Ogden, July 2, 1841, Deed Records of Bexar County, vol. A-2: 447–48; Nance, *After San Jacinto*, 431–34.

25. Nance, *After San Jacinto*, 434.

26. *Memoirs of Mary A. Maverick*, 59.

27. Corner, *San Antonio*, 113.

28. Harriet Smither, ed., "Diary of Adolphus Sterne," Part XV, *Southwestern Historical Quarterly* 33 (April 1930): 318.

29. Veatch to Lamar, February 23, 1848, Lamar Papers, doc. 2377, TSL.

30. Vernon, "Activities of the Seguíns," 36; 1850 Census of the United States, Bexar County (microfilm), #146, TSL.

31. *El Bejareño*, July 7, 1855; Santos, "Juan Nepomuceno Seguín," 563.

32. *El Bejareño*, July 21, 1855.

33. Santos, "Juan Nepomuceno Seguín," 564–65; Llerena Friend, *Sam Houston: The Great Designer* (reprint, Austin: University of Texas Press, 1969), 298–300.

34. Juan to Hardin R. Runnels, January 8, 1859, Hardin Richard Runnels Correspondence, Governors Papers, TSL.

35. Jack Jackson, *Los Tejanos* (Stamford: Fantagraphics Press, 1982), 121; Santos, in "Juan Nepomuceno Seguín," 565 (fn. 44), 566, cites the *Archivo de la Defensa Nacional*, where he examined a folder on "Juan N. Seguín." The author could not consult this folder as it is now unavailable.

36. *La Voz de Zaragoza*, 1 (December 1961): 27; Guillermo Colin Sánchez, *Ignacio Zaragoza: Evocación de un héroe* (Mexico: Editorial Porrúa, 1963), 41.

37. San Antonio *Light*, November 13, 1882; Clarksville *Northern Standard*, August 18, 1887.

*   *   *

Questions

1. According to Seguín, why and by whom is he being persecuted? How might his own perception of who he is differ from how others think of him?

2. On what grounds can we argue that geopolitical forces justify (or do not justify) the domination of indigenous people by others more economically, technologically, and militarily more powerful?

3. In what ways does or does not "The Making of a Tejano" fit with U.S. American stereotypes of Mexicans?

4. What might be alternative constructions of American Indian subjectivities, presented in this text as "hostile attackers of peaceful settlements"?

5. About the representation of others: This is primarily a male story and, therefore, the status of women, slaves, the working class, and American Indians is made obvious by their own invisibility. What voices are not being heard (in addition to Gertrudis Seguín and Juan López, the orphan who "looked like an Indian")?

∿

The United States War with Mexico
Francisco Hernández Vázquez

One cannot help but wonder, "Why or how did the United States and Mexico get into a war?" As mentioned in previous readings, after three hundred years of Spanish colonization, the nation-state of Mexico was born in 1821 out of the War of Independence. This new country soon found itself in a precarious position, with a devastated economy, warring political factions, and public debt, and in less than two decades it was dismembered (losing Texas and Central America). Meanwhile, the United States was fulfilling its desire for economic and territorial expansion through the Louisiana Purchase and the acquisition of Texas.

There are at least five interpretations of who was responsible for the war. One has already been mentioned: Manifest Destiny, the imperial expansion of the United States. From a purely economic perspective, commercial interests, New England merchants especially, are another explanation. Similarly, a third explanation blames sectional interests, like the Old South's attempt to extend slavery or the West's desire for further expansion. But if we want to blame individuals, the most likely character to blame in a fourth interpretation has been President James K. Polk. Finally, others put responsibility generally on one nation or the other, Mexico or the United States.[1]

In the case of Texas and the Seguín family, we already saw the process of an economic, political, and social seduction that promised to fulfill the desires of the Tejano elite. This same process was repeated throughout the northern provinces of Mexico, with General Mariano Vallejo in Northern California and Governor Manuel Armijo in New Mexico; later it occurred in

Cuba and Puerto Rico, creating what Louis A. Pérez calls "binding familiarities" (referring to early Cuban-U.S. relations). Besides the geopolitical perspective, however, it is helpful to gaze at the specific, cultural, interpersonal, almost invisible ways in which this seduction anticipates military intervention and the signing of treaties. As soon as Mexico became independent from Spain (1821), an enterprising William Becknell put together a trading party and traveled eight hundred miles from Franklin, Missouri, to what was then the Mexican border, Santa Fé, Nuevo México, where he was welcomed by Spanish-born Governor Facundo Melgares to sell his wares at a princely profit. As David J. Weber recounts,

> New Mexicans traded bullion, horses, and mules for American manufactured goods, becoming economically dependent upon the Americans. American trappers and merchants made New Mexico their permanent home . . . becoming Roman Catholics and citizens, learning Spanish, and marrying or living with New Mexican women. . . . New Mexicans learned that the "gringos," although often unpleasant, were not devils and that American rule over the territory would not be intolerable. At the same time, the Americans learned enough of local customs and of the power structure to serve as an effective fifth column when war erupted between the United States and Mexico.[2]

The Santa Fe Trail was soon connected to California via the Old Spanish Trail (which had never been used by the Spaniards) and a two-way trade of commodities flowed from the United States, through the northern provinces, and into the interior of Mexico. Thus, as in Texas, we see what appears to be a set of mutual economic and political interests but in reality they represent a sort of silent invasion, a cultural and economic colonization that points directly to the interior of Mexico.

It is not an exaggeration to say that this is the same process of economic seduction that more recently led to the signing of the North American Free Trade Agreement (NAFTA).[3] Then as now, not all Mexicans welcomed the U.S. Americans and the disagreement was usually along class lines, with the wealthy supporting relations with the Anglo-American neighbors. This is similar to what happened in the case of Cuba. On the contrary, in Puerto Rico the elite opposed the United States' intervention, whereas the poor supported it. Two final points need to be made here: One is that when it comes to an object of desire all parties become conspirators, and the other point is that, in this game of truth, the voice of the poor people often becomes deflected.

With the two documents discussed in the next section (Buchanan's letter to the U.S. Senate and excerpts from the Treaty of Guadalupe-Hidalgo),

Mexicans living in the conquered territories became territorial, involuntary citizens of the United States (although they were given a choice, in one way or another, they became subjects of the government). Unlike Cubans and Puerto Ricans, the Mexicans who lived in the conquered territories, received citizenship at the time of their military conquest. The term *Mexican*, however, applied to white Mexicans and not to Mexican Indians, though they were considered Mexican citizens according to Mexican law.

The U.S. Congress actually debated keeping all of Mexico. In the end it approved these two documents that represent the loss of half of Mexico, that is the loss of its Northern Territories including California, New Mexico, Arizona, and parts of Nevada, Wyoming, Kansas, Oklahoma, Colorado, and Utah as illustrated in the map. For purposes of comparison, Mexico received an indemnity of $15 million for what is now the Southwest of the United States; this same year President Polk offered Spain $100 million for Cuba. This is the harshest treaty in two hundred years of U.S. territorial acquisition, and the only U.S. national document addressing Mexican Americans.[4] As we will see later in this reader, the United States continued in its quest to acquire Cuba and as of 2008, with the decline of Fidel Castro and his appointment of his brother Raul, this remains a real possibility.

Notes and Suggestions for Further Research

1. Ramón Eduardo Ruiz, *The Mexican War: Was It Manifest Destiny?* (Hinsdale, IL: Dryden, 1963).

2. David J. Weber, *Foreigners in Their Native Land* (Albuquerque: University of New Mexico Press, 1973), 56. Governor Manuel Armijo sent word in 1827 to Mexico City "that every day the foreigners are becoming more influential over the miserable inhabitants of this Territory" and warning of an "evil of great consequence" should the foreigners not be dealt with. The new nation, however, lacked the resources to defend its northern frontier, so ultimately Armijo followed the example of other New Mexican oligarchs, formed a trading partnership with an American, and began importing goods from the United States. From Texas to California, Mexicans with capital welcomed the opportunity to trade with foreigners because the low cost of U.S. manufactured goods compared with the outrageous prices the Spanish had charged. Though the threat of invasion was real, as Weber points out, "ideology and diplomacy were not nearly as important as low-cost merchandise and the end of isolation" (135).

3. For a recent analysis on the negotiation of NAFTA, see Maxwell A. Cameron and Brian W. Tomlin, *The Making of NAFTA* (Ithaca, NY: Cornell University Press, 2000).

4. Juan Gómez-Quiñonez, *Roots of Chicano Politics, 1600–1940* (Albuquerque: University of New Mexico Press, 1994), 188–89.

CHAPTER SIX

~

Letter from James Buchanan and the Treaty of Guadalupe-Hidalgo

Included in this chapter are two kinds of texts. First is Secretary of State James Buchanan's letter to the minister of foreign relations of Mexico, explaining the U.S. Senate amendments to the treaty.[1] Secondly, there are articles eight to fifteen (out of the twenty-three articles) of the Treaty of Guadalupe-Hidalgo, that specifically affect the Mexicans who ended up in the territories taken over by the United States. To allow a comparison, we include copies of articles 9 and 10, before they were amended by the U.S. Senate (they deal with questions of landownership in the newly conquered territory and in Texas).

*   *   *

Letter from James Buchanan to the Minister of Foreign Relations of Mexico

To His Excellency, the Minister of Foreign Relations of the Mexican Republic.

Sir: Two years have nearly passed away since our Republics have been engaged in war. Causes, which it would now be vain if not hurtful to recapitulate, have produced this calamity. Under the blessing of a kind Providence, this war, I trust, is about to terminate, and, hereafter, instead of the two nations doing each other all the harm they can, their mutual energies will be devoted to promote each other's welfare by the pursuits of peace and of commerce. I most cordially congratulate you on the cheering prospect. This will become a reality as soon as the Mexican Government shall approve the treaty of peace between the two nations concluded at Guadalupe Hidalgo on the 2nd February, last, with the amendments thereto which have been adopted by the Senate of the United States.

The President, in the exercise of his constitutional discretion, a few days after this treaty was received, submitted it to the Senate for their consideration and advice as to its ratification. Your Excellency is doubtless aware that under the Constitution of the United States, "the advice and consent of the Senate" is necessary to the validity of all treaties and that this must be given by a majority of two thirds of the Senators present. Every Treaty must receive the sanction of this august Executive Council in the manner prescribed by the Constitution, before it can be binding on the United States.

The Senate commenced their deliberations on this Treaty on the 23rd February, last, and continued to discuss its provisions until the 10th instant (March) when they finally advised and consented to its ratification by a majority of 38 to 14. Your Excellency will perceive that a change of 4 votes taken from the majority and added to the minority would have defeated the Treaty.

I have now the honor to transmit you a printed copy of the Treaty with a copy, in manuscript, of the amendments and final proceedings of the Senate upon it. This is done to hasten with as little delay as practicable the blessed consummation of peace by placing in the possession of the Mexican Government at as early a period as possible all the information which they may require to guide their deliberations.

In recurring to the amendments adopted by the Senate, it affords me sincere satisfaction to observe that none of the leading features of the Treaty have been changed. Neither the delineation of the boundaries between the two Republics—nor the consideration to be paid to Mexico for the extension of the boundaries of the United States—nor the obligation of the latter to restrain the Indians within their limits from committing hostilities on the territories of Mexico nor, indeed, any other stipulation of national importance to either of the parties, has been stricken out from the Treaty by the Senate. In all its important features, it remains substantially as it was when it came from the hands of the negotiators.

The first amendment adopted by the Senate is to insert in Article 3 after the words "Mexican Republic" where they first occur, the words, "and the Ratifications exchanged."

Under this article, as it originally stood, the blockades were to cease and the troops of the United States were to commence the evacuation of the Mexican territory immediately upon the ratification of the Treaty by both Governments. The amendment requires in addition that these ratifications shall have been first exchanged.

The object of this amendment doubtless was to provide against the possibility that the American Senate and the Mexican Congress might ratify the

Treaty, the first in its amended and the latter in its original form: in which event peace would not thereby be concluded. Besides, it was known that this amendment could produce no delay, as under the amendment of the Senate to the 23rd article, the ratification of the Treaty may be exchanged at the seat of Government of Mexico the moment after the Mexican Government and Congress shall have accepted the Treaty as amended by the Senate of the United States.

The second amendment of the Senate is to strike out the 9th Article and insert the following in lieu thereof.

[Here follows the English version of Article 9]

This article is substantially the same with the original 9th article; but it avoids unnecessary prolixity and accords with the former safe precedents of this Government in the Treaties by which we acquired Louisiana from France and Florida from Spain.

The Louisiana Treaty of the 30th April, 1803 *[Document 28]*, contains the following article.

ARTICLE 3

The inhabitants of the ceded territory shall be incorporated in the union of the United States, and admitted as soon as possible, according to the principles of the Federal Constitution, to the enjoyment of all the rights, advantages and immunities of citizens of the United States, and in the mean time they shall be maintained and protected in the free enjoyment of their liberty, property, and the religion which they profess. Again, in the Florida Treaty of 22nd February, 1819 *[Document 41]*, the following articles are contained.

ARTICLE 5

The inhabitants of the ceded Territories shall be secured in the free exercise of their religion, without any restriction; and all those who may desire to remove to the Spanish Dominions, shall be permitted to sell or export their effects, at any time whatever, without being subject, in either case, to duties.

ARTICLE 6

The inhabitants of the territories which His Catholic Majesty cedes to the United States, by his Treaty, shall be incorporated in the Union of the United States, as soon as may be consistent with the principles of the Federal Constitution, and admitted to the enjoyment of all the privileges, rights and immunities of the citizens of the United States.

Under these Treaties with France and Spain, the free and flourishing States of Louisiana, Missouri, Arkansas, Iowa and Florida have been admitted into the Union; and no complaint has ever been made by the original or other inhabitants that their civil or religious rights have not been amply protected.

The property belonging to the different churches in the United States is held as sacred by our Constitution and laws as the property of individuals, and every individual enjoys the inalienable right of worshipping his God according to the dictates of his own conscience. The Catholic Church in this country would not, if they could, change their position in this particular.

After the successful experience of nearly half a century, the Senate did not deem it advisable to adopt any new form for the 9th Article of the Treaty; and surely the Mexican Government ought to be content with an article similar to those which have proved satisfactory to the Governments of France and Spain and to all the inhabitants of Louisiana and Florida, both of which were Catholic provinces.

I ought perhaps here to note a modification in the 9th article, as adopted by the Senate, of the analogous articles of the Louisiana and Florida Treaties. Under this modification, the inhabitants of the ceded territories are to be admitted into the Union, "at the proper time (to be judged of by the Congress of the United States") &c.

Congress, under all circumstances and under all Treaties are the sole judges of this proper time, because they and they alone, under the Federal Constitution, have power to admit new States into the Union. That they will always exercise this power as soon as the condition of the inhabitants of any acquired territory may render it proper, cannot be doubted. By this means the Federal Treasury can alone be relieved from the expense of supporting territorial Governments. Besides, Congress will never lend a deaf ear to a people anxious to enjoy the privilege of self government. Their application to become a State or States of the Union will be granted the moment this can be done with safety.

The third amendment of the Senate strikes from the Treaty the 10th Article.

It is truly unaccountable how this article should have found a place in the Treaty. That portion of it in regard to lands in Texas did not receive a single vote in the Senate. If it were adopted, it would be a mere nullity on the face of the Treaty, and the Judges of our Courts would be compelled to disregard it. It is our glory that no human power exists in this country which can deprive one individual of his property without his consent and transfer it to another. If grantees of lands in Texas, under the Mexican Government, possess valid titles, they can maintain their claims before our Courts of Justice. If they have forfeited their grants by not complying with the conditions on which they were made, it is beyond the power of this Government, in any mode of action, to render these titles valid either against Texas or any individual proprietor. To resuscitate such grants and to allow the grantees the same period after the exchange of the ratifications of this Treaty to which they were originally entitled for the purpose of performing the conditions on which these grants had been made, even if this could be accomplished by the power of the government of the United States, would work manifold injustice.

These Mexican grants, it is understood, cover nearly the whole sea coast and a large portion of the interior of Texas. They embrace thriving villages and a great number of cultivated farms, the proprietors of which have acquired them honestly by purchase from the State of Texas. These proprietors are now dwelling in peace and security. To revive dead titles and suffer the inhabitants of Texas to be ejected under them from their possessions, would be an act of flagrant injustice if not wanton cruelty. Fortunately this Government possesses no power to adopt such a proceeding.

The same observations equally apply to such grantees in New Mexico and Upper California.

The present Treaty provides amply and specifically in its 8th and 9th Articles for the security of property of every kind belonging to Mexicans, whether acquired under Mexican grants or otherwise in the acquired territory. The property of foreigners under our Constitution and laws, will be equally secure without any Treaty stipulation. The tenth article could have no effect upon such grantees as had forfeited their claims, but that of involving them in endless litigation under the vain hope that a Treaty might cure the defects in their titles against honest purchasers and owners of the soil.

And here it may be worthy of observation that if no stipulation whatever were contained in the Treaty to secure to the Mexican inhabitants and all others protection in the free enjoyment of their liberty, property and the religion which they profess, these would be amply guaranteed by the Constitution and laws of the United States. These invaluable blessings, under our form of Government, do not result from Treaty stipulations, but from the very nature and character of our institutions. . . .

James Buchanan
Department of State
Washington, 18th March, 1848

*   *   *

The Treaty of Guadalupe Hidalgo: Articles 8–15

Article VIII[2]

Mexicans now established in territories previously belonging to Mexico, and which remain for the future within the limits of the United States, as defined by the present treaty, shall be free to continue where they now reside, or to remove at any time to the Mexican Republic, retaining the property which they possess in the said territories, or disposing thereof, and removing the proceeds wherever they please, without their being subjected, on this account, to any contribution, tax or charge whatever.

Those who shall prefer to remain in the said territories, may either retain the title and rights of Mexican citizens, or acquire those of citizens of the United States. But they shall be under the obligation to make their election within one year from the date of the exchange of ratifications of this treaty: and those who shall remain in the said territories, after the expiration of that year without having declared their intention to retain the character of Mexicans, shall be considered to have elected to become citizens of the United States.

In the said territories, property of every kind, now belonging to Mexicans, not established there, shall be inviolably respected. The present owners, the heirs of these and all Mexicans who may hereafter acquire said property by contract, shall enjoy with respect to it, guarantees equally ample as if the same belonged to citizens of the United States.

Article IX

The Mexicans who, in the territories aforesaid, shall not preserve the character of citizens of the Mexican Republic, conformably with what is stipulated in the preceding article, shall be incorporated into the Union of the United States and be admitted, at the proper time (to be judged of by the Congress of the United States) to the enjoyment of all the rights of citizens of the United States according to the principles of the Constitution; and in the mean time shall be maintained and protected in the free enjoyment of their liberty and property, and secured in the free exercise of their religion without restriction.

[One of the amendments of the Senate struck out Article 10.]

Article XI

Considering that a great part of the territories which, by the present Treaty, are to be comprehended for the future within the limits of the United States, is now occupied by savage tribes, who will hereafter be under the exclusive control of the Government of the United States, and whose incursions within the territory of Mexico would be prejudicial in the extreme; it is solemnly agreed that all such incursions shall be forcibly restrained by the Government of the United States, whensoever this may be necessary; and that when they cannot be prevented, they shall be punished by the said Government, and satisfaction for the same shall be exacted, all in the same way, and with equal diligence and energy, as if the same incursions were meditated or committed within its own territory against its own citizens.It shall not be lawful, under any pretext whatever, for any inhabitant of the United States, to purchase or acquire any Mexican or any foreigner residing in Mexico, who may have been captured by Indians inhabiting the territory of either of the two Republics, nor to purchase or acquire horses, mules, cattle or property of any kind, stolen within Mexican territory by such Indians.

And, in the event of any person or persons, captured within Mexican Territory by Indians, being carried into the territory of the United States, the Government of the latter engages and binds itself in the most solemn manner, so soon as it shall know of such captives being within its territory, and shall be able so to do, through the faithful exercise of its influence and power, to rescue them and return them to their country, or deliver them to the agent or representative of the Mexican Government. The Mexican Authorities will, as far as practicable, give to the Government of the United States notice of such captures; and its agent shall pay the expenses incurred in the maintenance and transmission of the rescued captives; who, in the mean time, shall be treated with the utmost hospitality by the American authorities at the place where they may be. But if the Government of the United States, before receiving such notice from Mexico, should obtain intelligence through any other channel, of the existence of Mexican captives within its territory, it will proceed forthwith to effect their release and delivery to the Mexican agent, as above stipulated.

For the purpose of giving to these stipulations the fullest possible efficacy, thereby affording the security and redress demanded by their true spirit and intent, the Government of the United States will now and hereafter pass, without unnecessary delay, and always vigilantly enforce, such laws as the nature of the subject may require. And finally, the sacredness of this obligation shall never be lost sight of by the said Government, when providing for the removal of the Indians from any portion of the said territories, or for its being settled by citizens of the United States; but on the contrary special care shall then be taken not to place its Indian occupants under the necessity of seeking new homes, by committing those invasions which the United States have solemnly obliged themselves to restrain.

Article XII

In consideration of the extension acquired by the boundaries of the United States, as defined in the fifth Article of the present Treaty, the Government of the United States engages to pay to that of the Mexican Republic the sum of fifteen Millions of Dollars.

Immediately after this treaty shall have been duly ratified by the Government of the Mexican Republic, the sum of three millions of dollars shall be paid to the said Government by that of the United States at the city of Mexico, in the gold or silver coin of Mexico. The remaining twelve millions of dollars shall be paid at the same place and in the same coin, in annual installments of three millions of dollars each, together with interest on the same at the rate of six per centum per annum. This interest shall begin to run upon the whole sum of twelve millions, from the day of the ratification of the present treaty by the Mexican Government, and the first of the installments shall be paid at the expiration of one year from the same day. Together with each annual installment, as it falls due, the whole interest accruing on such installment from the beginning shall also be paid.

Article XIII

The United States engage moreover, to assume and pay to the claimants all amounts now due them, and those hereafter to become due, by reason of the claims already liquidated and decided against the Mexican Republic, under the conventions between the two Republics severally concluded on the eleventh day of April eighteen hundred and thirty-nine, and on the thirtieth day of January eighteen hundred and forty-three: so that the Mexican Republic shall be absolutely exempt for the future, from all expense whatever on account of the said claims.

Article XIV

The United States do furthermore discharge the Mexican Republic from all claims of citizens of the United States, not heretofore decided against the Mexican Government, which may have arisen previously to the date of the signature of this treaty: which discharge shall be final and perpetual, whether the said claims be rejected or be allowed by the Board of Commissioners provided for in the following Article, and whatever shall be the total amount of those allowed.

Article XV

The United States, exonerating Mexico from all demands on account of the claims of their citizens mentioned in the preceding Article, and considering them entirely and forever cancelled, whatever their amount may be, undertake to make satisfaction for the same, to an amount not exceeding three and one quarter millions of Dollars. To ascertain the validity and amount of those claims, a Board of Commissioners shall be established by the Government of the United States, who awards shall be final and conclusive: provided that in deciding upon the validity of each claim, the board shall be guided and governed By the principles and rules of decision prescribed by the first and fifth Articles of the unratified convention, concluded at the City of Mexico on the twentieth day of November, one thousand eight hundred and forty-three; and in no case shall an award be made in favour of any claim not embraced by these principles and rules.

If, in the opinion of the said Board of Commissioners, or of the claimants, any books, records or documents in the possession or power of the Government of the Mexican Republic, shall be deemed necessary to the just decision of any claim, the Commissioners or the claimants, through them, shall, within such period as Congress may designate, make an application in writing for the same, addressed to the Mexican Minister for Foreign Affairs, to be transmitted by the Secretary of State of the United States; and the Mexican Government engages, at the earliest possible moment after the receipt of such demand, to cause any of the books, records or documents, so specified, which shall be in their possession or power (or authenticated Copies or extracts of the same) to be transmitted to the said Secretary of State, who shall immediately deliver them over to the said Board of Commissioners: provided that no such application shall be made, by, or at the instance of, any claimant, until the facts which it is expected to prove by such books, records or documents, shall have been stated under oath or affirmation.

*   *   *

The Treaty of Guadalupe Hidalgo:
Articles 9 and 10 Before Senate Amendment

Article IX[3]

The Mexicans who, in the territories aforesaid, shall not preserve the character of citizens of the Mexican Republic, conformably with what is stipulated in the preceding Article, shall be incorporated into the Union of the United States, and admitted as soon as possible, according to the principles of the Federal Constitution, to the enjoyment of all the rights of citizens of the United States. In the mean time, they shall be maintained and protected in the enjoyment of their liberty, their property, and the civil rights, now vested in them according to the Mexican laws. With respect to political rights, their condition shall be on an equality with that of the inhabitants of the other territories of the United States, and at least equally good as that of the inhabitants of Louisiana and the Floridas, when these provinces, by transfer from the French Republic and the Crown of Spain, became territories of the United States.

The same most ample guaranty shall be enjoyed by all ecclesiastics and religious corporations or communities, as well in the discharge of the offices of their ministry, as in the enjoyment of their property of every kind, whether individual or corporate. This guaranty shall embrace all temples, houses and edifices dedicated to the Roman Catholic worship; as well as all property destined to its support, or to that of schools, hospitals and other foundations for charitable or beneficent purposes. No property of this nature shall be considered as having become the property of the American Government, or as subject to be, by it, disposed of or diverted to other uses.

Finally, the relations and communication between the Catholics living in the territories aforesaid, and their respective ecclesiastical authorities, shall be open, free and exempt from all hindrance whatever, even although such authorities should reside within the limits of the Mexican Republic, as defined by this treaty; and this freedom shall continue, so long as a new demarcation of ecclesiastical districts shall not have been made, conformably with the laws of the Roman Catholic Church.

Article X

All grants of land made by the Mexican Government or by the competent authorities, in territories previously appertaining to Mexico, and remaining for the future within the limits of the United States, shall be respected as valid, to the same extent that the same grants would be valid, if the said territories had remained within the limits of Mexico. But the grantees of lands in Texas, put in possession thereof, who, by reason of the circumstances of the country since the beginning of the troubles between Texas and the Mexican Government, may have been prevented from fulfilling all the conditions of their grants, shall be under the obligation to fulfill the said conditions within the periods limited in the same respectively; such periods to be now counted from the date of the exchange of ratifications of this treaty: in default of which the said grants shall not be obligatory upon the State of Texas, in virtue of the stipulations contained in this Article.

The foregoing stipulation in regard to grantees of land in Texas, is extended to all grantees of land in the territories aforesaid, elsewhere than in Texas, put in possession under such grants; and, in default of the fulfillment of the conditions of any such grant, within the new period, which, as is above stipulated, begins with the day of the exchange of ratifications of this treaty, the same shall be null and void.

The Mexican Government declares that no grant whatever of lands in Texas has been made since the second day of March one thousand eight hundred and thirty-six; and that no grant whatever of lands in any of the territories aforesaid has been made since the thirteenth day of May one thousand eight hundred and forty-six.

*   *   *

Notes

1. All of these documents were reprinted from Hunter Miller, ed., *Treaties and Other International Acts of the United States of America*, Vol. 5 (Washington, D.C.: Government Printing Office, 1937), 253–57.

*   *   *

Questions

1. What is your impression of the tone of Buchanan's letter?
2. Do you agree with Buchanan that the problem with the original article 9 was "unnecessary prolixity"?
3. How might a Puerto Rican react to Buchanan's claim that "Congress will never lend a deaf ear to a people anxious to enjoy the privilege of self-government. Their application to become a State or States of the Union will be granted the moment this can be done with safety"?

4. Again, according to Buchanan, "no human power exists in this country which can deprive one individual of his property without his consent and transfer it to another." A similar sentiment is expressed in article IX. What might have happened, then, that by 1923 most propertied Mexicans who remained in the United States had become destitute?
5. How can one explain the different perceptions regarding article X?

PART II C

~

The Fragile Political Status of Mexican Americans and Their Continued Quest for Democracy

Francisco Hernández Vázquez

In the fifty years after the U.S. conquest of Northern Mexico (despite the provisions of the Treaty of Guadalupe-Hidalgo) the political status of Mexicans in these territories as a dominant, governing, stratified people changed to that of an excluded, disenfranchised, propertyless, and despised minority ethnic group. Although the Mexican population in the United States grew from 116,000 in 1848 to 500,000 in 1900 because of massive immigration from Europe, this amounted to less than 1 percent of the entire population. Numerically and in many other ways, by 1900, Mexican human bodies in the United States were nearly insignificant.

As illustrated, political and economic upheavals in the United States (and in the rest of the world), during the first half of the twentieth century impacted the Mexican population in two related ways. There was a constant increase and decrease of the population and this, in turn, also had an impact on the social and political presence of the Mexican population. This led to the fragile political status of Mexican Americans that has continued up until the twenty-first century. It is important to note that this situation that has not been experienced by other conquered peoples or immigrant groups in the United States; keep this in mind when comparing Mexican immigrant with immigrants from other countries. Nevertheless, U.S. Mexicans have continued the struggle against the abuse of power and for a political and economic democracy.

Before we outline the ways in which the U.S. Mexicans have responded to the challenge, let us first try to understand how the material conditions in this dialectical (action-reaction) process created a vulnerable sociopolitical position. If you have major economic development in the Southwest of the United States, then you create a tremendous demand for labor from Mexico. If U.S. investments promote economic development in Mexico and you increase the railroad connection between the two economies, then this stimulates the displacement and migration of human bodies to where the jobs are. To intensify this situation, all you need is the first major social upheaval of the twentieth century: the Mexican Revolution (see chapter 3 for a personal account). If you want to rev up all the previous conditions, then just add the economic stimulus and labor demands of World War I. All this time, if you have inhumane living and working conditions, you have to deal with increased political and labor organizing activity among Mexicans and other U.S. workers. Middle-class U.S. Mexicans, especially those who fought in WWI, meanwhile, created organizations such as the still influential League of United Latin American Citizens (LULAC).[1] This dynamic system receives a sudden shock: the Great Depression of the 1930s. Now you have to get rid of all these bodies. Just send them back to Mexico. It does not matter if many of them are U.S. citizens. Another major event will eventually make your reverse your decision and bring thousands of Mexican bodies back to the U.S.: the beginning of World War II. By 1938, the U.S. Mexican population had increased fivefold, to 2.5 million (although it remained about 2 percent of the U.S. population).

Buffeted by this constant interplay of material conditions, U.S. Mexicans found it difficult to establish a solid sociopolitical presence, yet they have sustained a complex, multidimensional struggle for equity, justice, political, and economic democracy. Reflecting the diversity of their historical and intellectual formation, this struggle included many elements: immigration, labor exploitation and repression, rural-urban dichotomies, cultural reaffirmation, de-culturalization, educational segregation, increased politicization, labor conflict, intra-community factionalism, and transborder politics.[2] Briefly put, they lived a discourse in which an individual or a family "could be living three histories at once"[3] (a rather postmodern experience we might add!). Let us briefly expand on some of these elements that contribute to the political status of U.S. Mexicans as a way of providing a context for the contributions to this section of the reader and that are intended to illustrate the nature of the U.S. Mexican struggle to carve a rightful place in the United States.

As noted in the Chicanology piece and in the Conclusion, though the United States is a nation of immigrants, there is also a long history of ambivalent desire toward being "ethnic" at best, and rabid anti-immigrant sentiments at worst. This can be traced through the formation of the early colonies, the revolutionary period, the invitation and then exclusion of the Chinese in the nineteenth century and other legislative measures. Wilson Neate refers to these "troubled legislative efforts," noting that the "confused 1917 Immigration Act, detailed thirty categories [of immigrants] to be refused admission and ten classes of exceptions."[4] Mexicans were exempted from the literacy test and head tax, for example, when their labor was needed. Though when nativists realized this they were "shocked" and immediately tried to change the law to deny citizenship to Mexicans on the basis that they were really American Indians (and American Indians did not qualify for citizenship).[5] In addition, there was the 1924 National Origins Act, which denied entrance to human beings from Central, Eastern, and Southern Europe (because they were deemed racially inferior). At the same time, nativists tried to maintain "the American character" by facilitating continued Northwestern European immigration. The notion of a melting pot process itself includes the conflicting tension between the inclusion of ethnicity but its exclusion through assimilation.

This phenomenon is especially obvious in Mexican immigration to the United States, a process that is compared to a faucet that is turned on or off, depending on the needs of the U.S. economy. This is, again, a major factor in the construction of a fragile political status for Mexican Americans. This status is amply illustrated by the Repatriation Program of 1929–1939, which expelled one half to one million U.S. Mexicans during what is known as the "decade of betrayal." Though ironic, it is not surprising to learn that some repatriates arrived at their destination only to find labor contractors recruiting workers to pick cotton and other crops in Texas and Arizona![6] In the 1950s "Operation Wetback" rounded up and deported over one million Mexicans and U.S. Mexicans. In the 1990s, Proposition 187 in California attempted to turn every government official, including teachers and doctors, into official immigration agents for reporting the "undocumented" (a code word for "Mexicans") who may be using educational and health benefits reserved for U.S. citizens. Presently, the U.S. Congress has been unable to pass legislation to deal with the 12 million undocumented immigrants. Thus, in addition to vigilantes on the Mexican border, there is open discussion about deporting these 12 million undocumented people, and even of concentration camps to hold them until they can be deported.

If legislation is necessary to construct a solid political status, institutions are necessary to sustain the physical well-being of a people. In this respect, U.S. Mexicans did not receive support from U.S. institutions (unlike the first two waves of Cuban exiles, as noted in chapter 16). Though U.S. Mexican bodies belonged to categories such as "Catholics," "workers," "students," and "U.S. citizens," their quest for inclusion was not supported by the corresponding institutions, such as the Catholic Church, the American Federation of Labor, schools, or English-language newspapers. Protestant churches did try to help but only by demanding that U.S. Mexicans adopt Anglo American customs. Philanthropic institutions cared little for the welfare of U.S. Mexican bodies. In the final analysis, the effects of power during the first half of the twentieth century are evident in the bodies of the many U.S. Mexicans who were subjected "to terrorism, coercion, and murder in its most brutal form, lynching."[7]

Contrary to the stereotype of the illiterate, apathetic, passive Mexican, the people survived through their own institutions, such as the mutual aid societies, labor and political organizations, and through the abundant production of discourse through Spanish-language newspapers, music, corridos, and theater. Since the nineteenth century, Mexicans have engaged in resistance and radical movements and in organized labor, Masonic groups, and religious groups. The most prevalent and persistent were the cultural societies, the rudimentary unions and *mutualistas*, groups that are also found among Puerto Ricans and Cuban Americans (the latter refer to them as *municipios*). In effect, one of the key institutions at play in this particular game of truth is the mutualista. This is a mutual aid group that contributed to the organizing efforts of community forums, trade unions, and social and political associations, such as the *Congreso Mexicanista de 1911* (see chapter 7, especially the graph of the various organizations according to their politics). Present in almost every barrio in the Southwest, mutualistas maintained close links to other institutions, such as the Mexican consulate, and tried to use Mexican consulate services for lodging complaints against Anglo American authorities. Mutualistas also played an economic function: in return for dues, member families received a payment on the death of the wage earner and some unemployment benefits were available. Members were from the working and the lower-middle classes, with new immigrants making up a large number.[8]

The mutualistas also tried to establish a relationship with U.S. unions. One of their goals was to encourage U.S. Mexican workers to organize and protest because of low wages, poor treatment, and the desire for self-improvement. U.S. Mexican workers also promoted solidarity with Anglo American workers, who in most cases did not want to be associated with them. Non-Mexican workers defined power in terms of ethnocentric solidarity, exclusion of minorities, and identification with the Anglo American middle class. Often, white workers, not employers, persecuted nonwhite workers. Furthermore, U.S. Mexicans were often ineligible for union membership and, consequently, they were not hired for union-dominated jobs; this led to the practice of organizing separately.[9]

These events clearly illustrate how U.S. Mexicans struggled for inclusion in the United States, and that it was only when rejected that they found it necessary to retreat into their own communities and institutions. Unfortunately, this is a poorly understood dynamic that leads some people to assert that U.S. Mexicans prefer to have their own separate communities. On the contrary, the U.S. Mexican quest for an economic democracy has always included other U.S. Americans workers and workers in Mexico.

Because they were mostly involved in agricultural work, U.S. Mexicans did not play a major role in industrial areas. Yet many of them were significant participants in labor struggles in the South and the Midwest of the United States, even where they were systematically excluded from leadership or from union membership by exclusionist unions, such as the American Federation of Labor. Indeed a major chapter in Latino/a political thought is the important and often leading role of U.S. Mexican workers through the *Partido Liberal Mexicano* (PLM). This is especially obvious in the more militant sectors of the U.S. labor movement, such as the Industrial Workers of the World (IWW).[10] The PLM, led by Ricardo Flores Magón,

> represents an innovation in the political history of the Mexican people in the U.S. and in Mexico. It was an international, revolutionary, ideological, and clandestine party that fought for the destruction of the dictatorship in Mexico and capitalism in general.[11]

It had significant ties to U.S. American radicals, especially the IWW.

In its attempt to overthrow the Mexican dictator, the PLM can be compared to the nineteenth century *Partido Revolucionario Cubano* (Cuban Revolutionary Party, [PRC]), which under the leadership of José Martí operated in the United States to overthrow the Spaniards from Cuba. The active political discourse of U.S. Mexican workers was adversely affected not only by the Repatriation, but also by laws that were specifically used to deter militancy in the Mexican community. For example, the Taft-Hartley Act of 1947 allowed the U.S. president to order workers to go back to their jobs, gave states the right to eliminate union membership as a prerequisite for many jobs, and required union officials to sign affidavits pledging no Communist affiliation. The McCarran International Security Act of 1950, which makes a distinction between naturalized and native citizens, was used to deport citizens for political reasons—such as labor organizing.[12] In chapter 9, Chávez describes the trials and tribulations of union organizing among farm workers, who were left out of the National Labor Relations Act of 1932. Valle and Torres further elaborate on the fact that labor struggles not only continue but that they have also reached a new dimension of multi-ethnic collaboration that can only bode well in the quest for economic democracy (see chapter 12).

All this civic engagement by U.S. Mexicans in the struggle for economic democracy points to an undeniable truth: that an appreciation and pride in one's own heritage and culture definitely provides the foundation that is necessary for a healthy identity, for self-respect, and for meaningful and responsible participation in one's society. At the same time, is also important to acknowledge that the concept of cultural identity and affirmation covers a wide range. It may also lead, for example, to a kind of cultural nationalism that flirts with secessionist nationalism, as illustrated in chapter 10. There is, however, another aspect of cultural affirmation that points to factionalism within the U.S. Mexican community. Human history shows that the segment of *any* community that supports a tradition based on authoritarianism, hierarchy, and patriarchy, inevitably will come up against the modern, liberal culture that gives priority to the rights of the individual. As illustrated by Cherríe Moraga in chapter 11 within the U.S. Mexican culture one of these conflicts is manifested through gender wars.

These are, then, the historical political struggles for and against Mexican human bodies and their categorization according to pigment of skin, gender, class, nationality, ethnicity, and legal status. In other words, these are the power relations, the material conditions that construct a fragile political status for the U.S. Mexicans. These conditions happen to be the same ones that present a continuing challenge for anyone who cares about economic democracy in the United States. After one-and-a-half centuries since the Mexican American War, we continue to be faced with a cruel paradox: The demand for Mexican bodies is matched by the disregard for their well-being once they are on U.S. soil. Even if they become or are born U.S. citizens who are committed to democracy, even if they shed their blood for this country, apparently they do not fit the particular image of what constitutes the United States of America (see chapter 4). In fact, current research by the Pew Hispanic Center shows that the quality of life of Latinos/as suffers from the negative effect of the current anti-immigrant fervor. This situation will continue as long as there is no real regional integration based on ethical and environmental sustainability (i.e., beyond the North American Free Trade Agreement [NAFTA]) between Canada, the United States, Mexico, and the rest of Latin America.

In conclusion, Mexican American culture is not only alive and well but also its notion of *mestizaje* may offer an important lesson that the entire United States needs to learn, as pointed out in chapter 12 and, more recently by Gregory Rodriguez in *Mongrels, Bastards, Orphans, and Vagabonds: Mexican Immigration and the Future of Race in America*.

*   *   *

Notes and Suggestions for Further Research

1. Mario T. Garcia, *Mexican Americans: Leadership, Ideology, and Identity, 1930–1960* (New Haven, CT: Yale University Press, 1989), 25–61.

2. Juan Gómez-Quiñonez, *Roots of Chicano Politics, 1600–1940* (Albuquerque: University of New Mexico Press, 1994), 296.

3. Romano, I. R.-V., "The Historical and Intellectual Presence of Mexican Americans," *El Grito* (winter 1969): 32–46.

4. Wilson Neate, "Alienism Unashamed," *Latino Studies Journal* 8, no. 2 (Spring 1997): 68–91.

5. Gregory Rodriguez, *Mongrels, Bastards, Orphans, and Vagabonds: Mexican Immigration and the Future of Race in America* (New York: Pantheon, 2007), 165.

6. Francisco E. Balderrama and R. Rodríguez, *Decade of Betrayal: Mexican Repatriation in the 1930s* (Albuquerque: University of New Mexico Press, 1995), 118.

7. Gómez-Quiñonez, *Roots of Chicano Politics*, 299.

8. Juan Gómez-Quiñonez, *Mexican American Labor, 1790–1990* (Albuquerque: University of New Mexico Press, 1994), 57.

9. Gómez-Quiñonez, *Mexican American Labor*, 57–61.

10. Gómez-Quiñonez, *Roots of Chicano Politics*, 300.

11. Gómez-Quiñonez, *Roots of Chicano Politics*, 342.

12. Gómez-Quiñonez, *Mexican American Labor*, 174.

~

CHAPTER SEVEN

El Primer Congreso Mexicanista de 1911: A Precursor to Contemporary Chicanismo

José E. Limón

At the turn of the century we find a deterioration of the economic situation; a noticeable loss of the Mexican culture and the Spanish language; general social discrimination, particularly in education; and a pattern of officially tolerated lynching of U.S. Mexicans. It is particularly the unpunished brutality against the bodies of U.S. Mexicans that leads to this particular aspect of Latino thought represented by the *Congreso Mexicanista de 1911*. As the title of Limón's article indicates, these ideas are part of a radical, anti-assimilationist discourse of resistance that reappeared sixty years later. No wonder some Chicanos believed that they had invented this particular kind of radical resistance. Even before the advent of a global society, the Congreso also illustrated a discourse of transnational political and cultural identities discussed in chapter 15.

As exemplified by the League of United Latin American Citizens (LULAC), the tactics change in the 1920s.[1] But even then, a continuity in Latino/a political thought was maintained by the economic, physical, social, or psychic violence carried against Latino/a children, women, and men. There are similarities between the *Congreso* and the Cuban Patriotic League of Tampa.[2] A particularly invisible thread in Latino/a political thought is the presence of **Freemasonry** (a secret society) among many of the liberation groups discussed in these readings.[3] This system of lodges as a primary organizational base is also described by the Mason Benjamin Franklin in his autobiography. Another point of commonality between the Congreso, the Puerto Rican *independentistas*, the Cuban revolution, and the Chicano movement is the notion of separatism. After much human suffering there are indications that Latinos/as got to the point where, as the U.S. Declaration of Independence states, "it becomes necessary for one people to dissolve the political bands which have connected them with another."

Notes and Suggested Further Readings

1. Mario T. Garcia, *Mexican Americans: Leadership, Ideology, and Identity, 1930–1960* (New Haven, CY: Yale University Press, 1989), 25–61.

2. Enrique Collazo Pérez, "José Martí, the Cuban Patriotic League of Tampa and the Cuban Revolutionary Party," trans. and ed. K. Lynn Stoner, in *José Martí in the United States: The Florida Experience*, ed., Louis A. Pérez (Tempe: Arizona State University, Center for Latin American Studies, 1995), 71–80.

3. The role of Masons in Latino/a political thought has yet to be discussed comprehensively. Juan Gómez-Quiñonez, an authority on Chicano history, in his *Roots of Chicano Polities, 1600–1940* (Albuquerque: University of New Mexico Press, 1994), lists only one bibliographical entry on this topic: José Maria Mateos, *Historia de la Masonería en México desde 1806 hasta 1884* (Mexico City: 1884). One helpful source on Freemasonry in general is Stephen Knight, *The Brotherhood* (Dorset Press, 1986).

* * *

In its struggle for social change on behalf of the Chicano community, the contemporary Chicano movement has developed a broad coherent ideology to guide and legitimize its activity in the areas of schooling, labor, and organized politics. At least five major themes form the ideology that distinguishes this movement, composed largely of student groups such as MECHA [Movimiento Estudiantil Chicano de Aztlan] and MAYO [Mexican American Youth Organization]. This ideology consists of: (1) a critical attack on the social subordination of Chicanos as a holistic phenomenon; (2) a personal, artistic, and institutional affirmation of the special variant of Mexican culture found in the U.S.; (3) the assertion of a feminist position within the larger movement; (4) the search for a unified political solution to Chicano problems including at least a partial acceptance of radical politics; and (5) the somewhat unclear projection of a quasi-separate nation state as the final goal for this movement.[1]

Finding no adequate historical precedents within the community, scholars attribute a seeming novelty to this ideology. One influential study labels the 1848–1921 period as "apolitical." According to Alfredo Cuéllar, this period of organizational and ideological inactivity is followed by a series of organizations such as the Order Sons of America (1921), LULAC [League of

United Latin American Citizens] (1929) and the American G.I. Forum (1948). However, these groups follow an ideology of adaptation and accommodation to Anglo American society—a practice not substantially altered by later groups such as MAPA [Mexican American Political Association] (1959) and PASSO [Political Association of Spanish-Speaking Organizations] (1960). As such the 1921–1960 groups stand in marked contrast to the contemporary Chicano movement of the mid-sixties and its new ideology of Chicanismo. Or, as Cuéllar put it in 1970:

> Until recently no Mexican-American had tried to define the problems of the community in any terms except those of assimilation. It is precisely these ideas of assimilation and social "adjustment" that the Chicano militant rejects. As a new alternative, Chicanismo represents a conception of an autonomous and self determining social life for Mexican-Americans.
>
> It is interesting to note that it was not until the 1960's that the Chicano leaders emerged to question some of the oldest and most fundamental assumptions of Mexicans in American society.[3]

This history of ideologies needs to be revised on the basis of new evidence furnished by *El Primer Congreso Mexicanista de 1911*. In the present study I will argue that this early congress and its social milieu anticipate many of the major themes that define the supposedly new ideology of Chicanismo.

Background of the Congreso

El Primer Congreso Mexicanista was a political conference held in Laredo, Texas, on September 14–22, 1911.[4] It was convened by Texas-Mexicans to express and act upon a variety of social grievances which were the culmination of an encroaching Anglo-American domination of Texas-Mexicans during the latter half of the nineteenth century and into the early twentieth. This period was marked by the transfer of almost all Texas-Mexican land into Anglo-Texan hands through various legal and illegal means.[5] Coupled with an intensifying Mexican immigration, this loss of economic position started the conversion of the Texas-Mexican population into a cheap labor pool for the developing Anglo-Texan ranching and farming interests.[6] Protected by his nearly exclusive control of the political order and reinforced by his visible economic dominance, the Anglo-Texan, with his embedded sense of racial and cultural superiority, created a pattern of local, officially sanctioned segregation between the two peoples.[7] Finally, by suppressing acts of native resistance such as those of Juan Cortina and Catarino Garza and physically intimidating the Texas-Mexican population as a whole, law enforcement and military authorities reflected and supported the new socio-economic order.[8] In response to this developing climate of social oppression, Sr. Nicasio Idar and his family initiated a campaign of journalistic resistance that eventually led to El Primer Congreso Mexicanista.

The Idar Family and *La Crónica*

Born in Point Isabel, Texas, near Brownsville on December 26, 1853, Nicasio Idar moved to Laredo, Texas, in 1880, after living in Corpus Christi and attending schools there. He was primarily a journalist and commercial printer, although he also served as an Assistant City Marshall and a Justice of the Peace in Laredo. As a journalist he published *La Revista*, a Masonic review, and *La Crónica*, a weekly independent newspaper dedicated *"al beneficio de la raza méxico-texana."* In addition to his affiliation with the Mexican Masonry, he also belonged to the *Sociedad Mutualista Benito Juárez* in Laredo and was a vice president of a Mexican and Texas-Mexican fraternal lodge system known as *La Orden Caballeros de Honor*. According to his obituary he had also been active in labor organizing *"haste lograr la fundación de la primera associación de ferrocarrileros mexicanos . . . La Alianza Suprema de Ferrocarrileros Mexicanos."* He died on April 7, 1914, leaving his widow Jovita and eight children, one of whom eulogized him as a man who left a legacy of ideas *"sanas, nobles, benéfices, que forman un tesoro inacabable, pródigo siempre en beneficios y enseñanzas."*[9]

At least three children had shared, not only their father's ideas, but his enthusiasm and zeal in defending the rights of the Texas-Mexican community. Jovita (named after her mother), Clemente and Eduardo joined their father in his work as editor and publisher of *La Crónica*. This remarkable newspaper covered local and area news, México, and worldwide affairs, although it was centrally dedicated to *"el progreso y desarrollo industrial, moral e intelectual de los habitantes mexicanos en Texas."*[10] Eduardo covered Brownsville and the lower Rio Grande Valley as a traveling correspondent, while Jovita and Clemente served in a general capacity including considerable staff writing.[11] There were other writers for *La Crónica* including guest writers and the newspaper reprinted significant articles appearing elsewhere. It began publication sometime in the 1890s with Nicasio Idar as editor, although it is likely that he did not become its owner and publisher until 1910.[12]

La Cronica and Social Oppression

Throughout the period 1910–1911, *La Crónica* launched a series of attacks on particular manifestations of the social conditions oppressing Texas-Mexicans.

Five issues drew the Idar's interest and formed the immediate social context of El Primer Congreso Mexicanista: (1) the deteriorating Texas-Mexican economic condition; (2) the already perceptible loss of Mexican culture and the Spanish language; (3) general social discrimination; (4) the particular problem of educational discrimination; and (5) the pattern of officially tolerated lynchings of Texas-Mexicans. The latter two drew their principal attention.

On November 2, 1910, Antonio Rodriguez, probably a Mexican national, was arrested by sheriff's deputies near Rocksprings, Texas, and accused of having murdered an Anglo-American woman on a ranch near town. His guilt or innocence will never be known, because within hours a mob took him from the Rocksprings jail, tied him to a tree and burned him to death. The local coroner returned a verdict of death "at the hands of persons unknown."[13] A later investigation by the Texas Rangers would show that "the recent burning of the Mexican there was done entirely by Americans. . . ."[14] This atrocity had an impact on U.S.-Mexican relations and on the Texas-Mexican community.[15] *La Crónica* bitterly attacked the burning as a barbaric act, and denounced the inaction of the local authorities.[16]

On June 19, 1911, Antonio Gómez, age 14, was asked to leave a place of business in Thorndale, Texas. He refused, a fight ensued and a Texas-German was left dead with a wound from Gómez's knife. Gómez was arrested, but was taken from the authorities by a group of men who beat him to death and dragged his body around town with a buggy. *La Crónica* commented on this particular lynching and on the general condition of injustice:

> *Este hecho bárbaro fue communicado á todo el mundo civilizado causando la consternación consiguiente. Se espera saber que hará el Gobierno de Texas pero hay que suponer que se encausará a los lynchadores y se les dejará libres bajo fianza y despues de cansar la opinión pública con simulacros de juicios, se desechará completamente la causa; pues hasta ahora no recordamos de americano alguno que haya sido castigado por el lynchamiento de un mexicano, á pesar de que se han cometido algunas.*

La Crónica saw this incident as a particular case of the general racial hatred and contempt felt by most Anglo-Texans toward Mexicans.[17] In a later article, *La Crónica* attacked the Mexican consuls for timidity in entering the case and, noting that Thorndale Mexicans were retaliating by boycotting Anglo merchants, concluded:

> *. . . no queda a los mexicanos mas que un remedio; el que han adoptado los hombres de todas las razas para hacerse respetar: La asociación.*[18]

Later that month *La Crónica* took note of an Orden Caballeros de Honor meeting held in Bay City on the Texas Gulf Coast to discuss the Thorndale matter and the need to unify Texas-Mexicans. In attendance were delegates from Matagorda, Rockeye, Wharton, and Runge.[19]

La Crónica took interest in a third criminal case. León Cárdenas Martínez was arrested and tried for allegedly murdering two Anglo women near Reeves, Texas, in July, 1911. According to George Estes, his lawyer, a mob forced Martínez to confess at gunpoint. A single jury member who dissented on the "guilty" vote was threatened, and Martínez was finally sentenced to death. Under personal threats to his own life, Estes appealed the case and the death sentence was reduced to thirty years in the penitentiary.[20] Texas-Mexicans had sent several letters, including one from *La Crónica*, to Governor O. B. Colquitt asking for clemency for the 16 year old Martínez.[21] Governor Colquitt received pressure from the other side as well:

> . . . a petition said to bear the signature of nearly every Caucasian in Reeves County has been sent to Governor Colquitt asking him not to commute the Mexican's sentence.[22]

The Martínez case would receive attention at the Congreso.

The judicial injustices committed against Mexicans were a logical result of the general climate of social discrimination. According to *La Crónica*, even the *Houston Post* noted the effect of the Alamo syndrome on juries trying Mexicans. The *Post* concluded that there was very little sympathy for the "greaser" in this country. J. J. Mercado, the translator of the *Post* article commented:

> *Lo sabíamos ya nosotros antes de que el Post nos lo dijera y lo hemos sabido siempre, que millares de fallos judiciales en los tribunales de Texas en contra del Mexicano, han sido inspirados en la sangrienta venganza que entraña el grito "Remember de Alamo" y en el concepto de "greaser" que naciera de la eterna predisposición contra la raza mexicana.*[23]

Earlier in the year *La Crónica* had noted the general climate of racial discrimination particularly in central Texas where signs such as "No lots sold to Mexicans" and "No Mexicans admitted" were prevalent, and where, in Austin, State Representative J. T. Canales was called "the greaser from Brownsville" during a session of the legislature.[24]

The "greaser" concept particularly affected the educational process. Toward the end of 1910 and on through early 1911 Clemente Idar wrote a series of articles exposing glaring discrimination in Texas public schools, particularly in upper southern Texas. He argued that Texas-Mexicans paid school taxes, but were not permitted to participate in the educational system.

The Mexican consul in Laredo was asked to investigate, but confined his investigation to the largely Mexican counties of Webb, Starr, and Zapata and concluded there was no discrimination in Texas. Idar urged him to visit the rest of southern and central Texas as he himself had done, but this was never done. Idar continued to attack specific counties: Val Verde, Hays, González, Atascosa, Medina, Frío, La Salle, Dimmit, McMullen, Uvalde, and Wilson, and also the towns of Pearsal, Devine, Kingsville, Asherton, Kyle and Del Rio. In one significant article he interpreted this pattern of discrimination as a violation of the Treaty of Guadalupe Hidalgo. As a result of this extensive series *La Crónica* began to receive letters from its readers all over Texas confirming the existence of segregation in their communities.[25]

However, *La Crónica* also recognized that even in inferior and segregated schools, an ethnocentric educational process was starting to anglicize Texas-Mexican children. It expressed deep concern about the loss of the Spanish language and Mexican history and culture, and in a strikingly modern tone, argued for bilingual education:

> Con profunda pena hemos visto á maestros mexicanos enseñando inglés á niños de su raza, sin tomar para nada en cuenta el idioma materno que cada día se va olvidando más y cada día van sufriendo adulteraciones y cambios que hieren materialmente al oído de cualquier mexicano por poco versado que este en la idioma de Cervantes.[26]

English should also be learned, but Spanish was fundamental:

> . . . lo que quisimos significar simplemente es que no debe desatenderse el idioma nacional, porque es el sello caracteristico de las razas y las castas se hunden cuando se olvida la lengua nacional… No decimos que no se enseñe el inglés a la niñez mexico-texana, sea en hora buena, decimos que no se olviden de enseñarles el castellano.[27]

A second consequence of such mis-education would be a progressive cultural apathy and indifference:

> . . . si en la escuela americana á que concurren nuestros niños se les enseña la Biografía de Washington y no la de Hidalgo y en vez de hechas gloriosas de Juárez se le refieren las hazañas de Lincoln, por mas que estas sean nobles y justas, no conocerá ese niño las glorias de su Patria, no la amará y haste verá con indiferencia a los coterranos de sus padres.[28]

Late in 1910, *La Crónica* had proposed a dramatic solution for the cultural problem created by ethnocentric Anglo-U.S. schools: the creation of a separate school system staffed by imported Mexican teachers where the primary language of instruction would be Spanish. The expenses for such a school system were to be borne by the Texas-Mexican community.[29] Replying to a Texas-Mexican critic of this radical idea, *La Crónica* approvingly pointed to educational efforts of this kind already underway within the community:

> . . . en las cuales se propone la creación de escuelas donde se instruya á la juventud mexicana exclusivamente en la idioma de Cervantes, como una medida eficaz para que no pierda terreno y siga siendo todo el tiempo la hija de 'labradores pobres' y por tanto la bestia del trabajo, triste condición á la que se le quiere condenar . . . [30]

This was a strikingly modern linkage between the non-use of the child's native language and his progressive failure in the schools and in society. The notion of community created schools would appear again a month before the Congreso:

> La niñez mexicana en Texas necesita instruirse. Ni nuestro gobierno ni el de EEUU pueden hacer nada por ella, y no queda otro recurso que el de hacerlo por nuestro propio impulso á trueque de no seguir despreciados y vejados por los extranjeros que nos rodean.[31]

Another area of concern for the Idars was the steadily deteriorating economic position of Texas-Mexicans. They urged the people not to sell their land to the growing wave of,

> . . . agentes y compradores de terrenos, que hacen sus mejores especulaciones comprando propiedades de mexicanos á precios ínfimos, para traspasarlas á manos de otros individuos que nada tienen en común con nosotros, y el resultado lógico de esa actividad, inevitablemente será que en muy pocos años el numero de nuestros hombres acandalados de hoy se habrá reducido en grande proporciones, y entonces, sus descendientes y sus hermanos serán los que sufren las consequencias de su imprevisión.[32]

Idar felt now was the time to reverse the tide and hold on to the land. Only in this way could Texas-Mexicans reach *"el no lejano y glorioso provenir que espera á nuestra raza heróica y viril."*[33] As a result of this host of issues, the Idars begin making plans for El Primer Congreso Mexicanista.

El Primer Congreso Mexicanista—Organizational Techniques

The Idars were active members in the Orden Caballeros de Honor (OCH) a Texas-Mexican and Mexican fraternal lodge, and they utilized the Texas wide system of lodges as a primary organizational base. The largest groups were in Brownsville (200), Corpus Christi (80) and Laredo (90).[34] In January, 1911 through *La Crónica* the Idars began calling for a convention of the various lodges and special guests—*"los mexicanos mas ilustrados en las letras, residentes en Texas, a todos los periodistas mexicanos de Texas, y a todos los cónsules Mexicanos."* This convention to be held in Laredo, was to take up the questions of: (1) school discrimination; (2) the need for teaching Spanish in community controlled schools with Mexican teachers; (3) the Mexican consular system; (4) ways and means to protect Mexican lives and interests in Texas; (5) the role of the Orden; (6) formation of women's groups under the auspices of the Orden; (7) the need for Texas-Mexicans to acquire land and hold on to that which they had; and (8) organizing a future meeting to be known as El Primer Congreso Mexicanista.[35]

By February, 1911, the Idars changed their minds and asked each OCH lodge to send a special delegation to the OCH conventions. These special delegations would convene separately as El Primer Congreso Mexicanista so that immediate steps would be taken toward solving the Texas-Mexican problems. Arguing that Texas-Mexicans could not depend on change in the Anglo-Texan community or on external help from Mexico, *La Crónica* urged organization, unification, and education of the Mexican masses as the only solution to *"los problemas que afectan las vidas y los intereses de nuestros hermanos."* An open invitation was extended to all Texas-Mexican organizations, *"que en algo se preocupen por nuestro bienestar."* A special invitation was extended to the Texas-Mexican Masonic Lodges. Indeed, *La Crónica* urged Texas-Mexicans to organize themselves locally for the purpose of sending a delegation to the meetings.[36]

In the March 16th issue of the newspaper, the Idars printed letters of support from prominent individuals in various groups. They also received the support of the very important *sociedades mutualistas*. These self-help social groups existed extensively throughout Texas primarily to provide an insurance service, a place for socializing and an organizational base for the celebration of Mexican holidays in Texas. During this month the decision was also made to hold the dual convention during the week of September 14–22, 1911. The symbolic value of the date is, of course obvious, but *La Crónica* also took note of the tactical advantages—lower holiday train fares and the presence of large numbers of visitors in Laredo to celebrate *las fiestas patrias.*[37]

In July the proposed Congreso received the support of the *Agrupación Protectora Mexicana* of San Antonio, led by Doneciano Dávila and Emilio Flores and dedicated to the defense of Texas-Mexicans especially on the issue of lynchings. Dávila and Flores called for a nation-wide political unification of all Mexicans in the U.S. so that,

> . . . unidos todos bajo los vínculos más estrechos de compañerismo y con fraternidad nos pongamos á cubierto de los limites de la ley, de todo genero de infamias é injustícias que con nosotros se pretenda cometer.

Nicasio Idar thanked them for their support noting their previous efforts on behalf of Texas-Mexicans, particularly *"en el asunto de Cortez"* in obvious reference to the legal defense of Gregorio Cortez.[38] In this same month the Idars published the first estimate of the expected attendance at the meetings. We are told that *"la asistencia será de 300–400 personas."*[39] In August we learn that a *Mesa Directiva* was to be elected by a majority of those present and that after the Congreso, chapters were to be established *"en todos las poblaciones mexicanas"* under the central Mesa Directiva that would function as *"el centro de protección de todos los mexicanos de Texas, por medio de él se demandará justicia cuando sea necesario . . ."* [40] In early September, *La Crónica* also took note of growing local support in the form of financial contributions.[41] And, on the morning of the Congreso, *La Crónica* announced the presence of additional delegations from the Agrupación Protectora Mexicana of Houston and a Masonic lodge in México City.[42] That same morning a terse announcement entitled, *"Otra Víctima del Odio Yankee"* appeared in the paper:

> El lunes último fue muerto en Corpus Christi por un americano, el laborioso y digno mexicano José Olivares, hermano por parte materna del Sr. Nicasio Idar... [43]

No further explanation was given of this incident personally affecting the Idar family.

El Primer Congreso Mexicanista—The Meetings

On September 14, 1911 the delegates finally met on the second floor of a building in the town square known as Los Altos del Mercado. Roughly about this time the city of Laredo, located on the Rio Grande border approximately 200 miles from the Gulf port of Brownsville, was described in these terms:

> . . . a healthy and pleasant climate, an industrious and law abiding population, abundant and cheap labor, supplied with all the modern appliances for comfort, water works, electric lights, telephone exchange, costly public buildings, churches, schools, and private residences, smelters, and scapling works, ice fac-

tories, machine and car shops . . . a population of 15,000 souls and a taxable wealth of $3,000,000.[44]

More importantly a general review of Laredo newspapers from this time period tells us of a city whose political, educational, and cultural life were significantly influenced, if not dominated, by Texas-Mexicans—a situation which continues to the present.

As the Congreso met, a journalist covering the events would articulate the fundamental reason for the meetings:

Estar en tierra extraña, vivir á merced de la majoria que son los habitantes de la tierra en que están y no unirse y defenderse mutuamente es estar a merced de ellos, es entregarse manistados al primer explotador de conciencia elástica, pero unirse entre sí, formar una sola liga defensiva ofensiva es ser invulnerables, es triunfar en el campo de la razón y de la justicia.[45]

We do not have an exact count of the persons in attendance, although we do know the Idars were successful in gathering two delegates from each OCH lodge in twenty-four Texas localities. We can add to this an unspecified number of representatives from Masonic lodges, sociedades mutualistas, agrupaciones protectoras, other types of social groups such as *El Club Internacional* of Laredo, special visitors such as the delegations from México, the press, and of course an unspecified number of ordinary visitors.[46] The secretary of the Congreso spoke of *"una gran multitud"* present at the sessions.[47] After a welcoming address by Nicasio Idar, the convention moved to elect a Mesa Directiva for the Congreso and to express its gratitude to Clemente Idar for his leadership role in organizing the Congreso. The Mesa was composed of: José P. Reyes, President (Brownsville), Nicasio Idar, Vice President (Laredo), Lisandro Peña, Secretary (Laredo), and as vocales J. A. Garza (unknown), Isidro G. Garza (Kingsville) and Timoteo F. Gloria (Rio Grande).[48]

Unfortunately we do not have a detailed day to day account of the Congreso proceedings. We do have a program of events, short general descriptions of the sessions, and most importantly, a collection of the major speeches (see footnote 47). The remainder of the study will be based on this data.

The Congreso was composed of formal *discursos* rendered in a high oratorical style together with *discusiones* and *conferencias* or what we might call workshops. Music was used extensively and the Congreso opened with a chorus of children singing patriotic songs and the recitation of a patriotic poem by a young boy. The poem, and all of the major speeches are replete with extensive allusions to México and Mexican history and culture. This pervasive nationalistic style is one of the major themes of the Congreso.[49]

Eight other ideas emerged in the speeches. The call for unity against the oppressor was repeated again and again. Lisandro Peña, for example, exhorted the people so oppressed in the past to unite and claim that which was theirs in the face of *"malvados y tiranos."*[50] J. M. Mora also called for Unity:

> . . . cuando se hayan establecido relaciones de alianza y fraternidad en todas las sociedades mexicanas del Estado de Texas, será una liga tan fuerte y poderosa, revistiendo un carácter tan imponente ante el cual doblegarían la cerviz los politicos más astutos de la época, y sobre todo tendría gran representación social tanto aquí como en México, que llamaría la atención del mundo.[51]

A third major idea is a radical working class ideology again expressed by Mora representing *la Sociedad de Obreros Igualdad y Progreso*:

> En esta ciudad existió no hace mucho, una gran organización, y vimos como el capital persiguió a los obreros, hasta exterminarlos. El Capital como los politicos, ven un peligro amenazador para sus intereses cuando se trata, como en el asunto que nos ocupa, de unir el elemento obrero. Urge, pues, unir a la clase obrera y principalmente a los mexicanos que residimos en este país.[52]

A fourth idea was language and culture. S. G. Domínguez proposed the establishment of schools to teach both English and Spanish.[53] The Houston delegation sought discussion on the question of whether or not it makes more pedagogical sense to teach children in their native language first.[54] On the program we also find *discursos* and *conferencias* on topics such as *"Mexicanismo"* and *"Orígen y Civilización Azteca."*[55]

Several speakers addressed themselves to the question of criminal justice and bitterly denounced the lynchings.[56] They were, in fact, seen as one of the motivating reasons for the Congreso.[57] Hortencia Moncayo spoke explicitly on this issue and was congratulated by the Agrupación Protectora of San Antonio who saw her and other active women as *"las descendientes de Doña Josefa Ortiz de Domínguez, la Correjidora de Querétero y de Doña Leona Vicario."*[58]

Texas-Mexican women and their particular social problems received the attention of the Congreso. A special invitation had been extended to women in the Laredo area.[59] The education of women was a topic on the program and Prof. S. G. Domínguez supported the idea:

> . . . lo absolutamente indispensable es educar a la mujer de nuestra raza para que amolde la tierna inteligencia de sus hijos. . . [60]

Soledad Flores de Peña pursued this idea in addressing the assembly:

> *. . . es necesario comprender bien los dedeberes de cada uno y obrar según ellos: yo, como vosotros creo, que el mejor medio para conseguirlo es educar á la mujer, instruirla, darle ánimo a la vez que respetarla.*

In return, she promised, women would be true to the tradition of Mexican heroines and develop strength, pride, and intelligence in their children.[61]

A seventh major theme was the social discrimination experienced by Texas-Mexicans. A letter read at the meetings expressed this view:

> *Dia a dia se ve cruzar el Rio Bravo por grandes grupos de mexicanos que ansiosos de mejor salario para el sostenimiento de la familia van a Texas, y si bien es cierto que consiguen comer y vestir mejor... tambien es cierto que con frequencia son tratados con un vergonzoso desprecio de parte de los americanos trantandolos como a raza degenerada o inculta...* [62]

And, with regard to the particular case of school discrimination, the Houston delegation urged the Congreso to make a formal protest to the State Superintendent of Schools.[63]

Finally Telésforo Macías of Laredo urged Texas-Mexicans to practice sound economics so that the community would not find it necessary to go "*de rodillas a poner en el mercado de los traficantes del trabajo ajeno, nuestro sudor, nuestro esfuerzo y nuestras energias en publica subasta.*"[64] Macías also eloquently summarized all of the Texas-Mexican concerns that prompted the Congreso including the lack of criminal justice, discrimination, labor exploitation, cultural retention, and the need for unity.[65]

On September 20, 1911, this first state-wide gathering of Texas-Mexicans took a first small step in response to their social grievances. Appropriately enough, it donated $17.35 to the legal defense of León Cárdenas Martínez.[66]

The Role of Laredo

The success of the Congreso required at least four elements: dedicated organizers, a medium of communication, money and a protected environment. The Idars and their newspaper provided the first two. The City of Laredo contributed the others. Financial contributions totaling $118.77 had been obtained from small Texas-Mexican merchants in the city and these funds were used to pay for chairs, hall rental, decorations, music and printed materials.[67] The availability of funds, however, only revealed a more fundamental characteristic of the city. The Texas-Mexican influence in its political, social and cultural life provided a supportive context that would have been extremely difficult to obtain elsewhere in 1911 with the possible exception of

Brownsville. Laredo's distinctive characteristics had been noted in a March issue of *La Crónica*.[68]

Reception in Press

This narrative would not be complete without a discussion of the available newspaper coverage given to the Congreso. According to *La Crónica*, Spanish language newspapers such as *El Demócrata Fronterizo* (Laredo), *El Imparcial* (San Antonio), *El Gallo* (Falfurrias), *El Hachero* (Eagle Pass) and *El Porvenir* (Brownsville) supported the Congreso and its aims.[69] The Anglo-American press reacted somewhat differently, if we can judge this reaction using two major newspapers from the area. The *San Antonio Express* and the *Laredo Weekly Times* reported the general factual details of the Congreso such as the time and place of the meetings and the names of the speakers, but deliberately or otherwise, they missed or misrepresented the tone and content of the meetings.[70]

Throughout both newspapers we find the redundant use of the term *interesting* to describe the speeches. Almost nothing was said about their content and what was expressed does not correspond with the evidence presented in this study. According to the small notices buried in the back pages of both newspapers, the Congreso gathered to celebrate the "Mexican holidays" and to develop education and citizenship programs designed to elevate the "Mexican race." According to the *Express*, José Reyes, the president of the Congreso,

> . . . made an interesting speech in which he said the objects of the Mexican congress were of an uplifting character and that its principal work will be the enlightenment and elevation of the Mexican element in the State of Texas with a view of making them more desirable and better citizens and a credit to the Texas cities in which they make their homes. Several other addresses were made along similar lines and the Congreso seems determined in the work it has undertaken.[71]

The *Laredo Weekly Times* reported that J. M. Mora spoke on ways to relieve Mexican misery and,

> . . . maintained that the best way to bring about this condition was by the carrying out of moral and elevating ideas among the Mexican people, the bettering of their social positions by their own individual efforts to thereby obtain from them a position among the people with whom they make their homes.[72]

Unfortunately we do not have a text of José Reyes' speech, but it would seem improbable that a man expressing such views would have been elected to the presidency of a Congreso gathered to discuss lynchings, discrimination, the loss of land, labor exploitation and cultural nationalism. Mora, as I have shown, clearly spoke of the need for Mexican labor to unite itself over and against capital interests.

Post Congreso Developments

In an effort to provide a continuous long range solution to the multiplicity of Texas-Mexican problems, the Congreso decided to create an on-going state wide organization with local chapters, According to its constitution, *la Gran Liga Mexicanista de Beneficiencia y Protección* would have these objectives: (1) carry out culture and moral instruction among its members; (2) protect its members when treated unjustly by authorities; (3) protect them against unlawful acts by other persons; (4) create a fund for the organization; and (5) prevent the exclusion of Mexican children from Anglo-American schools, and its motto would be *"Por la Raza y Para la Raza."*[73] Structurally, la Gran Liga would be composed of a central governing mesa directiva and local chapters each with their own mesa. The central and local mesa would have the same official structure: Director, Vice Director, Secretary, Treasurer, and a Master of Ceremonies. The central mesa was to be elected annually by delegates from the local ligas to the annual convention on September 16th. The central mesa had only the power to carry out those policies already written into the constitution or adopted at the conventions, including the power to hire agents to start local ligas in places of its own choosing, although each delegate was supposed to carry out the task in his local community.[74] The rest of the constitution spelled out the requirements for membership and the rights and obligations of the members. The organization was not limited to U.S. citizens or to males.[75] The first Mesa Directiva of La Gran Liga Mexicanista was composed of: Nicasio Idar, *Presidente* (Laredo), Basilio Soto, *Vice Presidente*, (San Antonio), Gerónimo Jiménez, *Tesorero* (Laredo), Lisandro Peña, *Secretario* (Laredo). A Master of Ceremonies was not elected and all of the delegates were named as vocales.[76]

This was not the only organization produced by the Congreso. The women were to be heard from again. On October 15, 1911,

Un grupo de damas tan respetables como bellas se reunieron el domingo como a las diez de la mañana en el Salon de la Respetable Sociedad de Obreros "Igualdad y Progreso" y bajo los auspicios del Congreso Mexicanista organizaron la primera Liga Femenil

Mexicanista con el ardiente anhelo de luchar ellas tambien POR LA RAZA Y PARA LA RAZA.[77]

A debate was held to select a more specific name for this women's group and the biographies of several Mexican heroines were read including those of Josefa Ortiz de Domínguez, Leona Vicario, and Doña Manuela Aguado de Abasolo. Apparently no name was chosen. The officers of the new organization were: *Presidenta*: Jovita Idar, *Vice Presidenta*: Profa. M. de J. de León, *Secretaria*: Profa. Soledad F. de Peña, *Tesorera*: Profa. María Rentería, *Consejera General*: María Villarreal, *Vocales*: Sritas. Profas. Luisa Cabrera, Rita Tarvin, Aurelia Peña y Sra. de Silva.[78] Since a number of these women were teachers, the organization immediately undertook a project to provide free instruction for poor Mexican children who could not afford to attend school.[79]

This is as much as we presently know about El Primer Congreso Mexicanista and its offspring organizations. They do not appear to have met again in 1912. The issues of *La Crónica* that I have been able to locate run through December, 1911 with a single issue from April, 1914. No mention is made of the Congreso in this latter issue, nor is it mentioned in other local available newspapers from 1912 to1913. Although there were limited, scattered reports of efforts to organize ligas in a few communities, we must presume that La Gran Liga Mexicanista did not thrive.[80]

Analysis

The data presented permits us to argue that El Primer Congreso Mexicanista de 1911 represents an early organizational effort that anticipated many of the major themes of contemporary Chicanismo. Clearly we have the same pervasive concern for the socio-economic plight of Chicanos. To take three examples: (1) although far more subtle, the problem of social discrimination, particularly in the schools, continues to be a matter of intense interest to Chicanos; (2) the restoration of the land, particularly in Nuevo México, and the plight of Chicano labor, continue to attract contemporary attention; and (3) present day protest against police brutality in Chicano communities echoes the Congreso's denunciations of officially tolerated lynchings in 1910–1911. Yet taken by itself, the common concern with the subordinate socioeconomic position of Chicanos would not alone argue for the Congreso as a precursor to the Chicano movement. In their own way the post 1921 accomodationist groups, Order Sons of America, the LULACS, and the American G.I. Forum, were also generally committed to this basic cause.

The particularly firm and unique ideological parallels between the Congreso and the contemporary period are to be found in their mutual interest in cultural retention and a rejection of assimilation, the rights of women and political unification. Like today's insistence on a personal and institutional commitment to bilingual and bicultural education, the Congreso was equally dedicated to the teaching of the Spanish language and of Mexican history and culture. Indeed we can even find in the Congreso milieu a tendency toward alternative school systems controlled by the community bringing to mind contemporary Chicano efforts in Colorado, the lower Rio Grande Valley and Crystal City, Texas. Similarly today's activist Chicanas can find strong historical precedent for their work in the activity of the Congreso women and la Liga Femenil Mexicanista. Finally the cry for political unity can still be heard. The apparent failure of la Gran Liga Mexicanista to achieve the latter in no way diminishes its importance as an effort that anticipated the current struggle of the *Raza Unida* Party to provide a single unified Chicano political vehicle for obtaining the same basic goals of the Congreso.[81] The opening remarks of this study referred to the contemporary vision of a quasi-separate nation-state for Chicanos.[82] The Congreso did not evoke a utopian ideal paralleling the contemporary notion of Aztlán. Yet, given their insistence on cultural nationalism and a pure ethnic organization together with the developing Texas-Mexican numerical majority in south Texas, it seems likely that their hypothetical success would have led to a political and cultural Texas-Mexican domination of the area. If not Aztlán, at least a reasonable portion of that vision.

These common interests, the socioeconomic position of Chicanos, cultural retention, women's rights and the unity of the people, argue for the precursory character of El Primer Congreso Mexicanista de 1911. This relationship can perhaps be seen with greater clarity if approached with a conceptual framework.

Professor Ralph Guzmán has provided a simple and useful scheme for categorizing historical Chicano political organizations according to two variables—participation in the U.S. political system and intention to assimilate (table 7.1).[83] The data and analysis in the present study permit us to fill in some of the vacancies in his conceptual grid. All of the evidence gathered so far points to an extremely low almost non-existent assimilative intent in the Congreso and the ligas. The U.S. when mentioned was perceived as a problem, an obstacle, an enemy. Learning English, when it was mildly favored, if at all, was a purely utilitarian matter and seemed to have no intrinsic positive value as did the use of Spanish. Indeed we should note the exclusive use of Spanish in the Congreso and in *La Crónica*. Finally, we have a constant appeal to the Mexican cultural past.

Table 7.1. Social and Political Intent of Chicano Organizations as Posited by Ralph Guzmán

Social Intent (Assimilation)

		High	Medium	Low
Political Intent (Participation)	High		Mexican-American Political Association (MAPA), 1959 Political Association of Spanish-Speaking Organizations (PASSO), 1960	
	Medium	League of United Latin American Citizens (LULAC), 1927 The Order of the Sons of America (OSA),1927	Community Service Organization (CSO), 1947 American G.I. Forum, 1948	
	Low			Mexican Liberal Party (MLP), 1906

The potential and the organizational structure for political participation were clearly present in the Congreso and the ligas. Yet apparently they did not have the opportunity to participate directly in U.S. electoral politics. For these reasons they are characterized as "medium" in terms of this variable. Using low assimilative intent and medium political participation, the Congreso has been located in the appropriate square in a revised version of Guzmán's scheme (table 7.2).

Table 7.2. Revision of Social and Political Intent of Chicano Organizations

Social Intent (Assimilation)

		High	Medium	Low
Political Intent (Participation)	High		MAPA, 1960 PASSO, 1960	Gran Liga Mexicanista, 1911 Raza Unida Party, 1970
	Medium	LULAC, 1927 OSA, 1927	CSO, 1947 American G.I. Forum, 1948	
	Low			MLP, 1906

In both respects the Congreso and its milieu greatly resemble the 1967–70 Chicano movement ideologically, particularly in Texas. They were both phenomena marked by a strong sense of cultural nationalism, and, therefore, a low assimilative intent. Neither, however, actively and fully participated in the political process. On the same two criteria, the contemporary movement has been located in the same conceptual category with the Congreso.[84] Had la Gran Liga Mexicanista developed and participated in the U.S. political process on the same ideological grounds as the Congreso, it probably would have resembled the contemporary Raza Unida Party in Texas which developed directly from the Chicano movement.[85] Like Raza Unida, la Gran Liga would have been the institutionalized agency resulting from a formative ideological, organizational phase. The actual Texas Raza Unida Party and a hypothetically successful Gran Liga Mexicanista are conjoined in Table 7.2.

Conclusions

These findings permit us to fill in previously empty historical and conceptual slots thereby altering the political history of Chicanos in a significant manner. Whereas before it was probably correct to speak of a pre 1921 apolitical period and of a unique and novel post 1965 period, we now have to contend with an organized, militant, nationalist, pro-feminist social movement appearing in 1911.

The Congreso's scholarly importance is clear, but in arguing its precursory relationship to the contemporary scene, this study perhaps has accomplished more than a scholarly exercise. Professor Juan Gómez-Quiñones has called for a "union of history as discipline and history as action on behalf of a community in its struggle for survival."[86] If this new knowledge of historical ideological precedents lends moral and intellectual support to the contemporary struggle, this work has responded adequately to this call.

Notes

My appreciation to Linda X. Jiménez for her research assistance on this project.

1. Alfredo Cuéllar, "Perspective on Politics" in *Mexican Americans*, ed. Joan Moore (Englewood Cliffs, NJ: Prentice Hall, 1970), 137–58. See also Rodolfo Acuña, *Occupied America: The Chicano's Struggle Toward Liberation* (San Francisco: Canfield Press, 1972) particularly chps. 9 and 10, and Armando Rendón, *Chicano Manifesto* (New York: Macmillan, 1971).

2. Cuéllar, "Perspective on Politics," 137–56. For broader yet similar analyses, see Rodolfo Alvarez, "The Psycho-Historical and Socioeconomic Development of the Chicano Community in the United States," *Social Science Quarterly* 53, no. 4 (March 1973): 920–42; Jesús Chavarria, "A Precise and Tentative Bibliography on Chicano History," *Aztlán* I, no. 1 (Spring 1970), 133–41; Juan Gómez-Q. "Toward a Perspective on Chicano History," *Aztlán* II, no. 2 (Fall 1971), 1–49: Ralph Guzmán, "Politics and Policies of the Mexican-American Community," in *California Politics and Policies*, ed. Eugene P. Dvorin (Palo Alto, CA: Addison Wesley, 1966), 350–85, and Miguel D. Tirado, "Mexican-American Community Political Organization, the Key to Chicano Political Power," *Aztlán* I, no. 1 (Spring 1970), 53–78. Carey McWilliams' useful but incomplete *North From Mexico* (New York: Greenwood, 1968) has been superseded by Acuña's *Occupied America* and Matt Meir and Feliciano Rivera, *The Chicanos: A History of Mexican Americans* (New York: Hill and Wang, 1972). Neither of these general histories departs significantly from the analysis cited above. A study that sees cultural retention as a basic concern of the so-called assimilationist period is Charles Ray Chandler's, "The Mexican-American Protest Movement In Texas," Ph.D. dissertation, Department of Sociology, Tulane University, 1968. However, Chandler does not deal with the contemporary Chicano movement.

3. Cuéllar, "Perspective on Politics," 155.

4. David J. Weber has published a speech from the Congreso and a brief commentary. See "Por La Raza y Para La Raza—Congreso Mexicanista, 1911," in *Foreigners in Their Native Land: Historical Roots of the Mexican American* (Albuquerque: University of New Mexico Press, 1973), 248–51. This publication appeared independently and somewhat after my research note "El Primer Congreso Mexicanista de 1911: A Note on Research in Progress," *Aztlán* III, no. 1 (Spring 1972), 171. Weber's commentary misses some important issues discussed at the Congreso and incorrectly identifies León Cárdenas Martínez as the victim of the Thorndale lynching. (See pp. 222–23) To my knowledge this is the only scholarly work on the Congreso.

5. D. W. Meinig, *Imperial Texas: An Interpretive Essay in Cultural Geography*. (Austin: University of Texas Press, 1969), 54–56.

6. Victor Nelson-Cisneros, *"La Clase Trabajadora en Texas, 1920–1940,"* (Unpublished Ms., Center for Mexican-American Studies, University of Texas at Austin), 3–4.

7. Meinig, *Imperial Texas*, 98–101.

8. Américo Paredes, *With His Pistol in His Hand* (Austin: University of Texas Press, 1971), 31–32. See also McWillams, *North from Mexico*, 112–14.

9. *La Crónica*, April 18, 1914, 1–2.

10. See any masthead of *La Crónica* (1910–1911), Texas Newspaper Collection, University of Texas at Austin.

11. "El Primer Año de Vida" *La Crónica*, Jan. 1, 1910, 1. The author is currently at work on the preliminary research for a collective biography of this remarkable family whose members continue to be active participants in Chicano affairs today.

12. *The Chaparral*, Feb. 18, 1899, 3. "Mr. N. Idar, Assistant City Marshall and Editor of *La Crónica*, we regret to state has been quite sick the early part of this week." See "Progreso de 'La Crónica,'" LC, Sept. 3, 1910, 1.

Con elementos propios principiamos in publicación de nuestro semanario La Crónica en Enero del año pasado, viniendo a ser la segunda época de su existencia.

Nunca creimos que llegaría en un año de vida a sentar la reputación y popularidad de que hoy goza tanto en la frontera Norte de México como en Texas, California, Arizona, y Nuevo México.

13. *San Antonio Light and Gazette*, Nov. 4, 1910, 1.

14. "All Quiet in Edwards County—Lynching at Rock Springs Done By Americans, Says Ranger Captain." *San Antonio Daily Express*, Nov. 22, 1910, 10.

15. Stanley R. Ross, *Francisco I. Madero: Apostle of Democracy* (New York: Columbia University Press, 1955), 137.

16. "Barbarismos" *La Crónica*, Nov. 12, 1910, 1.

17. "*Cobarde Infame e Inhumano Lynchamiento de un Jovencito Mexicano en Thorndale, Milam Co., Texas*," *La Crónica*, June 29, 1911, 1. The accused were found not guilty. See "*Lo Mismo de Siempre*" *La Crónica*, Nov. 16, 1911, 1.

18. "*Valiente cobardia de los linchadores de Thorndale, Texas, Los Estados Unidos y Mexico nada pueden hacer para el castigo de los criminales—Represalias unica solución posible,*" *La Crónica*, July 13, 1911, 1.

19. "*Junta de Indignacion—El infame hecho de Thorndale gita á los Mexicanos de Bay City*" *La Crónica*, July 20, 1911, 6.

20. "*Traducción: Integra de la narración que hizo el Lic. George Estes á alungos periodicos como defensor del niño Leén Cárdenas Martínez, Jr., en el proceso que se le enstruyo en Pecos, Texas el 29 de Julio de 1911.*" *La Crónica*, Oct. 26, 1911, 2.

21. "*Solicitud de indulto,*" *La Crónica*, Aug. 24, 1911, 1.

22. "Claim Mexican Lad is Not Murderer" *San Antonio Light*, Sept. 12, 1911, 1.

23. J. J. Mercado, "*Facultad de perdonar—traducción*" *La Crónica*, Sept. 21, 1911, 4.

24. "*La Labor de La Crónica,*" March 2, 1911, 5.

25. "*Los niños Mexicanos en Texas*" *La Crónica*, Nov. 26, 1910, 3; "*La exclusión de los niños Mexicanos en la mayor parte de las escuelas oficiales de Texas es positiva.*" Dec. 17, 1910, 1; "*Tanto los niños Mexicanos como los Mexico-Americanos son excluídos de las escuelas oficiales—¿ya se Olvidaron los tratados de Guadalupe?*" Dec. 24, 1910), 1; "*La exclusión en el condado de Guadalupe,*" and "*Los Mexicanos de San Angelo demandan a los sindicos de las escuelas públicas,*" Dec. 31, 1970, 1; "*La exclusión de los niños Mexicanos de la escuela Americanas en algunas partes de Texas,*" Jan. 26, 1911, 3; "*La exclusión en las escuelas de los condados de Frio, Bee, Hays, Bastrop, Comal, Caldwell, Blanco, etc. etc.,*" Feb. 9, 1911, 1.

26. A. V. Negra, "*Por la raza—La niñez Mexicana en Texas,*" *La Crónica*, Aug. 10, 1911, 1. (See also J. J. Mercado, "*El Mexicano en Texas*" *La Crónica*, Sept. 14, 1911, 2, expressing concern for the linguistic deterioration already underway.)

27. A. V. Negra, "*La conservación del nacionalismo,*" *La Crónica*, Aug. 17, 1911, 1.

28. Negra, "*La conservación,*" 1.

29. *"En pro de la raza Mexicana del estado de Texas,"* La Crónica, Nov. 26, 1910, 1.

30. "A *'El Imparcial de Texas,'"* La Crónica, Dec. 10, 1910, 4.

31. Negra, *"Por la raza,"* 1.

32. Clemente Idar, *"Nuestro deber en este país: Solidaridad y altruismo,"* La Crónica, Dec. 24, 1910, 1.

33. Idar, *"Nuestro deber en este País,"* 1.

34. *"Excitativa del Gran Concillo de la Orden Caballeros de Honor á la raza Mexicana,"* La Crónica, Dec. 17, 1910, *oja suelta* inserted in newspaper.

35. *"A la Orden Caballeros de Honor de Brownsville, Texas,"* La Crónica, Jan. 12, 1911, 3.

36. *"Un Gran Excitativo al Gran Concilio de la Orden Caballeros de Honor,"* La Crónica, Feb. 2, 1911, 1.

37. *"Los elementos mas conspicuous de Laredo influyen cerca del G. Concilio de la Orden Caballeros de Honor,"* La Crónica, March 16, 1911.

38. Nicasio Idar, *"Agrupación Protectora Mexicana,"* La Crónica, July 13, 1911, 2. See Paredes, *With His Pistol,* for the full account of Gregorio Cortez.

39. *"Una Gran Convención Se Reúne en Laredo,"* La Crónica, Jul. 27, 1911, 4.

40. *"El Congreso Mexicanista. ¿Qué Es y Qué se Propone?"* La Crónica, Aug. 24, 1911, 2.

41. *"Para el Congreso Mexicanista"* La Crónica, Sept. 7, 1911, 4.

42. *"Mas delegados"* La Crónica, Sept. 14, 1911, 1.

43. *"Otra victima del odio Yankee"* La Crónica, Sept. 14, 1911, 4.

44. E. R. Tarver, *Laredo, the Gateway between the United States and Mexico* (Laredo: Immigration Society, 1889), 1.

45. *"El Congreso Mexicanista"* Fiat Lux, Sept. 15, 1911, 1.

46. That morning a general invitation to the public had appeared In La Crónica. *"Invitación"* La Crónica, Sept. 14, 1911, 1.

47. *Primer Congreso Mexicanista, verificado en Laredo, Texas, EEUU de A. los dias 14 al 22 de Septiembre de 1911. Discursos y conferencias por la raza y para la raza* (Tipografía de N. Idar, 1912), 1.

48. *Primer Congreso Mexicanista,* 5. We have no evidence concerning voting procedures and privileges.

49. *Primer Congreso Mexicanista,* 3–5, 10–13. The San Antonio Express, Sept. 17, 1911, 6, reports a number of patriotic speeches, the display of Mexican flags and shouts of *"¡Viva Mexico!"* and *"¡Viva Hidalgo!"* during the meetings on the 16th.

50. *Primer Congreso Mexicanista,* 13.

51. *Primer Congreso Mexicanista,* 17.

52. *Primer Congreso Mexicanista,* 16.

53. *Primer Congreso Mexicanista,* 19.

54. *Primer Congreso Mexicanista,* 31.

55. *Primer Congreso Mexicanista,* 4.

56. *Primer Congreso Mexicanista,* 26.

57. *Primer Congreso Mexicanista,* 1.

58. *Primer Congreso Mexicanista*, 26–27.

59. "A *La Mujer Mexicana de Ambos Laredos*" *La Crónica*, Sept. 14, 1911, 1.

60. *Primer Congreso Mexicanista*, 20.

61. *Primer Congreso Mexicanista*, 24.

62. *Primer Congreso Mexicanista*, 14.

63. *Primer Congreso Mexicanista*, 31.

64. *Primer Congreso Mexicanista*, 34.

65. *Primer Congreso Mexicanista*, 28–30.

66. "Al Beneficio de León Cárdenas Martínez," *La Crónica*, Sept. 21, 1911, 1.

67. "Corte de Caja," *La Crónica*, Sept. 28, 1911, 4.

68. "*La Labor de* La Crónica," *La Crónica*, March 2, 1911, 5.

69. See "*La convención de los Caballeros de Honor y El Primer Congreso Mexicanista*," *El Demócrata Fronterizo*, Sept. 23, 1911, 4; "*Congreso de Mexicanistas*" *La Crónica*, April 20, 1911, 4; and "*Comentarios de la Prensa Sobre el Congreso Mexicanista*," *La Crónica*, Sept. 28, 1911, 3.

70. There was only one exception. "Mexicans May Protest Against Separate Schools. Matter Is Placed Before *Congreso Mexicanista* in Session Now at Laredo" *San Antonio Express*, Sept. 17, 1911, 16.

71. "Form New Organization, *Congreso Mexicanista* Is Brought Into Existence" *San Antonio Express*, Sept. 16, 1911, 9. See also the *Express* for Sept. 15, 1911, 9; Sept. 18, 1911, 7; Sept. 19, 1911, 2; and Sept. 20, 1911, 7.

72. "The Mexican Congress—Interesting Subject Discussed" *Laredo Weekly Times*, Sept. 24, 1911, 4. See also the *Times* for Sept. 17, 1911, 10; and Sept. 24, 1911, 6, 8, 10.

73. "*Constitución de la Gran Liga Mexicanista de Beneficiencia y Proteccion*" in *Primer Congreso Mexicanista*, 39.

74. "*Constitución de la Gran*," 39–42.

75. "*Constitución de la Gran*," 39–40, particularly Cap. II, Art. 3 on 39.

76. "*Para Constituyentes de la Comisión Consejera Del Congreso Mexicanista*" *La Crónica*, Sept. 28, 1911, 4.

77. "*Liga Femenil Mexicanista*," *La Crónica*, Oct. 19, 1911, 1.

78. "*Liga Femenil Mexicanista*," 1.

79. "*La Liga Femenil Mexicanista*," *La Crónica*, Dec. 7, 1911, 1.

80. See "*La Crónica publicará Semanariamente los progresos del Congreso Mexicanista*," *La Crónica*, Sept. 28, 1911, 4, and "*Liga Mexicanista, No. 2*" *La Crónica*, Oct. 12, 1911, 1.

81. Acuña, *Occupied America*, 236–37.

82. Rendón, *Chicano Manifesto*, 168.

83. Guzmán, "Politics and Policies," 374.

84. There are also strong similarities in the social-behavioral determinants of these phenomena as social movements. The author is currently at work on a study of these relationships.

85. Acuña, *Occupied America*, 234–36.

86. Juan Gómez-Quiñones "Toward a Perspective on Chicano History" *Aztlán* 4 no. 2 (Fall 1971), 39.

*   *   *

Questions

1. In notes 4 and 5, Limón lists the many studies that see the Chicano movement as a new phenomenon. What can be said about such a game of truth? What are the political benefits and disadvantages of such "invisible" knowledge?
2. What is the process by which U.S. criminal, educational, and civil laws become tools for the oppression of a particular set of human bodies? Why would Texas Mexicans still demand "justice" and plan to have a nationwide political association to place themselves "under the protection of the law"?
3. How is the voice of the Texas Mexicans appropriated and suppressed? How is it invested with power and institutionalized to impact social reality?
4. Are there any hidden assumptions revealed in the description of the Mexican by the Anglo American press?
5. After reading the articles about the Chicano movement, do you agree with Limón that the Congreso anticipated its major themes? In particular, is it reasonable to argue that either one or both advocates separatism or, on the contrary, requesting equal treatment under the law or what we call public citizenship?

~

CHAPTER EIGHT

Epilogue from *Decade of Betrayal*
Francisco E. Balderrama
and Raymond Rodríguez

The word *repatriation* means that members of a society are "sent back to their *patria*" which means fatherland, country of origin. As a U.S. government policy sanctioned by the Mexican government, however, *Repatriation* is the name of a program that not only sent Mexican nationals back to Mexico it also expelled U.S. American citizens. As noted by the authors,

> [yet] the lessons of history appear to be lost in the turmoil besetting the question of legal and illegal immigration in the 1990s. Since massive repatriation is not a feasible alternative, other ingenious means are being proposed to halt the unwanted immigrant influx. It is suggested that steel walls, moats, fences, floodlights, and a beefed-up and well-equipped border patrol be deployed along the U.S.-Mexico border to deter entry from Mexico and Central America.

As discussed in chapter 26, this border games and immigration charade continues well into the twenty-first century.

Although questions of who, why, and how are a matter of debate, what is absolutely clear in this particular game of truth, is that this event illustrates the fragility of the political status of being a "Mexican" in the United States. If you were a Mexican entering the United States before 1908, there were no regulations on border crossing; in fact, there was no one to keep a record of your entry. If you entered before 1917 you were not required to pay a head tax or to pass a literacy test (unless your labor was needed, in which case you were exempt). If you entered before 1924 (when the Border Patrol was created) it was not even a crime to enter the United States "illegally." After

1924, however, these new laws would be applied retroactively and make you an "illegal" (or a "communist" if you were involved in union or social causes) and subject you to deportation or repatriation.[1]

How many Mexican human bodies were in the United States in 1930s when the Depression led to the repatriation? This is a difficult task, precisely because of the fragile status of the U.S. Mexican. In the 1920s, the U.S. Census Bureau counted U.S. Mexicans as members of the white population. In the 1930 census, however, Mexicans were defined as a separate "race," even as efforts were made to separate recent arrivals from those who were "territorial citizens." According to the census of 1930, there were 1,422,533 Mexicans in the United States. This number does not include undocumented Mexicans, and it is also marred by the thousands who were already on the move as a result of repatriation pressures. One calculation is that an additional one million Mexicans entered the United States without the proper documentation.[2] And how many were deported? Anywhere between one-half and one million Mexicans, many of whom were born in the United States and therefore were U.S. citizens. The actual bodies repatriated belonged in many categories: laborers, craftsmen, business people, merchants, shopkeepers, farmers, property owners, women (widows, single, abandoned), children, teenagers, children in county orphanages, the old and infirm, bedridden and terminally ill patients, and the mentally ill. The methods used ranged from seduction and inducement to threats of bodily harm, terrorism, and scare tactics.[3] By defining people along ethnic and cultural as opposed to national lines, U.S. officials deprived U.S. American children of Mexican descent of rights guaranteed them by the U.S. Constitution.

In these games of racial truths, even the undesirable Mexican, "who had no idea of becoming a citizen or a menace" (i.e., they were deportable), was preferred over the undeportable "Porto Rican Negro."[4] Indeed, most U.S. Mexicans did not become U.S. citizens, because they would still be viewed and treated as Mexicans anyway, and because as Mexican citizens they could seek the support of the Mexican Consul and secure justice. It is the same reason an American living in Mexico would prefer to remain a U.S. citizen.[5] What we see here is a quest for acceptance and belonging in the society in which one must live.

In terms of the role that institutions play, it is pertinent to note that the Bureau of Immigration was first placed in the U.S. Department of Labor. In 1933, its function was expanded to include naturalization and in 1940 the Immigration and Naturalization Service (INS), as it was by then called, was transferred to the Department of Justice. In effect, the root cause of the repatriation was the belief that getting rid of "aliens" would free up enough jobs for U.S. Americans. This illustrates the crisis that arises among members of a society when there are economic problems or the impact of the lack of production on social relations.

At this point it is pertinent to inject a personal account from Francisco Hernández Vázquez regarding his mother's repatriation:

> My grandparents immigrated to the United States as political refugees in 1914. Mother, born in the state of Colorado in 1926, was repatriated at the age of six, along with her parents and five siblings. According to U.S. Congressional Law, she would have had to live in the United States until she was fourteen years old in order for me to get my U.S. citizenship *jus sanguinis* (through bloodline). I argued with the Immigration and Naturalization Service (INS) for thirty years that I should be given a certificate of citizenship, because she *would have been here* if she had not been kicked out of her own country. After three decades, however, I had to obtain my U.S. citizenship through "naturalization." What strikes me about this event is its invisibility. Neither my grandparents, nor my mother, nor my in-laws ever talked about it. The clerk that dealt with my file told me that in over thirty years that she had worked in INS, she never heard about the Repatriation.

How do you hide one million experiences, many of which represent a violation of the civil rights of American citizens? It is all in the power of a discourse that erases memories that are not in agreement with the image of a freedom-loving country that is incapable of doing wrong. Memories of injustices, however, have a way of coming back. This is illustrated by Francisco E. Balderrama and Raymond Rodríguez's book, from which the following piece is excerpted, and other recent publications and movies such as *Mi Familia/My Family* and *Born in East L.A.* Space limitations, unfortunately, prevent us from including additional personal accounts regarding this truly apocalyptic event for individual U.S. citizens of Mexican descent.

In the following text, Balderrama and Rodríguez summarize the main issues, implications, and consequences of the repatriation. It is a mere glimpse of the trials and tribulations of the human bodies involved in one of the great mass movements in history. Their book inspired California legislators to draft Senate Bill 670 "Apology Act for the 1930s Mexican Repatriation Program." It became official in December 2005 and states, in part:

> The state of California apologizes . . . for the fundamental violation of their basic civil liberties and constitutional rights during the period of illegal deportation and coerced emigration.[6]

Earlier that year, the California Assembly voted 41-23 to approve the creation of a state fund that could be used to pay for reparations for the estimated 400,000 Californians that were repatriated, and to create a sixteen-member commission to make recommendations to the governor and Legislature on how to redress the deportations.[7]

Notes and Suggestions for Further Research

1. Abraham Hoffman, *Unwanted Mexican Americans in the Great Depression* (Tucson: University of Arizona Press, 1995), 50.
2. Francisco E. Balderrama and Raymond Rodríguez, *Decade of Betrayal: Mexican Repatriation in the 1930s* (Albuquerque: University of New Mexico Press, 1995), 7.
3. Balderrama and Rodríguez, *Decade of Betrayal*, 107–11.
4. Hoffman, *Unwanted Mexican Americans*, 29.
5. Hoffman, *Unwanted Mexican Americans*, 20.
6. Peter Hecht, "State to apologize for deportations," *The Press Democrat* (December 29, 2005).
7. "Reparation fund for Latinos OK'd," *The Press Democrat* (September 7, 2005).

*   *   *

No lloro, pero me acuerdo. [I don't cry, but I remember.]

—*Dicho Mexicano* [Mexican proverb]

The foregoing work chronicles the tragedy of a people who, in spite of being maligned and mistreated by American society, refused to surrender to adversity. Like other immigrant groups, they were proud of the contributions they made to their adopted country. However, during the Great Depression, American society chose to disregard the significant role that Mexicans had played in creating the nation's wealth. Instead, regardless of their place of birth, it became fashionable to blame Mexicans for the country's economic ills. A relentless campaign was launched to get rid of the pariahs by shipping them to Mexico. Since many of the Mexicans had been actively recruited to come and work in the United States, their ruthless expulsion was an ironic twist of fate. The vendetta created the first major contingent of displaced refugees in the twentieth century.

One of the most tragic aspects of the movement was the wholesale violation of basic human rights. When individuals were caught in INS raids, they were summarily deported without being informed of or accorded their legal rights. The wanton disregard of legal constraints in denying deportees their constitutional rights was so flagrant that groups as diverse as the Los Angeles Bar Association, the Wickersham Commission, industrialists, and ranchers felt compelled to condemn the illegal tactics, but to no avail. Protests about the injustice were drowned out by the roar of approval from opportune politicians, labor unions, and civic or patriotic groups. In 1942, another minority group, the Japanese, also learned the bitter lesson that constitutional guarantees are meaningless when mob hysteria is accorded institutional or legal status.

In many instances, the same charges of illegal action can be made regarding the repatriation efforts. As in the days of slavery, when families were split asunder by selling certain members "downriver," Mexican families suffered the same fate. Wives often refused to return to Mexico with their husbands because their children were American born and were entitled to remain in the United States. The situation became truly heart wrenching when older children refused to join their parents on the trek south. Younger children who had no choice but to accompany their parents suffered wholesale violations of their citizenship rights. This accounts for the fact that approximately 60 percent of those summarily expelled were children who had been born in the United States and were legally American citizens.

Lacking concrete or convincing substance were the three facetious claims often used to justify or at least to rationalize banishing the Mexicans: jobs would be created for "real Americans"; cutting the welfare rolls would save taxpayers money; and "those people" would be better off in Mexico with their "own kind." In every case, the allegations begged or ignored the question. With unemployment rates in the *colonias* averaging 50 percent or more, due to decrees forbidding their hiring in government or public projects, the Mexicans had been effectively eliminated as a rival working force. Many private employers were also scare headed by mobs into firing their Mexican workers. Furthermore, since the Mexicans constituted less than 1 percent of the nation's total population, few jobs would have been made available even if all of them had been shipped to Mexico.

The same false claims were made concerning welfare costs and projected savings. Mexican families with American-born children qualified for welfare assistance if the family could meet residency requirements and prove entitlement. However, even in Los Angeles and Detroit, the cities with the largest number of Mexicans on relief, they constituted 10 percent or less of the total number of welfare recipients. In truth, the anticipated savings were impossible to achieve for the simple reason that 85 percent of the approximately twenty million people on welfare were native-born or naturalized Americans. Yet politicians and the media adroitly created and nurtured the impression in the public's mind that Mexicans constituted the overwhelming majority of those on the public dole. The baseless and misleading charges were merely a ploy to inflame an overwrought public's anti-Mexican passions.

Equally inane were repeated attempts to justify the expulsion of the Mexicans by claiming that they would be better off in Mexico among relatives and friends. The irony was that Mexican families residing in *barrios* or colonias were already living among close relatives and friends. Many of them had resided in the United States for such a long time, often their entire adult life, that they did not have close friends or relatives in Mexico. Bearing the traumatic burden of being shipped "back" to Mexico were those least able to cope with their plight: the children. Shipping them to Mexico so they could be with "their own kind" was absolutely absurd. Although of Mexican ancestry, they considered themselves to be Americans and many of them spoke only a limited amount of Spanish. To them, historically and culturally, Mexico was a totally foreign country.

Nonetheless, welfare authorities reasoned that young children rightfully belonged with their parents and should accompany the family to Mexico. This convenient rationale relieved repatriation authorities of any blame or responsibility for failing to protect the rights of the American-born children. Regretfully, no one seemed to care about what was happening to them. Their personal identity and sense of self-worth were stripped from them without any qualms and hardly a ripple of protest in their behalf. The prevailing attitude was that "a Mexican was a Mexican," regardless of birthright.

The assumption that a Mexican was a Mexican prevailed in both the United States and Mexico, but for different reasons. The Mexican government accorded dual citizenship to children who were born abroad and whose parents were Mexican citizens. This dual citizenship was intended to enable them to move freely between the respective countries. It was also used as an inducement to relocate and settle in Mexico, with all the rights and privileges enjoyed by native-born individuals. It was hoped that they would not only augment Mexico's relatively small population, but would also contribute to the nation's socioeconomic stability.

In American society, the attitude of "once a Mexican, always a Mexican" enabled authorities to take collective action against the entire Spanish-speaking population. They were not hampered by the task of having to differentiate between Mexican Nationals and native-born Mexican Americans. This situation made racial and anti-Mexican propaganda easier to disseminate and more readily acceptable, and created a situation in which people blindly condoned illegal and discriminatory acts against a defenseless minority. The public's support dramatically eased the awesome task of expelling, with complete impunity, hundreds of thousands of people whose only crime was poverty.

Despite the odds arraigned against them, most Mexicans struggled to maintain their self-respect and independence. Three significant examples attest to their dauntless perseverance and their determination to survive. As has been previously stated, the overwhelming majority disdained applying for welfare and attempted to survive by a variety of innovative means. A resourceful lot, they often managed to cope with the relentless and bruising depression better than did their Anglo counterparts. Families who had lost their breadwinners were subjected to prolonged unemployment or were split apart by deportation or repatriation; or they were aided by extended families, friends, and neighbors. In most barrios and colonias, a common bond evolved in order to help each other survive. Families who had always paid their own way were reluctant to admit defeat and seek any type of government assistance. In many instances, that attitude served as the impetus for families who decided to return to Mexico voluntarily.

Disdaining any sort of government interference, the vast majority of Mexicans who lived adjacent to, or within driving distance of, the border simply loaded their personal belongings into the family sedan and headed south. Individuals who owned a truck and were returning to Mexico often found it convenient to take two or three families with them. This enabled the owner either to charge them a small fee or to share the trip's expenses. Women traveling alone or with young children welcomed the opportunity to hitch a ride with family or friends. Given the perilous nature of the journey, it was always best to travel with several companions. The highly individualistic Mexicans found it more to their liking to ignore the bureaucratic red tape on both sides of the border and to make their own arrangements.

The individualistic and philosophical attitude of the Mexicans illustrates the third aspect of their struggle to survive. Even during the darkest days of the Great Depression, they persevered in attempts to overcome racial discrimination, social injustice, segregated schooling, and unfair treatment in the workplace. Protests, demonstrations, and strikes were utilized in attempts to achieve their goals. In pursuing their aims, however, they were often set upon by hoodlums, goon squads, and local police and sheriff's deputies. Despite the beatings inflicted, barrio leaders repeatedly exhorted their compatriots not to abandon the struggle to improve the quality of life for themselves and for their children.

Exacerbating their plight and adding to their dilemma were the routine violations of legal rights by the judicial system. Basic procedural rights were commonly ignored as judges, sworn to uphold the law, turned their chambers into nothing more than kangaroo courts. The news media joined in discrediting the protestors and their goals by accusing them of being un-American or labeling them as communist agitators. With the willing connivance of the Labor Department and the Immigration Service, and the collaboration of police and the court system, trumped-up charges were used to justify deporting Mexicans who advocated ending discrimination, better working conditions, or desegregated schools.

Plagued by such adverse circumstances and envisioning little change for the better, many destitute and desperate Mexicans viewed returning to Mexico, if not as a boon, at least as a change for the better. Official releases on both sides of the border emphasized the benefits to be reaped by those who took advantage of the opportunity to return and colonize productive lands awaiting the plow. Using the work habits and skills acquired in *El Norte*, they would be able to help Mexico achieve new heights in agricultural and industrial production. The newcomers would also enrich the country's social development by augmenting the nucleus of the emerging middle class. Politically, they could infuse the nation with the ideals of a viable democratic system. Optimistic returnees and government officials envisioned Mexico assuming the role of *"los yanquis"* of Latin America. With the help of the repatriates, Mexico would be propelled into the twentieth century.

In actuality, the results were radically different from what the repatriates had envisioned. The dreams, hopes, and lofty aspirations failed to materialize. The task of resettling and assimilating the horde of people returning to *la madre patria* overwhelmed the Mexican bureaucracy. The sheer numbers and the enormity and complex nature of the vast undertaking taxed the government's ability to respond effectively. Farmland—vital to successful colonization and the crucial factor on which the nation's prosperity would be based—was not available in sufficient quantities. Despite the government's good intentions and its heroic efforts to build dams and irrigation canals, there were simply too many people who desperately needed help. Unfortunately, official edicts or decrees could not change the climate or the topography.

Lacking the opportunity to colonize and having no place else to go, most repatriates gradually drifted back into their native villages and *ranchitos*. Some opted to settle in the larger cities in the hope of earning a decent living. For the majority of the newcomers, the scenario they had foreseen when they made up their minds to go back to Mexico remained an illusion. Instead of being welcomed home with open arms, acquiring good land, and regaining their self-respect, they were trapped in a morass of grinding poverty rivaling the one they thought they had left behind in the United States.

Compounding their plight and adding to their misery was the fact that their status and well-being were issues that often became expedient political footballs. Politicos were aware that efforts to aid the resettlement of repatriates did not set well with rank-and-file Mexicans. Despite official policy, many politicians and their supporters believed that the nation's fiscal and material resources should be used to benefit loyal sons and daughters who had stayed home. Repatriates accused antagonists of conveniently overlooking the financial remuneration consisting of millions of dollars that they had remitted to families and relatives in Mexico during more prosperous times. Each group viewed the other as a bunch of ingrates.

Many Mexicans felt that the expectations and demands of the repatriates were unwarranted and that they should stop badgering the Mexican government, who could ill afford to grant them the aid they so desperately needed. Mexicanos believed those forced to return to Mexico should have exhausted all legal means available to them before succumbing to their fate. Instead, the repatriates had readily acquiesced in their own expatriation. By doing so, they had completely absolved the United States of any responsibility for their well-being, and this was especially true for those with American-born children. The children were deemed to be the responsibility of the American, rather than the Mexican, government.

In hindsight, the protestors were undoubtedly correct. The callous attitude of American authorities exposed the repatriated children to a cruel and virtually untenable fate. Ultimately, it was the children who bore the brunt of rejection and discrimination. They were neither Americans nor Mexicans as defined by their respective cultures. In the U.S. they were unilaterally classified as Mexicans, regardless of birthright. In Mexico they were regarded as *pochos, tejanos, or even gringos*. For teenagers, adjustment was especially difficult and they constantly badgered their parents to return to the United States.

The Mexican press reacted with hostility toward "ingrates" who sought to leave. Their departure was viewed as a slap in the face to Mexico's generous hospitality. The media failed to understand the urge that tormented the young repatriates and compelled them to return to their rightful homeland. The predictable reaction was an example of the perverse dilemma that beset the Mexican press. Failure to support and expound the government's official policy could have dire consequences. In commenting on the problems associated with the repatriates, the press had to be careful to absolve the government of any responsibility for the deplorable situation. While lauding the government's efforts, it unmercifully castigated the United States for its inhumane and racist actions.

Although not faced with the constraints that hindered the Mexican press, few English-language newspapers in the United States protested the injustices perpetrated against Mexican Nationals or against American citizens who happened to be of Mexican ancestry. While legal justification could be made for getting rid of unwanted aliens, it was an entirely different matter to deprive American citizens of their constitutional rights solely because of the accident of birth. Instead of protesting, the media acquiesced in the despicable action by commending authorities for their zeal and success in getting rid of as many Mexicans as possible. The failure to speak out in behalf of the Mexican community remains a black, irredeemable blot on the record of the American press.

In assessing the treatment accorded repatriation and deportation by the media, it must be borne in mind that neither the American nor the Mexican government was anxious to have its role in the tragedy publicly disclosed. The United States feared that the massive repatriation and deportation efforts could have negative repercussions upon its relations with countries in Latin America. It did not want to exacerbate the situation at a time when it was seeking to curtail immigration from the Western Hemisphere. To counter the adverse publicity, emissaries were sent abroad to convey assurances of America's goodwill. The United States was zealous in its efforts not to be perceived as a heartless society that turned its back on indigent immigrants in their hour of need.

The Mexican government also sought to minimize the repatriation issue in order not to alarm its own people about the magnitude of the problem. It diligently sought to avoid any embarrassment due to its inability to cope with the situation. Additionally, the Mexican government was caught between the horns of the proverbial dilemma: Since it was pursuing its own policy of expulsion against the Chinese and other unwanted individuals, it was not in a position to protest the expulsion of its Nationals from the United States. Mexico judiciously supported the right of every nation to determine who would be allowed to reside within its borders.

Obviously, authorities in both countries would have been acutely embarrassed if an accurate record of the number of Mexicans shipped to Mexico had been kept. However, a definitive body count is not essential to the essence of the tragic experience. Of greater importance were the consequences suffered by those forced to depart as well as those who remained behind. The loss of approximately one-third of the Mexican population in the United States augured an uncertain future for residents of *México de afuera*. Barrios and colonias were not only physically gutted; they lost a large cadre of dedicated community leaders. More significantly, they suffered the loss of a generation of young, intelligent minds.

The loss effectively stifled the socioeconomic development of Mexican colonias in the United States. Seemingly, the community had to await the coming of age of a new generation unencumbered by the stifling experience of a decade of betrayal before recovering from the ordeal. That may help to explain why the "Chicano movement" did not occur until twenty-five years after the end of the ominous decade. One can only speculate what might have been achieved in the intervening period if the Mexican community had not been devastated by the massive travesty unleashed against it. In truth, that may well constitute the ultimate tragedy of the anti-Mexican movement during the Great Depression.

Decade of Betrayal recounts what must be considered as the most significant and crucial event to befall *México de afuera* residents during the twentieth century. No other phenomenon, not even the issue of illegal immigration in the 1990s, has had such a far-reaching impact on the community. Following the tradition of Paul Taylor, Manuel Gamio, and Emory Bogardus, the work adds a new dimension to the study of Mexican Nationals and Mexican Americans in the United States. It delineates the consequences of deportation and repatriation on both sides of the border, from both the Mexican and American perspectives. However, the uniqueness of *Decade of Betrayal* lies in its focus on the calamitous experiences of the people who underwent the ordeal of the betrayal. This particular aspect constitutes an important historical contribution and a valuable insight for historians, students, and lay readers.

Yet the lessons of history appear to be lost in the turmoil besetting the question of legal and illegal immigration in the 1990s. Since massive repatriation is not a feasible alternative, other ingenious means are being proposed to halt the unwanted immigrant influx. It is suggested that steel walls, moats, fences, floodlights, and a beefed-up and well-equipped border patrol be deployed along the U.S.-Mexico border to deter entry from Mexico and Central America.

For those already in the United States, it is proposed that services encouraging people to emigrate be severely curtailed or totally eliminated. These services would include medical services, welfare eligibility, educational opportunities, drivers licenses, and similar benefits. Some states, including California, Texas, and New York, are contemplating or have sued the federal government in order to recover the billions of dollars they claim are being spent to serve the immigrant horde.

As in the 1930s, events beyond political control may again end the controversy. In this instance, rather than the ravages of war, it will be the ravages of old age. The population of the United States over sixty-five is aging twice as fast as the general population. That fact, and the nation's low birthrate, means that as the twenty-first century unfolds the United States

204 Part II: Mexicans and Americans

will be forced to import a labor force, as it has done traditionally in the past. Eventually, the tide will turn and immigrants again will be welcomed as a prime resource. As Mexicans are fond of saying about "what the fickle and unpredictable fates" have in store: *"Dios sabrá, Qué será, será!"*

Questions

1. Are there, ever, justifiable reasons to expel members or citizens of a particular society?
2. Is there an assumption regarding culture hidden under the phrase, "Once a Mexican always a Mexican"?
3. Consider the statement, "They were neither American nor Mexican as defined by their particular cultures." What are the implications of this statement for the present reality that a person has rights only when accorded by a particular state?
4. Are there any similarities between U.S. Mexicans' status and the status of Cuban Americans and Puerto Ricans?
5. How do the state interests of the United States and Mexico contribute to the construction of the Mexican American/Chicano subjectivity and its subsequent political economic development? Are there any similarities with the U.S./Cuban construction of *El Exilio* described in chapter 15?

CHAPTER NINE

∼

The Organizer's Tale

César E. Chávez

Largely invisible in the political memory of many people is the fact that U.S. workers fought long and hard for their right to speak collectively and negotiate with the bosses for what we now take for granted, such as the eight-hour work day, the elimination of child labor, and worker's compensation. It surprises many to learn that the right to organize into unions was not guaranteed until 1935, with the passing of the National Labor Relations Act. After learning this, it amazes some to learn that farm workers were not included in this act. So we must begin this particular story with the understanding that "labor unions and strikes in U.S. agriculture have been, for the most part, sporadic and scattered, except among Mexicans, who have waged strikes unmatched in scope, intensity or continuity for nearly one hundred years."[1] One example from the 1880s is their participation in the Knights of Labor.

Although we cannot review the entire history of the farm worker struggle for economic democracy, to understand the endurance of a quest for equality it is important to mention two labor institutions that preceded the United Farm Worker's union (UFW), organized by César E. Chávez. Although they were not successful in improving the working conditions of the farm workers, the National Farm Labor Union (NFLU), founded in 1946, and the Agricultural Workers' Organizing Committee (AWOC), begun in 1960, served as training grounds for many future labor leaders, such as Chávez and Dolores Huerta. Ernesto Galarza tells this fascinating story in *Spiders in the House and Workers in the Field*. From the words of the scholar Juan Gómez-Quiñonez:

In spite of all the union and governmental activity throughout the twentieth century, by the 1960s the socioeconomic condition of farm workers was still horrendous. Farm workers historically have labored in the most hazardous, dehumanizing, and oppressive conditions, and farm work has been the third most dangerous occupation in the United States because of accidents. While other workers have made gains, the situation for agricultural workers has remained the same. There was no minimum wage. Their wages provided for only the basic necessities of life and often even less than that. Thousands of impoverished laborers have been exploited, with low pay, abominable working conditions, lack of decent food, and continuous discrimination. The majority of farm workers have had no personal savings to fall back on in times of emergency, economic crisis, or layoffs. They have had no opportunity to make up lost wages, no fringe benefits, no basic insurance guarantees, and no retirement security.[2]

At this time César E. Chávez entered into the story. To help place the following piece by César in a chronological context, it will help to remember that he was born in Arizona on March 31, 1927. He joined the navy at seventeen and served in the South Pacific at the end of World War II. At the age of nineteen, he joined the agricultural workers' effort at Corcoran, California, and became involved in strike activities. Although the 1946 strike was for the most part unsuccessful, Chávez gained organizing experience. In the late 1940s, when the NFLU was formed, he became an active member. In the following piece, César begins his tale in 1950, describing how he had joined the Community Service Organization (CSO). The Battle of the Corcoran Farm Camp, an event he refers to as "thirty years ago" (meaning in October 1933), entailed one of the high points of California worker militancy and grower violence. In Pixley, the farmers opened fire on the striking farm workers, killing two and injuring eight.[3] Finally, the date when the NFLU and AWOC joined in a strike in Delano was Monday, September 20, 1965. The new union would be the UFW, which would be based on a "humanist" rather than a "business" basis. There is as yet no happy ending, however; this approach has apparently brought another set of problems.[4] The labor struggle continues in many fronts, as noted in chapter 12. As for the UFW, as of the time of this writing, it continues to struggle to recruit more members and even to keep the contracts it has gained.

Notes and Suggested Further Readings

1. Juan Gómez-Quiñonez, *Mexican American Labor, 1790–1900* (Albuquerque: University of New Mexico Press, 1994), 129.
2. Gómez-Quiñonez, *Mexican American Labor*, 242.

3. Ronald B. Taylor, *Chávez and the Farm Workers* (Boston: Beacon, 1975), 52–57.
4. Theo J. Majka and Linda C. Majka, "Decline of the Farm Labor Movement in California: Organizational Crisis and Political Change," *Critical Sociology* 19, no. 3 (1993): 11–36.

*   *   *

It really started for me 16 years ago in San Jose California, when I was working on an apricot farm. We figured he was just another social worker doing a study of farm conditions, and I kept refusing to meet with him. But he was persistent. Finally, I got together some of the rough element in San Jose. We were going to have a little reception for him to teach the *gringo* a little bit of how we felt. There were about 30 of us in the house, young guys mostly. I was supposed to give them a signal—change my cigarette from my right hand to my left, and then we were going to give him a lot of hell. But he started talking and the more he talked, the more wide-eyed I became and the less inclined I was to give the signal. A couple of guys who were pretty drunk at the time still wanted to give the *gringo* the business, but we got rid of them. This fellow was making a lot of sense, and I wanted to hear what he had to say.

His name was Fred Ross, and he was an organizer for the Community Service Organization (CSO) which was working with Mexican-Americans in the cities. I became immediately really involved. Before long I was heading a voter registration drive. All the time I was observing the things Fred did, secretly, because I wanted to learn how to organize, to see how it was done. I was impressed with his patience and understanding of people. I thought this was a tool, one of the greatest things he had.

It was pretty rough for me at first. I was changing and had to take a lot of ridicule from the kids my age, the rough characters I worked with in the fields. They would say, "Hey, big shot. Now that you're a *politico*, why are you working here for 65 cents an hour?" I might add that our neighborhood had the highest percentage of San Quentin graduates. It was a game among the *pachucos* in the sense that we defended ourselves from outsiders, although inside the neighborhood there was not a lot of fighting.

After six months of working every night in San Jose, Fred assigned me to take over the CSO chapter in Decoto. It was a tough spot to fill. I would suggest something, and people would say, "No, let's wait till Fred gets back," or "Fred wouldn't do it that way." This is pretty much a pattern with people, I discovered, whether I was put in Fred's position, or later, when someone else was put in my position. After the Decoto assignment I was sent to start a new chapter in Oakland. Before I left, Fred came to a place in San Jose called the Hole-in-the-Wall and we talked for half an hour over coffee. He was in a rush to leave, but I wanted to keep him talking; I was that scared of my assignment.

There were hard times in Oakland. First of all, it was a big city and I'd get lost every time I went anywhere. Then I arranged a series of house meetings. I would get to the meeting early and drive back and forth past the house, too nervous to go in and face the people. Finally I would force myself to go inside and sit in a corner. I was quite thin then, and young, and most of the people were middle-aged. Someone would say, "Where's the organizer?" And I would pipe up, "Here I am." Then they would say in Spanish—these were very poor people and we hardly spoke anything but Spanish—"Ha! This *kid?*" Most of them said they were interested, but the hardest part was to get them to start pushing themselves, on their own initiative.

The idea was to set up a meeting and then get each attending person to call his own house meeting, inviting new people—a sort of chain letter effect. After a house meeting I would lie awake going over the whole thing, playing the tape back, trying to see why people laughed at one point, or why they were for one thing and against another. I was also learning to read and write, those late evenings. I had left school in the 7th grade after attending 67 different schools, and my reading wasn't the best.

At our first organizing meeting we had 368 people: I'll never forget it because it was very important to me. You eat your heart out; the meeting is called for 7 o'clock and you start to worry about 4. You wait. Will they show up? Then the first one arrives. By 7 there are only 20 people, you have everything in order, you have to look calm. But little by little they filter in and at a certain point you know it will be a success.

After four months in Oakland, I was transferred. The chapter was beginning to move on its own, so Fred assigned me to organize the San Joaquin Valley. Over the months I developed what I used to call schemes or tricks—now I call them techniques—of making initial contacts. The main thing in convincing someone is to spend time with him. It doesn't matter if he can read, write or even speak well. What is important is that he is a man and second, that he has shown some initial interest. One good way to develop leadership is to take a man with you in your car. And it works a lot better if you're doing the driving; that way you are in charge. You drive, he sits there, and you talk. These little things were very important to me; I was caught in a big game by then, figuring out what makes people work. I found that if you work hard enough you can usually shake people into working too, those who are concerned. You work harder and they work harder still, up to a point and then they pass you. Then, of course, they're on their own.

I also learned to keep away from the established groups and so-called leaders, and to guard against philosophizing. Working with low-income people is very different from working with the professionals, who like to sit around talking about how to play politics. When you're trying to recruit a farmworker, you have to paint a little picture, and then you have to color the picture in. We found out that the harder a guy is to convince, the better leader or member he becomes. When you exert yourself to convince him, you have his confidence and he has good motivation. A lot of people who say OK right away wind up hanging around the office, taking up the workers' time.

During the McCarthy era in one Valley town, I was subjected to a lot of red-baiting [taunting people by calling them communists]. We had been recruiting people for citizenship classes at the high school when we got into a quarrel with the naturalization examiner. He was rejecting people on the grounds that they were just parroting what they learned in citizenship class. One day we had a meeting about it in Fresno, and I took along some of the leaders of our local chapter. Some redbaiting official gave us a hard time, and the people got scared and took his side. They did it because it seemed easy at the moment, even though they knew that sticking with me was the right thing to do. It was disgusting. When we left the building they walked by themselves ahead of me as if I had some kind of communicable disease. I had been working with these people for three months and I was very sad to see that. It taught me a great lesson.

That night I learned that the chapter officers were holding a meeting to review my letters and printed materials to see if I really was a Communist. So I drove out there and walked right in on their meeting. I said, "I hear you've been discussing me, and I thought it would be nice if I was here to defend myself. Not that it matters that much to you or even to me, because as far as I am concerned you are a bunch of cowards." At that they began to apologize. "Let's forget it," they said. "You're a nice guy." But I didn't want apologies. I wanted a full discussion. I told them I didn't give a damn, but that they had to learn to distinguish fact from what appeared to be a fact because of fear. I kept them there till two in the morning. Some of the women cried. I don't know if they investigated me any further, but I stayed on another few months and things worked out.

This was not an isolated case. Often when we'd leave people to themselves they would get frightened and draw back into their shells where they had been all the years. And I learned quickly that there is no real appreciation. Whatever you do, and no matter what reasons you may give to others, you do it because you want to see it done, or maybe because you want power. And there shouldn't be any appreciation, understandably. I know good organizers who were destroyed, washed out, because they expected people to appreciate what they'd done. Anyone who comes in with the idea that farmworkers are free of sin and that the growers are all bastards, either has never dealt with the situation or is an idealist of the first order. Things don't work that way.

For more than 10 years I worked for the CSO. As the organization grew, we found ourselves meeting in fancier and fancier motels and holding expensive conventions. Doctors, lawyers and politicians began joining. They would get elected to some office in the organization and then, for all practical purposes, leave. Intent on using the CSO for their own prestige purposes, these "leaders," many of them, lacked the urgency we had to have. When I became general director I began to press for a program to organize farmworkers into a union, an idea most of the leadership opposed. So I started a revolt within the CSO. I refused to sit at the head table at meetings, refused to wear a suit and tie, and finally I even refused to shave and cut my hair. It used to embarrass some of the professionals. At every meeting I got up and gave my standard speech: we shouldn't meet in fancy motels, we were getting away from the people, farmworkers had to be organized. But nothing happened. In March of '62 I resigned and came to Delano to begin organizing the Valley on my own.

By hand I drew a map of all the towns between Arvin and Stockton—86 of them, including farming camps—and decided to hit them all to get a small nucleus of people working in each. For six months I traveled around, planting an idea. We had a simple questionnaire, a little card with space for name, address and how much the worker thought he ought to be paid. My wife, Helen, mimeographed them, and we took our kids for two or three day jaunts to these towns, distributing the cards door-to-door and to camps and groceries.

Some 80,000 cards were sent back from eight Valley counties. I got a lot of contacts that way, but I was shocked at the wages the people were asking. The growers were paying $1 and $1.15 and maybe 95 per cent of the people thought they should be getting only $1.25. Sometimes people scribbled messages on the cards: "I hope to God we win" or "Do you think we can win?" or "I'd like to know more." So I separated the cards with the pencilled notes, got in my car and went to those people.

We didn't have any money at all in those days, none for gas and hardly any for food. So I went to people and started asking for food. It turned out to be about the best thing I could have done, although at first it's hard on your pride. Some of our best members came in that way. If people give you their food, they'll give you their hearts. Several months and many meetings later we had a working organization, and this time the leaders were the people.

None of the farmworkers had collective bargaining contracts, and I thought it would take ten years before we got that first contract. I wanted desperately to get some color into the movement, to give people something they could identify with, like a flag. I was reading some books about how various leaders discovered what colors contrasted and stood out the best. The Egyptians had found that a red field with a white circle and a black emblem in the center crashed into your eyes like nothing else. I wanted to use the Aztec eagle in the center, as on the Mexican flag. So I told my cousin Manuel, "Draw an Aztec Eagle." Manuel had a little trouble with it, so we modified the eagle to make it easier for people to draw.

The first big meeting of what we decided to call the National Farm Workers Association was held in September 1962, at Fresno, with 287 people. We had our huge red flag on the wall, with paper tacked over it. When the time came,

Manuel pulled a cord ripping the paper off the flag and all of a sudden it hit the people. Some of them wondered if it was a Communist flag, and I said it probably looked more like a neo-Nazi emblem than anything else. But they wanted an explanation. So Manuel got up and said, "When that damn eagle flies—that's when the farmworkers' problems are going to be solved."

One of the first things I decided was that outside money wasn't going to organize people, at least not in the beginning. I even turned down a grant from a private group—$50,000 to go directly to organize farmworkers—for just this reason. Even when there are no strings attached, you are still compromised because you feel you have to produce immediate results. This is bad, because it takes a long time to build a movement, and your organization suffers if you get too far ahead of the people it belongs to. We set the dues at $42 a year per family, really a meaningful dues, but of the 212 we got to pay, only 12 remained by June of '63. We were discouraged at that, but not enough to make us quit.

Money was always a problem. Once we were facing a $180 gas bill on a credit card I'd got a long time ago and was about to lose. And we *had* to keep that credit card. One day my wife and I were picking cotton, pulling bolls, to make a little money to live on. Helen said to me, "Do you put all this in the bag, or just the cotton?" I thought she was kidding and told her to throw the whole boll in so that she had nothing but a sack of bolls at the weighing. The man said, "Whose sack is this?" I said, well, my wife's, and he told us we were fired. "Look at all that crap you brought in," he said. Helen and I started laughing. We were going anyway. We took the $4 we had earned and spent it at a grocery store where they were giving away a $100 prize. Each time you shopped they'd give you one of the letters of M-O-N-E-Y or a flag: you had to have M-O-N-E-Y plus the flag to win. Helen had already collected the letters and just needed the flag. Anyway, they gave her the ticket. She screamed, "A flag? I don't believe it," ran in and got the $100. She said, "Now we're going to eat steak." But I said no, we're going to pay the gas bill. I don't know if she cried, but I think she did.

It was rough in those early years. Helen was having babies and I was not there when she was at the hospital. But if you haven't got your wife behind you, you can't do many things. There's got to be peace at home. So I did, I think, a fairly good job of organizing her. When we were kids, she lived in Delano and I came to town as a migrant. Once on a date we had a bad experience about segregation at a movie theater, and I put up a fight. We were together then, and still are. I think I'm more of a pacifist than she is. Her father, Fabela, was a colonel with Pancho Villa in the Mexican Revolution. Sometimes she gets angry and tells me, "These scabs—you should deal with them sternly," and I kid her, "It must be too much of that Fabela blood in you."

The movement really caught on in '64. By August we had a thousand members. We'd had a beautiful 90-day drive in Corcoran, where they had the Battle of the Corcoran Farm Camp 30 years ago, and by November we had assets of $25,000 in our credit union, which helped to stabilize the membership. I had gone without pay the whole of 1963. The next year the members voted me a $40 a week salary, after Helen had to quit working in the fields to manage the credit union.

Our first strike was in May of '65, a small one but it prepared us for the big one. A farmworker from McFarland named Epifanio Camacho came to see me. He said he was sick and tired of how people working the roses were being treated, and he was willing to "go the limit." I assigned Manuel and Gilbert Padilla to hold meetings at Camacho's house. The people wanted union recognition, but the real issue, as in most cases when you begin, was wages. They were promised $9 a thousand, but they were actually getting $6.50 and $7 for grafting roses. Most of them signed cards giving us the right to bargain for them. We chose the biggest company, with about 85 employees, not counting the irrigators and supervisors, and we held a series of meetings to prepare the strike and call the vote. There would be no picket line; everyone pledged on their honor not to break the strike.

Early on the first morning of the strike, we sent out 10 cars to check the people's homes. We found lights in five or six homes and knocked on the doors. The men were getting up and we'd say, "Where are you going?" They would dodge, "Oh, uh . . . I was just getting up, you know," We'd say, "Well, you're not going to work, are you?" And they'd say no. Dolores Huerta, who was driving the green panel truck, saw a light in one house where four rose-workers lived. They told her they were going to work, even after she reminded them of their pledge. So she moved the truck so it blocked their driveway, turned off the key, put it in her purse and sat there alone.

That morning the company foreman was madder than hell and refused to talk to us. None of the grafters had shown up for work. At 10:30 we started to go to the company office, but it occurred to us that maybe a woman would have a better chance. So Dolores knocked on the office door, saying, "I'm Dolores Huerta from the National Farm Workers Association." "Get out!" the man said, "you Communist. Get out." I guess they were expecting us, because as Dolores stood arguing with him the cops came and told her to leave. She left.

For two days the fields were idle. On Wednesday they recruited a group of Filipinos from out of town who knew nothing of the strike, maybe 35 of them. They drove through escorted by three sheriff's patrol cars, one in front, one in the middle and one at the rear with a dog. We didn't have a picket line, but we parked across the street and just watched them go through, not saying a word. All but seven stopped working after half an hour, and the rest had quit by mid-afternoon.

The company made an offer the evening of the fourth day, a package deal that amounted to a 120 per cent wage increase, but no contract. We wanted to hold out for a contract and more benefits, but a majority of the rose-workers

wanted to accept the offer and go back. We are a democratic union so we had
to support what they wanted to do. They had a meeting and voted to settle.
Then we had a problem with a few militants who wanted to hold out. We had
to convince them to go back to work, as a united front, because otherwise they
would be canned. So we worked—Tony Orendain and I, Dolores and Gilbert,
Jim Drake and all the organizers—knocking on doors till two in the morning,
telling people, "You have to go back or you'll lose your job." And they did.
They worked.

Our second strike, and our last before the big one at Delano, was in the
grapes at Martin's Ranch last summer. The people were getting a raw deal
there, being pushed around pretty badly. Gilbert went out to the field, climbed
on top of a car and took a strike vote. They voted unanimously to go out. Right
away they started bringing in strikebreakers, so we launched a tough attack on
the labor contractors, distributed leaflets portraying them as really low characters. We attacked one—Luis Campos—so badly that he just gave up the job,
and he took 27 of his men out with him. All he asked was that we distribute
another leaflet reinstating him in the community. And we did. What was unusual was that the grower would talk to us. The grower kept saying, "I can't pay.
I just haven't got the money." I guess he must have found the money somewhere, because we were asking $1.40 and we got it.

We had just finished the Martin strike when the Agricultural Workers Organizing Committee (AFL-CIO) started a strike against the grape growers, Di-
giorgio, Schenley liquors and small growers, asking $1.40 an hour and 25 cents
a box. There was a lot of pressure from our members for us to join the strike
but we had some misgivings. We didn't feel ready for a big strike like this one,
one that was sure to last a long time. Having no money—just $87 in the strike
fund—meant we'd have to depend on God knows who.

Eight days after the strike started—it takes time to get 1,200 people together
from all over the Valley—we held a meeting in Delano and voted to go out. I
asked the membership to release us from the pledge not to accept outside
money, because we'd need it now, a lot of it. The help came. It started because
of the close, and I would say even beautiful relationship that we've had with
the Migrant Ministry for some years. They were the first to come to our rescue,
financially and in every other way, and they spread the word to other benefac-
tors.

We had planned, before, to start a labor school in November. It never happened, but we have the best labor school we could ever have, in the strike. The
strike is only a temporary condition, however. We have over 3,000 members
spread out over a wide area, and we have to service them when they have problems. We get letters from New Mexico, Colorado, Texas, California, from farmworkers saying, "We're getting together and we need an organizer." It kills you
when you haven't got the personnel and resources. You feel badly about not
sending an organizer because you look back and remember all the difficulty you

had in getting two or three people together, and here *they're* together. Of course, we're training organizers, many of them younger than I was when I started in CSO. They can work 20 hours a day, sleep four, and be ready to hit it again; when you get to 39 it's a different story.

The people who took part in the strike and the march have something more than their material interest going for them. If it were only material, they wouldn't have stayed on the strike long enough to win. It is difficult to explain. But it flows out in the ordinary things they say. For instance, some of the younger guys are saying, "Where do you think's going to be the next strike?" I say, "Well, we have to win in Delano." They say, "We'll win, but where do we go next?" I say, "Maybe most of us will be working in the fields." They say, "No, I don't want to go and work in the fields. I want to organize. There are a lot of people that need our help." So I say, "You're going to be pretty poor then, because when you strike you don't have much money." They say they don't care about that.

And others are saying, "I have friends who are working in Texas. If we could only help them." It is bigger, certainly, than just a strike. And if this spirit grows within the farm labor movement, one day we can use the force that we have to help correct a lot of things that are wrong in this society. But that is for the future. Before you can run, you have to learn to walk.

There are vivid memories from my childhood—what we had to go through because of low wages and the conditions, basically because there was no union. I suppose if I wanted to be fair I could say that I'm trying to settle a personal score. I could dramatize it by saying that I want to bring social justice to farmworkers. But the truth is that I went through a lot of hell, and a lot of people did. If we can even the score a little for the workers then we are doing something. Besides, I don't know any other work I like to do better than this. I really don't, you know.

~

CHAPTER TEN

Brown Beret National Policies
David Sánchez

The Brown Berets not only provide an example of nationalism in practice, but they are also the closest that Chicanos have come to creating a formal, nationalist military force. The context for this chapter, nevertheless, is arguably symbolic of the quest for citizenship. It is a further illustration that Latino/a political thought is, to a large extent, a reaction to injustice. This story begins with the institution of Los Angeles City Hall led by a conservative mayor. The main character in the story is David Sánchez, who in early 1967 occupied the position of president of mayor Sam Yorty's Advisory Commission on Youth, a program that served as Sánchez's political training ground. The story of what happened in that year "clearly demonstrates how the powerful, omnipresent forces of racism can literally transform a young, innocent, politically naïve barrio Chicanito with a strong conscience into a fierce, competitive, militant leader fighting for justice for his people."[1] Indeed by the end of the year, Sánchez had severed his ties with the mayor's program and founded the Young Citizens for Community Action, which quickly evolved into the Young Chicanos for Community Action, and then into the Brown Berets. As founder and prime minister of the Brown Berets, Sánchez channeled young people, many of whom had been gang members or had been in juvenile hall or prison, into a political cause. This blurring of the line between what is criminal and what is political echoes nineteenth-century *Mexicano* resistance in the Southwest.

For example, *Las Gorras Blancas* of New Mexico (U.S. Mexicans who organized guerrilla-style attacks on the properties of wealthy ranchers and later a political party) issued a political platform that has been compared with the Brown Beret National Policies.[2] You may notice the feeling of solidarity with "the people" in general, a feeling that points to a sense of nationhood. We also find the usual anti-hegemonic discourse about the abuse of the judiciary and lack of justice, the suffering and persecution of the people, and the call for social change. There is also ambivalence in the call for justice within the existing system and a veiled threat for a violent break from it. Judging from the National Policies, U.S. Mexicans, Chicanos, indeed appear as a nation and (though it is not explicitly stated) a war of liberation is implicit in some of the statements. Among the major actions in which the Brown Berets were involved were the *Marcha de la Reconquista*, the *Chicano Moratorium Marches to protest the Viet Nam War* (the march of August 29, 1970, witnessed the death of Rubén Salazar), Expedition through Aztlán, and the takeover of Catalina Island. Probably the most significant were the student walkouts in 1968, the largest demonstration by high school students in the history of the United States.

* * *

Notes and Suggestions for Further Research

1. David Sánchez, *Expedition through Aztlán* (La Puente, CA: Perspectiva, 1978), vii.

2. Sánchez, *Expedition*, vii. See also Robert J. Rosenbaum, *Mexicano Resistance in the Southwest: The Sacred Right of Self-Preservation* (Austin: University of Texas Press, 1981), 111–79. For a historical fictional account of *Las Gorras Blancas*, see Daniel Aragón y Ulibarrí's *Devil's Hatband* (Santa Fe: Sunstone, 1999).

* * *

Let it be known to the universe that these are the policies of the Brown Beret National Organization, and any person who poses to be a Brown Beret and does not follow these policies and principles is not a Brown Beret and should not be respected as one.

For too long individuals have prostituted the good name of the Brown Beret National Organization for their own self advancement, or they have prostituted the Brown Beret name for other movements. And to prevent further foreign agent insurgency, these policies have been created.

ARTICLE I

Let it be recognized that the Brown Beret National Organization is an organization that relates its energies to the historical and geographical situation the

Chicano people are within. The situation the Chicano people are within is geographical because the land was stolen from the Chicano, and it is national because the Chicano people are a nation of combined abilities, both survival and cultural, of which we are a nation.

Fifteen million Chicanos are also within a sociological situation, where there is definite discrimination against Chicanos throughout the country. Whereas, wherever a Chicano is discriminated against and no matter where it may be, it is our cause to secure human rights as well as civil rights for all Chicanos.

The existing situation has not only left a people who have lost their land, but also the destruction of our people has taken place which is a detriment to our culture, heritage, and the existence of *la Raza*.

And because of the existing situation, we have created policies to not only create definite strategy, but also to prevent any threat to the coming nation. Whereas, we will halt any type of foreign intervention, by all means necessary.

ARTICLE II: HISTORY

Let it be known to all that the present invasion and occupation of the southwest was not by treaty, annexation, or purchase, as we have been told by the Treaty of Guadalupe Hidalgo of 1848. But, let it be known for historical record that in 1846, Brigadier General Stephen Kearney, along with other U.S. armed forces, took possession of the southwest by force. To prevent further battles between Anglo and Mexican gangs who fought against the occupation, a treaty was resolved in 1848 which guaranteed rights to those who remained in the southwest. And this same treaty of Guadalupe Hidalgo was violated when Rubén Salazar was not given the right of free assembly on August 29, 1970.

The treaty was broken, and two years before 1848, the land was stolen with malicious evil intent and malice. We have suffered, and we will never be free until the land is free from Anglo progress, which has been a detriment to the land, air, and water, as well as to our health.

Because the land purchase negotiations and annexation took place two years after the takeover of the southwest by U.S. forces, we declare the Treaty of Guadalupe Hidalgo invalid as well as its borders and promises. We also declare the invasion of the southwest a mistake, and an historical fraud which calls for attention. We will do all in our power to prove this historical mistake, because in history, the land always returns to the true inhabitants of that land.

ARTICLE III: WE ARE CHICANOS

We do not recognize any party which is affiliated with perpetuating white history. Left wing, right wing, socialists, democrats, and other foreign ideologies have attempted to prostitute the Chicano movement for the purpose of perpetuation of foreign movements. We are neither left wing nor right wing. We are Chicanos, and we denounce all white foreigners who try to put any other label on us, in order to create *la vida nueva de la Raza*.

ARTICLE IV: DEFENSE AGAINST FOREIGN MOVEMENTS

One side of the world is out to destroy the other side. The two great opposing ideologies both solicit nuclear destruction. The whole world is sucked into sick systems, and we wish to have no part in foreign movements. We will do everything in our power to prevent foreign agent persuasion. We are against insurgency by communists or republican parties or any other foreign political intervention.

ARTICLE V: EXPRESSION

Small scattered incidents and mobism in the past has led to lack of organization, turmoil, and some Chicano deaths. Perhaps, at that time, there was no way to control massive demonstrations by la Raza, from which we have already suffered not only loss of life, but also suffered at the hands of out-of-control police demonstrations.

Because of this, we wish to demonstrate in an orderly organized fashion with an organized disciplined body of people who can demonstrate without the problems of out-of-control mob violence.

We are on the move to show that we are right and to illustrate to all that anger and frustration can be directed towards constructive change. We will sacrifice our personal freedoms for significance, and to display how far we will go to make social change by the usage of the right of expression; whether that expression is military or otherwise. We have the right through peaceful means to show discontent toward local government by the use of free expression.

ARTICLE VI: PREPARATIONS

We must prepare for the escalation of massive coordination on a national scale, rather than on a local scale, including the development of academies necessary to prepare qualified officers to join our ranks.

All energies and resources must be directed toward preparations.

All education must be directed toward channeling students into a more skilled, technical, and qualified organization of the Brown Beret National Organization.

We must also make shelter and survival possible for Chicanos in case of disaster or evacuation.

ARTICLE VII: ABSOLUTE MILITARISM

In order to create massive organization within a society, and for that organization to control the conditions around it in order to survive conditions, it will take a sacrifice of our personal freedoms for absolute militarism, which is the fastest and strongest way to Chicano power. And in order to create real power for the people, discipline is necessary. We must understand that discipline is necessary in order to secure orderly action which alone can triumph over the seemingly impossible conditions of confrontation against any opposing force.

We must be able to recognize and face fear, because fear is the enemy of discipline. Fear unchecked will lead to panic, and a unit which panics is no longer a disciplined unit but a mob. Absolute militarism is needed to prevent out-of-control mob panic while allowing for effective massive coordination.

ARTICLE VIII: STRATEGY

By strategy, we are creating a movement by design to advance the Chicano movement five to ten years ahead of its time. *La caravana de la reconquista* is a tour and caravan of the southwest which is becoming a continuous migrating mass of people, and this continuous migration will revolve without end. During its travels, officers will be trained on this "Academy on Wheels."

Another strategy will be the reclamation of lands. This will begin first by the control of geographical areas taken place not by force, but rather by forms of occupation.

Further strategy also calls for the development of more chapters which will support the front line of *La caravana de la reconquista,* along with gathering resources from chapters to enforce and support special national projects of the Brown Beret National Organization.

ARTICLE IX: CULTURAL CUSTOMS

We are a nation with a definite culture and with a land that has been stolen. We are a state of *carnalismo,* we are not internationalist, we are nationalist. And those who come, or live in Chicano land must live and do as the Chicanos do.

ARTICLE X: BROWN BERET CHAPTERS

The chapters' first job will be to learn, instruct, and follow the Brown Beret National Policies.

The job of the chapter is one of community service and/or social action for change.

Another responsibility of the local chapter is to educate the *Raza* about these policies as well as getting the community involved with strategies of the Brown Beret National Organization.

Every Brown Beret Chapter is a local reserve organization.

It is also very important that each chapter understand that it is in itself a support office to reinforce the Brown Beret National Organization strategies with funds, reinforcements, and resources for greater national coordination.

ARTICLE XI: STOPPING FOREIGN INSURGENCY

We are a national organization and anyone who has associated himself with any international agency, organization, or other country is automatically terminated.

Anyone who does not accept and practice the Brown Beret National Policy will be terminated.

Any Brown Beret who is associated with the republicans or Anglo controlled Communist Party of the U.S.A., or is associated with the International Communist Party is hereby terminated. Any Brown Beret who identifies as being part of the small scattered incidents of the Chicano Liberation Front is terminated.

ARTICLE XII: SOCIAL SUPPORT

Despite age, profession, or income, it is of upmost importance that all Chicanos back each other in order to raise each other up, so that some Chicanos can have more resources for the purpose of channeling assistance to the Chicano movement.

It is also very important that all lay and professional Chicanos working in offices and organizations use their position as a vehicle to assist the Chicano Movement. Those holding such positions, as well as those without positions must back each other with support for all Chicanos in case anyone should encounter any problems while assisting the movement.

ARTICLE XIII: NEUTRALITY

We are a neutral state, because we have something to offer to the world.

ARTICLE XIV: WE DECLARE A NATION

We the Chicano people of the southwest, hereby declare ourselves a nation, and a nation that has been the subject of a profit-making invasion. We are a nation with a land that has been temporarily occupied.

And we are a nation with the ability to survive. We are a nation with great natural culturability. We are a nation, we who come from different ways, combining ourselves of one nation.

We are the good people who return nature back to its natural balance, and who bring justice to the universe.

ARTICLE XV: CHICANO AND INDIAN

Even though the Indian nation is somewhat unaware of the Chicano as being a people who all hold more than half Indian blood, we are of Indian-Mestizo descent, and we are of one Indian nation with similar and related cultures before the invasion of the primitive white man.

As far as all boundaries within the southwest which was once Mexico, we combine all people of Indian descent as being ONE, as well as its borders, boundaries, and perimeters of the southwest.

ARTICLE XVI: FURTHER POLICIES

Part A—Official

1) Anyone who states that he or she is a Brown Beret and does not conduct himself or herself with real discipline is not a Brown Beret.

2) Anyone who states that he or she is a Brown Beret, and does not have loyalty that is responsive to orders as well as ultimate respect towards the Prime Minister's Office, is not a Brown Beret.

3) Anyone who states that he or she is a Brown Beret and does not have loyalty to the National Prime Minister's Office, is not a Brown Beret.

4) Anyone who does not accept the Prime Minister's Office as Executive Chief of the Brown Beret Natural Forces, is not a Brown Beret.

Part B

The Brown Beret National Policy is to create unity within our own *barrios* without the alienation of our own people. We are Chicanos in a struggle for our rights and the eventual return of our land.

Anyone who attempts to apply any other label upon us is in violation of National Policy. The Brown Beret National Organization is based upon years of created organization capital, and anyone who causes a threat to the Foundation is in violation of National Policy.

The Brown Beret National Organization is based upon any funds that can be gathered for communications, transportation, demonstrations, and legal defense. Anyone who receives funds or other materials for the Organization, and does not turn in said funds or materials to the Organization is in violation of National Policy.

Part C

All violators of National Policy are subject to disciplinary action. Rank is for coordination, and those who do not respect rank (which was coordinated for the purpose of massive action) are in violation of National Policy.

During any event or action where there is no leadership in a community emergency situation, a Beret who does not attempt to take the burden of the emergency situation is in violation of National Policy.

Any unit or chapter who titles themselves, or claims affiliation with the name "Brown Beret" but does not actually affiliate with the Brown Beret National Organization, shall be denounced as violators of Brown Beret National Policy.

Any person who states that he or she is a Brown Beret and who is not actually affiliated with a registered chapter or unit, is in violation of National Policy.

Any person who mistreats any *soldado* by applying more stress and danger which is excessive to accomplish duties, is in violation of National Policy.

*   *   *

Note

These are the final Brown Beret National Policies adopted in 1972. They appeared in the last Brown Beret newsletter, *La Causa*, Los Angeles, California, 1972, 4–6.

Questions

1. Is there any basis on which these policies may be construed as a declaration of independence from the United States?
2. Is there any basis on which these policies may be construed as a quest for public citizenship, a demand for justice within the U.S. polity?
3. Are there historical and social contradictions that may be said to explain or to be reflected in the logical inconsistencies of the political positions of the Brown Berets?
4. If you were an American Indian, how would you feel about being included among the Chicano people?
5. Do the writing quality, style, and structure have any political effect of their own?

~

CHAPTER ELEVEN

Queer Aztlán:
The Reformation of Chicano Tribe
Cherríe Moraga

According to Moraga, "Chicanos are an occupied nation within a nation, and women and women's sexuality are occupied within [a] Chicano nation." Indeed, if the quest for cultural citizenship means being accepted by the dominant culture, what happens when the dominant culture is "your own culture" and, moreover, a traditional, patriarchal, and homophobic culture? Once again we are confronted by the question: Who are the people? In this essay, Moraga addresses one of the frontiers of political identity in Latino/a culture. When *El Plan de Aztlán* was conceived, "lesbians and gay men were not envisioned as members of the 'house.'" They were, and still are, considered illegitimate children of the Chicano family. As we have discussed, this position deploys a particular set of desire relations, "a critical position to address those areas within our cultural family that need to change." Moraga also touches on issues of bio-power: human bodies that are denied their rights as moral entities, who are raped physically and psychologically, and exposed to violence and illness. She raises a variety of critical questions about the degree of radicalism and acceptance of the Other, even within those who see themselves as oppressed; the good and the bad of Chicano and other nationalisms; relations with American Indians; sovereignty; and separatism.

*   *   *

How will our lands be free if our bodies aren't?

—Ricardo Bracho

At the height of the Chicano Movement in 1968, I was a closeted, light-skinned, mixed-blood Mexican-American, disguised in my father's English last name. Since I seldom opened my mouth, few people questioned my Anglo credentials. But my eyes were open and thirsty and drank in images of students my age, of *vatos* and *viejitas*, who could have *primos*, or *tíos*, or *abuelitas* raising their collective fists into a smoggy East Los Angeles skyline. Although I could not express how at the time, I knew I had a place in that Movement that was spilling out of *barrio* high schools and onto police-barricaded streets just ten minutes from my tree-lined working class neighborhood in San Gabriel. What I didn't know then was that it would take me another ten years to fully traverse that ten-minute drive and to bring all the parts of me—Chicana, *lesbiana*, half-breed, and *poeta*—to the revolution, wherever it was.

My real politicization began, not through the Chicano Movement, but through the bold recognition of my lesbianism. Coming to terms with that fact meant the radical restructuring of everything I thought I held sacred. It meant acting on my woman-centered desire and against anything that stood in its way, including my Church, my family, and my "country." It meant acting in spite of the fact that I had learned from my Mexican culture and the dominant culture that my womanhood was, if not despised, certainly deficient and hardly worth the loving of another woman in bed. But act I did, because not acting would have meant my death by despair.

That was twenty years ago. In those twenty years I traversed territory that extends well beyond the ten-minute trip between East Los Angeles and San Gabriel. In those twenty years, I experienced the racism of the Women's Movement, the elitism of the Gay and Lesbian Movement, the homophobia and sexism of the Chicano Movement, and the benign cultural imperialism of the Latin American Solidarity Movement. I also witnessed the emergence of national Chicana *feminista* consciousness and a literature, art, and activism to support it. I've seen the growth of a lesbian-of-color movement, the founding of an independent national Latino/a lesbian and gay men's organization, and the flourishing of Indigenous people's international campaigns for human and land rights.

A quarter of a century after those school walk-outs in 1968, I can write, without reservation, that I have found a sense of place among *la Chicanada*. It is not always a safe place, but it is unequivocally the original familial place from which I am compelled to write, which I reach toward in my audiences, and which serves as my source of inspiration, voice, and *lucha*. How we Chicanos define that struggle has always been the subject of debate and is ultimately the subject of this essay.

"Queer Aztlán" had been forming in my mind for over three years and began to take concrete shape a year ago in a conversation with poet Ricardo

Bracho. We discussed the limitations of "Queer Nation," whose leather-jacketed, shaved-headed white radicals and accompanying anglo-centricity were an "alien-nation" to most lesbians and gay men of color. We also spoke of Chicano Nationalism, which never accepted openly gay men and lesbians among its ranks. Ricardo half-jokingly concluded, "What we need, Cherríe, is a 'Queer Aztlán.'" Of course. A Chicano homeland that could embrace *all* its people, including its *jotería.*[1]

Everything I read these days tells me that the Chicano Movement is dead. In Earl Shorris' *Latinos*, the Anglo author insists that the Chicano *himself* is dead. He writes, "The Chicano generation began in the late 1960s and lasted about six or eight years, dying slowly through the seventies." He goes on to say that *Chicanismo* has been reduced to no more than a "handshake practiced by middle-aged men." Chicano sociologists seem to be suggesting the same when they tell us that by the third generation, the majority of Chicanos have lost their Spanish fluency, and nearly a third have married non-Chicanos and have moved out of the Chicano community. Were immigration from México to stop, they say, Chicanos could be virtually indistinguishable from the rest of the population within a few generations. My nieces and nephews are living testimony to these faceless facts.

I mourn the dissolution of an active Chicano Movement possibly more strongly than my generational counterparts because during its "classic period," I was unable to act publicly. But more deeply, I mourn it because its ghost haunts me daily in the blonde hair of my sister's children, the gradual hispanicization of Chicano students, the senselessness of barrio violence, and the poisoning of *la frontera* from Tijuana to Tejas. In 1992, we have no organized national movement to respond to our losses. For me, "El Movimiento" has never been a thing of the past, it has retreated into subterranean uncontaminated soils awaiting resurrection in a "queerer," more feminist generation.

What was right about Chicano Nationalism was its commitment to preserving the integrity of the Chicano people. A generation ago, there were cultural, economic, and political programs to develop Chicano consciousness, autonomy, and self-determination. What was wrong about Chicano Nationalism was its institutionalized heterosexism, its inbred *machismo*, and its lack of a cohesive national political strategy.[2]

Over the years, I have witnessed plenty of progressive nationalisms: Chicano nationalism, Black nationalism, Puerto Rican Independence (still viable as evidenced in the recent mass protest on the Island against the establishment of English as an official language), the "Lesbian Nation" and its lesbian separatist movement, and, of course, the most recent "Queer Nation." What I admired about each was its righteous radicalism, its unabashed anti-assimilationism, and its *rebeldía*. I recognize the dangers of nationalism as a strategy for political change. Its tendency toward separatism can run dangerously close to biological determinism and a kind of fascism. We are all horrified by the concentration and rape camps in Bosnia, falsely justified by the Serbian call for "ethnic cleansing." We are bitterly sobered by the nazism espoused by Pat Buchanan at the 1992 Republican Convention in which only heterosexual white middle-class voting Amerikans have the right to citizenship and heaven. Over and over again we are reminded that sex and race do not define a person's politics. Margaret Thatcher is a woman and enforces the policies of the Imperial whiteman and Clarence Thomas is Black and follows suit. But it is historically evident that the female body, like the Chicano people, has been colonized. And any movement to decolonize them must be culturally and sexually specific.

Chicanos are an occupied nation within a nation, and women and women's sexuality are occupied within Chicano nation. If women's bodies and those of men and women who transgress their gender roles have been historically regarded as territories to be conquered, they are also territories to be liberated. Feminism has taught us this. The nationalism I seek is one that decolonizes the brown and female body as it decolonizes the brown and female earth. It is a new nationalism in which *la Chicana Indígena* stands at the center, and heterosexism and homophobia are no longer the cultural order of the day. I cling to the word "*nation*" because without the specific naming of the nation, the nation will be lost (as when feminism is reduced to humanism, the woman is subsumed). Let us retain our radical naming but expand it to meet a broader and wiser revolution.

Tierra Sagrada: The Roots of a Revolution

Aztlán. I don't remember when I first heard the word, but I remember it took my heart by surprise to learn of that place—that "sacred landscape" wholly evident *en las playas, los llanos, y en las montañas* of the North American Southwest. A terrain that I did not completely comprehend at first, but that I continue to try, in my own small way, to fully inhabit and make habitable for its Chicano citizens.

Aztlán gave language to a nameless anhelo inside me. To me, it was never a masculine notion. It had nothing to do with the Aztecs and everything to do with Mexican birds, Mexican beaches, and Mexican babies right here in Califas. I remember once driving through Anza Borrego desert, just east of San Diego, my VW van whipping around corners, climbing. The tape deck set at full blast, every window open, bandana around my forehead. And I think, *this is México, Raza territory*, as I belt out the refrain . . .

"*Marieta, no seas coqueta*
porque los hombres son muy malos
prometen muchos regalos
y lo que dan son puro palos. . . ."

That day I claimed that land in the spin of the worn-out tape, the spin of my balding tires, and the spin of my mind. And just as I wrapped around a rubber-burning curve, I saw it: **"A-Z-T-L-A-N,"** in granite-sized letters etched into the face of the mountainside. Of course, I hadn't been the first. Some other Chicano came this way, too, saw what I saw, felt what I felt. Enough to put a name to it. *Aztlán. Tierra sagrada.*

A term Náhuatl in root, *Aztlán* was that historical/mythical land where one set of Indian forebears, the Aztecs, were said to have resided 1,000 years ago. Located in the U.S. Southwest, Aztlán fueled a nationalist struggle twenty years ago, which encompassed much of the pueblo Chicano from Chicago to the borders of Chihuahua. In the late sixties and early seventies, Chicano nationalism meant the right to control our own resources, language, and cultural traditions, rights guaranteed us by the Treaty of Guadalupe Hidalgo signed in 1848 when the Southwest was "annexed" to the United States at the end of the Mexican-American War. At its most radical, Chicano nationalism expressed itself in militant action. In the mid-1960s, Reies López Tijerina entered a campaign against the Department of the Interior to reclaim land grants for New Mexicans, resulting in his eventual imprisonment. In 1968, nearly 10,000 Chicano students walked out of their high schools to protest the lack of quality education in Los Angeles barrio schools. The same period also saw the rise of the Brown Berets, a para-military style youth organization regularly harassed by law enforcement agencies throughout the Southwest These are highlights in Chicano Movement history. To most, however, El Movimiento, practically applied, simply meant fair and equitable representation on the city council, in the union halls, and on the school board.

I've often wondered why Chicano nationalism never really sustained the same level of militancy witnessed in the Puerto Rican, Black, and Native American Movements. Certainly violence, especially police violence, was visited upon Chicanos in response to our public protests, the murder of journalist Rubén Salazar during the National Chicano Moratorium of 1970 being the most noted instance. And like other liberation movements, the Chicano movement had its share of FBI infiltrators.

In 1969, El Plan de Aztlán was drawn up at the First Annual Chicano Youth Conference in Denver, Colorado, calling for a Chicano program of economic self-determination, self-defense, and land reclamation, and including an autonomous taxation and judicial system. By the mid-1970s, such radical plans had gradually eroded in the face of a formidable opponent—the United States government—and Chicano nationalism as a political strategy began to express itself more in the cultural arena than in direct militant confrontation with the government.

Another reason for the brevity of a unified militant movement may be the heterogeneity of the Chicano population. Chicanos are not easily organized as a racial/political entity. Is our land the México of today or the México of a century and a half ago, covering thousands of miles of what is now the Southwestern United States? Unlike the island of Puerto Rico whose "homeland" is clearly defined by ocean on all sides, Aztlán at times seems more metaphysical than physical territory.

As a mestizo people living in the United States, our relationship to this country has been ambivalent at best. Our birth certificates since the invasion of Aztlán identify us as white. Our treatment by Anglo-Americans brand us "colored." In the history of African Americans, when the white slave owner raped a Black woman, the mixed-blood offspring inherited the mother's enslaved status. Over a century later, mixed-raced African Americans overwhelmingly identify as Black, not as mixed-blood. But the history of Mexicans/Chicanos follows a different pattern. The "Spanish-American" Conquest was secured through rape, intermarriage, the African slave trade, and the spread of Catholicism and disease. It gave birth to a third "mestizo" race that included Indian, African, and European blood. During colonial times, "Spanish-America" maintained a rigid and elaborate caste system that privileged the pure-blood Spaniard and his children over the mestizo. The pure blood *indio* and *africano* remained on the bottom rungs of society. The remnants of such class/race stratification are still evident throughout Latin America.

Chicano Nation is a mestizo nation conceived in a double-rape: first, by the Spanish and then by the Gringo. In the mid-19th century, Anglo-America took possession of one-third of México's territory. A new English-speaking oppressor assumed control over the Spanish, Mestizo, and Indian people inhabiting those lands. There was no denying that the United States had stolen Aztlán from México, but it had been initially stolen from the Indians by the Spanish some 300 years earlier. To make alliances with other nationalist struggles taking place throughout the country in the late sixties, there was no room for Chicano ambivalence about being Indians, for it was our Indian blood and history of resistance against both Spanish and Anglo invaders that made us rightful inheritors of Aztlán. After centuries of discrimination against our Indian-ness, which forced mestizos into denial, many Mexican-Americans found the sudden affirmation of our indigenismo difficult to accept. And yet the Chicano Indigenous movement was not without historical precedence. Little more than fifty years earlier, México witnessed a *campesino-* and Indian-led agrarian and labor movement spreading into the Southwest that had the potential of eclipsing the Russian Revolution in its vision. Political corruption, of course, followed. Today, the pending Free Trade Agreement with the United States and Canada marks the ultimate betrayal of the Mexican revolution: the final surrender of the Mexican people's sovereign rights to land and livelihood.

Radicalization among people of Mexican ancestry in this country most often occurs when the Mexican ceases to be a Mexican and becomes a Chicano. I have observed this in my Chicano Studies students (first, second, and third generation, some of whose families are indigenous to Aztlán) from the barrios of East Los Angeles, Fresno, and all the neighboring Central Valley towns of California—Selma, Visalia, Sanger, the barrios of Oakland, Sanjo, etc. They are the ones most often in protest, draping their bodies in front of freeway on-ramps and trans-bay bridges, blocking entrances to University administration buildings. They are the ones who, like their Black, Asian, and Native American counterparts, doubt the "American dream" because even if *they* got to UC Berkeley, their brother is still on crack in Boyle Heights, their sister had three kids before she's twenty, and *sorry but they can't finish the last week of the semester cuz Tío Ignacio just got shot in front of a liquor store.* My working-class and middle-class Mexican immigrant students,[3] on the other hand, have not yet had their self-esteem nor that of their parents and grandparents worn away by North American racism. For them, the "American dream" still looms as a possibility on the horizon. Their Mexican pride sustains them through the daily assaults on their intelligence, integrity, and humanity. They maintain a determined individualism and their families still dream of returning home one day.

A new generation of future Chicanos arrives everyday with every Mexican immigrant. Some may find their American dream and forget their origins, but the majority of México's descendants soon comprehend the political meaning of the disparity between their lives and those of the gringo. Certainly the Mexican women cannery workers of Watsonville who maintained a two-year victorious strike against Green Giant in the mid-eighties, and farm workers organized by César Chávez's UFW in the late sixties and early seventies are testimony to the political militancy of the Mexican immigrant worker. More recently, there are the examples of the Mothers of East Los Angeles and the women of Kettleman City who have organized against the toxic contamination proposed for their communities. In the process, the Mexicana becomes a Chicana (or at least a *Mechicana*); that is, she becomes a citizen of this country, not by virtue of a green card, but by virtue of the collective voice she assumes in staking her claim to this land and its resources.

Plumas Planchadas: The De-Formation of the Movement

> With our heart in our hands and our hands in the soil, we declare the independence of our mestizo nation.
>
> —*"El Plan Espiritual de Aztlán"*

El Movimiento did not die out in the seventies, as most of its critics claim; it was only deformed by the machismo and homophobia of that era and co-opted by "hispanicization" of the eighties.[4] In reaction against Anglo-America's emasculation of Chicano men, the male-dominated Chicano Movement embraced the most patriarchal aspects of its Mexican heritage. For a generation, nationalist leaders used a kind of "selective memory," drawing exclusively from those aspects of Mexican and Native cultures that served the interests of male heterosexuals. At times, they took the worst of Mexican machismo and Aztec warrior bravado, combined it with some of the most oppressive male-conceived idealizations of "traditional" Mexican womanhood and called that cultural integrity. They subscribed to a *machista* view of women, based on the centuries-old virgin-whore paradigm of *la Virgen de Guadalupe* and *Malintzin Tenepal*. Guadalupe represented the Mexican ideal of *"la madre sufrida,"* the long-suffering desexualized Indian mother, and Malinche was *"la chingada,"* sexually stigmatized by her transgression of "sleeping with the enemy," Hernán Cortez. Deemed traitor by Mexican tradition, the figure of Malinche was invoked to keep Movimiento women silent, sexually passive, and "Indian" in the colonial sense of the word.

The preservation of the Chicano *familia* became the Movimiento's mandate and within this constricted "familia" structure, Chicano políticos ensured that the patriarchal father figure remained in charge both in their private and political lives.[5] Women were, at most, allowed to serve as modern-day *"Adelitas,"* performing the "three f's" as a Chicana colleague calls them: "feeding, fighting, and fucking." In the name of this "culturally correct" familia, certain topics were censored both in cultural and political spheres as not "socially relevant" to Chicanos and typically not sanctioned in the Mexican household. These issues included female sexuality generally and male homosexuality and lesbianism specifically, as well as incest and violence against women—all of which are still relevant between the sheets and within the walls of many Chicano families. In the process, the Chicano

Movement forfeited the participation and vision of some very significant female and gay leaders and never achieved the kind of harmonious Chicano "familia" they ostensibly sought.

To this day, although lip service is given to "gender issues" in academic and political circles, no serious examination of male supremacy within the Chicano community has taken place among heterosexual men. Veteranos of Chicano nationalism are some of the worst offenders. Twenty years later, they move into "elderhood" without having seriously grappled with the fact that their leadership in El Movimiento was made possible by all those women who kept their "plumas planchadas"[6] at every political event.

A Divided Nation: A *Chicana Lésbica* Critique

> We are free and sovereign to determine those tasks which are justly called for by our house, our land, the sweat of our brows, and by our hearts. Aztlán belongs to those who plant the seeds, water the fields, and gather the crops and not to the foreign Europeans. We do not recognize capricious frontiers on the bronze continent.
>
> —From *"El Plan Espiritual de Aztlán"*

When "El Plan Espiritual de Aztlán" was conceived a generation ago, lesbians and gay men were not envisioned as members of the "house"; we were not recognized as the sister planting the seeds, the brother gathering the crops. We were not counted as members of the "bronze continent."

In the last decade, through the efforts of Chicana feministas, Chicanismo has undergone a serious critique. Feminist critics are committed to the preservation of Chicano culture, but we know that our culture will not survive marital rape, battering, incest, drug and alcohol abuse, AIDS, and the marginalization of lesbian daughters and gay sons. Some of the most outspoken criticism of the Chicano Movement's sexism and some of the most impassioned activism in the area of Chicana liberation (including work on sexual abuse, domestic violence, immigrant rights, Indigenous women's issues, health care, etc.) have been advanced by lesbians.

Since lesbians and gay men have often been forced out of our blood families, and since our love and sexual desire are not housed within the traditional family, we are in a critical position to address those areas within our cultural family that need to change. Further, in order to understand and defend our lovers and our same-sex loving, lesbians and gay men must come to terms with how homophobia, gender roles, and sexuality are learned and expressed in Chicano culture. As Ricardo Bracho writes: "To speak of my desire, to find voice in my brown flesh, I needed to confront my male mirror." As a lesbian, I don't pretend to understand the intricacies or intimacies of Chicano gay desire, but we do share the fact that our "homosexuality"—our feelings about sex, sexual power and domination, femininity and masculinity, family, loyalty, and morality—has been shaped by heterosexist culture and society. As such, we have plenty to tell heterosexuals about themselves.

When we are moved sexually toward someone, there is a profound opportunity to observe the microcosm of all human relations, to understand power dynamics both obvious and subtle, and to meditate on the core creative impulse of all desire. Desire is never politically correct. In sex, gender roles, race relations, and our collective histories of oppression and human connection are enacted. Since the early 1980s, Chicana lesbian feminists have explored these traditionally "dangerous" topics in both critical and creative writings. Chicana lesbian-identified writers such as Ana Castillo, Gloria Anzaldúa, and Naomi Littlebear Moreno were among the first to articulate a Chicana feminism, which included a radical woman-centered critique of sexism *and sexuality* from which both lesbian and heterosexual women benefited.

In the last few years, Chicano gay men have also begun to openly examine Chicano sexuality. I suspect heterosexual Chicanos will have the world to learn from their gay brothers about their shared masculinity, but they will have the most to learn from the "queens," the "*maricones.*" Because they are deemed "inferior" for not fulfilling the traditional role of men, they are more marginalized from mainstream heterosexual society than other gay men and are especially vulnerable to male violence. Over the years, I have been shocked to discover how many femme gay men have grown up regularly experiencing rape and sexual abuse. The rapist is always heterosexual and usually Chicano like themselves. What has the Gay Movement done for these brothers? What has the Chicano Movement done? What do these young and once-young men have to tell us about misogyny and male violence? Like women, they see the macho's desire to dominate the feminine, but even more intimately because they both desire men and share manhood with their oppressors. They may be *jotos*, but they are still men, and are bound by their racial and sexual identification to men (Bracho's "male mirror").

Until recently, Chicano gay men have been silent over the Chicano Movement's male heterosexual hegemony. As much as I see a potential alliance with gay men in our shared experience of homophobia, the majority of gay men still cling to what privileges they can. I have often been severely disappointed and hurt by the misogyny of gay Chicanos. Separation from one's brothers is a painful thing. Being gay does not preclude gay men from harboring the same sexism evident in heterosexual men. It's like white people and racism, sexism goes with the (male) territory.

On some level our brothers—gay and straight—have got to give up being "men." I don't mean give up their genitals, their unique expression of desire, or the rich and intimate manner in which men can bond together. Men have to give up their subscription to male superiority. I remember during the Civil Rights Movement seeing newsreel footage of young Black men carrying protest signs reading, "I AM A MAN." It was a powerful statement, publicly declaring their humanness in a society that daily told them otherwise. But they didn't write "I AM HUMAN," they wrote "MAN." Conceiving of their liberation in male terms, they were unwittingly demanding the right to share the whiteman's position of male dominance. This demand would become consciously articulated with the emergence of the male-dominated Black Nationalist Movement. The liberation of Black women per se was not part of the program, except to the extent that better conditions for the race in general might benefit Black women as well. How differently Sojourner Truth's "Ain't I a Woman" speech resonates for me. Unable to choose between suffrage and abolition, between her womanhood and her Blackness, Truth's 19th-century call for a free Black womanhood in a Black- and woman-hating society required the freedom of all enslaved land disenfranchised peoples. As the Black feminist Combahee River Collective stated in 1977, "If Black women were free, it would mean that everyone else would have to be free since our freedom would necessitate the destruction of all the systems of oppression." No progressive movement can succeed while any member of the population remains in submission.

Chicano gay men have been reluctant to recognize and acknowledge that their freedom is intricately connected to the freedom of women. As long as they insist on remaining "men" in the socially and culturally constructed sense of the word, they will never achieve the full liberation they desire. There will always be jotos getting raped and beaten. Within people of color communities, violence against women, gay bashing, sterilization abuse, AIDS and AIDS discrimination, gay substance abuse, and gay teen suicide emerge from the same source—a racist and misogynist social and economic system that dominates, punishes, and abuses all things colored, female, or perceived as female-like. By openly confronting Chicano sexuality and sexism, gay men can do their own part to unravel how both men *and* women have been formed and deformed by racist Amerika and our misogynist/catholic/colonized *mechicanidad*; and we can come that much closer to healing those fissures that have divided us as a people.

The AIDS epidemic has seriously shaken the foundation of the Chicano gay community, and gay men seem more willing than ever to explore those areas of political change that will ensure their survival. In their fight against AIDS, they have been rejected and neglected by both the white gay male establishment and the Latino heterosexual health-care community. They also have witnessed direct support by Latina lesbians.[7] Unlike the "queens" who have always been open about their sexuality, "passing" gay men have learned in a visceral way that being in "the closet" and preserving their "manly" image will not protect them, it will only make their dying more secret. I remember my friend Arturo Islas, the novelist. I think of how his writing begged to boldly announce his gayness. Instead, we learned it through vague references about "sinners" and tortured alcoholic characters who wanted nothing more than to "die dancing" beneath a lightning-charged sky just before a thunderstorm. Islas died of AIDS-related illness in 1990, having barely begun to examine the complexity of Chicano sexuality in his writing. I also think of essayist Richard Rodríguez, who, with so much death surrounding him, has recently begun to publicly address the subject of homosexuality; and yet, even ten years ago we all knew "Mr. Secrets" was gay from his assimilationist Hunger of Memory.[8] Had he "come out" in 1982, the white establishment would have been far less willing to promote him as the "Hispanic" anti-affirmative action spokesperson. He would have lost a lot of validity . . . and opportunity. But how many lives are lost each time we cling to privileges that make other people's lives more vulnerable to violence?

At this point in history, lesbians and gay men can make a significant contribution to the creation of a new Chicano movement, one passionately committed to saving lives. As we are forced to struggle for our right to love free of disease and discrimination, "Aztlán" as our imagined homeland begins to take on renewed importance. Without the dream of a free world, a free world will never be realized. Chicana lesbians and gay men do not merely seek inclusion in the Chicano nation; we seek a nation strong enough to embrace a full range of racial diversities, human sexualities, and expressions of gender. We seek a culture that can allow for the natural expression of our femaleness and maleness and our love without prejudice or punishment. In a "queer" Aztlán, there would be no freaks, no "others" to point one's finger at. My Native American friends tell me that in some Native American tribes, gay men and lesbians were traditionally regarded as "two-spirited" people. Displaying both masculine and feminine aspects, they were highly respected members of their community, and were thought to possess a higher spiritual development.[9] Hearing of such traditions gives historical validation for what Chicana lesbians and gay men have always recognized—that lesbians and gay men play a significant spiritual, cultural, and political role within the Chicano community. *Somos activistas, académicos y artistas, parteras y políticos, curanderas y campesinos.* With or without heterosexual acknowledgement, lesbians and gay men have continued to actively redefine familia, *cultura*, and *comunidad.* We have formed circles of support and survival, often drawing from the more egalitarian models of Indigenous communities.

Indigenismo: The Re-Tribalization of Our People

In recent years, for gay and straight Chicanos alike, our indigenismo has increased in importance as we witness the ultimate failure of Anglo-Americanism to bring harmony to our lives. In Ward Churchill's *Struggle for the Land*, he describes an "Indigenist" as someone who "takes the rights of indigenous peoples as the highest priority," and who "draws upon the traditions . . . of native peoples the world over." Many Chicanos would by this definition consider themselves Indigenists, subscribing to an indigenismo that is derived specifically from the traditions of *mechicano indio* peoples. Since the early seventies, Chicanos have worked in coalition with other Native American tribes and have participated in inter-tribal gatherings, political-prisoner campaigns, land-rights struggles, and religious ceremonies. Chicano Nation has been varyingly accepted as a tribe by other Native American peoples, usually more in the honorary sense than in any official capacity. The Indigenous Women's Network, for example, has included Chicanas since its inception in 1984.

Most Chicanos can claim, through physical traits alone, that we are of Native blood (we often joke that Chicanos are usually the most Indian-looking people in a room full of "skins"). The majority of us, however, has been denied direct information regarding our tribal affiliations. Since our origins are usually in the Southwest and México, Chicanos' Indian roots encompass a range of nations including Apache, Yaqui, Papago, Navajo, and Tarahumara from the border regions, as well as dozens of Native tribes throughout México. Regardless of verifiable genealogy, many Chicanos have recently begun to experience a kind of collective longing to return to our culture's traditional indigenous beliefs and ways of constructing community in order to find concrete solutions for the myriad problems confronting us, from the toxic dump sites in our neighborhoods to rape.

"Tribe," based on the traditional models of Native Americans, is an alternative socioeconomic structure that holds considerable appeal for those of us who recognize the weaknesses of the isolated patriarchal capitalist family structure. This is not to say that all Native Americans subscribe to the same tribal structures or that contemporary Indians fully practice traditional tribal ways. Few Native peoples today are allowed real political autonomy and self-determination. Tribal governments are corrupted by U.S. interference through the Bureau of Indian Affairs, the U.S. military, the FBI, and the U.S. Department of Energy. In essence, however, the tribal model is a form of community-building that can accommodate socialism, feminism, and environmental protection. In an ideal world, tribal members are responsive and responsible to one another and the natural environment. Cooperation is rewarded over competition. Acts of violence against women and children do not occur in secret and perpetrators are held accountable to the rest of the community. "Familia" is not dependent upon male-dominance or heterosexual coupling. Elders are respected and women's leadership is fostered, not feared.

But it is not an ideal world. Any Indian on or off the reservation can tell you about the obstacles to following traditional ways. The reservation is not indigenous to Native Americans; it is a colonial model invented to disempower Native peoples. The rates of alcoholism, suicide, and domestic violence are testimony to the effectiveness of that system. Chicanos, living in the colony of the U.S. barrio, have the same scars: AIDS, drugs, brown-on-brown murder, poverty, and environmental contamination. Nevertheless, the present-day values and organized struggles of traditional Native communities throughout the Americas represent real hope for halting the quickly accelerating level of destruction affecting all life on this continent.

Madre Tierra/Madre Mujer: The Struggle for Land[10]

Journal Entry

I sit in a hotel room. A fancy hotel room with two walls of pure glass and pure Vancouver night skyline filling them. I sit on top of the bed and eat Japanese take-out. The Canadian t.v. news takes us east to the province of Quebec, to some desolate area with no plumbing or sewage, no running water, where a group of Inuit people have been displaced. To some desolate area where Inuit children stick their faces into bags and sniff gas fumes for the high, the rush, the trip, for the escape out of this hell-hole that is their life. One young boy gives the finger to the t.v. camera. "They're angry," an Inuit leader states. "I'm angry, too." At thirty, he is already an old man. And I hate this Canada as much as I hate these dis-United States.

But I go on eating my Japanese meal that has somehow turned rotten on my tongue and my bloody culpability mixes with the texture of dead fish flesh and no wonder I stand on the very edge of the balcony on the 26th floor of this hotel looking down on restaurant-row Vancouver and imagine how easy and impossible it would be to leap in protest for the gas-guzzling Inuit children.

The primary struggle for Native peoples across the globe is the struggle for land. In 1992, 500 years after the arrival of Columbus, on the heels of the Gulf War and the dissolution of the Soviet Union, the entire world is re-constructing itself. No longer frozen into the Soviet/Yanqui paradigm of a "Cold" and invented "War," Indigenous peoples are responding en masse to the threat of a global capitalist "mono-culture" defended by the "hired guns" of the U.S. military. Five hundred years after Columbus' arrival, they are spearheading an international movement with the goal of sovereignty for all Indigenous nations.

Increasingly, the struggles on this planet are not for "nation-states," but for nations of people, bound together by spirit, land, language, history, and blood.[11] This is evident from the intifada of the Palestinians residing within Israel's stolen borders and the resistance of the Cree and Inuit Indians in northern Quebec. The Kurds of the Persian Gulf region understand this, as do the Ukrainians of what was once the Soviet Union. Chicanos are also a nation of people, internally colonized within the borders of the U.S. nation-state.

Few Chicanos really believe we can wrest Aztlán away from Anglo-Amer-ica. And yet, residing in those Southwestern territories, especially those ar-eas not completely appropriated by *gringolandia*, we instinctively remember it as Mexican Indian land and can still imagine it as a distinct nation. In our most private moments, we ask ourselves, *If the Soviet Union could dissolve, why can't the United States?*

Dreams of the disintegration of the United States as we know it are not so private among North American Indians. The dissolution of the Soviet Union has given renewed impetus to seccessionist thinking by Indians here in the United States. One plan, the "North American Union of Indigenous Nations," described in Ward Churchill's book, calls for the reunification of Indian peoples and territories to comprise a full third of continental United States, including much of Aztlán. Not surprisingly, Chicano Nation is not mentioned as part of this new confederacy, which speaks to the still tenuous alliance between Chicano and Native American peoples. Nevertheless, the spirit of the plan is very much in accord with Chicano nationalists' most rev-olutionary dreams of reclaiming a homeland, side by side with other Indian Nations.

If the material basis of every nationalist movement is land, then the reac-quisition, defense, and protection of Native land and its natural resources are the basis for rebuilding Chicano nation. Without the sovereignty of Native peoples, including Chicanos, and support for our land-based struggles, the world will be lost to North American greed, and our culturas lost with it. The "last frontier" for Northern capitalists lies buried in coal and uranium-rich reservation lands and in the remaining rainforests of the Amazon. The inhabitants of these territories—the Diné, the North Cheyenne, the Kayapó, etc.—are the very people who in 1992 offer the world community "living models" of ways to live in balance with nature and safeguard the earth as we know it. The great historical irony is that 500 years after the Conquest, the conqueror must now turn to the conquered for salvation.

We are speaking of bottom-line considerations. I can't understand when in 1992 with 100 acres of rainforest disappearing every minute, with global warming, with babies being born without brains in South *Tejas*, with street kids in Río sniffing glue to stifle their hunger, with Mohawk women's breast milk being contaminated by the poisoned waters of the Great Lakes Basin, how we as people of color, as people of Indian blood, as people with the same last names as our Latin American counterparts, are not alarmed by the destruction of Indigenous and mestizo peoples. How is it Chicanos cannot see ourselves as victims of the same destruction, already in its advanced stages? Why do we not collectively experience the urgency for alternatives based not on what our oppressors advise, but on the advice of elders and ancestors who may now speak to us only in dreams?

What they are telling us is very clear. The road to the future is the road from our past. Traditional Indigenous communities (our Indian "past" that too many Chicanos have rejected) provide practical answers for our survival. At the Earth Summit in Río de Janeiro in June 1992, representatives from "developing countries," and grassroots, Indigenous, and people-of-color organizations joined together to demand the economic programs necessary to create their own sustainable ecologically sound communities. In a world where eighty-five percent of all the income, largely generated from the natural resources of Indigenous lands and "Third World" countries, goes to twenty-three percent of the people, Fidel Castro said it best: "Let the ecological debt be paid, not the foreign debt."

And here all the connecting concerns begin to coalesce. Here the Marxist meets the ecologist. We need look no further than the North American Free Trade Agreement (NAFTA) to understand the connection between global ecological devastation and the United States' relentless drive to expand its markets. NAFTA is no more than a 21st-century plot to continue the North's exploitation of the cheap labor, lax environmental policies, and the natural resources of the South. The United States has no intention of responding to the environmental crisis. George Bush's decision to "stand alone on principle" and refuse to sign the Bio-Diversity Treaty said it all. Profit over people. Profit over protection. No sustainable development is possible in the Americas if the United States continues to demand hamburgers, Chrysler automobiles, and refrigerators from hungry, barefoot, and energy-starved nations. There is simply not enough to go around, no new burial ground for toxic waste that isn't sacred, no untapped energy source that doesn't suck the earth dry. Except for the sun . . . except for the wind, which are infinite in their generosity and virtually ignored.

The earth is female. Whether myth, metaphor, or memory, she is called "Mother" by all peoples of all times. *Madre Tierra.* Like woman, Madre Tierra has been raped, exploited for her resources, rendered inert, passive, and speechless. Her cries manifested in earthquakes, tidal waves, hurricanes, volcanic eruptions are not heeded. But the Indians take note and so do the women, the women with the capacity to remember.

Native religions have traditionally honored the female alongside the male. Religions that grow exclusively from the patriarchal capitalist imagination, instead of the requirements of nature, enslave the female body. The only religion we need is one based on the good sense of living in harmony with nature. Religion should serve as a justification against greed, not for it. Bring back the rain gods, corn gods, father sun, and mother moon and keep those gods happy. Whether we recognize it or not, those gods are today, this day, punishing us for our excess. What humankind has destroyed will wreak havoc on the destroyer. Fried skin from holes in the ozone is only one example.

The earth is female. It is no accident then that the main grassroots activists defending the earth, along with Native peoples, are women of all races and cultures. Regardless of the so-called "advances" of Western "civilization," women remain the chief caretakers, nurturers, and providers for our children and our elders. These are the mothers of East Los Angeles, McFarland, and Kettleman City, fighting toxic dumps, local incinerators and pesticide poisoning, women who experience the earth's contamination in the deformation and death occurring within their very wombs. We do not have to be mothers to know this. Most women know what it is to be seen as the Earth is seen—a receptacle for male violence and greed. Over half the agricultural workers in the world are women who receive less training and less protection than their male counterparts. We do not control how we produce and reproduce, how we labor and love. And *how will our lands be free if our bodies aren't?*

Land remains the common ground for all radical action. But land is more than the rocks and trees, the animal and plant life that make up the territory of Aztlán or Navajo Nation or Maya Mesoamerica. For immigrant and native alike, land is also the factories where we work, the water our children drink, and the housing project where we live. For women, lesbians, and gay men, land is that physical mass called our bodies. Throughout *las Américas*, all these "lands" remain under occupation by an Anglocentric, patriarchal, imperialist United States.

La Causa Chicana: Entering the Next Millenium

As a Chicana lesbian, I know that the struggle I share with all Chicanos and Indigenous peoples is truly one of sovereignty, the sovereign right to wholly inhabit oneself *(cuerpo y alma)* and one's territory *(pan y tierra)*. I don't know if we can ever take back Aztlán from Anglo-America, but in the name of a new Chicano nationalism we can work to defend remaining Indian territories. We can work to teach one another that our freedom as a people is mutually dependent and cannot be parceled out—class before race before sex before sexuality. A new Chicano nationalism calls for the integration of both the traditional and the revolutionary, the ancient and the contemporary. It requires a serious reckoning with the weaknesses in our mestizo culture, and a reaffirmation of what has preserved and sustained us as a people. I am clear about one thing: fear has not sustained us. Fear of action, fear of speaking, fear of women, fear of queers.

As these 500 years come to a close, I look forward to a new América, where the only "discovery" to be made is the rediscovery of ourselves as members of the global community. Nature will be our teacher, for she alone knows no prejudice. Possibly as we ask men to give up being "men," we must ask humans to give up being "human," or at least to give up the human capacity for greed. Simply, we must give back to the earth what we take from it. We must submit to a higher "natural" authority, as we invent new ways of making culture, making tribe, to survive and flourish as members of the world community in the next millennium.

Notes

An earlier version of this essay was first presented at the First National LLEGO (Latino/a Lesbian and Gay Organization) Conference in Houston, Texas, on May 22, 1992. A later version was presented at a Quincentenary Conference at the University of Texas in Austin on October 31, 1992.

1. Chicano term for "queer" folk.
2. To this day, there are still pockets of Chicano nationalists—mostly artists, poets, and cultural workers—who continue to work on a local and regional level.

3. UC Berkeley's Chicano/Latino immigrant students have not generally encountered the same degree of poverty and exploitation experienced by undocumented Mexican and Central American immigrants.

4. Further discussion of the "hispanicization" of the U.S. Latino can be found in Cherríe Moraga, "Art in *América con Acento*" in *The Last Generation*, (Cambridge, MA: South End Press).

5. The twenty-five-year-old Chicano *Teatro* Movement is an apt example. Initiated by Luis Valdez' *Teatro Campesino*, the teatro movement has been notorious for its male dominance even within its so-called collective structures. Over eighty percent of the Chicano Theatres across the country are directed by men. No affirmative-action policies have been instituted to encourage the development of Chicana playwrights, technicians, or directors. In recent years, however, there has been some progress in this area with the production of a handful of Chicana playwrights, including Josefina López, Evelina Fernández, Edit Villareal, and this author. To this day, gay and lesbian images and feminist criticism are considered taboo in most Chicano theatres.

6. The image alludes to Chicano cultural nationalists who during the seventies neoindigenist period sometimes wore feathers (*plumas*) and other Indian attire at cultural events.

7. In contrast to the overwhelming response by lesbians to the AIDS crisis, breast cancer, which has disproportionately affected the lesbian community, has received little attention from the gay men's community in particular, and the public at large. And yet, the statistics are devastating. One out of every nine women in the United States will get breast cancer: 44,500 U.S. women will die of breast cancer this year (*Boston Globe*, November 5, 1991).

8. See Rodríguez' essay "Late Victorians" in his most recent collection, *Days of Obligation: An Argument with My Mexican Father.*

9. This was not the case among all tribes nor is homosexuality generally condoned in contemporary Indian societies. See Ramón A. Gutiérrez "Must We Deracinate Indians to Find Gay Roots?" *Outlook: National Lesbian and Gay Quarterly*, Winter 1989.

10. I wish to thank Marsha Gómez, the Indigenous Women's Network, and the *Alma de Mujer* Center for Social Change in Austin, Texas, for providing me with statistical and other current information about Indigenous peoples' struggles for environmental safety and sovereignty, as well as published materials on the '92 Earth Summit in Brazil.

11. The dissolution of what was heretofore the nation-state of Yugoslavia, composed of Serbs, Slovenes, Croats, Albanians, and Macedonians, including the Muslim and Orthodox religions, represents the rise of bitter nationalist sentiment gone awry. It is a horror story of ethnic and cultural nationalism turned into nazism and serves as a painful warning against fascist extremism in nationalist campaigns.

*   *   *

Questions

1. Moraga claims that at the height of the Chicano movement in 1968 she was "a closeted, light-skinned, mixed-blood Mexican-American, disguised in [her] father's English last name." She also claims that she began her politicization, not through the Chicano movement, but through "the bold recognition of [her] lesbianism." This led to a "radical re-structuring of everything [she] thought [she] held sacred." And this, in turn, delivered her to political action "because not acting would have meant [her] death by despair."
   a. Is there some kind of connection between political action and despair?
   b. Do you recall other examples in which despair led to political action?
   c. Have you ever been confronted by some kind of realization that forces you to reexamine your most sacred beliefs?
   d. Have you ever felt that you must hide your beliefs (about anything) in front of your family or friends, as if you were wearing a "political disguise"?

2. It took Moraga a quarter of a century after the walkouts in 1968 to find a place "among la Chicanada" (the Chicano people). Though not a safe place, this is the "original familial place" from which she is compelled to write, to reach her audience, and which serves as a source of inspiration, voice, and struggle. Do you have or can you imagine a place that serves as a cradle for your thoughts and feelings and voice?

CHAPTER TWELVE

~

Class and Culture Wars in the New Latino Politics

Victor Valle and Rodolfo D. Torres

In this piece, Valle and Torres place Latino/a power and politics within a global and a metropolitan context. Thus they dispel any facile assumptions about a particular ethnic hegemony in Los Angeles. They note, among other things, the incipient political representation and the lingering invisibility to which Latinos/as are still subjected. At the same time, they point to the increasing political participation of the "postamnesty" Latino/a voter, a phenomenon that points to the quest for public citizenship. Focusing on the role of the working class, they provide a comprehensive point of view to understand what appears as interethnic or racial conflict. Of particular interest is their notion of genetic, political, and cultural *mestizaje* as a model for future democracy in the United States.

*   *   *

Population trends suggest that Latinos may have to wait until past the mid-century mark before their numerical dominance becomes irresistible. When and if that moment arises, increasing social differentiation and class divisions within the Latino community, complicated by globalism's unforeseen permutations, will make simple notions of ethnic cohesion problematic.

Rather, if Latino power is to have any real constructive and lasting meaning, it should be seen as both the catalyst for and the foundation of a new conception of the multicultural metropolis. Up to this point, we have suggested through our criticism that the only multiculturalism worth striving for should not disguise and obscure social inequalities with brotherly platitudes or allow the processes of racialization to continue reproducing themselves behind the benign facade of tolerance. Now we would like to be more explicit and focus our attention upon the immediate future. The Latino community, due to its current social composition, historical experience, and size, has the potential to play a crucial role in the construction of a new cosmopolitanism. Recent events suggest that such a building process is already under way in the political arena.

Spurred on by record levels of Latino voter registration and participation in California, twenty-four Latino and Latina candidates, or one in five members of the state legislature, were elected during the 1998 election cycle, an increase of eighteen over the 1996 election cycle.[1] More important for our study, most of the newly acquired seats were won in Los Angeles County. Yet several factors have distracted many analysts within and outside of the Latino community from grasping simultaneously the political *and* cultural significance of these electoral gains.

For one, dramatic increases in Latino political representation are recent. Not since the nineteenth century has Southern California's Latino community enjoyed such levels of political representation.[2] Still, there is something rather presumptuous about asking whether increased political representation should somehow translate into increased cultural influence. Latinos have viewed themselves as being in the minority for so long that the possibility of becoming the majority seems disorienting. The same goes for Latino leadership. Few Latino scholars have studied politics as an arena for cultural representation because, until relatively recently, it was assumed that, as a politically marginalized group, Latinos enacted their cultural lives in private, or at least in their neighborhoods. Now, however, Latino-elected leaders and their constituents have an opportunity to imagine and enact their cultural lives in public. We intend to show that the opportunities for increased cultural influence offered by enhanced public participation go beyond the simple administrative and legislative remedies available to Latino leadership. The political arena also offers a kind of stage upon which Latinos can construct new public identities. We intend to show that that transition has already been prefigured, and in many ways enabled, by the increasing reach and power of the various forms of Latino media, especially the Spanish-language media. When artists like Los Lobos create music that expresses a profound self-acceptance of their working-class and *mestizo* roots, when Spanish-language television broadcasters present illegal Latino border crossers as heroic survivors, when Mexican fans fill the Los Angeles Memorial Coliseum to capacity to root for the home team—*La Selección Nacional*—in a match against the U.S. national team, and when clubs like *La Conga* Room create a space where Latinos of all national origins can gather to enjoy the best in Afro-Cuban music, via Havana, one can already see the variety of cultural forms from which new public behaviors are being constructed.

As the presidential impeachment scandal of 1999 reminds us, politics is a kind of social practice where subjective, or cultural, forms are produced and circulated for public consumption. It is indeed a cliché of contemporary politics that elections and legislative battles are won or lost in the media. At both the national and the local levels, politicians increasingly debate questions once considered issues of private morality—gay marriage, abortion, adultery, school prayer—in the nation's virtual electronic town squares. And as the country has drifted further to the right, and the national political culture has fallen still more deeply under the sway of the corporate media and corporate dollars, political life, to the degree it is concerned with the production and consumption of moral discourse, is now dominated by the subjective. So it would seem that the same forces that have converted politics into cultural warfare would have further marginalized minority forms of counterrepresentation. Until recently, that judgment would have seemed especially applicable to Latinos, at least at the level of national discourse. Even though African Americans have lost discursive ground in recent decades, they, of all minorities, continue to play the lead role in the national political and cultural dialogue, especially as it concerns urban "race relations." By contrast, and with such notable exceptions as United Farm Workers labor and environmental struggles, Latino contributions to the national political discourse are usually obscured or absorbed by stronger voices. And but for the individual exceptions, it has been more common to conceive of Latino political leaders simply as creatures of their local political environments and not as shapers of the greater political culture.

Not surprisingly—and this is especially true of the practitioners of cultural studies—cultural and social historians have tended to privilege the analysis of marginal spaces and texts to understand how Latinos have contested hegemonic culture or constructed ethnic identities. Hence the recent studies that seek to understand, or read, how Latinos construct their lived cultures, and hence the emphasis on the texts of lived culture, from cookbooks to graffiti to low riders. But recent developments in cities such as Miami and Los Angeles now require a reconceptualization of the way Latinos negotiate the transition from political and cultural minority to political and cultural majority. In Los Angeles, the work of reconceptualization becomes especially urgent as Latino political leadership increases its policymaking role in the transition to an economy based upon cultural production, as evidenced by the explosion of such entertainment projects as the Staples Center, the proposed DreamWorks studio, and the city's first Catholic cathedral. Increased Latino political representation will mean greater access to the levers of government and, as a result, a larger niche in the state's ecology of representation. Now, for the first time since the city's founding, Latinos have the opportunity to acquire the institutional standing to open up what has been a closed dialogue on the matter of race and class.

In a strictly quantitative sense, then, the future already looks promising when considered in the light of recent political history. In the 1970s and 1980s, organizations such as the National Organization of Latino Elected and Appointed Officials measured success by counting electoral victories. Consistent with such thinking, most Latino officeholders replicated mainstream political thinking, making a religion of narrow political pragmatism. As in the major parties, raising money, winning elections, and holding onto political office were their method, objective, and reward. As apathy in the electorate broadened and deepened, ideas and issues played second fiddle to the art of deal making, fund-raising, polling, and media campaigning. Some of this narrowness was understandable. Increases in Latino voter participation had not kept pace with the quickened rate of Latino population growth during the 1970s and 1980s. As a result, Latino candidates remained dependent upon corporate donors, party bosses, and the demands of media campaigning. The dearth of Latino political ideas, however, also reflected weak leadership. The running rivalry between Councilman Richard Alatorre's and Supervisor Gloria Molina's political machines, the decision of Latino elected officials to soften their opposition to Proposition 187 to avoid alienating white voters, and the recent drug scandals engulfing Alatorre and Councilman Mike Hernandez illustrate some of the worst of the past generation of Latino political leadership.[3] By the late 1980s, and continuing until the mid-1990s, Latino population growth, coupled with the consequences of immigration legislation and California's attempt at ethnic cleansing, dramatically altered both the quantity and quality of Latino voter participation in state politics, and, as a consequence, the possibilities for new leadership.

The first tremors of the political earthquake were registered in Orange County when Democrat Loretta Sanchez defeated ultraconservative incumbent Republican Robert Dornan for a seat in the U.S. House of Representatives by a 984-vote margin in 1996. Although Dornan's defeat in the Forty-Sixth Congressional District rocked conservatives where it hurt most, in a seat long considered safe by Republicans, a growing Latino presence in Santa Ana made the upset foreseeable. Groups like La Hermandad Mexicana Nacional, a cross between an old-fashioned Mexican mutual-aid society and a labor and immigrant rights organization, helped translate that presence into votes, an achievement that quickly drew a reactionary response. In the already hostile climate created by the passage of Proposition 187 two years earlier, Dornan played up anti-Latino, anti-immigrant hysteria, accusing La Hermandad of a sinister conspiracy. Meanwhile, the *Los Angeles Times,* according to the O.C. *Weekly,* "manufactured incriminating evidence; declared *Hermandad* guilty months before a grand jury had even convened; and effectively sided with Dornan's laughable accusations that nuns, military men, residents of entire apartment buildings and 'thousands' of noncitizens quietly conspired to unseat him."[4] Local and federal authorities launched investigations, but two years later an Orange County grand jury, citing a lack of evidence, refused to hand down any indictments. In the end, all that could be established with any certainty was that "noncitizens who had passed all immigration tests and who were awaiting formal swearing-in ceremonies" had jumped the gun. They had improperly registered to vote and then exercised their franchise prematurely.[5] The most sinister charge that could be leveled against La Hermandad was that a pair of its voter registration volunteers may have been overzealous in their efforts to increase Latino political participation.

Ironically, the Dornan-manufactured media panic fueled new efforts to mobilize Latino voters. To protect their families, jobs, and civil liberties from continued Republican-led scapegoating, California's Latino immigrants took advantage of a period of immigration amnesty, became citizens, and then voted in record numbers. Although Latinos remain underrepresented at the polls, the 1996 election results show that newly enfranchised Latino immigrants voted "at a rate exceeding that of the state's voters as a whole." These new voters participated at rates that effectively surpassed the overall voter turnout, with "a little less than two-thirds" of them going to the polls.[6] Los Angeles County, where the 1996 turnout among both new and veteran Latino voters jumped from 11 percent to 18 percent, registered the biggest bounce. In Orange County, the setting for the Dornan-Sanchez race, the Latino vote rose from 6 percent to 9 percent.[7] 1996 elections marked two other historic firsts: Latino voter participation in the Los Angeles mayoral race hit 15 percent, which surpassed African American participation and matched the Westside Jewish turnout.[8] Not surprisingly, several recent studies show that Governor Pete Wilson, the most powerful and aggressive spokesman for the anti-immigrant backlash, did long-term damage to the Republican Party's credibility among new immigrant voters. But the Latino turnout, which rose at a time when Jewish political representation in Los Angeles County's top one hundred political of offices had declined by 30 percent since 1986, also gave the Westside's Democratic establishment much to ponder.[9]

Nativo Lopez, executive director of La Hermandad's Orange County branch, sees the emergence of the "postamnesty" Latino voter as a turning point in Southern California politics. The state's 1.7 million immigration applicants all became eligible to apply for amnesty at the end of 1995.[10] After January, February, and March 1996, these applicants became citizens in increasing numbers, and a growing cohort of high school-aged U.S.-born Latinos began voting thanks to the passage of President Clinton's "motor-voter" law. Equally important, groups such as the Southwest Voter Registration Education Project, La Hermandad, and the Los Angeles County Federation of Labor laid the organizational groundwork that translated legal opportunities into electoral gains. In 1996, their combined efforts succeeded in bringing as many as 1.3 million new potential Latino voters to the California polls.

"Certainly," Lopez said in an interview, "organization was a part of it, not just La Hermandad, but many others spurring people on to obtain their citizenship, and then registering them to vote." La Hermandad takes credit for qualifying anywhere from 175,000 to 180,000 people to enter the amnesty pipeline. "Many are still in the pipeline," Lopez added. "Locally, we have more than 10,000 applicants who have been waiting for twelve months to twenty-four months to get their final citizenship interview." And this trend will continue, "In the Los Angeles INS district," Lopez said, "there are more than a half a million people waiting for citizenship. By the year 2000 that backlog will be eliminated," which will produce another surge in Southern California's Latino vote just in time for the presidential election.[11]

During the 1998 election cycle, eleven Southern California Latino Democrats, most of whom can be classified as pro-labor progressives, rode this confluence of demographic and political forces into the California State Legislature. These victories helped Democrats regain a slim Assembly majority in Sacramento and lifted Antonio Villaraigosa from Assembly majority leader to the powerful position of Assembly speaker. In yet another portent of Latino political power, Los Angeles City Councilman Richard Alarcon handily won his San Fernando Valley State Senate seat after narrowly defeating former Assemblyman Richard Katz, a Westside political power broker, in a bitter Democratic primary. Other Latino candidates who lost close races in the last election cycle will be back for the next round, Lopez said: "There is no reason why in the year 2000, we shouldn't be close to 30 percent of the state assembly," or in other words, "close to parity with our numbers in the state's population."[12] Even Lopez, despite the onslaught of hostile media coverage, benefited from the postamnesty surge when he was elected president of the Santa Ana Unified School District Board of Education in 1996.

The city of Los Angeles—where Latinos are projected to constitute more than 49 percent of the population by 2001—promises future political opportunities, even though the charter reform movement, various City Council expansion schemes, and the San Fernando Valley secession movement have temporarily clouded that picture.[13] Latinos should continue to gain strength in the Valley, whichever way it goes, and in South-Central Los Angeles, where Latinos already made up 44 percent of the population in 1990.[14] There, Latinos will soon constitute as much as 60 percent of some districts. For the moment, few Latino or African American political leaders will publicly discuss that eventuality. But soon, Lopez said in another interview, "you are going to see Latinos running for those seats that have always been held by African Americans," competition that will increase tensions between Latino and African American political leaders.[15] Some analysts have already predicted that African American council member Rita Walters will be the first to be challenged by a Latino contender.[16] African American political leaders in Los Angeles must negotiate not only changing political demography but the growing fault line that divides a small but thriving African American middle class from the black urban poor. However, Latino office seekers and their supporters should resist the temptation to use ethnic loyalties to exploit the tenuous position of African American political leaders. Although such ploys may yield short-term gains, ethnically targeted appeals reinforce the city's divided political geography while leaving the Latino victors vulnerable to those who would exploit emerging class divisions among their own constituencies. Instead, African American and Latino elected officials representing inner-city districts need to develop strategies that address racialized class inequalities. By acknowledging, rather than obscuring, the class divisions in the Latino and African American communities, a new generation of leaders can build a movement based upon commonalities of class.

The anticipated growth of Latino populations in the suburbs and the unexpected consequences of legislative term limits will mean that "termed-out" Latino legislators will return from Sacramento or Washington to run in city districts both within and outside of the safe barrios now dominated by Latinos. Assembly Speaker Villaraigosa, State Senator Richard Polanco, Assemblyman Gil Cedillo, and Congressman Xavier Becerra, among others, may carpetbag into the seats vacated by Alatorre and Hernandez or run in the South-Central or Hollywood district, potentially doubling the number of Latinos on the City Council from three to six. Even a Villaraigosa mayoral challenge is conceivable if liberals and progressives can construct a viable post-Bradley-era coalition. The next census will also provide the numbers to translate a decade of Latino population growth into district reapportionment that increases Southern California's Latino congressional representation.

For the moment, however, many analysts appear preoccupied with calculating the new political math made possible by increased Latino participation while downplaying the content of the new postamnesty Latino leadership. Conventional political analyses still focus on identifying safe districts, reinforcing the conventional wisdom that the most important divisions in Los Angeles politics are racial or ethnic. Although these analytic prejudices are understandable, given the empiricist bias of professional political science and the racialized representation of the city's social divisions, both tendencies promote the Eastside-versus-Westside turf mentality that reinforces a fragmented status quo. But a closer examination of the postamnesty voter's role in the local and global economy offers important ways of reinterpreting the meaning of Latino voting patterns for the city and county as a whole.

In Nativo Lopez's view, "The most important demographic statistic left out of these discussions is that, in Los Angeles County, Latinos constitute more than 65 to 70 percent of the economically active workforce."[17] When Asian immigrant workers are factored into the equation, the emergence of new Latino and Asian leadership in the local labor movement seems logical. Already, Latino and Asian immigrant workers have begun to revive and expand decaying service sector unions into a new force in Los Angeles politics. The historic victories of the Service Employees International Union bear remembering in this context. An organizing practice that discovers the class interests of Latina, Asian American, and African American female home health-care workers shows how political alliances can be built across seemingly insurmountable local racialized boundaries.

Such victories, as well as union gains made earlier in the 1990s, have been felt far beyond the county line, providing the kinds of tactical and strategic knowledge that is transforming the AFL-CIO's national policies. At another level, the transformation of Los Angeles unionism bears comparison to the Irish immigrant takeover of New York's labor unions at the beginning of the twentieth century, except that now, Latino and Asian immigrants work under profoundly different economic and cultural circumstances.

Interpreting late capitalism remains tricky, however. The true believers in market solutions still promise that the emerging knowledge-based economy will eventually lift a sufficient number of boats, Latino vessels included, by providing a steady supply of new jobs. But increasing poverty in the midst of so-called full employment has, for the moment, disarmed their glib predictions and fueled postmillennial pessimism. Under the most noirish scenarios, the unequal development fostered by postindustrial society, with its concomitant transition to an information-based, post-Fordist industrial regime, will continue to produce massive economic and social dislocations. At the same time, the complex dialectics of capital, markets, and resources in the developing world will continue to make cities such as Los Angeles the destinations of choice for Latin American, Asian, Near Eastern, and African immigrants, thus creating a future theater of racialized conflict. Worse, during the next economic downturn, the opportunists will attempt to revive the anti-immigrant hysteria of the mid-1990s. Meanwhile, technological innovation will continue to demassify the media and facilitate the emergence of a knowledge elite whose job it will be to create and service the hardware and cultural software of an information/culture-based society. The new knowledge elites, we are told, will emerge as a dominant class of an economic regime based upon post-Fordist production, leaving behind those cultural and social sectors still dependent upon less efficient Fordist modes of production. Under post-Fordism, where information and culture industries emerge as the dominant productive force, the winners will either own or control the production of culture and information in all its economic and political applications. Everyone not owning or participating in these new knowledge-based industries stands to lose social prestige, not to mention financial and political viability. How the Latino community will fare in the ensuing transition to a society organized around digitized information and cultural production is hard to predict. But Latinos—either as members of a working and an incipient owning class—cannot expect to participate in, let alone influence, the knowledge-based industries except as consumers if they remain tied to inefficient Fordist industries. The emergent knowledge elites who serve at the pleasure of post-Fordist capital reserve the best roles for themselves.

Some may take heart in knowing that the *maquiladoras* concentrated along the northern Mexican border and scattered throughout Southern California's old and new suburbs will at least employ huge numbers of Latinos in the region's post-Fordist industries. The increased earning power of some Latinos has already tempted a few to mistake middle income for middle-class social position. But many middle-income Latinos, the pessimists say, have taken longer to acquire the social privileges and status that come with university-trained professions and upper-management corporate positions. Moreover, the Latinos who have joined the skilled, professional, and university-trained workforce remain in the minority. Most of the highly decentralized industries that employ Latinos do so at the lowest skill levels, offering them the lowest pay, benefits, and opportunities for educational advancement. For example, many of the low-skilled industries that employ Latinos in the Greater Eastside do not appear to have benefited from the globalization that has been so profitable for the knowledge industries, increasing their vulnerability to technological displacement and excess industrial capacity worldwide. The post-NAFTA international trade that has brought new investment and high-salary jobs into places like Santa Monica, Westlake Village, and Beverly Hills has not, according to one study, reached such Greater Eastside cities as Huntington Park, Cudahy, and Maywood, where minimum-wage jobs are plentiful.[18] Nor do the job niches Latinos currently hold in post-Fordist production promise greater access to the means of cultural representation; up to now, Latinos, with a few strategic exceptions, have been excluded from the means of mental production. The retrenchment of anti-affirmative action policies in higher education will act as a further drag on Latino integration in the knowledge-based economy.

Meanwhile, technological innovation will continue to facilitate the breakup of mass-media audiences into smaller, more socially isolated segments, while at the same time promoting the emergence of an information elite whose job it will be to create the information and cultural commodities that service a growing cybereconomy. The information elite will emerge as a dominant economic class of a social regime based upon post-Fordist production, leaving behind those cultural and social sectors still affiliated with Fordist modes of production. Under post-Fordism, where information and culture industries emerge as the dominant productive force, the winners will either own or create the production of knowledge. Everyone else, as Michael Rustin writes, stands to lose social prestige: "Insofar as mental labor does become more central to the production process, it is not surprising that those who live by it gain in social power, just as the depopulation of the countryside earlier had its consequences for class relations."[19]

According to some analysts, the noir scenarios are already visible in the inner city and in Greater L.A.'s aging near-in suburbs. The triple threat of a growing poverty-wage job sector, the steady evaporation of middle-income jobs, and meteoric salary increases for a select few knowledge workers at the top of the employment pyramid has already eroded the tax bases of Los Angeles and the older suburbs that Latinos have recently inherited. The crude inequalities of the new economy deliver the coup de grâce to a post-Proposition 13 history of disinvestment and physical decay in the recently Latinized suburbs. As Mike Davis notes in his latest book, *Ecology of Fear:*

> In addition to the dramatic hemorrhage of jobs and capital over the last decade, aging suburbia also suffers from premature physical obsolescence. Much of what was built in the postwar period (and continues to be built today)

is throwaway architecture, with a functional life span of 30 years or less. . . . At best, this stucco junk was designed to be promptly recycled in perennially dynamic housing markets, but such markets have stagnated or died in much of the old suburban fringe.[20]

And as these suburbs decay, white flight—at least for those with the skills to land higher-paying jobs in the knowledge-based and trade-based jobs of the edge suburbs—hastens the loss of tax revenues in the older suburbs.

The noir scenarios may underestimate the role Los Angeles will play in the regional, national, and global economy as well as the Latino community's resolve to salvage places written off as unredeemable, for Latinos will continue to seek social progress wherever they can obtain it. But compared to California's shameless boosters, the noir critique provides a sober corrective to unfounded optimism. For example, some analysts point with pride to increasing Latino household incomes as evidence of a growing Latino middle class. Gregory Rodriguez shows that in 1990 slightly more than 25 percent of Latino households in five Southern California counties earned incomes that exceeded $35,000, which was then the national median income. According to this income standard, slightly more than 25 percent of Latino households in Southern California's five counties were earning 1990 incomes that could be classified as middle-class. Recent immigrants, contrary to the underclass stereotype, constituted a significant portion (34 percent) of the Latino households earning at or above the median income level, registering some of the fastest income increases among Latinos. Latinos, both foreign-born and U.S.-born, showed rates of home ownership second only to Anglos and on par with Asians. Finally, Latino households earning at or above the middle-income level grew faster than the growth of Latino households living in poverty.[21]

Although impressive and important, studies that equate income with social status are nevertheless misleading. Latinos are indeed becoming more socially mobile, but the income numbers also show that 75 percent of Latino households earn below the national median, a proportion that is just as significant if one is interested in understanding the size of a low-wage, low-skilled Latino working class. And even for those Latinos categorized as middle-class, the high number of Latino households with three or more wage earners (more than 52 percent among the foreign-born and more than 25 percent among the U.S.-born, compared to 13.5 percent for U.S.-born whites and 19.4 percent for African Americans) suggests the pooling of several working-class salaries under what would appear to be a single middle-class roof.[22] To be contextualized accurately, studies of Latino social class need to look at per capita earning to understand how middle-income wealth is transmitted between generations. It is also important that researchers account for educational levels of wage earners when attempting to describe Latino social mobility. For example, as Rodriguez correctly notes, only 8.9 percent of foreign-born Latinos classified as middle-class had earned bachelor's degrees. Among U.S.-born Latinos categorized as middle-class, only 15.7 percent had earned bachelor's degrees, compared to more than 40 percent for both U.S.- and foreign-born whites.[23] When per capita income, education levels, and the working-class character of Latino labor force participation are taken into account, Latino movement into the middle class is more ambiguous than the household income figures would suggest. Although one can acknowledge that social mobility is occurring, one can also conclude that that progress is recent and still subject to the reversals produced by the transition to a knowledge-based, post-Fordist economy.

Still other analysts point with optimism to the growing number of Latino entrepreneurs as indicators of social mobility, for what better denotes middle-class social position than business ownership? Again, at first glance, the numbers appear impressive. The number of Latino-owned businesses in the Los Angeles area has grown three times faster than the population in recent years. In 1992, California led the nation in Latino-owned business, and Los Angeles County led the state with 109,104 Latino-owned firms employing 65,000 workers, earning $7.8 billion in revenues. Manufacturers of traditional Mexican and Latin American cheeses, such as Industry-based Cacique, Inc., and Paramount-based Ariza Cheese Co., represent a few of the county's multimillion-dollar successes, employing several hundred employees. The average Latino business owner, however, employed about three-fifths of an employee per business, underscoring the ambiguities of Latino entrepreneurship.[24] According to sociologists Ivan Light and Elizabeth Roach, many of the new Latino businesses were created as a defense against under-unemployment, especially among new immigrant arrivals. As employment opportunities for Latinos dropped during the 1990 recession, the number of marginal, unincorporated businesses owned by Latinos tripled to 54,768 from 18,480 in 1980.[25] Most of the unincorporated businesses were started by foreign-born Latinos, many of whom earned slightly below the national median income. In 1990, self-employed Latino entrepreneurs earned an annual mean of $29,599. By contrast, owners of incorporated businesses, most of whom were native-born Latinos, earned a mean of $44,981 a year. Likewise, the foreign-born Latinos realized a $4,737 average adjusted benefit for self-employment; native-born Latinos realized a $9,067 average adjusted annual benefit.[26] And although Latino entrepreneurship increased in Los Angeles, as a group Latinos ranked near the bottom, slightly below whites and slightly above African Americans. Self-employment rates among native- and for-eign-born Latino males averaged 8 percent, and between 4.5 percent and 6.1 percent for native- and foreign-born Latinas.[27] For Latinos at least, entrepreneurship is not a panacea that will deliver the American Dream, but neither has it failed to produce any rewards. Rather, the truth lies somewhere between these extremes. Light and Roach write that the

> growth of Hispanic entrepreneurs certainly drove down the rewards of business ownership among this group to a greater extent than any other. In a way, however, the Hispanic situation was superior to what the whites faced. They were developing new economic niches in garment manufacturing, gardening, and hotel and restaurant work as whites were losing their comfortable niches. Admittedly, the Hispanics were poorly paid, but getting a bad job may be easier to endure than losing a good one.[28]

Despite notable successes, which the media use to illustrate their model-minority narratives, most Latino businesses manage to employ only their entrepreneurs. Moreover, only a fraction of these entrepreneurs, available data show, have obtained the capital to invest in the knowledge-based businesses of the new economy. As a result, the Latino community cannot afford to put all its faith in market forces, when doing so would risk abandoning those with the least technical skills to combat poverty and despair. In other words, although the benefits of the market economy offer promise for a small but growing minority, the working-class Latino majority must preserve worker-oriented social and political action as a short- and long-term option if it hopes to address present and future structural inequalities. But the meaning of worker-oriented social and political action, as we have attempted to show, must be expanded and reconceptualized to incorporate new forms of struggle.

Toward a Class-Oriented Political Culture

To the degree that immigrant Latino and Asian workers continue taking control of local labor institutions, they will create a power base with the autonomy and human and financial resources to influence the electoral process and further diminish the clout of entrenched party machines. The Los Angeles County Federation of Labor, led by Miguel Contreras, together with immigrant rights groups, demonstrated this fact during Gil Cedillo's 1997 primary bid for the Forty-Sixth Assembly District. The federation, which had identified and canvassed nine thousand newly registered voters in the downtown district, brought an unprecedented 45 percent of these voters to the polls by emphasizing Cedillo's labor-organizing credentials and eagerness to fight Governor Wilson's political agenda.[29] Under Contreras's leadership, the 738,000-member federation also helped the Democrats recapture the State Assembly, enact school bond measures, and pass the living wage ordinance.[30]

Enlightened pragmatism, not leftist idealism, requires that present and future Latino leaders fashion an industrial and urban policy that transcends the worn-out discourses of race relations and identity politics. To achieve this, Latino elected leaders need to broaden and deepen their notions of representation to encompass the class interests of their constituents in the context of the new realities of globalized post-NAFTA Fordist production. The foregoing may sound too theoretical for some, but the post-economic realities that permit Mexican capital to invest in Southern California provide the concrete experiences that underlie these abstractions. Latino immigrant workers, Nativo Lopez explains, are "being employed more and more by other immigrants, other Latinos, and Asian immigrant entrepreneurs who are developing small and medium manufacturing or service plants." As these experiences become commonplace, immigrant workers will see through the mystification of ethnic or racial unity to discover that their "fundamental interests are class interests, not racial interests." At that moment of realization, Lopez argues,

> the possibility of developing multinational, multicultural coalitions will become easier. As a result of NAFTA, the owners of the plants will be Mexicans, and the workers in those plants will be Mexicans. The class lines will be more clearly established for our community. I think that's a very good development for fighting racism, and for fighting economic disadvantage.[31]

And as Latinos begin to make the transition from acting as a class in itself to thinking as a class for itself, they can begin to construct a political culture that represents and advances their interests. Lopez believes this sorting-out process has already begun. Cedillo, for example, received his political training while organizing students against Proposition 187 and leading the Los Angeles County Employees Union. Villaraigosa organized for the United Teachers of Los Angeles and served as president of the ACLU.[32] Becerra, leader of the Congressional Hispanic Caucus, demonstrated political courage by visiting Havana, without making apologies to the Cuban American members of the Congressional Hispanic Caucus, and by voting against moving Israel's capital from Tel Aviv to Jerusalem, without making apologies to Westside Democrats.[33] "This new crop of leaders is better educated, both academically, formally, and in their practical organizing experiences," Lopez said in an interview. "I think that we will have better-quality leadership and a greater ability to mobilize more broadly. I think it's possible, absolutely possible."[34]

Reorienting Latino political discourse toward a deeper appreciation of class issues will require Latino leaders, elected or not, to engage in the culture wars. As the Republicans recently demonstrated with their Contract with America and family values rhetoric, it is possible for one side to so dominate the political discourse that opponents are forced to speak that faction's language. Likewise, Latino elected leaders must be prepared to reframe the context of political dialogue in ways that are advantageous to their constituents. Whether at Whittier Narrows, in the heartland of the Greater Eastside, or in the newly won jurisdictions of the San Fernando Valley, reframing the political culture of Los Angeles demands a coherent long-term discursive strategy. The conventional functions of representation, such as lawmaking and issue-oriented debate, must be expanded to accommodate new tasks. The bully pulpit, in other words, must be reconceptualized as both political and cultural space. Timid Latino political leaders who cannot capture the cultural space to articulate a transnational human rights agenda, who fail to attack racialized media representations of immigrant workers and to advance an industrial policy that addresses the needs of their predominantly immigrant and working-class constituents, and who fail to utilize Latino-oriented media in a proactive manner risk reinforcing the existing hegemonic order.

Admittedly, the unequal power relations that define the Los Angeles political landscape, particularly the over concentration of media in the hands of local and transnational corporate elites, present formidable obstacles to Latino representation. But recent history also shows that the preamnesty generation of Latino elected leaders often failed to create a discursive umbrella under which coalition building among progressives and Latino-led grassroots organizations could occur. Although they had attained the bully pulpit, this generation of Latino political leaders rarely published or broadcast their ideas outside their districts or legislative chambers. Worse, their poor to mediocre Spanish-speaking skills hindered their ability to utilize the Spanish-language media effectively, which represents a serious failing.

These Latino leaders, particularly those second- and third-generation Mexican Americans with rudimentary Spanish-speaking skills, have been slow to acknowledge the fact that the local and national Spanish-language media, especially radio and television, have permanently changed the political and cultural landscape of Los Angeles. For better or for worse, Spanish-language media, particularly broadcast forms, increasingly function as the space where Latino panethnicity is modified and constructed. And although advertising and marketing decisions play a large role in how the broadcast media construct Latino ethnicity, the narrow marketing focus of these media also creates significant spaces for other forms of political and cultural dialogue to occur. The anecdotal evidence suggests that increases in local and network Spanish-language television news coverage have helped increase Latino political awareness and participation, especially among urban immigrant audiences. In turn, modest increases in news and public affairs coverage have aided urban Latino politicization in at least two ways.

First, although they lack the financial resources of their counterparts in the English-language media, Spanish-language journalists reporting for Spanish speakers in the United States feel a stronger obligation to inform their audiences. Latino journalists' more developed sense of social responsibility stems from pragmatic acknowledgment that their immigrant audiences rely upon their news reports to survive in a new society. But these journalists and their audiences also, even when using empiricized American news formats, expect to be addressed in different discursive forms. Media researcher Virginia Escalante, a former *Los Angeles Times* reporter who is writing a history of Spanish-language newspapers in the United States, argues that Latino-owned newspapers tend to address their readers as citizens, whereas the major English-language newspapers first view their readers as consumers.[35] Whatever factor predominates, economics or culture, recent content studies show a marked discursive difference between English-language and Spanish-language news styles. For example, Spanish-language television news appears to place a greater emphasis upon reporting the social context surrounding crime, which stands in dramatic contrast to the sensational, decontextualized crime-by-crime water torture practiced by English-language television news.[36]

Second, the Spanish-language news media continue to assume an advocacy role on behalf of their audience, but usually within a narrow range of immigration-related and urban issues. In a lucrative, immigrant-supported media market such as Los Angeles, the Spanish-language broadcast media have acquired the economic independence to take bold stances on certain issues, at least compared to their English-language counterparts. Language and narrow marketing focus, in other words, offer Spanish-language news media a degree of discursive freedom not enjoyed by English- language media. Future studies should determine whether this discursive freedom has produced measurable political results. For example, it would not be unreasonable to hypothesize that the Spanish-language broadcast media's coverage of the Proposition 187 policy debates and the televised beating of a truckload of undocumented Latinos by two Riverside police officers helped to mobilize a large Latino voter turnout.[37] The coverage of the Proposition 187 campaign thus represented a kind of discursive victory, one in which the Spanish-language media succeeded in framing the debate from a pro-immigrant perspective. The coverage became so intensely pro-immigrant that Governor Pete Wilson felt compelled at times to complain that he was being "vilified" by the Spanish-language media. By the time the governor had finished his campaigns for Proposition 187 and the anti-affirmative action initiative, the Spanish-language media had effectively transformed Wilson into the Latino community's number-one enemy, which made sense, especially in marketing terms.

Although some Spanish-language media owners contributed funds for and against the Proposition 187 campaign, the news and public affairs coverage rarely forgot which master the owners served: the immigrant audiences that bought the products advertised on their networks. Even the historically conservative Spanish-language newspaper *La Opinión* took a strong stand against the proposition, "running stories of how different segments of the community might be impacted and on the fear 187 was generating." Publisher Monica Lozano also "put a personal stamp on her opposition, reducing ad rates to solicit money for anti-Prop. 187 groups, helping host a fund-raiser for Taxpayers Against 187, and donating $5,000 of her own money."[38] The boost in voter turnout triggered by Proposition 187 pushed Latinos back into the Democratic camp at a time when a shrinking Republican Party most needed new immigrant blood. Latino leaders and pundits, for their part, treated the strong Latino rejection of Wilson's policies as a blessing. The governor and his Republican allies, they argued, had succeeded in mobilizing Latino voters where others had failed. Yet few pundits or scholars credited the role the Spanish-language media played in mobilizing the Latino vote, or in fixing Wilson's racist and anti-immigrant image in the minds of Latino voters.

Still, Spanish-language media, like other media, have maintained a reactive posture to events that limits their discursive independence. The event-oriented focus of daily news coverage is obviously a structuring influence independent of language, as are the symbiotic relations between the media and the state. Another inhibiting factor is the absence of a dynamic Spanish-language print media. *La Opinión*, still the dominant Spanish-language newspaper in Southern California, remains the weakest link in the city's Latino media ecology. Although the paper continues its historic mission as an important forum for Latin American policy and cultural debates and sports coverage, it has not developed an investigative or political reporting tradition that breaks the major stories that shape policy or precipitate government action. Ideally, a paper like *La Opinión* should have the resources to do the more complicated stories on local politics, economics, and culture that would influence the news budgets of other local Spanish-language media. Moreover, sustained, aggressive, in-depth print reporting could better prepare Latino readers to increase their levels of civic participation and lay the groundwork for more enterprising Spanish-language broadcast reporting. Many had hoped that *La Opinión*'s impressive circulation gains and the infusion of new capital following Times Mirror Corporation's purchase of a half interest in the paper would have resulted in greater editorial independence and a more pronounced improvement in editorial quality. Recently, however, its growth has stalled. The paper's circulation gains have not been able to go beyond the hundred thousand level. And despite the new energy brought to the paper by Associate Publisher Lozano, the conservative family-run paper has yet to make a significantly larger investment in its editorial product. *La Opinión*'s news staff remains small, low paid, and, some say, demoralized, and the paper's imitation of English-language news formats remains uncritical. Others point to an excessively timid management style hamstrung by corporate interference from Times Mirror.[39] Whatever the reasons, *La Opinión* remains an underachiever when it comes to local news. And as we saw in the arena policy debate, the local English-language broadcast or print media cannot be relied upon to provide critical coverage for their own target audiences, let alone underserved Latino, African American, or Asian American audiences.

A comparable disconnect also characterizes the Spanish-language broadcast media's weak ties to the more assimilated Latino intellectuals and political leadership. For the latter groups, success in the university, the publishing world, and legislative politics rests on the ability to communicate in English, not in Spanish. Success in one realm has not directly facilitated the Latino *intelligentsia*'s ability to cultivate support in the other. But given the Spanish-language news media's pro-immigrant stance, and its special access to the country's largest Latino community in Los Angeles, Latino leaders and intellectuals must make a systematic effort to bridge this gap. Latino academics can constructively engage the industry by investing more resources in the study and development of Latino-targeted media; by organizing conferences where academics, journalists, and progressives can discuss ways to improve news coverage; and by conducting workshops where community members can acquire media skills. Starting at the most elementary level, such dialogues could help the professional journalists expand their sourcing contacts in the academic community while providing journalists working in Latino-oriented media a chance to impress upon the academics and intellectuals the informational, rhetorical, and linguistic needs of their media. The Latino intelligentsia could also support the efforts of Spanish-language journalists to improve salaries and working conditions. All too often, journalists in the Spanish-language media are treated like second-class professionals; aside from its demoralizing effects, such treatment hinders the development of a Latino critical infrastructure. Addressing the concerns of Latino news editors who say that Spanish-language journalists lack the knowledge, skills, and contacts to cover local government effectively, Latino academics can use their institutional affiliations to organize special workshops on investigating City Hall and development politics. Better ongoing political and economic reporting could help shift the Spanish-language media from a relatively reactive to a more proactive discursive stance. Better coverage of the political economy could help immigrant audiences expand their levels of political participation beyond the immediate survival issues of immigration, health care, and gang violence.

Despite recent political gains, Latino elected officials in Greater Los Angeles represent another weak discursive link, especially when one contrasts them with the creative, vital, and varied Latino union leaders, community arts organizations, individual artists and intellectuals, church and environmental groups, and postamnesty political leaders who have begun to coalesce with non-Latino progressives on a range of issues. Coalitions such as the Los Angeles Alliance for a New Economy (LAANE) and the Bus Riders Union have reached across ethnic, gender, occupational, and neighborhood divisions to build social movements. As previously mentioned, LAANE and organizations like it continue to challenge the social relations of production within the region's largest cultural industry: the combined amusement, sporting, shopping, and multiscreen movie theater complexes packaged as megacultural destinations.[40] In another context, artists have joined forces with workers to engage important cultural empowerment. *Oficios Ocultos/Hidden Labor*, created by Common Threads Artists, stands out as one of the most interesting and creative of these collaborations. Inside department store windows, where displays formerly showed off women's high fashion, a collective of women artists, academics, and garment workers narrated the history of female garment workers in Los Angeles. The display, or rather counterdisplay, illustrated how workers and progressives can expand the arena of contestation by occupying, reinterpreting, and denaturalizing one of the spaces the garment and retail clothing industry has used for fetishizing women's bodies.

Fortunately, some of the discursive preconditions for building a progressive coalition in Los Angeles already exist. Buoyed by the emergence of a Latino and Asian working class in the nation's largest industrial area, the postamnesty Latino leaders are already promoting varying degrees of multiethnic, multigendered, and class-sensitive social justice agendas. This new cadre of leaders will need to develop strategies that reject the racializing identity politics of the present and previous decades and find ways to address Los Angeles residents who believe that their city is fatally fractured, especially for suburban home owners who assume reactionary postures when negotiating their demands for equality with other groups. Obviously, leadership that fails to address the increasing disparity between rich and poor, between racialized inner-city residents and multiethnic suburban home owners, between the landscapes of elite leisure and degraded places of industrial production, cannot expect much success. At the same time, these leaders will have to find ways to deconstruct the elite discourses that promote lopsided, top-down notions of corporate development under the aegis of multicultural tourism and economic empowerment. Moreover, the Latino and Latina leadership of the twenty-first century should begin preparing answers to the divisive, racializing initiatives the next recession is sure to spawn.[41] As LAANE and other groups have begun to demonstrate, an effective progressive agenda can advance simultaneously on political, economic, and cultural fronts because these seemingly distinct spheres are in fact mutually constitutive. So far, these movements have combined an updated class analysis of low-wage immigrant labor and the discourse of multicultural diversity to build tolerance and unity amid ethnic differences. The challenge of integrating class and cultural discourses is more than theoretical.

Latinos, who constitute the majority of industrial workers and residents in both the city of Los Angeles and Los Angeles County, currently endure a symbolic economy that devalues their labor, creativity, and political participation. Patterns of representation have material effects to the degree that they reinforce existing power arrangements. Conventional labor and political organizing alone cannot challenge the cultural discourses that keep immigrant workers isolated and alienated. Moreover, in the first decade of the twenty-first century, Latinos will gain only slim majority margins. And given the still-lagging rates of Latino voter participation and the prevailing class and ethnic divisions that fragment the regional political landscape, no one elite or social sector can attain dominance without building coalitions. The process of weaving a coalition along class lines will help, but it will not overcome the years of socially constructed distrust that divide potential allies along the fault lines of class, ethnicity, gender, and sexual orientation.

Descontructing "Race Relations"

Constructing the Latino metropolis must also demystify the culture industries that construct and reinforce the discourses of race itself. This task requires an understanding of the new linkages between culture industries and the new urban political economy, an understanding of the changing social relations within and between cultural sectors, and a deeper appreciation of the vitality of lived popular culture in the Latino metropolis.

Although Latinos engage the city's culture wars without moral advantages, are clearly susceptible to petty tribalism, and are capable of racializing themselves and others, they nevertheless possess a historic and cultural legacy that can, in the long term, help overturn two particularly divisive aspects of urban "race relations." First, Latinos must elaborate a critical discourse of cultural *mestizaje*, one shorn of essentializing romanticism, to disarm racialized discourses that disguise the economic causes of urban conflict and social inequality. If there is anything the lesson of mestizaje teaches, it is that pseudo-scientific racial categories are crisscrossed by the actualities of Latino genetic diversity and cultural hybridity. Second, a critical discourse of mestizaje grounded in the realities of the global city can be turned against those discourses of cultural production that treat ethnicity and race as commodities of "multicultural" tourism. As the vitality of popular culture continually reminds us, the freeways of cultural appropriation run in two directions. Edward W. Said emphasizes this point when he writes, "Cultural experience or indeed every cultural form is radically, quintessentially hybrid, and if it has been the practice of the West since Immanuel Kant to isolate cultural and aesthetic realms from the worldly domain, it is now time to rejoin them."[42]

What has not become sufficiently evident to Said and other cultural studies scholars, however, are the groundbreaking contributions of Latino intellectuals on the meanings and forms of mestizo hybridity, particularly when the discourse is expressed as one of the earliest critiques of Western colonialism.[43] In fact, *Chicana* feminist scholars have done some of the most ambitious work on this subject by resituating mestizaje in and along the borderlands.[44] The result has been to expand the meanings of mestizaje from a cultural to a political metaphor and, in the process, reconceptualize the meaning of culture itself.

Contrary to the construction of the southwestern borderlands and their Latinized cities as a zone of degradations, the Latinos who reside there, argues Renato Rosaldo, occupy one of the world's richest zones of "creative cultural production," which the dominant discourse renders as transitional and empty.

> Similarly, the borders between nations, classes, and cultures were endowed with a curious kind of hybrid invisibility. They seemed to be a little of this and a little of that, and not quite one or the other. Movements between such seemingly fixed entities as nations or social classes were relegated to the analytical dustbin

of cultural invisibility. Immigrants and socially mobile individuals appeared culturally invisible because they were no longer what they once were, and not yet what they could become.[45]

In many ways, journalists' nonresponsiveness to multiple Latino identities resembles the academy's attitude toward border regions. Academic institutions maintain "fields" of social science the way the media inscribe the "race relations" discourse—by creating and maintaining boundaries that mutually validate their discursive authority. Under such marginalizing circumstances, political *mestizaje* survives as an outlaw discourse, acknowledged by Latino intellectuals and lived by the Latino community, but ignored by the nation's dominant institutions. Marginalization, however, does not imply the absence of a documented history or discourses. Since the end of the nineteenth century, Latin American writers and intellectuals such as José Martí have translated lived *mestizaje* into written discourse.

Although Latino *mestizaje* in the United States has its antecedents in Mexican and Latin American history, its "lived" experience in the United States has produced discursive innovations. On the U.S. side of the border, immigration accelerates the process through which Latinos simultaneously encounter the First World and other immigrants from the developing world whom they would have been less likely to meet had they stayed at home. On the U.S. side, the meaning and experience of *mestizaje* have also evolved beyond the bounds of official ideology, such as Mexico's ruling PRI, which has historically constructed its meanings so as to maintain a one-party state. Whereas in Mexico the term *mestizaje* have been co-opted to legitimate and integrate the nation's mestizo middle class and regional cultures, in the United States its lived experience occurs beyond official sanction and outside of institutionalized urban "race relations."

In its most mundane form, *mestizaje* on the U.S. side of the border expresses itself as a refusal to prefer one language, one genome, one national or cultural heritage at the expense of others. Culturally speaking, then, *mestizaje* is radically inclusive, a stubborn refusal to make the Sophie's choice between cultural identities and races. At times, its inclusions take the form of a literal transgression of political borders. These transgressions can be, especially when expressed by artists and intellectuals, overtly ideological. Thus, in the manner of Caliban, who uses Prospero's language to blaspheme his colonial enterprise, mestizo hybridity makes a virtue of appropriating elite culture for popular ends. Publishing ethnographies of elite power, for example, represents one way of turning the methods of neocolonialism against the neoliberal global city, in a practice Guillermo Gómez-Peña aptly calls "reverse anthropology."

The day-to-day expressions of *mestizaje*, however, are adaptive. Stated in economic terms, the globalization of capital, with its power to penetrate and dominate regional markets and undermine native economies, obliges the Mexican peasant or Guatemalan worker to ignore certain rules and boundaries in order to survive. Sentimental loyalty to a particular nation-state and, by extension, that state's idealized "traditional" culture becomes an impoverishing, even life-threatening luxury. To this extent, then, the lived transcultural experience of mestizaje must also be considered transnational and potentially postnational. And policies such as granting voting status to immigrants in school board elections, for example, represent important ways of granting institutional recognition to Latino political *mestizaje*.

To again borrow Gómez-Peña's phrasing, the border crosser thus operates as a kind of cultural "cross-dresser" who willfully blurs political, racial, or cultural borders in order to survive in an unjustly constructed world. The lived experience of cultural *mestizaje* is not schizoid, nor does it lack the boundedness to produce identity. Instead, Latinos have evolved a countertradition, or anti-aesthetic, of juggling languages, music, clothing styles, foods, gender, anything with which to fashion a more meaningful social and cultural coherence. And it is this aspect of cultural *mestizaje* that allows Latinos to participate in and express the most contemporary manifestations of modernity.

Whatever the terminology, the "styles" of mestizo cultural construction evolve dialectically, generating adaptive responses to changing material conditions and forms of cultural representation. Contrary to the musings of some European postmodernists, who see the multicultural Americas as an orgy of limitless conjunctions, heterodoxy in this hemisphere occurs within materially and culturally defined combinatory systems. Some combinatories are identified with specific cultural spaces—Nuevo Laredo or New Orleans—whereas others, like thousands of migrant Mexican workers, float or migrate, as it were, from place to place, physical or virtual, as individual or communal stylistic expressions. Whether rooted or moving, mestizo border culture coheres, acquires integrity and patterning from its mode of construction, which, depending on the circumstances, may be pragmatic, strategic, or ideological in its orientation to the world. Over time, these strategies take on the appearance of what some would call tradition but could more properly resemble the dialectic between genetics and environment. Like an individual's DNA, cultural *mestizaje* obeys its own rules of inclusion and exclusion, conjunction and disjunction. Whatever internal consistency it achieves is derived over time from the culture's repertoire of responses to a specific landscape, its material conditions and social relations. Latinos may have evolved a particular style of border crossing, but they are not unique in this practice.

"All of us," Rosaldo writes, "inhabit an interdependent late-twentieth-century world marked by borrowing and lending across porous national and cultural boundaries that are saturated with inequality, power, and domination."[46] Chicanos who live in the borderlands know this instinctively when they acknowledge their cultural differences and similarities to Mexicans or other Latinos.

However, *mestizaje* is one of many strategic responses to the decline of the imperial West, and is thus symptomatic of a world in flux. The lived cultural experience of more and more people occurs outside the cultural norms idealized by the state and its enabling institutional apparatus. Cultural *mestizaje's* aggressive disregard for boundaries and unexpected inclusions should therefore be appreciated for its political possibilities in a context of global transformations.

Giving political expression to the praxis of mestizo border culture also offers a pragmatic alternative to representations that thwart coalition building in a multicultural city. The news media's reiteration of the "race relations" discourse has framed inner-city life as a competition in which contestants are defined by means of racial taxonomy. For Latinos, whose lived cultural experience spills beyond racialized boundaries, bending to or cooperating with the urban politics framed by the "race relations" discourse only delays the birth of a new political culture. Representations that encapsulate Latinos in essentialized racial or ethnic identities discourage use of the very tool—knowledge of their profound hybridity—with which they can unmask the lie of "race" and build an urban politics based upon commonalities of culture and class. Coalition builders in Los Angeles, Latino or not, will fail in imagining, let alone constructing, a new hegemony if they continue to represent their potential allies and friends in racialized terms and ignore the common interests created by the post-Fordist economy. The failure to deconstruct the discourse of "race relations" may make the attainment of Latino majority status, even when backed by political power, a cruel disappointment. Latino leaders who continue to perpetuate minority thinking by advancing their narrow ethnic interest in fact put off the moment when they might reap the fruits of majority power. Coming to this realization will mark the first step toward political maturity for Latino leadership. Acting upon this realization, by developing appropriate strategy and tactics, represents the second challenge.

Finally, a dialogue between journalists and intellectuals on cultural *mestizaje* could help reinforce certain healthy discursive tendencies already present in Latino journalism. Latino academics should acknowledge those moments when the Spanish-language media effectively counter the mainstream media's racializing representations of Latinos and criticize the Spanish-language media when they reaffirm "race" as an objective reality. Latino intellectuals should encourage the Spanish-language media's efforts to construct a pan-Latino political culture based upon a critical analysis of Latino multiethnicity and criticize those media when they commodify *mestizaje* as a means to mercenary marketing ends.

Constructing a political dialogue that mitigates the weaknesses and exploits the strengths of Latino media becomes all the more crucial if we remember that the discourses of dominance will continue to face crises of signification. Some crises will be triggered by social upheavals caused by the growing disparities of late postindustrial capitalism; whereas others will result from the "multicultural" conflict powered by migration, demographic change, and the continuing communication revolution. The blurring distinction between media programming and computer software will also continue to produce periods of discourse disequilibrium, as will the continuing decline of Fordist mass media and emerging post-Fordist demassified information industries. The atomization of media markets into ever smaller units will provide temporary tactical opportunities for Latino cultural workers to develop innovative progressive programming for economically viable ethnic audiences, but only if they can obtain needed technical assistance. The recent upsurge in computer purchases among Latinos suggests that some of the cultural benefits of Internet access may become more widely available to middle- and working-class Latinos than initially anticipated. In this way, members of the emerging ethnic pluralities in the nation's image-making cities, both as consumers and workers, may acquire the tools with which to mobilize discursive responses when social and cultural upheavals recur. Each moral panic constructed by the state and the media also presents an opportunity for critical analysis and community action when anticipated in the Latino metropolis. The Latino community's success at advancing a political as well as cultural discourse of *mestizaje* can thus acquire strategic significance, both for the community itself and for other communities disappeared by dominant media discourses. Counterdiscourse based upon inclusion, that renders hybridity, ambiguity, and border experience meaningful and empowering, and that makes racialized categories uninhabitable, will provide a nation as heterodox as the United States the acid with which to deconstruct its prisons of race and gender. To the degree a discourse of cultural *mestizaje* is not touted as a new orthodoxy, we believe it represents the greatest contribution Latinos will yet make to the United States. And Los Angeles, the nation's multicultural metropolis, will be the place where that contribution will first become evident.

Notes

1. George Skelton, "Now Latinos Are Changing the Face of Both Parties," *Los Angeles Times*, November 23, 1998, A1.

2. A recent study by the United Way of Greater Los Angeles found that as of September 1999 there were 240 Latinos holding elective office in L.A. County, most serving in city posts and on school boards. See United Way of Greater Los Angeles, Research Services, *American Dream Makers: Executive Summary* (Los Angeles, January 2000).

3. Gregory Rodriguez, "The Impending Collision of Eastside and Westside," *Los Angeles Times*, August 3, 1997, M1, M3.

4. R. Scott Moxley, "No Hits, One Run, 200 Errors: *Hermandad* Probes' Central Figure Returns from Mexico," O.C. *Weekly*, August 14–20, 1998, 14.

5. Moxley, "No Hits," 14.

6. Ted Rohrlich, "Latino Voting in State Surged in 1996 Election," *Los Angeles Times*, December 31, 1997, A1.

7. Rohrlich, "Latino Voting," A1.

8. Rodriguez, "The Impending Collision," M1, M3.

9. Rodriguez, "The Impending Collision," M3.

10. Nativo Lopez, interview by Victor Valle, tape recording, Occidental College, Los Angeles, October 14, 1998.

11. Lopez interview, October 14, 1998.

12. Lopez interview, October 14, 1998.

13. Beth Shuster, "New Latino Political Picture Offers Opportunity," *Los Angeles Times*, October 5, 1998, B12–B13.

14. David M. Grant, Melvin L. Oliver, and Angela D. James, "African Americans: Social and Economic Bifurcation," in *Ethnic Los Angeles*, ed. Roger Waldinger and Mehdi Bozorgmehr (New York: Russell Sage Foundation, 1996), 382.

15. Nativo Lopez, interview by Victor Valle, tape recording, Occidental College, Los Angeles, October 3, 1998.

16. Jim Newton, "Council Size Issue to Be Put to the Voters," *Los Angeles Times*, October 20, 1998, B2.

17. Lopez interview, October 14, 1998.

18. Manuel Pastor Jr., "Advantaging the Disadvantaged through International Trade" (Merril College, University of California, Santa Cruz, July 1998, photocopy), 11–13.

19. Michael Rustin, "The Politics of Post-Fordism; or, The Trouble with 'New Times,'" *New Left Review* 175 (May/June 1989): 66.

20. Mike Davis, *Ecology of Fear: Los Angeles and the Imagination of Disaster* (New York: Metropolitan, 1998), 404.

21. Gregory Rodriguez, "The Emerging Latino Middle Class," Pepperdine University Institute for Public Policy AT&T paper, October 1996, 7–12.

22. Rodriguez, "The Emerging Latino," 12.

23. Rodriguez, "The Emerging Latino," 12–13.

24. Robert A. Rosenblatt and Vicki Torres, "Number of Latino Firms Up 76 Percent in 5 Years; California Has Most," *Los Angeles Times*, July 11, 1996, D1; Lee Romney, "Hispanic Cheese: Haute Item," *Los Angeles Times*, June 16, 1998, A1, A32.

25. Ivan Light and Elizabeth Roach, "Self-Employment: Mobility Ladder or Economic Lifeboat?" in *Ethnic Los Angeles*, ed. Roger Waldinger and Mehdi Bozorgmehr (New York: Russell Sage Foundation, 1996), 198.

26. Light and Roach, "Self-Employment," 200–201, see Table 7.2.

27. Light and Roach, "Self-Employment," 205, see Table 7.4.

28. Light and Roach, "Self-Employment," 209.

29. Rohrlich, "Latino Voting," A1.

30. Sandra Hernandez, "Inside Agitators: The City's Most Effective Activists," *L.A. Weekly*, October 2–8, 1998, 38.

31. Lopez interview, October 3, 1998.

32. Harold Meyerson, "Activists Turned Elected Officials," *L.A. Weekly*, October 2–8, 1998, 30.

33. Rodriguez, "The Impending Collision," M1, M3.

34. Lopez interview, October 3, 1998.

35. Escalante cited in Melita Marie Garza, "Hola, America! Newsstand 2000," *Media Studies Journal* 8 (Summer 1994): 157.

36. Vivian Chavez and Lori Dorfman, "Spanish-Language Television News Portrayals of Youth and Violence in California," *International Quarterly of Community Health Education* 16, no. 2 (1996): 121–38.

37. Unfortunately, the underdeveloped state of Latino media studies means that cause-and-effect correlations between media coverage and political participation can still only be surmised.

38. Sandra Hernandez, "Stuck in Translation: *La Opinión* Searches for Readers— and a Mission—in the Times' Shadow," *L.A. Weekly*, June 11–17, 1999, 6.

39. Hernandez, "Stuck in Translation," 2–9.

40. For example, the Bus Riders Union, led by Eric Mann, the labor veteran who in the 1980s battled GM to stop it from shutting down its Van Nuys plant, organized a cross section of Los Angeles's working-class bus riders to launch a civil rights court battle that stopped the MTA from allocating hundreds of millions in public funds for sorely needed bus service to underground rail projects targeted for a tiny minority of suburban, middle-class commuters.

41. Sharon Zukin, *The Culture of Cities* (Cambridge, Mass.: Blackwell, 1995), 263.

42. Edward W. Said, *Culture and Imperialism* (New York: Alfred A. Knopf, 1993), 58.

43. Roberto Gonzalez Echevarria, "Latin America and Comparative Literature," in *Poetics of the Americas: Race, Founding, and Textuality*, ed. Bainard Cowan and Jefferson Humphries (Baton Rouge: Louisiana State University Press, 1997), 50.

44. See, for example, the incisive work of Sonia Saldívar-Hull, *Feminism on the Border: Chicano Gender Politics and Literature* (Berkeley: University of California Press, 2000).

45. Renato Rosaldo, *Culture and Truth: The Remaking of Social Analysis* (Boston: Beacon, 1989), 209.

46. Rosaldo, *Culture and Truth*, 217.

*　　*　　*

Questions

1. What are the changes that make it necessary to negotiate and reconceptualize the role of Latinos in the United States?
2. Do the conditions described by Valle and Torres lead to the possibility for Chicanos in southern California to establish regional autonomy?
3. How persuasive is the argument that class interests will override ethnic conflicts between Latino/as, African Americans, Asians, Anglos, and other groups?
4. If the Latino/a community "cannot afford to put all its faith in market forces," what other options are available? And what might be the implications of such options?
5. To what extent do or do not the views in this piece regarding culture and race echo other concepts of "culture"?

PART III

CUBANS AND AMERICANS

∽

The Treaty of Paris: Exchanging Colonial Masters or Establishing Relations of Mutual Desire?

Francisco Hernández Vázquez

While Secretary of State John Hay famously titled it a "splendid little war," Puerto Ricans and Cubans were not impressed by this significant historical shift from one colonial master to another. In effect, with this treaty they went from Spanish colonies, to independence, to U.S. American colonialism. The Treaty of Paris of April 11, 1898, however, also represents a major turning point in the history of the United States. This is when the United States itself was born as a twentieth-century world power, as an imperial democracy (engaged in cultural, economic, and political colonialism while ostensibly promoting democracy). When the United States won the Spanish-American War, which was fought mostly on Cuban soil, from April to August 1898, they "won" Puerto Rico, Guam, the Marianas, Samoa, Panamá, the Philippine Islands (until 1946 when they expelled U.S. troops), and Cuba (until 1959, when Fidel Castro took over). Even though this war took place a little over one hundred years ago, the implications for Puerto Ricans and Cubans are very much alive today. Will Puerto Rico remain a colony, become independent, or become the fifty-first state of the United States? Will Cuba continue to be independent or will Cuban Americans, given the opportunity, attempt to make Cuba part of the United States? But we are getting ahead of the story.

There are several different explanations of what led to the Spanish-American War. The benign view is that the United States was just responding to the cries for help on the part of oppressed peoples. (That sounds like the political debate regarding Iraq.) Another view is that the United States needed to control Puerto Rico and Cuba for military strategic reasons (see map) and provoked the war when it was clear that these countries were about to become independent. Others say that the expanding U.S. economy needed new markets. Indeed, within a wide historical context there seems to be two parallel tracks. One is the revolutionary war against Spain and the desire to become a modern society like the United States. The other, more problematic track is that the Cuban interests for freedom and democracy did not fit with the United States' plan for economic and political control of Cuba.

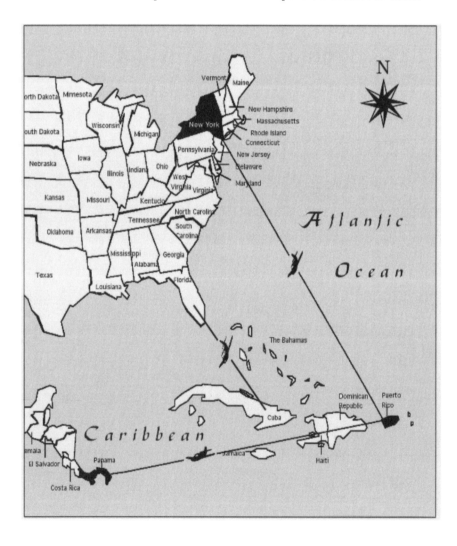

In this section, we look first at the historical context, then to the construction of close ties between the Cuban and U.S. American people, which are expanded on in chapters 13 and 14. Let us follow the stepping-stones that led these two peoples from what Pérez calls "relations of mutual desire" to the two governments becoming bitter enemies for the last half century to the point of bringing about a nuclear confrontation between the Soviet Union and the United States—this is the closest that the world has been to a nuclear war and the destruction of civilization as we know it!

The larger historical context is that Cubans, Puerto Ricans, and Filipinos were engaged in the latest round of struggles against European imperialism started by the Haitian African slaves under the leadership of François Dominique Toussaint L'Overure on May 6, 1794 (leading to Haiti's independence from France). In 1810, this war for independence continued with Father Miguel Hidalgo in Mexico and Antonio José de Sucre, José de San Martín, and Simon Bolívar in Spanish South America during the following three decades (see chapter 2). Unlike Mexico, which became independent in 1821, Cuba and Puerto Rico remained colonies of Spain throughout the nineteenth century. (The U.S. government did not allow the South American liberator Bolívar to free these two islands.) For several decades, however, the Cuban people themselves, *on their own*, rebelled against Spanish repression. First there was the Ten Years' War (1868–78), then the Little War (1879–80), and finally the War of Independence (1895–98). (Incidentally, this last one took the life of the great poet and liberator José Martí, the one individual who is admired by Cubans of every political persuasion and by people throughout the world. He wrote the poem that became the popular song *Juan Tanamera.*)

By 1898, it was clear to everyone that the Cuban insurgents were about to defeat the Spanish forces and gain independence. In April 1898, President William McKinley requested U.S. congressional authority to intervene militarily in Cuba, supposedly to serve as a neutral party to stop the fighting between Cubans and Spaniards (again, echoes with Iraq). Nevertheless, the Cuban revolutionary leaders considered this military intervention a declaration of war against them and vowed to fight against the United States. A compromise was reached through the Teller Amendment, which, after the war, led to the Platt Amendment, and this is discussed in more detail in chapter 14. It is precisely at this point that, mysteriously, the warship USS *Maine* just happen to explode while anchored in the Havana harbor (up until today, no one knows how it happened), and this was the pretext for the United States to declare war on Spain.

But there is another insidious game of truth going on here having to do with race and the fear of the masses of people (which is odd for a democracy to be afraid of "the people"). The U.S. government had earlier *supported* Spain in their war against the Cuban people, the same *independentistas* that they now wanted to help. Why would the United States forget its own revolutionary roots, its own struggle against European oppression and turn against those compatriots who struggled for freedom? Because the United States and the Cuban elite class had feared an independent Cuba for a long time: They believed that with the large number of Afro-Cubans, the country would experience political instability, social conflict, and economic chaos (as they saw happen in Haiti). This belief was based on the demographic numbers: By the 1850s, *criollos* (Spaniard born in Spanish America) were 44 percent and blacks were 56 percent of the population. In this tragic but common game of truth, that is, after its own Civil War, and as U.S. economic and political interests changed, villains turned into heroes at the snap of a finger. Unfortunately, one often finds such revolutionary discontinuities in the ongoing quest for economic democracy. Furthermore, one also finds distinct players in these games of truth; let us look closer at the role of the Cuban people.

The United States and Cuba: Relations of Mutual Desire

In many ways, shaped by their geopolitical position within a sugar global economy and strategic geographical location, Cubans were the first Latinos/as to become U.S. cultural citizens. Cubans were conceived as Cuban Americans as early as 1848, when U.S. president James K. Polk offered Spain $100 million for the island. (The same year, the United States paid Mexico $15 million for half of Mexico and as a war settlement.) Four years later President Franklin Pierce upped the offer to $130 million, without success. As for the Cuban people, their experience of the United States can be traced to the early 1850s. This is a time when Cubans in the United States and on the island were searching for ways to give expression to their own sense of nationality, and they found a model in the United States. And at the same time, the United States itself was undergoing fundamental geopolitical and economic change; it had just expanded its territory from sea to sea with the conquest of northern Mexico. Louis A. Pérez makes several key observations worth mentioning here.[1] Over three successive generations, Cubans of all classes and ages, men and women, and black and white emigrated to the Unites States to escape life in colonial Cuba and to plot the revolution against Spain. These included the people who would play a major role in the construction of *cubanismo*, of Cuban identity and nationality. More incisively, "they early developed the type of familiarity [with U.S. Americans] often reserved for a people of the same nation."[2]

As an alternative to Spanish rule, Cubans contemplated a life similar to the one they had experienced in the United States. Consequently, their sense of self and of nation and many of their values, such as the affirmation of modernity, progress, and above all civilization, were adopted from the United States. "At some point late in the nineteenth century," Pérez writes, "it became all but impossible for Cubans to contemplate their future, especially their future well-being, without pausing first to reflect on their relationship to North Americans." These circumstances paved "the way for the subsequent arrival of North Americans as bearers of more of the same truths after the U.S. intervention in 1898."[3] There are important implications here.

An important difference from the conquest of northern Mexicans, of all classes, is that although economic and political elements were obviously (and necessarily) involved, in the case of Cubans, it was more a case of cultural seduction. Pérez's thesis is, in effect, that "Cuban participation was indispensable to the success of U.S. hegemony and that Cubans bore some responsibility for their own domination, although it must be emphasized that few at the time would have remotely construed their condition as one of 'subjugation.'"[4] The same judgment may be said to apply to the Mexican elites from northern Mexico. Yet coercion and violence, low wages, and racism were a part of the relationship. Consequently, as with any political relation, the possibility for conflict is always there, ready to erupt when the economic and political conditions are ripe, such as they were in the late 1950s with the arrival of Fidel Castro. The following two chapters, the text by Pérez and the Platt Amendment, describe two contradictory aspects of the U.S.-Cuban relations of mutual desire: The Cuban people see the United States as a model to emulate, whereas the U.S. government sees Cuba as a colony to exploit.

Before we conclude, it is appropriate to compare the impact that the Treaty of Paris and its aftermath had on Cuba and Puerto Rico. Puerto Rico was immediately incorporated into the United States and governed by a military and then a civil government and to this day, by the U.S. Congress. On the other hand, Cubans had enough of a military presence to win the freedom to elect their own political representatives, as long as they did not threaten U.S. interests. Puerto Ricans were eventually declared U.S. citizens, whereas Cubans have always remained citizens of their country. So far.

Notes and Suggestions for Further Research

1. Louis A. Pérez, *On Becoming Cuban: Identity, Nationality and Culture* (Chapel Hill: University of North Carolina Press, 1999).

2. Pérez, *On Becoming Cuban*, 6.

3. Pérez, *On Becoming Cuban*, 7.

4. Pérez, *On Becoming Cuban*, 10.

~

CHAPTER THIRTEEN

Meanings in Transition
Louis A. Pérez

What Eduardo Galeano calls the "sugar-ocracy" (government by sugar), established since the English invasion of Cuba in 1762, is precisely what paved the way for the U.S. cultural and economic colonization of Cuba. This particular set of material conditions that ostensibly included commercial trade unique to each country's needs and a transfer of technology (steamships, railroads, telegraph) also led to the need for U.S.-trained personnel.

By 1850, the United States was absorbing one-third of all Cuban trade, selling it more and buying more from it than Spain, whose colony it was; the Stars and Stripes fluttered from more than half the ships arriving at the island. A Spanish traveler found U.S.-made sewing machines in remote Cuban villages in 1859. The main streets of Havana were paved with New England granite.[1]

U.S. Americans began to arrive in great numbers (doubling their numbers between 1846 and 1862) and to dominate the local economy. Incidentally, many of the newcomers to Cuba were transients on their way to the California gold rush. The reaction of the Spanish authorities was similar to that of the Mexican authorities with respect to Texas: to consider restricting the acquisition of land by U.S. Americans. To the chagrin of many Cubans, the English language also began to spread throughout the island. As in the case of northern Mexico, among the U.S. Americans settling in Cuba were drifters, deserters, fugitives, and escaped convicts.

In the following text, we see the other side of the two-way traffic between the United States and Cuba: Cubanization of the United States. This chapter provides details regarding the tens of thousands who went to the United States for tourism, for education, for employment, to escape political repression, or to plot the revolution against Spain and describes the many levels of their integration into U.S. society. Most importantly, it discusses how the emigration served to forge many vital elements of Cuban nationality. The discourse on nation benefited from the freedom to discuss, communicate, and publish. The discourse on nation also expanded from the *criollo* elite to include statements from the working class and the poor and also extended to include the role of women. We consider this as a further illustration of a quest for public citizenship.

Notes and Suggestions for Further Research

1. Eduardo Galeano, *Open Veins of Latin America: Five Centuries of the Pillage of a Continent* (New York: Monthly Review Press, 1977), 71.

*　　*　　*

Throughout the nineteenth century Cubans went to the United States by the tens of thousands, as tourists and travelers, vacationers and visitors, for education and employment, to escape political repression and plot colonial revolution. They represented a broad population: planters, merchants, manufacturers, workers, and members of the middle class, including attorneys, engineers, physicians, dentists, journalists, teachers, publishers, writers, and students. Among them were intellectuals José Antonio Saco and Rafael María Mendive; journalists Carmela Nieto de Herrera, Víctor Muñoz, Enrique Piñeyro, Julio Villoldo, Rafael Serra, and Raimundo Cabrera; labor leaders Carlos Baliño and Diego Vicente Tejera; historian Pedro José Guiteras; painter Leopoldo Romañach; poets Miguel Teurbe Tolón and Bonifacio Byrne; and novelists Cirilo Villaverde, Miguel de Carrión, Carlos Loveira, and Luis Rodríguez Embil.

Cubans integrated themselves at all levels of North American society. They attended school, obtained jobs, set up households, and raised families in communities across the United States. They established medical and dental practices and opened law offices. They engaged in all types of commercial activities. Many operated small business enterprises and retail stores. They adapted to North American ways of doing business, used local newspapers to advertise their goods and services, and learned that good business meant prompt service and competitive pricing. In local advertisements Antonio López, who owned the United States Laundry in Key West, assured prospective customers of "promptness in delivery and moderation in price [that] will prove satisfactory to all."[1] Luis M. Arredondo, who graduated from Manhattan College in 1882 subsequently worked as an interpreter for various New York hotels. The number of Cuban-owned hotels and boardinghouses increased throughout the nineteenth century; many served as the point of entry for newly arrived émigrés.[2]

Cubans bought countless retail stores, cafes and restaurants, pharmacies, barbershops, and *bodegas* (general stores). In New York, Manuel García Cuervo owned the *Bodega Cubana* and sold products of Cuba and *sanwiches* of all types. Julián Moreno was proprietor of the Restaurant Cubano, where "the food is Cuban, it's good, and moderately priced." Emiliano Pérez operated the barbershop in the lobby of Central Hotel. José Guillermo Díaz, who identified himself as an "ex-professor of the Faculty of Pharmacy at the University of Havana," operated the Columbia Pharmacy on Lexington and Eighty-seven Street. Echemendía and Company was a Cuban-owned publishing house. Néstor Ponce de León and Ignacio Mora owned bookstores. *Patria*'s roster of Cuban advertisers in New York between 1892 and 1895 listed forty cigar manufacturers, thirty-five physicians, twenty-five merchants, twenty attorneys, fifteen music teachers, six dentists, five bodegas, four restaurants, three drugstores, and two colegios.[3] In Key West, Gabriel Ayala owned the Nuevo Siglo grocery store, J. Avelino Delgado operated the Singer Sewing Machine agency, and D. Báez and Company managed a popular dry goods store. In Tampa, the Valdés Brothers operated a successful dry goods establishment. Manuel Moreno de la Torre, proprietor of El Bazar Americano, sold shoes, hats, and "Cuban style clothing"; Manuel Viñas's La María bakery sold "Cuban and American style bread." Marcos I. Sánchez operated a real estate office, Francisco Ysern was the proprietor of the Salón Central liquor store, and Antonio Salazar managed El Central restaurant.

Cubans were appointed to government positions and elected to political office at the municipal, state, and federal levels. In Key West, Alejandro Mendoza, Enrique Esquinaldo, Rogelio Gómez, and Juan María Reyes served as justices of the peace; Alfredo Reynoso was chief of police, and Juan Busto, Delio Cobo, Marcos Mesa, Juan Carbonell, Manuel Varela, and José Valdés were members of the city council. Isaac Carrillo received a federal appointment as southern district attorney, and Carlos Manuel de Céspedes and Manuel Govín were installed as officers in the U.S. customhouse in Key West. Céspedes subsequently won the mayoral seat in Key West, and Govín served as postmaster of Jacksonville. José Alejandro Huau was elected to four terms on the Jacksonville city council. Celestino Cañizares became mayor of Ocala. Manuel Moreno, Manuel Patricio Delgado, José Gonzalo Pompés, and

Fernando Figueredo Socarrás were sent to the Florida legislature. Figueredo Socarrás, a Rensselaer graduate, served as superintendent of schools in Hillsborough County and mayor of West Tampa. The first West Tampa city council included Vidal Cruz, S. Fleitas, Martín Herrera, J. D. Silva, and R. Someillán. In 1874 Aniceto G. Menocal was appointed chief engineer in the U.S. Navy and supervised all canal surveys in Panama and Nicaragua. He later designed the naval gun plant in Washington, D.C., and helped establish the naval base in the Philippines before retiring with the rank of commander. Joaquín Castillo Duany held a commission in the U.S. Navy and was assigned as surgeon to the 1881 Polar expedition. José Primelles Agramonte, who in 1887 graduated from Columbia University with a degree in civil engineering, obtained employment with the New York City Streets Department. Juan Guiteras served a tour of duty as a physician in the U.S. Army and subsequently joined the staff of the Marine Hospital Service. Charles Hernández was raised in Brockton, Massachusetts, where he attended public school, worked for the Brockton Electric Light Works, and served nearly a decade in the Massachusetts National Guard. Sotero E. Escarza graduated in civil engineering from Rensselaer in 1894 and for the next five years worked in the Pennsylvania Railroad Division of Bridges. José Agustín Quintero received a law degree from Harvard in 1849 and settled in New Orleans, where he was a member of the editorial staff of the *Picayune*. During the Civil War he served in the Confederate diplomatic corps in Latin America.

Still others fully integrated themselves into North American society, acquiring new identities and new careers, and went back to Cuba as representatives of U.S. interests. Pedro Bustillo graduated from the New York Business College, obtained U.S. citizenship, and returned to Havana in 1883 as the general agent of the Equitable Life Assurance Society. Another Business College graduate, Felipe Estrada, directed the *Departamento Hispano Americano* of the New York Life Insurance Company, also in Havana. Hipólito Dumois from Santiago de Cuba was educated at St. John's College in New York before taking a job with the American Ore Dressing Company copper mines in Oriente. Joaquín Chalons earned an engineering degree in North America, then returned to work for the Steel Ore Company in Santiago de Cuba. Esteban Duque Estrada graduated from the Stevens Institute of Technology in Hoboken, New Jersey, and in 1883 joined the Bethlehem Iron Company to supervise railroad construction in Santiago de Cuba. In Heredia's *Leonela*, John Valdespina studied engineering at William Penn College in Pennsylvania before returning to Cuba as chief engineer on the railroad construction project for Smithson Brothers.

Cubans found employment as educators and taught a generation of North Americans in a variety of fields. Luis A. Baralt Peoli and Antonio Franchi taught Spanish at Columbia University. Others included Mariano Cubí y Soler (Louisiana State University), Calixto Guiteras (Girard College), and Luis Felipe Mantilla (New York University). Federico Edelman Pinto served on the New York Board of Education and taught evening classes at DeWitt Clinton High School. Professors of medicine included Carlos J. Finlay (Columbia) and Juan Guiteras (University of Pennsylvania Medical School). Manuel González Echeverría was a professor of mental diseases at the State University of New York and founded the first asylum for epileptics and the mentally ill in the state. Gonzalo Núñez advertised his services as "professor of piano." Pianist Pablo Desvernine emigrated to New York in 1869 and taught piano to young adults, the most famous of whom was Edward MacDowell. Juan de Valera, the son of a sugar planter, earned a living teaching piano in New York, where he met and married Irish immigrant Catherine Coll. He died shortly after the birth of their son Eduardo, and Catherine returned to Ireland; she then gave the boy's name its Gaelic form: Eamon.

Some Cubans established private schools. In 1885 Tomás Estrada Palma founded a college preparatory school, *Instituto Estrada Palma*, in Central Valley, New York. Eduardo Pla directed an elementary school in Sussex County, New Jersey. Also in New York, Carlos de la Torre established *El Progreso* elementary school, Demetrio Castillo Duany opened a business school, *Inocencio Casanova* organized the *Instituto Casanova*, and N. A. Carbó and J. R. Parras operated the *Academia de Idiomas*. In Tampa, Cirilo Pouble founded the *Academia Pouble*.

A generation of Cuban musicians and performers spent their most productive years in the United States. In 1875 pianist Ignacio Cervantes, a student of Louis Gottschalk, arrived in New York, where his recitals earned him critical acclaim. Shortly after emigrating to New York in 1889, soprano Ana Aguardo was appointed soloist at the San Francisco Xavier Church. Opera singer Rosalía Díaz de Herrera performed on the Philadelphia and Washington stage under the professional name of Rosalía Chalía. Flutist Guillermo M. Tomás developed a following in New York during the 1880s and 1890s. Concert pianist Emilio Agramonte established the New York School of Opera and Oratory in 1893 and served as director of the Eight O'Clock Musical Club and conductor of the Gounod Choral Society of New Haven.

The emigration served as the crucible of nation, for many vital elements of Cuban nationality were forged and acquired definitive form in North America. Some of the most important leaders of independence emerged from this community. Martín Morúa Delgado, Enrique José Varona, Rafael Serra,

Manuel Sanguily, Diego Vicente Tejera, Francisco Vicente Aguilera, and José Morales Lemus all lived in the United States. Néstor Ponce de León resided in New York for thirty years before returning to the island in 1899. José Martí lived most of his adult life in the North. The principal leaders of the Cuban Revolutionary Party (PRC), Tomás Estrada Palma and Gonzalo de Quesada, were U.S. citizens and longtime residents of New York. Quesada received a law degree from Columbia.

Some of the most prominent military chieftains of the Liberation Army also emerged from this community. General Francisco Carrillo, commander of the Fourth Army Corps, and Colonel Julio Sanguily were U.S. citizens. General Pedro Betancourt, commander of the Matanzas division, was a U.S. citizen and a graduate of the University of Pennsylvania Medical School. Chief of Expeditions General Emilio Núñez, a naturalized U.S. citizen, and General Carlos García Velez both graduated from Penn in dentistry. General José Ramón Villalón, who served on the staff of Antonio Maceo, received an engineering degree from Lehigh University. General Eugenio Sánchez Argamonte (Fordham) was chief of the medical corps. General Carlos Roloff, a naturalized U.S. citizen, had previously worked for Bishop and Company in Caibarién. Colonel José Miguel Tarafa (New York Business College) was chief of staff for General Javier Vega of the Third Army Corps of Oriente. General Carlos María de Rojas (Harvard) served on the staff of General José María Rodriguez. The staff of General Calixto García was especially well represented with alumni of U.S. schools, including Chief of Staff General Mario G. Menocal (Cornell), Colonel Juan Miguel Portuondo Tamayo (Columbia), and Major Luis Rodolfo Miranda (Packard Business College).

Destierro was a transformative experience. For Cubans absorbed with matters of *patria*, the United States provided an environment in which the evolving discourse on nation was offered up freely at public forums among a vast number of participants. The proliferation of Cuban publications in exile—pamphlets, periodicals, and books, but mostly newspapers—was nothing less than extraordinary. Scores of newspapers, which appeared in almost every émigré community, were devoted primarily to the proposition of Cuba Libre in all of its ideological representations and programmatic manifestations. This was a free and frankly opposition press, defying—if from a distance—Spanish censorship and openly committed to overthrowing Spanish rule.

A mass readership emerged within émigré communities, and what concerned it most was the ongoing debate on nation. Some newspapers, most notably *Patria, El Yara,* and *El Avisador Cubano,* enjoyed national circulation. Many that were smuggled into Cuba were read daily by *lectores* (readers) to thousands of workers on hundreds of cigar factory floors.

The émigré press contributed to consciousness of nationality by creating open fields of exchange and expanding the modes of communication. These were local newspapers, to be sure, a source of local news and advertisements. But local news was also news of the nation and fostered community out of neighborhood, constituency out of community, and nationality out of constituency. This was a long-standing process of integration and inclusion, a narrative on nation that engaged Cubans of all social classes, men and women, black and white, conducted openly and in public.

The press contributed directly to a unified and informed constituency. Much of the exchange took place in editorials, letters to the editor, petitions, and public meetings—almost all of which would have been inconceivable inside Cuba. In expatriate communities from New Orleans to New York, the text of émigré newspapers resonated with renderings of nation. These were important conduits of the competing versions of patria debated in countless meeting halls and back rooms, on front porches and sidewalks, at factories and in homes, in barbershops and bodegas, in *cafés* and restaurants, and at hundreds of political clubs and patriotic *juntas*.

These were decisive developments, for the very process by which national identity formed was in large measure by way of discourse sustained outside Cuba by huge numbers of people who were daily subjected to North American influences, large and small, and who in the ordinary course of events drew on their environment to advance the cause of Cuba Libre. The circumstance of exile thus had a major impact on the elements used to define and defend patria. That these forms could themselves affect the character of identity was not readily apparent at the time, but increasingly the methods used to create nation also shaped the content of nationality.

The development of the émigré press was very much a product of this condition. Newspapers were in transition in the United States, as technological innovations reduced production costs and increased circulation. Improvements in communications by telegraph, cable, and telephone, as well as advances in transportation by road, rail, and sea, made for efficient collection of news and rapid distribution of newspapers. The cylinder presses that replaced the manually powered flatbed presses of the 1850s further reduced costs and increased efficiency. During the 1860s inexpensive newsprint made from wood pulp supplanted costly rag paper. These were the years, too, of the cheap penny press, popular urban-based newspapers focusing on social and economic issues, directed at specific readerships, and on which the émigré press was modeled.[4] Timing and circumstances made a network of émigré newspapers possible, allowing Cubans to publish at low cost for mass distribution at cheap prices.

That political dissidents could emigrate to the United States and enjoy comparative freedom of action all but guaranteed that much of the opposition to Spain would move to the North. The United States soon became the principal base from which to organize and sustain rebellion. The political leadership of almost all separatist uprisings between 1868 and 1898 was headquartered in New York. Indeed, often it was actually easier for Cubans in the western end of the island to join an insurrection in the eastern end by traveling north. The narrator of Raimundo Cabrera's partly autobiographical novel *Sombras que pasan* (1916) recalled the Ten Years War: "To conspire in Havana in 1870 and 1871 was a dangerous activity and all but absolutely impossible. More than an armed camp, the capital was a prison. On each street corner, a sentry post of armed guards; the cafés and grocery stores were under the surveillance of Volunteers; in every door way, a guard, an armed gatekeeper. In the homes, every Cuban man with a policeman near by. Three Cubans could not get together on a street corner or on the plazas without arousing suspicions."[5] Gustavo Robreño's historical novel *La acera del Louvre* (1925) similarly recalled the days when many Cubans "traveled abroad on the pretense of vacation or business" as a way to reach the rebellion. The "strict vigilance exercised by colonial authorities in the capital," Robreño remembered, "made it impossible for *habaneros* to join the insurrection and it was absolutely indispensable to go abroad, to return as members of an expedition."[6]

Much in Cuban political culture thus developed around the use of the United States as a surrogate site of opposition from which to plot conspiracies and plan for war, to raise funds and organize resistance, to publish opposition newspapers, and to establish hundreds of revolutionary clubs, patriotic juntas, and political associations. Inevitably, in the search for allies and assistance, Cubans involved North Americans in their affairs. And this also became a permanent feature of the Cuban practice of politics.

The circumstance of exile produced new ways to articulate discontent and to assemble power. Such mobilization for change, frankly subversive and revolutionary, could not have developed inside Cuba in the same way. Previous challenges to Spanish rule had originated from clandestine plots organized by small groups of conspirators, limited largely to representatives of creole elites.

The exile experience opened the discourse on nation to the participation of thousands of Cubans, for the discursive process itself functioned as a means of mobilization. The political base of the *independentista* constituency broadened, acquiring greater social diversity and ideological range, and eventually assumed the proportions of a populist mass-based movement. The incorporation of new social groupings guaranteed that the final rendering of patria, the one that would serve as the call to action, addressed the concerns of a vast and heterogeneous constituency. It was in exile that definition of national community broadened and the meaning of patria was transformed, the point at which a moral imperative insinuated itself into the final representation of patria. Nation was subsequently conceived in programmatic terms as national identity expanded to incorporate an explicit ideological content to free Cuba. These were not altogether new tendencies, of course. Much in these formulations had antecedents earlier in the nineteenth century. What was different after 1868, however, was a matter of degree, and eventually the difference in degree was sufficiently great to create a distinction in kind.

During the North American exile the meaning of national community expanded to include the working class, the poor—in the formulation of José Martí, *los humildes* and *los pobres de la tierra*. Martí understood the importance of incorporating los humildes into the separatist coalition; he also recognized that only by addressing working-class concerns explicitly as a function of nation could workers respond to patria. Indeed, Martí required the allegiance of workers to legitimize the construct of Cuba Libre as a representation of the whole nation and could plausibly find this endorsement only among the cigar workers of Florida. He detected in the Floridian communities the fullness of the ideal of nation: cigar workers organized in peculiarly North American small-town fashion—in Key West, Tampa, Jacksonville, and Ocala: entire townships of Cubans united by a vision of nation and governed by officials elected from among their own ranks. The creation of the Cuban Revolutionary Party in Tampa and Key West in 1892 gave institutional structure and political form to the inclusion of workers in the definition of nation. By 1892 Martí could proclaim that "the working people" were the "backbone of our coalition."[7]

The North was also the place where the process of nation formation was open to women. They shared with men many of the same patriotic concerns, often articulated in similar fashion, most of which had to do with the central issues of independence and sovereignty. Many enrolled in separatist ranks in response to opportunity, much of which arrived in the form of modernity. Women entered into the process of national liberation as a means of personal liberation and vice versa. In this period of transition and rapid change, old gender boundaries were difficult to sustain. For instance, in Wenceslao Gálvez's novel *Nicotina* (1898), set in Tampa during the early 1890s, Lucrecia contemplates the imminence of a new separatist war and regrets "not being a man so I too can go and fight." Reprimanded by her father—"Don't speak of those things, child, for women should not get involved in politics, that is unseemly"—Lucrecia retorts: "And why not? Those are backward views!"[8]

Women in exile became "involved in politics" at all levels—as fund-raisers, political organizers, and community leaders. They sponsored bazaars, picnics, and dances; organized theater groups; and collected clothing and medicine for insurgent forces in Cuba. Carolina Rodríguez, Emilia Casanova, Ana Aguardo de Tomás, María Josefa de Moya, Rosalía Hernández, Carmen Miyares, Magdalena Mayorga, and Paulina Pedrosa were only the most prominent women associated with the cause of Cuba Libre. Hundreds more served on the patriotic juntas and in the revolutionary clubs that were established in émigré communities. In sum, forty-nine women's clubs joined the PRC, representing more than 1,500 women, approximately 40 percent of the PRC delegates.[9]

The integration of women in the mobilization of patria introduced different issues about the nature of nationality, about who could participate and under what circumstances, much of which passed directly into the programmatic construct of nation. Although these developments were not entirely new, never before had conditions so favored the discussion of gender issues explicitly as a facet of nation. Patria may still have implied patriarchy, but it was no less true that women in exile contributed in fundamentally new ways to the assumptions from which the formulation and meaning of nation were derived. One émigré *programa político* in 1890 called for universal suffrage and "the progressive emancipation of women with the right to vote and to hold public and official positions." In 1897 Edelmira Guerra de Dauval, founder of Club Esperanza del Valle, issued a manifesto demanding equal rights for women, "the vote for single women and widows over the age of twenty-five, divorce for just cause, and access to public office in accordance with physiological and social laws."[10]

Destierro could be highly disruptive, for even the most commonplace assumptions were challenged daily, especially assumptions about gender roles. In many households the boundaries of production and "public," associated with men, and reproduction and "private," related to women, were blurred as the dislocation incurred by exile reduced the space between "work" and "home." It was but a short step from "public" in pursuit of patria to "public" in the pursuit of livelihood.

The position of bourgeois and middle-class women was particularly complex. They were deprived of status and experienced declining living standards. The same conditions that undermined the traditional male roles of husbands and fathers also transformed the traditional female roles of wives and mothers. Women formerly of comfortable means obtained work outside the home—in the factories, in sales positions, in service sectors. Large numbers of émigré households were headed by women, as men remained in Cuba to fight in a war or were killed or imprisoned. Men preparing to join an in-surrection often relocated their families in the United States and then re-turned to Cuba on an expedition. Women themselves emigrated, often alone or with small children, as widows or after abandonment, in search of oppor-tunities to support their families. Newly widowed Concha Agramonte, like many other women during the Ten Years War, immigrated to New York with her nine children and subsequently obtained work as a seamstress. Juan Pérez Rolo recalled his mother taking the four children to Key West in 1869 on the death of his father to find a job and security.[11]

Throughout the 1880s and 1890s increasing numbers of women joined the wage labor force in the United States. "There were Havana families . . . ," Juan Manuel Planas recounted of Key West, "who accepted the most humble employment in order to live. Housewives worked as laundresses and the daughters of good families were seamstresses or cooks." Data on employment patterns in the Florida cigar factories are incomplete but suggestive. Between 1887 and 1893 nearly 20 percent of the labor force in Key West (3,000 out of 15,000 workers) and Tampa (1,100 out of 5,900) were women.[12]

Criollas in the United States could not help but note the freedom of move-ment enjoyed by North American women, the ease and liberty with which they traveled alone, strolled, and shopped unaccompanied. These things were not done in Cuba, certainly not by white women with any real or pre-tended social status. "When we old-timers were children," Alvaro de la Igle-sia remembered, "one never saw a lady on the streets unless she was in her carriage." North American travelers to Cuba were slightly bewildered by the proscription against women in public. Women from the United States on Havana streets alone, observed one U.S. tourist, "were greeted in their progress by the half-suppressed exclamations of the astonished Habaneros, who seemed as much surprised to see a lady walk through their streets, as a Persian would to see one unveiled in his."[13]

These observations, of course, suggested larger issues. The encounter with the North could not but challenge the premises and the propriety of the con-straints of women of the colony. The experience contributed to new ways by which women came to reject the assumptions of the colonial condition and develop expectations of a new nationality. Certainly nothing caught the at-tention of criollas so quickly as the sight of North American women appear-ing alone in public. "What a pleasure it is to see women here driving their own carriages, often alone, sometimes with a girl friend or young daughter," exclaimed Aurelia Castillo de González, "to see also women alternate with their husbands, sometimes with her in the passenger seat, and sometimes him!" All this occurred without the reputation of the man "suffering in the slightest," commented Castillo de González, without anyone "caring about what they were doing, free and happy," in sharp contrast to those countries of "reclusion and preoccupation."[14]

These were customs that many women adapted to easily and, by implication, customs to which men adapted. Cuban men did not object to their wives and daughters traveling alone on North American city streets. One of the pleasures provided by family travel in the North was the opportunity for women to go out unaccompanied to shop, sightsee, and dine with other women. In New York, men conducted business, visited factories and banks, observed Eusebio Guiteras; their women shopped, attended the theater, and visited Central Park. These ways took hold among many Cuban women who lived in the United States. Carlos Loveira, who had himself spent many years in residence there, would write in Generales y doctores (1920) of "girls intoxicated with the feminine freedom that is inhaled in the North" and of the many criollas who "adopted American liberty, roots and all."[15]

These developments suggested other possibilities. Women found in the United States opportunities that were scarcely imaginable in Cuba, including education, professional training, and career possibilities. Few who traveled north failed to notice them. "Women in the United States," Eusebio Guiteras noted in 1883, "who receive a very complete education, have many options available to them to make a living." Aurelia Castillo de González made a similar observation. As in "every civilized country," she wrote, North American women are "formed by physical and intellectual education that create possibilities for an infinite number of lucrative occupations." Castillo de González marveled at conditions designed to assist women in their "campaign of emancipation," central to which was the opportunity for a "complete education."[16]

Women in exile did indeed pursue a variety of professional careers and business opportunities. The three daughters of Dr. Juan Fermín Figueroa and Angela Socarrás Varona graduated from pharmacy school in New York and opened the city's first pharmacy owned by women. Adela Campo de Grillo was the only female pharmacist in Key West. After graduating from the New York College of Pharmacy, María Dolores de Figueroa returned home and became the first woman licensed pharmacist in Cuba. Flora and Leopoldina Quesada ran a school for girls. Ana Otero and Isabel Salazar were self-employed music teachers. Herminia Andrade de Benech in New York advertised her skills as a seamstress of the "latest fashions," Dionisia Estrada in Tampa opened a dressmaking business, and Gertrudis Heredia de Serra operated the "Midwife Clinic of Havana" in New York. The Estenoz sisters ran a casa de familia, advertising "Cuban food, Cuban hospitality." After years of education and residence in

New York, Camagüey-born Rita Dunau returned to Havana and offered instruction in fencing, cycling, and riding as well as classes in French and English. Julia Martínez completed her secondary education at Notre Dame in Baltimore and subsequently received her doctorate in pedagogy at the University of Havana. María Josefa Granados, who lived in Key West and Tampa between 1886 and 1898, eventually went back to Cuba to establish the weekly *El Sufragista* of the Partido Sufragista Cubano in 1913 and subsequently participated in the founding of the Partido Femenista de Cuba.[17]

Samuel Hazard later told of women in Cuba looking "upon the United States as a country to be dreamed of as a fairy vision, where life and liberty are to be really enjoyed." Hazard recounted one conversation with "one sweet innocent": "'Everyone is free there now, Señor?' 'Oh yes,' I replied; 'we have no negro slaves there now.' 'No, no! Señor, you don't understand me. I mean the women, too—are they not free?' to which I was compelled to reply they were. . . . '*Es muy bueno, Señor;* it is not so here.'"[18]

Notes

1. *Daily Equator-Democrat*, March 26, 1889, 3.

2. In New York, these included the Hotel Central owned by Gervasio Pérez, Nuevo Boarding Cubano of Alfredo Du-Bouchet, Leopoldo Ortiz's Hotel Habana, Hotel Fénix owned and operated by F. Ferrer, Hotel América owned by Bernardo Pérez, Gran Boarding Cubano, Troncoso House, and *Casa de Huéspedes Cubana*. In Saratoga, Pedro M. Suárez owned the Everett House, offering "special arrangements for families," and Luis Baralt operated the Congress Park House—advertised as "a Cuban family hotel located at the best site in Saratoga." In Tampa, Miguel Montejo was proprietor of the Hotel Victoria, and the *Hotel de La Habana* passed through several ownerships before burning down in the early 1900s; in Key West, Martín Herrera owned the Hotel Monroe.

3. *Patria*, October 22, 1892, 4.

4. See Michael Schudson, *Discovering the News: A Social History of American Newspapers* (New York, 1978), 31–42; Robert A. Rutand, *The Newsmongers: Journalism in the Life of the Nation, 1690–1972* (New York, 1973), 240–62; and Sidney Kobre, *Foundations of American Journalism*, 2nd ed. (Westport, CT: 1970), 300–307.

5. Raimundo Cabrera, *Sombras que pasan* (1916; reprint, Havana, 1984), 109.

6. Gustavo Robreño, *La acera del Louvre* (Havana, 1925), 245.

7. José Martí, "El Partido Revolucionario Cubano," April 3, 1892, in Martí, *Obras completas*, ed. Jorge Quintana, 5 vols. (Caracas, 1964), 1, pt 2:303–307, and "La proclamación del Partido Revolucionario Cubano, el 10 de Abril," *Obras completas*, ed. Jorge Quintana, 5 vols. (Caracas, 1964), 1, pt. 2:307–13.

8. Wenceslao Gálvez, "Nicotina," *Revista Bimestre Cubana* 29 (May–June 1932): 409–410.

9. The juntas and clubs included: in New York, *Liga de las Hijas de Cuba*, *Club Mercedes de Varona*; in Tampa, *Club Estrella Solitaria, Discípulas de Martí, Club Gonzalo de Quesada, Club Justo Carrillo*; in Key West, *Club Hospitalarias Cubanas, Grupo Alegórico del Cayo, Protectoras de la Patria, Club A. Díaz-Marcano, Club Mariana Grajales de Maceo, Hijas de la Libertad*, and *Hermanas de Ruis Rivera*. For the activities of women's clubs in Key West, see Raoul Alpízar Poyo, *Cayo Hueso y José Dolores Poyo* (Havana, 1947), 26, 43–44; *Revista de Cayo Hueso*, May 19, 1897, 1–2; and K. Lynn Stoner, *From House to Streets: The Cuban Woman's Movement for Legal Reform, 1898–1940* (Durham, 1991), 24.

10. José Mayner y Ros, *Cuba y sus partidos políticos* (Kingston, Jamaica, 1890), 78; María Collado, "*La evolución femenina en Cuba*," *Bohemia*, December 11, 1927, 58.

11. Francisco Díaz Vólero, *Amor, patria y deber* (Havana, 1921), 87; Juan Pérez Rolo, *Mis recuerdos* (Key West, 1928), 6–9.

12. Juan Manuel Planas, *La corriente del golfo* (Havana, 1920); U.S. Congress, House of Representatives, *Tenth Annual Report of the Commissioner of Labor, 1894*, 54th Cong., 1st sess., H. Doc. 339, 2 vols. (Washington, DC, 1896), 1:138–49.

13. Alvaro de la Iglesia, *Cosas de antaño* (Havana, 1917), 180; A Physician, *Notes on Cuba*, p. 42.

14. Aurelia Castillo de González, *Un paseo por América: Cartas de Méjico y de Chicago* (Havana, 1895), 63–64.

15. Eusebio Guiteras, *Un invierno en Nueva York* (Barcelona, 1883), 134–40; Carlos Loveira, *Generales y doctores* (Havana, 1920), 189–200.

16. Guiteras, *Un invierno en Nueva York*, 88; Castillo de González, *Un paseo por América*, 64; and "*Cartes de Aurelia Castillo*," *Revista Cubana* 21 (April 1895): 307–29.

17. *Revista de Cayo Hueso*, March 27, 1898, 7; "*Farmacia cubana en Nueva York*," *Carteles*, September 18, 1955, 117; *El Fígaro*, March 3, 1895, 117; Ana Núñez Machín, *La otra María* (Havana, 1975), 24–110.

18. Samuel Hazard, *Cuba with Pen and Pencil* (Hartford, Conn., 1871), 84–85.

*   *   *

Questions

Several material conditions support the construction of Cuban subjectivities as U.S. cultural citizens. In other words, Cubans became integral members of the U.S. body politic through economic, political, and social channels.

1. To what extent are these conditions indications of a quest for U.S. cultural (and legal) citizenship and/or a desire to maintain a "Cuban" identity?
2. How do these conditions differ from those of Mexican Americans? Puerto Ricans?

3. How does one explain the paradox of a Cuban dual identity as U.S. citizens and, at the same time, Cuban revolutionaries developing a sense of *cubanidad*, of Cuban nationality?
4. Why would the exile experience promote the inclusion of diverse classes into the independence movement?
5. How does the exile experience affect the status of women? Are these circumstances similar to those Apodaca (see chapter 1) describes for Chicanas in terms of forces of production and social relations?

~

CHAPTER FOURTEEN

The Platt Amendment (1901)

On April 1898, President William McKinley requested U.S. congressional authority to intervene militarily in Cuba, supposedly to serve as a neutral party to stop the fighting between Cubans and Spaniards. But the Cuban revolutionary leaders considered this military intervention a declaration of war against them and vowed to fight against the United States. An agreement was worked out through the Teller Amendment, which promised "to leave the government and control of the island to its people."[2] The Cuban war for independence turned into the Spanish-American War when the USS *Maine* mysteriously exploded. Now we need to detail how the U.S. government stole the show. One immediate consequence of the war was that the Cuban revolutionaries were forced to take a back seat, not only in the conduct of the war but also in the negotiations for the Treaty of Paris. Another U.S. move was to put the old colonial elite that supported U.S. intervention take charge of the government. But the *independentistas* were much too popular, and their candidates kept on winning majorities of seats in the Cuban Constitutional Conventions.

Frustrated, U.S. officials resorted to a reinterpretation of the Teller Amendment. Now it was read as asserting the need for the United States to make sure that Cuba had a stable government. This new interpretation is what led to the interventionist Platt Amendment[1] (named after U.S. Senator Orville H. Platt). It was enacted into law by the U.S. Congress in February 1901 and imposed on the Cuban Constitutional Assembly. Protests were held throughout the island, and there was talk of taking up arms against the

United States. The Cuban Constitutional Assembly balked at enacting the amendment as part of their Constitution. But the threat of continued U.S. military intervention prevailed, and the Platt Amendment was accepted as an appendix to the new 1901 Cuban Constitution by a sixteen-to-eleven vote. (Once more there are similarities here with Iraq's efforts to establish a government under the military shadow of the United States in the twenty-first century.)

The end result is that Cuba came under the hegemony (indirect control) of the United States by virtue of the Platt Amendment, which gave the United States the right to intervene anytime it deemed it necessary "to maintain stability in the island". In actual political practice, this meant U.S. support for governments that sided with U.S. economic interests. This cycle of intervention ended when the United States supported the brutal dictator Fulgencio Batista against the wishes of the Cuban people and this precipitated the Fidel Castro revolution in 1959.

The Platt Amendment was repealed on May 29, 1934, but the United States kept the Guantánamo naval station, which, as of the year 2008, the Cuban government is still trying to get back. Incidentally, Guantánamo is also where the U.S. government keeps so called "enemy combatants" from Afghanistan, Iraq, and the "War on Terror." The U.S. government does not give these prisoners prisoners-of-war (POW) rights under the Geneva Convention. At any rate, a reciprocal trade agreement that reestablished U.S. hegemony over the Cuban economy was signed the same year that the Platt Amendment was repealed. Forcing the sugar-based Cuban economy to serve the interests of the U.S. economy despite the impact on the well-being of the Cuban people would prove to have disastrous results. These are discussed in part B, Cuban Self-Determination under U.S. Hegemony.

*   *   *

Notes and Suggestions for Further Research

1. This summary is based on Louis A. Pérez, "Intervention and Occupation," in *Cuba and the United States: Ties of Singular Intimacy* (Athens: University of Georgia Press, 1990), 82–112.

2. Pérez, *Cuba and the United States*, 96.

*   *   *

I. That the government of Cuba shall never enter into any treaty or other compact with any foreign power or powers which will impair or tend to impair the independence of Cuba, or in any manner authorize or permit any foreign power or powers to obtain by colonization or, for military or naval purposes or otherwise, lodgment in or control over any portion of said island.

II. That said government shall not assume or contract any public debt, to pay the interest upon which, and to make reasonable sinking fund provision for the ultimate discharge of which, the ordinary revenues of the island, after defraying the current expenses of government shall be inadequate.

III. That the government of Cuba consents that the United States may exercise the right to intervene for the preservation of Cuban independence, the maintenance of a government adequate for the protection of life, property, and individual liberty, and for discharging the obligations with respect to Cuba imposed by the Treaty of Paris on the United States, now to be assumed and undertaken by the government of Cuba.

IV. That all Acts of the United States in Cuba during its military occupancy thereof are ratified and validated, and all lawful rights acquired thereunder shall be maintained and protected.

V. That the government of Cuba will execute and as far as necessary extend, the plans already devised or other plans to be mutually agreed upon, for the sanitation of the cities of the island, to the end that a recurrence of epidemic and infectious diseases may be prevented, thereby assuring protection to the people and commerce of Cuba, as well as to the commerce of the southern ports of the United States and of the people residing therein.

VI. That the Isle of Pines shall be omitted from the proposed constitutional boundaries of Cuba, the title thereto being left to future adjustment by treaty.

VII. That to enable the United States to maintain the independence of Cuba, and to protect the people thereof, as well as for its own defense, the government of Cuba will sell or lease to the United States land necessary for coaling or naval stations at certain specified points, to be agreed upon with the President of the United States.

VIII. That by way of further assurance the government of Cuba will embody the foregoing provisions in a permanent treaty with the United States.[1]

Note

1. *U.S. Statutes at Large* 21, 897–98.

*   *   *

Questions

1. Did class struggle make Cubans really incapable of self-government?
2. Even if this was the case, was the United States justified in imposing its will over Cubans?
3. Can we separate good intentions from hegemonic ones?

PART III B

Cuban Self-Determination under U.S. Hegemony
Francisco Hernández Vázquez

As discussed in the previous section, in the second half of the nineteenth century Cubans established "ties of mutual desire" with the United States, and this relationship was used as a weapon in their fight for independence from the Spanish empire. This cultural seduction and economic oppression of the Cuban people represents a complex set of power relations that constructed Cubans as *Cuban Americans* long before the mass exodus to the United States in the 1960s.

At the turn of the twentieth century, the United States carved its hegemony in the very Constitution of Cuba. So how does a country function when it has been forced, militarily, to accept the intervention of another country? In this case, capitalism dictated the behavior of Cuban political institutions. We have here a case of a repetition that shatters the illusion of a linear progress. During the first decades that Cuba was under the power of the United States, the lives of the people of *Cuba Libre* (Free Cuba) resembled in many ways their situation during the last decades under Spain (as in Puerto Rico).[1] Who were "the people" according to their position in the class structure? The old colonial elite and the middle class became part of the economic and cultural structures of the United States. This dependency was manifested at all levels of everyday life, "through ties of sentiment and persuasion, by habits and self-interest."[2] Afro-Cubans, local manufacturers and industrialists, peasant farmers, small *colonos* (tenant farmers), and workers did not fare as well as the local elites. Racial discrimination, business failure as a result of unfair competition, loss of land, and displacement by U.S. corporations or

299

colonists was the most common experience for the former groups. The Cuban government served the interests of the United States and offered no protection from exclusionary racism, economic protection, or labor policies.[3]

In a familiar pattern throughout Latin America and other parts of the world, U.S. political and economic intervention led to waves of political and economic refugees leaving Cuba. This movement of human bodies was related to the ups and downs of the cigar and sugar industries. There were, furthermore, social and political struggles that created political exiles. These struggles also continued to influence the unfolding of events in the Cuban émigré community, which also grew over time. The pre-revolutionary Cuban population in the United States, however, was no more than thirty thousand.[4]

For many years Cubans lived under the illusion of a democracy that combined a dedication to the ideal of a Cuba Libre and a yearning for the United States. They felt equal to U.S. Americans. In fact, they were particularly optimistic about their future because in the 1940s they had achieved a decade of political stability after many years of cultural, political, economic, and class struggles. What Louis A. Pérez describes in On Becoming Cuban: Identity, Nationality and Culture, as "the lengthening shadows" of the days before the Castro revolution is in reality the will of the Cuban people that was ignored at a great cost in terms of human suffering, and that was just the beginning.

For a complete understanding of this situation, however, it is necessary to understand the nature of economic colonialism. We need to look at the contradictions generated by a growing population and a local economy based on the production of sugar and structurally dependent on, and therefore limited by, the U.S. economy. Once again we have here an illustration not only of the interaction between the forces of production and social relations, but also of the production of a nationalist discourse. The event that shattered this image of Cuba as a modern, civilized nation was the U.S. support of a coup d'état (literally "a blow to the State" meaning an illegal seizure of government) on March 10, 1952, by General Fulgencio Batista and the wave of political repression and persecution that followed.

After Fidel Castro's forces defeated the dictator Batista and took over the Cuban government in December 1959, the United States reacted with hostility to his modest reforms designed to help the working classes. This led to the elimination of the moderates, the political center, which was represented by Cubans who were trained in the United States and who were committed to democracy. And this, in turn, pushed the revolution to a more radical position. At the international level, Cuba became an ally of the Soviet Union from which it obtained nuclear missiles to forestall an attack from the United States. It was the struggle for the removal of said missiles that brought the two superpowers to the brink of a nuclear confrontation. At the domestic level, however, Castro was unable to forge an inclusive governing structure to accommodate the diverse groups that supported the revolution. As indicated by María de los Angeles Torres in chapter 15, these conflicting U.S. and Cuban national security interests provoked a massive Cuban exodus. Almost immediately after Castro's takeover, the first of three waves of Cuban exiles to the United States was under way, and it lasted until the end of the Cuban missile crisis of October 1962. The first wave of 248,070 Cuban human bodies was quite homogeneous: 94 percent white, they were an average of thirty-four years old, and had an average of fourteen years of schooling. Their political values were also homogeneous and similar to those of the conservatives in the U.S. Republican Party.[5] The second wave of exiles began in 1965, when the U.S. and Cuban governments negotiated an air bridge to transport the exiles, legally, from Camarioca, Cuba, to Miami, and lasted until 1973. Although whites were still in the majority, out of the 297,318 human bodies, 24 percent were of African, Chinese, Jewish, or mulatto ancestry. Though educated people still predominated, there were many members of the working class.[6]

Although the social status, citizenship, and civil rights of Latinos/as in the United States at that time was not, by any means, a government priority, the ideological struggle against communism worked wonders for the benefit of Cuban exiles. The Dwight D. Eisenhower and John F. Kennedy administrations added institutional support and millions of dollars of federal assistance to the already significant effort of a wide range of private social and charity institutions that offered relief programs to the Cuban exiles. The exiles received more support in terms of food, money, training, education, and relocation programs than was available to U.S. citizens. They also received special treatment from the U.S. Congress and the Immigration and Naturalization Service (INS). In this particular game of truth, African Americans in Miami "watched in disbelief as Cuban black and mulatto children attended 'white schools.'"[7]

Between April and September 1980, the third wave brought 124,776 additional Cubans to the United States. These Cubans differed from those of the previous two waves in several ways. Forty-two percent were single males or females, there was a large number of homosexuals, and there were many "street people" (prostitutes, petty thieves, con men, pimps), some with criminal records.[8] Consequently, their status was constructed differently, that is to say, they were portrayed and treated differently from that of previous exiles. This means their differences made them "undesirables"; they did not get as warm a reception from the U.S. government or the Cuban exile community as previous Cuban refugees did. García does not delve much into the specifics of racial relations among Cuban Americans in her book, *Havana USA*. She is not alone because the topic of racial relations among Latinos owes its invisibility to the historical attempt to subsume racial questions under nationalism. Still, we could also argue that *marielitos*, those who came to the United States in the third wave, were not "desirable" because of their racial makeup (15 percent to 40 percent were Afro-Cubans, compared to 3 percent of the 1959 to 1973 migration). At the same time, we cannot ignore the centrality of the forces of production: The marielitos arrived in the United States at a time of economic recession and consequent political turmoil.

What is not left out of García's discussion, however, is the violence perpetrated on Cuban bodies on both sides of the conflict. Cuban exiles engaged in killings under orders of the U.S. government or on their own, to the extent that Miami became known to the FBI as "the terrorist capital of the United States."[9] With reference to discourses that remain invisible or unsaid, it is pertinent to mention here an important point that is not included in the chapters on Cuba that follow. Even though a consistent, major concern of the entire exiled community has been the political prisoners in Cuba, women political prisoners in Cuba have received less attention than the men. In fact, the "roster of women who served time in prison for counterrevolutionary activities or ideological diversionism [meaning disagreement with the Revolution] has never been fully tabulated and it was not until the late 1980s that the women's experience even began to be told in the exile press in Miami."[10] This despite the fact that Dr. Elena Mederos established the organization *Of Human Rights* at Georgetown University in Washington, D.C., to monitor human rights abuses in Cuba, and despite the fact that women played a crucial role in that organization's campaign because it was their husbands, fathers and sons, and sisters and daughters who were held prisoner.

By 1990, there were 1,043,932 exiled bodies living in the United States, or 10 percent of Cuba's entire population. In a game of truth that continues into the twenty-first century, Cubans continue to migrate to the United States under the Cuban Adjustment Act, which grants Cubans—and only Cubans—the right to legal residency, to a work permit, and to citizenship one year after arriving. To regularize Cuban migration, this act was amended in 1994, and now it applies only if Cuban refugees reach dry land; those caught at sea who cannot prove political persecution by the Castro regime are returned. The amendment to the act includes the Cuban government agreement to allow twenty thousand people to come to the United States every year through a visa lottery system.[11] As a demonstration of the principle of uncertainty in power relations, it is pertinent to note that, in Miami the Cuban American quest for democracy apparently has become a quest for exclusivity. This is not a question of culture or ethnic "essence," but an exercise of power that needs to be confronted as any other hegemonic practice.

At any rate, the Cuban **diaspora** (and that of Puerto Rico, Mexico, and an increasing number of other countries) calls for the redefinition of the concepts of nation, state, and citizenship to include the needs and desires of human bodies according to the realities of a global economy.

Notes and Suggestions for Further Research

1. Louis A. Pérez, *Cuba and the United States* (Athens: University of Georgia Press, 1990), 147.

2. Pérez, *Cuba and the United States,* 148.

3. Pérez, *Cuba and the United States,* 148.

4. Alejandro Portes and Robert L. Bach, *Latin Journey: Cuban and Mexican Immigrants in the United States* (Berkeley: University of California Press, 1985), 84.

5. José Llanes, *Cuban Americans: Masters of Survival* (Cambridge, MA: Abt Books, 1982), 8–9.

6. Llanes, *Cuban Americans,* 98.

7. Maria Cristina García, *Havana USA* (Berkeley: University of California Press, 1996), 20–29.

8. Llanes, *Cuban Americans,* 183.

9. García, *Havanna USA,* 141.

10. García, *Havanna USA,* 159.

11. Derek Reveron, "Elian's Policy Legacy," *Hispanic Business Review* (October 2000).

~

CHAPTER FIFTEEN

El Exilio:
National Security Interests and the
Origins of the Cuban Exile Enclave
María de los Angeles Torres

The Cuban quest for inclusiveness came to a halt under U.S. political and economic colonialism in the 1950s and turned instead into the Cuban revolution led by Fidel Castro. In this piece, Torres illustrates a game of truth that constructs a new political reality for Cuban American people. Going beyond one-dimensional analyses, she considers three different players: the United States and Cuba and their respective national security interests and *El Exilio*, the exiled community, and its dynamics.

Strictly in terms of Cuban human bodies, it is of interest to note the many identities to which they are subjected. They support the revolution but, feeling excluded from it, become exiled and find themselves defined as enemies of the state—nonpersons in their own country. Once they leave Cuba, they receive special immigrant status and "fulfill the military, propagandistic, and symbolic needs of the United States." These bodies are trained for covert military operations (like the famous Bay of Pigs) under terrible conditions, but they are defined as "untrustworthy." They are useful as exiles, that is, as long as they are not part of the United States; when U.S. policy changes, their subjectivity changes from exiled/soldier/militant to "terrorist."

*   *   *

Prior to the revolutionaries' triumph in 1959, an estimated 124,000 Cubans had emigrated to the United States. Throughout the 1950s economic and political conditions on the island had spurred an exodus. A common practice among U.S. corporations was to recruit trained personnel straight from Cuban universities. Nor was it out of the ordinary for political refugees to enter the United States illegally. Yet, as much as postrevolutionary emigration represented a continuation of these trends, this exodus and the exile community, El Exilio, it created emerged from a unique set of circumstances.[1]

The origins of the postrevolution exile must first be understood in the context of the revolution itself and the dynamics it introduced on the island and abroad. Second, an analysis of the exodus and the subsequent communities it spawned must survey the international involvement of the United States as well as its domestic environment in the early 1960s. Finally, the exile community emerges from a society at war with itself, a war that had been carried out through battle with a foreign state. The community contributes to the shaping of its own politics and identity, which in turn influences the subsequent flow of émigrés, just as these successors leave their imprint on the politics and identity of the exile community.

Studies of Cuba and the Cuban community have been marked by some of the same ideological fault lines created by the cold war.[2] Although many factors have influenced the development of the community, studies of Cuban exile politics and identity have usually emphasized only one of many factors. In the early 1960s, with rare exception,[3] studies of the exile community had an island-based perspective. In studying the reasons why people left, scholars who had recently left Cuba explained that repressive conditions had spurred the massive exodus.[4] These analyses usually omitted U.S. policies as factors contributing to the exodus. In the 1970s, Cuban exile academics who were trained in the United States shifted the point of reference to the United States. These studies looked at the community as a minority group and emphasized the role that émigrés fulfilled for the U.S. state.[5] Unlike other Latinos, Cubans were seen as a privileged minority who had been afforded special immigration status because of their symbolic value in the cold war. Other studies looked at U.S. immigration policies as a determining factor in the development of the exile community.[6]

In the early 1980s, island-based academics linked to intelligence-gathering policy centers began to study the community that until then had been officially censured as an area of inquiry. Indeed, those studying the Cuban exile community were monitored closely. Internationally renowned sociologist Oscar Lewis was expelled from Cuba when, as part of his study of a Cuban family on the island, he interviewed family members who had emigrated to Miami. Officially sanctioned Cuban academics emphasized the part the United States played in fomenting immigration, claiming that the U.S. role had been an effort to sabotage the revolution while ignoring Cuban policies as well as the role of the community.[7]

While all these factors have contributed to the emergence and development of the Cuban exile community, our understanding of this community, particularly its origins, has been fragmented by the same ideological divide that so definitively demarcated people's political loyalties; it was either Cuba's fault or that of the United States. In this chapter I attempt a more comprehensive understanding of this period, beginning with an examination of the moment of rupture, taking into account the links between the opposition to Batista and Castro. I continue by looking at the role of the United States in facilitating and defining the movement and development of communities in the United States. I conclude by looking at the politics and identity of Cubans in the United States in the early years. Throughout this chapter I try to understand the unfolding of events within a context I assume has multiple players and states.

This is a difficult task. The fault line of the cold war is not just a theoretical proposition for people whose lives were ruptured by these historical events. For those of us who were young at the time of exile the memory of these early years is intricately interwoven with our childhood. The sharp contrast between our island existence and our U.S. existence has burned powerful images into our memories. The Cuban revolution stands as a monumental event in our lives, making it difficult to decipher the powerful myths it engendered. Many of our families were ardent supporters of the revolution, as was the vast majority of *el pueblo cubano*. U.S. government officials reacted in ways that facilitated the concentration of power on the island under the leadership of one man. This new leadership proved incapable of sustaining a governing structure that included the diverse groups that had supported the revolution. One of the consequences of this failure was the mass exodus of almost 300,000 Cubans in the two years following the revolution.

Revolution and Its Opposition

During the 1950s Cubans of all social classes organized into several coalitions demanding political change. Politicians willing to support change through an electoral process clustered around two parties, *Los Auténticos* and *Los Ortodoxos*. But this strategy lost its viability after Fulgencio Batista, a mulatto army sergeant, led a military coup in 1952 against President Carlos Prío Socarrás with the support of the United States.[8] On July 26, 1953, armed men attacked military barracks in Santiago de Cuba, signaling the commencement of an armed struggle against the island's military regime.

This act represented frustration over the inability to achieve political change through peaceful means.[9]

The revolutionary movement was composed of many organizations and sectors. It included a faction of the Auténticos that had gone underground after President Prío Socarrás had been deposed. *El Directorio Revolucionario*, composed mainly of university students heavily influenced by progressive Catholic thought, organized in Havana and advocated a strategy of *golpear arriba* (strike at the top). Their most dramatic act was a failed attempt to take over the presidential palace on March 13, 1957.[10] Fidel Castro's *Movimiento 26 de Julio* (M-26–7), named after the date of the assault on the *Moncada* military barracks, amalgamated an array of sectors that had settled on a strategy of guerrilla warfare in the countryside. The *Partido Socialista Popular*, Cuba's Communist Party, condemned the actions of both El Directorio and the M-26–7.

Seven anti-Batista organizations signed a unity pact in November 1957 forming a Cuban Liberation Council. Within a month Fidel had resigned from the council, claiming that it had not been sufficiently opposed to foreign intervention; years later he admitted that he did not believe that his group could control that many organizations.[11] Diverse ideologies, future visions, and strategies were included in this broad coalition, but all were united in their commitment to restore the Constitution of 1940 and to hold elections. The organizations opposed to Batista included:[12]

- Los Auténticos: Ramón Grau San Martin, Carlos Prío Socarrás (elected president in 1948 and 1952), removed by Batista military coup; initially advocated peaceful change but later financed various underground armed movements.
- *Partido del Pueblo Cubano Ortodoxo* (Los Ortodoxos): Offshoot of Los Ortodoxos, founded in 1947 by Eduardo Chíbas, congressman and later senator, who shot himself during his radio program in 1951.
- *Movimento Nacional Revolucionario*: Offshoot of Los Ortodoxos, headed by Rafael García Barcena, professor at the University of Havana and *La Escuela Superior de Guerra*; advocated armed coup led by military officers.
- Movimiento 26 de Julio (M-26–7): Headed by Fidel Castro, formally of Los Ortodoxos; armed movement focused on rural and mountain actions, named after its failed attempted takeover of a military barracks on July 26, 1953.
- *Directorio Revolucionario*: Founded in 1955 by members of the *Federación de Estudiantes Universitarios* (sole governing body of university students); headed by Antonio Echeverria; focused on urban armed ac-

tions, specifically at "hitting the top"; entered into a coalition with M-26–7 in 1956. Most of its leaders were killed in an attack on the presidential palace on March 13, 1957.
- Cuban Liberation Council: Formed on November 1, 1957; included, among others, M-26–7, Directorio, and Auténticos; Fidel Castro pulled out a month later.
- *Segundo Frente del Escambray*: Offshoot of El Directorio, headed by Eloy Gutiérrez Menoyo (other members of El Directorio joined M-26–7).
- *Legion Acción Revolucionaria*: Small group headed by Manuel Artime.
- Civic Resistance Movement: Civic group allied with M-26–7.
- *Agrupación Católica*: Headed by Juan Manuel Salvat and other Catholic students.

Despite the broad popular support enjoyed by these organizations, all met with brutal repression, resulting in an estimated twenty thousand deaths, according to *New York Times* correspondent R. Hart Phillips.[13] For Cubans of all walks of life the struggle was to regain the nation and the dignity they had lost at the hands of the military dictatorship. On January 1, 1959, Fidel Castro declared victory after a protracted guerrilla struggle in the mountains and began a march across the island that ended in Havana a week later. This marked the end of the movement that resulted in the ousting of Batista.

Disregarding the decisive participation of many organizations and sectors in the struggle against Batista, Castro quickly consolidated power under his command and his organization, the 26th of July Movement.[14] At first this was done by eliminating Batista supporters and bringing in representatives of the various sectors that had supported the revolution. A fairly representative cabinet was put in place in the early part of 1959, but before long it became evident that Castro would not tolerate differences in his government and an intense power struggle began. Frequent political purges characterized the new regime's administrative style. To the chagrin of many who had fought against Batista, Fidel began promoting members of the Partido Socialista Popular, the Cuban Communist Party, which had not supported the revolution and had advocated accommodation with Cuba's dictators since the 1930s.

Rapid and often unexpected political changes added to the daily turmoil.[15] Legal changes had the effect of concentrating power in the executive. A law passed by the cabinet in February vested legislative power in the cabinet.[16] Formal political institutions were bypassed as Castro overturned court decisions, often announcing his dictates on national television. In one renowned case a court in Santiago acquitted forty-four of Batista s airmen, only to have the case dismissed and a new trial ordered by Fidel.[17] Another major point of contention were elections that had been promised during the revolution but were never held.

In addition, the revolution caused a restructuring of power and class relations that led to a redistribution of land and resources. Once in power the government became increasingly radical. Initial reforms aimed at nationalizing large landholdings were extended to landowners with only moderate holdings. The *Instituto de Reforma Agraria* (Agrarian Reform Institute) became one of the institutional mechanisms through which Fidel and *los rebeldes* (the rebels) consolidated their power. Economic changes, such as the urban reform that included limits on the numbers of housing units that could be rented, also contributed to unrest.

Opposition to the new government grew. Fissures were evident in many sectors, and there were high-level defections. When Huber Matos, a former commander of the 26th of July Movement, tried to resign from his post with the Instituto de Reforma Agraria, he was arrested for counterrevolutionary activities and sentenced to twenty years in jail. Manuel Artime, who had been part of Agrupación Católica and later headed an armed group against Batista—and who would later play a leadership role in both the political and armed opposition to Fidel—resigned from the Agrarian Reform Institute and left the country before he could be arrested. Pedro Díaz Lanz defected from the air force, and many liberals started to resign from government, including Manuel Urrutia, who had been named provisional president; José Miró Cardona, prime minister; Elena Mederos, minister of social welfare; and later Manuel Ray, minister of public works.

Many of the organizations and sectors that had supported the revolutionary movement opposed the direction taken by Fidel Castro and his supporters. They resented his new alliance with the communists, whom they considered opportunists. They fought back by going underground and again taking up the arms they had used against Batista. The Auténticos regrouped under an organization named *Rescate Revolucionario* headed by Manual Antonio (Tony) de Varona and Ramón and Polita Grau. Agrupación Católica began publishing a newspaper titled *Trinchera*. Its members were closely allied with *El Directorio Estudiantil* headed by Juan Manuel Salvat and Alberto Müller. Manuel Artime went on to head *El Movimiento de Recuperación Revolucionaria*. All had varying degrees of contact with the United States.

By the middle of 1960 the various political and military organizations that had emerged following Castro's rise to power announced the formation of a coalition in Mexico City called the *Frente Democrático Revolucionario*. By then these groups were receiving help from the CIA in response to U.S. concerns about communist participation in the government but also for a series of other reasons that had little to do with Cuba. Under the auspices of the CIA the underground was organized under the banner of *Unidad Revolucionaria*.[18]

Repression and Exodus

For many who had supported the revolutionary movement it was the repressiveness of the new government that made them feel betrayed. Arrests, trials, and firing squads first used against Batista's former henchmen were now turned against anyone who was critical of Fidel. Arrests increased and revolutionary justice was quickly dispensed.

The day before the Bay of Pigs invasion the Cuban government made a massive series of arrests. Many adolescent boys were detained in collective jails for days. Detention and incarceration of political opponents became common practice.[19] Prisoners were summarily executed by firing squads. In a particularly dramatic case two young students, Virgilio Campaneria and Alberto Tapia Ruana, were executed on April 17, 1961.[20] Their execution drove a deep wedge into the broad support previously enjoyed by the revolution; the reason many people had joined the movement against Batista was because they rejected the arbitrary and repressive methods of his regime.

There was generalized uncertainty about what would happen next. Most people thought that the U.S. government would not sit by and let the situation continue. Rumors of invasion had begun to be heard as early as 1960, and many Cubans wanted to be outside the country when it happened. Cubans had begun leaving the island early in 1959. Most of these departures were undertaken without much fanfare. According to an analysis of the situation in Santiago de Cuba written by a consulate official, the demand for visas was increasing for a variety of reasons:

> Some wish to get away from the possibility of another revolution, others . . . "in case." Others think that the government is going to place further restrictions on travel, despite official denials. Still others are leaving because of the economic squeeze as a result of revolutionary laws . . . Some persons are going to considerable length to make trips appear casual, e.g., splitting up families or going by different routes to the U.S. or other countries. This, and leaving without publicity, are attempted because they do not want to attract attention which they think might bring intervention or confiscation of their properties.[21]

The exodus accelerated in response to one government action in particular. The government announced that all private schools would be closed, setting off panic among the middle class. This added fuel to rumors that the government was going to take over the *patria potestad* (legal authority) over children. The Catholic Church was particularly vehement in defending its right to provide private education. Priests in Cuba who had lived through the Spanish Civil War and witnessed the separation of families and children voiced their fears that the same would occur in Cuba. For parents whose children attended Catholic schools, this was a sure sign that they would lose power over what happened to their children. Simultaneously, the government initiated a literacy campaign to send all those who could read to the countryside to teach peasants how to read and write, further separating families and dispersing educated people. The rush to get out of Cuba grew. This is when many parents, including my own, decided to send their children—fourteen thousand of them—to the United States.

To Stay or Leave? Patriot or Traitor?

The issue of leaving or remaining in Cuba provided the new government with a political rallying point it could use to mobilize support for the revolution.[22] Leaving or staying, as well as one's position toward those who left, became a litmus test for loyalty to the revolution. For instance, when a great number of professionals began leaving and the loss started to have a noticeable impact on Cuba's economy, a political campaign was launched to link the act of remaining on the island with patriotism. During a rally at the University of Havana, Cuban president Osvaldo Dorticós asked those present to stand and take an oath that they would stay and give their services to the nation.[23] Those present complied. But pledging one's loyalty was not enough: revolutionary cadres were discouraged from staying in contact with relatives who had left the island. Party militants were explicitly prohibited from writing to relatives. In fact, writing to relatives was one of the criteria used to deny students entrance into the university.

In 1960 Raul Castro, Fidel Castro's younger brother and head of the Cuban Armed Forces, presented outgoing migration as "the normal exodus that takes place when the people take the power in their own hands and liquidate exploitation and the privileged classes. Their departure does not damage the revolution, but fortifies it as it is a spontaneous purification."[24]

Others had a much harsher view of the exiles. In the early days of the revolution Fidel Castro said, "Those who escape their duty, taking the road to the north, have lost the right to be worthy sons of la patria."[25] From the beginning the Cuban revolution considered leaving the island a treasonous act; the punishment was to strip the person who left of his or her national identity. People who left were called *gusanos* (worms), a reference to the duffel bags they carried with them.

Dissent was interpreted by Cuba's leadership as a threat to the nation's security. The closing of political space for peaceful or legal dissent meant that those on the island had few options for registering disagreement other than risk imprisonment or leave the country. For many leaving became a way of dissenting. Leaving thus acquired a symbolic value as a political act of defiance, which, in turn, reinforced the idea that those who left were enemies of the state. Furthermore, most Cubans who emigrated went to the United States—a host country that historically had been antagonistic to the homeland. Indeed, the participants in the 1961 U.S.-backed invasion of the island were Cuban émigrés. Thus, the concept of exile and enemy of the state were fused.

For a nationalist revolution the unrelenting exodus of people was indicative of profound systemic political and ideological problems. The revolution, which had been won precisely through the support of broad sectors of the nation, failed to remain inclusive when it came time to govern. Moreover, massive outgoing migration represented a tremendous loss of human resources. Externalizing dissent also had a high cost in that it led to a process of denationalization—the opposite of the goal of a nationalist revolution. In essence the exodus represented a crisis of legitimacy.

The painful rupture that accompanied leaving the country was extremely difficult to reconcile with the immediate past experience of many Cubans, who had been accustomed to being able to take a ferry from Cuba to Florida, honeymoon in Miami, and maintain a close relationship with friends and relations in the United States. Suddenly a trip that had been an easy weekend holiday had become a bureaucratic and political nightmare.

Eventually, the reaction of Cuba's leaders toward those who left was institutionalized in a series of policies that were enforced by government structures whose function was to guard the security of the nation. As early as 1961, a law was passed that authorized the Ministry of the Interior to grant exit and reentry permits to those wishing to leave the country. If a person had not returned by the date on the reentry permit, his or her leave was considered a "definitive abandonment" of the country and the state had the right to confiscate all of his or her property.[26] A law had been passed in 1959 calling for the confiscation of properties of those involved in counterrevolutionary activities, but the law of definitive abandonment included any person who overstayed the sixty-day limit.[27] Those who left the island were not allowed to return, even to visit. These policies marked a radical break with legal precedent, as Cuban law had guaranteed free travel to and from the island for all citizens. The use of exit and reentry permits and loss of property rights were justified by the government on the grounds of national security.[28] The effect was that those who left became classic exiles: nonpersons in their own country.

While the Cuban practice of exile has roots in its colonial past (Spain, too, had used it as a form of punishment), it contradicted contemporary immigration law that had been put into effect by a U.S. military governor in 1901. This law—an exact copy of U.S. immigration law at the time—does not recognize dual citizenship. Everyone born in Cuba or descended from a parent born in Cuba is defined as Cuban regardless of where they live. When traveling to Cuba, they must do so on a Cuban passport. Every Cuban constitution of this century also has stipulated, however, that anyone who acquires the citizenship of another country loses his or her Cuban citizenship. The law leaves room for regulations that define exactly how this is to occur. These regulations require that each case be processed individually; in other words, automatic stripping of citizenship is not allowed. In effect, there is a contradiction between law and practice, for a Cuban passport is required of any Cuban even if he or she has obtained citizenship in another country. Many of us in the Cuban diaspora now have two passports. But, while we may have Cuban passports, because of the postrevolutionary law of definitive abandonment, we have no property or social rights in Cuba.

Another major contradiction has tugged at Cuba's policy toward dissidents and émigrés. While the revolutionary government has maintained publicly that the construction of socialism is *"una tarea de hombres libres"* (a task of free men), it simultaneously set up legal mechanisms to punish those who left without authorization. In fact, departures not authorized by the government were considered political crimes. Leaving legally, even when the United States allowed massive immigration, has been very difficult. Once Cuban citizens filed the required papers at the Ministry of the Interior declaring their intent to leave the country, they generally lost their jobs, their property was inventoried, and their children were expelled from special educational programs.

Because of the politicization of emigration, Cuban émigrés have fulfilled several functions for the Cuban state. They have provided the government with ideological ammunition with which to rally their forces. For example, leaflets showing "lazy gusanos" were used to mobilize workers to cut sugar cane. Emigration also became the vehicle through which the government could rid itself of political opponents and consolidate power. If dissenters were externalized, competition for power would be reduced. State structures were created and often expanded to implement these governmental goals.

Massive emigration exacted a high toll on the state. It was living proof that the Cuban government could not effectively incorporate all parts of the nation. In addition, the sporadic and abrupt ways in which Cubans have left the country presented a security threat because these departures could ignite a rebellion against the government.

Once abroad, the ever-present threat of the counterrevolution from el exilio helped rationalize the need for strong national security agencies within Cuba charged with protecting the revolution. The conflict between the United States and Cuba required an expansion of Cuba's governmental capabilities to meet an external threat—an expansion that mirrored the post-World War II growth in the U.S. intelligence apparatus.[29] The expansion of the Cuban national security apparatus has been especially pronounced for those agencies dealing with Cubans who leave the island. Among the most important of these is the Ministry of the Interior, which encompassed both immigration services and the nation's internal and external intelligence agencies. Rapid growth has also been the case for offices within other departments, such as the Ministry of Foreign Affairs, the Cuban Communist Party, and the *Instituto de Amistad Con los Pueblos* (the Institute of Friendship with Other Countries),[30] an organization that supports solidarity with revolutionary movements throughout the world.

The violent postrevolutionary social rupture within Cuban society and the reaction of the United States to these events have found expression in Cuba's domestic and foreign policies. These policies have been conceived and developed in the realm of national security. In terms of foreign policy the overriding concerns are defense of territory and maintenance of sovereignty. In terms of the domestic agenda the preoccupation has been with economic and political stability.[31]

U.S. National Security Interests and Cuban Exiles

During the first years following the Cuban revolution U.S. policymakers operated with the unquestioned assumption that the leadership that had assumed power on the island would not last. The initial transfer of Cubans to the United States was not a mass movement of refugees but, rather, a response to military needs. U.S. government agencies involved in the fight against the Castro government needed ways to evacuate agents working for the underground opposition and their families. The story of how these programs evolved to become unprecedented immigration and relocation programs traverses the Eisenhower, Kennedy, and Johnson administrations; a contentious Congress; and a local and national backlash to unbridled immigration from the island to the United States. Furthermore, these years were marked by the failed invasion of the island and events that led to the brink of a nuclear war. Throughout the period Cuban exiles came to fulfill symbolic and political roles for the U.S. government as well as for the Cuban government—roles that in strange ways mirrored each other.

U.S. involvement in Cuban affairs was nothing new, and neither was the presence of Cubans in the United States. During the revolution the official U.S. representative in Havana, Earl Smith, had opted against supporting the popular will, choosing instead to try to help Batista until it became evident that his days were numbered.[32] After Batista was toppled, the Eisenhower administration reacted with hostility to the modest agrarian and urban reforms sponsored by the new Cuban revolutionary leadership.[33] Unlike interventions prior to World War II, however, U.S. reactions to the Cuban revolution were cast through the lens of the cold war and became intermeshed with the new crusade to stop communism from spreading in the Western hemisphere.[34]

Unquestionably, the Cuban revolution challenged U.S. hegemony in the Caribbean. It called for a reordering of political power to protect Cuban national interests rather than U.S. interests. It also called for exporting the revolution to other countries in Latin America. In the McCarthyite mood of the late 1950s, in which anticommunist hysteria permeated American public opinion, it was easy to see a revolutionary movement on an island ninety miles offshore as a test of wills between the United States and the Soviet Union. The immediate U.S. response was to attempt to remove the revolutionary leadership from power using military, political, and economic means.

But, unlike past incursions into Cuban affairs, a new mode of intervention was implemented—a foreign state-sponsored social movement.[35] Cuban émigrés became the conduit through which U.S. foreign policies were implemented. Used to try to overthrow and discredit the Cuban revolution,[36] these émigrés came to fulfill the military, propagandistic, and symbolic needs of the United States. The resulting relationship between the émigrés and their host country was forged within the evolving national security state.

Exiles: A Cover for U.S. Intervention

As early as spring 1959, during a National Security Council meeting, Vice President Richard Nixon proposed arming and otherwise supporting an exile force for direct military intervention against Fidel Castro.[37] He also succeeded in getting CIA and FBI approval of his recommendation.[38] On March 17, 1960, President Dwight Eisenhower approved a CIA policy paper that outlined the steps to be taken to "bring about the replacement of the Castro regime with one more devoted to the true interests of the Cuban people and more acceptable to the U.S. in such a manner as to avoid any appearance of U.S. intervention."[39] The document recommended a series of steps that could be taken, including the formation of an "exile" opposition whose slogan could be to "Restore the Revolution," which, it was to claim, had been lost to a "new dictatorship of Cuba subject to strong Sino-Soviet influence." It also included the provisions that individual freedoms must be restored and collectivism in commerce and education eliminated. The formation of a political opposition was to be accompanied by a military and propaganda operation.

Yet there were several concerns that needed to be addressed. One was the reaction of other Latin American countries to U.S. efforts to overthrow Castro. U.S. policymakers had been stung by Latin American protests, as evidenced among other things by CIA director Allen Dulles's testimony to a Senate Committee on Foreign Relations in 1958 regarding Nixon's tour of Latin America that year.[40] Thomas Mann, the assistant secretary for Interamerican affairs, wanted thoroughly to conceal U.S. sponsorship.[41] The White House and the CIA were also concerned about reactions from the press and other agencies (such as the State and Justice Departments) to the CIA's violation of its own charter by its anti-Castro activities in Miami.[42] When President John F. Kennedy took office he wanted to make sure that, if intervention in Cuba failed, it would not be perceived as his fault but, rather, that of the Cuban exiles directly involved; "plausible deniability," the ability to hide the CIA's direct involvement, was critical.[43]

The CIA promoted multiple organizations at the same time that it tried to get these organizations to form a united front. There were disagreements within the bureaucracy and Congress about the appropriate nature of the organizations that should be supported, with some promoting less ideologically driven politicians and others the more liberal and nationalist groups. But agreements were finally reached, and by early 1960 the CIA had facilitated a meeting of organizations it deemed necessary for a united front. Whether or not this coalition would be considered a government in exile was a point hotly contested by the State Department's lawyers, who were concerned about formal recognition because the United States still had full diplomatic relations with the Castro government. In addition, official recognition would break with past policy in that it would recognize a "government" that existed outside national territory and one that did not control the state apparatus.[44] Nonetheless, the *Frente* (Front), as it was first called, was formed in the spring of 1960 at a meeting at New York's Statler Hotel hosted by CIA agent Frank Bender.[45] The formation of the group was announced publicly in Mexico City on June 21, 1960; it included the following men, described to the president by the State Department as follows:[46]

- Manuel Antonio de Varona, leader of a large faction of the Auténticos, the official political party during the administration of Ramón Grau San Martin and Carlos Prío Socarrás (1944–52);
- Justo Carrillo, head of the Montecristi Group formed in 1952 by wealthy professionals and businessmen in opposition to the Batista dictatorship;
- José Ignacio Rasco, head of the Christian Democratic Movement (MDC) formed in late 1959 by young Catholic groups in opposition to the Castro regime;
- Manuel Artime, nominal head of the *Movimiento Recuperacion Revolucionaria*, an underground anti-Castro movement formed in 1959 whose members consisted principally of defectors from the July 26 Movement; and
- Rafael Sardiña Sanchez, former vice president of the *Asociación de Colonos Cubanos* (Cuban Association of Sugar Cane Cutters). (He is not identified as a member of this group in any lists.)

The fifth member of the group was Aureliano Sanchez Arango, a member of the United Front of National Liberation who had served as minister of education and state in the Prío administration. Both his closeness to the communists and his attitude—he was described by the Americans as a prima donna—made him a controversial figure in Washington.[47] Curiously, one of the CIA operators on the Cuban case listed Antonio Maceo, the grandson of one of the generals of the War of Independence, as the fifth person. Apparently, there was either confusion or disagreement (or both) within the U.S. bureaucracy regarding the composition of the group.

At the same time, military training had begun two months earlier, when President Eisenhower authorized the CIA to attempt to overthrow the Castro government. Cuban émigrés provided the human resources to implement a military strategy against Cuba that would appear to be Cuban in origin. Estimates of the number of Cubans who received military training from the United States range from two thousand to fifteen thousand.[48] The most dramatic action would be an invasion, training for which took place in the United States, Guatemala, and Nicaragua. Operatives received a monthly pension from the U.S. government for themselves and their families: $175 for themselves, $50 for the first child, and $25 for each additional child.[49]

Conditions were terrible for those in training. Kept in the dark about the political maneuvering taking place behind the scenes in Washington and Miami, the men in the camps, many of whom had fought for the revolution, felt underrepresented and marginalized. One of their concerns was that the more liberal sectors of the opposition had been excluded from the political organization. Conflicts erupted, and the men went on strike. On March 18, 1961, Tony de Varona and Manuel Ray, at one time described as the Frente's coordinators for the island,[50] met to negotiate the expansion of the Frente and agree on a spokesman. The strike had resulted in the dissolution of the Frente and the formation of a new civic political structure called *El Consejo Revolucionario Cubano* (Cuban Revolutionary Council).[51]

This expansion was also supported by liberals in the Kennedy administration such as Arthur Schlesinger Jr., whose candidate, José Miró Cardona, former law professor and the first prime minister of the revolutionary government, was elected as coordinator over Felipe Pazos, Ray's candidate.[52] Tracey Barnes of the CIA described the members' political leanings, underlining the names of the original members of the Frente; there was a discrepancy about Aureliano Sanchez Arango, who at the time did not join the Consejo in protest over the inclusion of former politicians in a provisional government (see table 17.1).[53]

The group's platform consisted of twelve points, including the reestablishment of the 1940 Constitution as well as a commitment to hold elections within eighteen months.[54] The new organization, however, had its opponents in the U.S. government, among them Senator Thomas Dodd from Connecticut, at the time vice chairman of the Internal Security Subcommittee. On March 23, 1961, he wrote to Secretary of State Dean Rusk about his concerns that José Miró Cardona, Manuel Ray, and Felipe Pazos were anti-American and had socialist leanings, calling them left-wing turncoats. In addition, he was extremely concerned about the amount of money being paid to the various organizations directly under the control of the CIA, saying that, "this operation meant that some Cubans had never had it so good as during exile and consequently acquired a financial interest in preserving the Castro regime."[55]

After months of training, the Bay of Pigs invasion was launched.[56] Despite the demand from the soldiers that Cuban exile political organizations and

Table 15.1.   Exile Groups

Left	Left of Center	Center	Right
Carrillo Jesus Fernandez (Labor, 30 November)	Artime Collada (Labor for Fraginals)	Varona Rasco Fernandez Travieso (students for Müller) Alvarez Diaz Sergio Carbo Pepin Bosch	Maceo Vargas Gómez Carlos Hevia Goar Mestre

not the CIA be in charge of the operation, the role of the exile organizations continued to be essentially propagandistic. On April 17, 1961, the day of the invasion, the members of El Consejo were locked in barracks at a military camp in Opa-Locka, Florida, unable to communicate with "their" soldiers; in fact, they were not even told that the invasion was under way. This, however, was not surprising given the CIA's view that Cubans were not to be trusted. The CIA's psychological profile of Cubans described them as follows:

> From a management point of view the Cuban may seem disappointing in long-range performance and at the same time overly sensitive to criticism. . . The biggest problem appears to be that of long-term loyalty and control. Essentially, the Cuban is loyal only to himself.[57]

Disregard for the exiles was again apparent when council members tried to see the president after the invasion had failed. Arthur Schlesinger Jr. was worried about the impact of such a visit and warned in a memo:

> Exiles who see the President are likely to try to make capital of this when they return to the Cuban community. FBI clearance is not enough. If this should turn out to be a responsible and representative group, I see no objection. Indeed such a presentation might help in composing the feelings of the Cuban exile community. We do not, however, regard this as a high priority.[58]

Schlesinger did, however, urge the president to call Dr. Miró Cardona, who was afraid that his son, captured in the invasion, would be executed. "The feeling is that his anguish would be relieved if you were to call him and express sympathy." His concern with negative press is reflected in the postscript: "Cardona is holding a press conference from 11:30 to 12:30."[59]

The U.S. attempt to hide its military actions behind a Cuban exile screen failed. But the consequences of having trained a secret army would be felt throughout the next decade. The CIA now had highly specialized small teams with which to carry out a covert war against Castro and other governments.[60] The military actions had their influence on politics as well.

Foreign Policy Contours of Exile Politics

The *origins* of the Cuban exile are anchored in both the foreign policy objectives of the U.S. state and the internal policies of the Cuban state. Exiles provide the United States with military resources and ideological cannon fodder. As long as Cuban émigrés were exiles and not a part of the United States, the administrations in Washington could deny involvement in the military actions taken by them against the revolution. Because of their exile status, they provided plausible deniability to the CIA and other agencies involved in the covert war against the Castro regime. Exiles also fulfilled the ideological functions of providing evidence that communism is a repressive system; they had shown that they preferred to flee to a free country. Legal definitions within the United States as well as U.S. aid to the exile community contributed to this distinct exile identity. These international, bureaucratic, and political concerns all contributed to institutionalizing practices that in effect *created* Cuban exiles and turned Miami, where most exiles landed, into a foreign city on U.S. soil.

Cuban state policies also influenced the formation of the exile community. By equating fleeing with treason, the Cuban government used (and continues to use) the exiles as a rallying point. Externalizing opposition allows the Cuban government to get rid of its dissidents in a way that renders them impotent to launch legitimate challenges to the government.

Such has been the case for most exiles of the twentieth century, including those from the Spanish Civil War, Vietnamese, and Chileans.[61] Often home country governments equate abandoning the regime with treason, and thus the process of exodus becomes one of delegitimation. This is particularly effective if the host country is at war with or is antagonistic to the home country. A force tied to one of the nation's historical enemies has little chance of mounting a popular claim against the government. The Cuban revolution delegitimized those who left by defining their exit as "definitive." They were no longer considered part of the nation. Worse, they migrated to the United States, a host country that was a historical as well as a contemporary enemy of Cuba. The revolution fueled an exile that, in the short run, may have externalized opposition but, in the long run, institutionalized exile as a persistent feature of the Cuban and American landscape.

The interaction between U.S. foreign policy objectives and Cuban domestic security policies fueled the creation of a Cuban community abroad in exile. The close interaction of national security agencies within Cuba and the United States created political organizations and ideologies that were then consolidated within the community. In effect, Cuba's need to divide the opposition and the U.S. need to control it may have contributed to the proliferation of the many groups operating in exile.

From 1960 on the CIA's strategy to defeat Castro relied on military action.[62] These actions institutionalized a series of practices that cemented the military functions Cuban émigrés continued to fulfill for the United States. On the one hand, Cuban émigrés were part of U.S. foreign policy, since they received monies and training from the CIA and carried out orders. On the other hand, émigrés were kept away from the centers of power and treated as nationals of another state. Through this distancing, the United States could avoid taking responsibility for the émigrés' actions. The militarization of this opposition by the United States and the promotion of hard-line policies on both sides of the Florida Straits encouraged antidemocratic tendencies within the community and contributed to the politics of intolerance.[63] This had a negative influence on the political culture of the exile.

Once outside national territory and without links to the internal opposition, exile activism became exaggerated and out of touch with the internal dynamics of the island. The United States promoted the exile/soldier as a militant, but, when the United States disengaged from active opposition to the Castro regime, the militant activist came to be considered a terrorist.[64]

Politics is articulated through political organizations. In the case of post-revolutionary Cubans in the United States it was the national security apparatus and policies that had a dominant influence on exile politics. U.S. foreign policies directed at overthrowing and discrediting the Cuban revolution were implemented in part by Cuban émigrés. Having arrived in the United States, many Cuban émigrés participated in military actions backed by the United States, such as the Bay of Pigs invasion in 1961. Through these dynamics the U.S. intelligence network gave life to the first political organizations and leaders in the Cuban community. This connection continued after the failure of Bay of Pigs as the U.S. government again tried to engage exiles in its war against Castro.

Notes

1. "Analysis of the Opposition Movement to the Castro Regime," *Foreign Service Dispatch*, American Embassy, Havana, December 6, 1960; reported by W. C. Bowdlering.

2. For an extensive review of the debates about Cuban studies, see Marifeli Perez-Stable, "The Field of Cuban Studies," *Latin American Research Review* 26, no. 1 (1991): 239–50.

3. An exception to this was the seminal study of Cuban exile political attitudes by Richard Fagen, Richard Brody, and Thomas J. O'Leary, *Cubans in Exile: Disaffection and the Revolution* (Stanford: Stanford University Press, 1968).

4. See the work of Juan Clark, "The Exodus from Revolutionary Cuba (1959–1974): A Sociological Analysis" (Ph.D. diss., University of Florida, 1975).

5. I include my own work in this, along with that of Lourdes Argüelles, "Cuban Miami: The Roots, Development, and Everyday Life of an Émigré Enclave in the National Security State," *Contemporary Marxism* 5 (Summer 1982): 27–44; and Pedraza-Bailey, *Political and Economic Migrants*, 146.

6. Jorge Domínguez, *Cuba: Order and Revolution* (Cambridge, MA: Belknap Press, Harvard University, 1978), 140.

7. Rafael Hernández, *"La política imigratoria de Estados Unidos y la revolución cubana"* Centro de Estudios Sobre America, La Habana, Serie Avances de Investigacione no. 3, (1980).

8. For a detailed account of the various attempts to hold elections, see both Hugh Thomas, *The Cuban Revolution* (New York: Harper and Row, 1971); and Thomas G. Paterson, *Contesting Castro: The United States and the Triumph of the Cuban Revolution* (New York: Oxford University Press, 1994).

9. Marifeli Pérez-Stable, *The Cuban Revolution: Origins, Course, and Legacy* (New York: Oxford University Press, 1993), has an excellent account of the emergence of the armed struggle strategy.

10. Jaime Suchlicki, *University Students and Revolution in Cuba, 1920–1968* (Miami: University of Miami Press, 1969).

11. Suchlicki, *University Students,* 84.

12. Composed with information from Suchlicki, *University Students;* Thomas, *The Cuban Revolution.*

13. R. Hart Phillips, *Cuba: Island of Paradox* (New York: McDowell, Oblensky, 1957), quoted this figure although the numbers have been contested and may be as low as eight thousand.

14. After the early 1960s, few references to the revolutionary movement include any organization except *Movimiento 26 de Julio.* In fact, Jesús Díaz's fictional film, *Cladestino,* caused quite a stir in Havana upon its release because it legitimized the urban struggle.

15. See Domínguez, *Cuba,* chap. 6.

16. Thomas, *The Cuban Revolution,* 416.

17. Thomas, *The Cuban Revolution,* 423.

18. Jay Mallin, Sr., *Covering Castro: Rise and Decline of Cuba's Communist Dictator* (New Brunswick: Transaction Publishers, 1994).

19. Estimates of the number of political prisoners vary widely depending on the method of counting "political" crimes, but they range from 10,000 to 20,000. See María Cristina García, *Havana, USA: Cuban Exiles and Cuban Americans in South Florida* (Berkeley: University of California Press, 1996), 156–57.

20. Tomas Fernández-Travieso, *"Los ocho fusilados,"* El Nuevo Herald, April 17, 1991, 4.

21. *Foreign Service Dispatch* no. 100, April 21, 1960.

22. For an extensive review of the literature of postrevolutionary immigration, see Lisandro Pérez, "Migration from Socialist Cuba: A Critical Analysis of the Literature," in Miren Uriarte and Jorge Cañas, eds., *Cubans in the United States* (Boston: Center for the Study of the Cuban Community, 1984), 12–22.

23. In Pedraza-Bailey, Political and Economic Migrants, 151.

24. Quoted in Pedraza-Bailey, Political and Economic Migrants, 150; from *New York Times,* July 23, 1961.

25. Quoted in Pedraza-Bailey, Political and Economic Migrants, 149; from *New York Times*, November 12, 1960.

26. Law no. 989, *Gaceta Oficial de la Republica de Cuba, miercoles*, December 1, 1962, 23705.

27. Abel Enrique Hart Santamaría, *Delitos contra la seguridad del estado* (Havana: Editorial de Ciencias Sociuales, 1988), 76.

28. See the work of Hugo Azcuy, *"Los derechos fundamentales de los Cubanos y la cuestion de la emigracion en las relaciones Cuba-Estado Unidos,"* Paper presented at the Latin American Studies Association, Cuban-Community Research group meeting, Chicago, April 1995.

29. Domínguez, *Cuba*, 37.

30. Rex A. Hudson, "Castro's America Department" (Washington, DC: Cuban-American National Foundation, *Departamento de las Americas* pamphlet, 1991).

31. Santamaría, *Delitos contra la seguridad del estado*, 171.

32. Earl Smith, *El Cuarto Piso: Relato sobre la revolucion comunista de Castro* (Santo Domingo: *Editora Corripio*, 1983).

33. Fidel Castro, *La historia me absolvera* [speech given at his trial after the failed assault on the military garrison, Moncada, 1953], (Havana: *Editorial Ciencias Sociales*, 1973).

34. Barnet, *Roots of War; and Saul Landau, The Dangerous Doctrine: National Security and U.S. Foreign Policy* (Boulder: Westview Press, 1988).

35. Carlos Forment, "Caribbean Geopolitics and Foreign State Sponsored Social Movements: The Case of Cuban Exiles Militancy, 1959–1979," in Miren Uriarte and Jorge Cañas, eds., *Cubans in the United States* (Boston: Center for the Study of the Cuban Community, 1984), 65–102.

36. Argüelles, "Cuban Miami," 27–44.

37. Philip Brenner, *From Confrontation to Negotiations: U.S. Cuba Relations* (Boulder: Westview Press, 1988), 12.

38. William Appleman Williams, *The United States, Cuba, and Castro* (New York: Monthly Review Press, 1962), 122.

39. CIA document titled "A Program of Covert Action against the Castro Regime," March 16, 1960, 1 (approved for release June 18, 1988, MR Care No. 88–21).

40. U.S. Congress, Senate Committee on Foreign Relations Executive Sessions of the Senate Foreign Relations Committee (Historical Series), vol. 10, 85th Cong., 2nd sess., 1958, in Lars Schoultz, *National Security and the United States Policy toward Latin America* (Princeton: Princeton University Press, 1987), 16.

41. Peter Wyden, *Bay of Pigs: The Untold Story* (New York: Touchstone, 1979), 100.

42. Wyden, *Bay of Pigs*, 76.

43. Williams in *United States, Cuba, and Castro*, adds that "he was also concerned for his power, his externalization of evil, and his urge to control the future while still in the present" (152).

44. Correspondence between Joseph Scott, December 2, 1960, and Mr. Hager, December 7, 1960, addressed to Mr. Merchant; obtained from the State Department's

Freedom of Information Office, identified as being from the State Department's Cuba file, 1960, 737.00/12/2/60.

45. Haynes Johnson, with Manuel Artime, José Pérez San Román, Erneido Oliva, and Enriquez Ruíz-Williams, *The Bay of Pigs: The Leaders Story of Brigade 2506* (New York: W. W. Norton, 1964), 29.

46. A memo to the secretary from Mr. Mann on the subject of the President's Inquiry Regarding Cuban Opposition groups, dated October 28, 1960; obtained from State Department's Freedom of Information Office.

47. Department of State, Memorandum of Conversation, Cuba Series; participants, Ambassador Philip Bonsal and Dr. Aureliano Sanchez Arango, February 3, 1961, 737.00/2–361.

48. Argüelles "Cuban Miami," 31.

49. Wyden, *Bay of Pigs,* 49.

50. Johnson and others, *Bay of Pigs,* 62.

51. Department of State, Cuba Series, *Foreign Service Dispatch* no. 397, American Embassy, Mexico, D.F., October 1960, Report of Conversation with Jose (Pepin) Bosch reported by R. G. Cushing and J. J. Montilor, 737.00/10–1160.

52. Department of State, Cuba Series, Memorandum of Conversation, February 4, 1961; participants, Carlos Piad and Ambassador Philip W. Bonsal, 737.00/2–461.

53. Memorandum for director of Central Intelligence Agency (CIA) from Tracy Barnes, March 21, 1961, John F. Kennedy (JFK) Presidential Library, National Security Council Files, Cuba, box 48.

54. Memorandum for director of CIA from Tracy Barnes, March 21, 1961, JFK Presidential Library, National Security Council Files, Cuba, box 48

55. Report sent to Dean Rusk, secretary of state, from the Department of State, Cuba Series, March 23, 1961, 737.00/3–2361.

56. Johnson and others, *Bay of Pigs,* 62.

57. Andrew Wilson, "Portrait of a Cuban Refugee," *Central Intelligence Agency, Studies in Intelligence* (Summer 1964): 35–41.

58. Arthur Schlesinger, Jr., memorandum for Kenneth O'Donnell, May 8, 1961, JFK Presidential Library, White House Papers, Arthur Schlesinger Jr. files, box 5.

59. Arthur Schlesinger, Jr., April 21, 1961, box 115, Presidential Papers, JFK Presidential Library.

60. "Alleged Assassination Plots Involving Foreign Leaders: An Interim Report of the Select Committee to Study Governmental Operations with Respect to Intelligence Activities," United States Senate, 94th Cong., November 20, 1975, report no. 94–465.

61. Yossi Shain, *Frontiers of Loyalty: Political Exiles in the Age of the Nation State* (Grand Rapids, MI: William B. Eerdmans, 1977), 23.

62. Paterson, *Contesting Castro.*

63. Forment, "Caribbean Geopolitics."

64. Forment, "Caribbean Geopolitics," 66.

*　　*　　*

Questions

1. If the political conditions in the 60s, 70s, and 80s affected the studies of Cuba and the Cuban community, what can be said about the political conditions affecting Torres's own study?

2. In what ways did U.S. government officials facilitate "the concentration of power on the island under the leadership of one man"? To what extent is this a case of unintended consequences?

3. With so many organizations involved in the ousting of the dictator Batista, how was Castro able to consolidate power? To what extent can we say that Castro intended to create a dictatorship if his original objective was to restore the Constitution of 1940 and to hold elections? To what extent can we say he was a victim of circumstances?

4. The political situation in the 60s allowed the formation of a Cuban American exiled community. Were Cubans justified in leaving Cuba?

5. Imagine that Cubans had been not been accepted into the United States. Would Cubans have migrated to other countries in the same numbers? How might the history of Cuba be written if that was the case?

CHAPTER SIXTEEN

~

Havana USA
María Cristina García

Expanding on the previous chapter, García explains the unique political and economic processes by which the Cuban American quest for democracy was achieved for many, if not all, of the exiles. She provides an account of the transition period in Cuban American politics from terrorism to working within the political system of the host country. She also gives us a peek at the future relations between Cuba and the Cuban American community and at how the quest for democracy may turn into a practice of exclusivity and intolerance. We are left with conjectures: Will Cuba remain independent or will it be annexed by the United States? If the latter, will it be annexed Puerto Rican style or Hawaiian style? Or will it be annexed by the United States as requested by one group of exiles?[1]

Note

1. María Cristina García, *Havana USA* (Berkeley: University of California Press, 1996), 165.

*　　*　　*

The Emergence of a Cuban American Identity

As early as the 1970s, there was evidence of a shift in the emigré community, as Cubans began to perceive themselves as permanent residents rather than temporary visitors, as immigrants rather than refugees. This shift in con-sciousness—attributable, in part, to the termination of the freedom flights, which forced many emigrés to come to terms with their status in the United States—was especially evident in three areas: the economic success of the Cuban community in south Florida; the growing number of exiles seeking naturalization; and their new involvement in domestic politics and civic af-fairs.

As the Cubans bought homes, built businesses, paid taxes, and sent their children to school, they established ties to their communities in spite of their original intentions. In south Florida they created a thriving economic en-clave that absorbed each new wave of immigration from Cuba as well as from elsewhere in Latin America.[1] By 1980, emigrés in Dade County generated close to $2.5 billion in income each year. Forty-four percent of the nearly five hundred thousand Cubans living in greater Miami were professionals, com-pany managers, business owners, skilled craftsmen, or retail sales and clerical personnel, and eighteen thousand businesses were Cuban-owned. Sixty-three percent of emigrés owned their own homes.[2] The figures improved with each year, and by the early 1990s over twenty-five thousand businesses in Dade County were Latino-owned, making south Florida home to the most prosperous Latino community in the United States.[3] In both the 1980 and 1990 censuses, Cubans also exhibited the highest income and educational levels of the three major Latino groups, levels only slightly below the na-tional average—a notable accomplishment for a community of first-genera-tion immigrants.[4]

The Cubans' success could be attributed to several factors. Cuban women had a high rate of participation in the labor force; as early as 1970, they con-stituted the largest proportionate group of working women in the United States.[5] Women expanded their roles to include wage-earning not as a re-sponse to the feminist movement or the social currents of the 1960s but to ensure the economic survival of their families. The structure of the Cuban household, with three generations living under one roof, also ensured success because it encouraged economic cooperation.[6] The elderly contributed to the family's economic well-being both directly, with salaries, refugee aid, and Social Security checks, or indirectly, by raising children and assuming house-hold responsibilities. These factors, along with the Cubans' low fertility rates and high levels of school completion, facilitated the family's structural as-similation.

In the community, the Cubans created prosperous businesses, built with the skills and capital of the middle- and upper-class emigrés who comprised the first wave of immigrants. The wealthy elite had money invested in American banks at the time of the revolution, and when they settled in Miami they invested that capital in new business ventures. The middle-class emigrés lacked that kind of capital, but they did have the skills and business know-how with which to create lucrative businesses. They identified the needs in the community and built businesses catering to those needs, with the assistance of loans from local banks or the Small Business Administration and long hours of work by family members. As their businesses expanded, these emigrés took on additional employees, almost always their compatriots. Thus, south Florida became home to a thriving business community that provided job opportunities for the new immigrants who arrived each year, easing their assimilation into the economic mainstream.[7]

The Cuban presence attracted international investment and helped convert Miami into a major trade and commercial center linking North and South America. By 1980, thirteen major banks and over one hundred multinational corporations had established regional offices in the Miami area. Between 1977 and 1980 the port of Miami, which had already replaced New Orleans as the chief port of trade with Latin America, tripled its ship passenger traffic. From 1975 to 1980, air passenger traffic at Miami International Airport increased 100 percent and air cargo traffic 250 percent, making it the ninth busiest airport in the world in passenger traffic and sixth busiest in cargo traffic. During the same period, exports and imports increased by close to 150 percent.[8]

As early as the 1960s, the national news media, particularly popular magazines such as *Life*, *Fortune*, and *Newsweek*, celebrated the Cubans' business acumen and mythologized the "Cuban success story." Articles with titles like "To Miami, Refugees Spell P-R-O-S-P-E-R-I-T-Y" and "Cuban Refugees Write a U.S. Success Story" proclaimed the Cubans to be "golden immigrants" and the newest Horatio Algers.[9] In an era of social upheaval and disillusionment, when Americans questioned and discarded old values and perspectives, the Cubans seemed to prove that the American Dream was strong and intact. News of the Cubans' apparent success helped ease any misgivings Americans might have had about giving these people asylum or spending millions of taxpayers' dollars on refugee aid.

The "Cuban success story," however, overlooked the fact that many Cubans did not share in the community's wealth, as well as the fact that their success, while substantial, was less spectacular than the rags-to-riches stories promoted by the popular media.[10] Despite the large middle and upper classes and the comprehensive federal assistance pumped into the community, Cuban income still remained below the national average (albeit slightly) and a significant percentage of Cubans lived in poverty.[11] Working class emigrés, like other Americans, struggled for better wages, benefits, and working conditions, as well as job security, particularly if they were women. Black Cubans experienced discrimination from both their white compatriots and the larger society, and as late as 1990 their income lagged behind that of white Cubans by almost 40 percent.[12] As one editorial in an exile newspaper said:

> Many think that all exiles are rich; and it's not that way. . . . Ninety percent of exiles in Miami work in the factories or other such workplaces. They are all workers—some at a higher rank—but they are all workers. It is for these people that we publish our newspaper, so that they will learn American laws and realize that they don't have to be exploited . . . and many of them are exploited, especially by Cuban bosses.[13]

Nevertheless, the Cuban success story enjoyed wide circulation within the exile community: the Cubans made the story an essential element of their collective identity. Rather than focusing on those who had not assimilated economically, they focused on those who had—and there *were* plenty Horatio Algers in the community. To do otherwise would have been to give Fidel Castro propaganda to use against them. They wanted to prove to their compatriots back home what could be accomplished. That the community had accomplished so much in so little time, they argued, was a testimony to the old-fashioned values of thrift, hard work, and perseverance, and a symbol that God was on their side. The U.S. news media celebrated the Cubans' adoption of the Puritan work ethic, but for the emigrés it was simply the exile work ethic. Their strong anticommunism and their economic prosperity were the two characteristics they took the most pride in and promoted about themselves. Their success within the American mainstream was an indictment of the revolution, the best revenge a *gusano* could have.

But not all Cubans were comfortable with the community's success. Some emigrés accused their countrymen of sacrificing *la causa cubana* for the comforts of exile: if they had invested as much time in assisting the counterrevolution as they had in climbing the economic ladder, went the argument, they could have all returned to Cuba within a matter of years. "The dollar sign has destroyed the patriotic values of many," lamented one editorial.[14] Another warned that economic success was "prostituting the combative spirit of the exile community . . . distracting our youth from working on behalf of our slave country."[15] Yet another editor wrote, "We exchanged the committed, militant exile of [1961] for the present apathetic exile, committed only to dances and festivities."[16] For these and other exiles, the economic success of the community signified a denial of their responsibilities toward Cuba.

Nowhere was the theme of national allegiance more evident than in the debate over naturalization, a debate carried out in homes and offices, in newspapers and on the radio, throughout the 1960s and 1970s. Many Cubans were completely opposed to the idea of applying for U.S. citizenship. Some even resented that their children were forced to swear allegiance to the American flag at school. Many Cubans believed that becoming an American citizen meant assuming a new identity, emotionally erasing any memory of life prior to taking the oath of citizenship. The oath was a symbolic act by which they renounced allegiance to their homeland, their heritage, and their people; as one individual wrote, "How can I ever forget my language, my customs, my folklore? How can I honestly forget my past?"[17] Becoming a citizen meant that they had failed la causa cubana and compromised their ideals. They would no longer be exiles but rather ethnic Americans. In an effort to remind exiles of their responsibilities, the *periodiquitos* dedicated a number of issues in the early 1970s to defining the concepts of *patria* (nation) and *cubanidad*.

College students were particularly caught up in this debate over identity and national allegiance. Many had left Cuba as teenagers, and they were acutely aware that they straddled two cultures. At the University of Miami, Miami-Dade Community College, the University of Florida at Gainesville, and other universities around the country, Cuban students joined organizations such as the *Federación de Estudiantes Cubanos and the Agrupación Estudiantil Abdala* (known more commonly as *Abdala*)[18] to discuss issues of nationality, identity, culture, and their responsibilities toward Cuba. They tried to define cubanidad for themselves. "Young people who wish to identify themselves as Cuban face many difficulties in exile," wrote one student in *Antorcha*, the Cuban Students Federation publication at the University of Miami:

> I am not referring to the obvious problem of having to choose whether one is Cuban or American, but rather to a more subtle (and perhaps more dangerous) conflict, which is distinguishing between *cubanía* and being Cuban-like. It is one thing to be concerned about the people who share one's language and origin, to be genuinely concerned with Cuba. It is quite another thing to think that one is Cuban simply because one likes *arroz con frijoles* or reads a Spanish-language newspaper in the afternoons. It is best to do both.[19]

Some students became more staunchly nationalistic than their parents, and they castigated the community for forfeiting its ideals. One editorial in *Antorcha* challenged its readers: "We must ask ourselves why we came to Miami. To contribute to its growth? To become involved in its politics? To make money? Did we leave Cuba as emigrants? . . . While we should be proud of being Cubans we should be ashamed of not having a country."[20] Others appealed to their compatriots' sense of cubanidad, warning them that the traditions and values they took most pride in would eventually die in the United States. "The Cuban family will be destroyed on foreign soil. . . . It is only in Cuba that we can preserve her."[21] Not surprisingly, many students, particularly those affiliated with Abdala, became more deeply involved in the war against Castro.

Many Cubans, however, saw no contradiction in being both exiles and citizens of the United States. Tangible legal, professional, and economic benefits could be derived from U.S. citizenship; Cuban professionals in particular realized that in order to practice their careers they had to meet state licensing requirements, and permanent residency or citizenship was always a prerequisite. But it was more than just economic considerations that led many Cubans to apply for citizenship. As they resigned themselves to a lengthy stay in the United States, they developed a sense of loyalty to the country that gave them refuge, and citizenship seemed a logical step.

The Miami Herald reported in 1974 that approximately two hundred thousand Cubans had sought U.S. citizenship.[22] In late 1975, Cuban professionals, led by media personality Manolo Reyes initiated a citizenship drive, the Cubans for American Citizenship Campaign, with the goal of registering ten thousand new citizens in celebration of the United States Bicentennial. Members of the steering committee recruited exiles, helped them fill out the necessary papers, and taught courses in schools to help them prepare for the examinations. The campaign surpassed its goal: on just one day—July 4, 1976—more than sixty-five hundred Cubans swore the oath of citizenship, and by the end of the year 26,275 exiles had become U.S. citizens.[23] The campaign continued throughout the late 1970s. By 1980, 55 percent of the eligible Cubans in Dade County were American citizens, compared to just 25 percent in 1970.[24] Even with their new legal status, however, these new citizens continued to regard themselves as Cuban exiles—and they would always maintain this dual identity. Their ties to Cuba were unseverable.

During the 1970s, the local news media, and in particular the Miami Herald, monitored the sentiments of the exile community. In the aftermath of the Civil Rights Movement, the media tried to reflect the concerns of ethnic minorities and to study the relationships between the different groups in the community. The Herald commissioned various polls and surveys to determine how well the Cubans were adapting to life in the United States. Did they feel accepted? Did they want to return to Cuba? Did they object to the reestablishment of diplomatic relations with the Castro government? Many of the surveys yielded surprising results: a 1972 poll revealed that while 97 percent of the Cubans interviewed felt that they had been accepted in Miami, 62 percent were less satisfied with their lives in the U.S. than with the lives they had led in Cuba.[25] The termination of the freedom flights, however, proved to be a turning point in the exiles' attitudes toward Cuba and the United States. A study by sociologists Clark and Mendoza in 1972 showed that close to 79 percent of the Cubans interviewed wanted to return to Cuba once Castro was overthrown, but two years later, less than half expressed the same desire.[26] Another study by Portes and Mozo yielded similar results: in 1973, 60 percent of those interviewed reported plans to return to Cuba once Fidel Castro fell, but by 1979 less than one-fourth wanted to return.[27]

The Cubans' growing involvement in civic affairs and local politics also revealed a shift in consciousness. In 1965, seventeen Cuban businessmen created the *Cámara de Comercio Latina* (Latin American Chamber of Commerce), or CAMACOL, to lobby on behalf of Dade's Latino business community before the Metro-Dade County Commission and the state legislature. In 1970, emigrés created the Cuban National Planning Council to study domestic (U.S.) issues that were important to Cubans, including language, education, health care, and employment. A Cuban ran for the mayoral seat as early as 1967, two ran for the city commission in 1969, and another five ran for various public offices in 1971. All were unsuccessful, but in 1973 two veterans of the Bay of Pigs invasion were elected to public office, Manolo Reboso to the City Commission and Alfredo Duran to the Dade County School Board. The city of Sweetwater also became the first city in south Florida to elect a Cuban-born mayor.

Another example of the Cubans' growing influence in Dade County was the Bilingual-Bicultural Ordinance of April 1973. The resolution designated Spanish as the county's second official language and called for the establishment of a Department of Bilingual and Bicultural Affairs, the translation of county documents into Spanish, and increased efforts to recruit Latinos to county jobs.[28] The passage of such an ordinance by a board comprised entirely of non-Latinos demonstrated a recognition of the role Cubans and other Latinos were playing in the local community, and would play in the years to come. As the resolution declared, "Our Spanish-speaking population has earned, through its ever increasing share of the tax burden, and active participation in community affairs, the right to be serviced and heard at all levels of government."[29] (The resolution was repealed in 1980 in the aftermath of Mariel, but reinstated in 1993.)

Over the next decade, the Cubans' political accomplishments were even more impressive. Cubans came to occupy positions in the local, state, and national government, as well as key positions in the key institutions of Miami and Dade County. At the same time, they continued to be actively concerned with the political affairs of their homeland just ninety miles away. Whether they called themselves Cuban exiles or Cuban Americans, it was clear that the emigrés had carved a niche for themselves in their country of refuge and were satisfactorily resolving the question of identity—at least for themselves.

The 1970s: A Transition Period

During the 1970s, the exile community in south Florida seemed to be developing along parallel courses, one of adjustment and acceptance, the other of increasing militance and desperation. It was a decade of social and economic progress. The number of emigrés seeking American citizenship increased. The Latino business community of Dade County became one of the most productive in the nation. Emigrés became involved in domestic politics: by 1976, they comprised 8 percent of registered voters in Dade County and occupied important elected offices in city and county governments. There was an indication that some Cubans were developing an ethnic (as opposed to purely national) identity, as seen by their growing membership in pan-Latino organizations such as the League of United Latin American Citizens (LULAC) as well as in the creation of groups such as the Cuban National Planning Council, the Spanish American League Against Discrimination (SALAD), and the National Coalition of Cuban Americans, which focused on voting rights, employment, housing, education, health, and other domestic concerns. All signs seemed to indicate that the emigrés had psychologically unpacked their bags and settled into their new society.

Alongside newspaper headlines celebrating the emigrés' success, however, was news that the war against Castro had taken a menacing turn. Propaganda and paramilitary groups decreased in number in the late 1960s, victims of a lack of funding and growing apathy in the community—an apathy generated, in part, by suspicions that many of these political groups were embezzling funds. But at the same time, new, more militant organizations emerged, committed to overthrowing Castro at whatever the cost. Most had no specific political vision for Cuba, no particular leader they wanted to see occupy the presidency; their goal was simply to eliminate Castro. As these groups became desperate their tactics became more radical, drawing international attention to the exile community in south Florida and polarizing emigrés further.

A shift in American foreign policy catalyzed this radicalism. Under the guidance of Secretary of State Henry Kissinger, the Nixon and Ford administrations adopted a policy of detente. Negotiations concentrated on the Soviet Union and China, but the U.S. government also turned its attention to improving relations with Cuba. In 1973, both countries signed an antihijacking treaty. In 1975, the United States supported the OAS's vote to lift the eleven-year-old embargo of Cuba. For the first time, the U.S. government also allowed subsidiaries of U.S. corporations in foreign countries to trade with the island.

During the Carter administration, the United States and Cuba moved further towards rapprochement. The countries negotiated a fishing rights agreement and a maritime boundary agreement. The U.S. lifted its ban on transferring American currency to Cuba as well as on using an American passport to travel there. In April 1978, the first commercial flight between Miami and Havana in sixteen years departed from Miami International Airport, and the federal government also granted visas to Cubans to come to the U.S. on a temporary basis.[30] An unprecedented number of scholars, artists, writers, and scientists traveled to and from Cuba in the interest of cultural and scholarly exchange. The Cuban government also allowed a group of fifty-five young Cuban exiles of the *Brigada Antonio Maceo* to witness first-hand the accomplishments of the revolution—the first exiles since the revolution to be permitted to return to the island. The most important development, however, was the creation of American and Cuban "interests sections," which provided limited diplomatic representation.

Many emigrés of course were enraged by this new climate of tolerance. Polls conducted by the *Miami Herald* showed that more than 53 percent remained opposed to reestablishing diplomatic and trade relations with Cuba and felt betrayed by the U.S. government.[31] Emigrés expressed their anger in the exile news media and staged rallies and demonstrations in Miami, Union City, Washington, and other cities. A "Congress Against Coexistence" was held in San Juan, Puerto Rico, in 1974, attended by representatives from some seventy exile organizations. When the OAS announced that member nations would debate the lifting of sanctions against Cuba, emigrés traveled to the meeting as a protest lobby, and in Miami emigrés destroyed the Torch of Friendship, a monument to hemispheric solidarity at Bayfront Park. When the sanctions were finally lifted a year later, in 1975, exile organizations organized a "Liberty Caravan," a thousand-car parade through Little Havana culminating in a boisterous rally at the Orange Bowl condemning the OAS's action.[32]

At the same time, polls indicated that a growing number of emigrés supported some type of rapprochement with the Castro regime. A 1975 *Herald* poll, for example, revealed that 49.5 percent of Cuban emigrés were at least willing to visit the island; a surprising revelation to hardliners in the community. Letters to newspaper editors revealed that some favored reestablishing diplomatic and trade relations—not for the idealistic goal of furthering world peace but for more practical considerations: the normalization of relations would allow them the opportunity to visit their family and friends in Cuba. Many questioned the value of the U.S. embargo, which instead of weakening Cuba's revolutionary fervor only seemed to tighten its ties to the Soviet Union. Polls revealed a generational difference in attitudes: Cubans raised and educated in the United States were more likely to approve of some form of rapprochement than their elders were. While they shared their parents' suspicion of—perhaps even their contempt for—the Castro regime, they tended to favor a diplomatic solution to the problems in Cuba rather than continued military or economic aggression.

A handful of organizations emerged during the 1970s to lobby for the diplomatic approach, among them the Cuban Christians for Justice and Freedom, the National Union of Cuban Americans, and the Cuban American Committee. In 1979, the latter group sent a petition with over ten thousand signatures to President Jimmy Carter requesting that the United States normalize relations with the Castro government.[33] A few individuals established careers as advocates of a new diplomacy, the most controversial being the Reverend Manuel Espinosa, pastor of the Evangelical Church in Hialeah. Espinosa, a former captain in Castro's military and a former member of several anti-Castro organizations, used his weekly sermons to preach reconciliation and to advocate the normalization of diplomatic relations with Cuba.

The number of emigrés that joined these organizations, or who supported these activists, was not significant enough to serve as an effective lobby—at least during the 1970s. Those who favored the normalization of relations kept silent, for the most part, because they feared being branded *comunistas*. In this politically conservative community, such a tag inevitably affected careers, businesses, relationships, and even lives. Espinosa's activism brought him a severe beating at the hands of militant Cuban exiles in 1975, and other activists had their businesses boycotted, their homes vandalized, their families harassed, and their reputations ruined.[34]

Many emigrés believed that an accommodation of the Cuban government was an endorsement of Castro-communism. They could not understand why *exilados* would even speak to the individuals who had tortured, imprisoned, and executed tens of thousands of their compatriots. As one exile wrote, "Those who speak of coexistence demonstrate that they have forgotten our language."[35] Another had harsher words: "Those who physically or intellectually support the Castro regime are traitors, as are those who support a *fi-*

delismo sin Fidel, a nationalist communism, or who surreptitiously plant the idea of coexistence. Those who forgive, accept, or befriend the traitors are also traitors. Yes, one can be a Cuban by birth, but if one's heart is not Cuban one is a traitor."[36] When Manuel Espinosa publicly admitted (years later, in 1980) that he was an agent for the Cuban government, most emigrés were not surprised; his admission simply confirmed the popular belief that active supporters of renewed relations with Cuba had to be in some way connected to the regime.

Even the shipment via third countries of medicine and food parcels to Cuba was considered by hardliners to be an accommodation of the Castro government.[37] Radio talk show hosts attributed Castro's continued hold on Cuba to the "economic subsidies" Cubans received in the form of packages from the exile community—estimated at hundreds of thousands of dollars a year. If exiles stopped sending their relatives food, clothing, and medicines, they argued, discontent on the island would grow and ultimately lead to Castro's overthrow. For those emigrés who had elderly relatives or children in Cuba, though, maintaining a hard line against Cuba came at great personal and psychological cost. Those who sent packages to Cuba preferred to keep it secret, to avoid censure.

Angered by the new developments in American foreign policy and what they perceived to be a growing complacency in the exile community, the militant extremists escalated the war against Castro. As one militant explained: "It is to be expected that after eighteen years in exile a frustrated generation would emerge whose impatience would lead them to use extreme methods."[38] Their methods were so extreme that even the exile community feared to speak out against them. Groups such as *El Condor, Comandante Zero, Movimiento Neo-Revolucionario Cubano-Pragmatista, Coordinación de Organizaciones Revolucionarias Unidas* (CORU), *Poder Cubano, Acción Cubana,* M-17, the *Frente de Liberación Nacional de Cuba,* and Omega 7 bombed Cuban embassies and consulates around the world, murdered Cuban diplomatic employees, harassed and threatened individuals and institutions alleged to have ties to the Castro government, and placed bombs aboard planes heading for Cuba.

1976 was a particularly violent year. As thousands of emigrés celebrated the U.S. Bicentennial by taking the oath of citizenship, others waged war against Cuba. In April, commandos attacked two Cuban fishing boats, killing one fisherman, and bombed the Cuban Embassy in Portugal, killing two persons. In July, bombs exploded at the Cuban mission at the United Nations, at the offices of the British West Indian Airways of Barbados (which represented Cubana Airlines, the national airline), and inside a suitcase that was about to be loaded onto a Cuban jet in Kingston, Jamaica. Later that summer, two employees of the Cuban Embassy in Buenos Aires disappeared; the Cuban consul in Mérida, Mexico, was almost kidnapped; and a bomb exploded in the Cubana Airlines office in Panama. In October, bombs exploded on a Cuban jet minutes after it left Barbados; all 73 passengers died. In November, a bomb destroyed the Madrid office of Cubana Airlines.[39] The violence increased further in 1977 and 1978 as a result of the Carter administration's new policies towards Cuba and the *diálogo*.

While the paramilitary organizations of the 1960s had limited their actions to Cuba and its allies, the militant extremists targeted all those they perceived to be their enemies, including members of their own community, and many did not care how many innocent victims got in the way. They bombed Little Havana travel agencies, shipping companies, and pharmacies that conducted commercial transactions with Cuba. They harassed and threatened all who favored political coexistence. Extremists bombed the offices of *Réplica*, a popular Spanish-language news magazine, because its editor, Max Leznick, advocated lifting the trade embargo.[40] They harassed and ultimately murdered crane operator Luciano Nieves and Hialeah boatbuilder Ramón Donestevez because of their suspected ties to the Castro government.[41] In 1973, they assassinated Cuban exile leader José de la Torriente, who was suspected of embezzling funds from a liberation effort he had established, the *Plan Torriente*.[42] From 1973 to 1976, more than one hundred bombs exploded in the Miami area alone, and the FBI nicknamed Miami "the terrorist capital of the United States";[43] but the groups also operated in (and out of) New York, Union City, Los Angeles, Madrid, Santo Domingo, Mexico City, and Caracas. During the late 1970s, a Cuban exile tabloid in Puerto Rico, *La Crónica*, published interviews with the controversial leaders of these militant groups, whose identities were disguised. They warned the exile community to watch their backs.

Many emigrés spoke out against the terrorism of their compatriots, condemning these acts not only as immoral but also as tactically stupid. "They are politically and militarily incapable of producing a change in the regime," wrote a former member of the CRC of the terrorists: "[They will] cost human lives, create immense anxiety in the community, and, more importantly, discredit the exile community before U.S. public opinion. . . . Whether one likes it or not, these acts do not serve the liberation cause but, rather, serve subversive Marxist elements in this country."[44]

Sadly, many who spoke out against the terrorism became victims themselves. In 1976, extremists murdered José Peruyero, president of the Brigade 2506 Veterans Association, because he condemned the participation of Brigade veterans in terrorist activities.[45] Journalists became popular targets;

they were frequently threatened and their homes and offices vandalized. Three months after Peruyero's death, a bomb exploded in the car of WQBA news and program director Emilio Milián. Milián, who denounced acts of terrorism on his radio program *Habla el pueblo*, miraculously survived the explosion, but he lost both his legs. A few weeks later, he courageously returned to his job at WQBA and resumed his critical editorials, but a year later he was fired by the station because his editorials were allegedly too incendiary.[46]

A joint committee of local, state, and federal agencies investigating these terrorist acts learned that membership in the terrorist groups interlocked— that is, those who committed acts of violence often worked on behalf of three or four different groups. Organizations frequently disbanded and their members created splinter groups, giving the impression that there were more terrorists than there actually were. When a congressional subcommittee asked the Dade County Public Safety Department to identify the number of groups operating in the Miami area, one investigator revealed the frustration of tracking these organizations: "I can say that we have more than 10 militant groups with hard-core militants. . . . those 10 groups may be 12 tomorrow, and next week there may be 50. And then week after next it may be [down] to eight, because there is a constant change in the staffing of these groups and there is constant exchange."[47]

While the terrorist groups received some funding from sympathetic individuals in the community, more often than not they resorted to extortion, threatening wealthier emigrés with death or property damage if they did not supply the necessary funds.[48] A few militants received financial assistance from foreign agents—agents who later used the Cubans in their own domestic plots. The Chilean state police, for example, reportedly hired Cubans to assassinate the former Chilean ambassador Orlando Letelier in Washington in 1976.[49]

Investigations were made especially difficult by the Cuban intelligence network in Miami. American law enforcement agencies had to determine whether the violence and terrorism were actually committed by emigrés or by *infiltrados* who tried to destroy exile organizations by framing them. The Castro government had reportedly infiltrated hundreds of spies into Miami, most of them arriving in the U.S. as small-boat escapees, "fence-jumpers" at the U.S. base at Guantánamo, or immigrants arriving from third countries.[50] So extensive was this network that Castro's spies often served as the FBI's informants on the emigrés' illegal activities: when Alpha 66, for example, hired a gunman to assassinate Fidel Castro during a planned speech at the United Nations, Cuban spies uncovered the plot and notified American authorities.[51] Interviews in the Cuban press with emigrés who defected back to Cuba also revealed the inner workings of the top militant groups operating in south Florida.[52]

Emigrés hotly debated who was responsible for the wave of terror. Most preferred to interpret it as a Castro plot to divide and demoralize the community,[53] arguing that these acts of terrorism were too professional to be done by the "weekend warriors." Castro also stood to gain the most by the campaign of intimidation, which divided and silenced his opponents. In the meantime, while Justice Department officials tried to track down the culprits, emigrés with unpopular views or in visible positions took extra precautions. The exile press carried advertisements for security devices, including remote-control gadgets that could start cars from a distance of one hundred meters.

The FBI eventually tracked down fifteen terrorists associated with the New Jersey-based Omega 7, regarded as the most dangerous of the organizations; all fifteen were ultimately convicted. The FBI also arrested dozens of other militants, including five emigrés accused of assassinating Letelier.[54] Many cases, however, remain unsolved.

The wave of violence that rocked the community during the 1970s arose in part out of the secret war of the 1960s. Several of those convicted for terrorism and government espionage were former CIA protégés. The skills they had learned to destabilize and overthrow the Castro government were now used against their own community and their host society. According to some newspaper accounts, some of the Cubans involved in organized crime in south Florida, particularly in drug trafficking, also had CIA connections. Three of the Watergate burglars, Bernard Barker, Virgilio González, and Eugenio Martínez, were Cuban exiles with ties to the CIA.[55]

Some in the émigré community regarded the extremists as heroes and *patriotas*. One editor of a *periodiquito* wrote:

> I know there are many Cubans who don't like these tactics and criticize them, but I have to ask myself, "What have these compatriots done all these past years, and what has been their contribution to the struggle for liberation?" Most of them have simply enjoyed the comforts of living in the land of liberty. . . . No, my friends. A Cuban is not merely someone who was born in Cuba. A Cuban is someone who thinks about the seven million compatriots who are living as slaves.[56]

A well-known journalist wrote, "The realities of world politics leave no alternative but to use violence. Only when the exiles destroy the lives and interests of our enemies will Washington, Moscow, the OAS, or whoever take our views into account."[57]

Some exiles raised funds to help the militants in their cause—and later in their legal defense.[58] In 1974, Cuban radio stations in Miami helped raise over twelve thousand dollars for the families of two militants associated with the Frente de Liberación Nacional de Cuba who had been injured while constructing a bomb.[59] In 1978, *La Crónica* printed an advertisement for the Cuban Defense League, Inc., which raised funds for the legal defense of "Cuban political prisoners in the United States, Mexico, and Venezuela."[60] That same year, a New York-based publication entitled *Desde las Prisiones* began publishing articles by or in support of the "Cuban freedom fighters." The White House and the Department of Justice frequently received letters and petitions asking the government to commute sentences. In August 1979, for example, a Chicago exile coalition called the Federación de Organizaciones Cubanas de Illinois wrote Attorney General Benjamin Civiletti on behalf of ten men detained for various acts. "Now that the Cuban Communist authorities are releasing political prisoners," they wrote, ". . . we believe the United States Department of Justice should also grant benevolent concessions to the exile patriots incarcerated in this country, who acted according to the best interest of what traditionally has been a struggle to restore freedom and democracy in Cuba."[61]

The most famous militant was Orlando Bosch, a Miami pediatrician who in 1968 was sentenced to ten years in prison for firing on a Polish freighter with a bazooka. Released on parole after four years in a federal penitentiary, Bosch fled the country in 1974 when he became a chief suspect in the assassination of Cuban exile leader José Elias de la Torriente. Over the next two years, he served as leader of the militant group *Acción Cubana*, which claimed responsibility for the bombings of several Cuban embassies and consulates throughout Latin America. In 1976, the government of Venezuela charged Bosch with conspiracy in the Cubana Airlines bombing that killed seventy-three people, including the entire Cuban national fencing team. Although a Venezuelan judge found insufficient evidence to charge him in the bombing, Bosch remained in prison while his case was reviewed in civil and military courts.[62] Although he was acquitted two more times, he was not released from prison until 1987.

Over the years, Bosch's supporters staged marches and demonstrations to protest his incarceration. They organized exhibitions of his drawings in art galleries in Little Havana, Tampa, Union City, Chicago, and New York City to raise money for his defense and to assist his family. Miami mayoral candidates, hoping to garner a few votes, even visited Bosch in prison in Caracas. The emigré press in particular rallied to his defense. "[Bosch] has done some things which the U.S. government could call terrorism," said WQBA news director Tomás García Fusté, "but he is fighting for the liberation of our country. It is not terrorism but self-defense. We, the Cubans, are at war with Fidel Castro."[63]

Not all emigrés regarded Bosch as a hero, of course. When Miami City Commissioner Demetrio Pérez introduced a resolution in 1983 for an Orlando Bosch Day, both his office and the *Miami Herald* were swamped with letters, as many opposed to the motion as in favor of it. "I am a Cuban, and proud of it," wrote one woman, ". . . but I do not support someone whose idea of patriotism is to attack a Polish freighter, who has violated parole in the United States, and who has been accused of killing 73 innocent people."[64] The federal government was also unsympathetic. When Bosch returned to the United States in February 1988 following his release from prison, he was arrested by U.S. marshalls for having violated his parole. Deportation proceedings were begun, but the Justice Department was unable to find any country willing to grant Bosch entry. Finally, in late 1990, he was placed under house arrest.

For many emigrés, the wave of violence posed a moral dilemma that forced them to seriously reconsider their heroes as well as the methods they considered acceptable in the war against Castro. They learned that the line that divided revolutionary activities from terrorist activities could be a very thin one. The violence of the 1970s, then, led some emigrés to disassociate themselves completely, in fear or disgust, from exile politics. For others the negative media attention focused on the community, plus the realization that even the militant groups were impotent in bringing about change, forced them to reevaluate strategy, and slowly they realized that if they wanted to evoke meaningful change in Cuba they had to work within the political machinery of their host country. The war against Castro took a new direction in the 1980s, and the election of Ronald Reagan facilitated that redirection.

Conclusion

Those intrigued by the community of Cuban exiles and Cuban Americans in south Florida frequently ask what will happen in Miami once there is a changing of the guard in Cuba. Will the emigrés return to their homeland? Or will thousands more Cubans immigrate to the United States? The answer is yes—to both questions. Once Fidel Castro is no longer in office (for whatever reason)—and assuming that democratic reforms are enacted—some percentage of the community will return to Cuba. The numbers are difficult to predict: a poll conducted in 1993 by Florida International University revealed that 29 percent of Cuban-born heads of households wanted to return to live permanently in Cuba, while a similar poll conducted in 1990 showed that only 14 percent would actually return.[65] Among those born or raised in the United States the percentages are probably much lower. The emigrés talk a great deal about returning to their homeland, but few will actually pack up and leave when the opportunity arises. As several interviewees told me, "Why uproot yourself twice in one lifetime? The first time was hard enough." They have invested time and hard work in the United States. They have re-built their lives and careers; they bought homes and raised their children here. They have developed ties to the United States in spite of their original intentions. Most do not want to start all over again, especially in a society that will undoubtedly experience social, economic, and political turmoil in the post-Castro years.

The length of time spent in the United States and family ties in the two countries are the principal factors that will influence the decision to stay or to return. For Cubans who grew up in the U.S., "returning" to Cuba would be akin to moving to a foreign country, notwithstanding the culture they claim to share with those on the island. The emigrés most likely to return will be the elderly, eager to spend their remaining years in their homeland. Also likely to return are those who feel alienated in the U.S. and have found it impossible to adapt. The majority of emigrés, however, will want to stay close to their families. Many of the first generation are now grandparents and even great-grandparents; they will not want to move too far away from their children.

Nevertheless, Cubans in south Florida will always maintain an interest and play a role in the affairs of Cuba. Cuba is closer to Miami than Tampa, Orlando, or the state capital at Tallahassee, and the interest in Cuba is as much geopolitical as cultural. South Florida, like the rest of the Caribbean, has a stake in the political and economic stability of the island, and thus Cuba will play a role in public debate on the streets of Havana USA as well as in the corridors of Tallahassee and Washington.

Travel back and forth across the Florida Straits will be guaranteed. Emigrés who remain in the U.S. will want to travel to Cuba to visit relatives, or for a vacation, or for a variety of other reasons. In much the same way that former refugees from Eastern Europe and the Baltic states are presently investing in their homelands, the more entrepreneurial among the emigrés will want to in-vest in or establish businesses in Cuba—both to help their former country and to increase their own fortunes. In the early 1990s, U.S. airline and shipping companies were already plotting ways to corner this new travel market. Ac-cording to the *Miami Herald,* some companies were even drafting models for hydrofoils that might transport people back and forth in a couple of hours. It is conceivable that some emigrés might divide their time between the two countries, working in one country and making their homes in another, much as many Americans commute between, say, New York and Connecticut, or as others commute back and forth across the U.S.-Mexico border. The first generation's dual citizenship will facilitate this development.

Migration from Cuba will continue regardless of what happens in Cuba. In September 1994, in order to force the Cuban government to curtail the traffic of homemade rafts across the Florida Straits, the Clinton administration agreed to allow the immigration of a minimum of twenty thousand Cubans each year, not including the immediate relatives of United States citizens.[66] Even with the installation of a more democratic government, migration from Cuba will continue. Some Cubans will choose to emigrate to be reunited with their families in the United States, while others, impatient with the sluggish Cuban economy, will want to try their luck in the U.S. The number of migrants in such a scenario will depend as much on U.S. immigration policy as on the political and economic conditions in Cuba; but whatever the number, the influx of immigrants will continually revitalize Cuban identity and culture in the United States. Cuban American culture in south Florida will continue to define itself in relation to two countries and two cultures.

The most difficult challenge in the post-Castro era, both on the island and in Florida, will be learning to forgive. The exile community remains divided thirty-five years after the revolution by political differences. Emigrés are unable to forgive each other for their role (or lack thereof) in the revolution and later the counterrevolution. From the comfort of exile, they criticize their compatriots on the island for allowing the government of Fidel Castro to endure, and while they applaud the *balseros* for taking to the seas to escape Castro's Cuba, many wonder suspiciously why they didn't do it sooner. Conversely, many Cubans on the island continue to regard the emigrés as gusanos and cannot forgive them for exploiting, and later abandoning, their country. A great deal of cooperation (and, perhaps, time) is needed before Cuban societies on opposite sides of the Florida Straits are tolerant, peaceful, and democratic.

The Cubans of south Florida will play a major role in the civic, cultural, and political life of the area in the years to come. Their principal challenge will be to share their power base with the many different groups that call south Florida home. Over the past three decades, a growing tension—even hostility—has emerged in south Florida, the product of rapid demographic transformation and the perceived dominance of Cubans in the local economy and local politics. The 1990 U.S. census revealed that Latinos comprised 49.2 percent of Dade County's total population of 1.9 million. In the city of Miami, 62.5 percent of the population was of Latino origin; in Hialeah, 88 percent.[67] Despite a near-doubling in total population over the past thirty years, the percentage of non-Latino whites had fallen from 80 percent in 1960 to 37 percent in 1990. Such measures as the 1980 English Only amendment ultimately proved unsuccessful in controlling the Latino population (and in May 1993, voters overturned the 1980 ruling).[68] Unable to compete in a bilingual economy and angered by the cultural changes in south Florida, many non-Latino whites have moved to the counties immediately north of Dade, where they can maintain their cultural and political dominance.

The non-Latino black population has remained more rooted to the area, but blacks, too, are resentful. For thirty-five years, they have watched Cubans grow wealthier and more powerful. They resent the federal government's early assistance to the refugees—the grants and loans that helped them go to school or start small businesses, the remedial education and job retraining programs, the health benefits. Blacks resent that these non-English-speaking foreigners could receive so much while the native-born were overlooked. These benefits helped the Cubans assert their economic and political power. By 1990, three of the five members of the Miami City Commission, including the mayor, were Cuban; by contrast, only one member was African American. Blacks in Dade County have fared better economically than their counterparts elsewhere around the state—in part because of the economic transformation brought on by Cuban immigration—but many feel that they have been shut out from the most important local institutions.[69]

This resentment was obvious as early as 1968, when blacks rioted during the Republican National Convention in Miami Beach. Riots took place again in 1980, 1982, and 1989, each spurred by a specific incident involving police brutality, but each also an expression of the deep-seated resentment towards whites and Latinos.[70] In the wake of the riots the city created an antidiscrimination coalition entitled Greater Miami United to address the concerns of the various racial and ethnic communities. There are many ill feelings, however, and groups from the Nation of Islam to the Ku Klux Klan have tried to capitalize on the tension in the community.

The class, racial, ethnic, and national diversity within the Latino community is also the source of much tension. While the Cubans helped produce the economic prosperity that attracted large-scale immigration from the Caribbean and Latin America, the newer immigrants resent the Cubans' dominance in local institutions, from the Spanish-language media to city hall. Latinos complain of Cuban powerbrokers who refuse to allow others into their inner circle, of the neverending anti-Castro diatribes on the radio, and of the media's lack of sensitivity to issues that are important to them. "They think they're the only Hispanics in Miami," said one disgruntled Puerto Rican. Many of the complaints filed with the FCC in the past decade have been filed by Latinos who perceive the Cuban radio shows to be bigoted.[71] At times,

Latino resentment has been expressed through violence—as in December 1990, when Puerto Ricans in the Wynwood neighborhood rioted. Like the black riots of the 1980s, the episode was a reaction to a specific case of police brutality; but it too was a manifestation of the larger ethnic and racial tensions in south Florida.[72]

Latinos also express concern about the climate of censorship in Miami, a concern shared by whites and blacks as well. Individuals who support Fidel Castro or the Sandinistas or who favor tolerance and dialogue are branded comunistas and suffer discrimination, and sometimes even verbal or physical abuse. In past years, Latin American entertainers who have performed in Cuba have been banned from appearing at the annual *Festival de la Calle Ocho* because the organizers claim that to allow them to perform would be to risk a confrontation, endangering the two million people who attend the weeklong festivities. In December 1990, under pressure from the Cuban community, the city of Miami withdrew its official welcoming of Nelson Mandela because of his support of Fidel Castro. In January 1991, Miami city commissioners told members of the local Haitian community that they could celebrate the inauguration of their country's new president at Bayfront Park only if Fidel Castro was not invited to the inauguration in Haiti.[73] For Latinos, Haitians, and others, these incidents are just the most recent examples of the censorship in south Florida that violates their civil rights. Miami, they argue, has become a city where the needs and interests of the dominant group outweigh the needs and interests of the rest of the population.

The Cubans, however, will be forced to make concessions. While they are the largest immigrant group in south Florida, others are growing rapidly. In the early 1990s Central and South Americans, and in particular immigrants from Nicaragua and Colombia, had replaced Cubans as the fastest-growing Latino groups. Emigrés are slowly realizing that it is to their benefit to try to foster a more inclusive vision of community. Just as others accommodated them, they must now accommodate others. Hopefully, the Cuban Americans—particularly the second generation—will play a mediating and conciliatory role in community relations. As the children of emigrés, they can relate to the immigration experience of others; as Americans, they are bound to the local community and to the country that offered them safe haven. They do not share the exile generation's obsession with Cuba; rather, their energies are invested in the hybrid borderland society that produced them. It is the Cuban Americans who will ultimately help determine south Florida's future.

Notes

1. Among the first to write about the Cuban economic enclave were sociologists Alejandro Portes and Robert L. Bach. They defined the economic enclave as "a distinctive economic formation, characterized by the spatial concentration of immigrants who organize a variety of enterprises to serve their own ethnic market and the general population." According to Portes and Bach, the enclave economy allowed Cubans to avoid the economic disadvantages that usually accompany segregation. See Alejandro Portes and Robert L. Bach, *Latin Journey: Cuban and Mexican Immigrants in the United States* (Berkeley and Los Angeles: University of California Press, 1985), and Alejandro Portes, "The Social Origins of the Cuban Enclave Economy of Miami," *Sociological Perspectives* 30 (October 1987): 340–71. A study by Portes and Jensen found that ethnic enterprises were effective avenues for economic mobility, particularly for men; although few women were self-employed, they earned higher incomes working within the enclave economy. See Alejandro Portes and Leif Jensen, "The Enclave and the Entrants: Patterns of Ethnic Enterprise in Miami before and after Mariel," *American Sociological Review* 54 (December 1989): 929–49.

For another interpretation of the enclave economy, and more specifically the role of Cubans in the U.S. labor movement, see Guillermo J. Grenier, "The Cuban American Labor Movement in Dade County: An Emerging Immigrant Working Class," in Grenier and Stepick, eds., *Miami Now!* 133–59. Grenier explores the role class-based organizations such as labor unions have played in fostering group solidarity and group consciousness.

2. "Cuban and Haitian Arrivals: Crisis and Response," June 30, 1980, 6, in File "ND16/CO38 1/20/77-1/20/81" Box ND-42, White House Central File, Subject File: National Security–Defense, Carter Library. See also Carlos Arboleya, *The Cuban Community, 1980: Coming of Age as History Repeats Itself* (Miami, 1980).

3. Carlos Arboleya, *El impacto cubano en la Florida* (Miami, 1985). Arboleya, former president and CEO of Barnett Bank, Miami, periodically published reports on the Cuban community in south Florida. Arboleya's report also included the following statistics for Dade County: over 4,500 Cuban doctors, 500 lawyers, 17 bank presidents and 390 vice presidents, and 25,000 garment workers. See also "Dade Latin Businesses Top U.S.," *Miami Herald,* October 23, 1986, 1A.

4. In 1990, the median family income for Cubans was $33,504, which was higher than the median family income for Latinos in the U.S. ($27,972) but lower than the median national income ($37,403). 18.5 percent of Cubans had four or more years of college education, as compared to 9.7 percent for Latinos and 23.7 percent for the nation as a whole. 21.6 percent of Cuban males and 20 percent of Cuban females were professionals or executives (as compared to the national averages of 26.3 and 27.2 percent). See Alejandro Portes, *"¿Quienes somos? ¿Qué pensamos? Los cubanos en Estados Unidos en la década de los noventas," Cuban Affairs/Asuntos Cubanos* 1, no. 1 (Spring 1994): 5.

For an analysis of the 1980 census, see Lisandro Pérez, "The Cuban Population of the United States: The Results of the 1980 U.S. Census of Population," *Cuban*

Studies/Estudios Cubanos 15 (Summer 1985): 1–18; Joan Moore and Harry Pachón, *Hispanics in the United States* (Englewood Cliffs, NJ: Prentice-Hall, 1985), 69–78. The 1980 census did not include the Cubans who arrived during the Mariel boatlift.

5. Lisandro Pérez, "Immigrant Economic Adjustment and Family Organization: The Cuban Success Story Re-Examined," *International Migration Review* 20 (Spring 1986): 4–20. See also Pérez, "The Cuban Population of the United States," 8–9. The 1980 census revealed that more Cuban women worked outside the home than any other group, 55.4 percent as compared to the national average of 49.9 percent. For an analysis of Cuban women's roles in the economic, political, and cultural affairs of the community, see García, "Adapting to Exile." For an economic analysis see Myra Marx Ferree, "Employment without Liberation: Cuban Women in the U.S.," *Social Science Quarterly* 60 (January 1979): 35–50. See also Dorita Roca Mariña, "A Theoretical Discussion of What Changes and What Stays the Same in Cuban Immigrant Families," in José Szapocznik and María Cristina Herrera, eds., *Cuban Americans: Acculturation, Adjustment, and the Family* (Washington: The National Coalition of Hispanic Mental Health and Human Services Organization, 1978).

6. Pérez, "Immigrant Economic Adjustment." See also Portes and Jensen, "The Enclave and the Entrants."

7. Portes and Jensen found that 34 percent of their Mariel respondents (excluding the self-employed) were working for Cuban-owned firms. See Portes and Jensen, "The Enclave and the Entrants."

8. Arboleya, *The Cuban Community, 1980.* See also Raymond A. Mohl, "An Ethnic 'Boiling Pot': Cubans and Haitians in Miami," *Journal of Ethnic Studies* 13 (Summer 1985): 51–74.

9. "To Miami, Refugees Spell P-R-O-S-P-E-R-I-T-Y," *Business Week*, November 3, 1962, 92; "Cuban Refugees Write a U.S. Success Story," *Business Week*, January 11, 1969, 84.

10. In his article "Immigrant Economic Adjustment and Family Organization," Lisandro Pérez challenges the "myth of the golden exile." He concludes that comparisons of economic achievements between Hispanic groups are inconclusive because they ignore the differences in the structural conditions within which economic adjustment takes place. See also Alejandro Portes, "Dilemmas of a Golden Exile: Integration of Cuban Refugee Families in Milwaukee," *American Sociological Review* 34 (August 1969): 505–18.

11. In 1990, 16.9 percent of Cuban Americans lived in poverty, as compared to 13.5 percent of the general population; Portes, "¿Quienes somos?" 5. See also note 60.

12. Alfonso Chardy, "'Invisible Exiles': Black Cubans Don't Find Their Niche in Miami," *Houston Chronicle*, September 12, 1993, 24A.

13. "Temas," *Impacto*, March 11, 1972. Translation mine. The concerns of the Cuban working class are articulated in the exile newspapers *El Trabajador*, *Trabajo*, and *Impacto*.

14. "Editorial," *Cubanacan: Asociación de Villaclareños en el Exilio*, 9, no. 106 (January 1975), 1. Translation mine.

15. "Editorial," *Martiano*, November 1972, 2. Translation mine.

16. "*Temas,*" *Impacto*, May 20, 1973, 2. Translation mine.

17. "Are We to Become Citizens?" *Antorcha*, January 1968, 5.

18. Founded in 1967, Abdala took its name from a fable by the nineteenth-century independence leader José Martí. Abdala, a prince from the imaginary land of Nuvia, renounces all material comforts and pleasures in order to defend his nation. Prince Abdala ultimately dies for his beliefs.

19. "*Entre dos banderas,*" *Antorcha*, April 1973, 2. Translation mine.

20. "Editorial," *Antorcha*, October 1969, 1. Translation mine.

21. "Editorial," *Antorcha*, December 1969, 1. Translation mine.

22. Roberto Fabricio, "The Cuban Americans: Fifteen Years Later," *Tropic Magazine* (*Miami Herald*), July 14, 1974, 30–36.

23. Miguel Pérez, "10,000 New Americans Is Exile Group's Goal," *Miami Herald*, November 24, 1975, 8B; George Volsky, "Cuban Exiles Now Seek U.S. Citizenship," *New York Times*, July 4, 1976, 19; Helga Silva, "The Cuban Exiles: Landmarks of an Era," *Miami Herald*, April 8, 1979, 22A.

24. Arboleya, *The Cuban Community, 1980*, 3.

25. Roberto Fabricio, "Cubans at Home, but Homesick," *Miami Herald*, October 29, 1972, 1B.

26. Humberto Cruz, "Dade Cubans Won't Return, Study Shows," *Miami Herald*, June 10, 1974. The *Herald* published part of a study by sociologists Juan Clark and Manuel Mendoza of Miami-Dade Community College. Clark and Mendoza conducted interviews with 151 Dade Cubans fifty-five years or older—the group most likely to have failed to adapt to life in the United States—and less than half of these stated that they would return to Cuba if Castro were overthrown.

27. Alejandro Portes and Rafael Mozo, "The Political Adaptation Process of Cubans and Other Ethnic Minorities in the United States: A Preliminary Analysis," *International Migration Review* 19 (March 1985): 35–63.

28. Metro-Dade County, Board of County Commissioners, Resolution no. R.-502–73; Chuck Gómez, "In Cases of Emergency, Latins Can Lose Out," *Miami Herald*, June 3, 1974, 1A.

29. Resolution no. R.-502–73, as cited in Castro, "The Politics of Language in Miami," 116.

30. Myles R. R. Frechette, "Cuban-Soviet Impact on the Western Hemisphere," *Department of State Bulletin* 80 (July 1980): 79–80.

31. *Miami Herald*, December 29, 1975.

32. Roberto Fabricio, "Torch Ruins Show Rising Exile Anger," *Miami Herald*, October 13, 1974, 1B; Roberto Fabricio, "Exiles Protest Lifting of Cuba Sanctions," *Miami Herald*, November 4, 1974, 1B; Roberto Fabricio, "Cubans' OAS Protest Cooled by Downpour," *Miami Herald*, May 11, 1975, 1D.

33. *"El exilio pide relaciones entre Cuba y Estados Unidos,"* Arcíto 5, nos. 19–20 (1979): 7–8; *"10 mil exiliados piden Carter reanude relaciones con Cuba,"* El Mundo, June 25, 1979, 8.

34. See, for example, the Miami Herald, April 2, 1975, July 23, 1975, and August 22, 1978.

35. "Editorial" in Martiano, n.d. Translation mine.

36. Carlos López-Oña, Jr., *"Los traidores,"* Antorcha, July 1970, 4. Translation mine.

37. The shipment of food and medicine to Cuba was always hotly debated in the community. See, for example, ¡Fe!, December 15, 1972, 1. Even burial in Cuba—which was allowed beginning in 1979—was strongly discouraged because such arrangements benefitted the Cuban government financially. Ana E. Santiago, *"Más restos cubanos llevados a la isla,"* El Nuevo Herald, April 4, 1991, 1A, 4A.

38. *"Desde la cárcel denuncia La Cova al exilio Cubano,"* La Nación, October 15, 1976, 14. Translation mine.

39. "Exiles Say They Planted Bomb on Cuban Airliner," New York Times, July 16, 1976, 8; "Terrorism Charged to Cubans in Testimony by Miami Police," New York Times, August 23, 1976, 12; "Nine Cuban Refugees Go on Trial in Miami Tomorrow, Putting Focus on Terrorists' Activity in South Florida," New York Times, November 28, 1976, 35. See also Cuba Update (Center for Cuban Studies) 1, no. 1 (April 1980).

40. Jay Clarke, "Cubans in Miami Fearful," Washington Post, May 23, 1976, E1.

41. Edna Buchanan, "Foes Stalked Slain Exile," Miami Herald, February 23, 1974, 1B; *"Acusa Nieves de agresión a líder pragmatista,"* ¡Fe!, April 7, 1973, 3; *"No permitiremos que juege con Cuba un puñado de traidores,"* ¡Fe!, June 15, 1973, 2. See also Internal Security Hearings, 1976, 615.

42. Hilda Inclán, "Six Cuban Exiles Marked for Death by 'Zero,'" Miami Herald, April 15, 1974; *"Dara plazo a Torriente,"* ¡Fe!, February 24, 1973, 7; *"Torriente es el farsante mas grande que ha parido este exilio corrompido y timorato,"* ¡Fe!, May 19, 1973, 10.

43. "Nine Cuban Refugees Go on Trial in Miami Tomorrow, Putting Focus on Terrorists' Activities in South Florida," New York Times, November 28, 1976, 35.

44. José Ignacio Lasaga, *"El terrorismo en Miami,"* Krisis 1 (Spring 1976): 23, 30. Translation mine.

45. On August 31, 1977, a group of men claiming to represent the Brigade 2506 Veterans Association announced that they would continue "all kinds of actions to fight against the communist tyranny."

46. Hilda Inclán, "I Am Not Afraid," Nuestro, April 1977, 46–47; Benjamin de la Vega, *"Estrepitosa caida de las WQBA en el survey de la Arbitron,"* Alerta, August 1980; Larry Rohter, "Dissenting Voice Fights to Stay on Air," New York Times, March 2, 1993, A14. As a side note, Milián organized the first Three Kings Day parade in Little Havana in 1971. See Miami Herald, January 7, 1975, 1B.

47. Internal Security Hearings (1976), 615–16.

48. Internal Security Hearings (1976), 632, 651.

49. Internal Security Hearings (1976), 652. Letelier, ambassador to the U.S. during Salvador Allende's government, was a vocal critic of the Pinochet military regime. Cuban militants claimed that he was a subversive furthering the cause of international communism. See *El Imparcial*, May 7, 1981, 1.

50. For a sample of newspaper articles dealing with this topic see *"El espionaje del G-2 en Miami," Bohemia Libre*, November 13, 1960, 83; *"Lleno el exilio de agentes G-2," Patria*, July 25, 1961, 4; "Castro Spies Prowl Miami, Defector Says," *Miami News*, December 18, 1971; Joe Crankshaw, "500 Castro Agents Operate in Miami, Witness Testifies," *Miami Herald*, August 19, 1976; Jim McGee, "Exiles Wage Silent War with Castro Spies," *Miami Herald*, June 19, 1983, 1A. Cuban exile newspapers claimed that the number of spies in Miami was much larger than that supposed by local authorities. One exile newspaper, for example, claimed that as many as seventy-five hundred Cuban spies operated in south Florida. See *Látigo*, January 1979, 10. Most newspapers never explained how they arrived at these figures. The tabloid *Patria* published pictures of suspected G-2 police hiding in exile. See also *"Aumento alarmante de infiltrados," Impacto*, December 30, 1971, 1.

51. McGee, "Exiles Wage Silent War with Castro Spies."

52. For example, a 1974 interview by *Prensa Latina* with defector Carlos Rivero Collado, (a former *brigadista* and the son of Andrés Rivero Agüero, Batista's chosen successor) discussed his work with the *Pragmatistas* and the Cuban Nationalist Movement. A Radio Havana interview with 1976 defector Manuel de Armas discussed the alleged involvement of the group Abdala in the assassination of exile leader Rolando Masferrer. Internal Security Hearings (1976) 626–27, 631–32, 649–56.

53. For one such interpretation see Lasaga, *"El terrorismo en Miami."* See also *El Clarín*, May 27, 1976.

54. In 1990 and 1991, the FBI arrested two more Cubans connected to the plot. Two former Chilean military officials remain in hiding at the time of writing. In July 1991, the Chilean Supreme Court reopened the Letelier case. See Gloria Marina, "Five Cubans and an American Figure in the Letelier Case," *Miami Herald*, May 6, 1978, 11A; and *"A investigación aspecto chileno del caso Letelier," El Nuevo Herald*, September 24, 1990, 1A.

55. Many in the exile community did not understand why Americans were making such a fuss about Watergate, and they continued to support President Nixon in his "struggle against subversion." See Frank Calzón, *"El exilio cubano y la crisis norteamericana," ¡Cuba Va!* 1 (Winter 1974): 3–5; Pedro Moreno, "Watergate *y los cubanos," Joven Cuba* 1 (February 1974): 11–12; Roberto Fabricio, "Watergate Had Ironic Twists for Cubans," *Miami Herald*, June 12, 1982, 1B.

56. *Guerra* (New York), November 19, 1976, 3. Translation mine. See also the August/September 1973 issue of *Abdala*, in which the editors pay tribute to a young Cuban who died while putting together a bomb in his Paris hotel room: "From a very young age he was attracted by his patriotic duty. . . ."

57. Gaston Baquero, *"No hay mas alternativa que la violencia,"* reprinted in *Impacto*, October 14, 1972, 5. Translation mine.

58. *El Imparcial*, May 7, 1981.

59. Internal Security Hearings (1976), 636–37.

60. *La Crónica*, October 10, 1978, 18.

61. Federación de Organizaciones Cubanas de Illinois, "Petition to the United States Department of Justice," Box 17, Staff Offices, Papers of Esteban Torres, Carter Library.

62. Merrill Collett, *"Absuelto Bosch en Venezuela,"* *El Herald*, July 22, 1986, 1A.

63. Reinaldo Ramos, *"Exiliados reflexionan sobre* Orlando Bosch," *El Herald*, July 27, 1986, 1, 3. Translation mine.

64. Letter to the editor, *Miami Herald*, April 2, 1983, 16A.

65. Deborah Sontag, "The Lasting Exile of Cuban Spirits," *New York Times*, September 11, 1994, 1E.

66. "U.S.-Cuba Joint Communiqué on Migration," *U.S. Department of State Dispatch* 5, no. 37 (September 12, 1994), 603.

67. Richard Wallace, "South Florida Grows to Latin Beat," *Miami Herald*, March 6, 1991, 1A; Sandra Dibble, "New Exiles Flocking to Dade," *Miami Herald*, April 11, 1987, 1D; Celia W. Dugger, "Latin Influx, Crime Prompt 'Flight' North," *Miami Herald*, May 3, 1987, 1B.

68. "Dade County Commission Repeals English-Only Law," *New York Times*, May 19, 1993.

69. Sergio López-Miró, ". . . While Hispanics Become the Area's Scapegoats," *Miami Herald*, October 11, 1990, 27A.

70. Jeffrey Schmalz, "Disorder Erupts Again in Miami on Second Night after Fatal Shooting," *New York Times*, January 18, 1989, 1; Jeffrey Schmalz, "Miami Mayor Apologizes to Police for Actions at Scene of Disorder," *New York Times*, January 19, 1989, 1.

71. Jay Ducassi, "Stations Seldom Face Libel Suits or FCC Action," *Miami Herald*, June 22, 1986, 2B.

72. Steven A. Holmes, "Miami Melting Pot Proves Explosive," *New York Times*, December 9, 1990, E4.

73. Nancy San Martín, "Castro Clause on Inaugural Upsets City's Haitian Leaders," *Miami Herald*, January 31, 1991, 3B.

*   *   *

Questions

1. To what extent can the status of Cuban Americans as a model Latino minority be attributed to individual drive to succeed and to what extent can it be attributed to the institutional support and material resources provided by the U.S. government?

2. Under what circumstances might we expect other minority groups to become as successful as Cuban Americans if they received the same level of material support? What are the implications for future policy and the nature of social change?
3. Cuba produces the New Men and New Women. The United States produces the Cuban American "golden immigrants." Given the evidence provided by García, can we say that one system produces a "better" citizen in terms of critical thinking, diversity, and self-motivation?
4. Keeping in mind that during the Revolutionary War English American patriots terrorized their fellow colonists who remained loyal to the king, under what circumstances can we assign Cuban and Puerto Rican "terrorists" the subjectivity of "patriots" or "freedom fighters"?
5. Anglos move out of the area, African American and non-Cuban Latinos riot to protest Cuban-American domination, censorship, and intolerance. To what extent does this situation have to do with the nature of Cuban culture and to what extent does it have to do with the nature of power relations? What are the implications for a pluralistic society?

~

CHAPTER SEVENTEEN

Last-Mambo-in-Miami
Gustavo Pérez-Firmat

Soy un ajiaco de contradicciones.
I have mixed feelings about everything.
Name your *tema*, I'll hedge;
name your *cerca*, I'll straddle it
like a *cubano.*
I have mixed feelings about everything.
Soy un ajiaco de contradicciones.
Vexed, hexed, complexed,
hyphenated, oxygenated, illegally alienated,
psycho *soy, cantando voy:*
You say tomato,
I say *tu madre;*
You say potato,
I say *Pototo.*
Let's call the hole
un hueco, the thing
a *cosa,* and if the *cosa*
goes into the *hueco,*
consider yourself *en casa,*
consider yourself part of the family.
(Cuban-American *mí:*
I *singo* therefore I am, *sí.*)

Soy un ajiaco de contradicciones,
un puré de impurezas,
a little square from Rubik's Cuba,
que nadie nunca acoplará.
(Cha-cha-chá.)

PART IV

PUERTO RICANS AND AMERICANS

PART IV A

~

Under Two Empires:
A 400-Year Struggle
Francisco Hernández Vázquez

People in Puerto Rico have their own national Olympic Team and each year contestants vie for the title of Miss Universe.[2] Puerto Ricans are U.S. citizens by birth, they do not, however, get to vote for president, have no representation in the U.S. Senate and no proportional representation in the House of Representatives. Because there is no taxation without representation for U.S. citizens, Puerto Ricans do not pay federal taxes. Depending on whom you ask, Puerto Rico is a colony or a Commonwealth of the United States.

To understand the development of this unusual situation for this group of Latino and Latina people, Section A provides a historical and political context. This is followed by excerpts from three U.S. Congressional laws known as the Foraker Act, the Jones Act and Public Law 600; these are the symbolic "birth certificates" that incorporated Puerto Ricans into the United States. There is also a historical context and a discussion of how these laws were used as tools for the economic and cultural colonization of Puerto Rico. Then, to illustrate the Puerto Rican evolution of tactics in the struggle for democracy (see table 2.1) there are two texts on revolutionary nationalism, one by Corretjer. His focus is on Pedro Albizu Campos, a central figure in the fight for Puerto Rican Independence in the 1930s, and on the Ponce Massacre, which illustrates how the United States dealt with the *independentistas*. The other text takes us to New York where decades later in the late 1960s, Nuyo Rican youth, create a group known as the Young Lords to express their desire for Puerto Rican independence and extend their revolutionary zeal to include all third world peoples. These strategies in Section A contrast with those of Section B, where in chapter 21 Grosfoguel points to a different tactic that goes beyond nationalism and colonialism and the focus is on a better life, not a better citizenship. In chapter 22, Duany addresses a more personal kind of struggle that takes place at the level of everyday life and often causes "a traumatic racial experience." The colonization methods, ostensibly based on some kind of legality, illustrate the point made in Chicanology about how domination reaches beyond the law to extract wealth from human bodies.

The Expectation of Independence

Of all Spanish colonial possessions in the Americas, Puerto Rico is the only territory that has never gained its independence. In fact, Puerto Rico is, arguably, the oldest colony in the world. Many of the same internal and geopolitical dynamics that we saw affecting Cuba during the last quarter of the nineteenth century are also involved in Puerto Rico. The island's value to U.S. policy makers was as an outlet for excess manufactured goods; but primarily its value was as a key naval station in the Caribbean. One important difference, however, is that Puerto Rico did not have the benefit of technological modernization. The railroads, for example, were operating in Cuba by 1837, but Puerto Rican construction had barely begun by 1878. When the U.S. Americans conquered the island, they saw trains pulled by oxen; no one had capital to buy locomotives.[3] This difference in material conditions is a key factor in the difference in the relations of these two groups with the U.S. government and the dominant U.S. society.

By the 1830s the "Colossus of the North" (as the United States was called) had begun to emerge as an important potential market for Puerto Rican products, and through economic exchanges, started to influence Puerto Rican politics. This is how "binding familiarities" are established; the same binding familiarities that in previous chapters Pérez identifies in the early U.S.-Cuban relationship and that we also saw operating in U.S. relations with northern Mexicans. Similar to the people of the United States just before independence from England, Puerto Rican political opinion was divided between those who supported the Spanish Crown and those who supported independence. After 1850, however, the differing stakes of the various groups on the island complicated the political issues. There were those fundamentally loyal to Spain and who accepted Puerto Rico's dependent status under the Crown. There were others who desired greater autonomy, the abolition of slavery, and a stronger orientation to the United States. Finally, there were the separatists, those who sought in varying degrees an autonomous or independent Puerto Rico.

By 1867, Puerto Rico had 656,328 inhabitants, with 346,437 recorded as whites and 309,891 as "of color" (which included blacks, mulattoes, and *mestizos*). Out of this heterogeneity, a common national culture had been established, as represented in music, the arts, colloquial language, and architecture. Though the rural population were relegated to the mountainous areas and barely lived at a subsistence level, it is from these rural highland folk that the term *jíbaro* originated. This term functions variously as an image, stereotype, or symbol of either all that is great or all that is wrong about the people of Puerto Rico, depending on your political orientation (similar to the term *Chicano* for U.S. Mexicans). In the Indian language, jíbaro means "being free."

Frustrated by the lack of political and economic freedom, and enraged by the continuing Spanish repression on the island, Puerto Ricans organized a pro-independence movement and staged an armed rebellion; a call of independence known as "*Grito de Lares*" broke out in September 23, 1868. The rebellion was planned by a group led by Dr. Ramón Emeterio Betances and Segundo Ruiz Belvis, who on January 6, 1868, founded the *Comité Revolucionario de Puerto Rico* from their exile in the Dominican Republic. Within the context of a struggle for democracy, it is ironic that between 1869 and 1873, the establishment of a liberal government in Spain led to ample liberties in the Caribbean. This included the rights of Puerto Ricans and Cubans to send representatives to the Spanish Cortes (the institutions that governed the Spanish-American Colonies). The point is that these liberal reforms granted Puerto Rico the status of *diputación provincial*, this means the island became *a province of Spain or the equivalent of a state in the United States*, and this paved the way for the establishment of the first national political parties.

Two central points in the discussion of the political status of Puerto Rico need to be emphasized here. One is that Puerto Ricans did clearly have a track record of political struggle for democracy; and the other one is that their efforts resulted in their getting, if not independence, at least equal status with their mother country. Yet, as the public and government records of the time clearly indicate, U.S. officials considered Puerto Ricans incapable of self-government and, after one hundred years, the nature of the relationship between the Unites States and Puerto continues to be debated in Congress and by political factions in the mainland and on the island (see chapter 21).

Toward the end of the 1880s, the island's population suffered from a severe economic crisis. Consequently, there were many violent incidents, particularly looting and arson, against Spanish commercial establishments. The government and its Civil Guard responded with a series of raids and imprisonments, applying severe torture measures that became known as *compontes*. The social conditions of the island were also critical to events during this period. In addition to a lack of civil liberties, approximately 85 percent of the population remained illiterate. Malnutrition and extreme poverty were widespread. On the positive side, Puerto Ricans and Cubans finally were granted self-government by Spain when the *Carta Autonómica* (a form of constitutional autonomy) was approved by the Spanish Cortes on November 25, 1897. However, by the time of the first elections in March 1898, tensions were already building between Spain and the United States, and the freedoms for which Puerto Ricans and Cubans had fought for hundreds of years would come to an abrupt end one month later with the advent of the Spanish-American War.

There are two initial actions on the part of the United States that do not bode well for its future relations with Puerto Rico. Although Spanish surrender was certain by July 1898, the United States occupied Puerto Rico in an effort to secure a presence on the island before the initial discussions of a peace settlement. On July 18, General Nelson A. Miles and eighteen thousand U.S. troops landed at Guánica Bay and immediately moved to the city of Ponce and other towns on the southern part of the island. Many Puerto Ricans welcomed U.S. troops, *trusting* they would end colonialism. The U.S. troops then proceeded north toward San Juan, Puerto Rico's capital, and the main military post of Spanish forces on the island. But before they could reach San Juan, Spain agreed to sign a peace treaty on August 13, putting an end to all military hostilities. The formal transfer of Puerto Rico to the United States took two months, from August 13 to October 18, 1898, when the last Spanish troops sailed back to Spain and the U.S. flag was raised in most public buildings on the island. Symbolic of the arbitrary power exercised by the United States, Miles changed the official name of the country "Porto Rico" though the word *porto* does not exist in the Spanish language.[4] It took 34 years and literally an act of the U.S. Congress on May 7, 1932, to change the name back to Puerto Rico.

In 1898, immediately after the occupation of Puerto Rico, a military government was established under the command of General John R. Brooke. Thus begins the construction of a peculiar, ambiguous and contradictory political status for Puerto Rico through a series of Congressional Acts. The reaction to the United States takeover and the establishment of a military government reflected the various political positions in Puerto Rico. Beginning with the distinguished Puerto Rican philosopher, Eugenio María de Hostos, there was widespread demand for independence. Nevertheless, there was also support for U.S. occupation from surprisingly contradictory political players. The sugar plantation owners and the professional classes and individuals from the political left, such as Santiago Iglesias and his Socialist Party, were relentless advocates for statehood. So was Luisa Capetillo, the feminist and anarchist popularly known as the first woman in Puerto Rico to wear pants in public.[5]

A Power Play in Three Acts and a Call for Independence

Under the authority of the U.S. Congress, the Foraker Act (1900) replaced the military government with a unique civilian one. Unlike the U.S. system of checks and balances, it had both legislative and judicial functions with the executive appointed by the U.S. president. Despite the annexation of Puerto Rico, the U.S. Supreme Court decided (*De Lima v. Bidwell*, 1901) that Puerto Ricans were not citizens and in *Downes v. Bidwell*, 1901 that U.S. constitutional rights did not apply to Puerto Ricans. Incidentally, these legal precedents arising from challenges to the Foraker Act provide the legal discourse by which the United States holds on to colonies today. Basically, the implication is that the United States may take over any land in the world by treaty or by force and give its inhabitants only the rights that Congress considers appropriate.

When the administration of Puerto Rico under the Foraker Act failed, and the people were becoming more restless as a result of the deteriorating economic situation, and as World War I approached, the Jones Act (1917) was enacted. A main significance of this act is that it allowed for a system of checks and balances; it provided, for example, for an elected Puerto Rican Senate. This governing body, however, is subjected to the governor's veto, the U.S. president's final say, and the right of the U.S. Congress right to annul any Puerto Rican law at any time. In fact, Congress continued control of the governorship, the Department of Justice, the Department of Education, and the Office of the Auditor, all generally filled by nonresident Americans until the 1940s. Also, the U.S. Congress had the power to stop any action taken by the legislature in Puerto Rico. The United States maintained control over fiscal and economic matters and exercised authority over mail services, immigration, defense and other basic governmental matters. The judicial branch was also kept out of Puerto Rican hands under greater supervision than under the Foraker Act. The other significant part of the Jones Act of 1917 is that it grants U.S. citizenship to Puerto Ricans but for the reasons just noted, without the full protection of the U.S. Constitution. Thus, some felt that the purpose of this Act was to securely tie the Puerto Rican people to the United States, others, more cynically, argue it was just in time to induct eighteen thousand Puerto Ricans into service for the war with Germany. As indicated in chapter 19, failure of these two Acts, coupled with the Great Depression of 1930 led to an incipient revolutionary movement headed by Albizu Campos. As Ronald Fernández puts it:

> Four hundred years of Spanish rule and no colonial government had ever managed to create a serious and widespread push for independence. But within fifteen years of taking over the island, Americans produced such a desire for independence that Congress gave the islanders U.S. citizenship to permanently eliminate their then ardent desire for a divorce.[6]

These factors, when added to poor living conditions may spur a movement for independence. On the one hand, one of the main purposes of U.S. colonization was to control the economy and laboring bodies of Puerto Rico to serve U.S. American interests. As noted by Eduardo Galeano, in his classic *Open Veins of Latin America: Five Centuries of Pillage of a Continent*, this is particularly the case when it comes to the sugar cane industry:

> It was the fate of the "sugar islands" [such as Puerto Rico and Cuba] to be incorporated one by one into the world market and condemned to sugar until our day. Grown on a grand scale sugar spreads its blight on a grand scale and today unemployment and poverty are these islands' permanent guests.[7]

In chapter 19, Corretjer does an excellent job of describing the relationship between sugar and the colonization of Puerto Rico. He notes, for example: "In 1900, Senator Foraker made the following statement in Congress: 'The sugar and tobacco trusts are already practically the owners of all sugar and all tobacco in Puerto Rico.'"

On the other hand, the colonization of Puerto Rico was also carried out through education and the law not only for economic reasons, but, as Grosfoguel points out, to create a supportive block among the Puerto Rican people for military and symbolic reasons. There were many criticisms of the U.S. administration of Puerto Rico under the Foraker Act: (1) the imposition of the U.S. educational system (including requiring instruction in the English language); (2) the concentration of power in the hands of U.S. individuals, (as opposed to institutions that represented the various segments of the Puerto Rican people); and (3) the Americanization of Puerto Rican law, which was a powerful force in the drive toward assimilation.[8] The Americanization project failed. By the 1930s the economy of the island remained in a shambles and social conditions were little better than at the end of the nineteenth century.[9]

Juan Antonio Corretjer, former national secretary of the Puerto Rican Nationalist Party, enriches our understanding of the specific economic, political, and cultural steps that created these poor social conditions. He also describes the various roles that the Puerto Rican people, the U.S. government, and unions played in the almost forgotten tragic event, known as the Ponce Massacre. His personal role, in these revolutionary times, as we see in chapter 19, led him to a U.S. prison along with Albizu Campos, that party's president, in 1937, and he served six years of a ten-year term.

Though Puerto Rico did not engage in open guerrilla warfare like the Philippines did when they fought against U.S. control, Puerto Rican independentistas were active enough to provoke the enactment of *La Ley de la Mordaza*, the gag law signed in 1948 by Jesús Piñero, the first Puerto Rican governor appointed by President Harry S. Truman. *La Mordaza* makes it illegal to display a Puerto Rican flag, to sing a patriotic tune; more to the point, it makes it a felony to engage in any act that could lead to Puerto Rico's independence, which would necessarily involve the overthrow of the U.S.-controlled Puerto Rican government. It is a felony to talk, "print, publish, edit, circulate, sell, distribute, or publicly exhibit any writing or publication which encourages, pleads, advises, or preaches the necessity, desirability, or suitability of overthrowing the insular government."[10] It was also known as "the Little Smith Act" because it was patterned after a similar fascist law passed for the mainland. Later that year, Puerto Ricans exercised the right to elect their own governor (under the Elective Governors Act) and so, they elected Popular (People's) Party candidate Luis Muñoz Marin. He is the man behind Operation Bootstrap, designed to bring economic prosperity to the island. But there was trouble in this paradise island.

Under continuing pressure from the Puerto Rican people and from the United Nations, to decolonize Puerto Rico, on July 4, 1950, President Truman granted what to some seemed like a further concession but others saw as a trap to keep Puerto Rico under the domination of the United States. This is known as Public Law 600 of 1950, and it allows Puerto Rico to draft its own Constitution. Of course the U.S. Congress (like the Spanish Cortes did before for the Spanish Empire) exercises ultimate authority over U.S. possessions. Three months later, on October 30, five armed nationalists attacked the Governor's mansion; uprisings erupted in other island towns, causing twenty seven dead and ninety wounded. On November 1, two New York Puerto Ricans tried to kill President Truman; a White House policemen and one assailant died in the attempt. Campos and other nationalists received long prison sentences for complicity. Two years later, on March 3, 1952, the new Constitution was approved in a referendum, and through this vote

Puerto Rico's legal status changed from that of a colony to a Free Associated State or the Commonwealth of Puerto Rico. This satisfied the United Nations, which took Puerto Rico off the list of states that were not free, but it enraged some independentistas four of whom shot at congressmen in the U.S. House of Representatives on March 1, 1954.

Not only ardent revolutionaries felt that the U.S. control over Puerto Rican people was unjust, but others did also. The distinguished jurist José Trías Monge, Attorney General of Puerto Rico (1953–1957) and Chief Justice of Puerto Rico (1974–1985), reflects on the fact that by the 1950s there were no "civilizing" or economic reasons to keep Puerto Rico as a colony. Using a striking metaphor, he asks, "What was the reason then for the [U.S] pathological insistence on keeping Puerto Rico on parole, with electronic devices on hands and feet to forewarn of any suspicious movement, claiming that the self-governing powers so far granted could at any time be unceremoniously taken away?"[11] His answer is similar to Grosfoguel's: The United States has a symbolic interest that goes beyond legal or economic logic.

One way to deal with the failure of its Americanization policies and yet to set Puerto Rico as a model of capitalist liberal democracy, the U.S. government decided to promote migration of Puerto Ricans to mainland U.S.A. By 1960, as a consequence of increasing rates of migration, by 42 percent (one million) of all Puerto Ricans lived on the mainland United States. By the year 2000, 46 percent (2.8 million), of all Puerto Ricans lived on the mainland, and 3.8 million remained on the island.[12] This adds up to a total of 6.6 million Puerto Ricans in both the United States and Puerto Rico. Though some demographers predict that by the end of the first decade of the new century, off-island Puerto Ricans will exceed the number living on the island, by the latter part of 2008 the ratios remain the same.

In addition to chapter 19, this section includes a text of another kind of Puerto Rican or rather "NewYoRican" revolutionary strategy. The "Young Lord's Party: 13 Point Program and Platform" calls for the liberation of all oppressed people in the world focusing first on Puerto Ricans on the island and inside the United States. In point #12, there is specific mention of peaceful demonstrations conducted by those engaged in the struggle for equality, which is reminiscent of the peaceful march that led to the Ponce Massacre. The call, however, is for armed struggle.

Notes and Suggestions for Further Research

1. The most important source for bibliography of books and articles concerning the Commonwealth of Puerto Rico is the annual Handbook of Latin American Stud-

ies (http://lcweb2.loc.gov/hlas/) produced by over 130 contributing editors under the editorship of the Hispanic Division of the Library of Congress. Additional coverage of journal articles can be found through a subscription to the Hispanic American Periodical Index (http://hapi.gseis.ucla.edu/). Both the Handbook and HAPI are available in selected libraries in book form. One of the major aggregators for links to a wide variety of subjects relating to regional resources for Latin America is the University of Texas' LANIC (http://lanic.utexas.edu/la/cb/other/pr/). Another site one should especially note is the site prepared by the Law Library of the Library of Congress for international and multinational information on their Guide to Law Online (www.loc.gov/law/guide/us-pr.html).

2. On July 23, 2006, Zuleyka Rivera Mendoza, representing Puerto Rico, not the United States, was crowned Miss Universe.

3. Ronald Fernández, *The Disenchanted Island,* 2nd ed. (Westport, CT: Praeger, 1996), 30.

4. Fernández, *Disenchanted Island,* 9.

5. Juan Gonzalez, *Harvest of Empire* (New York: Viking, 2000), 61.

6. Fernández, *Disenchanted Island,* 33.

7. (New York: Monthly Review Press, 1997), 65.

8. Pedro A. Cabán, "The Colonizing Mission of the United States in Puerto Rico, 1898–1930" in *Transnational Latina/o Communities,* ed. Carlos G. Vélez-Ibáñez, et al. (Lanham, MD: Rowman and Littlefield, 2002).

9. José Trías Monge, *Puerto Rico: The Trials of the Oldest Colony in the World* (New York: Yale University Press, 1997), 98. For another distinguished jurist who specialized in Puerto Rican citizenship is José A. Cabranes, *Citizenship and the American Empire: Notes on the Legislative History of the United States Citizenship of Puerto Ricans* (New Haven: Yale University Press, 1979).

10. Fernández, *The Disenchanted Island,* 178.

11. Trías Monge, *Puerto Rico,* 120.

12. Juan Gonzalez, *Harvest of Empire* (New York: Viking, 2000), 81.

~

CHAPTER EIGHTEEN

Excerpts from the Foraker and Jones Acts and Public Law 600: The Commonwealth of Puerto Rico

We welcome the new citizen, not as a stranger but as one entering his father's house.

President Woodrow Wilson, April 1, 1917
(on the signing of the Jones Act)

The three documents below represent a symbolic "birth certificate" for the political birth of the Puerto Rican people as subjects of the United States. For over a century they have constructed a peculiar, ambiguous, and contradictory political status for the Puerto Rican nation. They have also created a particular sociopolitical and cultural identity for the millions of people who live in Puerto Rico and the mainland United States (see chapter 22). By dictating how millions of people must live, this particular discourse of power has a direct impact on human bodies, on the well-being of the people. Corretjer and Grosfoguel, in their respective chapters, present two different positions with respect to ultimate effect of the political status given to Puerto Ricans by these Congressional Acts.

Because the historical context and significance of these three U.S. congressional laws are discussed in the previous section, the excerpted texts are presented after a brief explanation. They are intended to familiarize you with the way language is used by an empire for the administration of a colony. Notice, for example, how general concepts such as "ruling over" are delicately articulated in an attempt to encompass every possible behavior or interpretation.

The Foraker Act

On April 2, 1900, the Foraker Law, officially the Organic Act of 1900, established a civil government and free commerce between Puerto Rico and United States. As described, the new government had a U.S. governor with five Puerto Rican Cabinet members. It is named after Senator Joseph B. Foraker, and it makes this island the first "unincorporated" territory of the United States.

The Foraker Act

Fifty-Sixth Congress Session I Chapter 191, April 12, 1900.
CHAP. 191.—An Act Temporarily to provide revenues and a civil government for Porto Rico, and for other purposes.

Be it enacted by the Senate and House of Representatives of the United States of America in Congress assembled, That the provisions of this Act shall apply to the island of Porto Rico and to the adjacent islands and waters of the islands lying east of the seventy-fourth meridian of longitude west of Greenwich, which were ceded to the United States by the Government of Spain by treaty entered into on the tenth day December, eighteen hundred and ninety-eight; and the name Porto Rico, as used in this Act, shall be held to include not only the island of that name, but all the adjacent islands as aforesaid.

SEC.2. That on and after the passage of this Act the same tariffs, customs, and duties shall be levied, collected, and paid upon all articles imported into Porto Rico from ports other than those of the United States which are required by law to be collected upon articles imported into the United States from foreign countries: *Provided*, That on all coffee in the bean or ground imported into Porto Rico there shall be levied and collected a duty of five cents per pound, any law or part of law to the contrary notwithstanding: *And provided further*, That all Spanish scientific, literary, and artistic works, not subversive of public order in Porto Rico, shall be admitted free of duty into Porto Rico for a period of ten years, reckoning from the eleventh day of April, eighteen hundred and ninety-nine, as provided in said treaty of peace between the United States and Spain: *And provided further*, That all books and pamphlets printed in the English language shall be admitted into Porto Rico free of duty when imported from the United States.

GENERAL PROVISIONS

SEC.6. That the capital of Porto Rico shall be at the city of San Juan and the seat of government shall be maintained there.

SEC.7. That all inhabitants continuing to reside therein who were Spanish subjects on the eleventh day of April, eighteen hundred and ninety-nine, and then resided in Porto Rico, and their children born subsequent thereto, shall be deemed and held to be citizens of Porto Rico, and as such entitled to the protection of the United States except such as shall have elected to preserve their allegiance to the Crown of Spain on or before the eleventh day of April, nineteen hundred, in accordance with the provisions of the treaty of peace between the United States and Spain entered into on the eleventh day of April, eighteen hundred and ninety-nine; . . .

SEC.11. That for the purpose of retiring the Porto Rican coins now in circulation in Porto Rico and substituting therefore the coins of the United States...

THE GOVERNOR

SEC.17. That the official title of the chief executive officer shall be: "The Governor of Porto Rico." He shall be appointed by the President, by and with the advice and consent of the Senate; he shall hold his office for a term of four years and until his successor is chosen and qualified unless sooner removed by the President;...

THE EXECUTIVE COUNCIL

SEC.18. That there shall be appointed by the President, by and with the advice and consent of the Senate, for the period of four years, unless sooner removed by the President, a secretary, and attorney-general, a treasurer, an auditor, a commissioner of the interior, and a commissioner of education, each of whom shall reside in Porto Rico during his official incumbency and have the powers and duties hereinafter provided for them respectively, and who, together with five other persons of good repute, to be also appointed by the President for a like term of four years, by and with the advice and consent of the Senate, shall constitute an executive council at least five of whom shall be native inhabitants of Porto Rico . . .

HOUSE OF DELEGATES

SEC.27. That all local legislative powers hereby granted shall be vested in a legislative assembly which shall consist of two houses; one the executive council; as hereinbefore constituted, and the other a house of delegates, to consist of thirty-five members elected biennially by the qualified voters as hereinafter provided; and the two houses thus constituted shall be designated "The legislative assembly of Porto Rico."

THE JUDICIARY

SEC.33. That the judicial power shall be vested in the courts and tribunals of Porto Rico as already established and now in operation . . .

. . . *Provided, however,* That the chief justice and associate justices of the Supreme Court and the marshal thereof shall be appointed by the President, by and with the advice and consent of the Senate, and the judges of the district courts shall be appointed by the governor . . .

*   *   *

The Jones Act of 1917

On March 2, 1917 President Woodrow Wilson signed the Jones-Shafroth Act, better known as the Jones Act. It is named after Congressman William A. Jones and Senator John D. Shafroth. With this law: (1) Puerto Rico became a territory of the United States ("organized but unincorporated,"); (2) A bill of rights was created; (3) Separated the three governmental powers into: the legislative, executive, and judicial branches; (4)The United States granted Puerto Ricans U.S. statutory citizenship, which means that Puerto Ricans were granted citizenship by act of Congress, not by the Constitution and citizenship is therefore not guaranteed by it (the Puerto Rican citizenship was abolished and it was not until 1927 that it was reestablished for residency purposes only.); (5) Established that elections were to be celebrated every four years; (6) English is decreed the official language of Puerto Rico. On the other hand, the Foraker Act still applies to economic and fiscal aspects of government. On May, U.S. President Woodrow Wilson signed compulsory military service act into law. Twenty-thousand islanders are drafted into World War I. On July 6, the first elections under Jones Act were celebrated.

The Jones Act. Sixty-Fourth Congress.

Session II. Chapter 145, March 2, 1917. (H.R. 9533)[Public, No. 368]
CHAP. 145.—An Act To provide a civil government for Porto Rico, and for other purposes.

Be it enacted by the Senate and House of Representatives of United States of America in Congress assembled, That the provisions of this Act shall apply to the island of Porto Rico and to the adjacent islands belonging to the United States, and waters of those islands; and the name. Porto Rico as used in this Act, shall be held to include not only the island of that name but, all the adjacent islands as aforesaid.

BILL OF RIGHTS.

Sec. 2. That no law shall be enacted in, Porto Rico which shall deprive any person of life, liberty, or property without due process of law, or deny to any person therein the equal protection of the laws.

That in all criminal prosecutions the accused shall enjoy the right to have the assistance of counsel for his defense, to be, informed of the nature and cause of the accusation, to have a copy thereof, to have a speedy and public trial, to be confronted with the witness against him, and to have compulsory process for obtaining witnesses in his favor.

That no person shall be held to answer for a criminal offence without due process of law; and no person for the same offense shall be twice put in jeopardy of punishment, nor shall be compelled in any criminal case to be a witness against himself.

That all persons shall before conviction be bailable by sufficient sureties, except for capital offenses when the proof is evident or the presumption great.

That no law impairing the obligation of contracts shall be enacted.

That no person shall be imprisoned for debt.

That the privilege of the writ of habeas corpus [protection against unlawful detention] shall not be suspended unless when in, case of, rebellion, insurrection, or invasion the public safety may require it, in either of which, events the same may be suspended by the President, or by the governor, whenever during such period the necessity for such suspension shall exist.

That no ex post facto law or bill of attainder shall be enacted.

Private property shall not be taken or damaged for public use except upon payment of just compensation ascertained in the manner provided bylaw.

Nothing contained in this Act shall be construed to limit the power employees of the legislature to enact laws for the protection of the lives, health, or safety of employees.

That no law granting a title of nobility shall be enacted, and no person holding any office of profit or trust under the government of Porto Rico shall, without the consent of the Congress of the United States, accept any present, emolument, office or title of any kind whatever from any king, queen, prince, or foreign State, or any officer thereof.

[Note: Section 2 continues to guarantee the rights of no excessive bail, unreasonable searches, issue of warrants, involuntary servitude (slavery), freedom of speech, religious liberty and many others. We now move to the section on citizenship.]

SEC. 5. That all citizens of Porto Rico, as defined by section seven of the Act of April twelfth, nineteen hundred, "temporarily provide revenues and a civil government for Porto Rico, and for other purposes," and all natives of Porto Rico who were temporarily absent from that island on April eleventh, eighteen hundred and ninety-nine, and have since returned and are permanently residing in that island, and are not citizens of any foreign country, are hereby declared, and shall be deemed and held to be, citizens of the United States: Provided, That any Person hereinbefore described may retain his present political status by making a declaration, under oath, of his decision to do so within six months of the taking effect of this Act before the district court in the district in which he resides, the declaration to be in form as follows:

"I,   , being duly sworn, hereby declare my intention not to become a citizen of the United States as provided in the Act of Congress conferring United States citizenship upon citizens of Porto Rico and certain natives permanently residing in said island."

In the case of any such person who may be absent from the island during said six months the term of this proviso may be availed of by transmitting a declaration, under oath, in the form herein provided within six months of the taking effect of this Act to the executive secretary of Porto Rico: *And provided further*, That any person who is born in Porto Rico of an alien parent and is permanently residing in that island may, if of full age, within six months of the taking effect of this Act, or if a minor, upon reaching his majority or within one year thereafter, make a sworn declaration of allegiance to the United States before the United States District Court for Porto Rico, setting forth therein all the facts connected with his or her birth and residence in Porto Rico and accompanying due proof thereof, and from and after the making of such declaration shall be considered to be a citizen of the United States.

*   *   *

Public Act 600

On July 4, 1950, President Harry S. Truman signed Senate Law 3336, known as Public Act 600. The U.S. Congress thus "upgraded" Puerto Rico's political status from protectorate to the Commonwealth of Puerto Rico. By allowing Puerto Ricans to draft their own Constitution, it quieted the demands of the United Nations and some Puerto Ricans for the United States to free Puerto Rico but it also sparked *independentista* attacks on President Truman and the U.S. congressmen.

Public Law 600

81st Congress 2nd Session, Chapter 446 June 30, July 3, 1950 [S.3336]

AN ACT

To provide for the organization of a constitutional government by the people of Puerto Rico.

Whereas the Congress of the United States by a series of enactments has progressively recognized the right of self-government of the people of Puerto Rico; and

Whereas under the terms of these congressional enactments an increasingly large measure of self-government has been achieved: Therefore

Be it enacted by the Senate and House of Representatives of the *United States of America in Congress assembled*, That, fully recognizing the principle of government by consent, this Act is now adopted in the nature of a compact so that the people of Puerto Rico may organize a government pursuant to a constitution of their own adoption.

SEC.2. This Act shall be submitted to the qualified voters of Puerto Rico for acceptance or rejection through an island-wide referendum, to be held in accordance with the laws of Puerto Rico. Upon the approval of this Act, by a majority of the voters participating in such referendum, the Legislature of Puerto Rico is authorized to call a Constitutional convention to draft a constitution for the said island of Puerto Rico. The said constitution shall provide a republican form of government and shall include a bill of rights.

SEC.3. Upon adoption of the constitution by the people of Puerto Rico, the President of the United States is authorized to transmit such Constitution to the Congress of the United States if he finds that such Constitution conforms with the applicable provisions of this Act and of the Constitution of the United States.

Upon approval by the Congress the constitution shall become effective in accordance with its terms.

Except as provided in section 5 of this Act, the Act entitled

"An Act to provide a civil government for Porto Rico, and for other purposes", approved March 2, 1917, as amended, is hereby continued in force and effect and may hereafter be cited as the "Puerto Rican Federal Relations Act".

~

CHAPTER NINETEEN

Albizu Campos and
the Ponce Massacre
Juan Antonio Corretjer

This chapter was originally published in 1965 and distributed as a pamphlet in the United States to let the U.S. American people know about a massacre of Puerto Ricans who were dedicated to the independence of Puerto Rico. Corretjer (1908–1984) casts the massacre against a backdrop of the struggle between the United States, as an imperial liberal democracy, and the oppressed peoples of the world symbolized by the Puerto Rican revolutionary Pedro Albizu Campos. He vividly describes the economic and cultural colonization through the peso devaluation, the refusal to aid the coffee industry after the hurricane, and exodus to the city, all effects that continue to affect Puerto Rico today. As an exposé, not only does he describe the specific steps that led to this tragic event, he reveals the involvement of U.S. officials high up in the government. An effort has been made to reproduce this pamphlet *as originally published,* including the note about the author and the introduction by Vincent Copeland (1916–1993) a cofounder of the Workers World Party, former labor officer, and a leader of protests against the Viet Nam War. Grammatical errors in the original have not been indicated by the term *sic* to avoid unnecessary interruption of the text, and the street map has also been reproduced with minor revisions for clarification purposes. A few editing comments in brackets are from editor Vázquez.

*   *   *

[Preface and Introduction by Vincent Copeland]

About The Author

Juan Antonio Corretjer is one of the Old Guard of Puerto Rico's anti-Yankee revolution, and at the same time a prophet and fighter for the country's revolutionary future.

The national secretary of the Puerto Rican Nationalist Party at the time of imperialism's Ponce Massacre, he went to a U.S. prison along with Albizu Campos, that party's president, in 1937 and served six years of a ten-year term. The remaining time he was under parole in New York City and barred for visiting his native land.

In 1934 he had borne arms in the Cuban revolution against dictator Machado. (A revolutionary "*junta*" took power from Machado, but a traitor-member of the junta, strong in the army, was able to defeat the other members later, and with the backing of the U.S., set up his own dictatorship. His name was Batista.)

Today, Señor Corretjer leads the Socialist League of Puerto Rico, a Marxist-Leninist organization which solidarizes with Fidel Castro and predicts that the Puerto Rican struggle for independence will to a large degree follow the Cuban example.

His party is based on the working class, and his ideas for Puerto Rican liberation are rooted in Marxism. While he sees the road to Puerto Rican independence going at the same time to socialism, he has nothing in common with those pseudo-Marxists who say there can be no independence for Puerto Rico until the U.S. is socialist. (And then, they say, no independence will be necessary!)

He is a vigorous man in his middle fifties respected by all shades of radical and nationalist opinion in Puerto Rico and much loved by his friends and followers. He resides with his wife, Consuelo, in Guaynabo (very near to San Juan). He edits "*Pabellon*" (the organ of the Socialist League), the newsletter, "*Quincena*" and other literary material.

Introduction

The Ponce Massacre is little known to North Americans but long remembered by Puerto Ricans who love their country.

The story must have been told many times in Spanish. But it seems to us that this is the most complete account in English—at least in recent years. Of course, this event is not included in any official history and needless to say, the public school system of Puerto Rico does not include it in its curriculum—in either Spanish or English. The lengthy New York obituaries at the death of Albizu Campos on April 21, 1965 are replete with the accounts of his alleged "terrorism," but singularly forgetful about the U.S. terror against his unarmed followers at Ponce.

The present pamphlet [i.e., chapter] contains the story of the massacre itself and in addition, pins the responsibility where it belongs: on Yankee imperialism, led at that time by Franklin D. Roosevelt. The necessarily abridged comments of the author about the Nationalist Party and its great leader, Albizu Campos, are an indispensable guide to the understanding of the larger Puerto Rican liberation struggle as well as the massacre of 1937. The same goes for the author's brief recapitulation of the decades of Yankee tyranny.

There will be those North Americans who wonder why the massacre of 1937 is so important today in the light of the much bloodier events that now shake the world and why this pamphlet should be on their required reading list when the 28-year-old atrocity [as of 1965; 71 years as of 2008] has paled before the more recent crimes of Hiroshima, Sharpeville, Stanleyville and Vietnam. The importance lies mainly in the relationship of the U.S. rulers to the ruled and in the fact that the U.S. treatment of its "own" colony gives the clue to its real intentions in Africa, Asia, etc.

The story is especially important to the understanding of the role of imperialist *liberalism*.

Engineered by appointees of Franklin D. Roosevelt in the very heyday of the "Good Neighbor" era inaugurated by that liberal President, the massacre tells us volumes about the true nature of FDR's liberalism—and imperialist liberalism in general. (Since FDR was the very model and prototype of imperialist liberalism!)

Those who have been, brought up in the aura of Roosevelt's alleged friendship to labor, his "humanitarianism" etc., may not easily believe Señor Corretjer's story of Roosevelt's involvement and responsibility in this classical act of colonial repression.

The workers of the Republic Steel Company in Chicago during that same year of 1937, however, had occasion to question Roosevelt's dedication to the cause of labor and would have readily understood Roosevelt's responsibility for the Ponce Massacre had they known, even a few of the facts.

On Memorial Day of that year, a peaceful parade of unarmed steel-workers trying to organize a union, was fired upon by policemen. Without provocation, in broad daylight, these cops killed ten marchers and wounded scores of others.

Roosevelt was asked to make a statement condemning the slaughter and he cheered the widows and orphans with the often-quoted remark: "A plague on both your houses!" (i.e. the houses of capital and labor). John L. Lewis, then head of the militant C.I.O [Congress of Industrial Organizations], publicly condemned Roosevelt for this and all but broke with him. Lewis well understood that beneath an apparently intemperate and thoughtless brutality on Roosevelt's part was a calculated and deliberate signal to the U.S. ruling class that his "pro-labor" bias went just so far and no farther.

Now Roosevelt's callousness to the massacred steelworkers did not materially affect his popularity in other quarters. And the myth of his great benefactions to labor was rather fortified in later years (mostly by the leadership of the same labor movement he tamed and so to speak, "legalized"). Both liberals and reactionaries, each in their own way and each with their own reasons, continued to build up Roosevelt's reputation.

But the point is that if Roosevelt could get away with such an attitude in the case of workers in Chicago, how much easier it was for him to do so in the case of distant and "foreign" Puerto Rico—even though his complicity was much greater!

Puerto Rico was an open colony of the U.S. at that time without even *the* fig leaf of commonwealth status or the euphemistic subtitle of "Free Associated State." Few North Americans paid any attention to it.

And most of those who did were chauvinists and racists who regarded Puerto Ricans as automatically inferior to "Americans."

The man now occupying the White House is now organizing a far bigger massacre in Vietnam than Roosevelt's henchmen did in Puerto Rico. He would be no less ready than Roosevelt to massacre Puerto Ricans if they should, like the Vietnamese, choose freedom.

It is partly in the hope of preventing such an eventuality that this pamphlet has been written for the North American public. The Puerto Ricans will fight as bravely for their independence as any other nation on earth when their time comes. But the active sympathy of all progressives in the United States is clearly a key requirement for the freedom of this little country, virtually occupied as it is by U.S. troops and often surrounded by U.S. battleships.

At the moment, it is true, the freedom struggle in Puerto Rico does not indicate any immediate large-scale drive for independence. But as the author says, "What is real is often not visible."

This is not a statement of faith in mysticism, but an assertion of the profound driving forces of liberation which move beneath man's consciousness, so to speak, and only push their way to the surface—to the "visible"—on special occasions.

These special occasions are known to history as *revolutions*. The Puerto Rican revolution is not now so visible as it was just prior to March 21, 1937.

But it is real, nevertheless, and it will win in spite of everything.—Vincent Copeland

*   *   *

Contents

[The original pamphlet includes a table of contents with the following items that correspond to the divisions in the text: 1.Meet Bolivar. 2.Disorganization of the Economy. 3.The Cultural Tension. 4.Persecution. 5.The Nationalist Party. 6. Albizu Campos. 7.The Cadets. 8.General Winship. 9.The Road to Ponce. 10.The Ponce Massacre. 11.Music and Fire. 12.The First Shot. 13.The Blood and the Spirit. 14.Appeasement. 15.The Unseen Reality.]

Meet Bolivar

On sunny Palm Sunday afternoon, a young Puerto Rican dragged his dying body over the hot pavement of a Ponce Street. It was March 21, 1937. Summoning all his strength, he reached the sidewalk. His finger moistened in his blood, he wrote:

> *"Viva la República!*
> *Abajo los asesinos!"*

He was one of 21 who were dying at this same moment. His name was Bolivar: Bolivar Marquez. The coincidence of names evokes Neruda's poem:

> I met Bolivar on a long morning . . .
> "Father," I said, "Are you, or are you not, or who are you?"
> And he said:
> "I rise every hundred years when the people wake up."

Around Bolivar Marquez, rifle and machine gun fire were wounding 150 more—men, women, children. This was the Ponce Massacre.

Was this happening in a social vacuum?

It was not.

A good understanding of the events reported here requires a previous knowledge of the general environment, historical and social as well as political, in which they took place.

The general background was the impact of the 1929 crash of American capitalism on a country—Puerto Rico—which since 1898 had been cynically deprived of political sovereignty and brutally exploited by American vested interests under the protection of the military, the cordial consent of the "democratic alliance" for colonialism (U.S.A., Britain, France, Holland, Belgium, etc.), the traitorous policy of the Latin American governments, the impotent sympathy of the Latin American people, and the tragic ignorance or indifference of the international Left.

Moreover, to underline this general panorama, something of paramount importance must be added. What U.S. imperialism had and has been pursuing in Puerto Rico is not merely deprivation of sovereignty, but the destruction of Puerto Rico as a Spanish American nation.

By the 1930's, the anti-Puerto Rican offensive had penetrated deeply. Yet, due to this same penetration, the Puerto Rican forces for a counter-attack developed. The instrument which shaped these forces from out of colonial chaos was the Nationalist Party of Puerto Rico. Its leader was Pedro Albizu Campos.

Disorganization of the Economy

In 1900, Senator Foraker made the following statement in Congress: "The sugar and tobacco trusts are already practically the owners of all sugar and all tobacco in Puerto Rico." (Congressional Record, Vol. 33, Part 3, Page 2649.)

But just one year earlier, 93 per cent of all the farms (consisting of 91 per cent of all the land in Puerto Rico) were the property of those who lived on them. The size of the average farm was 45 acres. Coffee was the main product, and there were 21 sugar centrals and 249 individual sugar-raising farms.

The use of Puerto Rican money (which was then at par with the American dollar) was abolished in 1899 and United States currency substituted on the basis of 60 U.S. cents for one peso. Thus were the Puerto Ricans robbed of 40 Percent of their money by a simple order of the Government of the United States.

At the time, coffee was the economic mainstay of the Island, which exported 58 million pounds. The coffee planters, encouraged by a consistent demand for their product in Europe during the latter half of the Nineteenth Century, had gone into an orgy of production. They mortgaged their properties in order to buy more land, and the change of currency automatically increased their mortgage burden.

The San Ciriaco Hurricane of August 8, 1898, had devastated the coffee country, and it was on this main sector of the economy that the forty per cent loss in currency fell heaviest. To recover from this double blow, a proposition was made by the Puerto Ricans to borrow several million dollars, to be loaned through the banks for private needs of the Island. This was incorporated in a bill presented to the Executive Council (created by the invaders and composed of six Americans and five Puerto Ricans, all named by the President of the United States) with the primary purpose of increasing money circulation in the Island; but it was generally understood to be a plan for aiding the coffee planters whose estates had been ruined by the cyclone of August, 1898. The bill was twice defeated by a solid American vote. With the coffee crop fallen from 50 million pounds to five million and the value from $10,000,000 to $600,000, and a coincidental fall of the price of coffee in the world markets, the disaster reached every Puerto Rican home. It was a death blow to the coffee economy, whose breakdown effectively achieved the economic disorganization pursued by American imperialism in behalf of its investors. The ruin of the industry, which afforded work to more than half the population, was only one dramatic effect of the ruin that devaluation of the local currency brought about.

Losing their properties, the planters were forced to migrate to the cities where they added to the prevailing bureaucratic servitude and political cynicism. The coffee workers followed than and were forced to squat on the outskirts of urban communities, giving rise to the malodorous slums still in existence to this day.

North American capital began invading Puerto Rico. The tobacco and sugar industries, protected by the tariff, were among the first to be expanded. Sugar displaced coffee as Puerto Rico's dominant industry, its fortune linked with the U.S. tariff. Plantation-factories making moscavado sugar ["*muscovado*" is raw, brown with a taste of molasses] on individual estates gave way to modern sugar *centrales* where cane sugar from thousands of acres could be ground. By 1900, the twenty-two centrales and the 249 individual haciendas reported in 1899 had been merged into forty-one highly modernized (80 per cent U. S.-owned) sugar centrales.

The workingman's lot became worse. As a result of the economic dislocation under the domination of an invading imperialist army, and as a result of the substitution of one ruling class by another, there followed the total deprivation of the masses.

An accomplice of imperialism in the camp of labor, Samuel Gompers (then President of the American Federation of Labor) fearful of an explosion, could not but observe in 1904:

"The salaries being paid now in Puerto Rico are 50 per cent under those that were paid under Spanish rule in most of the industries and in agriculture, and sometimes less. The price of meat is impossible for workers, being higher than it was under the Spaniards. Rice is also expensive, so expensive that to many unhappy workers it has become a delicacy."

The high price of meat might also be traced to the fantastically criminal concept of Nineteenth Century theoreticians of British-American imperialism, which asserted that a people with a low diet of meat was necessarily docile and, of course, easy to deal with. Puerto Rican cattle were bought at a conqueror's price and shipped away, especially to Texas, with the inevitable shortage of meat in the market and the promotion of imported codfish and canned foods to the Puerto Rican table.

In the 1930's, when the wave of disaster brought to the world by the U. S. crash of October, 1929, swept over Puerto Rico, our country had been under its impact even earlier. Capitalism first inflicts its crisis upon the colonial peoples before it throws the crisis on its own working class. This crisis found a Puerto Rico that for years had been submitted to a one-crop *latifundia* [large tracts of land owned by] absentee [landlords] economy and to American monopoly in commerce.

We had, at the time, 55,519 farms and 52.9 per cent of the total number of farms were less than ten acres in size. They occupied 7.6 per cent of the total farm area, 10.6 per cent of the cultivated land, and their worth amounted to 6.9 per cent of the total value of all lands, buildings, agricultural implements and machinery of all the country's farms.

Three hundred forty-two farms, that is to say, 0.6 per cent of all farms, consisted of 500 or more acres, accounting for 30.9 per cent of the total farm area and 25.8 per cent of land under cultivation.

They represented 44.1 per cent of the value of all land and agricultural implements and machinery of the total farming area of the country.

Seventy per-cent of the population lived in the countryside: over 230,000 families consisting of 1,302,898 people. Over eighty percent of the families living in the rural areas were landless; they were the families of workers living on a salary, *agregados*, (a semi-feudal relationship or peonage).

A few years later (1941-2), with 70,000 men in the Army and an increase in the construction of military public works, "the coefficient derived from a study of 4,999 workers' families in Puerto Rico was 218 persons working for every 1,000 inhabitants", counting even those working for a living who were between ten and fourteen years old. Sixty per cent of the workers were jobless!

The 1940 census accordingly showed a drop between the ages of twenty-five and thirty-four—the most productive period in the life of laborers—a characteristic which was not present in the 1899 census. This was attributed to tuberculosis which, in 1936, was killing 305 out of every 1,000 Puerto Ricans.

The Cultural Tension

A public school system was organized in Puerto Rico in 1900 shaped after the one current in U. S. Army camps. The introduction to the text of the 1901 School Law of Puerto Rico, approved by Governor Allen, said: "The most important dispositions of the Military Orders are here embodied". So English, not Spanish, was the official language in the schools. The military heroes and deeds of the armed forces of the United States were presented to Puerto Rican children as their own, and even foreign languages were taught in English to a Spanish-speaking nation! Puerto Rican history was ignored: all relations of the Puerto Rican historical and cultural heritage with the Latin American sister nations was ignored. And the dislodging of all national consciousness was pursued with the cultivation of an inferiority complex as its fellow traveler.

In the year of 1937, the year of the Ponce Massacre, President Franklin Delano Roosevelt addressed the following letter (the equivalent of a Tsarist ukase) [a Russian imperial order or decree passed down from top officials to officers] to his underling, the Commissioner of Education of Puerto Rico:

> "I desire at this time to make clear the attitude of may administration in the ex-tremely important matter of teaching English in Puerto Rico. It is an indispen-sable part of American policy that the coming generation of American citizens in Puerto Rico grow up with complete facility in the English tongue. It is the language of our nation. It is only through familiarity with our language that the Puerto Ricans will be able to take full advantage of the economic opportunities which became available to them when they were made American citizens.
>
> "Bilingualism will be achieved by the forthcoming generations of Puerto Ri-cans only if teaching of English throughout the insular educational system is entered into at once with vigor, purposefulness and devotion, and with the un-derstanding that English is the official language of our country."

This despotism over Puerto Rico's cultural life reached into all educa-tional spheres. In the very year of the Ponce Massacre, this tyrannical order was delivered by the President of the United States, and General Winship imported one hundred Americans to teach English in the Puerto Rican grade schools.

Persecution

Early in 1932, the usual government "observation" of the pro-independence groups began to be transformed into provocation and persecution. The first of these provocations of really great magnitude was made through the colonial legislature where Gompers' associate, Santiago Iglesias, on petition of Colonel Theodore Roosevelt, Jr., introduced a bill to convert the Puerto Rican national flag to a colonial banner. *A people's mass attack on the colonial capitol building left one killed, dozens wounded.*

The registration period (it was an election year) was marked by violence everywhere. Provocation against the *Independentistas* (Nationalists and Liberals) was the order of the day.

With the intensification of the Independentista movement came new persecutions. The credit for initiating modern, streamlined methods of political persecution in Puerto Rico belongs to Mr. Ernest Gruening [Famous Liberal Senator from Alaska, he was the Director of Division Territories and Island Possessions].

In March, 1936, Gruening sent off a series of letters to influential Americans on the Island, requesting confidential information concerning any anti-American activity in general and specifically within the National Guard and at the University. One of the most "documented" informers of Mr. Gruening was Atherton Lee, Director of the Federal Experimental station in Mayaguez. At Mr. Gruening's request, two special agents from the Division of Investigation of the Department of the Interior were sent to Puerto Rico and, on his request also, the FBI extended its activities to our country.

The Department of the Interior men were to investigate Independentista infiltration of the Puerto Rico Reconstruction Administration (PRAA). Under Governor Winship's instructions, the Legislature named a special investigating commission with the same task. Under Gruening's orders, a "test on independence" was established.

When this question hit the press (*El Mundo* in San Juan and through this, the New York Times), Gruening double-talked that "The PRAA does not propose to intervene in the belief of its employees even though those beliefs may occasionally appear to be in conflict with a minimum of common sense."

So it was Gruening also who inaugurated the theory of the intellectual emptiness of patriotism. In his anti-independence campaign, as in every other one of his activities in Puerto Rico, Gruening was (as Secretary Ickes declared) responsible only to the President of the United States. And it is revealing that in his mistrust of everything and everybody in Puerto Rico, the only exception he made was General Blanton Winship, the great assassin at the Ponce Massacre, *who was also responsible only and directly to the president of the United States.* His appointment to the Division of Territories and Island Possessions, which was so much acclaimed by American liberals, led Albizu

Campos to remark, "Puerto Rico is the graveyard of American liberalism." (This is just as true of Franklin Roosevelt as it is of Gruening.)

Not happy with such lackeys of American policy as Dr. Jose Padin, the Commissioner of Education appointed by President Roosevelt, a similar secret investigation of the Department of Education was taking place. The situation forced Padin's resignation in November, 1936. It was Dr. Gruening who presented the resignation letter to President Roosevelt and who secured immediate acceptance from him.

A similar "cleaning up" operation against suspected Independentistas was being carried on throughout the whole colonial government apparatus.

All this tends to show that the independence movement was strong and growing. Let us turn now to the general political development of the 30's. The protagonist of this development was the Nationalist Party which became the center that attracted the main weight of the repression.

The Nationalist Party

The Nationalist Party had been organized for several years without becoming a significant group. It did become just that in May, 1930, when Pedro Albizu Campos, backed by the Party's youth (he was 39 years of age) was elected president.

Under Albizu's leadership it rapidly developed into a real revolutionary vanguard attempting to show the way out of the reigning misery and chaos. Thanks mainly to imperialist maneuvering, intimidation, and bribery, but also to clear-cut class and sectional differentiations, it always remained small in numbers. But its influence readied far beyond its organized force. It was, in reality, a powerful mass movement.

This could not have happened without the situation we have described. But the importance of the leadership should not be under-estimated. Albizu came forward as the movement's brilliant and courageous leader at a moment when the influx of the people into the independence movement required precisely such brilliant and courageous leadership. The pitiless persecution he has suffered ever since has been the highest recognition of this fact. That he did not succeed in leading Puerto. Rico into independence could not be charged to any incapacity on his part.

Somewhere else I have pointed out that during the two different periods of his leadership Albizu led the independence movement during two corresponding periods of imperialist development and world reaction: first during the period of the rise of fascism and then during the period when U. S. imperialism reached the summits of atomic monopoly power. These two periods were from May, 1930, when he was elected his party's president, to June 7, 1937, when he entered the Atlanta Penitentiary, and from December 15, 1947, when he came back home, to November 2, 1950, when he was again taken into custody.

In this particularly difficult situation, his party and his leadership were additionally crippled by the absence of a regularly developed Marxist movement in Puerto Rico. It was too late in Puerto Rican history for the national bourgeoisie to take the full leadership—most of it was already compromised by collaboration with the foreign oppressor—and the lack of a Marxist ally accentuated the petty bourgeois shortcomings of the whole situation. Albizu himself, with all of his genius, was a bourgeois leader without a bourgeoisie to follow him.

A few facts about the Nationalist Party's mass character and vanguard role follow: Under its pressure, another and more conservative petty bourgeois party (the Liberal, later to be transformed into the Popular [People's] Party) was organized. In the 1932 election, the Popular Party gained thirty-six per cent of the electorate and in 1936, forty-eight per cent. Under the Nationalist Party's pressure, the Republican Party (traditionally a colonial appendage to the *American* G.O.P.) added "independence" to its program.

After a strong campaign of the Nationalists, the Asociacion de Colonos de Cana was organized. [An organization of small farmers who own land but are totally dependent on the big corporation's "sugar central" to get their cane ground and prepared for the market. The central further dominates the farmer by lending him money on his crop in advance of the harvest.] The Nationalists' campaign to expose and discredit Governor Colonel Theodore Roosevelt [Jr.] led to his removal in 1932.

In 1934, workers in the sugar fields went on a spontaneous strike. Slaking the shackles of the A.F.L. [American Federation of Labor], the workers at Fajardo (the Armstrong, New York, sugar empire which had been an A.F.L. stronghold since the start of the century) kicked out the collaborationist A F.L. leaders and called Albizu to lead the strike to victory, which he did. Following this, Albizu led the whole industry strike into which the Fajardo outburst had spread.

Finally, with anti-Nationalist repression at its highest peak, the U.S. Court indicted Albizu Campos and seven other party leaders in April, 1936. And his followers raised thousands of dollars by collections of nickels and dimes from the broad masses and paid the million dollar bail on the very day of the indictment.

The Cadets

The youth organization of the Nationalist Party was called the Army of Liberation—or Cadets of the Republic. They wore white pants, black shirts (symbolizing mourning for the Country's colonial bondage), and overseas caps. Some of the battalions (groups, in reality, as there was no regularity in the numbers) used wooden rifles for drilling and parades.

Officers wore white pants and a white coat over a black shirt and a tie, and a regular officer's cap. They also used parade swords.

The girls' organization was called the Women's Auxiliary Corps, and their uniform was a skirt, blouse, and cap, with colors matching the uniform of the Cadets.

Albizu Campos

Pedro Albizu Campos was born at Barrio de Tenerias, a rural area in the neighborhood of Ponce on "the Day of Saint Peter and Saint Paul", as he was fond of repeating, in 1891. He was seven years old when the U.S. invaders went through his native city late in July, 1898.

He received his early education in the public schools of Ponce, up to high school. At that time a scholarship offered to the brilliant teenager by the Logia Aurora (Ponce's Freemasons) enabled him to go to college at the University of Vermont.

It was during his studies at Vermont that two Harvard professors, while teaching a summer course there, took note of his talents. Because his scholarship did not cover his full college education, the Harvard professors got him a small job at Cambridge, explaining to him that it would be easier for him to advance his studies in the Harvard environment, and so he left Vermont for Cambridge.

He graduated from Harvard's College of Sciences and Letters and the Harvard Law School. It was in Harvard that two powerful influences in his life developed: His conversion to Catholicism (He had left Ponce very much impressed by the current theosophical ideas at that time in that city) and Irish nationalism. A Catholic priest, Father Ryan, appears to have been his guide to communion, while a Catalonian sage, an astronomer that was for many years was to be the director of the Ebro Observatory, Father Luis Rodes, apparently gave him the peculiar clue to combine faith and science, mysticism and common sense. (The Irish rebellion during this period further raised the prestige of Catholicism; since in Ireland, at least, it was an oppressed church and appeared to favor the national revolution.)

At the outbreak of the First World War, he joined the Harvard Cadet Corps, organized and trained as a source of officers by the French Military Mission under Colonel Paul Azan. (As a general, and under Marshall Petain, this same Azan was to become the butcher-pacifier of French Morocco.) As a commissioned officer, Albizu asked to serve with Puerto Rican troops and was transferred to the 375th Infantry Regiment in San Juan, as a Staff Second Lieutenant. So as he came back to Puerto Rico after the war and after graduation at Harvard, all the elements combining the personality he was to project into Puerto Rican history were present: the blend of catholicism and patriotism, mysticism and self-sacrifice typical of Irish nationalism; the necessary degree of practical materialism for an objective approach to politics: juridicism and a military as well as a providentialist conception of history.

Of all the vulgarities thrown against him by his enemies and foes of Puerto Rico's independence I will only demur briefly on one, because that tends to belittle his patriotism at the same time that it sneers at his racial origin—that is to say, that his political career has been the consequence of his mistreatment as a Black Man, both in Harvard and in the Army.

I have the personal testimony of persons who knew him in Ponce before he left for the United States as an adolescent, testimonies to his radical independentist attitude while a high school student in his native town. Such testimonies include a distinguished American who lived in P.R. from early youth to his death a few years ago, who as principal of schools in Ponce was one of the persons who obtained [NOTE: STREET MAP WAS ORIGINALLY HERE]the Freemasonry scholarship that sent him to Vermont and who remained his friend to the last moment, Mr. Charles Terry. Others are the famed Ponce theosophist Don Andres Corazon; Don Rafael Rivera Esbri; the reknowned laywer Don Rafael Marchand who was in the third and fourth years of the Ponce high school while Albizu was in his first and second, and lawyer Guillermo Atiles Moreu, for many years of great regard among anti-Trujillo and anti-Franco forces. To this I must add Albizu's himself, who once and again, in public but also in private, intimate conversations always defended Harvard against the charge of having mistreated him.

(Since the above lines were written, Albizu Campos has died. His obituaries in the imperialist press have referred to his alleged personal "hatred" for the United States as the motivation for devoting his whole adult life to the cause of his country's liberation. Only a hopelessly provincial and narrow-minded parochialism could come up with such an evaluation of a great revolutionist. But the metropolitan dailies of New York City did not really make an evaluation; they only mouthed a slander.

Not content with their persecution of Albizu Campos living, they continued to attack Albizu Campos dead. The New York Times even exhumed the old story that Albizu was ashamed of his racial origin—his mother was black—and that the U.S. treatment of him as a Black Man made him so angry he then became a nationalist.

Without giving these slanders the dignity of a detailed reply, it is still necessary in the interest of preserving a great revolutionist's memory, to condemn the slanderers.—ed.[of the original publication])

General Winship

In January 1934, President Roosevelt appointed General Blanton Winship of Macon, Georgia, to the Governorship of Puerto Rico. Winship was not, as it had been many times said, newly acquainted with Puerto Rican realities. Indeed, he was not unfamiliar with Nationalist activities either

Late in 1930, the Nationalist Party launched on the Wall Street market a sale of bonds to raise money to establish the Republic of Puerto Rico. They had five denominations, the largest being $100. The first public sale was one of $200,000, announced in April, 1931, in San Juan. The hope was that if the first sale met with success the issue would grow to $5 million. The first sale of the bonds on the continent was attempted in the summer of 1932. Governor Colonel Roosevelt, consulted by Washington, advised the War Department to ignore the question. A year later, when the issue moved to Wall Street, General Walker asked the Judge Advocate of the U.S. Army for legal opinion. *The Judge Advocate was General Blanton Winship.* His advice was for prosecution. However, diplomatic opinion prevailed and no action was taken.

It was in January that General Winship was appointed—in the midst of a very militant period on the Island. *Strike* was the key word during all of 1933. At the turn of the year, following police suggestions, a group of propertied stools for imperialism began making plans for the organization of a so-called "Citizens Committee of One Thousand For the Preservation of Peace and Order."

This alarmist group cabled President Roosevelt that "a state of actual anarchy exists. Towns in state of siege. Police impotent, Business paralyzed." Jorge Bird Arias, general manager and vice president of the Fajardo Sugar Company (the Armstrong, New York, capitalists) and one of the most esteemed Puerto Rican traitors in Washington, wired secretary of War, Stern, that "existing conditions, both economic and political, demand . . . an exceptionally good, *strong* and capable man."

In this opinion the War Department concurred. It was Colonel James Beverley, a Texan sugar corporation lawyer and former governor of Puerto

Rico, who mentioned General Winship. In a letter to his friend General Cox, Beverley wrote January 1, 1934:

> "I strongly favor an ex-army officer for the next governor . . . appointed at once, one who has sufficient experience to know how to size up and handle delicate situations and who has the courage to do his duty whether it is popular or not. Is not General Winship available for a position of this kind?"

This letter had just reached Washington when the great strike in Fajardo began. The traditional A.F.L. leadership was rejected by the workers. They called Albizu Campos to lead them. On the 12th day of January, General Winship was appointed.

This General Blanton Winship was the "strong" man requested by Fajardo sugar stooge Bird Arias; the man "who has the courage to do his duty whether it is popular or not", requested by Texan-colonel sugar-lawyer Beverley. This was the man who was to order the Ponce Massacre.

His kind was sprouting all over the world at the time. That year of 1934 was the year Hitler rose to power. In 1935, Mussolini invaded Ethiopia. In 1936, the Spanish general rebelled against the Republic. Batista was in Cuba. Trujillo next door . . .

The Road to Ponce

The sugar industry workers' strike of January, 1934, is the starting point whose continuation, politically speaking, is the line that takes us directly to the Ponce Massacre. This great strike marks the point at which Puerto Rico, for the first time in history, represented by the Nationalist Party and with Albizu Campos in the leadership, contended man to man with inperialism to wrest the direct control of the masses out of foreign hands.

The immediate consequence was an imperialist retreat.

This maneuver paralyzed the Puerto Rican offensive, leaving a vacuum the Nationalist Party could not immediately fill. The law of polarity resolved itself into a strengthening of imperialism by its adopting a defensive position. It was at this crucial moment that the petty-bourgeois weakness of the Independentista movement was revealed and the whole situation cried out for a Marxist ally, embodied in a staff of cadres able to transform the immense sympathy and popularity won by Albizu Campos into a solid labor revolutionary organization. But that ally did not exist.

Counting on the impossibility of the Nationalists organizing their natural reserves, imperialism gave in to the demands of the workers. The effect was a general and immediate demobilization of the aroused masses. The Nationalists were deprived, at the same time, of maintaining contact with the working masses and of achieving, even by the torturous trial-and-error method, an elementary labor organization.

The bloody and amazing revolutionary development which followed became, of necessity, a competitive struggle between Albizu's brilliant mind and his courageous followers on one side, and American total power on the other. The Nationalist recovery, of which the Cadets' concentration in Lares, September 23, 1935, and the United Front days of 1936 are examples; the popular emotion in behalf of the Nationalists because of the police assassination of five of their leaders in Rio Piedras, on October 24,1935; the Utuado street fighting for the flag in January, 1936; the counter-attack in February with the revolutionary execution of Colonel Riggs; the people's indignation at the assassination of Beauchamp and Rosade [accused of killing Colonel Riggs] at Police Headquarters on February 23, 1936; demonstrations against the Federal raids and subpoena citations and the sympathy with the incarcerated Nationalist General Secretary on April 2, 1936; the great de Diego birthday celebration on April 16, 1936; the patriotic rejoicing on the Tydings Bill that same month [proposing independence to Puerto Rico]; the emotional solidarity which accompanied Albizu Campos and his comrades to prison. . . , all of these were episodes, glorious episodes, of Puerto Rican history. But the reaction prevailed. The imperialists punished the Nationalist leadership in court July the 30th, 1936. And in Ponce, the 21st of March, 1937, the people were given punishment through government-sponsored terror.

The Ponce Massacre

On or about March 14th, Plinio Graciany and Luis Castro Quesada, Nationalist leaders of Ponce, notified the township government that the Nationalist Junta (Committee) would hold a meeting, preceded by a parade, on Sunday, March 21st. Even in those stormy days of 1937, Nationalist parades and meetings were a great popular attraction; even the police respected than because of their discipline and order. The mayor of Ponce, Jose Tormos Diego, promptly gave permission. It should be noted that the request for permission was a courtesy the Nationalists extended to the municipal government. According to Puerto Rican law, permission was not needed for the use of plazas and parks for meetings or parades. This colonial Supreme Court ruling of 1926 was also valid for the streets.

On Friday, March 19th, the Insular Chief of Police, Colonel Orbeta arrived in Ponce to study the situation. (Orbeta was the brother-in-law of

Dionisio Trigo, [Spanish Dictator] Franco's representative in Puerto Rico. When Trigo died in a Berlin hospital, he was sent to Madrid with a Luftwaffe [Nazi German Air Force] escort.) Orbeta went back to San Juan and talked with General Winship. There, at that moment, the Massacre was planned and ordered.

Winship ordered Orbeta to go back to Ponce and convince (or coerce) the Mayor to stop the parade.

On March 20th, the *day* before *the parade was to be held,* the district po-lice chief of Ponce, Captain Felipe Blanco, wrote the following letter to Na-tionalist leaders Luis Castro Quesada and Plinio Graciany:

"I have the pleasure of acknowledging your letter, dated yesterday, at 7:40 P.M., informing me of the parade of the Cadetes de la Republica and the meeting to be held by the Junta Nacionalista next Sunday, March 21st, in this city of Ponce, the program of which I have read on Page 3 of El Mundo yesterday, which says in part:

"'2:00 P.M.—Divisional Concentration of the Liberation Army, District of Ponce and neighboring towns, to parade along the streets of Ponce!'

"I wish to inform you that, according to instructions from my superiors, the Police will not permit this celebration, and by this letter, in fulfilment of my duty, I so notify you."

On March 21st, and for some days before, a significant concentration of police was taking place in Ponce. They were well armed: rifles, carbines, Thompson sub-machine guns, tear gas bombs, hand grenades, plus the usual police clubs, etc., a force of 200 men in addition to the routine Ponce police garrison.

Colonel Orbeta talked things over with Captain Blanco. They decided to see Mayor Tormos and convince him to cancel the permit. It was not until after midday that they located the Mayor, who made it very clear that he had granted the permit.

Colonel Orbeta tried to impress the Mayor with the dangers involved. He said that he had information that the Nationalists planned to come armed and that he had particular information concerning armed groups coming from Mayaguez. Nevertheless, under later cross-examination by the Investigation Committee, the Colonel said that he had told the Mayor that such a parade was scandalous, that he had no information, but any one of the Nationalists might act *as* an insane man and throw stones at the shop windows or commit any number of disorderly acts. As a matter of fact it was proved beyond doubt that the group of 50 persons from Mayaguez (composed of women and chil-dren, as well as men) was unarmed, as were all the other Nationalists.

After long discussions the Mayor gave in. He immediately called the Nationalist's leaders and told them he had overlooked the fact that it was a religious holiday, Palm Sunday, and that the Paulist Fathers had asked him not to allow the parade.

The Nationalists knew he was lying, but ignoring this, they told him that the people coming to the parade were already in Ponce, that the parade would be held in orderly silence, and that they would inform the Paulist Fathers to that effect. At this point the Mayor cut the interview short and said that the permit was canceled.

Present at the last interview, in addition to the formerly mentioned Ponce leaders, were the Acting President of the Nationalist Party, lawyer Julio Pinto Gandia, and the Acting Secretary General, lawyer Lorenzo Pineiro.

From this moment until 3:00 P.M. a series of discussions took place between Colonel Orbeta and Captain Blanco on one side and the Nationalist leaders on the other. While these discussions were taking place the police concentrated heavily on all streets around the Nationalists Club and at the corner of Marina and Aurora Streets. The Nationalists were entering the club with their wives and children. There is plenty of evidence that those who were not Nationalists were told by the police not to go into the area between Marina, Aurora and Jobos Streets.

But Nationalists (easily recognizable because many were in uniform and those in civilian clothes were wearing insignias were allowed to go across the police lines. About 80 uniformed Cadets were permitted among them.

Shortly before the shooting, Colonel Orbeta and Captain Blanco visited the area. The very air was tense. The police were already there and the Nationalists were surrounded. Colonel Orbeta and Captain Blanoo then left. They said afterwards that they had given no orders to the police. According to Colonel Orbeta's story, they went around Ponce and its surroundings in a police car, looking at the beautiful scenery.

They returned after the shooting was over.

Music and Fire

At about 3:15 the Cadets lined up for the march in a column of three abreast. Behind them was the Nurses' Corps in white uniforms. Trailing the Nurses was the band, which consisted of only four musicians. The band played the National Anthem, "La Borinquena" and Cadets and Nurses stood at attention.

The reader can now study the small map which shows the relation between the police, the cadets, the nurses and the public. Marina Street runs from north to south. It is first crossed by Luna Street here. A little farther up, it is crossed by Aurora Street. On this corner the Nationalists had their club. Then comes Jobos Street. Between Luna and Aurora, a group of police were lined up on the east side of Marina. Just off Marina a large group of police was standing ready in the middle of Aurora Street. Other groups formed on both sides of Aurora. On the west side of Marina, another group of Police stood in front of the Nationalist Club. All were armed with rifles, tear gas bombs, carbines, etc. The Cadets were standing at attention on the south side of Aurora.

Behind the Nationalist formation, there was another group of policeman armed with Thompson sub-machine guns. Eye-witnesses and photographs show how completely trapped and cornered the Nationalist were—and how weaponless. Two news photographers had taken positions on the balcony of the home of a prominent Ponce family, the Amy family, (George Amy, an outstanding Puerto Rican artist, had worked for the old New York Globe for many years.) These photographers took many pictures. One, taken by Jose Luis Conde, seconds before the shooting, shows the police coming in toward the people from the north, that is, from Aurora Street. It also shows large groups of people, men, women and children—nearly all of them gathered at the corner of Aurora and Marina, almost in front of the Nationalist Club. The photo also shows the Cadets in formation, followed by the nurses, and right behind them the police detachment with machine-guns under the command of Chief Perez Segarra.

Just remember that Colonel Orbeta and Captain Blanco, who had apparently expected ferocious acts from the Cadets, had left for a sight-seeing drive around town. Captain Blanco later declared that nobody was left in command of the police and that the auxiliary chiefs, Soldevila, Bernal and Perez Segarra, each one commanding a separate group of policemen, had not received any instructions.

The Cadets were completely surrounded with no chance of escape. It is obvious from the police formation that it had but one purpose. And that purpose was not simply to break up the Cadets' parade or dissolve a riot. The classical dispersion and anti-riot tactic is to give those being attacked a chance to disperse. This chance was deliberately denied to the Puerto Rican Nationalists on that fateful Palm Sunday afternoon of March 21st, 1937.

The purpose was to frighten the whole Puerto Rican people with a show of crude brutality, a massacre.

The First Shot

In a situation like this, anyone might shoot first. And each side would naturally claim to have been the victim of the first shot. But in his report to the American Civil Liberties Union, Mr. Arthur Garfield Hayes, who investigated the Ponce Massacre, writes:

"Carlos Torres Morales, a photographer for El Imparcial, being aware of the menacing attitude of the police, raised his camera to his eyes. Before he had focused, a shot was fired, perhaps two, he was not sure. He took the picture.

"In his photo we can see practically all the policemen at Aurora and Marina Streets (maybe 17 or 18) ready to fire against the people. All of them have weapons in their hands. We also see a policeman at the moment he fires his revolver. Although we have used the testimony of experts, it was really unnecessary, as the firing policeman appears with the upper part of his arm toward the flying crowd. His forearm is hidden by another person, but in accord with the direction of his arm and beyond the other person there is a white cloud and the smoke of the shot. The shot is being fired directly at the people on the sidewalk. The firing policeman can be clearly seen.

"This Committee has not been able to understand why this policeman and other officers fired at the crowd and not the Cadets, unless they wanted to clear out the front side of the Nationalist Club on whose sidewalk and surroundings they were standing. Or perhaps the purpose was to terrorize them.

"We are not saying that this photo shows the first shot. In fact, the testimony of another witness directly identified another policeman as having fired the first shot.

"We have tried to understand why the government did not use these photographs, all of them widely published. They show the police in action. They show the Nationalist Cadets—the Army of Liberation—50 to 70 in number, standing in silence and motionless, their hands hanging at their sides. At their front stands their commander in white uniform. Beside them there is a boy, black-shirted, his arm around a comrade's shoulder. Behind them is the Cadets' flag-bearer. All of them look somewhat surprised, patiently waiting for the disaster to strike. No one looks ready to run, not ready to even make a movement. Behind them are the girls, in white, some of them running away. One of them has almost reached the sidewalk. This in itself corroborates the photographer's statement that he took the photo immediately after the shooting began. Behind the band is a police platoon, some 15 men, armed with machine-guns and rifles. Nationalists and non-Nationalists were murdered."

The Blood and the Spirit

At the first shot the police went crazy. Volleys from all sides fell on the Cadets and the people. For about ten minutes they were submitted to cross-fire. When the last volley had done its work, twenty lay dead. More than 150 were wounded. Another boy died in a nearby hospital; some were maimed for life.

That half hour before the shooting and those murderous ten minutes of the killings have gone down in history as an unsurpassed example of serenity and courage of people under fire.

Bolivar Marguez, a cadet, fell mortally wounded, dragged himself towards the sidewalk and on the wall of a house wrote with his blood, "Long Live the Republic! Down with the assassins!"

Carmen Fernandez, 35 years old, saw the flag-bearer killed. As she tried to take the flag from him she received a volley of carbine fire. She fell, seriously wounded.

Dominga Cruz Becerril, a girl from Mayaguez, had already reached cover when she saw the flag on the pavement. She left her protected cover, ran to the flag, raised and waved it, and ran with it to the Pila Hospital. She was not wounded. Asked why she had done this she answered quietly: "Our Master has said the flag should always be flying." (The Master was Pedro Albizu Campos, the Nationalist leader.)

Genaro Lugo did not stay in the place after he saw the girl's murder. As he ran, he saw the police under Chief Perez Segarra s sub-machine squad firing on the terrified public.

Julio Conesa was the owner of the then only radio station in Ponce. He had parked his car at the Marina and Jobos street corner. He saw the police sub-machine detachment shooting against the people. He did not know the Rodriguez family at the time, but he recognized them in the photos. He had no doubts that he saw the Police sub-machinegunning the father and two sons of this family.

The Rodriguez's were standing in front of a shoemaker's shop south of Jobos Street Rafael, 18 years old, had just taken a couple of shots with his little camera. As he was preparing for another, the firing began. They fell on their faces for protection. There was a general discharge. He heard his brother say, "ay . . . !"and he saw his father immediately raising himself to protect his son. He saw his head was bleeding. He was fatally wounded. He died in a matter of seconds. His brother also. Rafael himself was wounded. Two policemen picked him up a quarter of an hour later. They threw him like a bag into a police wagon.

A young man was walking down Jobos Street. Suddenly he saw a policeman coming towards him. He was at least 50 feet away from the center of the shooting. As he read murder in the policeman's face and saw a gun in his hand, he cried out:—"I am not a Nationalist, I am a National Guard. I am . . . "—until death silenced him forever.

He was really a National Guard. He had drilled that same morning at the El Castillo esplanade, some 100 meters from the place where he was killed. His name was Jose Delgado and he was 20 years old.

Such a socialite as Don Luis Sanchez Frasqueri (he is the father of Roberto Sanchez Vilella, who last November was named, through the polls, to the governorship) saw a man was going to be killed and yelled, "Don't kill him!" A police lieutenant, recognizing who he was, and not willing to have such a respectable witness against himself, stopped his men. The man was pushed unharmed into the police patrol, When Sr. Sanchez Frasqueri saw him again he was wrapped in bandages. He told him that in the police wagon first and at headquarters afterwards, he had been brutally beaten.

A fruit vendor, by the side of his car (Sanchez Frasqueri's car), was 75 yards away from the Nationalist Club. A policeman passing by saw him, turned back and opened his head with his riot club. This was also part of Sanchez Frasqueri's statement. At the same distance from the Club, on Luna Street, Sr. Sanchez Frasqueri saw a corpse. The body was filled with holes. In the man's agony he had tried to write with his blood the word valor, but he only lived to write V A L . . .

> "When we began our investigation—wrote the Investigating Committee headed by Arthur Garfield Hays—we objected to naming our Committee The Committee For the Investigation of the Ponce Massacre. To refer to the Ponce tragedy, we used the Ponce Case, the riot, or any other phrase that should demonstrate our intention of dealing objectively with the facts. Now that we have heard all the proofs we agree that the people of Ponce had given this tragedy the only title it can possibly have: The Ponce Massacre."

Appeasement

That night the Berlin radio had something to say. Nazi virulence was fed with flesh of martyrs. The trumpets resounded at all ends of the Axis. Mussolini's loudspeakers were taking revenge for all of America's hypocrisy on Ethiopia. Tokyo was giving the Asian peoples the truth about Franklin D. Roosevelt's humanitarianism. But, above all else, they were telling Latin America about the tenderness in the Good Neighbor's heart.

On March 27, 1937, the *New York Post* demanded:

> "We expect Congress to make an independent investigation of the increasing unrest in Puerto Rico. The suppression of the Nationalist Party seems to become bloodier, and it is thought that it will eliminate the softening effect of the Good Neighbor Policy and of its last obstacles, just removed, with Ambassador Caffery out of Havana . . . if Puerto Rico wants independence our answer should be to grant it. To answer her demand with machine guns is dishonorable for a people who love the memory of its own seditious nationalists of 1776."

Congressman Vito Marcantonio, sincerely on our side, wanted such an investigation. Senator Borah indicated some interest. Nothing came from Congress. In Puerto Rico itself, the American residents, some 1500, with the exception of half a dozen, were solidly behind Winship and joyful for the massacre. It is good to keep this in mind, because there are 65,000 U. S. residents in Puerto Rico today, who are here only as exploiters and agents of exploiters. In a similar event, one can venture to say that the half dozen of 1937 would not be much bigger now. A portent of this was given ten years ago when Americans at the Teatro Tapia fanatically *cheered the police* during the presentation of Rene Marques' PALM SUNDAY, a drama on the Ponce Massacre.

But the American Civil Liberties Union, of which Secretary of the Interior Harold Ickes was an officer, did make a thorough investigation, on request of its Puerto Rican representative Don Miguel Mondragon. It was presided over by Mr. Arthur Garfield Hays, whom we have quoted.

Because of Puerto Rico's plight, the deprivation of outside justice, and the high tension of the moment, the ACLU [American Civil Liberties Union] report has been generally taken as sympathetic. But it is not. There is some justice in it, but no sympathy. We know the ACLU officials have no sympathy for us, not a single bit of interest in what really counts, that is Puerto Rico's independence, which is the first and greatest of all civil rights for Puerto Rico, and the source of all others. We know that Roger Baldwin, the Committee's chairman, had wanted the Nationalist leadership indicted for murder and incitement to commit murder, so that imperialism could be whitewashed of all accusation of political persecution.

But there is justice in it because Hays saw the truth. He was shown the truth by his associates in the investigating committee. Because, yes, there is always something that is overlooked when quoting the Report: the ACLU Report is the consequence of an investigation carried on, not only by Dr. Hays, but by other members of the Committee as well—Antonio Ayuso Valdivieso, Emilio S. Belaval, Fulgencio Pinero, Francisco M. Zeno, Jose Davila Ricci and Mariano Acosta Velarde. Behind this group of distinguished Puerto Ricans was the whole people of Puerto Rico, to the very District Attorney of Ponce, R.V. Perez Marchand, who resigned his rather than carry out Winship's wish to indict for murder the innocent survivors of the Massacre.

The assassin general was left alone in his palace, with his pretorian guard, his little bunch of killers and sycophants, his resident countrymen. Washington was the center of world accusations.

So appeasement became the order of the day. And appeasement came to Puerto Rico. The ACLU Report places the blame for the Massacre squarely on the shoulders of General Winship. That did not embarrass Washington. Had the President of the United States wanted to remove his assassin-appointee he had only to do so, as he did two years afterward for other reasons. But Franklin Roosevelt did not want to do this at the time. Unmoved by the

ACLU Report, he was equally unmoved by the coinciding McCaleb Report, the result of a secret investigation made by the Department of the Interior. General Winship, backed by Gruening, had found secure protection in the White House.

To do justice to Hays, it must be said that he grasped the inner meaning of the situation which the Nationalists faced in Ponce. On May 23, 1937, he wrote to a Miss Mason:

> "Now I will tell you something about Ponce, which I did not even suggest for our report since perhaps it is my individual view. If I were a Nationalist and had been notified a few days in advance that a parade was prohibited, I would have called it off. Nobody but a people with a martyr complex of a lunatic would lead a crowd to face machine guns. But if I had arranged a parade and there was an attempt to stop it at the last minute, my self-respect would make me see it through. It may be just as crazy, but that is the way we human beings are. When the issue is drawn, we refuse to be intimidated. If I had been the leader, I too would have said, Forward march!' At least I hope I would."

But appeasement succeeded. Because Mr. Hays was an American, because the ACLU is an American institution, because Secretary Ickes was one of its officials, and because of the Tydings Independence Bill, the Report was generally interpreted as a signal of approval by the Administration.

Because the liberal-reformist tendency was dominant in the Independentista intelligentsia, because there was no Marxist-guided workers' organization to back the unconvinced Nationalists, because it appeared to offer a way out of the nightmare of police terrorism, the ACLU Report was paramount in restoring faith in an American solution of Puerto Rico's independence.

Late in May, the 10-year sentence pending an appeal in Washington, by Albizu Campos and seven other top party leaders, came down from the Supreme Court as approved. On June 7, 1937, the bars of Atlanta Penitentiary closed behind them.

The Unseen Reality

Apparently, all was darkness. In political life, what is real is often not visible. The doors of history were opening wider for what was, and has been, the core of Albizu Campos' life: the independence of Puerto Rico. He himself still had new chapters to add to Puerto Rico's national struggle. And in the very years ahead, going through the abyss and the heights of this century, whose historic task our Hostos[1] predicted as the liquidation of colonialism, socialism broadens its domains, and its torch goes on bringing light among the working masses and nations, which only socialism can make really free. Its flag waves triumphantly in Puerto Rico's most beloved sister nation, Cuba.

Of those 21 killed and 150 wounded that Palm Sunday afternoon in Ponce, not one was a propertied person. It was to their own class they really offered their lives and sufferings.

But the illegal foreign government power which indicted their leaders in a foreign court, in a foreign language; the President of the United States in whose name *as* head of a foreign government they were indicted; the foreign judge, the foreign marshall, the foreign prosecuting attorneys, the jurors, mainly foreign or representatives of foreign corporations, the foreign prison into which they were sent, the assassin-general, the weapons, all this, yes, all of them belong, in their own right to the exploiter class. And it is their class that is doomed by history's justice.

That time will come, and soon. As for today, the recent bombings of North Vietnam prove, the whole world is aware that U.S. imperialism is the main enemy of all the people of the world.

When for Puerto Ricans, the hour of decision comes we will not be alone in the world. And here in Puerto Rico a workers' organization will be the revolutionary standardbearer of independence. The Puerto Rican Socialist League struggles to achieve this end.

Guaynabo, Puerto Rico
February 24, 1965

Notes

1. Eugenio M. de Hostos, Puerto Rican philosopher, 1839–1903. Died in exile. Predicted among other things, the emergence of China as a great power, bringing with its revival a new creative spirit for modern times.

~

CHAPTER TWENTY

Young Lords Party:
13-Point Program and Platform
Michael Abramson

As the legend goes, until 1967, the Young Lords were a street gang. Like the Brown Berets, they are an example of the blurring of the line between criminal and political activity (and thus between illegitimate and legitimate knowledge). The emergence of the Young Lords Party (YLP) in 1968 took place within the context of the second generation of Puerto Rican migrants who had achieved some social and economic advances and had started attending college in large numbers. Beyond the legend, though, the YLP was a combination of working-class college students from the *Sociedad de Albizu Campos* in New York and, indeed, gang members, too. They got their charter from the Chicago Young Lords Organization.

Like their Chicano counterparts in the Southwest, the Puerto Rican youth took a militant and aggressive stand. They took a leading part in the demonstrations that shut down the City College of New York in the spring of 1969 and in the militant action at Queens, Brooklyn, and Lehman Colleges that resulted in the establishment of Puerto Rican studies programs. They occupied a church in East Harlem in the spring of 1970, engaged in militant action around Metropolitan and Gouverneur Hospitals, and were involved in aggressive demonstrations around Lincoln Hospital in the Bronx in the autumn of 1970. The Young Lords Party evolved from an organization with fraternal relations with the Black Panther Party to become a Maoist coalition of groups in the early 1970s seeking to create a new, multiracial revolutionary party. By the early 1970s, it had transformed itself into the Puerto Rican Revolutionary Workers Organization. The following document is presented here as it was originally written (capitalization and spelling purposeful) in October 1969 and revised in May 1970, when the organization started to grow nationally.

* * *

Young Lords Party: 13-Point Program and Platform

The Young Lords Party is a revolutionary political party fighting for the liberation of all oppressed people.

1. WE WANT SELF-DETERMINATION FOR PUERTO RICANS, LIBERATION ON THE ISLAND AND INSIDE THE UNITED STATES.

For 500 years, first spain and then the united states have colonized our country. Billions of dollars in profits leave our country for the united states every year. In every way we are slaves of the gringo. We want liberation and the Power in the hands of the People, not Puerto Rican exploiters. *¡QUE VIVA PUERTO RICO LIBRE!*

2. WE WANT SELF-DETERMINATION FOR ALL LATINOS.

Our Latin Brothers and Sisters, inside and outside the united states, are oppressed by amerikkkan business. The Chicano people built the Southwest, and we support their right to control their lives and their land. The people of Santo Domingo continue to fight against gringo domination and its puppet generals. The armed liberation struggles in Latin America are part of the war of Latinos against imperialism. *¡QUE VIVA LA RAZA!*

3. WE WANT LIBERATION OF ALL THIRD WORLD PEOPLE.

Just as Latins first slaved under spain and the yanquis, Black people, Indians, and Asians slaved to build the wealth of this country. For 400 years they have fought for freedom and dignity against racist Babylon. Third World people have led the fight for freedom. All the colored and oppressed peoples of the world are one nation under oppression. NO PUERTO RICAN IS FREE UNTIL ALL PEOPLE ARE FREE!

4. WE ARE REVOLUTIONARY NATIONALISTS AND OPPOSE RACISM.

The Latin, Black, Indian and Asian people inside the u.s. are colonies fighting for liberation. We know that washington, wall street, and city hall will try to make our nationalism into racism, but Puerto Ricans are of all colors and we resist racism. Millions of poor white people are rising up to demand freedom and we support them. These are the ones in the u.s. that are stepped on by the rulers and the government. We each organize our people, but our fights are the same against oppression and we will defeat it together. POWER TO ALL OPPRESSED PEOPLE!

5. WE WANT EQUALITY FOR WOMEN. DOWN WITH *MACHISMO* AND MALE CHAUVINISM.

Under capitalism, women have been oppressed by both society and our men. The doctrine of machismo has been used by men to take out their frustrations on wives, sisters, mothers, and children. Men must fight along with sisters in the struggle for economic and social equality and must recognize that sisters make up over half of the revolutionary army: sisters and brothers are equals fighting for our people. FORWARD SISTERS IN THE STRUGGLE!

6. WE WANT COMMUNITY CONTROL OF OUR INSTITUTIONS AND LAND.

We want control of our communities by our people and programs to guarantee that all institutions serve the needs of our people. People's control of police, health services, churches, schools, housing, transportation and welfare are needed. We want an end to attacks on our land by urban renewal, highway destruction, and university corporations. LAND BELONGS TO ALL THE PEOPLE!

7. WE WANT A TRUE EDUCATION OF OUR AFRO-INDIO CULTURE AND SPANISH LANGUAGE.

We must learn our long history of fighting against cultural, as well as economic genocide by the spaniards and now the yanquis. Revolutionary culture, culture of our people, is the only true teaching. *¡JIBARO SI, YANQUI NO!*

8. WE OPPOSE CAPITALISTS AND ALLIANCES WITH TRAITORS.

Puerto Rican rulers, or puppets of the oppressor, do not help our people. They are paid by the system to lead our people down blind alleys, just like the thousands of poverty pimps who keep our communities peaceful for business, or the street workers who keep gangs divided and blowing each other away. We want a society where the people socialistically control their labor. *¡VENCEREMOS!*

9. WE OPPOSE THE AMERIKKKAN MILITARY.

We demand immediate withdrawal of all u.s. military forces and bases from Puerto Rico, VietNam, and all oppressed communities inside and outside the u.s. No Puerto Rican should serve in the u.s. army against his Brothers and Sisters, for the only true army of oppressed people is the People's Liberation Army to fight all rulers. U.S. OUT OF VIETNAM, FREE PUERTO RICO NOW!

10. WE WANT FREEDOM FOR ALL POLITICAL PRISONERS AND PRISONERS OF WAR.
No Puerto Rican should be in jail or prison, first because we are a nation, and amerikkka has no claims on us; second, because we have not been tried by our own people (peers). We also want all freedom fighters out of jail, since they are prisoners of the war for liberation. FREE ALL POLITICAL PRISONERS AND PRISONERS OF WAR!

11. WE ARE INTERNATIONALISTS.
Our people are brainwashed by television, radio, newspapers, schools and books to oppose people in other countries fighting for their freedom. No longer will we believe these lies, because we have learned who the real enemy is and who our real friends are. We will defend our sisters and brothers around the world who fight for justice and are against the rulers of this country. *¡QUE VIVA CHE GUEVARA!*

12. WE BELIEVE ARMED SELF-DEFENSE AND ARMED STRUGGLE ARE THE ONLY MEANS TO LIBERATION.
We are opposed to violence—the violence of hungry children, illiterate adults, diseased old people, and the violence of poverty and profit. We have asked, petitioned, gone to courts, demonstrated peacefully, and voted for politicians full of empty promises. But we still ain't free. The time has come to defend the lives of our people against repression and for revolutionary war against the businessmen, politicians, and police. When a government oppresses the people, we have the right to abolish it and create a new one. ARM OURSELVES TO DEFEND OURSELVES!

13. WE WANT A SOCIALIST SOCIETY.
We want liberation, clothing, free food, education, health care, transportation, full employment and peace. We want a society where the needs of the people come first, and where we give solidarity and aid to the people of the world, not oppression and racism. *¡HASTA LA VICTORIA SIEMPRE!*

* * *

Questions

1. Under what conditions does the definition of "nation" fit the statement "All the colored and oppressed peoples of the world are one nation under oppression"?
2. What contradictions do you detect in this platform? How would the Young Lords respond to your observation(s) regarding these contradictions?
3. Was there a feeling among the Young Lords similar to that among Chicanos at the time, that they were charting new ground and had no predecessors?
4. In what ways might or might not the revolutionaries who had been fighting for Puerto Rico's independence be predecessors?

~

Searching for the Best Life, Not the Best Citizenship
Francisco Hernández Vázquez

In chapter 21, Grosfoguel indicates a possible turning point in the struggle by going beyond nationalism and colonialism and towards the affirmation and demand for a radical economic and political democracy. Chapter 22 by Duany extends the discussion to include Dominicans and brings the discussion full circle to the question of racial identity, or the *mestizaje*, discussed in the introductory and concluding chapters and specifically by Valle and Torres in chapter 12. This discussion of the reconstruction of racial identity in the Caribbean paves the way for the subsequent Part V History of the Present.

By now it should be clear that the exercise of colonial power (like any attempt at total and absolute oppression) elicits a reaction against it; and that this reaction can take many, sometimes contradictory, forms.[1] In other words, the people will look after their own interest whether or not they conflict with those of their countries or their governments. For example, when it came to women's right to vote Puerto Ricans used the U.S. Congress to fight their own Puerto Rican government. After more than one hundred years of struggle, women in the United States got the right to vote in 1919. Because Puerto Rican women had become U.S. citizens in 1917 thanks to the Jones Act, one would think, logically, that they also would be able to vote in 1919. For sixteen years, though, this particular "truth" was caught in a political game between Puerto Rican feminists supported by the Socialist Party *and* the U.S. Congress against the Puerto Rican legislature and the Catholic Church. This is but one of the many instances illustrated in the reader where gender equality comes up against nationalism. Overcoming the patriarchy and classism of church and state, Puerto Rican women finally won universal suffrage in 1935.[2]

Once again we are confronted with the question that keeps emerging throughout this reader, "What other strategies beyond liberal reforms and revolution are there?" Customs and traditions may at times provide the ammunition for people to defend their interests. The effectiveness of the traditions and customs of a people in the fight against domination can be measured by the force that the government uses against it. In effect, overt demonstrations of Puerto Rican cultural identity, such as waving the Puerto Rican flag, were once regarded as subversive.[3] Thus, culture becomes an important site of struggles, some of which are overtly "political" and others of which are not obviously so, as with Puerto Rican *jaiba* politics[4] or the *choteo* in Cuba, or with *cantinflismos* in México. Unfortunately, any such forms of political struggle by marginalized people (such as Afro-Latinos/as, the elderly, gays, lesbians, women, workers, and youth) remain invisible because they are considered illegitimate knowledges or they are not recognized as tactics for social change. We need to increase our understanding of how these particular tactics and strategies form part of the quest for democracy.

Another form of struggle against colonial oppression is provided by Ramón Grosfoguel's discussion of citizenship as the affirmation of the rights of the Puerto Rican people against narrow nationalism or the interests of the state. This critical notion of the possibility of choosing the best citizenship merits some discussion. For example, we already saw early in this reader how *Tejanos* struggled for self-government, first within Mexico, then within the Republic of Texas, and now, as "Latino," within the United States (chapter 5). Similarly, U.S. Mexicans, who historically have preferred to remain Mexican citizens, have done so because they have had more access to justice through the Mexican consulates. Abraham Hoffman makes the following statement:

> Mexicans who crossed their northern border were *looking for a better life, but not necessarily a better citizenship.* [Emphasis mine]

The same goes, he adds, for the increasing number of U.S. Americans who choose to live or retire in Mexico and who prefer to retain their U.S. citizenship.[5] In agreement with Grosfoguel, this is precisely the same sentiment that is expressed by Wilfredo Mattos-Cintron:

> Above all, they [the Puerto Rican *independentistas*] must finally learn that it is not independence per se that the masses are after, but a political status that will clearly fulfill their aspirations to a better life.[6]

This notion helps to understand the ambivalence that Puerto Ricans feel regarding U.S. versus Puerto Rican citizenship. The following are a few historical examples of this ambiguity. Almost immediately after annexation the Union Party, under the leadership of Luis Muñoz Rivera, insisted on having a "government founded on the will of the governed" and that this could be achieved through either statehood or independence (even if it was obtained under a protectorate status). The central point of contention was (and continues to be one hundred years later) that the Puerto Rican people have never been given the right to vote (other than symbolically) on the relationship they want to have with the United States. Supposedly, on the other side of the political spectrum, the Puerto Rican Republican Party, under the leadership of Afro-Puerto Rican José Barbosa, welcomed U.S. annexation and even statehood. From the 1920s to 1950s, however, the party expressed ambivalence about the issue and eventually questioned statehood after repeated rejections from Washington. These major parties represented the propertied classes leaving the workers outside of traditional politics, until Spanish-born Santiago Iglesias founded the Socialist Party in 1915, which clearly supported statehood.

The Puerto Rican people are not the only ones who are ambivalent. So is the U.S. government. With the 1940 U.S. Nationality Act, which became effective January 13, 1941 (ratified by the Nationality Law in 1952), the U.S. Congress amended the statute on naturalization, expanding the applicability of the *jus soli* (where you are born) rule to Puerto Rico. This means that under this Act, all persons born in Puerto Rico after that date are considered natural born U.S. citizens, and therefore, their U.S. citizenship is protected under the 14th Amendment of the U.S. Constitution. (In 1917, U.S. citizenship granted to Puerto Ricans was a naturalized legislative or statutory citizenship; Congress can revoke this statutory citizenship under certain conditions).[7]

This ambivalent discourse on the part of the U.S. government and the Puerto Rican people continues in the twenty-first century. For example, on October 25, 2006, Juan Mari Brás became the first person to receive *a Puerto Rican citizen certificate* from the Puerto Rico State Department. Among the many factors involved in this ambivalence is fear: the Puerto Rican fear of cultural assimilation,[8] and the U.S. fear of adding a poor, Spanish-speaking, and mostly democratic state to the Union. Nevertheless, the referendums in 1963, 1993, and 1998 indicate an increasing preference for maintaining the status quo of a Commonwealth (about 48 percent in 1998) over (about 46 percent) and a decreasing percentage (4 percent and 2.5 percent in the last two referendums) for independence. These are nonbinding referendums, meaning they do not affect U.S. congressional law. Again, Grosfoguel provides an excellent explanation for this situation. The major positions are represented, among others, by the Popular (People's) Democratic Party, which backs continued Commonwealth status (and elected Sila Caldererón as the first woman governor in 2000); and by the New Progressive Party, which supports statehood for Puerto Rico.

Table IVB.1 indicates the degree of ambivalence as a 0.2 percentage points, if measured by the recent votes for governor.

A recent survey, apparently shows that *now* is the best chance for statehood:

The possibility of Puerto Ricans overwhelmingly supporting Statehood has never been more of a reality than in today's political environment. A November 2006 telephone poll of residents of the island showed when faced with the decision, 74% would choose Statehood over the 12% in favor of Independence. With 65% of respondents favorable to Luis Fortuño winning PNP's [*Partido Nuevo Progresivo* (New Progressive Party)] gubernatorial race in 2008, "now" may very well be Puerto Rico's best chance at moving towards true representation in Washington.

According to the poll, 43% of respondents believed a plebiscite vote [a binding vote] for Statehood would provide more job opportunities, better living conditions and an overall better quality of life. The benefits of Statehood were also on the minds of 28% who said the economy was the biggest problem facing Puerto Rico today. In addition, 20% gave the public schools a failing grade citing the need for federal help necessary to improve public education.[9]

Over one hundred years after incorporation into the United States, Puerto Rico's level of poverty is atrocious. It has fallen below that of several other

Table IVB.1.   Puerto Rican Positions on the Status of Their Nation

Political parties	In favor of	1998 Referendum	2004 Votes for governor
Partido Popular Democrático (Popular Democratic Party [PPD])	Commonwealth (current) Status (Public Law 600)	48%	953,459 or 48.4% (a thin win for Aníbal Acevedo Vilá)
Partido Nuevo Progresivo (New Progressive Party [PNP])	U.S. statehood	46%	949,579 or 48.2%
Partido Independentista Puertorriqueño (Puerto Rican Independence Party [PIP])	Independence	2.5%	52,660 or 2.7%

Caribbean countries and unemployment is between two and four times that of the United States. The high school dropout rate is 30 percent and the homicide rate is 27.5 per 100,000 residents, as opposed to 9 percent for the mainland United States.[10]

Furthermore, just like the Mexican Americans, despite their treatment as second-class citizens, Puerto Rican men and women have met the responsibilities of U.S. citizenship in full measure. Over 200,000 have served in its wars with distinction, and some 2,000 have paid the ultimate sacrifice, and the number is growing. Since the beginning of hostilities in Iraq, some 7,600 troops from Puerto Rico have served in harm's way and 24 soldiers with island addresses or roots in Puerto Rico have been killed as of February 2005. Thus, no matter what their political orientation almost all Puerto Ricans opt for U.S. citizenship for themselves and future generations. This is obvious in the platforms of the two major parties and it includes those wishing for independence but who lobby for dual citizenship.[11]

Puerto Rican scholars observe that, shaped by the colonial relationship, Puerto Ricans have become an "ethno-nation" that encompasses the mainland United States and Puerto Rico.[12] This sort of transnational political and cultural identity is actually becoming the reality for many people as a result of an increasingly interconnected world and the effects of the global economy (see chapters 25 and 26). This is illustrated by Duany in chapter 22, who bridges the experience of Dominicans in Puerto Rico and mainland United States and thus brings the conversation full circle to the question of racial identity, or the mestizaje, discussed by Valle and Torres in chapter 12. This discussion of the reconstruction of racial identity in the Caribbean also paves the way for the next part on the History of the Present.

*   *   *

Notes and Suggestions for Further Research

1. This struggle is illustrated by many scholars, among them are: J. Gómez-Quiñonez, "Toward a Concept of Culture," *Revista Chicano-Riqueña* 5, no. 2 (1977): 29–47; and William V. Flores and Rina Benmayor, eds., *Latino Cultural Citizenship: Claiming Identity, Space and Rights* (Boston: Beacon Press, 1997).

2. Yamila Azize-Vargas, "The Emergence Of Feminism In Puerto Rico, 1870–1930," in Vicky L. Ruiz and Ellen Carol DuBois, eds., *Unequal Sisters* (New York: Routledge, 1994), 260–67.

3. Arlene Davila, *Sponsored Identities* (Philadelphia: Temple University Press, 1997), 1.

4. Ramón Grosfoguel and others, "Beyond Nationalist and Colonialist Discourses," 26. The terms *jaiba, choteo,* and *cantinflismos* refer to the practice of mocking authority and power as a counterhegemonic tactic, that is, a tactic against domination.

5. Abraham Hoffman, *Unwanted Mexican Americans in the Great Depression* (Tucson: University of Arizona Press, 1974), 19–20. See part V, section B for further discussion of this point.

6. Wilfredo Mattos-Cintrón, "The Struggle for Independence: The Long March to the Twenty-first Century," in Edwin Meléndez and Edgardo Meléndez, eds., *Colonial Dilemma* (Boston: South End, 1993), 214.

7. www.votelaw.com/blog/archives/003917.html Accessed January 11, 2008.

8. José Trías Monge, *Puerto Rico: The Trials of the Oldest Colony in the World* (New York: Yale University Press, 1997), 61.

9. "Statehood: Is Now the Best Chance?" *The Puerto Rico Herald*, February 1, 2007, www.puertoricoherald.org/issues2/2007/vol11n01/PRR0201-Puerto-Rico-Report-en.html. Accessed on January 14, 2008.

10. Trías Monge, *Puerto Rico*, 160.

11. "A Second Look at Second-Class Citizenship," *The Puerto Rico Herald*, www.puertoricoherald.org/issues2/2005/vol09n08/Poll0908-en.html. Accessed January 11, 2008.

12. Ramón Grosfoguel, Frances Negrón-Muntaner, and Chloé Georas, "Beyond Nationalist and Colonialist Discourses: The *Jaiba* Politics of the Puerto Rican Ethno-Nation" in Frances Negrón-Muntaner and Ramón Grosfoguel, eds., *Puerto Rican Jam: Rethinking Colonialism and Nationalism,* (Minneapolis: University of Minnesota Press, 1997), 17. According to Roberto P. Rodriguez-Morazzani, one of the characteristics of this ethno-nation is the myth of racial harmony, the "Rainbow People thesis" that he considers an attempt to deny racism by masking it behind cultural nationalism thus perpetuating a "conspiracy of silence in the Island." See "Beyond the Rainbow: Mapping the Discourse on Puerto Ricans and 'Race'" *Centro* VIII, nos. 1, 2 (1996): 163.

~

CHAPTER TWENTY-ONE

The Divorce of Nationalist Discourses from the Puerto Rican People

Ramón Grosfoguel

Grosfoguel agrees with the general view that for over a century Puerto Rico has served the military, economic, and symbolic interests of the United States. His explanation of this fact, however, challenges the reader to depart from the usual colonial or nationalist explanations and thus represents an important contribution to the quest for democracy. This explanation consists of three main points. First, in terms of the difficulty in understanding why social justice is so difficult to attain (see chapter 4), Grosfoguel's analysis goes beyond the usual revolutionary versus conservative rhetoric, and beyond the pro- or anti-U.S. discourse. This is what he means by "(non)essentialist interpretations," and they challenge the reader to wrestle with new ways to see not only the Puerto Rican struggle but also the concept of a radical democratic perspective.

Secondly and more specifically, he clarifies the reasons why the nationalists are having a difficult time gathering mass support for the independence of Puerto Rico from the United States. He is dealing here with a question of bio-power, the well-being of the people, that is, those options of the Puerto Rican working class that best guarantee the basics of life, such as the federal minimum wage, food stamps, housing subsidies, unemployment insurance, social security, civil rights, and abortion rights. To become an independent nation-state like Haiti and the Dominican Republic (or Cuba, some will surely point out) may lead into unknown territory at best and dictatorship at worse. To remain associated as a state or a commonwealth, he suggests, does not necessarily imply the elimination of language and culture.[1]

Thirdly, Grosfoguel argues that the people's position is not necessarily a selling out or evidence of a "colonized mentality." And this leads to his insightful conclusion that the Puerto Rican working class is actually practicing a political pragmatism, a "subversive complicity" that leaves open the possibility for what he calls "a democratization of democracy." In other words, as has been pointed out throughout this reader, Latino/a thought is not so much the struggle of Mexican Americans and Puerto Rican or Cuban independence against the United States government, as it is the struggle of all "the people" for the idea of democracy itself based on human rights.

Notes

1. For a similar argument regarding Chicanos, see Mario Barrera, *Beyond Aztlán: Ethnic Autonomy in Comparative Perspective* (New York: Praeger, 1988), 157–76.

*　　*　　*

The referendum of November 14, 1993, concerning the political status of Puerto Rico provides a critical opportunity to analyze the historically consistent rejection of independence by Puerto Ricans. More than 70 percent of the electorate participated in the referendum. The breakdown of the results by alternatives was as follows: 48 percent voted in favor of maintaining the Commonwealth (the current colonial status), 46 percent voted for statehood, and only 4 percent voted for independence. A significant feature of the outcome was the increase of the pro-statehood vote, which grew by 7 percent, as compared to the 1967 plebiscite where statehood received 39 percent of the vote. There can be no doubt that the great majority of the Puerto Rican people expressed an interest in consolidating some form of "permanent union" with the United States.

Historically, nationalist discourses have put forward several explanations to account for the failure of the independence movement. Certain discourses claim that traditional colonialist leaders have developed a campaign to misinform and instill fear about independence, some blame the "ignorance" of the Puerto Rican people, and still others point to the cultural/ideological colonization by, or assimilation to, the United States as the culprit. Even if we give these arguments the benefit of the doubt, the failure of the pro-independence movement cannot be reduced to a problem of "alienation." Elitist claims that people are "assimilated/alienated" obscure relevant questions such as: Why does independence have minimal support among the Puerto Rican people despite the offer of double citizenship? Why do the overwhelming majority prefer a political status that consolidates the union with the United States? Why has the pro-statehood alternative received massive support among Puerto Ricans despite the "English Only" precondition?

To understand the unpopularity of the independence movements in Puerto Rico, it is important to understand the shifting relationship of Puerto Rico to the United States since 1898. I propose that the United States has made political and economic concessions to working classes in Puerto Rico (which have rarely been made to any other colonial or postcolonial peoples) primarily because of the *military* and *symbolic* strategic importance of the island.

This essay [i.e. chapter] attempts to address these questions and to suggest other ways of articulating the status issue within a radical democratic perspective. The first section consists of a historical overview of Puerto Rico's peculiar modes of incorporation to the United States. The second part critically places the unpopularity of independence discourses within the context of the postwar Caribbean "modern colonies." The last section is an attempt to provide a nonessentialist interpretation of the status alternatives.

Puerto Ricos' Modes of Incorporation (1898–1995)

The colonization of Puerto Rico by the United States has had three dominant interests, namely, economic, military, and symbolic.[1] Despite the simultaneity of these three interests throughout the century, one interest has acquired priority over the others at times, depending on the historical context. It is important to note that these interests can either reinforce or contradict each other. Contrary to the economic reductionism of some dependency/mode of production approaches, the economic interests did not always dominate the core-periphery relationship between Puerto Rico and the United States. Instead, state geopolitical considerations such as symbolic or military interests have dominated the U.S.-Puerto Rico relations over extensive periods during the twentieth century.[2] The importance of these geopolitical interests was such that in some instances they actually contradicted corporate economic interests of the United States in Puerto Rico.

The economic interests have been embodied by U.S. corporations. The dominant industries have shifted through different historical periods. From 1898 through 1940, U.S. sugar corporations were the dominant economic actors. During the 1947–70 period, labor-intensive light industries (apparel, textile, shoes, etc.) became dominant. As of 1973, U.S. capital-intensive, high-tech, transnational industries (i.e., pharmaceutical and electronic) have controlled the production sphere.

Military interests are represented by the Pentagon. Puerto Rico has served as a beachhead for U.S. invasions and military operations in the Caribbean region. The island has been a naval training ground for joint exercises of the North Atlantic Treaty Organization (NATO) and Latin American naval ships. Because of the island's tropical weather, it has served as a training ground for counterinsurgency operations deployed in countries such as Vietnam, Grenada, and Haiti. U.S. military interests in Puerto Rico ruled from 1898 through 1945.

Symbolic interests were inscribed in the actions taken by the State Department and the Department of the Interior. For instance, Puerto Rico became a symbolic showcase of the capitalist model of development that the United States presented to the "Third World" vis-à-vis the competing Soviet model.[3] Thus, Puerto Rico became an international training ground for President [Harry S.] Truman's Point Four Program. Through this program, thousands of members of the peripheral countries' elites visited Puerto Rico to receive technical training and learn firsthand the lessons of the first experiment in capital import-export-oriented industrialization. This model of development was based on attracting foreign capital through cheap labor, development of industrial infrastructure, and tax-free incentives for corporations. Billions of dollars in federal aid were transferred from the core state to the colonial administration in order to make Puerto Rico a "success story."[4]

The dialectical dynamics among the interests just outlined are crucial to understanding the specific relationship the United States has with Puerto Rico. For example, as will be discussed later, political concessions to the Puerto Rican population as a result of military or symbolic considerations sometimes clashed with U.S. corporations' economic interests during certain historical periods. Thus, I prefer to conceptualize Puerto Rico's modes of incorporation as the hierarchical articulation (harmonious and/or contradictory) between the economic, military, and symbolic interests of the United States spanning different historical contexts. The consequent periodization of Puerto Rican history during the twentieth century is, then, as follows: a period of agrarian capitalism in which the U.S. military interests predominated (1898–1940), a labor-intensive export-oriented industrialization period in which the U.S. State Department's symbolic interests were dominant (1950–70), a capital-intensive export-oriented industrialization period[5] in which both the transnational corporations and military interests shared the dominant position (1973–90), and an era of overtly economic interest dominating over all geopolitical interests, thus significantly reducing the strategic importance of the island (1991–?). Despite the predominance of one or two actors' interests (the Pentagon, U.S. corporations, the State Department) at a specific historical period, the three have been simultaneously present throughout these periods. The peculiar manifestations of each interest and the articulation among them has, however, changed historically.

Early-Twentieth-Century Puerto Rico (1898–1930)

The geopolitical strategies of core countries in the world interstate system have been crucial determinants of the peripheral incorporation of Caribbean societies. The interest of the United States in seizing Cuba and Puerto Rico from Spain in 1898 was a response mainly to state security interests. Several years before the Spanish-American War, American naval strategist Alfred T. Mahan stressed the strategic importance of building a canal in Central America in order to solve a major problem of U.S. mainland defense: the forced division of its naval fleet between the Atlantic and Pacific coasts. A U.S.-controlled canal in Central America would make possible a unified fleet. The fleet would move with greater speed and security from one ocean to the other by way of a canal, thus eliminating the trip around the tip of South America through the Strait of Magellan. Otherwise, 13,000 miles between San Francisco and Florida had to be navigated, taking more than 60 days.[6]

In addition to building and controlling a canal, Mahan added that it would be necessary to control the canal's eastern and western strategic maritime routes before construction. Mahan foresaw that the construction of a canal would attract the interest of other imperial powers, forcing the United States to enter international conflicts. According to Mahan, foreign control of the canal could be used as a beachhead to attack the United States. This foreign control would destroy the major U.S. asset against foreign aggression, namely, its geopolitical isolation.[7] As a means to achieve geopolitical control, he recommended the acquisition of Hawaii and the naval control of four Caribbean maritime routes before building the canal. The four routes were *Paso de Yucatán* (between Mexico and Cuba), *Paso de los Vientos* (the principal U.S. access route to the canal between Cuba and Haiti), *Paso de Anegada* (near St. Thomas, an island off Puerto Rico's eastern coast), and *Paso de la Mona* (between Puerto Rico and the Dominican Republic).[8] Mahan advised that naval bases be established in each of these zones as necessary steps for the United States to become a superpower. Mahan's influence was strongly felt among key political elites headed by Theodore Roosevelt and Henry Cabot Lodge.[9]

The only islands with access to the four maritime routes mentioned by Mahan were Cuba and Puerto Rico. Moreover, they were more amenable to foreign control when compared to Haiti and the Dominican Republic, which had already become nation-states. Cuba and Puerto Rico were still colonies of Spain, a weak and declining imperial state. Because the United States feared other imperial countries would take advantage of Spain's weakness by seizing its last two colonies in the Western Hemisphere,[10] these islands became targets. At the time, this belief was not farfetched, because the Germans had a military plan to attack the United States wherein the first step was to seize Puerto Rico.[11] Another strategic consideration in terms of timing was to intervene before Cuban nationalist rebels defeated Spain in their war of independence. A sovereign nation-state could make the negotiation process difficult for the United States.[12] Thus, in the mid-1890s the United States began to plan a conflict with Spain. In 1898, Puerto Rico and Cuba were seized by the United States during the Spanish-American War.

The geopolitical interests of the United States and the local relation of forces in Puerto Rico and Cuba set the conditions for the different modes of incorporation of the two islands. The United States encountered important local differences between Cuba and Puerto Rico. Cuba had a strong nationalist movement pressuring for the departure of the Americans. The negotiations between the United States and Cuba established a protectorate treaty as well as the right of the United States to build a naval base in Guantanamo.

Two salient features of the internal power relations in Puerto Rico affected its mode of incorporation to the United States. First, all political parties supported the annexation of Puerto Rico to the mainland immediately after the 1898 invasion. Shortly after the landing of U.S. troops in Puerto Rico, General Nelson Miles proclaimed that the war against Spain occurred for humanitarian reasons such as justice and freedom.[13]

Second, Puerto Rico did not have a strong nationalist movement at the time of the U.S. invasion. This allowed the United States to make Puerto Rico a colonial possession without difficulties, thus providing the best conditions to safeguard the military strategic use of the island. Accordingly, the U.S. military prescribed that Puerto Rico remain a colonial possession and that a naval base be built off the northeastern coast of Puerto Rico in Culebra.[14]

A few years after the U.S. invasion, the Orthodox Party and Liberal Party exchanged political programs.[15] The Orthodox Party, linked to the sugar landowners who were radical autonomists under Spain, became an annexationist force under U.S. domination. This transition was marked by a name change from the Orthodox Party to the Puerto Rican Republican Party. The Liberal Party, linked to the coffee *hacendados* who were moderate autonomists under Spain, initially assumed an annexationist position with autonomist tendencies, but later, because of the U.S. pro-sugar policies,[16] became a radical autonomist party, ultimately flirting with pro-independence positions. These transitions were marked by name changes from the Liberal Party to the Federal Party and subsequently to the Union Party.

The Union Party represented those social forces with the greatest potential for building a pro-independence movement. However, the local hacendados were never supported by the popular classes. Because of the hacendados' alliance with the Spanish colonial administration's authoritarian repressive measures against the rights of peasants and workers, many among these sectors perceived the hacendados as their class enemies. Workers and peasants associated the hacendados' pro-independence positions with a romantic nostalgia for the forms of labor coercion and authoritarianism of the Spanish regime, under which the hacendados' social and economic position had not been threatened. Under U.S. domination, on the other hand, many workers saw an opportunity to establish civil and labor rights by pressuring the U.S. government to extend their legislative laws to the island. These sectors adopted the Americanization discourse promoted by the new imperial power as a strategy to weaken the political power of the local hacendados and gain democratic rights recognized in the metropolitan constitution. Despite the negative effects on U.S. sugar corporations of extending labor rights to Puerto Rico, the American state extended these rights to the Puerto Rican working class. The U.S. government wanted to gain popular support for the island's colonial incorporation. By extending labor rights to Puerto Rican workers, the pro-annexationist position of the labor movement was strengthened. This encouraged the formation of a pro-colonial bloc, which in turn impeded the possibility of a pro-independence alliance. The U.S. government's extension of civil and labor rights to Puerto Rico proved to be an important deterrent to the development of a collective national demand for self-determination.

The concessions to the Puerto Rican working classes by the U.S. government mark a distinctive feature of Puerto Rico's incorporation. Different from other U.S. military occupations of Caribbean countries such as Cuba, the Dominican Republic, and Haiti, where the U.S. government relied on authoritarian alliances with the landowners and/or the political/military elites to protect its interests, the U.S. strategy in Puerto Rico relied on a populist-democratic alliance with the working classes and progressive liberal middle-class sectors at the expense of the coffee landowners. The extension of democratic rights to the colony precluded the working classes sympathizing with a nationalist solution to the colonial question. The weakening of the hacendados' power base also debilitated the pro-autonomy forces and accelerated wage-labor relations in Puerto Rico. By contrast, the U.S. invasion in a country like Haiti relied on a class alliance with the local commercial elites and the coffee landowners, which strengthened noncapitalist forms of labor coercion.[17]

In sum, the evidence suggests that Puerto Rico's re-peripheralization from a Spanish possession to a U.S. colony was predominantly due to the American government's security interests. Puerto Rico's geopolitical location was strategically important for the U.S. government's defense against possible European aggression against the Panama Canal and the U.S. mainland. In contrast to the peripheral incorporation of other countries, where the economic interests in mining or agriculture were predominant, Puerto Rico's incorporation to the United States in the early twentieth century was primarily geopolitical. As illustrated earlier, the secondary status of the economic interests of the United States was such that certain state policies such as the extension of civil and labor rights to the local population contradicted the immediate interests of U.S. corporations investing in the island at the time.

The End of the Sugar Plantations (1930–45)

During the Great Depression, the United States developed the "Good Neighbor" foreign policy toward Latin America. The decline in sugar production, the spread of poverty, unemployment, and hunger throughout Puerto Rico, along with the emerging popularity of pro-independence ideas among many sectors had become shameful examples for U.S. foreign policy in the region. To counteract the impact of Puerto Rico's situation upon its international reputation, the United States extended to Puerto Rico certain New Deal reforms and supported an industrialization program (the Chardón Plan). This change of policy was marked by the transfer of the U.S. colonial administration in Puerto Rico from the Department of War to the Department of the Interior. However, the local power bloc hegemonized by U.S. sugar plantations presented many obstacles for the extension of these reforms. This period in U.S.-Puerto Rico relations (when symbolic interests of the United States dominated Puerto Rico's incorporation) was short-lived because of the imminent possibility of war, which made military interests dominant again.

During the late 1930s and early 1940s, the U.S. government supported a local populist power bloc at the expense of U.S. sugar corporations. The mortal blow to the sugar plantations, however, was the implementation of the 500-acre law in 1941. This law forced U.S. corporations to sell all land exceeding 500 acres to the colonial government. These lands were used to enforce the agrarian reform that eradicated the *agregados* (peasants forced to pay in rent, kind, or labor for living on the landowner's property) and mitigated the housing needs of thousands of peasants.

State military considerations during World War II fundamentally structured these policies. The state understood that a local population angry at the exploitation and abuses of U.S. sugar corporations was completely undesirable because it could represent a security problem for the military use of the island in times of war. The new governor of Puerto Rico in 1941, the reformist liberal Rexford Tugwell, confirms the military priority of Puerto Rico in his memoirs:

> My duty as a representative of my country in Puerto Rico was to shape civil affairs, if I could, so that military bases, which might soon (before they were ready) have to stand the shock of attack, were not isolated in a generally hostile environment.[18]

In short, the U.S. strategy in Puerto Rico was one of exchanging basic democratic rights for Puerto Ricans for the military exploitation of the island.

Postwar Puerto Rico (1945–95)

The U.S. symbolic interest in Puerto Rico gained dominance immediately after World War II. Puerto Rico became a token in the symbolic battleground between the Soviet Union and the United States, particularly in the United Nations. The Soviets claimed that Puerto Rico symbolized U.S. colonialist and imperialist aims in the world. Concerned about the image of the United States in the eyes of newly independent Third World countries, the State Department pressured for concessions to Puerto Rico. These concessions developed into a strategy to make Puerto Rico a showcase of democracy and capitalism during the 1950s and 1960s.[19] The first concession was the appointment of a Puerto Rican as governor in 1946. The right to elect a local governor was established shortly after, in 1948. Following this, the metropolis fostered the creation of a new status called *Estado Libre Asociado* (Commonwealth), which was approved in 1952. Lastly, a program of industrialization through massive foreign capital investments (i.e., the model of industrialization by invitation) was implemented, thus radically improving the island's infrastructure.

To enable the fulfillment of Puerto Rico's symbolic role and to foster a successful economic program, the U.S. government cooperated with local elites to support a massive labor migration of the marginalized Puerto Rican labor force.[20] The creation of the institutional framework to facilitate migration through the availability of cheap airfares between Puerto Rico and the United States as well as an advertisement campaign for jobs in the United

States provided the conditions of possibility for Puerto Rico's "success story" during the 1950s and 1960s.

These transformations allowed the U.S. State Department to designate Puerto Rico in 1950 as the Point Four Program's international training ground for technical development of Third World elites. This program was more ideological than technical to the extent that these elites learned first-hand about the American model of development for "Third World" countries as opposed to the competing Soviet model.

Puerto Rico's important symbolic role during the Cold War explains the massive U.S. federal assistance given to Puerto Rico in areas such as housing, health, and education.[21] Puerto Rico was treated like any other state in need of federal assistance. The main difference between Puerto Rico and other states was that Puerto Rico's residents did not have to pay federal taxes. It is important to note that this "privileged" status was not granted to any other U.S. colonial territories.

Recent events have transformed once again the United States interest in Puerto Rico. The disappearance of the Soviet Union has changed the priorities of the core powers and the articulation among the different global logics. Today, U.S. economic interests have primacy over geopolitical considerations, and domestic economic concerns over foreign policy. As Anthony P. Maingot states in an excellent article about the Caribbean in the post-Cold War era, "geopolitics have given way to geoeconomics."[22] Therefore, the symbolic and military importance of Puerto Rico for the United States has become a secondary concern. In this sense, Puerto Rico is perceived by U.S. political elites more as an expense to the state than as an important military bastion or symbolic showcase. Economic crisis in the United States (such as the huge U.S. public debt) has created the context for Congress to eradicate 936 benefits for U.S. corporations in Puerto Rico, reduce federal transfers, and (among several factions of the U.S. political elites) articulate a sympathetic position toward a more autonomous status for the island. These trends suggest that a change in Puerto Rico's colonial status could result in the formation of a neocolonial relationship with the United States. If Puerto Rico becomes a neocolony, the United States would be relieved from the expenses of a modern colony, creating a "colony without any expenses." Particularly affected by this redefinition are Puerto Rican working classes.

Modern Colonies in the Postwar Caribbean

Modern colonialism is the term that addresses the dramatic change of the colonialism implemented by core countries in the postwar Caribbean.[23] In terms of standard of living and civil rights, postwar Caribbean colonial incorporations to the metropolises have been more beneficial to working classes than neocolonial relationships. This can be illustrated by comparing U.S., French, and Dutch postwar modern colonies to neocolonial republics.

Anticolonial struggles and Cold War geopolitical military and symbolic considerations forced western metropolises to make concessions to their colonies. While certain colonies became nation-states, such as Jamaica, Guyana, and most of the English Caribbean, other territories remained colonial possessions because of their strategic location and/or symbolic/ideological importance. U.S., French, and Dutch colonies such as Puerto Rico, Martinique, and Curaçao, respectively, were granted economic and democratic reforms in order to preclude the success of any potential anticolonial struggles. The benefits enjoyed by these modern colonial populations (vis-à-vis their neocolonial neighbors) include annual transfers of billions of dollars of social capital from the metropolitan state to the modern colony (e.g., food stamps, health, education, and unemployment benefits), constitutional recognition of metropolitan citizenship and democratic/civil rights, the possibility of migration without the risks of illegality, and the extension of Fordist social relations that incorporated the colonial people to metropolitan standards of mass consumption.

Given Puerto Rico's importance as a symbolic showcase and a strategic military location, the United States responded to the 1974 economic crisis with federal assistance aimed to guarantee political stability and the survival of the "industrialization by invitation" model of development. The federal transfers were increased by extending several programs to individuals on the island. Federal transfers to individuals increased from $517 million in 1973, to $2.5 billion in 1980, to $4 billion in 1989. Federal aid represented 8 percent of the gross national product (GNP) in 1973, 23 percent in 1980, and 21 percent in 1989. Federal transfers to individuals were 10 percent of personal income in 1973, 22 percent in 1980, and 21 percent in 1989. While approximately 60 percent of families in Puerto Rico qualified for food stamps, only 11 percent of families in the United States qualified for the same program. This countercyclical "shock absorber" is crucial to understanding how the Puerto Rican lower classes survived the crisis.

These economic benefits account in part for why hardly any significant segment of the population from Puerto Rico, Martinique/Guadeloupe, or Saint Martin/Curaçao is willing to renounce U.S., French, or Dutch citizenship.[24] The fact that half of the Surinamese population moved to the Netherlands when the Dutch imposed, for economic reasons, the formation of Surinam as a nation-state supports this argument.[25]

There is no doubt that the colonial administration of these modern colonies developed ideological and cultural colonization strategies. The people of these modern colonies, however, are neither passive recipients of colonial policies nor ignorant about what is happening in the region. On the contrary, observing the situation of neighboring neocolonial republics, speaking with immigrants from these countries (e.g., people from the Dominican Republic in Puerto Rico, from Grenada in Curaçao, and from Haiti and Dominica in Guadeloupe), and listening to the authoritarian and elitist discourses of pro-independence leaders, modern colonial peoples of the Caribbean fear the authoritarian and exploitative potential of a nation-state. It is not a coincidence that a constant comment made by Puerto Ricans, Guadeloupeans, and Martinicans in the streets is, "To be independent like Haiti or the Dominican Republic, better to be a colony."

Although authoritarianism is not intrinsic to independence, these issues continue to worry those who enjoy democratic and civil rights under modern colonial arrangements vis-à-vis neocolonial relationships. Their preoccupation should not be underestimated in light of the clientelistic/*caudillista* political traditions and the weak peripheral economies of small Caribbean islands. The possibilities of a dictatorship under these conditions are relatively high, especially considering the long-term dictatorships of Cuba, Haiti, and the Dominican Republic during this century. Moreover, even the recently formed independent Caribbean states like Surinam, Dominica, Guyana, and Grenada have suffered military coups and/or authoritarian regimes.

The anti-independence and pro-permanent union political positions of most modern colonial peoples of the Caribbean should not be caricatured as the product of a "colonized" or "ignorant" people. Given the drastic difference between the situation of working classes in modern colonies and neocolonial nation-states of the region, these people prefer a modern colony that benefits from metropolitan transfers over a neocolonial nation-state with the same colonial exploitation of a modern colony but no benefits from the metropolitan state. Rather than the assumption that modern Caribbean colonial peoples are "alienated" or "assimilated," their position suggests a political pragmatism rooted in conditions where options are extremely limited. In the current Caribbean context there is no space external to U.S. hegemony over the region. Even the most "independent" republic cannot escape U.S. control. Any attempt to subvert this order is militarily or economically destroyed, as occurred in Grenada, Nicaragua, and Jamaica.

The Puerto Rican people's strategy has been pragmatic rather than utopian; that is, they are not struggling to be freed from imperialist oppression (which is highly improbable and perhaps even undesirable under the present circumstances) but are instead attempting to struggle for a milder version of this oppression. They would rather be exploited with some benefits (as in Curaçao and Martinique) than be exploited without any benefits (as in the Dominican Republic and Haiti). In this sense, the unpopularity of the independence movement is a pragmatic rejection of a neocolonial independence. Puerto Rican workers in many instances throughout the century have followed a strategy of *subversive complicity* with the system. This is a subversion from within the dominant discourses. A good example is the use and abuse of the discourse of Americanism by the early-twentieth-century working class movement in Puerto Rico. As a Puerto Rican pro-statehood worker recently stated,

> In the name of democratic and civil rights as citizens of the United States we should struggle for equality by becoming the 51st state. We cannot let the Americans enforce an independence status on us in order to cut their budget deficit. Through independence they will keep controlling us but without the commitment to extend welfare benefits and civil rights. After destroying our economy and exploiting the best energies of the Puerto Rican workers during this century, now they want to get rid of us. That is unacceptable. After the Americans ate the meat, let them now suck the bones.[26]

I am not suggesting that colonialism is the solution to Third World problems nor that we should stop struggling against colonial oppression. These islands are no paradise.[27] Instead, I am trying to understand, without resorting to traditional nationalist moralization or colonialist explanations, why the people from modern colonies like Puerto Rico, Curaçao, and Martinique prefer a status of permanent union with the metropolis to independence. Considering the history of imperialist exploitation and destruction of the local economies, it is legitimate to pose the following questions: On whose shoulders would the sacrifices required by the economic reconstruction for an independent state fall? Whose salaries and wages would be reduced for local and transnational industries to compete favorably in the world economy? Who would be affected by the reduction of state assistance (e.g., food stamps, housing subsidies) in favor of the republic's economic reconstruction? Obviously, the sacrifice will not be made by the lawyers, merchants, doctors, and professors of the pro-independence leadership but instead will be made by the working classes. Does the rejection of this scenario imply a "colonized" mentality?

When people ask pro-independence militants how they will survive if Puerto Rico becomes a nation-state, the response usually refers to the new equality and justice for all that will be achieved under the republic. This vague response does not address the legitimate concern that Puerto Rico imports approximately 80 percent of its food. Those who demand a serious answer are aristocratically accused of being colonized, assimilated, or ignorant. However, people eat neither flags nor hymns; nor do they outlive the eternity of sacrifices necessary to reach the future "paradise republic."

The romantic rhetoric of the pro-independence movement cannot conceal the dire reality awaiting a future republic. In the contemporary world system, where no space is external to global capitalism,[28] the transition toward an independent nation-state will entail overwhelming sacrifices for the working classes.

Toward a Nonessentialist Treatment of the Status Question: Challenges and Options

Irrespective of whether Puerto Rico becomes an independent republic, a reformed commonwealth, the fifty-first state, or an associated republic, the island will remain under U.S. hegemony. Thus, the relevant question is, Which status alternative will be more favorable to the protection, deepening, and expansion of the social and democratic rights already recognized under the current colonial status (e.g., federal minimum wage, unemployment benefits, social security, abortion rights, civil rights)?

The failure of the independence movement in the past referendum (only 4 percent of the votes) manifests the historical divorce between nationalist discourses and the Puerto Rican people. If the pro-independence movement[29] wants to convince the Puerto Rican people of their project, they need to offer a political-economic-ecological-sexual program superior to that of other status alternatives. Their alternative program would have to significantly improve the standard of living and the democratic and civil rights that Puerto Ricans already enjoy. This challenge is difficult to meet, however, within the present context of global capitalism. The free-trade agreement between Mexico and the United States, the increased opening of Cuba, the incorporation of the Central American economies after a decade of civil wars, the absence of a Puerto Rican "national" economy, the island's extreme dependence on federal assistance, and the competition of other low-wage countries in the Caribbean region make the economic viability of an independent Puerto Rico extremely questionable in this historical conjuncture. An independent Puerto Rican nation-state would have to pauperize its population in order to compete in the capitalist world economy by reducing the minimum wage and government transfers to individuals, by submitting to neoliberal policies of the International Monetary Fund to subsidize the trade and balance of payment deficits, and by reducing environmental controls. Thus, given the impossibility in the present historical conjuncture of offering a pro-independence project superior to that of the other status options at this moment in history, the progressive forces within the pro-independence movement have three alternatives. First, they can continue to support the independence project but can speak openly to the people about the necessary sacrifices and risks of a transition to an independent state. Second, they can abandon the independence project and support one of the two remaining status alternatives, submitting to their currently conservative programs and leadership. Third, they can stop understanding the status issue in essentialist terms or as a question of principle. Instead, the movement could struggle for a "democratization of democracy" in all spheres of everyday life, pressure the other parties to develop progressive programs, and open the pragmatic question of which status alternative will do better (or the least evil) in protecting and improving the island's ecology, quality of life, and democracy. This could channel their efforts beyond the limits set by the status debate. Although it is important to assume a position concerning the status issue, progressive forces should not reify it at the expense of democratic struggles. The reification of the status question precludes the emergence of alternative forms of radical politics.

Given the unconvincing platform of the pro-independence movement, the third option, that is, a radical democratic project,[30] could become a more viable alternative than the second alternative, which basically supports the traditional conservative programs and colonialist leadership of the pro-commonwealth and pro-statehood options. The political practice of a radical democratic project would privilege the improvement of oppressed subjects' qualify of life in the present rather than in a distant future "paradise." This movement would include a multiplicity of projects to promote and support the struggles of diverse oppressed subjects such as blacks, women, youth, gays, lesbians, and workers. Coalitions between these groups can only be possible if differences and organizational autonomy are respected without privileging the demands of one group at the expense of another.

Although these demands may not entail the destruction of capitalism, they can at least weaken the power bloc and improve the quality of life of different social groups. I call this strategy subversive complicity with the system against capitalism, patriarchy, racism, heterosexism, and authoritarianism. A meta-narrative (totalizing discourse) articulated to struggle against the system from the vantage point of a utopian space beyond capitalism makes the movement vulnerable to an authoritarian response from the state. By contrast, the strategy of subversive complicity would imply the radical resignification of the symbols of U.S. hegemonic discourses in the Caribbean region such as democracy, civil rights, and equal opportunities. This means using a democratic discourse rather than a socialist discourse but resignifying it in a radical democratic direction.

A radical democratic project in Puerto Rico would "democratize democracy" through the deepening of democratic and civil rights for oppressed subjects and the increasing of their control over the conditions of everyday life. Several struggles could exemplify a radical democratic project:

1. A struggle against environmental pollution. Currently, the colonial government's *Junta de Calidad Ambiental* (Board of Environmental Control), in alliance with transnational capital, has a pernicious effect on the island's environment. The *Junta* overlooks pollution increases and allows the destruction of the island's natural resources. A radical democratic project could struggle for the right to a healthy life by demanding legal measures that criminalize harmful industrial practices. The focus would be the democratization of political power over the environment.

2. A struggle for women's rights. Stronger social measures to transform the sexual division of labor that subordinates thousands of women could be developed in the name of equality of opportunities. For instance, the creation of child-care centers combining public and private funds would significantly reduce the amount of work women do in Puerto Rico.

3. Struggles to improve the quality of life. Two measures that would radically improve the quality of life are the construction of a monorail in the major cities and a train route throughout the whole island. This form of transportation would decrease the use of cars (Puerto Rico has one of the highest numbers of cars per capita in the world) and would in turn immediately improve the quality of life by eradicating traffic jams, lowering pollution levels, and indirectly increasing salaries due to the decrease in car expenses (e.g., gas, auto parts, insurance, and loans).

4. A struggle to decrease the crime rate. Most homicides and robberies in Puerto Rico are a result of two factors: unemployment and drugs. First, the legalization of highly addictive drugs (e.g., heroin) and the free distribution of drugs among the addicted population would eliminate the need to kill or steal to gather the necessary money to maintain a heroin addiction. Experimental programs in England and the Netherlands have had impressive results using this strategy. Second, the reduction of the workday while keeping constant the eight-hour workday salary

would increase the job supply, enabling the massive incorporation of unemployed workers in the formal economy. Given the trend toward automation and technological development, global capitalism cannot continue to expand or create new jobs indefinitely. Thus, it is meaningless to plead for the creation of new eight-hour workday jobs. Moreover, these measures would decrease the importance of illegal informal economic activities (e.g., selling drugs) for a large number of unemployed workers. These activities, criminalized by the state, constitute the economy of a large unemployed and underemployed sector of Puerto Rican society.

To gain legitimacy, the Left needs to dissociate itself from essentialist discourses regarding the status issue, namely, to stop defending independence as a matter of principle. Contrary to the discourses and practices of Puerto Rican political culture, status alternatives are not essentially progressive or reactionary. The progressive or reactionary character of a status alternative is contingent on the relation of forces, the strengths or weaknesses of social movements, and the discourses articulating the status options in a specific conjuncture of the global capitalist system. Just as nation-states can be either reactionary or progressive, states or associated republics can be either reactionary or progressive. For instance, compare Hawaii's or Vermont's progressive health-care policies to Pennsylvania's reactionary policies in the United States, or compare the Russian state's authoritarian control over the "autonomous" republics to the democratic autonomous regions of Spain.

The pro-statehood movement in Puerto Rico has been hegemonized by conservative and right-wing factions.[31] However, the statehood alternative is not inherently reactionary. One can imagine an antimilitarist and a radical-democratic pro-statehood movement in Puerto Rico that makes alliances with and defends the democratic struggles of other oppressed groups (e g., Latinos, African Americans, women, gays and lesbians) in the United States. The early-twentieth-century movement of Puerto Rican workers is a good example. This socialist pro-statehood movement built coalitions with U.S. workers' unions and defended Americanism as a strategy to make civil and labor rights recognized in the mainland extend to Puerto Rico.

Similarly, we can imagine an autonomous status, called the Associated Republic, that could eliminate certain federal laws to improve the quality of life of the population instead of pauperizing it. Examples are increased autonomy from federal environmental laws so that stricter regulations could be developed, and the elimination of the federal minimum wage so that it could be increased.

In a more progressive direction, the transformation of the Puerto Rican party system, traditionally organized in terms of status alternatives, presupposes the development of a popular radical democratic movement that defies the boundaries of current debates by undoing the correspondence between status alternatives and political parties. This movement could garner people with diverse political positions regarding the status issue who want to protect and expand the existing democratic, sexual, civil, and social rights. They could struggle for the decolonization of the island by demanding the right of self-determination for the Puerto Rican people without imposing a status option that would unnecessarily divide the movement. This mass democratic movement could struggle against any potential turn toward authoritarianism irrespective of the eventual political status of the island. All in all, the status is not a matter of principle and, consequently, remains secondary in relation to the primacy of radical democratic struggles.

Discourses warning against the threat of losing our "national" identity and language under the actual colonial status or statehood are mainly employed by nationalist groups in Puerto Rico to justify their defense of independence as a matter of principle. To speak Spanish at school and in public administrative life was achieved through the struggles of the Puerto Rican people more than fifty years ago. Moreover, the Quebecois in Canada, the Catalans in Spain, Guadeloupeans under France, and the Curaçaoans under the Netherlands are also "nations" without independent states. These "nations" without nation-states have not lost their languages or their "national cultures" although their cultures and languages have been transformed by the influence of the metropolises. This transformation can be seen, however, as an enrichment rather than a hindrance. Thus, statehood or some other form of union with the metropolis does not necessarily entail cultural or linguistic genocide. Puerto Ricans can be part of the struggle, together with other Latinos, for the recognition of cultural and linguistic diversity in the United States.

The Puerto Rican people share a feeling of nationhood that has not translated into traditional nationalist claims to form a nation-state. Puerto Ricans have formed an "imaginary community" with an imaginary belonging to a territory that spans the island as well as certain areas on the mainland (e.g., South Bronx, Spanish Harlem, North Philadelphia). This imaginary community oscillates between feelings of nationhood and ethnicity; that is, Puerto Ricans simultaneously imagine themselves as a nation and as an ethnic group. Puerto Ricans' self-perception does not fit either the concept of a "nation" or that of an "ethnic group." I believe the concept of "ethno-nation"[32] accommodates the Puerto Ricans' diverse and peculiar subject positions better than that of "nation."

Pro-independence ideologies that attempt to equate the status debate to a matter of principle constitute the political project of a minority seeking to become a national elite and/or bourgeoisie. This movement's emphasis upon the purportedly inevitable cultural and linguistic genocide has precluded a serious discussion of the socioeconomic consequences of independence for working classes today. Their struggles could be more effective if they concentrated on the development of a radical democratic movement that protects, expands, and improves the quality of life and the democratic and civil rights Puerto Ricans have today.

*   *   *

Notes

1. Ramón Grosfoguel, "World Cities in the Caribbean: The Rise of Miami and San Juan," *Review (Journal of the Fernand Braudel Center)* 17, 3 (summer 1994).

2. Ramón Grosfoguel, "Puerto Rico's Exceptionalism: Industrialization, Migration and Housing Development" (Ph.D. diss., Temple University, 1992).

3. Grosfoguel, "Puerto Rico's Exceptionalism."

4. Grosfoguel, "Puerto Rico's Exceptionalism."

5. Public Law 936 (passed in 1976) enabled transnational corporations in Puerto Rico to repatriate their profits to the mainland without paying U.S. federal taxes.

6. María Eugenia Estades Font, *La presencia militar de Estados Unidos en Puerto Rico: 1898–1918* (Río Piedras: Ediciones Huracán, 1988), 27–28.

7 Estades Font, *La presencia militar de Estados Unidos en Puerto Rico*, 27–28.

8. Estades Font, *La presencia militar de Estados Unidos en Puerto Rico*, 29.

9. See Estades Font, *La presencia militar de Estados Unidos en Puerto Rico*, 31; and Jorge Rodríguez-Beruff, *Política militar y dominación* (Río Piedras: Ediciones Huracán, 1988), 149.

10. See Estades Font, *La presencia militar de Estados Unidos en Puerto Rico*, 40.

11. Helger Herwig, *Politics of Frustration: The United States in Naval Planning* (Boston: Little, Brown and Company, 1976), 61–65, 86–87.

12. Wilfredo Mattos Cintrón, *La política y lo político en Puerto Rico* (Mexico: Serie Popular ERA, 1980), 58.

13. See Estades Font, *La presencia militar de Estados Unidos en Puerto Rico*, 89–90.

14. Estades Font, *La presencia militar de Estados Unidos en Puerto Rico*, 36; and Alfred T. Mahan, *Lessons of the War with Spain and Other Articles* (Boston: Little, Brown and Company, 1899), 28–29.

15. Mattos Cintrón, *La política y lo político en Puerto Rico*.

16. Mattos Cintrón, *La política y lo político en Puerto Rico*; Angel Quintero Rivera, *Conflictos de clase y política en Puerto Rico* (Río Piedras: Ediciones Huracán, 1976).

17. Suzy Castor, *La ocupación norteamericana de Haiti y sus consecuencias (1915–1934)* (Mexico: Siglo XXI, 1972).

18. Rexford G. Tugwell, *The Stricken Land* (New York: Doubleday, 1947), 148.

19. Grosfoguel, "Puerto Rico's Exceptionalism."

20. Ramón Grosfoguel, "The Geopolitics of Caribbean Migration: From the Cold War to the Post-Cold War," in Jorge Rodriguez-Beruff and Humberto García-Muñiz, eds. *Security Problems and Policies in the Post-Cold War Caribbean* (London: Macmillan Press, 1996).

21. Grosfoguel, "Puerto Rico's Exceptionalism."

22. Anthony P. Maingot, "Preface," *Annals of the American Academy of Political and Social Sciences* 533 (May 1994): 8–18.

23. Gerald Pierre Charles, *El Caribe Contemporáneo* (Mexico: Siglo XXI, 1981).

24. The most absurd campaign recently pursued by some pro-independence leaders is the rejection of their U.S. citizenship. This "revolutionary" luxury can only be enjoyed by individuals with enough income to sustain their families without working or who do not depend on the welfare state. This campaign shows the elitist character of the pro-independence leadership and their "alienation" from the Puerto Rican people. See also *"E.U. impediría ingreso Mari Bras a Puerto Rico," Claridad*, Feb. 18–24, 1924, 12.

25. Grosfoguel, "The Geopolitics of Caribbean Migration." In a referendum held on Nov. 19, 1993, 76.3 percent of the people of Curaçao voted for the present status. Only 0.5 percent voted for independence.

26. This quote is taken from ethnographic work done by the author in Puerto Rico during the summer of 1990.

27. There has been a cost to this special relationship. In the Puerto Rican case, the high crime rate suggests an acute social polarization.

28. Immanuel Wallerstein, "Dependence in an Interdependent World: The Limited Possibilities of Transformation within the Capitalist World Economy," in *The Capitalist World Economy*, essays by Immanuel Wallerstein (Cambridge and Paris: Cambridge University Press and *Editions de la Maison des Sciences de l'Homme*, 1979).

29. Although the Left and nationalist movements are not inherently equivalent, they have been linked in Puerto Rico since the founding of the Nationalist Party during the 1920s.

30. Ernesto Laclau and Chantal Mouffe, *Hegemony and Socialist Strategy* (London: Verso, 1985).

31. The only exception has been the socialist pro-statehood movement of the 1910s and early 1920s.

32. For a discussion of the concept of "ethno-nation," see the introduction in Frances Negrón-Muntaner and Ramón Grosfoguel, eds., *Puerto Rican Jam: Rethinking Colonialism and Nationalism* (Minneapolis: University of Minnesota Press, 1977).<notes>

*   *   *

Questions

1. How does one explain the lack of widespread nationalism at the time of the U.S. invasion of Puerto Rico and its growth and development in subsequent years?
2. Why did the United States use a strategy of making alliances with the elite among northern Mexicans and Cubans, but not among the Puerto Ricans, preferring instead an alliance with the working class and progressive-liberal middle class?
3. For economic reasons, the Dutch let Surinam become an independent nation-state. According to Grosfoguel, the United States may do that with Puerto Rico if it becomes an "expensive colony." What does he mean by Puerto Rico becoming a neocolony, and what may be some of the consequences?
4. Can Grosfoguel's idea of "subversive complicity" be classified as class analysis or nationalism? In what sense is this analysis a "radical democratic project"?
5. In what ways may or may we not compare the notion of a Puerto Rican "ethno-nation" with that of a Chicano Aztlán?

~

CHAPTER TWENTY-TWO

Reconstructing Racial Identity: Ethnicity, Color, and Class among Dominicans in the United States and Puerto Rico

Jorge Duany

The notion of *mestizaje*, a mixed ethnic, racial, and political mixed identity is discussed at various points in this reader (Introduction, chapter 12, and the concluding chapter). Here Duany discusses a variation on mestizaje, a situation affecting the fourth largest Latino/a group in the United States: the Dominican immigrants to the mainland United States and Puerto Rico. He argues, specifically, that the massive migration from the Dominican Republic has culturally redefined the migrant's racial identity, causing a "traumatic racial experience." There is a contradiction between the public perception and the self-concept of Dominican immigrants, and this is a main problem for their adaptation to U.S. society. There is also an apparent paradox: Though Puerto Rico's racial classification is different from that of the United States and similar to that of the Dominican Republic, Dominicans in Puerto Rico are viewed as black or colored. Unfortunately, this is not unique to these two groups, pigmentocracy is prevalent throughout Latin America.

*   *   *

When people move across state borders, they enter not only a different labor market and political structure but also a new system of social stratification by class, race, ethnicity, and gender. Migrants bring their own cultural conceptions of their identity, which often do not coincide with the ideological constructions of the receiving societies. As a mulatto Dominican colleague told me recently, she "discovered" that she was black only when she first came to the United States; until then she had thought of herself as an *india clara* (literally, a light Indian) in a country whose aboriginal population was practically exterminated in the 16th century.

For most Caribbean immigrants in the United States, race and color have played a crucial role in the formation of their cultural identities. Two different models of racial hegemony are juxtaposed in the process of moving from the Caribbean to the United States. On one hand, Caribbean migrants—especially those coming from the Spanish-speaking countries of Cuba, the Dominican Republic, and Puerto Rico—tend to use three main racial categories—black, white, and mixed—based primarily on skin color and other physical characteristics such as facial features and hair texture (Seda Bonilla, 1980). On the other hand, the dominant system of racial classification in the United States emphasizes a two-tiered division between whites and nonwhites deriving from the rule of hypodescent—the assignment of the offspring of mixed races to the subordinate group (Harris, 1964; Winant, 1994). This clear-cut opposition between two cultural conceptions of racial identity is ripe for social and psychological conflict among Caribbean migrants, many of whom are of African or mixed background and are therefore defined as black or colored in the United States (Kasinitz, 1992; Safa, 1983).

I will argue that the massive exodus from the Dominican Republic has culturally redefined the migrants' racial identity. Whereas North Americans classify most Caribbean immigrants as black, Dominicans tend to perceive themselves as white, Hispanic, or other (including the folk term *indio*, to be discussed later). This contradiction between the public perception and the self-concept of Dominican migrants is one of their key problems in adapting to North American society. In Puerto Rico, although the traditional system of racial classification is similar to that of the Dominican Republic, most Dominican immigrants are viewed as blacks or colored (in local lore, *prietos*, *morenos*, and *trigueños*). Thus, in both receiving countries, Dominicans face the intense stigmatization, stereotyping, prejudice, and discrimination to which all people of African origin are subjected.

The argument is organized in four main parts. [Only the first part is included below.—Ed.] First, I will briefly review the extensive literature on race relations in the Caribbean and the United States, with special attention to the Dominican Republic and Puerto Rico. This background will help to clarify the different ideological constructions of racial identity in the sending and receiving countries. Second, I will summarize two field studies I directed among Dominican immigrants in the United States and in Puerto Rico. These studies will provide empirical support for the claim that migration has restructured the cultural conceptions of racial identity among Dominicans living abroad. Third, I will compare the Dominican communities of Washington Heights in New York City and Santurce, Puerto Rico. The data will reveal different patterns of racial and ethnic segregation, prejudice and discrimination, cultural adaptation, and identity, despite the similarity of many of the migrants' socioeconomic characteristics. Finally, I will assess the incorporation of Dominicans into North American and Puerto Rican societies and its potential impact on the Dominican Republic. My main thesis is that the racialization of Dominican immigrants in the United States and Puerto Rico has reinforced the persistence of an ethnic identity against the prevailing racial order and has largely confined them to the secondary segment of the labor and housing markets.

The theoretical framework for my argument owes much to the discussion of the racial formation of the United States by Michael Omi and Howard Winant (1994). According to these writers, race is not a fixed essence, a concrete and objective entity, but rather a set of socially constructed meanings subject to change and contestation through power relations and social movements. Hence, racial identity is historically flexible and culturally variable, embedded in a particular social context (see Winant, 1994, for a recent attempt to reconceptualize the study of race relations from a Gramscian and poststructuralist perspective). I would argue that the dominant racial ideologies in the United States, the Dominican Republic, and Puerto Rico categorize and interpret race in different ways. Consequently, Dominican immigrants in the United States and Puerto Rico tend to be treated as blacks, although most of them do not define themselves as such.

My comparative analysis of the Dominican diaspora is also informed by recent thinking on transnationalism (Basch, Schiller, and Szanton Blanc, 1994; Schiller, Basch, and Blanc-Szanton, 1992; Rouse, 1991). For present purposes, Schiller, Basch, and Blanc-Szanton (1992) provide the most useful definition of transnationalism as the process whereby migrants establish and maintain sociocultural connections across geopolitical borders. The migrants' social relations, cultural values, economic resources, and political activities span at least two nation-states. Such transnational links are often sustained by a constant back-and-forth movement of people facilitated by rapid transportation and communications systems. As a result, migrants have multiple identities that link them simultaneously to more than one nation. Transnationalism interacts with ethnicity, race, class, gender, and other variables, complicating the process of identity formation. Among other consequences, transnational migration often transforms the cultural definition of racial identity.

In this context, the wider significance of the Dominican experience in the United States and Puerto Rico is twofold. On one hand, the reconstruction of racial identity among Dominican immigrants confirms that all systems of racial classification are arbitrary and contingent on varying forms of cultural representation. As a terrain of ideological contestation, the perceived racial identity of individuals and groups does not necessarily coincide with their self-perception (Omi and Winant, 1994). On the other hand, the racialization of Dominicans in the United States and Puerto Rico is part of a larger phenomenon affecting Caribbean communities in the diaspora. The prevailing definition of these migrants as black and colored tends to exclude them as biologically different from and culturally alien to the receiving societies (Basch, Schiller, and Szanton Blanc, 1994). To the extent that Caribbean migrants are racialized, their efforts to become integrated into the host countries face more obstacles than those of other ethnic groups that are not so labeled.

Caribbean versus U.S. Racial Discourses

Much of the academic literature on Caribbean race relations is now several decades old (but see Oostindie, 1996, and Carrión, 1997, for recent collections revisiting the topic). The pioneering essays of the 1950s (Wagley, 1958), 1960s (Harris, 1964; Hoetink, 1967), and 1970s (Lowenthal, 1972; Mintz, 1974) contrasted the social construction of race in the Caribbean, the United States, and other countries of the Americas. The clearest picture emerging from these classic studies is that Caribbean societies tend to be stratified in terms of both class status and color gradations ranging from white to brown to black. Color distinctions in the Caribbean involve a complex inventory of physical traits such as skin pigmentation, hair form, and facial structure (Lowenthal, 1972; see also Smith, 1984). Phenotype and social status rather than biological descent define a person's racial identity, especially in the Spanish-speaking countries.

The Dominican Republic

Historians have shown that the present-day population of the Dominican Republic is the result of the intense mixture of peoples of European, African, and, to a lesser extent, Amerindian origin. By the end of the 18th century, the majority of Dominicans were classified as colored—that is, mulattos and blacks or, in contemporary parlance, *pardos* and *morenos*. Free blacks and mulattos displaced creole whites, African slaves, and Taíno as the leading sector of the colony of Hispaniola (Moya Pons, 1986; Franco, 1989). Today, informed sources agree that approximately 75 percent of the Dominican population consists of mulattos, with about 10 percent black and 15 percent white (compare Encyclopaedia Britannica, 1994; Ferguson, 1992; Black, 1986; Wiarda and Kryzanek, 1982). Like all racial statistics, these estimates reveal more about the official views of race than about the actual extent of racial mixture or the presence of blacks in the country.

Regardless of the exact demographic composition of the Dominican Republic, the dominant discourse on national identity defines it as white, Hispanic, and Catholic. Scholars have traced the origins and development of a racist and xenophobic ideology in the Dominican Republic since the mid-19th century. This ideology has produced an idealized view of the indigenous elements in Dominican culture, a systematic neglect of the contribution of African slaves and their descendants, increasing animosity toward Haitians and other black immigrants (such as the so-called *cocolos* from the eastern Caribbean), and a marked preference for Hispanic customs and traditions (Hoetink, 1994; Sagás, 1993; 1997; Alcántara Almánzar, 1987). As in other Hispanic Caribbean countries, racial prejudice and discrimination have been central features of the conventional wisdom on Dominican identity.

Under Rafael Trujillo's dictatorship (1930–1961), the pro-Hispanic and anti-Haitian discourse became the official ideology of the Dominican state. The Cibao region—with its traditional peasantry, popular music, Hispanic folklore, and "white" physical appearance—became the romantic symbol of an "authentic" Dominican culture (Hoetink, 1994). Thus, the Dominican merengue, particularly in its *Cibao* variant, became a powerful icon of national identity (Duany, 1994). Meanwhile, Dominican politicians and intellectuals associated with the Trujillo regime defined Haiti as the antithesis of the Dominican Republic. If Dominicans were supposed to be white, Haitians were black; if Dominicans were Hispanic, Haitians were African; if Dominicans spoke Spanish, Haitians spoke Créole; and if Dominicans were Catholic, Haitians were voodoo practitioners. This binary opposition represented Haitians as the other—as inferior, foreign, and savage. The category "black" disappeared altogether from the official and popular discourses on race in the Dominican Republic, except in reference to foreigners (Baud, 1996; Charles, 1992; del Castillo, 1984).

Nowadays, even the darkest-skinned Dominican is considered not black but *indio oscuro* (dark Indian) or trigueño. As a result of this cultural conception, most Dominicans are declared to be white (*blanco*), Indian (*indio*), or a mixture of the two races (*mestizo*); only Haitians are considered "pure" blacks. A recent essay by Peter Roberts (1997) has analyzed the importance of the concept of indio for the construction of national identity in the Dominican Republic, as well as in Cuba and Puerto Rico. Stressing the indigenous roots of the Dominican nation helped to distinguish it from the Spanish metropolis as well as from neighboring Haiti. According to Ernesto Sagás (1993), the Dominican government now classifies the majority of Dominican citizens as indios. Thus, the term has become an official racial category in the Dominican Republic. The equivalent term *mulato*, referring to a mixture of white and black, is rarely used.

The academic literature contains numerous studies on the hostile relations between the Dominican Republic and Haiti (see the extensive bibliography in Lozano, 1992). The key historiographic issue has been the impact of the Haitian occupation of Santo Domingo (1822–1844) on the formation of the Dominican nation-state (Moya Pons, 1992; Franco, 1989). Whereas most historians traditionally considered this period a traumatic collective experience, Harry Hoetink (1971) emphasized the positive impact of the Haitian occupation on Dominican race relations and cultural identity. One of the recurring themes of the sociological literature is the massive migration of Haitians to the Dominican Republic and their slavelike working conditions on the sugar and coffee plantations (see Báez Evertsz, 1986; Lozano and Báez Evertsz, 1992). An invidious system of occupational segregation has isolated Haitians in the worst-paid and least desirable jobs, such as cane cutting and construction work. In both instances, directing racial and ethnic prejudice at a foreign enemy—Haitians—helped to define and consolidate a Dominican nationalist project conceived by the dominant elite and filtered down to the popular sectors.

Although many Dominican intellectuals in the post-Trujillo era have rejected the myth of Haitian inferiority, the popular sectors continue to repudiate Haitian immigrants and Haiti in general. Lower-class Dominicans attribute all kinds of social problems and negative situations to the Haitian "invasion," including racial "degeneration." According to a young Dominican cook living in Puerto Rico, "All Dominicans were blonde and blue eyed before they got dark and mixed with the Haitians." The Haitian has acquired a mysterious and legendary status in Dominican folklore as a practitioner of obscure rites such as black magic and cannibalism. It will take time to eradicate firmly held beliefs and practices that exclude Haitians (and, by extension, blacks) from the accepted definition of national identity in the Dominican Republic (see Torres-Saillant, 1992–1993; 1997; Sagás, 1993; 1997). Anti-Haitianism pervades the dominant discourse on Dominican identity, from popular religion, music, and literature to economic affairs, public policies, and party politics. One of the main problems faced by the presidential candidate of the Dominican Revolutionary party, José Francisco Peña Gómez, has been his Haitian origin and black appearance. Although racism was not the only reason for Peña Gómez's defeat in 1996, it played a key role in the electoral campaign.

In sum, the Dominican system of racial classification has two peculiar features in a comparative Caribbean context. First, it does not identify local blacks as a separate category within the color spectrum but instead reserves that category for Haitians. Second, it blurs the distinctions among creole whites, light coloreds, and mulattos, thereby creating the impression of a predominantly white and Indian population. Through these discursive strategies, the system fosters the racial and cultural homogenization of the Dominican Republic vis-à-vis Haiti. Thus, the social construction of race and ethnicity is characterized by a strong reactive or oppositional identity. It is this sense of national pride and rejection of their own negritude that many Dominican migrants bring with them and must reevaluate when they confront the U.S. model of racial stratification.

Puerto Rico

The best empirical study of Puerto Rican race relations remains Eduardo Seda Bonilla's pioneering fieldwork, conducted in the late 1950s and 1960s, although several essays have dealt with the racial question on the island and the U.S. mainland since then (see Sagrera, 1973; Zenón Cruz, 1974; Ginorio, 1979; Picó de Hernández et al., 1985; Díaz Quiñones, 1985; Rodríguez-Morazzani, 1996; V. Rodríguez, 1997). Seda Bonilla (1973) argued convincingly that most Puerto Ricans use phenotype rather than hypodescent as the main criterion for racial identity. Puerto Ricans tend to think of three main physical types—white, black, and mulatto—defined primarily by skin color, facial features, and hair texture (see also C. Rodríguez, 1989). Furthermore, whereas North Americans pay close attention to national origin in defining a person's ethnic identity, Puerto Ricans give a higher priority to birthplace and cultural orientation.

Thus, when Puerto Ricans move to the U.S. mainland, they confront a different construction of their racial identity (Seda Bonilla, 1980). In the United States, Puerto Ricans are often grouped together with black and colored people. Those with mixed racial backgrounds lose their intermediate status in a white-nonwhite dichotomy. Light-skinned immigrants are sometimes called "white Puerto Ricans," whereas dark-skinned immigrants are often treated like African Americans. Most are simply classified as "Pororicans" as if this were a distinct racial category. Like other ethnic minorities, Puerto Ricans in the United States have been thoroughly racialized (see V. Rodríguez, 1997; Rodríguez-Morazzani, 1996).

Statistically, the majority of the Puerto Rican population is white by local standards. Estimates of the white group on the island range from 73 percent

(Seda Bonilla, 1980) to 80 percent of the population (Encyclopaedia Britannica, 1994), with an additional 8 percent black and 19 percent mulatto in Seda Bonilla's count. These statistics are open to debate because of the fluid definition of racial groups as well as the lack of recent official data on the island's racial composition. (In 1970, the Census Bureau dropped the racial identification question for Puerto Rico.) However, the available figures confirm that most Puerto Ricans perceive themselves as white rather than as black or mulatto.

In any case, study after study has shown that blacks are a stigmatized minority on the island, that they suffer from persistent prejudice and discrimination, that they tend to occupy the lower rungs of the class structure, and that they are subject to an ideology of progressive whitening (blanqueamiento) through intermarriage with lighter-skinned groups and a denial of their cultural heritage and physical characteristics (Seda Bonilla, 1973; Zenón Cruz, 1974; Picó de Hernández et al., 1985). Thus, the main difference between the Puerto Rican and North American models of racial stratification is not the treatment of blacks—who are accorded a subordinate status in both societies—but rather the mixed group. In Puerto Rico, light mulattos often pass for whites, whereas in the United States, this intermediate racial category does not even exist officially. The symbolic boundaries among whites, mulattos, and blacks seem more porous in Puerto Rico than in the United States.

New York-based Puerto Rican sociologist Clara Rodríguez reports that many members of the so-called Neo-Rican community resist being classified as either black or white and prefer to identify themselves as "other." In the 1980 Census, 48 percent of New York's Puerto Rican population chose this category, including alternative ethnic labels such as Hispanic, Spanish, and Boricua (C. Rodríguez, 1989; 1992; Rodríguez and Cordero-Guzmán, 1992). Hence, many Puerto Rican migrants and their descendants continue to employ a tripartite rather than a bipolar system of racial classification. Contrary to Seda Bonilla's (1980) prediction that the Neo-Rican community would split along color lines, most migrants reject their indiscriminate labeling as members of a single race (see also Ginorio, 1979). Rather than dividing themselves into white or black, most Puerto Ricans recognize that they are a multiracial or—to use Rodríguez's (1989) apt image—a "rainbow" people.

In sum, the Puerto Rican model of race relations has several distinguishing features. In contrast to North Americans, most Puerto Ricans consider racial identity not primarily a question of biological descent but rather one of physical appearance. As a result, a person of mixed racial background is not automatically assigned to the black group in Puerto Rico. Rather, racial classification depends largely on skin color and other visible characteristics such as the shape of the mouth, nose, and hair. Puerto Ricans have developed an elaborate racist vocabulary for referring to these characteristics. Socio-economic variables such as occupation and education can also affect a person's racial identity. Furthermore, Puerto Ricans usually distinguish between blacks and mulattos, whereas North Americans tend to view both groups as colored or nonwhite. Finally, because of the proliferation of multiple and fluid physical types, Puerto Rico has not established a two-tiered institutionalized system of racial discrimination such as that of the United States. For example, neither the occupational nor the residential structures of Puerto Rican society segregate its members exclusively by color. As we shall see, the island's system of racial classification has distinct implications for the racial identity of Dominican migrants.

The United States

The preceding discussion has already alluded to the key features of the dominant model of racial formation in the United States. Scholars have debated whether this model resembles a caste system, especially as it operated in the Old South prior to the abolition of the Jim Crow laws in the 1950s. In any case, the North American system is unusual (comparable to South Africa's apartheid) in its terminological simplicity and intense separation between subordinate "racial" minorities and dominant ethnic groups. Historically, the black/white division has been rigidly defined in the United States through the rule of hypodescent (Omi and Winant, 1994). North American race relations have been characterized by institutionalized discrimination against so-called racial minorities such as African Americans, Native Americans, Latinos, and Asians, defined partly by their skin color and partly by their geographic origin.

The dominant racial discourse in the United States assigns an upper status to white groups of European origin and a lower status to black and brown groups from other regions, including the Caribbean and Latin America. Racial minorities such as Haitians and Chinese are stereotyped and marginalized more acutely than other ethnic groups in North American society. As a result, the social distance between such groups is much greater than that between, say, the Irish or Italians and English or Germans, who are all defined as "white ethnics." The racialization of Caribbean immigrants has slowed their structural and cultural assimilation into North American society. Recent studies have coined the terms "*segmented assimilation*" and "*oppositional identity*" to refer to the fate of racially defined minorities in the contemporary United States (see Portes, 1994, for a conceptual discussion and empirical data focusing on second-generation immigrants).

Residential segregation is a fundamental aspect of racial and ethnic relations in the United States (Massey and Denton, 1993). Black Americans have been subjected to the highest degree of racial segregation in major urban centers over the past five decades, and so have most Caribbean immigrants, who tend to be considered black or colored (Kasinitz, 1992). Recent studies have shown that Latinos, especially Puerto Ricans and dark-skinned immigrants, suffer from a similar disadvantage in the housing market of metropolitan areas such as New York, Philadelphia, Chicago, and Hartford (Santiago and Wilder, 1991; Santiago, 1992). Some scholars have even predicted that Latinos will become a "middle race" between whites and blacks in the United States (Domínguez, 1973).

Until now, no empirical study has systematically examined the impact of the North American system of racial stratification on the Dominican diaspora. The major publications have neglected the cultural redefinition of the migrants' racial identity in the United States (see Guarnizo, 1994; Grasmuck and Pessar, 1991; Portes and Guarnizo, 1991; Georges, 1990; Georges et al., 1989; del Castillo and Mitchell, 1987). An exception to this trend is Virginia Domínguez's (1973; 1978) comparative assessment of Cubans, Dominicans, and Puerto Ricans in Washington Heights during the 1960s. One reason for this oversight may be that researchers have usually focused on Dominican migrants as lower-class workers rather than as members of a "racial" minority. Most studies have underestimated a key variable in the incorporation of Dominican immigrants into the secondary segment of the U.S. labor and housing markets: their public perception as blacks, colored, or nonwhite. . . .

Conclusion

Transnational migration often calls into question immigrants' conceptions of ethnic, racial, and national identities. In the Dominican Republic, most people perceive themselves as dark-skinned whites or light mulattos; only Haitians are considered black. The Dominican system of racial classification, labeling people along a wide color continuum ranging from black to white, clashes with the racial dualism prevalent in the United States. For most Dominican migrants, who have some degree of racial mixture, the rule of hypodescent means that they are considered black, nonwhite, or colored. Through a profound ideological transformation, the so-called indios suddenly become black, Hispanic, or "other." The data presented here suggest that most of the Dominicans who identify themselves as blacks in New York would probably call themselves indios in their home country. This process of self-redefinition is, in Frank Moya Pons's (1986: 247) graphic expression, a "traumatic racial experience."

Dominicans in Puerto Rico encounter less cognitive dissonance regarding their racial identity than in the United States. Immigrant Dominicans, like native Puerto Ricans, are classified in terms of a complex system that takes into account skin pigmentation, hair texture, facial features, and social class. This cultural conception does not automatically assume that all Dominicans are black or that they can be divided neatly along color lines. Rather, Puerto Ricans traditionally adopt a flexible definition that recognizes multiple and heterogeneous racial groups, especially among intermediate types. Still, the dark skin color and other "African" features of most Dominican immigrants, together with their low occupational status, place them at the bottom of the Puerto Rican stratification system.

The racialization of Dominican immigrants has been a prime obstacle to their successful incorporation into the labor and housing markets of the United States and Puerto Rico. Although many Dominicans oppose their classification as colored, some have become increasingly aware of themselves as an Afro-Caribbean people. Migrants' general response to external labels has been to emphasize racial diversity within their community as well as the cultural bonds of solidarity among Dominicans of different skin colors. The persistence of a Dominican identity in the United States may be interpreted in part as resistance to the prevailing racial order.

The incorporation of Dominican immigrants into Puerto Rican society has been hampered by their class composition as well as their racial identity. Xenophobia and racism have increased with Dominican immigration over the past three decades. The age-old stereotypes of black Puerto Ricans are now extended to Dominican immigrants, who in turn attribute them to Haitians—for example, stupidity, uncleanliness, and ugliness (see Zenón Cruz, 1974, for a complete catalogue of racial infamies in Puerto Rico). The social construction of race and ethnicity in contemporary Puerto Rico increasingly conflates black with Dominican. Still, Puerto Rican society segregates Dominicans not primarily by skin color or national origin but by social class. *Barrio Gandul* is neither a black ghetto like Harlem nor an ethnic neighborhood like Washington Heights.

The theoretical implications of this comparative case study are numerous, but I can only underline three of them here. First, transnational migrants face different, often conflicting, definitions of their racial identity in the sending and receiving societies. This ideological discrepancy confirms the absence of any essential characteristics or fixed meanings in racial discourses and focuses attention on the socially constructed and invented nature of racial classification systems. Second, regardless of their imaginary and arbitrary character, cultural conceptions of racial identity have a practical and material impact when they are applied to concrete groups and individuals in social interaction. The racialization of Caribbean immigrants in the United States and elsewhere places them in a disadvantageous position in the labor and housing markets and excludes them from the hegemonic cultural practices of the receiving nation-states. Finally, the immigrants' lower-class standing reinforces their public perception as ethnic and racial outsiders. This intersection of ethnicity, color, and class makes it harder for Caribbean diaspora communities to shed their multiple stigmas.

At this point, it is difficult to assess the impact of the cultural redefinition of the migrants' racial identity on the Dominican Republic. A decade ago, the distinguished Dominican historian Frank Moya Pons (1986) claimed that massive migration had not eroded the island's sense of identity. More recently, the New York-based Dominican literary critic Silvio Torres-Saillant (1992–1993) went beyond this to propose that Dominican identity is reasserted in the diaspora against a backdrop of ethnic and racial oppression. In my view, increasing numbers of Dominicans in the United States and Puerto Rico are being forced to confront racially exclusive conceptions and practices, framed in the language either of biological descent or of physical appearance.

By and large, the Dominican diaspora has actively resisted its subordination as a racialized other and attempted to redefine the terms of its incorporation into the host societies. Whether this effort results in asserting that Dominicans are part of a middle race such as Latinos or Hispanics (Domínguez, 1973), making common cause with African Americans on the basis of their colored status, or embracing a wider pan-Caribbean identity that includes Haitians has yet to be determined. For the moment, transnational migration has transformed the cultural conceptions of racial identity among Dominicans in the United States and Puerto Rico. For many racially mixed immigrants, coming to America has meant coming to terms with their own, partially suppressed, sometimes painful, but always liberating sense of negritude.

*   *   *

Note

Jorge Duany is an associate professor of anthropology and director of the *Revista de Ciencias Sociales* at the University of Puerto Rico in Río Piedras. He has published widely on Caribbean migration, ethnic identity, and popular culture and has recently coauthored (with José A. Cobas) *Cubans in Puerto Rico: Ethnic Economy and Cultural Identity* (1997) and (with Luisa Hernández Angeira and César E. Rey) *El Barrio Gandul: Economía subterránea y migración indocumentada en Puerto Rico* (Caracas: Nueva Sociedad, 1995). The author thanks Ramona Hernández, Helen Safa, Carlos Severino, Constance Sutton, Emelio Betances, and Jeff Tobin for useful comments on earlier drafts. The Puerto Rican study was conducted with the collaboration of César A. Rey and Luisa Hernández and cosponsored by the U.S. Census Bureau and the University of the Sacred Heart in Santurce, Puerto Rico. The New York study was sponsored by the Dominican Studies Institute of the City University of New York, under the direction of Silvio Torres-Saillant. The author is grateful for his colleagues' intellectual support and for the financial support of these institutions.

∗   ∗   ∗

References

Alcántara Almánzar, José. 1987. "Black Images in Dominican Literature." *New West Indian Guide* 61(3, 4): 161–73.

Báez Evertsz, Franc. 1986. *Braceros haitianos en la República Dominicana*, 2nd ed. Santo Domingo: *Instituto Dominicano de Investigaciones Sociales*.

Basch, Linda, Nina Glick Schiller, and Cristina Szanton Blanc. 1994. *Nations Unbound: Transnational Projects, Postcolonial Predicaments, and Deterritorialized States*. Basel: Gordon and Breach.

Baud, Michiel. 1996. "'Constitutionally White': The Forging of a National Identity in the Dominican Republic," in Gert Oostindie, ed., *Ethnicity in the Caribbean: Essays in Honor of Harry Hoetink*, pp. 121–51. London: Macmillan Caribbean.

Black, Jan Knippers. 1986. *The Dominican Republic: Politics and Development in an Unsovereign State*. Boston: Allen and Unwin.

Carrión, Juan Manuel, ed. 1997. *Ethnicity, Race, and Nationality in the Caribbean*. San Juan: Institute of Caribbean Studies, University of Puerto Rico.

Charles, Carolle. 1992. *"La raza: una categoría significativa en el proceso de inserción de los trabajadores haitianos en República Dominicana,"* in Wilfredo Lozano, ed., *La cuestión haitiana en Santo Domingo: migración internacional, desarrollo y relaciones inter-estatales entre Haití y República Dominicana*, pp. 145–68. Santo Domingo: *Facultad Latinoamericana de Ciencias Sociales*.

del Castillo, José. 1984. *Ensayos de sociología dominicana*. Santo Domingo: Taller.

del Castillo, José, and Christopher Mitchell, eds. 1987. *La inmigración dominicana en los Estados Unidos*. Santo Domingo: CENAPEC.

Diaz Quiñones, Arcadio. 1985. *"Tomás Blanco: Racismo, historia, esclavitud,"* in *El prejuicio racial en Puerto Rico*, pp. 13–91. Río Piedras: Huracán.

Domínguez, Virginia. 1973. "Spanish-Speaking Caribbeans in New York: 'The Middle Race.'" *Revista/Review Interamericana* 3(2): 135–42.

————. 1978 "Show your colors: Ethnic divisiveness among Hispanic Caribbean migrants." *Migration Today* 6(1): 5–9.

Duany, Jorge. 1994. "Ethnicity, Identity, and Music: An Anthropological Analysis of the Dominican Merengue," in Gerard Béhague, ed., *Music and Black Ethnicity: The Caribbean and South America*, pp. 65–98. Miami: North-South Center, University of Miami.

Encyclopaedia Britannica 1994 "1994 Britannica World Data," in *1994 Book of the Year*. Chicago: Encyclopaedia Britannica.

Ferguson, James. 1992. *Dominican Republic: Beyond the Lighthouse*. London: Latin America Bureau.

Franco, Franklin J. 1989. *Los negros, los mulatos y la nación dominicana*, 8th ed. Santo Domingo: *Editora Nacional*.

————. 1990. *The Making of a Transnational Community: Migration, Development, and Cultural Change in the Dominican Republic*. New York: Columbia University Press.

Georges, Eugenia, and others. 1989. *Dominicanos ausentes: Cifras, políticas, condiciones sociales*. Santo Domingo: *Fundación* Friedrich Ebert.

Ginorio, Angela Beatriz. 1979. "A Comparison of Puerto Ricans in New York with Native Puerto Ricans and Native Americans on Two Measures of Acculturation: Gender Role and Racial Identification." Ph.D. diss., Fordham University.

Grasmuck, Sherri, and Patricia R. Pessar. 1991. *Between Two Islands: Dominican International Migration*. Berkeley: University of California Press.

Guarnizo, Luis E. 1994. "Los Dominican Yorks: The Making of a Binational Society." *Annals of the American Academy of Political and Social Science* 533, 70–86.

Harris, Marvin. 1964. *Patterns of Race in the Americas*. New York: Norton.

Hoetink, Harry. 1967. *Caribbean Race Relations: A Study of Two Variants*. London: Oxford University Press.

————. 1971. "The Dominican Republic in the 19th Century: Some Notes on Stratification, Immigration, and Race," in Magnus Mörner, ed., *Race and Class in Latin America*, pp. 96–121. New York: Columbia University Press.

————. 1994. *Santo Domingo y el Caribe: Ensayos sobre cultura y sociedad*. Santo Domingo: *Fundación Cultural Dominicana*.

Kasinitz, Philip. 1992. *Caribbean New York: Black Immigrants and the Politics of Race*. Ithaca, NY: Cornell University Press.

Lowenthal, David. 1972. *West Indian Societies*. New York: Oxford University Press.

Lozano, Wilfredo, ed. 1992. *La cuestión haitiana en Santo Domingo: migración internacional, desarrollo y relaciones inter-estatales entre Haití y Republica Dominicana*. Santo Domingo: *Facultad Latinoamericana de Ciencias Sociales*.

Lozano, Wilfredo, and Franc Báez Evertsz. 1992. *Migración internacional y economia cafetalera: Estudio sobre la migración estacional de trabajadores haitianos a la cosecha cafetalera en la República Dominicana*, 2nd ed. Santo Domingo: *Centro de Planificación y Acción Ecuménica*.

Massey, Douglas S., and Nancy A. Denton. 1993. *American Apartheid: Segregation and the Making of the Underclass*. Cambridge: Harvard University Press.

Mintz, Sidney W. 1974. *Caribbean Transformations*. Chicago: Aldine.

Moya Pons, Frank. 1986 *El pasado dominicano*. Santo Domingo: *Fundación* J. A. Caro Alvarez.

———. 1992. *"Las tres fronteras: Introducción a la frontera domínico-haitiana,"* in *Wilfredo Lozano*, ed., *La cuestión haitiana: Migración internacional, desarrollo y relaciones inter-estatales entre Haití y República Dominicana*, pp. 17–32. Santo Domingo: *Facultad Latinoamericana de Ciencias Sociales*.

Omi, Michael, and Howard Winant. 1994. *Racial Formation in the United States: From the 1960s to the 1990s*, 2nd ed. New York: Routledge.

Oostindie, Gert, ed. 1996. *Ethnicity in the Caribbean: Essays in Honor of Harry Hoetink*. London: Macmillan Caribbean.

Picó de Hernández, and others. 1985. *Discrimen por color, sexo y origen nacional en Puerto Rico*. Río Piedras: *Centro de Investigaciones Sociales, Universidad de Puerto Rico*.

Portes, Alejandro, ed. 1994. *The New Second Generation*. International Migration Review 28(4).

Portes, Alejandro, and Luis E. Guarnizo. 1991. *Capitalistas del trópico: La inmigración en los Estados Unidos y el desarrollo de la pequeña empresa en la República Dominicana*. Santo Domingo: *Facultad Latinoamericana de Ciencias Sociales*.

Roberts, Peter. 1997. "The (Re)Construction of the Concept of 'Indio' in the National Identities of Cuba, the Dominican Republic, and Puerto Rico," in Lowell Fiet and Janette Becerra, eds., *Caribe 2000: Definiciones, identidades y culturas regionales y/o nacionales*, pp. 99–120. Río Piedras: *Facultad de Humanidades, Universidad de* Puerto Rico.

Rodríguez, Clara E. 1989. *Puerto Ricans: Born in the U.S.A.* Boston: Unwin Hyman.

———. 1992 "Race, Culture, and Latino 'Otherness' in the 1980 Census." *Social Science Quarterly* 73(4): 930–37.

Rodríguez, Clara E., and Héctor Cordero-Guzmán. 1992. "Placing Race in Context." *Ethnic and Racial Studies* 15(4): 523–42.

Rodríguez, Víctor M. 1997. "The Racialization of Puerto Rican Ethnicity in the United States," in Juan Manuel Carrión, ed., *Ethnicity, Race, and Nationality in the Caribbean*, pp. 233–73. San Juan: Institute of Caribbean Studies, University of Puerto Rico.

Rodríguez-Morazzani, Roberto P. 1996. "Beyond the Rainbow: Mapping the Discourse on Puerto Ricans and 'Race.'" *Centro* 8(1, 2): 151–69.

Rouse, Roger. 1991. "Mexican Migration and the Social Space of Postmodernism." *Diaspora* 1(1): 8–23.

Safa, Helen I. 1983. "Caribbean Migration to the United States: Cultural Identity and the Process of Assimilation," in Edgar Gumbert, ed., *Different People: Studies in Ethnicity and Education*, pp. 47–73. Atlanta: Center for Cross-Cultural Education, Georgia State University.

Sagás, Ernesto. 1993. "A Case of Mistaken Identity: *Antihaitianismo* in the Dominican Republic." *Latinamericanist* 29(1): 1–5.

———. 1997. "The Development of *Antihaitianismo* into a Dominant Ideology during the Trujillo era," in Juan Manuel Carrión (ed.), *Ethnicity, Race, and Nationality in the Caribbean*, pp. 96–121. San Juan: Institute of Caribbean Studies, University of Puerto Rico.

Sagrera, Martín. 1973. *Racismo y política en Puerto Rico: La desintegración interna y externa de un pueblo*. Río Piedras: Edil.

Santiago, Anne M. 1992. "Patterns of Puerto Rican Segregation and Mobility." *Hispanic Journal of Behavioral Sciences* 14(1): 107–33.

Santiago, Anne, and Margaret G. Wilder. 1991. "Residential Segregation and Links to Minority Poverty: The Case of Latinos in the United States." *Social Problems* 38(4): 492–515.

Schiller, Nina Glick, Linda Basch, and Cristina Blanc-Szanton, eds. 1992. *Towards a Transnational Perspective on Migration: Race, Ethnicity, and Nationalism Reconsidered*. New York: New York Academy of Sciences.

Seda Bonilla, Eduardo. 1973. *Los derechos civiles en la cultura puertorriqueña*, 2nd ed. Río Piedras: Bayoán.

———. 1980 *Réquiem para una cultura*, 4th ed. Río Piedras: Bayoán.

Smith, M. G. 1984. *Culture, Race, and Class in the Commonwealth Caribbean*. Mona, Jamaica: Department of Extra-Mural Studies, University of the West Indies.

Torres-Saillant, Silvio. 1992–1993. "*Cuestión haitiana y supervivencia moral dominicana.*" *Punto y Coma* 4(2): 195–206.

———. 1997. "*Hacia una identidad racial alternativa en la sociedad dominicana.*" Op. Cit.: *Revista del Centro de Investigaciones Históricas* (University of Puerto Rico, Río Piedras) 9: 235–252.

Wagley, Charles. 1958. *Minorities in the New World*. New York: Columbia University Press.

Wiarda, Howard H., and Michael Kryzanek. 1982. *The Dominican Republic: A Caribbean Crucible*. Boulder: Westview.

Winant, Howard. 1994. *Racial Conditions: Politics, Theory, Comparisons*. Minneapolis: University of Minnesota Press.

Zenón Cruz, Isabelo. 1974. *Narciso descubre su trasero: El negro en la cultura puertorriqueña*. 2 vols. Humacao: Furidi.

* * *

Questions

1. How is it possible to adopt an identity of white, indio or mestizo if in fact you are a mulatto, of African descent? What are the processes involved in the creation of such a fictional identity?
2. If, as it is claimed, U.S. white identity is dependent on U.S. black identity, to what extent is Dominican "nonblack" identity dependent on

Haitian black identity? What are the implications of this comparison for the definition of race?

3. Which human bodies can be said to benefit from the different racial classifications in Puerto Rico and the United States? How do these benefits shift as these bodies cross national or territorial (U.S./Puerto Rican) borders? How does class affect these "benefits" in different nations or territories?

4. In terms of the impact on the socioeconomic status of human bodies, what difference does it make to consider racial identity a question of biological descent as opposed to physical appearance?

5. Although admittedly a matter of speculation, given the factors for the construction of ethnic and racial identities discussed in this and other chapters in this book, do you believe that Dominicans will (a) become a part of a Latino/Hispanic "middle race" in the United States; (b) join the African American identity; or (c) embrace a pan-Caribbean identity? Why?

~

CHAPTER TWENTY-THREE

native of nowhere
Chloé S. Georas

stranded between vanishing islands
floating on an endless sea of receding coasts
my body is my only land
my hands navigate my skin
mapping the currents with my fingers
abysses fields mountains deserts oceans
so many oceans
echoes and cemeteries

transnational orphan
with feet full of memories
of running barefoot along volcanic cliffs
lightning between my breasts
of sitting on hot asphalt in the rain
watching the steam and the fog exchanging masks
of hurting somewhere
deep outside
everywhere

my feet
the corridors to places i lived places i died places i never went places
    i can't remember
populated by voices of missing people
some dead some i killed some gone some i left behind some i never met
nor did i touch

nor did i caress
people i never traveled
native of nowhere
a ticket to the wind on my back
i swallow hurricanes
my skeleton floats wildly in my body of floods
earthquakes vibrate through my limbs
reconfiguring my desires

my body
a disaster zone of erotic wastes
a white wooden house lies wrecked
my father pulls the curtains

my body is my only land
a land without homes nor hosts
a land of humidity, edges and edges
a land of volcanoes submerged in quicksand
a land of roaming scars

my land
a body from which i remove the earth with each step
i travel that territory called myself
before i become extinct

once again

PART V

HISTORY OF THE PRESENT

~

Comparative Thumbnail Sketch of the Status of Mexicans, Cubans, and Puerto Ricans in the United States
Francisco Hernández Vázquez

The texts in this part are intended to provide a current, transnational larger context for the three separate Latino/a groups and at the same time to focus on specific intractable issues that stubbornly continue to confront not only these groups but also society in general. Already addressed by Apodaca and Moraga in chapters 3 and 11, respectively, one of these issues is gender. In this section, chapter 24 by Córdova serves as a forum for a wider variety of Latina voices to define and present the feminist position on the quest for democracy. Latinos/as in the United States fulfill Simon Bolívar's dream of all Latin Americans under one nation. What he did not foresee is that *that* nation would be the United States.

In other words, as de los Angeles Torres points out in chapter 25 Latinos/as come into the United States from a variety of countries and this reality points to the need to come up with new legal arrangements, that is, new forms of citizenship to accommodate them. This is already being addressed in Canada and in the European Union. Robinson's focus in chapter 26 is precisely on the latest development of global capitalism as the main reason why masses of people are increasingly migrating to other countries, the negative effects of this new phenomenon on human rights, and the mass demonstrations against this new form of dehumanization. Gomez-Peña paints a startling picture of this dehumanized "postdemocratic" world in chapter 27 and illustrates the difficulty in even finding the language to raise the obvious, vital, critical questions that need to be raised about the well-being of the most vulnerable members of our society. The final piece by Vázquez attempts to

define the role of Latinos/as within the larger human quest for economic democracy and its implications for a sustainable society on the American continent. The definition includes a discussion of the archetypal struggle between the people and the state and the difficult issues involved in the pursuit
of justice for all.

To weave the three separate histories into a discussion of the present, it is
useful to briefly summarize and compare the Puerto Ricans, Cubans, and U.S.
Mexicans based on the texts thus far. But first a warning about such a comparative thumbnail sketch: The advantage is that it puts lots of information
in a capsule so the comparison can be made at a glance; the disadvantage is
that summaries are based on generalizations that may appear as stereotypes,
and thus have negative unintended consequences. With that caveat in mind,
we begin with the three separate stories and then compare them according
to seven categories.

The United States established a special relationship with Puerto Rico, a
Commonwealth that, according to Public Law 600, is free to govern itself but
must check with the U.S. Congress before making any final decisions. Puerto
Rican nationalists engage in violent actions to protest this judicial sleight of
hand. Class, gender, and pigmentocracy issues, however, lead to the emergence of two majoritarian social movements, one for U.S. statehood and another for keeping the Commonwealth status, whereas support for independence decreases to 2.7 percent of the electorate.

Historically, Cuba and the United States have a stormy but intimate relationship. The relationship became strained as a result of the weakening
of its economic and political colonial structure; it descended into name-
calling and finally collapsed after sixty years. In the process of getting a divorce and protecting their security interests, these two nation-states gave
birth to the Cuban Americans. This group continues a paradoxical Cuban
discourse of desire for assimilation into U.S. culture and *cubanidad,* a cultural nationalism that at times reaches extremes of chauvinism and terrorism. At the same time, there is some effort at healing the rupture within
the Cuban people, which is presently divided between two rival nation-
states. After health reasons forced Fidel Castro to cede power to his brother
Raul, everyone is holding their breath to see what is going to happen. Will
Cuba be taken over by Cuban Americans and be incorporated into the
United States? Will Cubans fight to keep their socialist society? Castro,
however, remains a player in Cuban politics, as a continuing member of the
Council of State (the island's governing body). As of January 2008, 8.4 million voters cast their ballots for a slate of parliamentary candidates that in-
cludes Castro.

Mexicans in the United States started the twentieth century with a small population. They battled their assigned status and portrayal as strangers and aliens in their own land, and as being genetically or culturally inferior and therefore incapable of progress and inclusion in U.S. society. (This battle continues in the new millennium with publications such as the "Hispanic Challenge" by Samuel Huntington.) Depending on the political and economic forces in Mexico and the United States at a given time, Mexican bodies are subjected to cycles of importation and deportation. U.S. Mexicans have, nevertheless, created their own social, labor,, national, and international organizations to build strong, active communities. As is true of people from other ethnic and cultural backgrounds, Puerto Ricans, U.S. Cubans, and U.S. Mexicans also struggle within their own communities—against internal forms of domination based on gender, class, and skin pigmentation.

These three different groups and their distinct stories can be compared according to the following categories: (1) The exercise of U.S. colonial power, (2) institutional support and relations, (3) inclusive/exclusive citizenship practices, (4) integration into (the electoral and other) politics, (5) (de)construction of status and identities, (6) role of the U.S./global economy, and (7) cultural nationalism.

The Exercise of U.S. Colonial Power

From a historical perspective, for Cubans, U.S. colonial power was exercised hegemonically, that is, indirectly through the control of the economy and the attempt to control the political system. In Puerto Rico, it was done through Congress and the judiciary. Although, to be sure, military power was also present. This power was exerted on these peoples while they remained on their own islands, away from the mainland. For Mexicans, the exercise of colonial power was more violent and coercive because of the struggle for the land and, to some extent, to the categorization of Mexicans as Indians (so that the practice of extermination was also applied to them). Colonial power was exercised through the state legislatures and courts, vigilantism, and manipulation of the law.

Institutional Support and Relations

Education in Cuba remains in Cuban hands. Education is imposed on U.S. Mexicans and Puerto Ricans based on the theories and practices that, at the very least, implicitly assume the inferiority of these peoples. The Anglo Catholic Church is not particularly helpful to U.S. Mexicans or the majority of Puerto Ricans. Cubans were political refugees at a critical point in a nuclear confrontation, so they received political and economic support even greater than what is provided for U.S. citizens. U.S. Mexicans had to rely on the Mexican consulate offices and mutual aid societies to survive. Puerto Ricans are U.S. citizens and negotiate for the acquisition of benefits that are given to other U.S. citizens.

Inclusive/Exclusive Citizenship Practices

Puerto Ricans are U.S. citizens, more or less. Cubans are accepted into the United States with no questions asked and given citizenship as soon as possible. Mexicans are in constant danger of being deported, whether they are U.S. citizens or not.

Integration into (the Electoral and Other) Politics

U.S. Cubans continue their tradition of political involvement, especially because they come primarily from the upper and middle classes. In the past some have engaged in terrorism against Castro and their own community in the United States. Puerto Ricans participate in politics within the limits imposed by the U.S. Congress and the courts. Those engaged in *independentista* "terrorist" activities are, of course, subjected to persecution by the state. U.S. Mexicans have been kept out of the electoral process through a variety of mechanisms, including laws to deport militant workers, literacy standards, and head taxes. At the start of the twenty-first century, however, thirty-two million Latinos/as in the United States represented 7 percent of the one million votes cast in the November 7, 2000, elections. Approximately two-thirds of these voters were of Mexican descent.

(De)Construction of Status and Identities

Cubans arrived in waves and to a particular place, south Florida, mostly from the white upper and middle classes, and created an economic, political, and cultural enclave that has supported additional arrivals (also mostly *en masse*), even if they are from working, dark-skinned classes. Cubans are portrayed as the "golden immigrants." In addition to the Mexicans who were already in what is now the United States at the time of the conquest, others arrived in waves (although these waves were more diffuse in terms of time, geography, and class, compared with Cuban exiles). However, most Mexican migration came from peasant stock and this fed the image of "the Mexican" in the United States that still survives today. Puerto Ricans also arrived in waves and, like Cubans who go to Miami, they go to particular places—New York and New Jersey—and they represent working-class and peasant segments of the population. Cubans have Ricky Ricardo, Puerto Ricans have Maria from *West Side Story*, Mexicans have "Hey Pancho," "Hey Cisco," or "Speedy Gonzalez." These are the symbols that most U.S. Americans, across generations, associate with these ethnic groups.

Role of the U.S./Global Economy

The United States economy has become increasingly integrated with the economies of Puerto Rico (especially through Operation Bootstrap), Cuba (until 1960), and Mexico (through the North American Free Trade Agreement [NAFTA]). Unlike Puerto Ricans and Cuban Americans, who were constructed by issues of national security, the Mexican immigrant population was constructed by the interplay between the U.S. and Mexican political economies. For all three groups, this means subsequent dislocation and movement of human bodies to the United States and back (when they can or when they must). The proliferation of identities and forms of struggles must be understood against the corresponding proliferation of forms of subjectification and oppression created by the increasing globalization of the economy. Such is the postmodern condition.

Cultural Nationalism

All three peoples have kept a core of customs and traditions, their culture, despite, or because of, the forces of assimilation, or rather "normalization." This is the one constant that underlies the quest for an economic democracy. When the going gets rough, it is within the *ethnos*, the people, the extended family, the *paisano/as*, where we find inclusiveness, respect, and justice. This is also the shield, the flag that comes up whenever the well-being of the people is threatened. Thus, vulnerable populations wear their identity as a badge of honor, from the gang members who tattoo it in their bodies, to the Mexicans who wave the Mexican flag, to the millions of U.S. Americans who brought out their flags after the attack on September 11, 2001. The ultimate resort is personal justice, taking justice into one's own hands, the willingness to die and to shed blood, as illustrated by the increasing number of suicide bombers in the current war on terrorism.

~

CHAPTER TWENTY-FOUR

Fields of Knowledge for Democracy, Justice, and Community: A Latina Quest

Teresa Córdova

This chapter consists of a special contribution to this second edition. Written from a personal perspective, it chronicles, illustrates, and models a feminist quest for the status of truth and justice. Rather than a comparative study, Córdova's *testimonio* provides an inside story of the struggle expressed by various groups of Latinas. More than a representation of Latina thought, it is a presentation of a treasure of sources that point to a rich field of knowledge and the need for further research. Here Córdova traces the emergence of power/knowledge fields among groups of Latinos/as and notes the shift away from community-based research and the need to expand research that addresses issues facing Latino/a communities. Thus, Córdova, lifts the veil of invisibility regarding the contributions of Latinas to the quest for an economic democracy, and focuses Latino/a thought on the well-being of our communities.

*　　*　　*

I remember the first time that I met Francisco H. Vázquez. It was 1982, in Tempe Arizona, at the annual conference of the National Association for Chicano Studies (NACS). He was on a panel presenting his ideas on Power, Chicano Studies, and Public Policy. I attended the panel because, at the time, I was deeply engrossed in the study of ideology and the importance of "counterhegemonic" (Gramsci) efforts in the battle of what constitutes legitimate knowledge. As I left the room, I passed a note to Francisco letting him know about the panel that we were organizing to discuss Chicana issues within NACS.

Being the organizer that I was (and am), my invitation to Francisco was also an invitation to attend a party that we held as a way to build interest in what would become a historic panel that set into motion the formation of the Chicana Caucus within NACS and the transformation of the organization. The conversations at that party were hard work. I remember well how so many of the guys resisted the notion that there were even issues to be discussed. Did we not know that we were being divisive, that we were being duped by white women and their middle class interests, and that we were distracting Chicanos from the real issues at hand?

These were the questions that we addressed in our panel. As Mujeres en Marcha, a group of Chicana social science graduate students and faculty at Berkeley, we organized our panel to challenge the presumptions and conditions that Chicanas faced within NACS. Though we were placed at the end of the day on the last day of the conference, we packed the room. The panel served as a declaration of sorts: As Chicanas, we could not and would not accept a relegated position within the organization; our issues were distinct, though at times coalesced, from the white feminist movement; and Chicano studies and our communities would benefit by improving the position of our women.

In my concluding statement of the panel, I noted, "there is a systematic body of knowledge that oppresses Chicanas. We need to identify both a Chicanology and a Chicanalogy. [Today we have begun] to enumerate together the assumptions, the actions, and the consequences of dominance by men over women." We emphasized that it is a process, and we made the commitment to continue the conversation regarding sexism and how to elevate Chicanas within the networks of Chicano Studies. "What is in it for the women, is in it for the men—cooperation, humanization, friendship, and liberation."[1]

Throughout the conference, Francisco and I engaged in remarkable exchanges about the power of discourse and the potential significance of our work as Chicano Ph.D.s. Unmistakably we shared a passion for the importance of discourse as an explanatory variable and the importance of a political effort that challenged dominant discourse. We were both reading Michel Foucault and understood the use of historically structured meaning to both perpetuate and challenge relations of power. Francisco's concept of *Chicanology* was his term for the invisible narrative that limited the power of Chicanos. We agreed on the need for a consciously counterhegemonic articulation and actualization of our political and intellectual efforts. Chicano studies was, we agreed, a key strategy to create this counterhegemonic body of knowledge that had the potential of altering power relations. Later, I wrote an article "Power and Knowledge: Colonialism and the Academy," which was influenced by the many conversations that Francisco and I had over the years.[2] That conference marked the beginning of a twenty-six year friendship with Francisco and his family.

It is thus with great pleasure that I contribute this chapter to Francisco's book on Latino/a political thought. Intellectual trends ebb and flow but it is important that Francisco has maintained the pursuit of his concept of Chicanology and the need to challenge this powerful force.[3] Narratives that ignore or dismiss Chicano or Latino experiences are designed to reinforce power relations that undermine the strengths of our communities. A book on Latino social political thought counters those master narratives. To include Latina feminist thought is critical, not only because it gives voice to the perspectives of women in our communities, but also because of its challenges to colonialism and patriarchy, both of which are fundamentally anti-humanitarian and anti-democratic.[4]

The voices of Latina feminists or *feministas*, can be viewed as counter-hegemonic by virtue alone of our insistence to define and interpret our own experiences, establish truths and thus challenge those discourses that define our identities as illegitimate, inferior or infuriating. Yet it is in the critiques of anti-democratic and unjust conditions, and in the narratives that support and justify those conditions, that we find the greatest value of Latina voices. These critiques become the basis for further action to change the power relations involving decision making and the distribution of resources.

Before, and since that NACS conference in 1982, I ask the question of how our presence in academia makes a difference. It has always been my opinion, that if we are here because of a social movement, then we have a responsibility to serve the communities that put us here. The Preamble of NACS is a call to that social obligation. That call has become a quest for the betterment of our communities. It is our communities, I believe that we as Latino academics serve. In a world confounded by disenfranchisement and injustice, the quest for community is also a quest for democracy and justice. In this chapter, I describe how the pursuit of Latina feminist thought can be described as a quest for that democracy, justice, and the betterment of our communities. Though my voice is one of a Chicana feminist, this chapter describes the many convergences with Puerto Rican, Cuban, and other Latina women in the United States.

Establishing Fields of Knowledge

Francisco Hernández Vázquez quotes an excerpt from Foucault's *Discipline and Punishment* in which he says, there "is no power relations without the correlative constitution of a field of knowledge, nor any knowledge that does not presuppose and constitute at the same time power relations" (see chapter 4). In the formation of Chicano and Puerto Rican studies, graduate students and faculty members consciously and intentionally sought to create a "field of knowledge." The Preambles of the NACS and *El Centro de Estudios Puertorriqueños* demonstrate the consciously articulated strategy to establish fields of knowledge that represented our experiences and to tie that production of knowledge to the needs of our communities.[5]

The final paragraph of the NACCS Preamble clearly articulates the connection between ideas, inequality and policy.

> Accordingly, the association also recognizes and emphasizes the broader scope and significance of Chicano research. We must not overlook the crucial political role of ideas in the construction and legitimization of social reality. Dominant theories, ideologies, and perspectives play a significant part in maintaining structures of inequality. It is imperative that Chicano scholars struggle against these structures on a theoretical as well as on a policy level. Thus it is urgent that we construct theories and perspectives, which explain the basic dynamics of the Chicano past, present, and future. Since ideas can point to possible directions for our people, they are of fundamental importance in defining and shaping our future.

Puerto Rican scholars reflect a similar philosophy that shaped the formation of the Centro de Estudios Puertorriqueños at Hunter College in New York City. Their statements reflect awareness of the history of colonialism in Puerto Rico, the conditions that gave rise to migration to the United States, an awareness of racism, and an awareness of the university as an arena of struggle. They state,

> Departments of Puerto Rican Studies are not simply places of learning but new and valuable institutions for our community. We believe a proposal such as the present one must convey as lucidly and emphatically as it can the urgency of our need, the sacrifices that have been made to underwrite our emerging presence in the university and the seriousness of our purpose. To create new knowledge and quickly and comprehensibly transfer it to a long denied community is the principal goal of all our efforts undertaken within the university.</ext>

Creating knowledge was a mission for Chicano, Puerto Rican and other Latino scholars. The very creation of these fields of study themselves originate with social movements such as the Chicano movement and Puerto Rican rights movements, including perspectives supporting Puerto Rican independence. Chicana and Puerto Rican women were part of those movements, so when they spoke up for their rights and the legitimacy of their voices, they interfaced those struggles with a fight for community. The "roots and resistance"[6] of Chicana feminism were based in an understanding of "triple oppression,"[7] that is, the "intersections of class, race and gender."[8] Puerto Rican women were especially keen in their understanding and concern for issues of colonialism, labor force status, forced sterilization and the politics and difficulties of migrating from the island to the mainland. Other Latinas who became self-identified feministas tended also to have their political roots in the various social movements of their time.

Because of this connection to social movements, early Latina feminists were focused on the issues facing their communities. For many Puerto Rican feminists, an understanding of issues of Puerto Rican women in the United States was tied to an understanding of the political economy of the island. A history of the island reveals the colonial legacy and its social, cultural, and economic impacts. It is precisely because of the ways that colonialism changed the economy of the island that led to U.S. and Puerto Rican government policies regarding population control of the "surplus labor" that was created because shifts in the economy made opportunities for employment scarce. The two major government strategies for population control were to encourage migration from the island to the mainland and the mass sterilization of Puerto Rican women. Puerto Rican scholars and activists were engaged in both issues.

Puerto Rican activists, understandably, were outraged by the countless stories of forced sterilization both on the island and in the United States. In fact, the practice was also used on Mexican women in Los Angeles, a topic that Chicanas also wrote about in the early 1970s. The issue of reproductive policies was especially noteworthy because investigation revealed that Puerto Rican women were also being used as guinea pigs for research on birth control pills and devices so as to make them available to middle class women in the United States. This exemplifies the ways that interests of poor women of color do not converge with those of middle class white women and why articulations of a feminist agenda as it relates to reproductive health would be different for the Puerto Rican woman than for the white middle class woman in the United States.

In New York City, organizations and coalitions were formed to deal with reproductive rights and issues of sterilization. The National Latina Health Organization, for example, worked on issues of forced sterilization. Several annotated bibliographies are available with a wealth of listings on this topic. Florita Z. Louis de Malave[9] provides a partially annotated listing of research that covers several disciplines and addresses sterilization within the context of class structure, population control policies over time, political economy, psychological impacts, and "the ideology of health care systems." According to material in her bibliography, Malave reports that between the 1930s and the 1970s, approximately one-third of Puerto Rican women of childbearing age had been sterilized by *la operación,* as the surgery is commonly called. *Operation Bootstrap,* an experimental economic policy of corporate tax breaks and incentives, exacerbated poverty and unemployment on the island and led to a concerted government campaign to encourage migration to the United States to work as sources of cheap labor, primarily in service industries, but also in some manufacturing jobs. We can see from the writing of Puerto Rican women that they were concerned with the many difficulties that arose in the transition of moving from the island of Puerto Rico to places like New York City. Much of the early writing of Puerto Ricans addressed the social, psychological, and economic issues that families faced. In 1983, noted Puerto Rican historian, Virginia Sanchez Korrol, wrote about Puerto Ricans in transition. She wrote *From Colonia to Community: The History of Puerto Ricans in New York City, 1917–1948;* Korrol also wrote articles on the "Work Experiences of Early Puerto Rican Migrant Women" and what it was like "Between Two Worlds" (for the) educated Puerto Rican migrant. Clara Rodriguez, another important Puerto Rican scholar, wrote about assimilation in the Puerto Rican communities of the United States. Rodriguez also edited with Virginia Sanchez Korrol and José Alers, an important collection of essays on the struggles of survival of Puerto Ricans in the United States.[10] In 1982, Ruth Zambrana compiled a volume of essays in *Work, Family, and Health: Latina Women in Transition.*

Many manuscripts and research papers were produced at the Hispanic Research Center at Fordham University. Lloyd Rogler helped train many Puerto Rican researchers in the area of psychology and mental health. Much of this research was tied directly to the experience of migration including the transition and adaptation of families. Rogler and Rosemary S. Cooney wrote a book they called, *Puerto Rican Families in New York.* I have a fondness for the work of Rogler that goes back to 1974 when he gave me a tour of Division Street in Chicago and introduced me to the city's vibrant Puerto Rican neighborhood. By the time I moved to that same neighborhood twelve years later, it had suffered decline and economic disinvestment. Today the neighborhood is gentrified and hardly resembles the place where Puerto Ricans obtained their *café bustelo* and *arroz con bacalou.*

It was precisely the lives of neighborhoods and families that interested many of the Puerto Rican researchers and literary writers. What was the status of health care, child care, and employment opportunities? What were the conditions facing the working mother? And how did changing economic conditions affect the living conditions in that neighborhood? How then did those conditions impact the individuals and families? Social psychological research today is returning to issues of race and class related traumas and their impacts of mental and behavioral health.

Thus, it is important to note that early writings and activism by Puerto Rican women in the United States were directly connected to the issues facing their communities.[11] In 1972, women formed the National Conference of Puerto Rican Women.[12] This advocacy group still promotes solutions to address issues faced in Puerto Rican communities. They use research to address some of those issues. El Centro Puertorriqueños at Hunter College under the direction of Frank Bonilla was also a hotbed of research addressing issues of the Puerto Rican community. Unfortunately, with even more shifts in the economy as a result of dynamics of economic restructuring and globalization, the issues that families face in their communities have worsened rather than improved.

The difference in experiences of Latinas in the U.S. and their communities was directly related to when (and if) they immigrated and under what conditions. For example, in an article that I wrote with Juan Betancur and Maria de los Angeles Torres[13] we traced the connection between the politics of the immigration of Latino workers, their role in the labor force, and their levels of educational attainment and income levels. Cubans, for example, who immigrated to the United States in the late 1950s and early 1960s, came under different circumstances than the Puerto Ricans who left at approximately the same time. For Cubans, they were fleeing the Cuban Revolution, and with financial assistance from the U.S. government, relocated in several parts of the United States, particularly in southern Florida. Politics of Cuban American women, therefore, was closely tied to their views with respect to the revolution and their particular economic interests. Nonetheless, there were a number of Cuban feministas who joined the wave of Latina feminism. Early writing address the experience and impact of immigration and the heartaches related to leaving the homeland. There is, of course, an extensive network of feminists in Cuba who are deeply engaged in the politics of the island.

The early Chicana identity was distinctly working class, with the name itself reflecting the class roots. Similar to Puerto Ricans, Chicana activists of the 1970s, expressed concerns about a number of social issues facing women in their communities. The working class perspective of many Chicana feminists, for example, led them to an analysis of Chicana employment issues and labor struggles. Yolanda Nava wrote, in *Regeneración and Encuentro Femenil* on "The Chicana and Employment: Needs Analysis and Recommendations for Legislation" and "Employment Counseling and the Chicana." Anna Nieto-Gómez also wrote "Chicanas in the Labor Force" and "the Needs of the Spanish Speaking *Mujer* (woman) in Woman-Manpower Training Programs.". Laura Arroyo wrote one of the few articles by a Chicana appearing in *Aztlán*, "Industrial and Occupation Distribution of Chicana Workers." A 1971 volume of *Regeneración* contained a testimonial by Maria Moreno, an agricultural worker. She titled her statement, "I'm Talking for Justice."

As Chicanas in the late 1970s continued to write about feminism and the importance of "breaking out of silence"[14] Martha Cotera published her booklet, *The Chicana Feminist*. By the 1980s, there was more of a critical mass of Chicanas and Latinas in universities. Shortly after the 1982 NACS conference and the panel on "Unsettled Issues: Chicanas in the 80s," women within NACS formed the Chicana Caucus during the annual conference at Ypsilanti and then demanded that the next conference of NACS (to be held in Austin) would be dedicated to *Voces de la Mujer*. The book, *Chicana Voices: Intersections of Class, Race, and Gender*, marked this historical moment, with essays on feminism, higher education, literary criticism, and historical figures and movements. The volume is an important reminder of the emergence of the Chicana scholar to take her rightful place within academia. As a result of insistence by Chicana activists within the organization, the name is now The National Association for *Chicana and Chicano Studies*.

In summer 1982, Chicana academics, spurred by the leadership of Ada Sosa Riddel, formed the *Mujeres Activas en Letras y Cambio Social* (MALCS). In meetings that took place in Berkeley and Davis, California, the women of MALCS formed its Preamble. The MALCS Preamble originates from theory about origins and the commitment that comes from making ties to roots. "Our values, our strength, derive from where we came." This Preamble explicitly states a class identity and embraces a history of struggle as working class daughters.

As Chicanas in universities, we recognized the value of research, "We document, analyze, and interpret the Chicano/Mexicano experience in the United States." We do so, however, because "we are particularly concerned with the conditions women face at work, in and out of the home." Once again, our research is tied to the potential of its usefulness and recognizes the urgency of issues that women in our communities face. "We continue our mothers' struggle for social and economic justice." Expressing a collective identity, MALCS founders proclaimed, "The scarcity of Chicanas in institutions of higher education requires that we join together to identify our common problems, to support each other and to define collective solutions." Similar to the NACS Preamble, Chicana scholars said, "We reject the separation of academic scholarship from our communities." Research and action are again seen as inseparable. One can sense in the MALCS Preamble, the passion and commitment to the finding the potential relevance in connecting our lives in the universities with the roots of our communities. Being daughters of our mothers was the cord that connected us. Transforming this tie into political action was the dream that the pioneering Chicanas pronounced.

An important struggle of civil rights movements was access to education. Demands for this access often included sit-ins, demonstrations, and political pressure. With the rise of Latinas in higher education, we began to see a proliferation of writings in the 1980s, through the 1990s and to the present. This is also the point when we begin to see a divergence from those scholars whose work was community-based research and those doing academic-disciplined based research. Some writers captured the activism of both historical and contemporary efforts. These studies clearly demonstrate that Latinas are not passive but continue their historical actions as agents of change.

Carol Hardy-Fanta wrote about grassroots politics in Boston. Her book is an interesting depiction and comparison of Latino men and women engaged in local politics. Through interviews and participant observation of Puerto Rican, Dominican, and Central American women, she notes differences between men and women on what they view as important features of political engagement. "Making connections" seemed to be an important part of politics for Latinas. They used these connections to advance their political efforts.[15] This is similar to the work of Mary Pardo on the Mothers of East L.A. in which she describes their fight against an incinerator and a prison in their neighborhood. Pardo points out that in their organizing, the *mexicanas* turned their preexisting gender based networks into political benefits; bringing forward previously "invisible" women into leadership positions; transforming the identity of "mother" into a force for political opposition; developing their own cultural and political identities; and developing a sense of entitlement on behalf of their communities.[16]

Chicanas have documented resistance efforts of Chicana activists, especially labor organizers.[17] The historian Vicki Ruiz wrote about the labor activism of cannery workers in California. After describing the work and union activism of these workers, she concludes that their efforts reveal a "struggle of proud, courageous men and women joining together whenever possible to counter economic and ethnic oppression."[18]

The examples of unrecorded labor activism, however, are countless, leaving room in the Chicana studies literature for more accounts of historical and contemporary efforts.

Lourdes Santiago, with the help of Felix Padilla, gave a penetrating account of her life as the wife of a gang member serving a seventy-year prison term for killing a rival gang member. In *Outside the Wall: A Puerto Rican Woman's Struggle*, Santiago and Padilla also describe her fight for prison reform.[19]

Cynthia Orozco writes on the participation of women within the League of United Latin American Citizens (LULAC).[20] Chicanas have written about involvement of Chicanas/Mexicanas in social movements showing that they are critical actors in fights for social justice. They have, nonetheless, also fought within their organizations on issues of how the men treat the women.[21] There are even fewer written documentations of Chicana activism that is community or neighborhood based. There are, however, numerous accounts of strength and survival.[22]

In my article on Chicana grassroots organizers in the environmental justice movement, I characterize the work of the Southwest Organizing Project.[23] Chicanas in the organization display a sophisticated knowledge base including an understanding of socioeconomic conditions and their causes; function with a high level of "oppositional consciousness" and a sense of the "collective good"; engage in principled strategies designed to directly confront the logic of their opposition; work in coalition with other groups but still maintain a specific cultural and regional identity; and as gender conscious Chicanas, use organizations that are not gender based to impact issues facing their communities, suggesting the inseparability of gender from issues of family and community. The principles of the movement include addressing issues affecting women and provide an arena where feminist issues can be raised (e.g. process, leadership development, and child and youth development).

> grassroots activists are inserting themselves into questions of international economic integration, local economic development, neighborhood change including issues of gentrification, infrastructure, tax abatements, natural resource management, zoning, and an array of other development issues. The potential of these activities and this social movement are enormous, as grassroots organizations define questions of social change as their realm in their struggle for environmental and economic justice.[24]

The work of grassroots organizers alerts us to the many issues facing Chicanas today. Corporate welfare is replacing social welfare. The gap is increasing between the rich and the poor with Latinos continuing to comprise the largest segment of the working poor. Labor force segmentation enhances the concentration of Chicanas/Mexicans in low wage employment often under toxic working conditions. Rates of certain diseases increase while access to adequate health care, housing, and education erode. Communities are experiencing impacts of displacement, contamination, and depletion of natural resources. Chicana activists express their views on these issues through newsletters, magazines, correspondence, and newspaper editorials.[25] The fundamental challenge posed by these activists is the challenge against antidemocratic and patriarchal power expressed through corporate power.

The increasing internationalization of the economy has also created even more pressing issues for Latinas and their families. Issues of work, transnational migration, and cultural citizenship are issues that are intensifying in Latino communities. Lourdes Argüelles, a Cuban American feminist, has continued her work over the years and has conducted research on human immunodeficiency virus (HIV) among Latinas and stress and health risks. She and Anne Rivero have also explored issues of gender and sexual orientation, violence, and transnational migration in which they interview "women we think we know."[26] Other Latina feminist writers contribute to the extensive literature on transnational migration. Frances Aparicio and Candida Jaquez have edited a volume on transnational migration and "cultural hybridity."[27] Another volume of rich essays is *Border Women: Writing from la Frontera*, edited by Debra Castillo and Maria Socorro Tabuenca Córdoba.[28] Edna Acosta-Belén continues to write on Latina feminism in her article on the cultural interface of Latina and Latin American feminisms.[29] The topic of cultural citizenship has gained popularity in explaining the complexities of the immigration experience. Antonia Darder edited *Culture and Difference: Critical Perspectives on the Bi-Cultural Experience*.[30]

Angie Chabram-Dernersesian has edited a cultural studies reader that contains articles that capture some of these dynamics of culture and politics. Several Latinas have written books on the topics of popular culture. Alicia Gaspar de Alba wrote about the CARA exhibition in Chicano Art; Frances R. Aparicio has creatively intertwined a feminist/popular culture analysis of *Listening to Salsa: Gender, Latin Popular Music, and Puerto Rican Cultures*; and Michelle Habell-Palian with her creative title, *Loca Motion: The Travels of Chicana and Latina Popular Culture*, has raised insights on Latina identity.[31]

Education, psychology, public health, and law are just some of the other disciplines that we find Latinas in universities researching and writing about issues facing Latinas and their communities. I encourage students that are interested in learning more about issues of schools, health care, substance abuse, adolescent sexuality, and legal justice to use their academic search engines to explore works of Angela Valenzuela, Elena Flores, Maria Alaníz,

Yvette Flores Ortiz, Antoinette Sedillo Lopez, Iris Ofelia Lopez, Magdalena Avila, Nancy Lopez, and many more. It is exciting that there are so many more Latinas doing research. Yet we need more research and policy analysis to deal with the increasing social problems being faced in our communities.

I would love, for example, to see more students follow the path of community and regional planning or urban planning to address issues of economic development, housing, infrastructure development, youth development, neighborhood planning, and other community issues. My work with the Resource Center for Raza Planning at the University of New Mexico, exemplifies the value of community based research and policy analysis to local communities. Communities can benefit from the work that we do in the university. For example, University of New Mexico Anthropologist, Sylvia Rodriguez, recently published her book *Acequia Culture: Water Sharing, Sanctity and Place*, which she wrote in close collaboration with the Taos Acequia Association; it provides an important analysis toward the efforts to save this valuable irrigation, cultural, and political system.[32]

Latina Collaborations

A rich and powerful body of literary works can also be found among Latina feminist writing. Novels, poetry, autobiographical essays and books, plays, and *testimonios* are among the outlets that Latina writers use to express their voice and to create the field of knowledge about who they are. Happily, the amount of writing is so extensive that it is impossible to tell you about it in this brief chapter. It will not be hard to find, though, because a journey through your academic search engine or a trip to your library will yield an almost overwhelming array of writings. Many literary critics and essayists will include bibliographies in their writing. Nicholasa Mohr, a Puerto Rican from New York, for example, has won the New York Times Book of the Year Award and several other literary awards for her books. Ruth Behar, a Cuban American has also written extensively, and the list of Chicana writers will definitely include Cherríe Moraga.

There are several anthologies that bring together some of these Latina voices.[33] Evangelina Vigil edited a volume on Latina writers, *Woman of Her Word*. In 1989, Norma Alarcon, Norma, Ana Castillo, and Cherríe Moraga, edited a volume on the sexuality of Latinas. Also in 1989, several Latinas, Asuncion, Horno-Delgado, Eliana Ortega, Nina M. Scott, and Nancy Saporta Sternbach, joined forces to compile *Breaking Boundaries: Latina Writings and Critical Readings*. Roberta Fernandez produced *In Other Words: Literature by Latinas of the United States* in 1994, and Lillian Castillo-Speed edited

Latina: Women's Voices from the Borderlands in 1995. To add to this list of compilations, Alvina E. Quintana created a teaching guide on U.S. Latina writers, *Reading U.S. Latinas Writer: Remapping American Literature.* In 2005, Vicki Ruiz and Virginia Sánchez Korrel published a volume of essays on Latina legacies.[34] These aforementioned edited volumes are collaborations among Latinas: Puerto Rican, Chicana, Cubana, Central American, and Caribbean voices blending to create a Latina identity, while celebrating the specificities of each cultural experience.

In a particular instance, the desire for collaboration among Latinas led to a proposal to the Inter University Program (IUP) for Latino Research, which at that time was located at El Centro de Estudios Puertorriqueños at Hunter College. IUP was in the practice of providing seed funding for groups of Latino researchers to convene. The Latinos in a Changing U.S. Economy project was one of such collaborative research projects among Latinos.[35] In the proposal to convene a research working group, Latinas made the case for comparative research where the project had the potential "to have an impact in the realms of public policies directed towards women, institutional resources at the university level, and the overall difference [made by] politics of feminist research and practice in various areas." The Puertorriqueña/Chicana Comparative Research Project received the seed money for a gathering of Latina women. Celia Alvarez, Rina Benmayor, Antonia Castañeda, and Caridad Souza served as a planning committee and convened sixteen women at the Asilomar Retreat Center in Monterrey Bay, California, June 20–22, 1993.[36]

I flew into San Francisco and drove to Monterrey with Elena Flores. The meeting began at noon with introductions and a roundtable where each participant addressed the questions posed to us, "What research, community action and institutional development issues are you grappling with? How can this comparative dialogue move these agendas forward? It was an interesting way to learn about one another and our current endeavors. I was involved with the environmental justice movement and spoke about issues of disproportionate impacts of toxic contamination in communities of color. But I also had a pressing issue with which I was grappling. We were in a somewhat isolated retreat center with no television, and I wanted to figure out how I was going to get to watch game six of the NBA championship series between the Chicago Bulls and the Phoenix Suns. As I posed the question, Liza Fiol-Matta, enthusiastically ushered a resounding desire to join my quest.

By game time, we had identified the sports bar on the main drag. Several of us piled into vehicles and watched an exciting game and what became a notable game winning three point shot by John Paxson. Everyone expected

Michael Jordan to take the shot. It was one of those moments in basketball that gets replayed among the best plays in NBA history. The excitement of the Bulls victory of the game and their third straight NBA Championship was matched by the excitement of watching this game with these women. To this day, I remember how rowdy and animated we were. What I remember most is how we bonded and created what Puerto Ricans call, *revolu*—a synergistic energy that permeates the surroundings. This energy fueled our work for the next two days.

Before our meeting, the women who brought us together stated in their proposal:

> This is a particularly appropriate moment to initiate such collaboration, as scholars from both groups and in wide range of fields have expressed the need to engage in a structured and sustained exchange. There now exists a critical mass of seasoned Chicana and Puertorriqueña scholars who are asking similar questions of politics, theory and method and who are investigating parallel historical and contemporary issues in their respective communities.[37]

The authors of the proposal noted that Chicanas and Puertorriqueñas are "national minorities" and as such, "have special colonized historical relationships to the United States. These histories are commonly marked by the taking of and displacement from lands, as well as formal but second-class citizenship . . ." This commonality, we believed, was an important basis for forming our connections as Latina feminists. The proposal goes on, "these histories have had specific impact on Chicanas' and Puertorriqueñas' location in organizations, their visibility or invisibility in terms of public leadership, and their claims to dual identities, languages and cultures as formal citizens of the United States."

What seemed a natural alliance between Chicanas and Puertorriqueñas was the basis for a shared Latina identity. Extending the network to other Latinas was a next step. We met many of our goals for the meeting: define research issues of mutual concern and address the politics of such research, identify a framework for comparative focus; discuss and decide an appropriate format for carrying out this research agenda including an institute for the following year; discuss translating theoretical/methodological issues into the policy arena; and develop funding strategies, and assigning tasks. As the group developed, new women joined and others fell off. What is exciting is that a group of eighteen women (nine from the original group) met together over a period of seven years.[38] The result was a beautiful collaborative volume of testimonios, which reflected an identity of *latinidad*—a merged identity of Mexican, Puerto Rican, Cuban, Dominican, American Indian, and mixed heritage women "located at the borderlands of a reconfigured Latin(a) America." The book, published in 2001, is appropriately titled, *Telling to Live: Latina Feminist* Testimonios.[39]

I began the story in this chapter by reiterating the need to create alternative fields of knowledge. The identity of latinidad that these women sought was tied to their desire to create an alternative intellectual space,

> The flesh and blood theory many of the narratives deploy marks the Latina feminist subject in process as a new type of intellectual whose knowledge of the political economy of cultural constructions serves to decenter what counts as theory and who can engage in theorizing. The testimonios offer the language of Latina intellectuals as an alternative site of knowledge[40]

> We have become convinced that the emotional force and intellectual depth of testimonio is a springboard for theorizing about *latinidades* in the academy, in our communities, and in our lives.[41]

> Creating space for Latina feminisms—*latinidades feministas*—means confronting established and contested terms, identities, frameworks, and coalitions that have emerged in particular historical contexts. In charting our own course through these contested terrains as Latina feminists, we have attempted to expand traditional notions of ethnicity and nationalism, question Euro centric feminist frameworks, and situate ourselves in relation to the activism and writings by women of color. At the same time, as Latina feminist we have felt the need to create our won social and discursive spaces.[42]

> Our group histories and lived experiences are intertwined with global legacies of resistance to colonialism, imperialism, racist, anti-Semitism, religious fundamentalist, sexism and heterosexism. When theorizing about feminist latinidades, we reveal the interrelationships among these systems of power.[43]

Chicana Feminism

When Chicanas speak about their experiences they find themselves in opposition with those that would define them otherwise. The result, as evident in the writings of Chicana feminists, is an *identity of opposition*[44] or what Chela Sandoval calls, "oppositional consciousness"[45] against destructive discourses of domination. In 1994, when I wrote "Roots and Resistance," I suggested that,

> [the] very essence of Chicana writings is to establish Chicanas as subjects and to replace all previous representations with self-representations. The act of

redefining the experiences of Chicanas through their own voices is an expression of resistance against all other definitions. When Chicanas confront
hegemonic representations they question the symbolic bases of power relationships. The expression from the margins is a fundamental challenge to the
orderings of power.[46]

Chicana Studies, therefore, was born out of resistance. The critical mass of
Chicana feminist scholars established a space and a voice, *un sitio y una
lengua*,[47] to express our identity of opposition. We created our organization
(MALCS), Chicana and lesbian caucuses within NACCS, a body of writings
and research that constitutes the "field" of Chicana studies, a Chicana studies journal, and several academic positions. Since 1992, Chicanas published
several anthologies of feminist writings. In 1992, *Chicana Voices: Intersections
of Class, Race, and Gender* was reprinted. An updated forward describes why
the essays in the volume are still relevant and includes an analysis of the activities of Chicanas within NACCS since the original publication in 1986.
MALCS's *Chicana Critical Issues*, and Pesquera and de la Torre's *Building with
our Hands: New Directions in Chicana Studies* were both published in 1993.
Mexican American Perspectives featured a special issue on Chicanas.[48] Alma
Garcia edited *Chicana Feminist Thought: Basic Historical Writings* (1997).
Carla Trujillo edited two significant volumes, *Chicana Lesbians: The Girls
Our Mothers Warned Us About* in 1991 and *Living Chicana Theory* in 1998.

More recently, we can laud the anthology edited by Gabriela F.
Arredondo, Norma Klahn, and Aída Hurtado *Chicana Feminisms: A Critical
Reader* (2003). Arredondo, Hurtado, Norma Klahn, Loga Nájera-Ramírez,
and Patricia Zavella, combined efforts and published an important set of essays that "disrupt dialogues" in *Chicana Feminisms: Disruptions in Dialogue*
(2003). Vicki L. Ruiz and Virginia Sánchez Korrel, edited *Latina Legacies:
Identity, Biography, and Community* (2005).[49]

Chicanas not only disrupted dialogues but also replaced them with discourse that is counter to the *Chicanology*, the master narratives of dominance. It is in the fundamental challenge to colonialism and one of its instruments, patriarchy, that we find the punch of Chicana feminism. Emma
Pérez tells us we need to break the addiction to the patriarchal power that
destroys us. We need to side with those who attempt to defy the social sexual power of the patriarchy, rather than turn our backs on those who have
the courage to resist. Indeed we need to join that resistance to form a collective community that is free of the colonizer's power over us.[50]

The most important potential of Chicana feminist political thought is the
refusal to participate in colonial activity. Instead, we must replace an adher-

ence to the values and practices of colonialism with values of community, humanity, democracy, and justice.

Refusing Colonialism: Democracy, Justice, and the Betterment of Our Communities

The combination of our Latina voices constitutes fields of knowledge that pose potential for successful engagement against the forces that would prefer us subordinate and subjugated. The potential of a Latina identity and alliances of *latinidades feministas*, is that we can combine our voices to speak more loudly about identities and conditions that arise from historical and contemporary similarities. Latina feminist thought is critical, not only because it gives voice to the perspectives of women in our communities, but also because of its challenges to colonialism and patriarchy, both of which are fundamentally anti-humanitarian and anti-democratic.[51]

Colonialism feeds on the brutalities against those it colonizes. We see its results in the faces of undocumented, segmented, and worn-out labor; residents of disinvested neighborhoods; mothers of children born without brains; under/unemployed parents who can barely, if at all, sustain their families; high rates of poverty related disease; alienated youth and adults addicted to alcohol, drugs, or violence; diving graduation rates, and skyrocketing incarceration. Global restructuring is making all these problems worse, making our resistance against this dehumanization all the more important. We can resist at every level: in our households, our workplaces, our organizations, our communities etc. As limited interests seek decentralization of regulations and privatization of services, our local community involvement becomes more critical. We need to continue our previous efforts to establish collective, truly democratic, humane ways of treating one another. We must not confuse what is authoritarian and what is democratic.

Colonialism feeds on dehumanization. If we build healthy local communities, where humanity and humanization is our main priority, then we can challenge the nature of colonialism and colonial relationships. Our strategy and our struggle against colonialism should be to replace it with the struggle for community. Part of a humanizing agenda is to build community. Building community opposes domination and injustice. In this effort, we can find allies and build coalitions. Coalitions become critical for our survival.

The voices of *feministas latinas* serves a counterhegemonic function by defining and interpreting our own experiences, speaking "truth to power," and challenging those discourses that define our identities in ways designed to subjugate our interests. The critique of anti-democratic and unjust conditions and the narratives that support and justify those conditions offer the greatest value of Latina voices. The critiques become the basis for further action to change the power relations involving decision making and the distribution of resources.

The Chicana studies scholar is concerned with research "rooted in the political life of communities" and rejects "the separation of academic scholarship and community involvement" According to the Preamble of MALCS, "We document, analyze, and interpret the Chicana/Mexicana experience" and see ourselves "developing strategies for social change—change emanating from our communities . . . We continue our mothers' struggle for social and economic justice." How might the Latina scholar collaborate in developing strategies for social change as she conducts her research?

Research is a worthy mission for the Latina scholar who wants to address "pressing problems and issues affecting our communities." From this point of view, creating fields of knowledge has two major purposes: (1) to reconstruct ideology—"Our research efforts are aimed at directly confronting such tenuous images and interpretations and challenging" structured inequality and (2) guide action (i.e., "Our research should generate information that can lead to effective problem-solving action.") Our fields of knowledge should help us to address the problems in our communities and build communities where we can thrive. Returning to the roots of Chicana, Puerto Rican, and Latina feminism will affirm our agency, our relevance, and our connection to community.

* * *

Notes and Suggestions for Further Research

1. Mujeres en Marcha, *Unsettled Issues: Chicanas in the 80's*, (Berkeley: Chicano Studies Library Publication Unit, University of California, 1983). Partially reprinted in Alma Garcia, ed., *Chicana Feminist Thought: The Basic Historical Writings* (New York: Routledge, 1997), 253–70.

2. Teresa Córdova, "Power and Knowledge: Colonialism in the Academy" in Carla Trujillo, ed., *Living Chicana Theory* (Berkeley: Third Woman Press, 1997), 17–45

3. See chapter 4 of this volume.

4. See Teresa Córdova, "Anti-Colonial Chicana Feminism," *New Political Science: A Journal of Politics and Culture* 20, no. 4 (December 1998): 379–97.

5. For a discussion of the NACS and MALCS Preambles, see Teresa Córdova "Agency, Commitment and Connection: Embracing the Roots of Chicano and Chi-

cana Studies," in *The International Journal of Qualitative Studies in Education* 18, no. 2 (March-Spring 2005).

6. Teresa Córdova, "Roots and Resistance: The Emergent Writings of Twenty Years of Chicana Feminist Struggle," in Felix Padilla, ed., *The Handbook of Hispanic Cultures in the United States: Sociology* (Houston: Arte Público Press, 1994), 175–202.

7. Velia G. Hancock, "La Chicana, Chicano Movement and Women's Liberation" *Chicano Studies Newsletter* (February-March, 1971): 1, 6.

8. Teresa Córdova and others, eds., *Chicana Voices: Intersections of Class, Race, and Gender* (Austin: Center of Mexican American Center, University of Texas, 1984). (Incidentally, this text was reprinted by University of New Mexico Press in 1993.)

9. "Sterilization of Puerto Rican Women: A Selected, Partially Annotated Bibliography" May 1999. http://womenst.library.wisc.edu/bibliogs/puerwom.htm (accessed 7/29/2008). Included in it is the pertinent Vanessa Bauza, "Puerto Rico: The Covert Campaign to Sterilize Women." MS [new series] 5, no. 2 (September/October 1994):14. See also Maria Gonzalez L., Victoria Barrera, Peter Guarnaccia, and Stephen L. Schensul "*La Operación*: An Analysis of Sterilization in a Puerto Rican Community in Connecticut" in Ruth E. Zambrana, ed., *Work, Family and Health: Latina Women in Transition* (New York: Hispanic Research Center, 1982), 47–61.

10. Clara Rodriguez, Virginia Sanchez Korrol, and Jose O. Alers, eds., *The Puerto Rican Struggles: Essays on Survival in the U.S.* (New York: Puerto Rican Migration Research Consortium, 1980). A second edition appeared in 1986, *Historical Perspectives in Puerto Rican Survival in the U.S.*

11. See also Edna Acosta-Belén, ed., *The Puerto Rican Woman: Perspectives on Culture, History, and Society*, 2nd ed. (New York: Praeger, 1986).

12. National Conference of Puerto Rican Women. *Puerto Rican Women in the United States: Organizing for Change* (Washington, D.C.: NACOPRW, 1977).

13. Juan Betancur, Teresa Córdova, and Maria de Los Angeles Torres, "Economic Restructuring and The Process of Incorporation of Latino Workers into the Chicago Economy," in Frank Bonilla and Rebecca Morales, eds., *Latinos in the Changing U.S. Economy* (Thousand Oaks, CA: Sage Publications, 1993), 109–32.

14. Rita Sánchez, "Chicanas Breaking out of Silence" in *La Cosecha: Literatura y la mujer chicana. De Colores* 3, no 3. (Albuquerque, NM: Pajarito Publications, 1977).

15. Carol Hardy-Fanta, *Latina Politics, Latino Politics: Gender, Culture, and Political participation in Boston* (Philadelphia: Temple University Press, 1993).

16. Mary Pardo, *Mexican American Women Activists: Identity and Resistance in Two Los Angeles Communities* (Philadelphia: Temple University Press, 1998).

17. See for example, Vicki L. Ruiz, *Cannery Women Cannery Lives: Mexican Women, Unionization, and the California Food Processing Industry, 1930–1950* (Albuquerque: University of New Mexico Press, 1987); "The Watsonville Women's Strike, 1986: A Case of Mexicana Activism," in Ana Castillo, *Massacres of the Dreamers: Essays on Xicanisma* (Albuquerque: University of New Mexico Press, 1994), 43–62. In Magdalena Mora and Adelaida Del Castillo, eds. *Mexican Women in the United States: Struggles*

Past and Present (Los Angeles: Chicano Studies Research Center Publications, 1980) see the following articles: Maria Moreno, "I'm Talking for Justice," 181–82; "Lucy Durán-Wife, Mother, and Organizer," 183–84; Irene Castañeda, "Personal Chronicle of Crystal City," 185–88; Clementina Durón, "Mexican Women and labor Conflict in Los Angeles: The ILGWU Dressmakers' Strike of 1933," *Aztlán* 15, no. 1 (Spring 1984): 145–61; Magdalena Mora, "The Tolteca Strike: Mexican Women and the Struggle for Union Representation" in Antonio Rios Bustamante, ed., *Mexican Immigrant Workers in the U.S* (Los Angeles: Chicano Studies Research Center, University of California, Los A), 111–17; Bertha Romero, "The Exploitation of Mexican Women in the Canning Industry and the Effects of Capital Accumulation on Striking Workers," *Revista Mujeres* 3, no. 2 (June 1986): 16–20. For more stories of strength and survival see endnote 22.

18. Ruiz, *Cannery Women*, 123.

19. Felix M. Padilla and Lourdes Santiago, *Outside the Wall: A Puerto Rican Woman's Struggle* (New Jersey: Rutgers University Press, 1993). Santiago and Padilla also describe her fight for prison reform.

20. Cynthia Orozco, "Beyond *Machismo, La Familia,* and Ladies Auxiliaries: A Historiography of Mexican-Origin Women's Participation in Voluntary Association and Politics in the United States, 1870–1990" in *Perspectives in Mexican American Studies* 5 (1995): 1–34.

21. See Elizabeth Martínez "'Chingón Politics' Die Hard: Reflections on the First Chicana Activist Reunion," in Carla Trujillo, ed., *Living Chicana Theory* (Berkeley: Third Woman Press, 1997), 123–35. See also Alma Garcia, ed., *Chicana Feminist Thought: The Basic Historical Writings,* (New York: Routledge, 1997).

22. Vicki Ruiz, "By the Day or the Week: Mexicana Domestic Workers in El Paso," in Vicki Ruiz and Susan Tiano, eds., *Women on the U.S.-Mexican Border: Responses to Change* (Boston: Allen and Unwin, 1987), 61–76. In the same volume, see Rosalía Solórzano-Torres, "Female Mexican Immigrants in San Diego County," 41–59; Alicia Chavira, "'Tienes que ser valiente': Mexicana Migrants in a Midwestern Farm Labor Camp," in Margarita Melville, ed., *Mexicanas at Work in the United States* (Houston: Mexican American Studies Program, University of Houston, 1988), 64–74; in the same volume, see Julia E. Curry-Rodríguez, "Labor Migration and Familial Responsibilities: Experiences of Mexican Women," in Margarita Melville, ed., *Mexicanas at Work in the United States* (Houston: Mexican American Studies Program, University of Houston, 1988), 47–63; Adela de la Torre, "Hard Choices and Changing Roles among Mexican Migrant Campesinas," in Adela de la Torre, and Beatríz Pesquera, eds., *Building with Our Hands: New Directions in Chicana Studies* (Berkeley: University of California Press, 1993); Mary Romero, *Maid in the USA* (New York: Routledge, 1992); Raquel Rubio-Goldsmith, "Shipwrecked in the Desert: A Short History of the Adventures and Struggles for Survival of the Mexican Sisters of the House of Providence," in Vicki Ruiz and Susan Tiano, eds., *Women on the U.S.-Mexican Border: Responses to Change* (Boston: Allen and Unwin, 1987); "Women in the U.S.-Mexican," in Vicki Ruiz and Susan Tiano, eds., *Women on the U.S.-Mexican*

Border: Responses to Change (Boston: Allen and Unwin, 1987), 177–95; Lourdes Argüelles, "Undocumented Female Labor in the United States Southwest: An Essay on Migration, Consciousness, Oppression and Struggle" in Adelaida Del Castillo, ed., *Between Borders: Essays on Mexicana/Chicana History* (Encino, CA: Floricanto Press, 1990), 299–312; Pat Zavella, *Women's Work and Chicano Families: Cannery Workers of the Santa Clara Valley* (Ithaca, NY: Cornell University Press, 1987).

23. Teresa Córdova, "Grassroots Mobilizations by Chicanas in the Environmental and Economic Justice Movement," Voces: A *Journal of Chicana/Latina Studies* 1, no. 1 (1997): 31–55

24. Córdova, "Grassroots," 49.

25. For example Jeanne Gauna, Co-Director of the SouthWest Organizing Project wrote regularly in *Voces*, the organization's newsletter; Elizabeth "Betita" Martinez writes for *Z Magazine*; and Patrisia Gonzalez, a syndicated columnist, writes regularly with her husband Roberto Rodriguez in their *Column of the Americas*. See also Betita's book, *Elizabeth Martinez, De Colores Means All of Us: Latina Views for a Multi-Colored Century* (Cambridge, Mass: South End Press, 1998) and *500 Years of Chicana Women's History* (New Jersey: Rutgers University Press, 2008).

26. Lourdes Argüelles and Anne M. Rivero, "Gender/Sexual Orientation Violence and Transnational Migration: Conversations with Some Latinas We Think We Know," *Urban Anthropology and Studies of Cultural Systems and World Economic Development* 22 (Fall/Winter1993): 259–75.

27. Frances R. Aparicio and Cándida Jáquez, eds., *Musical Migrations: Transnationalism and Cultural Hybridity in Latin(o) America* (Philadelphia: Temple University Press, 2001.

28. Debra Castillo and Maria Soccorro Tabuenca Córdoba, *Border Women: Writing from La Frontera* (University of Minnesota Press, 2002).

29. Edna Acosta-Belen and Christine E. Bose, "U.S. Latina and Latin American Feminisms: Hemispheric Encounters," *Signs* 25, no. 4 (Summer 2000): 1113-19.

30. Antonia Darder, ed., *Culture and Difference: Critical Perspectives on the Bi-Cultural Experience* (Westport, CT: Greenwood Publishing Group, 1995).

31. Angie Chabram-Dernersesian, *Chicana/o Cultural Studies Reader: Critical and Ethnographic Practices* (New York: Routledge, 2006); Alicia Gaspar de Alba, *Chicano Art Inside/Outside the Master's House: Cultural Politics and the CARA Exhibition* (Austin: University of Texas Press, 1998); Frances R. Aparicio, *Listening to Salsa: Gender, Latin Popular Music, and Puerto Rican Cultures* (Hanover, NH: Wesleyan University Press, 1998); Michelle Habell-Palian, *Loca Motion: The Travels of Chicana and Latina Popular Culture* (New York: New York University Press, 2005). Rosalinda Fregoso has written on Latinas in film.

32. Sylvia Rodriguez, *Acequia: Water Sharing, Sanctity, and Place* (Santa Fe: School for Advanced Research Scholar Book, 2006).

33. Norma Alarcón, Ana Castillo, and Cherrie Moraga, eds., *Third Woman: The Sexuality of Latinas* (Berkeley: Third Woman Press, 1989); Evangelina Vigil, *Woman of Her Word* (Houston: Arte Public Press, 1987); Asuncion Horno-Delgado, Eliana

Ortega, Nina M. Scott, and Nancy Saporta Sternbach, eds., *Breaking Boundaries: Latina Writings and Critical Readings* (Amherst: University of Massachusetts Press, 1989); Roberta Fernandez, ed., *In Other Words: Literature by Latinas of the United States* (Houston: Arte Público Press, 1994); Lillian Castillo-Speed, ed., *Latina: Women's Voices from the Borderlands* (New York: Touchstone, 1995). Alvina E. Quintana, *Reading U.S. Latina Writer: Remapping American Literature* (New York: McMillan, 2003); Vicki L. Ruiz and Virginia Sánchez Korrel, *Latina Legacies: Identity, Biography, and Community* (New York: Oxford University Press, 2005).

34. There are also several more recent compilations of Chicana literature. Sonia Saldívar-Hull, *Feminism on the Border: Chicana Gender Politics and Literature* (Berkeley: University of California Press, 2000) in which authors explore their connection to the U.S. Mexico border. Teresa McKenna provides her literary analysis of Chicano Literature in her book *Migrant Song: Politics and Process in Contemporary Chicano Literature* (Austin: University of Texas, Press, 1997).

35. This working group, which spanned several years, produced a volume of studies comparing the impacts of economic restructuring on Latino communities in major U.S. Cities. Frank Bonilla and Rebecca Morales edited the volume, *Latinos in the Changing U.S. Economy* (Thousand Oaks, CA: Sage Publications, 1993).

36. The Latinas who attended this meeting (and their institutional affiliations at the time) were Luz del Alba Acevedo (SUNY Albany), Celia Alvarez (Arizona State University, West), Rina Benmayor (CUNY, Hunter College), Liza Fiol Matta (La Guardia Community College, Union Institute), Aurora Levins Morales (Union Institute), Iris Lopez (CUNY, CCNY), Caridad Souza (SUNY, Oneonta, UC Berkeley), Norma Alarcon (UC Berkeley), Teresa Córdova (University of New Mexico), Julia Curry-Rodriquez (UC Berkeley), Maria Chacon (IUP), Elena Flores (University of San Francisco), Alicia Gaspar de Alba (University of New Mexico), Deena Gonzalez (UC Riverside), and Clara Lomas (Colorado College).

37. I obtained this proposal from my personal files from this meeting.

38. The participants in *Telling to Live* include Luz del Alba Acevedo, Norma Alarcón, Celia Alvarez, Ruth Behar, Rina Benmayor, Norma E. Cantú, Daisy Cocco De Filippis, Gloria Holguín Cuádraz, Liza Fiol-Matta, Yvette Flores-Ortiz, Inés Hernández-Avila, Aurora Levins Morales, Clara Lomas, Iris Ofelia López, Mirtha N. Quintanales, Eliana Rivero, Caridad Souza, Patricia Zavella

39. Latina Feminist Group, *Telling to Live: Latina Feminist* Testimonios (Durham, NC: Duke University Press, 2001). The group consciously rejected the idea of comparative research and focused instead on the intellectual journey of testimonios.

40. Latina Feminist Group, *Telling to Live*, x.

41. Latina Feminist Group, *Telling to Live*, 2.

42. Latina Feminist Group, *Telling to Live*, 2.

43. Latina Feminist Group, *Telling to Live*, 10.

44. Córdova, "Roots and Resistance."

45. Chela Sandoval, "U.S. Third World Feminism: The Theory and Method of Oppositional Consciousness in the Postmodern World," *Genders* no. 10 (Spring

1991): 1–24. For more recent work by Sandoval, see Chela Sandoval, *Methodology of the Oppressed* (Minneapolis: University of Minnesota Press, 2000).

46. Córdova, "Roots and Resistance."

47. Emma Pérez, "Sexuality and Discourse: Notes from a Chicana Survivor" in Carla Trujillo, ed., *Chicana Lesbians: The Girls Our Mothers Warned Us About* (Berkeley: Third Woman Press, 1991), 174

48. *Perspectives in Mexican American Studies* 5 (1995).

49. For recent anthologies on Chicana feminism, see Gabriela F. Arredondo, Norma Klahn, and Aída Hurtado, eds., *Chicana Feminisms: A Critical Reader* (Durham, NC: Duke University Press, 2003); Gabriela F. Arredondo, Aída Hurtado, Norma Klahn, Loga Najera-Ramirez, and Patricia Zavella, eds. *Chicana Feminisms: Disruptions in Dialogue* (Durham, NC: Duke University Press 2003); and Vicki L. Ruiz and Virginia Sánchez Korrel, *Latina Legacies: Identity, Biography, and Community* (New York: Oxford University Press, 2005).

50. Emma Pérez, "Sexuality and Discourse," 169.

51. Teresa Córdova, "Anti-Colonial Chicana Feminism," *New Political Science: A Journal of Politics and Culture* 20, no. 4 (December 1998): 379–97.</notes>

*   *   *

Questions

1. To what extent did the separation of Chicana and Chicano as two different fields of knowledge help or hinder the social struggle of Mexican Americans/Chicanos?

2. Can a social movement be part of the mission of a university or social advocacy be the main activity of faculty members?

3. To what extent is university research able to make a difference in the lives of the poor? How does it become public or social policy?

4. To what extent do you see faculty in your university involved in social action research and including such research in their courses?

CHAPTER TWENTY-FIVE

~

Transitional Political and Cultural Identities: Crossing Theoretical Borders

María de los Angeles Torres

Political identities are assigned to human bodies who "belong" to a particular nation-state; for example, if you are a human body from a Communist country (say Cuba), you are welcomed as a "refugee," but if you are a human body from a friendly (and non-Communist) country (say Mexico or Haiti), you are expelled as an "illegal alien." In this text, de los Angeles Torres raises several pertinent questions regarding the need to redefine the concept of citizenship for peoples who "have crossed political borders," or we might add, people who have been crossed by political borders. She also addressed the need to redefine the concept of assimilation as a desirable and even possible objective. In this context, de los Angeles Torres considers the nationalist movements as "an affective return to the homeland," but also as something that may be interpreted as a search for inclusion, for belonging, and as a quest for dignity and respect.[1]

The Latino/a diaspora, however, often do not find inclusiveness in their homelands either. Their nation-states of origin have their own exclusive definitions of citizenship. A 2006 survey of Latino immigrants indicates that only a small share of immigrant population regularly engages in all three of the following activities measured in the survey. Only one in ten (9%) of all Latino immigrants send remittances, make phone calls at least once a week, and have traveled back to their country or origin in the past two years. Meanwhile, nearly three in ten (28%) do not engage in any of these activities. Most Latino immigrants (63%) engage in one of two of these activities.[2] Nevertheless, as Robinson points out in chapter 26, the corporate global economy produces illegal immigration to the point that the question of immigrant rights is the civil and human rights issue for the new millennium. Under these circumstances, there is a critical ethical need to construct a multicultural space in both home and host countries. This has been considered a threat to the idea of the nation-state based on a single culture. We are left facing the monumental task of expanding the concepts of "citizen" and "nation" to accommodate an increasingly global migratory phenomenon.

Notes

1. The notion of respect is a central issue in the claim for cultural citizenship. See William V. Flores and Rina Benmayor, eds., *Latino Cultural Citizenship: Claiming Identity, Space and Rights* (Boston: Beacon, 1997).

2. Roer Waldinger, "Between Here and There: How Attached Are Latino Immigrants to Their Native Country?" Washington: The Pew Hispanic Center (October 25, 2007).

* * *

Political borders—a defining feature of nation-states during the twentieth century—are changing, being reinforced at the same time that they are eroding. These increasingly porous frontiers suggest that, like economies, the nature of politics and of political participation may also change.[1] One reason is that people, particularly in diaspora communities, are affected by decisions made by governments in which they have only a limited voice or no voice at all. In home countries, governments make decisions that affect diaspora communities residing beyond the state's geographic jurisdiction. In host countries, diaspora communities often have a restricted role in public affairs because of their newcomer status. Ironically, while some countries are extending voting rights to their communities abroad, most host countries are limiting or even reversing some of the avenues immigrants have used to express their opinions in the past. There are few analytical and legal concepts that go beyond the nation-state as the parameter for political participation, making it difficult to envision immigrant political participation in both host and home countries.

In addition, the cultural identities of diaspora communities are not only informed by the host country, but also have many points of reference to home country culture. Past cultural and familial connections are not severed by crossing political borders. Immigrant flows from home countries have added new layers to existing diaspora communities. Yet the prevailing social science framework used to study the immigrant experience assumes that the nation-state is the principal organizational unit of politics and cultural identity. In this framework, public power is organized and contested within the geographic boundaries of nation-states, which also define the economies and social organization of societies. It is the state that regulates the affairs of the nation.

Citizenship: Who Is Entitled?

The notion of citizenship is deeply interwoven with the rise of the nation-state. With the formation of nation-states came a new set of conditions that defined the rights of individuals, particularly in relation to the state. These included a definition and legal categorization of who was entitled to these rights. Citizenship became something to be granted or denied by the state. Although there are many legal variations in how citizenship is acquired—for instance, under German law it is passed from parent to child, while under Spanish, French, and British law the place of birth is the determining factor[2]—nation-states make citizenship and residency a requirement of political participation.

Furthermore, citizenship assumes loyalty to a state. In order to acquire U.S. citizenship, for example, emigres must swear an oath of exclusive allegiance to the United States. Yet the identities of many immigrants are too complex to allow this. Diaspora communities often reside in multiple states or have traveled through them. Restricting loyalty to one state flattens immigrants' experiences and limits their political options, particularly when they are affected by the decisions of many states.

The "nation" side of the nation-state concept also carries built-in assumptions. In regard to citizenship, the nation was conceived from the start as socially and culturally homogeneous. Those who are citizens are assumed to have a common cultural base. Even in the United States, where property, gender, and race were used initially to define who was included in the body politic, a romanticized abstraction of the androgynous, raceless citizen prevailed. Naturalized citizens—that is, those not born in the United States—were expected to leave their homeland behind when it came to public affairs.

Those born in other countries are not automatically entitled to U.S. citizenship. The state can choose whether and when to grant this right to those who apply. Moreover, participation in public affairs depends on one's legal status. Undocumented residents and legal residents who are not naturalized are not allowed to vote, nor do they enjoy the same rights as citizens.

The Assimilation Model: Politics and Identity

Assimilation, the prevailing model of immigrant political development, is shaped by a geographically determined definition of political space and agenda. The assimilation model predicts that recent immigrants do not participate in politics immediately after their arrival in the host country because they are still preoccupied with home country issues and with trying to adapt to a new environment. By the second generation, ties to the homeland have weakened. Political involvement begins at the local level, moving to the national level within another generation. By the third generation, the political agenda of immigrant groups may include international issues; by this time the focus of international affairs is not confined to the country of ancestry because the connection with the homeland has effectively been broken. Although there is a distinction between assimilation (becoming the other) and acculturation (adapting to the other), assimilationist views now dominate the public discourse.[3]

This view of political participation fits well within a pluralist framework that conceived of politics as a product of individual and organizational effort. Individuals organized to exert pressure on the political system, which provided outputs needed by the community. This model of politics was based primarily on the experiences of immigrants who came to the United States at the turn of the century—a time of extraordinary industrial growth and relatively weak government structures, particularly at the local level. Communities first became integrated economically, facilitating their political incorporation. (It is not clear whether these earlier immigrant communities genuinely cut their ties to the homeland or whether such ties simply were difficult to maintain. For example, in a study of ethnic Chicago, historians of various immigrant communities noted a persistent interest in homeland issues even at the turn of the century.[4] Models of political development that suggested an assimilationist path to political participation have failed to explain this persistence.)

The assimilation model is less useful in explaining the political development of groups that came to the United States at a time when the economic structure was different and the state had become much more expansive. European immigrants and emigres from countries in neocolonial situations—countries that were politically or economically dominated by the United States, like many in Latin America and the Caribbean—have had different relationships to the United States. When emigre communities did not succeed in achieving formal political incorporation, the unquestioned validity of this model forced social scientists to focus their inquiries not on what was wrong with the model (whose validity was unquestioned), but on what was wrong with these communities. The answer usually was that they resisted assimilation. A group of Latino political scientists set out to disprove this claim by documenting the attitudinal similarities between "Americans" and immigrant groups, such as Mexican-Americans. As a result, for years the study of Latino politics sought to dispel the importance of ethnicity as a factor in political mobilization and to counter the assumption that home country issues were part of the agenda for such immigrant communities.[5]

How is the political identity of diaspora communities evolving in light of changes in the nation-state? Identity is a social construction that requires continuous negotiation among the individual, the community, and the society at large. Social and political identities have at least two important dimensions: how societies construct an individual's or a group's identity, and how the individual or community constructs its own identity.

Social and political identities are closely tied to each other precisely because the nation and the state are coupled. The nation embodies culture, history, and social structures, while political identities are defined and regulated by the state. The concept of citizenship does not exist in a vacuum; rather, it is related to other aspects of a society, particularly when a society is marked and divided by racism and when race and national origin have determined who is awarded citizenship. Nor is the definition of citizenship isolated from questions of politics, as is the case in totalitarian regimes, which demand loyalty not just in return for citizenship, but in return for a national identity. It is in this intersection that social identities, including ethnic and national identities, become critical in understanding who has access to a political system.

The assimilationist view of immigrant identity predicts that, by the second generation, immigrant communities will have lost their affective and cultural ties to their homeland and identify themselves with the host country. In the United States, the second generation will have become "American." However, many first-generation Latinos, their children, and even grandchildren retain a level of interest in home country politics and culture. Like the political assimilation model, the prevalent model of identity assumes a singular identity tied to one geographic space. It also assumes that this identity is fixed and does not change over time.

The notion of assimilation itself assumes not only that integration is desirable, but also that it is possible. Shedding one's ethnicity is taken as a sign of leaving behind that which is old and replacing it with something new. This act suggests that individuals and communities can somehow discard their past and incorporate into a new culture. But this predictive model does not take into consideration the fact that in many host countries, immigrants are neither welcomed nor allowed to assimilate socially or, at times, even legally.

Another serious limitation of the assimilation model is that it cannot explain the persistence and reappearance of ethnicity and the desire to reconnect with the homeland in the sons and daughters of immigrants. These movements may be stronger in the second and third generations, particularly at times when anti-immigrant feelings are on the rise. Such has been the case, for instance, for third-generation Mexican-Americans born on Chicago's South Side. One of the country's strongest and most vibrant neighborhood museums, the Mexican Fine Arts Museum in Chicago's Pilsen neighborhood, was founded by the grandchildren of Mexican immigrants who had come to work in Chicago's steel mills. Their struggles to provide education to the Mexican community included bringing to that community the art and culture of their country of ancestry. (Later on, the museum's goal expanded to include bringing to Mexico culture created by Mexicans in the United States.)

In addition, reconnecting to the identity of one's parents may be more important at certain stages of the life cycle. The passage from adolescence to adulthood is generally accompanied by a reassessment of one's heritage and values. For second-generation immigrants, this can manifest itself as an awakening of interest in the homeland and culture of one's parents.

The prevailing vision of politics and identity insists on a uniform public culture while permitting political pluralism. While a wide array of cultures and even languages is permitted in the private spaces of U.S. society—religious, private educational, and cultural institutions—public (political) discourse demands cultural homogeneity.

The assimilation model itself may be a myth that developed in the United States between the two World Wars. Immigration to the United States from Western Europe was at its peak. When the United States went to war with Europe, patriotism and loyalty to the United States were expected. People rallied publicly under the banner of "Americans." Ethnic communities, particularly those from countries with which the United States was at war, such as Germans, Italians and Japanese, suffered varying degrees of repression. It was during this period that the public myth arose that immigrant communities actually had cut their ties to the homeland and were now as "American" as the native-born. (Curiously, Mussolini's government was the first to develop a state-sponsored project to reach out to Italian communities abroad and encourage them to influence U.S. policies toward their home country.)[6] But racism persisted. For example, after World War II Mexican-Americans formed organizations of veterans to show their loyalty to the United States. But racism was so severe that even Mexican-Americans who had been killed in the war were not buried in the same cemeteries as "white" soldiers. In response to such discrimination, organizations like the GI Forum and the League of United Latin American Citizens (LULAC) began advocating for equality and integration.

The Emergence of Alternative Views of Latino Reality

History and Homeland: The 1960s to the Mid-1970s

Integrationist movements of the post-World War II era failed to bring equality and were met with disdain. Although the federal government eventually responded to internal and international pressure to abolish segregationist laws, racism remained entrenched in states and local communities. The persistence of racism contributed to the emergence of more radical movements. In the United States, the civil rights movement of the 1960s led communities that had been excluded from the political process on the basis of race or national origin to demand inclusion on the same grounds. Unlike the integrationist movement of the 1950s, which sought entrance and equality, the movements of the 1960s sought to change the rules of the game as well. This included a vision for transforming the cultural and political spaces in which immigrant communities exist.

Instead of trying to prove that they were loyal Americans, immigrant organizations in the 1960s sought to define their identities in terms of *difference*. Difference was celebrated in a search for roots that had been severed by oppression and denied by shame. One of the results of this search for identity was an affective return to the homeland. Some groups, such as the Colorado-based Crusade for Justice, founded by Corky González, initially sought a mythical homeland, Aztlán; and even organizations with a U.S.-based agenda, such as *Raza Unida*, later sought relations with Mexico. In the Cuban exile community, groups like the Antonio Maceo Brigade and *Areíto* sought connections to Cuba.

At the same time, radical movements in Mexico and Puerto Rico reached out to communities abroad. For example, connections were established between Mexican-Americans and the Mexican left after governmental repression in Mexico forced many political activists to flee to the United States. Organizations like *Central de Acción Social Autónoma* (CASA) represented the merger of the struggles against repression in Mexico and racism in the United States. Pro-Puerto Rican independence organizations bridged communities on the island and the mainland.

Radical politics in the various Latino communities challenged the prevailing paradigms of identity and politics by crossing borders. Scholars became critical links in this crossing as they began to redefine the paradigms within which the politics and identity of Latinos in the United States were studied. Chicano scholars, for example, played an important role in challenging ahistorical accounts of the origins of the Chicano community.[7] The recovery of history led to a growing awareness in the Southwest of the connections between the Chicano community and Mexico.[8] Alternative frameworks like the internal colonial model looked at the connections between the U.S. conquest of Mexico's northern territory in the mid-1800s and labor exploitation to understand the persistence of poverty and racism in the Southwest.[9]

Parallel critical studies emerged in the Puerto Rican and Cuban exile communities. Studies of Puerto Rican labor migration to the United States examined the connections between the colonization of the island and the migratory response of labor.[10] Cuban exile scholars sought to understand how U.S. foreign policy toward Cuba influenced the formation of Cuban communities in the United States.[11] Yet many of these studies were still bound by nation-state perspectives. An exception was the geopolitical model Carlos Forment suggested to analyze terrorist politics in the Cuban exile community.[12] In this model the unit of analysis is the region, and hegemonic politics finds expression through regional blocs. In the field of sociology, Marisa Alicea's dual-home-base model began to depart from the culturally accepted notion that immigrants have a single "home."[13] (Bi-national experiences were seen under the assimilation model as potentially destructive to the formation of community. Indeed, the ability to move back and forth from the island to the mainland was often cited as the reason for Puerto Ricans' low wages and low voter turnout.)

In addition to the search for homeland, another phenomenon emerged. Various groups of similar national origins began to come together as a means to mobilize community and political resources. Félix Padilla initially documented this phenomenon in Chicago, the first U.S. city to witness the coexistence of communities from several Latin American countries.[14] While retaining its individual ethnic identification, under certain circumstances a community would also adopt the label of "Latino," a broader ethnopolitical identity that coexisted with other ethnic identities.

In 1984 four university-based research centers dedicated to the study of the Latino experience in the United States came together to form the Inter-University Program for Latino Research.[15] This was the first academic endeavor to bring together Latino scholars from different disciplines and communities. Underlying many of its research projects was the assumption that Latino groups in the United States share a common legacy because the United States had intervened in some way in their countries of origin. Yet each group, and each subsequent immigration wave, was unique.

Growing organizational unity at the community level also found expression nationally. Organizations such as the National Association of Latino Elected and Appointed Officials (NALEO) and the Hispanic Institute (the research arm of the Congressional Hispanic Caucus) attempted to present a unified voice in national politics. Since it was harder to find consensus on foreign policy than on domestic issues, these organizations often avoided the former. Other groups, such as Policy Alternatives for the Caribbean and Central America (PACCA), the Southwest Voter Registration and Education Project, and the Cuban American Committee, advocated changes in U.S. policies toward Mexico, Central America, and the Caribbean.[16]

Ambivalent Homelands: The 1970s to the Mid-1980s

Just as attempts to assimilate to the host country encountered limits, so did movements to reconnect with countries of origin. For example, U.S.-based Mexicans experienced a mixed welcome in their homeland, where they were often referred to as *pochos* (wetbacks), and where they found the government's repressive politics intolerable.

Nevertheless, as the number of Mexican-Americans taking part in U.S. political life rose, the Mexican government began to consider the possible implications for its interests in the United States, hoping to create a Chicano lobby similar to the Jewish-American organizations that supported Israel within the United States. In the 1980s, the Mexican government institutionalized this interest in an office dedicated to the *Mexicans de Afuera* (Mexicans Abroad) in its Ministry of Foreign Relations.[17] This office was responsible for developing and maintaining ties with Mexican-American communities in the United States; activities, organized through Mexico's consular offices, included cultural events and arranging for scholarships to study medicine in Mexico.

Cuban exiles, called *gusanos* (worms) in their homeland, had similar experiences with the island government, although this relationship unfolded within a much more politicized climate, both on the island and in the United States. Cuban exiles who tried to return to their homeland were told by government officials that they would better serve the interests of the revolution by remaining abroad and arguing for the lifting of the U.S. embargo imposed on Cuba in the early 1960s.[18] The Ministry of the Interior was put in charge of the *Comunidad Cubana el Exterior* (COCUEX) project.[19] Like Mexican-Americans,

Cuban exiles found that their relationship to the homeland was placed within the context of state interests, particularly foreign and security affairs. Both homeland governments considered those who had left not as nationals, but rather as resources to be used in the "national" interest.

The relationship of Puerto Ricans on the mainland to those on the island was also ambiguous. Although the independence movement at times has been stronger in U.S. cities such as Chicago and New York than in Puerto Rico, those on the island arguing for independence did not support efforts to include Puerto Ricans living in the United States as part of the electorate. On this issue, supporters of independence found allies in the pro-statehood forces, who were also leery of the politics of U.S. Puerto Ricans. When the question of a referendum on the island's status was debated in 1990, groups on the island, including the *independentistas*, lobbied against allowing mainland Puerto Ricans to vote. It became clear that home country governments and political organizations ultimately held a very narrow definition of who was to be considered part of the nation.[20]

The movement to reconnect with homelands failed just as the assimilationist path had. Homeland governments were mainly interested in the political clout, symbolic or otherwise, that their communities abroad could offer. Even when remittances sent home by immigrants began to provide critical economic resources—in some cases becoming the most important or the second most important contribution to the gross national product—communities abroad were still not entirely welcome in the body politic. In many cases, the resentment deepened.

Identity Redefined: The 1980s to the Mid-1990s

Latinos had found that while they shared some common ground with their countries of origin, there were important differences as well. Being in and out of place in both home and host country gave rise to the exploration of border identities. Border identities are unique because they contain elements of various cultures coexisting side by side. Community organizations have played a central role in the creation of border identities, but it is artists and writers—unconstrained by the slow production mode of academia or the structures of the electoral arena—who have redefined the parameters of the debate and offered more radical notions about identity and, consequently, politics.

In the Southwest, Gloria Anzaldúa proposed the notion of border identities, which forced a reexamination of the prevailing rigid categories of ethnicity and gender that had emerged from the 1960s.[21] In Cristina García's novel *Dreaming in Cuban*, Pilar returns for a visit to the forbidden island to

The search for a more complex understanding of identity was in part a response to the rigid categories of identity that emerged from the radical movements of the 1960s. It was also a response to the postmodern prediction that, as cultural spaces became increasingly homogenized through easy transportation and communication, all human beings would in effect move toward a single identity. Instead, communities at the "margins" came to witness an accelerated fragmentation of identity. As nation-states eroded, they were not replaced by a homogeneous superstate or a single identity. Rather, societies became more diverse as immigration from one part of the world to another rushed ahead, giving rise to the movement for a recognition of the multicultural character of societies. At the same time, receiving societies became less open. While the 1960s movement for equality—that is, political and civil rights—asked for representation in the host country, and the movements of the 1970s witnessed demands to reconnect with the homeland, the multicultural movement of the 1980s sought to transform the public spaces in both home and host countries.

Institutionalization and Backlash

The backlash against the multicultural movement emerged in the late 1980s and early 1990s at a time when U.S. society was witnessing a major transformation of its economy as well as its position in the world. The new service-based economy provided few high-paying and many low-paying jobs, a structure that exacerbates social inequality. At the same time, an unprecedented number of minorities had begun to enter what had been previously almost exclusively "white" institutions, signaling the end of white dominance within them. A backlash ensued, met by newcomers' demands for the transformation of these institutions. Racial and ethnic tension in the United States increased.

Minorities entering U.S. institutions played a critical role in demanding their transformation. But their demands were met with hostility, even by traditional allies, such as supporters of the civil rights movement of the 1960s. In universities, for example, white progressives were insulted when the African-Americans and Latinos they had helped bring into the academy demanded radical change. For many progressive whites, the question of equality was defined as one of representation, not necessarily sharing power with minorities.

In some universities, administrators embraced the rhetoric of multiculturalism. New faculty members were allowed to create courses and even programs devoted to the study of minority communities, although these generally were not funded at the same level as traditional programs. Ethnic studies often have been marginalized or exoticized, with universities and other institutions packaging courses about minorities, women, and gays under the banner of multiculturalism. Instead of mainstreaming these topics, this process marginalized these communities further. The reduction of "otherness" to an exotic location in academia tended to distort the discourse. Instead of deconstructing "otherness," such strategies reinforced it.

Furthermore, conservatives unleashed a backlash against diversifying the public sphere. Many conservative intellectuals have questioned whether democratic societies could have a multicultural public space. For example, Richard Bernstein, an early promoter of the phrase "*politically correct*," maintains that there should be a separation between private identities, which can be diverse, and the public realm.[28] In part, he bases his vision on the need to keep religion and ethnicity out of the public space, noting that historically (as in the European Jewish experience) when religion has entered the public discourse, it has been used for repressive purposes.

Arthur Schlesinger, Jr., views the multicultural movement as dangerous to democracy because it sabotages the unity of the nation. In *The Disuniting of America*,[29] he presents the argument that democracies need a uniform public identity in order to grant equal status to all citizens. But while in theory all individuals are equal, citizens who were not white, rich, and male historically have not had equal access to the political system. Schlesinger's vision of the United States thus ignores the fact that many communities were never considered part of the unified whole. Similar arguments have been made in Great Britain by John Rex,[30] who sees multiculturalism as incompatible with a democratic state. Like Schlesinger, he equates the public persona to the "citizen," who in theory should have a shared cultural identity, and calls for "privatization" of other aspects of identity.

For proponents of the idea that citizens should share a cultural identity, the basic unit of politics is, again, the nation-state: the public persona is defined as a citizen of a specific nation-state. Individuals who are not born in the nation-state where they reside may or may not be eligible to obtain the status and protections of citizenship.[31]

Many opponents of the multicultural movement also call for the closing of borders, arguing that increased immigration poses a threat to a culturally unified nation. The same forces call for English-only policies. What began as a conservative intellectual backlash in the 1980s found expression at the voting booth a few years later. In the early 1990s, candidates from both the Republican and Democratic parties ran successfully on anti-immigrant platforms with distinctly racial and ethnic overtones. Only mayors of large urban areas like Chicago and New York spoke up in defense of immigrants. In these cities, the undocumented population included significant numbers of European immigrants.

Transnational Cultural and Political Identities

The alternative to the notion of a culturally homogeneous public space confined within the border of a nation-state is the multicultural paradigm. In this paradigm, the public space can accommodate many cultures; the teaching of a variety of cultures and languages is encouraged and it is recognized that the imposition of any one culture oppresses the others. Even so, the multicultural paradigm in its first instance proposed a transformation of the public space within the confines of the nation-state, leaving unchallenged the notion of the nation-state itself.

Increased worldwide immigration coupled with ease of transportation has brought people into more direct contact with multiple cultures. In addition, rapid changes in communications and transportation have contributed to a global economic transformation. Political institutions thus far have resisted these changes. Nonetheless, paradigmatic changes in the definition of identity and the resulting vision of politics are taking place.

With increased contact between people and cultures, we may be witnessing the rise of transnational identities. Such identities are likely to be more visible in communities where people have crossed many borders. Diaspora communities where people are grounded in multiple cultures also produce hybrid identities.[32] The notion of a transnational or hybrid identity presents an interesting personal and political vision for diaspora communities. It proposes not only that communities be transformed, but that their host *and* home countries undergo transformation as well. Both home and host countries are often leery of these propositions.[33] This proposition would also encourage a political hybridity that expands not only the objects of politics, but the forms as well.[34] A transnational framework that accepts hybrid cultural formations brings to the forefront questions of what is home and what is exile. It also creates what others have called a "third space" beyond the confines of any one nation-state.[35]

Such a transnational framework also raises the problem of political bi-focality. Purnima Mankekar, for instance, asks "how we conceive of a political space that enables us to subvert the binaries of homeland and diaspora, while simultaneously allowing us to build alliances with struggles for social justices in both places?"[36] Throughout the 1900s, various immigrant communities have participated in both home and host country politics. Sometimes homeland issues have taken priority, while at other times host country problems have dominated the agenda. The contestation of power has crossed borders. The Southwest Voter Registration and Education Project has struggled with this dilemma for years. On questions involving the encroachment of U.S. foreign policy on Mexico and Central America, it has been an ally of the Mexican government; on questions of human rights, it often has challenged that government. In the Southwest, the project's ongoing work to increase voter registration and mobilize Chicano voters has often pitted it against local power structures.

The expansion of the political space to include multiple states suggests that the concept of a citizen bound to a single nation-state also must change. A transnational political identity, or citizenship, would better accommodate the rights of individuals who for a myriad of reasons cross the frontiers of multiple nation-states and whose lives are affected by decisions made by more than one state.

This discussion raises enduring dilemmas. For one, the realm of the political is still organized along the lines of nation-states, and within the international order, some nation-states are more powerful than others. This means that discussion of a global society or a global notion of rights emerging from more powerful nation-states can be read as another form of domination. Nonetheless, regardless of how the language of "globalness" is used by those in power, the reality is that there are human rights that do cross the borders of nation-states, and these need to be protected. Against the backdrop of an interconnected world, it would be shortsighted simply to dismiss any discussion of global rights as impossible to conceptualize. Such a discussion, of course, will involve difficult questions. What is the balance between specific national or ethnic rights and global human rights? Who determines the limits of such rights? Through what institutions are these issues to be discussed and decided upon?

What is clear is that, today, much of what is done in one part of the world affects other parts of it. Because of their transnational experiences, diaspora communities have long struggled against the restrictions of "one identity, one state." The reconceptualization of identity and power emerging from these communities is an important point of departure for a broader discussion that challenges the nature and exercise of power in this century.

Notes

1. Frank Bonilla, "Migrants, Citizenship, and Social Pacts," in Edwin Meléndez and Edgardo Meléndez, eds., *Colonial Dilemma: Critical Perspectives on Contemporary Puerto Rico* (Boston: South End Press, 1993), 181–88.

2. Douglas B. Klusmeyer, "Aliens, Immigrants and Citizens: The Politics of Inclusion in the Federal Republic of Germany," *Daedalus* 122 (Summer 1993): 84.

3. See, for instance, essays in Laurence Halley, ed., *Ancient Affections: Ethnic Groups and Foreign Policy* (New York: Praeger, 1985); Abdul Aziz Said, *Ethnicity and U.S. Foreign Policy* (New York: Praeger, 1977); Mohammed E. Ahrari, *Ethnic Groups and U.S. Foreign Policy* (New York: Greenwood, 1982).

4. Mervin Holli and Peter d'A. Jones, eds., *Ethnic Chicago* (Grand Rapids: William B. Eerdmans, 1977).

5. See, for example, Rodolfo de la Garza, Robert Winckle, and Jerry Polinard, "Ethnicity and Policy: The Mexican American Perspective," in Chris F. García, ed., *Latinos and the Political System* (Notre Dame, IN: University of Notre Dame, 1988), 426–41.

6. Yossi Shain, *The Frontiers of Loyalty: Political Exiles in the Age of Nation-States* (Middletown: Wellesley University Press, 1992).

7. Juan Gómez-Quiñonez, "On Culture," *Revista Chicano-Riqueña* (1977): 29–46.

8. See Juan Gómez-Quiñonez, "Notes on the Interpretation of the Relations between the Mexican Community in the United States and Mexico," Carlos Vasquez and Manuel Garcia y Griego, eds., *Mexican/U.S. Relations: Conflict and Convergence* and Carlos Zazueta, "Mexican Political Actors in the United States and Mexico: Historical and Political Contexts of a Dialogue," in Carlos Vasquez and Manuel Garcia y Griego, eds., *Mexican/U.S. Relations: Conflict and Convergence* (Los Angeles: University of California Press, 1983), 417–83.

9. See the work of Tomas Almaguer, "Toward a Study of Chicano Colonialism," in *Aztlán: Chicano Journal of Social Sciences and the Arts* 1 (Fall 1970): 7–21; Rudy Acuna, *Occupied America: A History of Chicanos* (New York: Harper and Row, 1988); and Mario Barrera, *Race and Class in the Southwest* (Notre Dame, IN: University of Notre Dame Press, 1979).

10. History Task Force of the *Centro de Estudios Puertorriqueños*, *Labor Migration Under Capitalism: The Puerto Rican Experience* (New York: Monthly Review Press, 1979); Manuel Maldonado-Dennis, *The Emigration Dialectic: Puerto Rico and the USA* (New York: International, 1980).

11. See for example, Lourdes Casal, "Cubans in the United States," in Martin Weinstein, ed., *Revolutionary Cuba in the World Arena* (Philadelphia: Institute for the Study of Human Issues, 1979); Lourdes Argüelles, "Cuban Miami: The Roots, Development and Everyday Life of an Émigré Enclave in the National Security State," *Contemporary Marxism* 5 (Summer 1982): 27–44.

12. Carlos Forment, "Caribbean Geopolitics and Foreign State-Sponsored Movements: The Case of Cuban Exile Militancy 1959–1979," in Miren Uriarte-Gastón and Jorge Canas, eds., *Cubans in the United States* (Boston: Center for the Study of the Cuban Community, 1984), 65–102.

13. Marisa Alicea, "Dual Home Bases: A Reconceptualization of Puerto Rican Migration," *Latino Studies Journal* 1, no. 3 (1990): 78–98.

14. Félix Padilla, *Latino Consciousness: The Case of Mexican Americans and Puerto Ricans in Chicago* (Notre Dame, IN: University of Notre Dame Press, 1985).

15. Frank Bonilla, "Brother Can You Paradigm?" Inter-University Program on Latino Research, Milenio Series, 1997.

16. María de los Angeles Torres, "Latinos and U.S. Policies: Foreign Policy Toward Latin America," *Latino Studies Journal* 1 (September 1990): 3–23.

17. David Ayon and Ricardo Anzaldua Montoya, "Latinos and U.S. Policy," in Abraham F. Lowenthal, ed., *Latin America and the Caribbean Contemporary Record* (Baltimore: Johns Hopkins University Press, 1990).

18. Jesús Díaz, *Del exilio a la Patria* (La Habana: UNEAC, 1977).

19. María de los Angeles Torres, *"Encuentros y encontronazos: nación y exilio,"* *Diaspora: A Journal of Transnational Studies* 4 (1995): 211–39.

20. Angelo Falcón, "A Divided Nation: The Puerto Rican Diaspora in the United States and the Proposed Referendum," in Edwin Meléndez and Edgardo Meléndez, eds., *Colonial Dilemma: Critical Perspectives on Contemporary Puerto Rico* (Boston: South End Press, 1993), 173–80.

21. Gloria Anzaldúa, *Borderlands—La Frontera: The New Mestiza* (San Francisco: Spinster/Aunt Lute, 1987).

22. Cristina García, *Dreaming in Cuban* (New York: Knopf, 1992).

23. Rubén Martínez, *The Other Side: Fault Lines, Guerrilla Saints and the True Heart of Rock 'n' Roll* (New York: Verso, 1992).

24. Richard Rodríguez, *Hunger of Memory: The Education of Richard Rodriguez, an Autobiography* (Boston: D. R. Godine, 1981).

25. Gustavo Pérez-Firmat, *Life on the Hyphen: The Cuban-American Experience* (Austin: University of Texas Press, 1994).

26. Tato Laviera, *AmeRican* (Houston: Arte Public Press, 1985).

27. Madelin Camara, "The Third Option: Beyond the Border," in Ruth Behar, ed., *Bridges to Cuba* (Ann Arbor: University of Michigan Press, 1995).

28. Richard Bernstein, *Dictatorship of Virtue: Multiculturalism and the Battle for America's Future* (New York: Knopf, 1994).

29. Arthur M. Schlesinger, Jr., *The Disuniting of America: Reflections on a Multicultural Society* (New York: Norton, 1991).

30. John Rex, "Ethnic Identity and the Nation-State: The Political Sociology of Multi-Cultural Societies," *Social Identities* 1, no. 1 (1995): 21–34.

31. Milton Esman, "The Political Fallout of International Migration," *Diaspora: A Journal of Transnational Studies* 2 (1992): 3–38.

32. For an extensive study of transnational communities, see Linda Basch, Nina Glick Schiller, and Cristina Szanton Blanc, *Nations Unbound: Transnational Projects, PostColonial Predicaments and Deterritorialized Nation-States* (Amsterdam: Gordon and Breach, 1994). See also David Skidmore and Valerie M. Hudson, eds., *The Limits of State Autonomy: Societal Groups and Foreign Policy Formulation* (Boulder: Westview Press, 1993).

33. David Lipscomb, "Caught in a Strange Middle Ground: Contesting History in Salman Rushdie's *Midnight's Children*," *Diaspora: A Journal of Transnational Studies* 1 (1991): 163–90.

34. Ellen Dorsey, "Expanding the Foreign Policy Discourse: Transnational Social Movements and the Globalization of Citizenship," in David Skidmore and Valerie M. Hudson, eds., *The Limits of State Autonomy: Societal Groups and Foreign Policy Formulation* (Boulder: Westview Press, 1993), 237–67.

35. Homi Bhabha, "The Third Space," in Jonathan Rutherford, ed., *Identity, Community, Culture and Difference* (London: Lawrence & Wishart, 1990), 207–22.

36. Purnima Mankekar, "Reflections on Diasporic Identities: A Prolegomenon to an Analysis of Political Bifocality," *Diaspora: A Journal of Transnational Studies* 3 (1994): 366.

* * *

Questions

1. Does a democracy need both cultural and political pluralism? Why?
2. Can a state or its people (or you?) overcome the fear that some of its citizens may identify with a culture from another country?
3. Regarding multiple political identities: Is it possible to have one political identity that encompasses two different countries? Or does this imply two political identities? Why does this issue arise among some people and not others?
4. What is the balance between specific national or ethnic rights and global human rights?
5. Through what institutions and/or individuals are the definition and implementation of such rights determined?

~

CHAPTER TWENTY-SIX

"Aquí estamos y no nos vamos!":
Global Capital and Immigrant Rights
William I. Robinson

In this article Robinson provides a clear and comprehensive explanation of the role that Latinos/as play in the immigration debate in the United States at the start of the new millennium. In doing so, he clarifies and illustrates many of the themes such as the insidious workings of power relations, the struggle between the people and the nation-state/government, and the need for economic democracy. Furthermore, he places the immigration issue in the context of an emerging struggle between the new structures of global capitalism and the transnational immigrant working class it creates. [Note: This article is reproduced, with English spellings and grammar modified to American English.]

Although this new stage of global capitalism is indeed a new phenomenon, this preface to Robinson's text is designed to provide a historical context and also to flesh out the ethical implications of this political economic system. In a way, the immigration issue in the United States is both easy and impossible to understand. It is easy because we know that a sustainable regional, continental economic democracy similar to the one being developed in the European Union would go a long way to address if not solve the problem. On the contrary, it is impossible because, so far, any attempt to solve it smashes against an absurd wall of contradictory interests.

For those who are familiar with the history of immigration, the current debate evokes phrases like déjà vu and the plot of the film *Groundhog Day* where the main character wakes up to a day that repeats what happened the day before. Not surprisingly, recent publications have titles such as *Border*

Games[1] and "The Immigration Charade"[2] and we will refer to these in a moment. For a historical context, however, we need to refer to the work of the immigration scholar Jorge A. Bustamante.[3] He quotes the following words from John Garner, Vice-President of the United State in 1926.

> Mr. Chairman, here is the whole problem in the nutshell. Farming is not a profitable industry in this country, and, in order to make money out of this you have to have cheap labor . . . in order to allow land owners now to make a profit on their farms, they want to get the cheapest labor they can find, and if they can get the Mexican labor it enables them to make a profit. That is the way it is along the border and I imagine that it's the way it is anywhere else.[4]

The significance of this date is that it is *two years after the establishment of the border patrol*, which started the differentiation between legal and illegal immigrants (a distinction that has expanded into citizens and immigrants and that Robinson points out as a key factor in the exploitation of labor worldwide).

Bustamante adds that over a quarter of a century later, in 1953, the same attitude is expressed by Senator McCarran:

> Senator (Elender) I think you will agree with me that on this side of the border there is a desire for these wetbacks . . . Last year when we had the Appropriations Bill up, the item that might have prevented them from coming over to some extent, was stricken from the bill . . .we might just as well face this thing realistically. The agricultural people, the farmer along the Mexican side of the border in California, in Arizona, in Texas . . . wants this help. They want this farm labor. They just cannot get along without it.[5]

As noted in part II, this constant economic "pull factor" that attracts Mexican immigrants changes into a political "push factor" when the U.S. economy or political expediency calls for the deportation of Mexicans (even if they are U.S. born American citizens such as the 1930 Repatriation Program, Operation Wetback). In the 1990s, there have been legislative propositions such as 187 in California to deny health and education rights to undocumented and to require all social service personnel to turn them in. By 2006, a combination of the war on terrorism, the growth and visibility of the Latino/a population, and economic uncertainty, have led the U.S. Congress to discuss the possible deportation of 12 million undocumented people.

Professor Christopher Jencks believes that the core issue in what he calls "the immigration charade" is precisely the inability of the U.S. government to mediate effectively between these pull-push factors. This inability has generated distrust of the government and increased hostility toward immigrants. From Robinson's perspective, of course, it is not necessarily the government helplessness that is to blame. It is, rather, a logical position within the logic of global capitalism. In effect, Jencks admits that the "collapse of this year's [2007] bipartisan push for immigration reform suggests that ending the charade will be extremely hard."[6] Both of them agree with most observers, though, that this creates a volatile situation in which civil society breaks down into warring factions.

The brutal implication of this charade is that human bodies are exchanged for short-term political posturing and image crafting. In *Border Games: Policing the U.S.-Mexico Divide*, for example, Peter Andreas observes that the dominant border narrative suffers from "historical amnesia" and that border policing is more a "ritualistic performance" then it is a deterrence.

> My narrative of policing the U.S.-Mexico border is to a significant extent *a story about the political success of flawed and failing policies*. Yet, as I have also stressed, the enforcement buildup had done far more than simply project an appearance of "doing something," for the collateral damage has been substantial. In the case of U.S. immigration control, the death toll along the border continues to rise as migrants are pushed to attempt entry in more difficult and hazardous terrain away from urban areas. (Emphasis mine)[7]

Since Andreas published this in the year 2000, border-crossing deaths have reached obscene levels. Between 1990 and 1999, there were 125 deaths, compared to 802 from 2000 to 2005. Since 1994, when the Southwest Border Strategy was implemented under the Clinton administration, 4,500 Mexicans have died crossing the border. This figure does not include immigrants from Central America and other regions.[8]

From this sobering perspective, the immigration debate is an abstraction that feeds on the human beings who often pay with their lives for the consequences of misguided policies. This poses a serious ethical challenge to all of us. In effect, this sadistic merry-go-round of immigration is reminiscent of "The Ones Who Walk Away from Omelas." This is the story of a Utopian society whose survival depends on the existence of a child who is locked in a small room and mistreated. Although all of the citizens of Omelas are aware of the child's situation, most of them accept that their happiness is dependent on the child's "abominable misery." Sometimes, however, a few people, after visiting the child and seeing the deplorable conditions under which it lives, leave Omelas forever.[9]

If the child in the Omelas represents the illegal immigrants, and if we want to know what kind of "abominable misery" they are exposed to, Luis

Urrea in his book *Devil's Highway* describes what death from "exposure" really entails:

> Your heart pumps harder and harder to get fluid and oxygen to your organs. Empty vessels within you collapse. Your sweat runs out. . . . Your temperature redlines—you hit 105, 106, 108 degrees. Your body panics and dilated all blood capillaries near the surface, hoping to flood your skin with blood to cool it off. You blush. Your eyes turn red: blood vessels burst, and later, the tissue of the whites literally cooks until it goes pink, then a well-done crimson. Your skin gets terribly sensitive. It hurts, it burns. Your nerves flame. Your blood heats under your skin. Clothing feels like sandpaper. Some walkers at this point strip nude. Originally, BORSTAR rescuers thought this stripping was a delirious panic, an attempt to cool off at the last minute. But often, the clothing was eerily neat, carefully folded and left in nice little piles beside the corpses. They realized the walkers couldn't stand their nerve endings being chafed by their clothes.
>
> Once they're naked, they're surely hallucinating. They dig burrows in the soil, apparently thinking they'll escape the sun. Once underground, of course, they bake like a pig at a luau. Some dive into sand, thinking it's water, and they swim in it until they pass out. They choke to death, their throats filled with rocks and dirt. Cutters can only assume they think they're drinking water. Your muscles, lacking water, feed on themselves. They break down and start to rot. Once rotting in you, they dump rafts of dying cells into your already sludgy bloodstream. Proteins are peeling off your dying muscles. Chunks of cooked meat are falling out of your organs, to clog your other organs. The system closes down in a series. Your kidneys, your bladder, your heart. They jam shut. Stop. Your brain sparks. Out. You're gone.[10]

Notes and Suggestions for Further Research

1. Peter Andreas, *Border Games: Policing the U.S.-Mexico Divide* (Ithaca, NY: Cornell University Press, 2000).

2. Christopher Jencks, "The Immigration Charade," *New York Review of Books* (September 27, 2007).

3. Jorge A. Bustamante, "The Historical Context of Undocumented Mexican Immigration to the United States," *Aztlán-International Journal of Chicano Studies Research* 3 no. 2 (1972). Reprinted in Jorge José Ríos-Bustamante, ed., *Immigration and Public Policy: Human Rights for Undocumented Workers and their Families* (Los Angeles, California: UCLA Chicano Studies Center Publications, 1977.

4. Bustamante, "The Historical Context," 272.

5. Bustamante, "The Historical Context," 273.

6. Jencks, "The Immigration Charade," 52.

7. Peter Andreas, *Border Games: Policing the U.S.-Mexico Divide* (Ithaca, NY: Cornell University Press, 2000), 142–48 passim.

8. Shannon Jones, "US: More immigrant deaths in desert border crossings," July 18, 2007 at www.wsws.org/articles/2007/jul2007/immi-j18.shtml, accessed February 1, 2008.

9. Ursula K. LeGuin, *The Wind's Twelve Quarters* (New York: Harper, 1975). See also www.bookrags.com/The_Ones_Who_Walk_Away_From_Omelas

10. onto, (sic) "US border policy increases migrant deaths 20-fold in Arizona desert," March 1, 2007 at http://deletetheborder.org/node/2016/print, accessed February 3, 2008.

*   *   *

Abstract: The recent mass demonstrations by millions of Latino immigrant workers in the [United States], against planned legislation that could lead to the criminalization and deportation of, literally, millions of workers shook the [George W.] Bush administration and took commentators by surprise. The upsurge has been dubbed the new civil rights movement. It marks a new stage in globalization and the phenomenon of mass, transnational migration that such globalization has engendered. Unprecedented in size and scope, the movement challenges the structural changes bound up with capitalist globalization and points to the necessity of transnational popular and democratic struggles against it.

*   *   *

A specter is haunting global capitalism—the specter of a transnational immigrant workers' uprising. An immigrant rights movement is spreading around the world, spearheaded by Latino immigrants in the [United States], who have launched an all-out fight-back against the repression, exploitation, and racism they routinely face with a series of unparalleled strikes and demonstrations. The immediate message of immigrants and their allies in the United States is clear, with marchers shouting: *"aquí estamos y no nos vamos"* (we're here and we're not leaving!). However, beyond immediate demands, the emerging movement challenges the structural changes bound up with capitalist globalization that have generated an upsurge in global labor migration, thrown up a new global working class, and placed that working class in increasingly direct confrontation with transnational capital.

The U.S. mobilizations began when over half a million immigrants and their supporters took to the streets in Chicago on March 10, 2006. It was the largest single protest in that city's history. Following the Chicago action, rolling strikes and protests spread to other cities, large and small, organized through expanding networks of churches, immigrant clubs and rights groups, community associations, Spanish-language and progressive media, trade unions and social justice organizations. Millions came out on March 25 for a "national day of action." Between one and two million people demonstrated in Los Angeles—the single biggest public protest in the city's history—and millions more followed suit in Chicago, New York, Atlanta, Washington DC, Phoenix, Dallas, Houston, Tucson, Denver, and dozens of other cities. Again, on April 10, millions heeded the call for another day of protest. In addition, hundreds of thousands of high school students in Los Angeles and around the country staged walk-outs in support of their families and communities, braving police repression and legal sanctions.

Then on the first of May, International Workers' Day, trade unionists and social justice activists joined immigrants in "The Great American Boycott 2006/A Day Without an Immigrant." Millions—perhaps tens of millions—in over 200 cities from across the country skipped work and school, commercial activity, and daily routines in order to participate in a national boycott, general strike, rallies and symbolic actions. The May 1 action was a resounding success. Hundreds of local communities in the South, Midwest, Northwest, and elsewhere, far away from the "gateway cities" where Latino populations are concentrated, experienced mass public mobilizations that placed them on the political map. Agribusiness in the California and Florida heartlands—nearly 100 percent dependent on immigrant labor—came to a standstill, leaving supermarket produce shelves empty for the next several days. In the landscaping industry, nine out of ten workers boycotted work, according to the American Nursery and Landscape Association. The construction industry suffered major disruptions. Latino truckers who move 70 percent of the goods in Los Angeles ports did not work. Care-giver referral agencies in major cities saw a sharp increase in calls from parents who needed last-minute nannies or baby-sitters. In order to avoid a total shutdown of the casino mecca in Las Vegas—highly dependent on immigrant labor—casino owners were forced to set up tables in employee lunch-rooms and hold meetings to allow their workers to circulate petitions in favor of immigrant demands. International commerce between Mexico and the United States ground to a temporary halt as protesters closed Tijuana, Juarez-El Paso, and several other crossings along the 2,000-mile border.[1]

These protests have no precedent in the history of the [United States]. The immediate trigger was the passage in mid-March by the House of Representatives of HR4437, a bill introduced by Republican representative James Sensenbrenner with broad support from the anti-immigrant lobby. This draconian bill would criminalize undocumented immigrants by making it a felony to be in the [United States] without documentation. It also stipulated the construction of the first 700 miles of a militarized wall between Mexico and the [United States] and would double the size of the U.S. border patrol. And it would apply criminal sanctions against anyone who provided assistance to undocumented immigrants, including churches, humanitarian groups, and social service agencies.

Following its passage by the House, bill HR4437 became stalled in the Senate. Democrat Ted Kennedy and Republican John McCain cosponsored a "compromise" bill that would have removed the criminalization clause in HR4437 and provided a limited plan for amnesty for some of the undocumented. It would have allowed those who could prove they have resided in the [United States] for at least five years to apply for residency and later citizenship. Those residing in the [United States] for two to five years would have been required to return home and then apply through U.S. embassies for temporary "guest worker" permits. Those who could not demonstrate that they had been in the [United States] for two years would be deported. Even this compromise bill would have resulted in massive deportations and heightened control over all immigrants. Yet it was eventually jettisoned because of Republican opposition, so that by late April the whole legislative process had become stalled. In May, the Senate renewed debate on the matter and seemed to be moving toward consensus based on tougher enforcement and limited legalization, although at the time of writing (late May 2006) it appeared the legislative process could drag on until after the November 2006 congressional elections.

However, the wave of protest goes well beyond HR4437. It represents the unleashing of pent-up anger and repudiation of what has been deepening exploitation and an escalation of anti-immigrant repression and racism. Immigrants have been subject to every imaginable abuse in recent years. Twice in the state of California they have been denied the right to acquire drivers' licenses. This means that they must rely on inadequate or nonexistent public transportation or risk driving illegally; more significantly, the drivers' license is often the only form of legal documentation for such essential transactions as cashing checks or renting an apartment. The U.S.-Mexico border has been increasingly militarized and thousands of immigrants have died crossing the frontier. Anti-immigrant hate groups are on the rise. The [Federal Bureau of Investigation] FBI has reported more than 2,500 hate crimes against Latinos in the [United States] since 2000. Blatantly racist public discourse that, only a few years ago, would have been considered extreme has become increasingly mainstreamed and aired in the mass media.

More ominously, the paramilitary organization Minutemen, a modern day Latino-hating version of the Ku Klux Klan, has spread from its place of origin along the U.S.-Mexican border in Arizona and California to other parts of the country. Minutemen claim they must "secure the border" in the face of inadequate state-sponsored control. Their discourse, beyond racist, is neo-fascist. Some have even been filmed sporting T-shirts with the emblem "Kill a Mexican Today?" and others have organized for-profit "human safaris" in the desert. One video game discovered recently circulating on the Internet, "Border Patrol," lets players shoot at Mexican immigrants as they try to cross the border into the [United States]. Players are told to target one of three immigrant groups, all portrayed in a negative, stereotypical way, as the figures rush past a sign that reads "Welcome to the United States." The immigrants are caricatured as bandolier-wearing "Mexican nationalists," tattooed "drug smugglers" and pregnant "breeders" who spring across with their children in tow.

Minutemen clubs have been sponsored by right-wing organizers, wealthy ranchers, businessmen, and politicians. But their social base is drawn from those formerly privileged sectors of the white working class that have been "flexibilized" and displaced by economic restructuring, the deregulation of labor and global capital flight. These sectors now scapegoat immigrants—with official encouragement—as the source of their insecurity and downward mobility.

The immigrant mobilizations have seriously threatened ruling groups. In the wake of the recent mobilizations, the Bush administration stepped up raids, deportations, and other enforcement measures in a series of highly publicized mass arrests of undocumented immigrants and their employers, intended to intimidate the movement. In April 2006 it was revealed that KBR, a subsidiary of Halliburton—Vice-President Dick Cheney's former company, which has close ties to the Pentagon and is a major contractor in the Iraq war—won a $385 million contract to build large-scale immigrant detention centers in case of an "emergency influx" of immigrants.

Latino immigration to the [United States] is part of a worldwide upsurge in transnational migration generated by the forces of capitalist globalization. Immigrant labor worldwide is conservatively estimated at over 200 million, according to [United Nations] data.[2] Some 30 million are in the [United States], with at least 20 million of them from Latin America. Of these 20 million, some 11 to 12 million are undocumented (south and east Asia are also significant contributors to the undocumented population), although it must be stressed that these figures are low-end estimates.[3] The [United States] is by far the largest immigrant-importing country, but the phenomenon is global. Racist attacks, scapegoating, and state-sponsored repressive controls over immigrants are rising in many countries around the world, as is the fightback among immigrant workers wherever they are found. Parallel to the

U.S. events, for instance, the French government introduced a bill that would apply tough new controls over immigrants and roll back their rights. In response, some 30,000 immigrants and their supporters took to the streets in Paris on May 13, 2006 to demand the bill's repeal.

The Global Circulation of Immigrant Labor

The age of globalization is also an age of unprecedented transnational migration.[4] The corollary to an integrated global economy is the rise of a truly global—although highly segmented—labor market. It is a global labor market because, despite formal nation-state restrictions on the free worldwide movement of labor, surplus labor in any part of the world is now recruited and redeployed through numerous mechanisms to where capital is in need of it and because workers themselves undertake worldwide migration, even in the face of the adverse migratory conditions.

Central to capitalism is securing a politically and economically suitable labor supply, and at the core of all class societies is the control over labor and disposal of the products of labor. But the linkage between the securing of labor and territoriality is changing under globalization. As labor becomes "free" in every corner of the globe, capital has vast new opportunities for mobilizing labor power where and when required. National labor pools are merging into a single global labor pool that services global capitalism. The transnational circulation of capital induces the transnational circulation of labor. This circulation of labor becomes incorporated into the process of restructuring the world economy. It is a mechanism for the provision of labor to transnationalized circuits of accumulation and constitutes a structural feature of the global system.

While the need to mix labor with capital at diverse points along global production chains induces population movements, there are sub-processes that shape the character and direction of such migration. At the structural level, the uprooting of communities by the capitalist break-up of local economies creates surplus populations and is a powerful push factor in out-migration, while labor shortages in more economically advanced areas is a pull factor that attracts displaced peoples. At a behavioral level, migration and wage remittances become a family survival strategy, made possible by the demand for labor abroad and made increasingly viable by the fluid conditions and integrated infrastructures of globalization.

In one sense, the South penetrates the North with the dramatic expansion of immigrant labor. But transnational migratory flows are not unidirectional from South to North and the phenomenon is best seen in global capitalist rather than North-South terms. Migrant workers are becoming a general category of super-exploitable labor drawn from globally dispersed labor reserves into similarly globally dispersed nodes of accumulation. To the extent that these nodes experience labor shortages—skilled or unskilled—they become magnets for transnational labor flows, often encouraged or even organized by both sending and receiving countries and regions.

Labor-short Middle Eastern countries, for instance, have programs for the importation (and careful control) of labor from throughout south and east Asia and north Africa. The Philippine state has become a veritable labor recruitment agency for the global economy, organizing the export of its citizens to over a hundred countries in Asia, the Middle East, Europe, North America, and elsewhere. Greeks migrate to Germany and the [United States], while Albanians migrate to Greece. South Africans move to Australia and England, while Malawians, Mozambicans and Zimbabweans work in South. African mines and the service industry. Malaysia imports Indonesian labor, while Thailand imports workers from Laos and Myanmar and, in turn, sends labor to Malaysia, Singapore, Japan, and elsewhere. In Latin America, Costa Rica is a major importer of Nicaraguan labor, Venezuela has historically imported large amounts of Colombian labor, the Southern Cone draws on several million emigrant Andean workers and an estimated 500,000 to 800,000 Haitians live in the Dominican Republic, where they cut sugar cane, harvest crops, and work in the *maquiladoras* under the same labor market segmentation, political disenfranchisement and repression that immigrant workers face in the United States and in most labor-importing countries.

The division of the global working class into "citizen" and "noncitizen" labor is a major new axis of inequality worldwide, further complicating the well-known gendered and racialized hierarchies among labor, and facilitating new forms of repressive and authoritarian social control over working classes. In an apparent contradiction, capital and goods move freely across national borders in the new global economy but labor cannot and its movement is subject to heightened state controls. The global labor supply is, in the main, no longer coerced (subject to extra-economic compulsion) due to the ability of the universalized market to exercise strictly economic discipline, but its movement is juridically controlled. This control is a central determinant in the worldwide correlation of forces between global capital and global labor.

The immigrant is a juridical creation inserted into real social relations. States create "immigrant labor" as distinct categories of labor in relation to capital. While the generalization of the labor market emerging from the consolidation of the global capitalist economy creates the conditions for global migrations as a world-level labor supply system, the maintenance and strengthening of state controls over transnational labor creates the conditions for immigrant labor as a distinct category of labor. The creation of these distinct categories (immigrant labor) becomes central to the global capitalist economy, replacing earlier direct colonial and racial caste controls over labor worldwide.

But why is this juridical category of immigrant labor reproduced under globalization? Labor migration and geographic shifts in production are alternative forms for capitalists to achieve an optimal mix of their capital with labor. State controls are often intended not to prevent but to control the transnational movement of labor. A free flow of labor would exert an equalizing influence on wages across borders whereas state controls help reproduce such differentials. Eliminating the wage differential between regions would cancel the advantages that capital accrues from disposing of labor pools worldwide subject to different wage levels and would strengthen labor worldwide in relation to capital. In addition, the use of immigrant labor allows receiving countries to separate reproduction and maintenance of labor, and therefore to "externalize" the costs of social reproduction. In other words, the new transnational migration helps capital to dispose of the need to pay for the reproduction of labor power. The interstate system thus acts as a condition for the structural power of globally mobile transnational capital over labor that is transnational in actual content and character but subjected to different institutional arrangements under the direct control of national states.

The migrant labor phenomenon will continue to expand along with global capitalism. Just as capitalism has no control over its implacable expansion as a system, it cannot do away in its new globalist stage with transnational labor. But if global capital needs the labor power of transnational migrants, this labor power belongs to human beings who must be tightly controlled, given the special oppression and dehumanization involved in extracting their labor power as noncitizen immigrant labor. To return to the situation in the [United States], the immigrant issue presents a contradiction for political and economic elites: from the vantage points of dominant group interests, the dilemma is how to deal with the new "barbarians" at Rome's door.

Latino immigrants have massively swelled the lower rungs of the U.S. workforce. They provide almost all farm labor and much of the labor for hotels, restaurants, construction, janitorial and house cleaning, child care, gardening and landscaping, delivery, meat and poultry packing, retail, and so on. Yet dominant groups fear a rising tide of Latino immigrants will lead to a loss of cultural and political control, becoming a source of counterhegemony and instability, as immigrant labor in Paris showed itself to be in the late 2005 uprising there against racism and marginality.

Employers do not want to do away with Latino immigration. To the contrary, they want to sustain a vast exploitable labor pool that exists under precarious conditions, that does not enjoy the civil, political, and labor rights of citizens and that is disposable through deportation. It is the condition of deportability that they wish to create or preserve, since that condition assures the ability to super-exploit with impunity and to dispose of this labor without consequences should it become unruly or unnecessary. The Bush administration opposed HR4437 not because it was in favor of immigrant rights but because it had to play a balancing act by finding a formula for a stable supply of cheap labor to employers with, at the same time, greater state control over immigrants.

The Bush White House proposed a "guest worker" program that would rule out legalization for undocumented immigrants, force them to return to their home countries and apply for temporary work visas, and implement tough new border security measures. There is a long history of such guest worker schemes going back to the Bracero program, which brought millions of Mexican workers to the [United States] during the labor shortages of the Second World War, only to deport them once native workers had become available again. Similar guest worker programs are in effect in several European countries and other labor-importing states around the world.

The contradictions of "immigrant policy reform" became apparent in the days leading up to the May 1 action, when major capitalist groups dependent on immigrant labor—especially in the agricultural, food processing, landscaping, construction, and other service sectors—came out in support of legalization for the undocumented. Such transnational agro-industrial giants as Cargill, Swift and Co., Perdue Farms, Tyson Foods, and Goya Foods, for instance, closed down many of their meat-packing and food processing plants and gave workers the day off.

Neoliberalism in Latin America

If capital's need for cheap, malleable and deportable labor in the centers of the global economy is the main "'pull factor" inducing Latino immigration to the [United States], the "push factor" is the devastation left by two decades of neoliberalism in Latin America. Capitalist globalization-structural adjustment, free trade agreements, privatizations, the contraction of public employment and credits, the break-up of communal lands and so forth, along with the political crises these measures have generated—has imploded thousands of communities in Latin America and unleashed a wave of migration, from rural to urban areas and to other countries, that can only be analogous to the mass uprooting and migration that generally takes place in the wake of war.

Just as capital does not stay put in the place it accumulates, neither do wages stay put. The flip side of the intense upsurge in transnational migration is the reverse flow of remittances by migrant workers in the global economy to their country and region of origin. Officially recorded international remittances increased astonishingly, from a mere $57 million in 1970 to $216 billion in 2005, according to World Bank data. This amount was higher than capital market flows and official development assistance combined, and nearly equaled the total amount of world FDI (foreign direct investment) in 2004. Close to one billion people, or one in every six on the planet, may receive some support from the global flow of remittances, according to senior World Bank economist Dilip Ratha.[5] Remittances have become an economic mainstay for an increasing number of countries. Most of the world's regions, including Africa, Asia, Latin America, and southern and eastern Europe report major remittance inflows.

Remittances redistribute income worldwide in a literal or geographic sense but not in the actual sense of redistribution, meaning a transfer of some added portion of the surplus from capital to labor, since they constitute not additional earnings but the separation of the site where wages are earned from the site of wage-generated consumption. What is taking place is a historically unprecedented separation of the point of production from the point of social reproduction. The former can take place in one part of the world and generate the value—then remitted—for social reproduction of labor in another part of the world. This is an emergent structural feature of the global system, in which the site of labor power and of its reproduction have been transnationally dispersed.

Transnational Latino migration has led to an enormous increase in remittances from Latino ethnic labor abroad to extended kinship networks in Latin America. Latin American workers abroad sent home some $57 billion in 2005, according to the Inter-American Development Bank.[6] These remittances were the number one source of foreign exchange for the Dominican Republic, El Salvador, Guatemala, Guyana, Haiti, Honduras, Jamaica, and Nicaragua and the second most important source for Belize, Bolivia, Colombia, Ecuador, Paraguay, and Surinam according to the Bank. The $20 billion sent back in 2005 by an estimated 10 million Mexicans in the [United States] was more than the country's tourism receipts and was surpassed only by oil and *maquiladora* exports.

These remittances allow millions of Latin American families to survive by purchasing goods either imported from the world market or produced locally or by transnational capital. They allow for family survival at a time of crisis and adjustment, especially for the poorest sectors—safety nets that replace governments and fixed employment in the provision of economic security. Emigration and remittances also serve the political objective of pacification. The dramatic expansion of Latin American emigration to the [United States] from the 1980s onwards helped to dissipate social tensions and undermine labor and political opposition to prevailing regimes and institutions. Remittances help to offset macroeconomic imbalances, in some cases averting economic collapse, thereby shoring up the political conditions for an environment congenial to transnational capital.

Therefore, bound up with the immigrant debate in the [United States] is the entire political economy of global capitalism in the western hemisphere—the same political economy that is now being sharply contested throughout Latin America with the surge in mass popular struggles and the turn to the Left. The struggle for immigrant rights in the [United States] is thus part and parcel of this resistance to neoliberalism, intimately connected to the larger Latin American—and worldwide—struggle for social justice.

No wonder protests and boycotts took place throughout Latin America on May 1 in solidarity with Latino immigrants in the [United States]. But these actions were linked to local labor rights struggles and social movement demands. In Tijuana, Mexico, for example, *maquiladora* workers in that border city's in-bond industry marched on May 1 to demand higher wages, eight-hour shifts, an end to "abuses and despotism" in the *maquila* plants and an end to sexual harassment, the use of poison chemicals, and company unions. The workers also called for solidarity with the "Great American Boycott of 2006 on the other side of the border" and participated in a protest at the U.S. consulate in the city and at the main crossing, which shut down cross-border traffic for most of the day.

The Nature of Immigrant Struggles

Labor market transformations driven by capitalist globalization unleash what McMichael calls "the politics of global labor circulation"[7] and fuel, in labor-importing countries, new nativisms, waves of xenophobia and racism against immigrants. Shifting political coalitions scapegoat immigrants by promoting ethnic-based solidarities among middle classes, representatives of distinct fractions of capital and formerly privileged sectors among working classes (such as white ethnic workers in the [United States] and Europe) threatened by job loss, declining income and the other insecurities of economic restructuring. The long-term tendency seems to be toward a generalization of labor market conditions across borders, characterized by segmented structures under a regime of labor deregulation and racial, ethnic, and gender hierarchies.

In this regard, a major challenge confronting the movement in the [United States] is relations between the Latino and the Black communities. Historically, African Americans have swelled the lower rungs in the U.S. caste system. But, as African Americans fought for their civil and human rights in the 1960s and 1970s, they became organized, politicized, and radicalized. Black workers led trade union militancy. All this made them undesirable labor for capital—"undisciplined" and "noncompliant."

Starting in the 1980s, employers began to push out Black workers and massively recruit Latino immigrants, a move that coincided with deindustrialization and restructuring. Blacks moved from super-exploited to marginalized—subject to unemployment, cuts in social services, mass incarceration and heightened state repression—while Latino immigrant labor has become the new super-exploited sector. Employers and political elites in New Orleans, for instance, have apparently decided in the wake of Hurricane Katrina to replace that city's historically black working class with Latino immigrant labor. Whereas fifteen years ago no one saw a single Latino face in places such as Iowa or Tennessee, now Mexican, Central American, and other Latino workers are visible everywhere. If some African Americans have misdirected their anger over marginality at Latino immigrants, the black community has a legitimate grievance over the anti-black racism of many Latinos themselves, who often lack sensitivity to the historic plight and contemporary experience of blacks with racism, and are reticent to see them as natural allies. (Latinos often bring with them particular sets of racialized relations from their home countries.)[8]

White labor that historically enjoyed caste privileges within racially segmented labor markets has experienced downward mobility and heightened insecurity. These sectors of the working class feel the pinch of capitalist globalization and the transnationalization of formerly insulated local labor markets. Studies in the early 1990s, for example, found that, in addition to concentrations in "traditional" areas such as Los Angeles, Miami, Washington DC, Virginia, and Houston, Central American immigrants had formed clusters in the formal and informal service sectors in areas where, in the process of downward mobility, they had replaced "white ethnics," such as in suburban Long Island, the small towns of Iowa and North Carolina, in Silicon Valley, and in the northern and eastern suburbs of the San Francisco Bay Area.[9]

The loss of caste privileges for white sectors of the working class is problematic for political elites and state managers in the [United States], since legitimation and domination have historically been constructed through a white racial hegemonic bloc. Can such a bloc be sustained or renewed through a scapegoating of immigrant communities? In attempting to shape public discourse, the anti-immigrant lobby argues that immigrants "are a drain on the US economy." Yet, as the National Immigrant Solidarity Network points out, immigrants contribute $7 billion in social security a year. They earn $240 billion, report $90 billion, and are only reimbursed $5 billion in tax returns. They also contribute $25 billion more to the U.S. economy than they receive in health care and social services.[10] But this is a limited line of argument, since the larger issue is the incalculable trillions of dollars that immigrant labor generates in profits and revenue for capital, only a tiny proportion of which goes back to them in the form of wages.

Moreover, it has been demonstrated that there is no correlation between the unemployment rate among U.S. citizens and the rate of immigration. In fact, the unemployment rate has moved in cycles over the past twenty-five years and exhibits a comparatively lower rate during the most recent (2000–2005) influx of undocumented workers. Similarly, wage stagnation in the United States appeared, starting with the economic crisis of 1973 and has continued its steady march ever since, with no correlation to increases or decreases in the inflow of undocumented workers. Instead, downward mobility for most U.S. workers is positively correlated with the decline in union participation, the decline in labor conditions and the polarization of income and wealth that began with the restructuring crisis of the 1970s and accelerated the following decade as Reaganomics launched the neo-liberal counterrevolution).[11]

The larger backdrop here is transnational capital's attempt to forge post-Fordist, post-Keynesian capital-labor relations worldwide, based on flexibilization, deregulation and deunionization. [This means relations that go beyond the previous agreements among corporations, unions and government.] From the 1970s onward, capital began to abandon earlier reciprocities with labor, forged in the epoch of national corporate capitalism, precisely because the process of globalization allowed to it break free of nation state constraints. There has been a vast acceleration of the primitive accumulation of capital worldwide through globalization, a process in which millions have been wrenched from the means of production, proletarianized and thrown into a global labor market that transnational capital has been able to shape.[12] As capital assumed new power relative to labor with the onset of globalization, states shifted from reproducing Keynesian social structures of accumulation to servicing the general needs of the new patterns of global accumulation.

At the core of the emerging global social structure of accumulation is a new capital-labor relation based on alternative systems of labor control and diverse contingent categories of devalued labor—subcontracted, outsourced, casualized, informal, part-time, temp work, home-work, and so on—the essence of which is cheapening and disciplining labor, making it "flexible" and readily available for transnational capital in worldwide labor reserves. Workers in the global economy are themselves, under these flexible arrangements, increasingly treated as a subcontracted component rather than a fixture internal to employer organizations. These new class relations of global capitalism dissolve the notion of responsibility, however minimal, that governments have for their citizens or that employers have toward their employees.

Immigrant workers become the archetype of these new global class relations. They are a naked commodity, no longer embedded in relations of reciprocity rooted in social and political communities that have, historically, been institutionalized in nation states. Immigrant labor pools that can be super-exploited economically, marginalized and disenfranchised politically, driven into the shadows and deported when necessary are the very epitome of capital's naked domination in the age of global capitalism.

The immigrant rights movement in the [United States] is demanding full rights for all immigrants, including amnesty, worker protections, family reunification measures, a path to citizenship or permanent residency rather than a temporary guest worker program, an end to all attacks against immigrants and to the criminalization of immigrant communities. While some observers have billed the recent events as the birth of a new civil rights movement, clearly much more is at stake. In the larger picture, this goes beyond immediate demands; it challenges the class relations that are at the very core of global capitalism. The significance of the May 1 immigrant rights mobilization taking place on international workers' day—which has not been celebrated in the [United States] for nearly a century—was lost on no one.

In the age of globalization, the only hope of accumulating the social and political forces necessary to confront the global capitalist system is by transnationalizing popular, labor and democratic struggles. The immigrant rights movement is all of these—popular, pro-worker and democratic—and it is by definition transnational. In sum, the struggle for immigrant rights is at the cutting edge of the global working-class fight-back against capitalist globalization.

Notes and Suggestions for Further Research

1. For these details, and more, see, inter alia, summaries of press reports from around the United States compiled by *CIS-DC Info Digest* (Vol. 41, no. 17), "Tally of Plant Closings and Demonstrations," available by request at www.mutualaid.com .

2. Manuel Orozco, "Worker Remittances in an International Scope," *Working Paper* (Washington, DC, Inter-American Dialogue and Multilateral Investment Fund of the Inter-American Development Bank. March 2003), 1.

3. For this and more data and links to different academic and foundation reports and government census agencies, see the University of California at Santa Barbara website http://aad.english.ucsb.edu.

4. On migration and globalization. and more generally on capitalism and migration, see, among others, Peter Stalker, *Workers Without Frontiers* (Boulder: Lynne Riener, 2000); Robin Cohen, *The New Helots: Migrants in the International Division of labour* (Aldershot: Ashgate, 1987); Nigel Harris, *The New Untouchables: Immigration and the New World Worker* (London: I. B. Tauris, 1995); Stephen Castles and Mark J. Miller, *The Age of Migration: International Population Movements in the Modern World* (New York: Palgrave Macmillan, 1993); Lydia Potts, *The World Labor Market: A History of Migration* (London: Zed, 1990). For discussion of current topics and new directions in the sociology of migration, see Alejandro Portes, "Immigrant Theory for a New Century; Some Problems and Opportunities," *International Migration Review* 3, no. 4 (1997): 799–825. See also Alejandro Portes and Jozsef Borocz, "Contemporary Immigration: Theoretical Perspectives on Its Determinants and Modes of Incorporation," *International Migration Review* 23, no. 3, (1990): 606–30.

5. For these details, see Richard Boudreaux, "The New Foreign Aid: The Seeds of Promise," *Los Angeles Times* (14 April 2006), IA.

6. Inter-American Development Bank, *Remittances 2005: Promoting Financial Democracy* (Washington DC: IDB, 2006).

7. Philip McMichael, *Development and Social Change: A Global Perspective*, (Thousand Oaks, CA: Pine Forge Press, 1986), 189.

8. In a commentary observing that mainstream Black political leaders have been notably lukewarm to the immigrant rights movement. Keeanga-Yamahtta Taylor writes: "The displacement of Black workers is a real problem—but not a problem caused by displaced Mexican workers . . . if the state is allowed to criminalize the existence [of] immigrant workers this will only fan the flames of racism eventually consuming Blacks in a back draft of discrimination. How exactly does one tell the difference between a citizen and a non-citizen? Through a massive campaign of racial profiling, that's how . . . In fact, the entire working class has a stake in the success of the movement." She goes on to recall how California building owners and labor contractors replaced Black janitors with largely undocumented Latino immigrants in the 1980s. But after a successful Service Employees International Union drive in the "Justice for janitors" campaign of the late 1980s and 1990s, wages and benefits went up and the union's largely Latino members sought contractual language guaranteeing African Americans a percentage of work slots, See Taylor, "Life Ain't Been No Crystal Stair: Blacks, Latinos and the New Civil Rights Movement," *Counterpunch* (May 9, 2006), downloaded May 18, 2006, www.counterpunch.org/ taylor05082006.html.

9. See the special issue of *NACLA Report on the Americas*, "On the Line: Latinos on labor's cutting edge," 30, no. 3, (November/December 1996).

10. For this data, further information and links, see the Network's website at www.immigrantsolidarity.org.

11. For these details see http://stad.english.ucsb.eduieconimpacts.html.

12. In drawing on migrant workers, dominant groups are able to take advantage of a global reserve army of labor that has experienced historically unprecedented growth in recent years. For instance, the entry of China, India, and the former Soviet bloc into the global economy led to a doubling of the global labor market, from 1.46 to near 3 billion workers by 2000, which resulted in a decline in the global capital-to-labor ratio to just 55 to 60 percent of what it otherwise would have been. See Richard Freeman, ' "China, India and the Doubling of the Global Labor Force: Who Pays the Price of Globalization," *The Globalist* (June 3, 2005), posted at *Japan Focus*, August 26, 2005, and downloaded on October 13, 2005, www.japanfocus. org/article.asp?id—377.

*　　*　　*

Questions

1. Should people who cross the border be treated as committing a felony crime?
2. Should the people who are in the United States be deported or provided with a path toward citizenship?
3. What kind of rights do illegal aliens or undocumented workers have?
4. In what sense are the mass protests for immigration legislation a new civil rights movement and in what sense are they not?
5. If illegal immigration is a byproduct of the global economy, what does this imply for policies to deal with illegal immigration?

∾

CHAPTER TWENTY-SEVEN

A Postdemocratic Era
Guillermo Gómez-Peña

This brief text raises an important question, one that we have been trying to discern out of the many identities that are forced on human bodies: "Who are we?" Appropriately enough, this chapter is part of a collection, under the general title *Reflections on the Culture of Despair,* in which Gómez-Peña attempts to articulate the philosophical and political complexities at the turn of the millennium. In a concise manner, he touches on the topics covered by previous chapters in this collection: the difficulty of finding a language to express our fears or desires in a postsomething era in which concern for human bodies is not a government concern or even on the political agenda. In such a world, Gómez-Peña calls for new models of citizen collaboration and multilateral cooperation, or what we have called a quest for democracy.

*   *   *

We experience the end of the world . . . and the word, as we know them, and the beginning of a new era. Perhaps our main frustration is our total inability to envision the characteristics and features of the coming age. It's a bit like being drunk in the middle of an earthquake, and not having a language to express our fears. But who are *we* anyway?

We now live in world without theory, without ethics, without ideology. Our spiritual metahorizons are rapidly fading, and so are our geopolitical borders. Nation-states collapse in slow motion before our swelling eyes. As they crumble, they are immediately replaced by multinational macro-communities governed by invisible corporate boards, "trading partners," and media trusts. Composed of cold-blooded technocrats and clean-cut neoliberals who position themselves at the center of the center of nothingness, the new political class believes—or perhaps pretends to believe—that free trade and a healthy economy are the solutions to all our problems, even the cultural and social ones. They have no (visible) blood on their hands. They simply press buttons and computer keys. They silently exchange and transfer capital, products and weapons, from continent to continent.

In this unprecedented "postdemocratic era" (if I may call it that), basic humanistic concerns are no longer part of the agenda for these politicos. Civic, human and labor rights, education, and art are perceived as minor privileges, expendable budget items, and dated concerns. Both the politicians and the media seem to have lost (or willingly abandoned) the ability to address the fundamental issues and ask the crucial questions: with all their rhetoric of globalization, why are the US and Western Europe retrenching to isolationist and xenophobic positions, advocating nativist policies and criminalizing immigrants? Why do they advocate open borders from North to South, and closed borders from South to North? Why is Washington still bombing small nations in the post cold-war era? Why are all types of guns freely available to the citizenry of the US? Why does the death penalty still exist in certain so-called "First World" nations? Why are policemen so rarely punished when they engage in acts of brutality? Why are most educational systems bankrupt and dysfunctional? Why are the homeless living in the streets? Why have the arts been defunded? Why aren't these questions being asked in national forums?

In our crumbling postdemocracies, humanism has become a mere corporate "interest" or "goal," a quaint topic explored by the Discovery Channel, a trendy marketing strategy for computer firms. In this new context, artists and intellectuals don't seem to perform any meaningful role other than that of decorators of the omnipresent *horror vacui* and entertainers of a new, more tolerant and cynical consumer class.

As far as I am concerned, we have no real government looking after the human being. The homeless, the elderly, our children and teens, and the newly arrived immigrants from the South are completely on their own. Alone and abandoned in the virtual jungle of advanced capitalism, it is entirely up to us to figure out what can be the new models of citizen collaboration and multilateral cooperation, the new terms for a new social and cultural contract, the new artistic rituals to give voice to our rage, shape our eclectic spiritualities and our fragmented identities. In this sense, citizen responsibility, community action and the creation of a civilian *logos* have been for me the most crucial issues of the 90s. This presentation is a humble expression of a search for new metaphors and images to begin articulating our new place in a foreign world, as well as a humble call for community action. But the main question remains unanswered: who are the remaining *we*? Who is left to listen and respond to this call?

~

Latino U.S.A.: A Canary in the Mine of Continental Democracy

Francisco Hernández Vázquez

The history of the incorporation of Mexican, Cubans, and Puerto Ricans into the United States and the issues that have emerged as a result of this incorporation, point to an important, and potentially crucial historical role for Latinos/as in the new millennium. Based on this history, the purpose of this chapter is to explore this Latino/a role in the evolution of a democratic society not only in the United States but also across the entire American continent.

This chapter is divided into eight parts: (1) a conceptual and metaphorical vocabulary that serves as a template for the subsequent discussions; (2) the evolution of the city-state into imperial democratic nation-states and most recently, into a corporate global economy; (3) inclusive and exclusive citizenships in the United States; (4) Latino/a struggle to democratize the United States; (5) contradictions and paradoxes in the struggle for social justice; (6) crucial difference between "we the people" and "we the state"; (7) survival in the twenty-first century; and (8) inclusive cultural citizenships in a continental democracy.

The Furies, Apollo, and the Social
Contract between the People and the Government

Greek mythology, as it appears in Aeschylus' *The Oresteia*,[1] provides a striking conceptual and metaphorical vocabulary that serves as template throughout the subsequent discussion. There are three reasons for this choice. First, it reminds us of the deep historical and archetypal roots of the eternal clash that occurs when different cultures are brought under one civilization. In other words, it reflects the struggle between the customs of diverse peoples and the rule of law imposed over them by one government. It should be noted in passing that this Greek tragedy is also considered a symbol of the emergence of patriarchy.[2] The second reason is the striking imagery. The Furies represent the people and their ecology. Apollo represents the nation-state, civilization, the federal government, and the global economy. This imagery facilitates the understanding of the social contract by making it easier to keep track of the main actors and forces involved in the struggle for a government of, by, and for the people, that is, the quest for an economic democracy. More concretely, the drama and the characters of this myth serve as a point of departure for the discussion of the role of Latinos/as in the United States. Let us then become a bit more acquainted with the antagonism between the Furies and Apollo.

The Furies are three goddesses that are responsible for the people: this means, human bodies, *familia,* clan, tribe, nation, and the elements that support their survival: blood, the earth, nature, and the economy of the household. Significantly, they are also responsible for the memories of the past, of "what really happened." They protect and avenge the people against the injustices that have not been addressed. Some of these injustices may come from the city-state, the *polis* (from where we get our word "polity" or political system), which today is the government in the form of nation-state and increasingly the corporate global economy. Represented by Apollo this polis, nation-state, or governing political system has a preference for civic duty over family allegiance; it prefers historical amnesia than remembering old feuds; it requires a justice based on written contracts, constitutions, and abstract laws that are supposed to guarantee the equality of all peoples; and it demands for order and democratic law for its own preservation, the preservation of the polis, the nation-state/government.[3]

With this in mind, this chapter entertains the following line of reasoning. Throughout history, a variety of peoples and cultures agree, through a social contract, to forgo their own definitions of justice based on revenge (an eye for an eye is literally bloodletting) and let the polis, that is the nation-state apply one standard of justice for all the different peoples on an equal basis. This is, in other words, how a healthy democracy functions. Whenever the social contract is broken, when there is inequality among the different peoples, and injustices are committed against human bodies, then the Furies appear to demand justice through bloodshed. Or to put succinctly, as the protest chant goes: "No justice, no peace." Sadly, this dynamic is reflected not only by the centuries-long conflicts in the Middle East, but also by the worldwide rise of terrorism.

Now, when we apply this line of reasoning to the social contract between Latinos/as and the U.S. nation-state, the following key factors emerge. First, there is a tendency to perceive U.S. Latinos/as as "illegals" (regardless of their real status); this tendency makes them the most vulnerable human bodies in the United States in the sense that they are subject to deportation or criminalization (again, *regardless* of their status). Secondly, there are objective factors that make Latinos/as the focus of public and government attention, such as their exponential demographic growth and their racial and cultural diversity. Thirdly, over time, Latinos/as will play a role in U.S.-Latin American international policy and potentially, in the development of a continental inter-American union. Finally, as we enter a new millennium, the United States is the only military superpower, and ostensibly, it is committed to democracy. These four key factors lead to the following conclusion: If the United States is really committed to democracy, then that commitment should be revealed by how it treats its own citizens, especially those who are most vulnerable, which at this time it happens to be Latinos/as. In metaphoric terms, this implies that Latinos/as represent the canary in the mine of world democracy. (Miners take a canary with them to detect dangerous gasses; when the canary dies, the mine is no longer safe.)

In political science terms, there are those who care first about the state and secondly about individual or group rights, democracy, or equality (xenophobic U.S Americans like the vigilantes are an example of this position). A variation of this position is promoted by a group of people who care about interpersonal relations but only if they are based on a homogeneous identity, and furthermore, they resent a government that allows for cultural differences that may threaten that identity. Scholars like Samuel P. Huntington, champion this position with the claim that Mexican immigrants are fundamentally different from U.S. Americans, and they threaten the identity of the nation-state. He even foresees the possibility of bloodshed from clashes between white supremacists and Mexican nationals. In the context of this discussion, it is necessary to point out that among the many problems with Huntington's analysis of the "Hispanic challenge" is that he does not take into consideration the role of economic inequality in the creation of stable identities. As noted elsewhere by Vázquez, this problem also undermines his previous "Clash of Civilizations," which supposedly warned about the war in Iraq.[4] There are others, who believe that the health of a democracy and its political institutions is measured by the well-being of human bodies, that is in terms of personal freedom and security, respect for their rights, economic security, and sustainable prosperity. This chapter represents this position.

From City State to Imperial Democracy Theological Global Economy

We have come a long way, however, from the submission of tribes to the Greek city-state to the modern nation-state, whose authority seems to be shifting, slowly but surely to the corporate global economy. The main shift can be attributed to the industrial revolution (see chapters 3 and 4). Among the first indigenous people on the Earth to rebel against its impact were the English people known as the Luddites. Though they fought back with their sledgehammers against the biggest militarization of England at that time, their communal way of life was destroyed by a new way of production that has, over the last two hundred years grown to overwhelming proportions.[5] At the same time, it must be noted that this enormous productive capacity also led to the development of a political technology (i.e., the writing of Constitutions) in the eighteenth century that allowed for the establishment of democracies.

In the nineteenth, twentieth, and start of the twenty-first centuries, the United States has come to embody all these material and cultural changes. In addition, in the process of developing into a world power and an imperial democracy, the United States appropriated Mexican, Cuban, and Puerto Rican territory and citizens (among others). This is not just a story of Latinos/as as victims of the world's superpower. The capitalist system of production, anywhere, turns human bodies from all over the world into commodities that serve the political and economic needs of the state and of the corporations. In one hundred years, this global political economy has expanded all over the world to such an extent that by the twenty-first century it is no longer subject to any authority and had turned all aspects of life itself into a commodity for the sake of profit making.

> Even the movements of subatomic particles, the genetic codes of germ plasms, the information of human discovery, the unconscious regions of the id, and the reaches of human technology towards the stars are appropriated for money-profit rule. *Any opposition to this rule is perceived as heresy and condemned as a threat to freedom.* [emphasis mine][6]

It seems as if history is moving back to a situation somewhat similar to what the English American and Spanish American patriots faced over two hundred years ago. As Eduardo Galeano implies in *Upside Down: A Primer on the Looking Glass World*, instead of fighting the Monarchy, now it is the "[twin] totalitarianisms [of] . . . the dictatorships of consumer society and obligatory injustice."[7] Unlike Alice in Wonderland, who had to go down a rabbit's hole to see the world upside down, Galeano says that to update his *Primer* all we have to do is look at our local newspaper.[8]

Indeed, in the daily newspapers we can see the increases in: slavery of women and children; U.S. incarceration of progressively younger citizens (in most states of the United States a felony is grounds for disenfranchisement); state executions; the gentrification of low-income neighborhoods; the school push-out rates; regional and international bloody conflicts that threaten the stability of the entire world. At the heart of these growing problems is the issue of income inequality worldwide. Let us focus on the United States because it is the wealthiest country in the world. The congressional budget office reports that an increase in incomes of the top 1 percent of U.S. Americans from 2003 to 2005 exceeded the total income of the poorest 20 percent. Furthermore,

> [the] poorest fifth of households had total income of $383.4 billion in 2005, while *just the increase in income for the top 1 percent came to 524.8 billion, a figure 37% higher.* Total income of the top 1.1 million households: $1.8 trillion, or 18.1 percent of all Americans, up from 14.3 percent of all income in 2003. The income of 3 million individual Americans at the top was roughly equivalent to that of the bottom 166 million Americans. [emphasis mine][9]

According to previous reports, the top 10%, top 1%, and fractions of the top 1% enjoyed their greatest share of income since 1928 and 1929 (is this perhaps another indication that history is moving backward?).

What we do not see in the newspapers, what remains invisible is that this "moral absolutism" of a global market is portrayed as "freedom":

> The global market system is a more totalized regime of prescribing how to live than any in history. Its sweeping demands are imposed on societies around the world on a continuous, twenty-four hour basis. Its threats and punishment for violations of its laws exceed in their severity the most punitive of theological fundamentalisms.[10]

To reiterate a previous point, it is precisely the growing presence of Latinos/as within the United States, that is, *within a country that embodies both democracy and unbridled global capitalism,* that makes them a canary in the mine of democracy. We need to ask at this point: Are the Furies still content with their agreement with Apollo? Social unrest in the form of religious, race or ethnic wars, terrorist attacks, the consequent war on terror, and ecological disasters suggest that they may not be too happy. Consider the provocative book titles such as *The Next World War: Tribes, Cities, Nations, and Ecological Decline* and a 2007 bestseller titled *The World Without Us*.[11] Because nation-states still claim sovereignty, and they provide both legitimacy to, and ostensibly, protection for human bodies in the form of citizenship, we can measure the status of the relationship between the people and the nation-state, by looking at the human bodies that are considered worthy of citizenship and those that are *not*.

Inclusive and Exclusive Citizenships in the United States

Focusing on the United States, the leading polis or nation-state world superpower, let us see how human bodies that come under its jurisdiction have been treated. Apparently, they have been categorized

> into a bewildering range of categories, including not just birthright and naturalized citizens and state and U.S. citizens but also nonvoting citizens, "jurisdictional" citizens, "commercial" citizens, citizens subject to incarceration or deportation without due process owning to their race, denizens, U.S. nationals, and even colonial subjects.[12]

Here are some examples. The wording in the U.S. Treaty with France for the acquisition of Louisiana in 1803, which was also used for the acquisition of Florida from Spain in 1819 and to replace article IX in the Treaty of Guadalupe Hidalgo that ended the Mexican American War, states:

> The inhabitants of the ceded territory will be incorporated in the union of the United States and admitted as soon as possible according to the principles of the Federal constitution, to the *enjoyment of all the rights advantages and immunities of citizens of the United States* . . . [emphasis mine][13]

The treaty with Russia for Alaska, however, excludes certain categories of human bodies: "the inhabitants of the ceded territory . . . *with the exception of uncivilized native tribes*, shall be admitted to the enjoyment of all the rights . . ." [emphasis mine]. Not only are human bodies classified as " uncivilized natives" excluded from citizenship, but also in the case of Puerto Rico, a new form of *territorial exclusion* is invented. Compare the different status accorded to Hawaiians compared to Puerto Ricans. On one side, the Joint Congressional Resolution of 1898, stated regarding Hawaii: "the said Hawaiian Island

and their dependencies be and are hereby *annexed as a part of the territory of the United States . . .*) [emphasis mine]. On the other side, the U.S. Treaty with Spain in 1898, that made Puerto Rico an unincorporated territory states: "the civil rights and political status of the native inhabitants . . . *shall be determined by the Congress . . .*" [emphasis mine]. Furthermore, the Foraker Act of 1900 provided that the former Spanish subjects "will be deemed and held to be *citizens of Puerto Rico . . .* " [emphasis mine].[14] As of today, Puerto Ricans are U.S. citizens but cannot vote in presidential elections and have no representation in Congress.[15] Indeed,

> [it] is striking that Americans structure access to their civic identity via terminology and institutions that harken back to political systems their Revolution was meant to overthrow.[16]

Exclusive citizenship was practiced, however, even if initially the wording was inclusive. Take the Treaty of Guadalupe Hidalgo as an example. Under Mexican law, black and indigenous peoples were considered citizens. According to article IX of the Treaty of Guadalupe Hidalgo, those who did not choose to remain Mexican citizens would be considered "to have elected" to become U.S. citizens. The California delegates to the state constitutional convention, including six native *Californios*, constructed a category that would exclude blacks and American Indians from citizenship while including "Mexicans." Suffrage was extended to "every white, male citizen of Mexico who shall have elected to become a citizen of the United States."[17] In New Mexico, following the pattern established under the Northwest Ordinances of 1787 and Wisconsin Organic Act of 1836, the people residing in new territories were "citizens-in-waiting." (For Puerto Ricans, the differences indicated previously, mean that their waiting is forever.) Light-skinned Mexican citizens residing in New Mexico, got full U.S. citizenship rights with statehood in 1912. Their fellow Indian Mexican citizens, however, like the Pueblo Indians, lost their citizenship rights in 1848. American Indians did not get full U.S. citizenship until 1953.[18] In the decades of the 1920s and 1930s, to deal with the "menace of Mexicanization" there was an attempt to deny U.S. citizenship to Mexicans with Indian blood.[19] Even Latinos/as who were "whites of a different color,"[20] who considered themselves part of the privileged "we the people," who saw themselves as part of the discourse of progress, civilization, and the U.S. American Dream (like the elites in northern Mexico, Cuba, and Puerto Rico); all of these eventually found themselves dispossessed of property, political status, and, respect.[21]

In 1849, California exemplifies the bloody, even genocidal consequences of the combination of an incipient global economy and a citizenship that rests on weak or nonexistent juridical protection: Hordes of "forty-niners" from all over the world in their desperate search for gold stabbed, extorted, or lynched native Californios, primarily the dark-skinned ones.

The complex, ongoing process of making and unmaking both, citizenship and "criteria of belonging," for human bodies has been discussed at length by many scholars.[22] This deplorable historical experience clearly points to the need for a citizenship that gives priority to the rights of human bodies over exclusive categories that benefit the privileged classes, the privileged few, and/or the interests of states and the free market. As attacks on immigrants increase and as efforts to change the U.S. Constitution to curtail the rights of citizenship continue today (as they usually do, in response to economic crisis), this becomes an increasingly urgent task.[23]

Evidently, the individual Latino/a bodies that came under the jurisdiction of the United States as a result of armed intervention in 1848 and 1899 have not fared well. As a group, U.S. Mexicans were portrayed as "greasers" and foreigners in their own land and are subjected to periodic deportations and repatriations; Puerto Ricans became a possession but are not yet citizens with equal rights; and Cubans were subjected to U.S. political and economic intervention and are now split by the competing security interests of two nation-states. To explain these events there are the usual theories and analyses: imperialism, capitalism, sexism, and racism.[24] These analyses, as pointed out in chapter 4, are necessary but not sufficient. In addition, in public or private conversation one often hears reference to the abused notion of human agency or lack of it ("Latinos/as don't try hard enough") and the deficiency theories based on biological or cultural determinism ("it's their genes or their culture that is to blame").[25] People, however, do fight back.

Latino/s Struggle to Democratize the United States

As illustrated by the contents of this reader, Latinos/as have indeed organized anticolonial, antiracist, class, and sexist struggles to fight against these oppressive circumstances making use of a variety of analytical tools, tactics, and strategies. The political history of Mexican Americans reveals a series of defensive struggles based on the right of self-preservation: uprisings, including guerrilla warfare and social banditry; mutual aid societies and unions to care for the human bodies that the political and economic system used and discarded; a movement for civil rights. Cubans had a revolution to oust the U.S.-backed dictator Fulgencio Batista and many later turned against it.

Some Puerto Rican *independentistas* continue to engage in insurgent or terrorist activities (depending on who is doing the defining). All the while the vast majority of Latinos/as have also been proactive, attempting to exercise their duties of citizenship through productive activities.

Noted in the Introduction but worth repeating is the notion that shedding your blood, giving your life up for your country, is considered the highest form of commitment. Consequently, it is especially significant to note the participation of Mexican Americans in the armed forces: In World War II, in proportion to their percentage of the population, more Mexican Americans served in combat divisions than any other ethnic group; in the Allied invasion of the European mainland, they died in battle at a rate out of proportion to their numbers.[26] Mario Barrera's documentary, *Latino Stories of World War II* is the first to tell the stories, in their own words, of four veterans who served in the Air Force, the Army, and the Marines. The 1960 movie *Hell to Eternity* describes the exploits of one of them, Guy Gabaldon, although the film did not mention he was a Latino.[27]

The same commitment is evident today; from 1992 to 2001, while the overall end strength of the military dropped by 23 percent from 1,775,000 to 1,369,000, the number of Hispanics in uniform grew by a staggering 30 percent from 90,600 to 118,000.[28] Latinos/as have also increased their participation in the electoral process (in the United States and in their countries of origin, with which, through migration they still retain strong ties). More recently, in response to the lack of immigration policies, Latinos/as have marched in unprecedented numbers throughout the United States.

No matter how much commitment they show to the United States, however, or how hard they work and contribute to U.S. American society, most Latinos/as believe and feel that they get no respect. As John Rawls points out in A *Theory of Justice*, respect is a key component in a just society.[29] As discussed in chapter 5, Mexicans who fought for Texas independence for almost two hundred years were not only excluded form political participation, but also in the case of Juan N. Seguín, their lives were threatened and they were forced to leave Texas. This pattern of discriminations has continued up until today. In 1997, a major research project in New York, Texas, and Los Angeles found a consensus among Latinos/as, whether they are U.S. citizens or immigrants, that they do not feel fully included and accepted by U.S. Americans. The authors of this study assert the right of a cultural citizenship and call for the creation of a sociopolitical space to accept cultural differences alongside citizenship.[30] In addition to these Latino/a contributions to the definition of cultural citizenship, there are specific policy proposals for the rights of cultural groups and for transnational citizenship. These are being developed at a worldwide level by the United Nations Educational, Scientific, and Cultural Organization (UNESCO), and closer to home, by the Canadian scholar Will Kymlicka.[31]

In 2007, a decade after the aforementioned major research on Latino/a cultural citizenship, another nationwide survey of Latinos by the Pew Hispanic Center found that just over half of all Hispanic adults in the United States worry that they, a family member, or a close friend could be deported. Nearly two-thirds say the failure of Congress to enact an immigration reform bill has made life more difficult for all Latinos/as. Smaller numbers (ranging from about one in eight to one in four) say the heightened attention to immigration issues has had a specific negative effect on them personally. These effects include more difficulty finding work or housing; less likelihood of using government services or traveling abroad; and more likelihood of being asked to produce documents to prove their immigration status.[32] Indeed, bodies continue to be abused: Parents of undocumented soldiers killed in Iraq are deported,[33] families are being separated, and children are especially impacted by immigration raids.[34] It is not surprising, then, that respect for Latinos/as is not forthcoming even from the candidates for the U.S. 2008 presidential election.[35]

Clearly, as the title of the Pew Report states it: As Illegal Immigration Issue Heats Up, Hispanics Feel A Chill. In part this is as a result of the Chicanology effect (a deep-rooted anti-Mexican sentiment discussed in chapter 4). In part, it is because all Latinos/as or Hispanics are often categorized automatically as "aliens," and as Robinson points out in chapter 26, the undocumented workers are the ones with the least rights. Again, it is the treatment of its most vulnerable and unprotected members of society that reveal the health of a democracy.

Contradictions and Paradoxes in the Struggle for Social Justice

E Pluribus Unum, diversity in unity, is the goal. A sober look at the quest for democracy, however, shows that this is easier said than done. This is because under some circumstances there is a desire and a demand for equal treatment, whereas under other circumstances, the emphasis is on the right to be different. To attempt to untangle the various contradictory and paradoxical threads of this knot, let us look first at it from the perspective of the state and the global economy. On the one hand, they both insist that everyone is equal, the same: either under the law or under private enterprise. Under their influence, there is a tendency to deny ethnic or cultural differences (Lady Justice is blind) or to turn them into commodities. The goal is to erase, homogenize, and normalize differences and create loyal citizen or consumers, respectively.

On the other hand, the state and the global economy also categorize people according to their differences: In this case, the goal is to define and organize (allegedly to protect and provide services), but when necessary, they divide society, by categorizing some of the people as Others who do not belong. This happened with Mexicans during the 1930s repatriation program, the Zoot-Suit riots in 1942, and the Operation Wetback in the 1950s. Presently, this is going on with the overlapping of terrorism and immigration issue and the targeting of all Latinos/as as a potential threat to the United States. This serves to divert the power of a unified Latino/a civil society, and preserve private, white-nationalist or class interests. The global economy, of course, sees differences as the opportunity to create niche markets!

Now, looking at this knotty issue from the perspective of the people and of individuals, it is abundantly clear that what people want is a just life that guarantees their survival, their safety, and their well-being. Thus, they work at *integrating, even assimilating,* themselves into the society or government that best serves that purpose (this is an important point that will be amplified in this chapter). They want to be treated as equals, with the same respect as everyone else. This is their quest for justice and democracy. Yet depending on the circumstances, they also assert their cultural differences, sometimes through nationalist, and even separatist, movements. As in the case of some Puerto Ricans and Mexicans, they may *resist,* and even refuse, citizenship if it provides no justice or security or if it threatens their identity and self-respect. Thus, echoing the dictates of the Furies, Chicana writer Gloria Anzaldúa contends:

> I am visible—see this Indian face—yet I am invisible. I blind them with my beak nose and am their blind spot. But I exist, we exist. They'd like to think I have melted in the pot. But I haven't, we haven't. . . . The whites in power want us people of color to barricade ourselves behind our separate tribal walls so they can pick us off one at a time with their hidden weapons; so that they can whitewash and distort history. Ignorance splits people, creates prejudices. A misinformed people is a subjugated people.[36]

The words and phrases that were just used (*exclusion, rejection, prejudice, hidden weapons* and *distorted history*) make it sound as if we are dealing here with a simple "Us against Them." That is not necessarily the case. There are also democratic spaces in the United States in which marginalized people can find justice. That makes our search for understanding of the status of Latinos/as in the United States even more complex. For example, for *some* marginalized

Latino/a populations, the U.S. government and culture have proved beneficial. Puerto Rican women used the U.S. Congress to circumvent the island's sexist and classist (anti-working class) local government and obtain universal suffrage.[37] Cuban exiles received unprecedented moral and material support (even beyond what is given to U.S. citizens) to help them become the "golden minority."[38] Many Latino/a gays, known as "sexiles" migrate to the United States because of the homophobia in their countries of origin.[39] Even Mexicans in Mexico (who are usually portrayed as "prickly" nationalists by the media), would prefer U.S. citizenship if that meant better living conditions (59 percent of the people, according to a 1991 survey of Mexican people).[40] Does this mean that Mexicans (in Mexico) have no loyalty to their own country? Not necessarily; it means they have more loyalty to themselves as a people.

Crucial Difference between "We the People" and "We the State": In Search of a Better Life, not a Better Citizenship

The question remains, "What do we all want: equal, different or diverse?" To get a handle on these seeming contradictions and paradoxes we need to take a more detailed look at the relationship between the people and the nation-state/government. We also need to keep in mind that the compass orienting us out of this mess of contradictions is the consent of the people, which is the basis for a democracy. Previously we noted that people work at *integrating, even assimilating,* themselves into the society or government that best takes care of them. This means, in brief, that the loyalty is to the people, not to the nation-state/government.

The historian Juan Gómez-Quiñonez observes that Mexican people do not see much difference between the U.S. and the Mexican governments. More incisively, he states:

> Unlike North Americans, Mexicans can *distinguish between nation and state* and know that the interests of the people and the government do not coincide. [emphasis mine][41]

This distinction between the *nation* and the *state* is not, of course, only made by Mexicans. Yet if a democracy is truly a government of the people, by the people and for the people, then this is an excellent point to help us assess the quest for democracy. It also helps to understand the reason why many Mexicans in the United States have been reluctant at times to become U.S. citizens in the same proportion as other immigrants. For example, in his book on the repatriation of half to one million Mexicans, many of whom were U.S. citizens, Hoffman makes the following statement: "Mexicans who crossed their northern border were *looking for a better life, but not necessarily a better citizenship.*" [emphasis mine]⁴²

From the perspective of a quest for democracy, this is the crux of the matter: Looking for a better life *is* looking for a better citizenship, one that fulfills the desires, and physical and moral needs of the people. Thus, Hoffman finds it paradoxical that Mexicans protected themselves by *not* becoming U.S. citizens. The privileges of U.S. citizenship were meaningless in a society in which the dominant belief was that "once a Mexican always a Mexican." By remaining a Mexican citizen she or he could call on the Mexican Consul for assistance and often secure justice. As a U.S. citizen she or he did not understand the courts and was not able to secure as adequate a hearing as if she or he was a Mexican citizen. The same dynamics would apply to U.S. Americans in Mexico.⁴³ To prove that the people know their own interest, during the late 1990s, however, millions of Mexicans became U.S. citizens to preserve their economic, health, and educational rights that were being threatened by propositions such as 187 in California.

It sounds as if Latinos/as are actually a conservative people. So here is another paradox: Although the media's most popular image is of minorities protesting for their rights, militants question why Mexican American and Puerto Rican working classes have not supported nationalist, separatist, or independent movements.⁴⁴ One hears charges that present-day or previous generations of Latinos/as are assimilated, colonized, ignorant, or have false consciousness.⁴⁵

As Ramón Grosfoguel bluntly puts it, Puerto Ricans "would rather be exploited with some benefits (like people in Curaçao and Martinique) than be exploited without any benefits (like people in the Dominican Republic and Haiti)?" Does this mean Puerto Ricans like to be exploited? Not so, argues Grosfoguel. He calls this attitude *"subversive complicity,"* meaning the Puerto Rican people's pragmatic rather than utopian strategy "for the protection, deepening, and expansion of the social and democratic rights."⁴⁶ In agreement with Grosfoguel, this is precisely the same sentiment that is expressed by Wilfredo Mattos-Cintron:

> Above all, they [the Puerto Rican *independentistas*] must finally learn that it is not independence per se that the masses are after, but a political status that will clearly fulfill their aspirations to a better life.⁴⁷

So, one answer to the question that opened this section is: What people want is justice not a better citizenship.

We the Peasants: Survival in the
Global Economy of the Twenty-First Century

Whether Latinos/as are radicals or conservatives, one main point is that if we are to have a government of the people, by the people, and for the people, as Abraham Lincoln put it, then we need to have confidence on the wisdom of the people. This may sound romantic but today, this confidence is being threatened and this is leading to a fragmentation of "we the people" into tribes. As noted previously, it becomes evident that the Furies are loose, when the topic of conversation is a world war among tribes, cities, and nations, and we have painted an image of the world without humans.[48] Let us briefly explore the nature of this wisdom of the people. John Berger makes an important distinction between the conservatism associated with the ruling class (or the Republican Party) and "peasant conservatism." (Because the word *peasant* carries a pejorative connotation, we must remember that the word comes from the French *païsant*, which in Spanish and Italian means *paisano* or a fellow country person. Technically, it means an agricultural worker).

At any rate, Berger claims that this is "a conservatism not of power but of meaning."[49] In other words, it is *a conservatism of survival* in a world that offers no protection (a reality for increasing numbers of people world wide).[50] He also anticipates the question: "What do peasants have to do with a global economy?" Sounding much like the Furies, Berger states that, conservatism of meaning "represents a depository (a granary) of meaning preserved from lives and generations threatened by continual and inexorable change." It is similar to what McMurtry calls the "civil commons" or the underlying life organization of society.[51] This "conservatism of meaning" becomes important now that the same forces that threaten the peasants threaten all of us, as Berger points out:

> Productivity is not reducing scarcity. The dissemination of knowledge is not leading unequivocally to greater democracy. The advent of leisure has not brought personal fulfillment but greater mass manipulation. The economic and military unification of the world has not brought peace but genocide.[52]

To be sure, this is not a suggestion to go back to the pre-Enlightenment dark ages of superstition when knowledge was based on religion and folklore. Nor is it intended to romanticize the peasant. The point is that nation-states and the global corporate economy are increasingly more concerned with their own survival than they are with the survival of the people. As a consequence, for the sake of their physical survival and their own identity, the people find ways to resist this new kind of domination. According to Castells, it is precisely the resistance to what he calls an "information network society," which is a contributor to the fragmentation of civil society, into specific, often oppositional ethnic, tribal, or religious identities.[53]

Previously I mentioned the Luddites as a people who fought against the dehumanization of the industrial revolution. This is the case for some Latinos/as also. Let us review two examples from two different historical periods. Historically, vast social sectors in Puerto Rico have struggled to remain outside of the market. The law known as *Ley Libreta of 1849* was one of the instruments used by landholders and the government to force "idle" peasants to work. On January 1, 1994, Mexican Maya peasants, the Zapatistas, rose up in arms against the Mexican government and the North American Free Trade Agreement (NAFTA). The [Mexican] government's commitment to neoliberal macroeconomic policies and free trade had badly shaken the peasantry. Many have rightly concluded that with the Article 27 reforms and NAFTA that they were being deleted from the script for Mexico's future. The amendment to Article 27 of the Mexican Constitution ended the land distribution program and opened the way for *ejido* privatization. Ejido is a community-based system of land tenure dating back to pre-Conquest times. As we enter into a new millennium, we are witnessing another chapter in the peasant Zapatista revolt in Mexico, with a different government for the first time in almost eight decades. For the sake of comparison among Latino/a groups, this is the appropriate place to note that the first waves of Cuban exiles in the 1960s are the least peasant of all U.S. Latinos/as; the material formation of the cultural identity, of *cubanidad*, of this particular social class has been wrapped up with the notion of progress and civilization since the middle of the nineteenth century.[54]

Presently, as Robinson points out in chapter 26, as a result the U.S. or economic global capitalism, increasing numbers of displaced peoples are becoming the refugees, migrants, or exiles of tomorrow. Regrettably, recent research indicates that although most people in the world welcome the global economy, they do not want to extend rights to the immigrants that this trade produces.[55] Faced with the likely future of "further extension of world capitalism in all its brutalism" or the uncertain victory of a protracted struggle against it, Berger's bleak conclusion is that the peasant experience of survival may be better adapted than the reformist progressive hope of an ultimate victory. In short, ultimately we are all potential peasants and this is not necessarily an exaggeration.[56]

Although it remains to be seen what, if any, options remain open, it is precisely the wisdom of the people, this "peasant conservatism" that includes the necessity of a sustainable economy, which is not represented in our current political-economic systems. Consequently, we the people need to move toward a politics of sustainability not only in ecological terms but also in terms of governance and in term of an ethics of care and responsibility. Our present theories of justice that assume an even playing field for all human bodies are not adequate to address the reality of the differences that characterize human beings.[57]

Latinos/as seem to play the role of the Furies within the Apollonian United States. This role is demonstrated by Latinos/as historical claims of the right of self-preservation against the manipulation of the law; in their emphasis for the concrete care of the human bodies; the economic survival and the dignity of the people, through their social, cultural, worker, and political organizations; and in their concern for the environment.[58] They do not, however, tend toward tribalization. On the contrary, they promote a harmony of differences. This is evident in their genetic, social, and political *mestizaje* as Valle and Torres point out in chapter 12. The most recent comprehensive exposition of *mestizaje* as a significant Mexican contribution to race relations in the United States is Gregory Rodriquez's *Mongrels, Bastards, Orphans, and Vagabonds: Mexican Immigration and the Future of Race in America.*[59]

The struggle for democracy and more specifically for an inclusive political representation, directs our attention once again toward citizenship, the one concept that still provides a foundation for some kind of protection for human bodies and the implications for an inclusive system of governance across the American continent.

Toward Inclusive Cultural Citizenships in a Continental Democracy

Two visions appear before us. One is a continental American democracy similar to the European Union. Here, inclusive forms of cultural citizenship integrate human bodies in the political process, that is, nation-states based on economic and political democracy facilitate the people's participation in making the decisions that affect society in general, and their communities in particular. Unfortunately, free trade agreements between the United States and other countries in the American continent focus on the exchange of commodities and exclude labor, environmental, social, and ethical elements. This situation points to the other, darker vision in which light-skin minorities create totalitarian, fascist states to rule over dark-skin majorities that are divided against each other in perpetual struggle. Again, this becomes a more urgent issue in view of the increasing size of the Latino/a population in the

United States (up to 25 percent by 2050), which remains the most powerful country in the world. Let us first address an expanded notion of citizenship.

Traditional, liberal democratic theory narrowly defines community as a collection of individuals with a mutual geographical or ethnic basis or as "merely a group of individual interest maximizers." Consequently, as Carol Hardy-Fanta states, citizenship is

> narrowly defined to mean legal status bestowed upon the individual by the sovereign state and conferring certain rights within the legal/political system . . . as a social contract between the citizen and the state, [under which] the political expression of citizenship is reduced to a limited set of behaviors.[60]

Feminist theories of citizenship are based instead on equality, mutuality, and consensual, face-to-face relationships, to develop collectivity while respecting diversity. A Latina feminist vision also calls for the inclusion of groups commonly excluded from the official definition of citizenship: women and immigrants and especially "illegal aliens" or rather "undocumented workers." This is of particular interest to Latinos/as who attempt to build community on the basis of diversity and often, to include undocumented members of the community. Hardy-Fanta argues that these human bodies "do not so much *belong* to a 'found' (or ascribed) community but seek to create a community." This perspective calls for nation-states/governments to provide an inclusive citizenship.

Although Hardy-Fanta categorizes this view as feminist, there are similar positions with respect to the rights of underrepresented groups and their inclusion in the larger society that are not necessarily labeled *feminist*. For example, Kymlicka, a leading theorist of cultural rights, argues that "liberalism also contains a broader account of the relationship between the individual and society—and, in particular of the individual's membership in a community and a culture."[61] There is also a remarkable implicit agreement among Latinos/as that illustrate an inclusive citizenship. Some of them extend the concept of inclusion within one state to people who are caught between two or more states.

From a personal Cuban-American position:

> For years I felt that I had neatly put away pieces of my identity in different parts of the world, but more recently I have come to understand that I need not accept the categories that divide who I am. Instead, I must construct new categories, new political and emotional spaces, *in which my multiple identities can be one.* [emphasis mine][62]

From a Dominican American perspective:

> I have argued in favor of placing primacy on contextual factors influencing migration processes, such as patterns of residence and the legal and political mechanisms existing in both countries. It is difficult to understand how migrants negotiate their existence between two countries and many cultures without analyzing the ongoing communication and relationships that take place across the border, and the ongoing influences of economic and political conditions in both countries.[63]

According to a Puerto Rican point of view:

> The political practice of a radical democratic project would *privilege the improvement of oppressed subjects' quality of life* in the present rather than in a distant future "paradise." This movement would include a multiplicity of projects to promote and support the struggles of diverse oppressed subjects such as blacks, women, youth, gays, lesbians, and workers. [emphasis mine][64]

A Chicano perspective:

> *[The] globalization of capital, with its power to penetrate and dominate regional markets and undermine native economies,* obliges the Mexican peasant or Guatemalan worker to ignore certain rules and boundaries *in order to survive.* Sentimental loyalty to a particular nation-state and, by extension, that state's idealized "traditional" culture becomes an impoverishing, even life-threatening luxury. To this extent, then, the lived, transcultural experience of *mestizaje* must also be considered transnational and potentially postnational. And policies such as granting voting status to immigrants in school board elections, for example, represent important ways of granting institutional recognition to Latino *mestizaje*. [emphasis mine][65]

Although the notion of letting immigrants vote in the United States seems far-fetched, given the current strong anti-immigrant bias, there is an international trend toward cultural rights and cultural citizenship. As Kymlicka points out, and Robinson corroborates in chapter 26, there is an increasing sense, among people all over the world, that they are entitled to their rights not as a matter of charity or favors from the dominant groups but as their legitimate right.[66] He cites three main reasons for this change in consciousness: demographics (the Other is here to stay), knowledge of their rights, and the confidence to speak out that is provided by a democratic society. In terms of cultural rights, a distinction is made between national groups and immigrant groups. Because Mexicans, Puerto Ricans, and Cubans were incorporated into the United States through war, historically, they are national groups, and because they continue to migrate to mainland United States, however, they are also immigrants at the same time.

Now, in many parts of the world, multinational federalism (providing autonomy to different groups within a country) is common practice and it is considered successful in terms of providing protection of minority rights. In the United States, however, perhaps the most controversial aspect of cultural rights is the argument that true equality requires different treatment for different groups. This is the case with American Indians and, arguably, with natives of Alaska and Hawaii.

Multinational federalism as a form of cultural citizenship is successful in terms of providing peace and individual security, democracy, individual rights, intergroup equality and economic prosperity. It should also be noted that multinational federalism, like the European Union, is among the wealthiest in the world. It is not so successful in terms of the actual experience of the minorities, which ranges from ignorance or indifference from and toward the dominant group to resentment and annoyance. As noted before, recent studies show that this is the case with Latinos/as in the United States. One other failure of multinational national federalism or cultural citizenship is that secession remains for some groups as part of the political agenda.[67] As noted by Grosfoguel, to a limited extent this is the case for Puerto Ricans.

As for Mexican American, Mario Barrera explored the possibility of multinational federalism in *Beyond Aztlán: Ethnic Autonomy in Comparative Perspective*. Although there has never been a clear nationalist movement among Mexican Americans, nativists, xenophobes and even scholars like Huntington, raise the possibility that Mexican Americans plot to take back the land they lost to the United States in 1848. Despite the dire predictions of scholars, like Huntington or right wing political pundits like Patrick Buchanan, an inclusive citizenship does not necessarily mean tribal anarchy or ethnic wars, rather, it can be the foundation for the strengthening of the civil society, the reconstruction of democracy *through a democratic process*.

In terms of world historical trends, however, it is evident that cultural citizenship in one form or another, within the United States and throughout the entire American continent, remains a viable goal in the quest for democracy. As Kymlicka points out, this is not a perfect solution but it is the best of all possible worlds.[68] Cultural democracy, research clearly shows, is the best antidote to deal with the failure of the North American Free Trade Agreement (NAFTA) and the Central American Free Trade Agreement (CAFTA) to address social, ethical, and environmental issues. In chapter 26, Robinson points out the correlation between Latinos/as protests for fair immigration legislation and the democratic movements in Latin America.

Sooner or later we need to adopt a democratic integration at a continental level to cope with the increasing negative integration at the continental level through the spread of violent gangs, like the Mara Salvatrucha, and organized crime that infiltrates and takes over governments.[69] This is supported by Peter Hakim, President of the Inter-American Dialogue, a Washington-based center for policy analysis and exchange on Western Hemisphere affairs:

> Regardless of how successful these bilateral and subregional agreements are [between the United States and Latin American countries], none of them can offer the economic gains that would come with a comprehensive, hemispheric accord that brings together every economy in the Americas. A European-style trade arrangement is what would most benefit the nations of the Western Hemisphere. Too bad hemispheric negotiations remain stymied.[70]

More immediately, he notes that the most critical challenge for a continental America is the social agenda, namely, poverty and inequality. Hakim believes that the United States can make a difference here. He also recommends that the next president stop the Cuban embargo and work with other Latin American countries to integrate Cuba into the Inter-American system and collaborate with Latin American partners to define a multilateral strategy to combat drugs and criminal activity.

There appears to be a solid foundation for a continental-wide democratic alliance. All fourteen recent presidential elections in Latin America were judged to be free and fair by international observers. Only in Mexico was it contested. Elections were competitive, and turnout was high.[71] At the grassroots level, there are organizations that work to oppose the free trade area of the Americas and provide an alternative political economic agenda based on democratic processes. One of them is the Hemispheric Social Alliance, a transnational coalition of civil society organizations (labor unions, social movements, indigenous, environment, and citizen organizations from throughout the Americas).[72]

Another strategic tool for continental integration is "cosmopolitan legality," an emerging new field of policy oriented legal studies. It is similar to critical race theory, which focuses on racism and on judicial judgments as social construction based on power relations. Cosmopolitan legality extends this challenge beyond racism and considers liberal and conservative assumptions about justice and civil rights, as social constructions. By doing so, it points to the reconstruction of human rights beyond the model of neoliberal institutions. In the American continent, for example, labor and immigrant rights become sites for cosmopolitan legality involving a community in Tennessee and undocumented workers from Mexico and Central America.[73]

U.S. Latinos/as are also beginning to stake their position in inter-American diplomacy. On May 29, 2002, in Washington, DC, the Tomás Rivera Policy Institute (TRPI) and the Inter-American Dialogue (IAD) convened a select group of Latino/a leaders from Boston to Miami. The purpose of this meeting was to talk about ways to increase U.S. Latino/a engagement into U.S. foreign policy and thus to build a Latino/a base on foreign policy. Such a base could, for example, add another dimension to the struggle for immigrant rights in the United States and promote policies that improve the quality of life in Mexico. The future clearly points toward increased "integration of Mexico in U.S. interests." Another salient point is that although U.S. Latinos/as have focused on the domestic agenda, there are economic and security issues in Latin America that require the attention of the U.S. Latino/a elite and leadership.[74]

The history of Latino/a political thought clearly indicates, and the many studies included here provide abundant evidence for the claim that, the only hope for survival depends, as always, on the people, the subjects of civil society, or the civil commons. Strategically, that means a focus on an inclusive citizenship and a corresponding reconfiguration of (male? Western?) dominant political and economic theory in such a way that the care of the human body and its ecology become the main objective. But here is another key point: The state will only do so much for the people; the people must practice democracy at the level of everyday life to make a difference.

Tactically, this means we need to promote public dialogue among individuals across all levels to sort out the mystification that language brings into any struggle for liberation. This will encourage coalitions, such as the ones going on in the Latino/a Metropolis of Los Angeles. The goal is to eliminate exclusive categories that make public interest invisible and therefore impossible to protect. Whether or not the category of class is among the "worn-out discourses of race relations and identity politics" depends on how much it actually contributes to an inclusive citizenship. The struggle for justice as the care of human bodies and the preservation of all life demands an imaginative use of existing discourses and the invention of new ones. It should be clear by now that the principle of uncertainty reigns over any notion of physical or social immutable laws. As Nietzsche put it: "What sacred games shall we have to invent?"[75]

*　　*　　*

Notes and Suggestions for Further Research

1. Aeschylus, *Oresteia: Agamemnon, The Libation Bearers, The Eumenides*, trans. Richmond Lattimore (University of Chicago Press, 1953).

2. There are several ways to approach the historical event that signals the beginning of patriarchy, the state, and the idea of progress. From a mythological perspective, two of them are based on Aeschylus' trilogy of plays, Aeschylus, *Oresteia*. Riane Eisler in *The Chalice and the Blade* [(Cambridge: Harper and Row, 1987), 78–85] sees it as the denial of full female participation in all aspects of society. James Hersh in "From *Ethnos* to *Polis*," *Spring: An Annual of Archetypal Psychology and Jungian Thought* (1985), sees it as the imposition of state rule over independent peoples. The readable novel by Daniel Quinn *Story of B: An Adventure of the Mind and Spirit* (New York: Bantam Books, 1996) suggests that *totalitarian agriculture* allowed one culture to take over others and to replace their 200,000 year-old tribal rules with written constitutions intended to provide justice for the diverse peoples contained within the nation-state. The unintended result, he argues, is the current social injustice and ecological crisis. An academic treatment is provided by Kirkpatrick Sale in *Rebels against the Future: The Luddites and Their War on the Industrial Revolution, Lessons for the Computer Age* (New York: Addison-Welsley Publishing Company, 1995). He places this historical confrontation between the values of the human community and the values of a technological society based on progress in the nineteenth century and the Luddites war against the industrial revolution and notes that this uprising led to the unprecedented militarization of England.

3. Hersh, "From *Ethnos* to *Polis*."

4. Francisco Hernández Vázquez, "The Political Economy of Culture and The Birth of A Civil Society after NAFTA," *Latino Studies Journal* 8, no. 1 (1997), 62–93; Samuel P. Huntington, "The Clash of Civilizations," *Foreign Affairs*, 72, no. 3 (1993): 22–49; "The Hispanic Challenge," *Foreign Policy*, (March/April 2004), 30–45 which is part of his, *Who Are We?: The Challenges to America's National Identity* (New York: Simon & Schuster, 2004). See critique by Alan Wolfe, "Native Son: Samuel Huntington Defends the Homeland" (*Foreign Affairs*, May/June 2004) and debate in "Creedal Passions" (*Foreign Affairs*, September/October 2004).

5. Sale, *Rebels against the Future*.

6. John McMurtry, *Unequal Freedoms: The Global Market as an Ethical System* (West Hartford, CT: Kumarian Press, 1998), 279.

7. Eduardo Galeano, *Upside Down: A Primer for the Looking-Glass World*, trans. Mark Fried (New York: Metropolitan Books, 2000), 25.

8. Galeano, *Upside Down*, 337.

9. David Cay Johnston, "Richest in U.S. See Fast Rise in Income," *The Press Democrat* (December 17, 2007).

10. McMurtry, *Unequal Freedoms*, 279.

11. Roy Woodbridge, *The Next World War: Tribes, Cities, Nations, and Ecological Decline* (Toronto: University of Toronto Press, Inc., 2004) and Alan Weisman, *The*

World Without Us (New York: St. Martin's Press, 2007). For additional references regarding the ecological crisis see endnotes 49, 50.

12. Rogers M. Smith, *Civic Ideals: Conflicting Visions of Citizenship in U.S. History* (New Haven, CT: Yale University Press, 1997), 14.

13. The point is made by Roberta Ann Johnson in *Puerto Rico: Commonwealth or Colony?* (New York: Praeger, 1980), 58n.

14. Johnson, *Puerto Rico: Commonwealth or Colony?*, 58–59.

15. One of the last actions of exiting president Bill Clinton was to authorize yet another study of the political status of Puerto Rico.

16. Smith, *Civic Ideals*, 13.

17. Richard Griswold del Castillo, *The Treaty of Guadalupe Hidalgo: A Legacy of Conflict* (Norman: University of Oklahoma Press, 1990), 66–69.

18. Griswold del Castillo, *The Treaty of Guadalupe Hidalgo*, 70–72.

19. Gregory Rodriguez, *Mongrels, Bastards, Orphans and Vagabonds: Mexican Immigration and the Future of Race in America* (New York: Pantheon Books, 2007), 164–72 passim.

20. See Matthew Frye Jacobson, *Whiteness of a Different Color: European Immigrants and the Alchemy of Race* (Cambridge: Harvard University Press, 1998) for a discussion of the factors involved in the subjectification of human bodies to the category of the color white.

21. Jesus de la Teja, ed., *A Revolution Remembered: The Memoirs and Selected Correspondence of Juan N. Seguín* (Austin: State House Press, 1991). Rosaura Sánchez, "Constructs of Ethnicity," *Telling Identities: The Californio Testimonios* (Minneapolis: University of Minnesota Press, 1995). Robert J. Rosenbaum, *Mexicano Resistance in the Southwest: The Sacred Right of Self Preservation* (Austin: University of Texas Press, 1981). The familiar feeling of "being a stranger in his own land" for which Seguín is often quoted, is also found in the Cuban experience, see Louis A. Pérez, *On Becoming Cuban: Identity, Nationality and Culture* (Chapel Hill: University of North Carolina Press, 1999), 136. Regarding Puerto Ricans, the dispossession of the Puerto Rican coffee and sugar plantation owners is one of the first traumatic experiences as a possession of the U.S. polity. See for example Ronald Fernandez, *The Disenchanted Island* (Westport, CT: Praeger, 1996), 4–7.

22. Aihua Ong, "Cultural Citizenship as Subject Making: Immigrants Negotiate Racial and Cultural Boundaries in the United States," in Rodolfo D. Torres, Louis F. Mirón, and Jonathan Xavier Inda, eds., *Race, Identity and Citizenship* (Malden, MA: Blackwell Publishers, 1999), 262–93.

23. Richard Delgado, "Citizenship" in Juan F Perea, ed., *Immigrants Out! The New Nativism and the Anti-Immigrant Impulse in the United States* (New York: New York University Press, 1997), 318–23.

24. Juan Antonio Corretjer, *Albizu Campos and the Ponce Massacre* (New York: World View Publishers, 1975), Guillermo Flores and Ronald Bailey "Internal Colonialism and Racial Minorities in the United States: An Overview," in Frank Bonilla and Robert Girling, *Structures of Dependency* (1973), 149–58. Antonio Rios-Bustamante, *Mexicans*

in the United States and the National Question: Current Polemics and Organizational Positions (Santa Barbara: *Editorial La Causa*, 1978). Gloria Anzaldúa, *Borderlands* La Frontera: *The New Mestiza* (San Francisco: Aunt Lute Foundation Book, 1999). Raymund Paredes, "The Origins of Anti-Mexican Sentiment in the United States." in R. Romo and R. Paredes, ed., *New Directions in Chicano Scholarship* Chicano Studies Monograph Series (San Diego: University of California, 1978).

25. Nick C. Vaca, "The Mexican American in the Social Sciences 1912–1970," *El Grito* 4, no. 1, (1970): 17–51.

26. Rodriguez, *Mongrels, Bastards, Orphans and Vagabonds*, 182.

27. Available at www.odysseyproductions.info/.

28. Hispanic Center Fact Sheet, "Hispanics in the Military," (Washington D.C.: March 27, 2003). Available at www.pewhispanic.org

29. John Rawls, *A Theory of Justice* (Cambridge: Harvard University Press, 1971). This remains, arguably, a valid argument despite the questionable assumptions this theory makes in other areas (e.g., Amartya Sen, "Equality of What?" in his *Choice, Welfare and Measurement* (Cambridge: MIT Press, 1982), 353–72; Eva Feder Kittay, *Love's Labor: Essays on Women, Equality, and Dependency* (New York: Routledge, 2000) and McMurtry's *Unequal Freedoms*.

30. William V. Flores and Rina Benmayor, eds., *Latino Cultural Citizenship: Claiming Identity, Space and Rights*, (Boston: Beacon Press, 1997).

31. See for example, Colin Mercer and others, *Toward Cultural Citizenship: Tools for Cultural Policy and Development* (Stockholm: Swedish International Development Cooperation Agency, 2002); Will Kymlicka, *Multicultural Citizenship: A Liberal Theory of Minority Rights* (Oxford: Clarendon Press 1995). For a critique of the attempt to develop international standards of minority rights, see Will Kymlicka, "Multiculturalism and Minority Rights: West and East," *Journal on Ethnopolitics and Minority Issues in Europe* no. 4, (2002).

32. Pew Hispanic Center, *2007 National Survey of Latinos: As Illegal Immigration Issue Heats Up, Hispanics Feel A Chill* (Washington, D.C., December 2007).

33. Domenico Maceri, *New America Media, Commentary*, Posted: September 4, 2007.

34. Randy Capps and others, *Paying the Price: The Impact of Immigration Raids on America's Children*, Urban Institute Report (Washington: National Council for La Raza, 2007).

35. Ruben Navarrette, "Where's the Respect?" 11/13/2007, at www.postwritersgroup.com/navarrette.htm, accessed November 14, 2007.

36. Gloria Anzaldúa, "*La Conciencia de la Mestiza*: Towards a New Consciousness," in *Borderlands* La Frontera: *The New Mestiza* (San Francisco: Aunt Lute Foundation Book, 1999), 108.

37. Gladys M. Jiménez-Muñoz, "So We Decided to Come and Ask You Ourselves": The 1928 U.S. Congressional Hearings on Women's Suffrage in Puerto Rico," in Frances Negrón-Muntaner and Ramón Grosfoguel, eds., *Puerto Rican Jam: Rethinking Colonialism and Nationalism* (Minneapolis: University of Minnesota Press, 1997),

Yamila Azize-Vargas, "The Emergence of Feminism In Puerto Rico, 1870–1930." *Radical America* 23, no. 1 (1989).

38. Maria Cristina García, *Havana USA* (Berkeley: University of California Press, 1996), 29.

39. Ramón Grosfoguel, Frances Negrón-Muntaner, and Chloé S. Georas, "Beyond Nationalist and Colonialist Discourses: The *Jaiba* Politics of the Puerto Rican Ethno-Nation," in Frances Negrón-Muntaner and Ramón Grosfoguel, eds., *Puerto Rican Jam: Rethinking Colonialism and Nationalism* (Minneapolis: University of Minnesota Press, 1997), 26.

40. Roger Bartra, *"La Venganza de la Malinche: Hacia una identidad posnacional," Oficio Mexicano* (Mexico: *Editorial Grijalbo*, 1993), 93–97.

41. Juan Gómez-Quiñonez, "On Culture" (Los Angeles: University of California, Chicano Studies Center Publications, 1977), 10.

42. Abraham Hoffman, *Unwanted Mexican Americans in the Great Depression* (Tucson: University of Arizona Press, 1974), 19. For a more extensive discussion of this event see also Francisco E. Balderrama and R. Rodríguez. *Decade of Betrayal: Mexican Repatriation in the 1930s* (Albuquerque: University of New Mexico Press, 1995).

43. Hoffman, *Unwanted Mexican Americans*, 20.

44. Fred A. Cervantes, "Chicanos as a Post Colonial Minority: Some Questions Concerning the Adequacy of the Paradigm of Internal Colonialism," in R. Flores Macias, ed., *Perspectivas en Chicano Studies I* (Los Angeles: University of California, Chicano Studies Center, 1977), 123–35; Ramón Grosfoguel "The Divorce of Nationalist Discourses from the Puerto Rican People," in Frances Negrón-Muntaner and Ramón Grosfoguel, eds., *Puerto Rican Jam: Rethinking Colonialism and Nationalism* (Minneapolis: University of Minnesota Press, 1997), 57–76, and Mariano Negrón-Portillo "Puerto Rico: Surviving Colonialism and Nationalism," in Frances Negrón-Muntaner and Ramón Grosfoguel, eds., *Puerto Rican Jam: Rethinking Colonialism and Nationalism* (Minneapolis: University of Minnesota Press, 1997), 39–56.

45. See for example the claims that people in the past have not been very active in, *El Plan De Santa Barbara* (Santa Barbara: La Causa Publications, 1971) and *The Spanish Land Grant Question Examined* (Albuquerque, 1966); and discussions of this issue by José E. Limón, *"El Primer Congreso Mexicanista de 1911:* A Precursor to Contemporary Chicanismo." *Aztlán* 5, nos. 1 & 2 and Mario T. Garcia, *Mexican Americans: Leadership, Ideology, and Identity, 1930–1960* (New Haven, CT: Yale University Press, 1989). And yet, it should be noted, when the U.S. Republican Party attacked immigration and bilingual education, they provoked a pan-Latino/a movement of sorts that cost them many positions in the 1996 elections including the presidency.

46. Grosfoguel, "The Divorce of Nationalist Discourses," 68–70 passim.

47. Wilfredo Mattos-Cintrón, "The Struggle for Independence: The Long March to the Twenty-First Century," in Edwin Meléndez and Edgardo Meléndez, eds., *Colonial Dilemma* (Boston: South End, 1993), 214.

48. Woodbridge, *The Next World War*, and Weisman, *The World Without Us*.

49. John Berger, *Pig Earth* (New York: Vintage International, 1979), xxiii.

50. Zygmunt Bauman, *Wasted Lives* (Cambridge: Polity Press, 2004).

51. McMurtry, *Unequal Freedoms*, 26.

52. Berger, *Pig Earth*, xxii–xxvi passim.

53. Manuel Castells, *The Power of Identity*, 2nd ed., vol 2: *The Information Age: Economy, Society, and Culture* (Malden, MA: Blackwell, 2004).

54. See Mariano Negrón-Portillo, "Surviving Colonialism and Nationalism," in Frances Negrón-Muntaner and Ramón Grosfoguel, eds., *Puerto Rican Jam: Rethinking Colonialism and Nationalism* (Minneapolis: University of Minnesota Press, 1997), 52; Tom Barry, *Zapata's Revenge* (Boston: South End Press, 1995), 233; Louis A. Pérez, *On Becoming Cuban: Identity, Nationality & Culture* (Chapel Hill: University of North Carolina Press, 1999), especially the first two chapters.

55. Pew Research Center. *World Publics Welcome Global Trade—But Not Immigration* (October 4, 2007).

56. A sober look at this possibility is provided by an abundant number of publications, among them are: Donella H. Meadows, Jørgen Randers, and Dennis L. Meadows, *Limits to Growth: The 30-Year Update* (White River Junction, VT: Chelsea Green Publishing Company, 2004) and Lester R. Brown, *Plan B 3.0: Mobilizing to Save Civilization*, 3rd ed. (New York: W. W. Norton, 2008).

57. Martha Nussbaum, "Disabled Lives: Who Cares?" *New York Review of Books* XLVIII, no. 1 (January 11, 2001), 34–37.

58. See, Laura Pulido, *Environmentalism and Economic Justice* (Tucson: University of Arizona Press, 1996) and the extensive work of Devon G. Peña: *Chicano Culture, Ecology Politics* (Tucson: University of Arizona Press, 1998), *Chicano Culture, Ecology, Politics: Subversive Kin* (Tucson: University of Arizona Press, 1999), *Mexican Americans And The Environment: Tierra Y Vida* (Tucson: University of Arizona Press, 2005).

59. (New York: Pantheon Books, 2007)

60. Carol Hardy-Fanta, *Latina Politics/Latino Politics: Gender, Culture and Political Participation in Boston* (Philadelphia: Temple University Press, 1993), 99.

61. Will Kimlicka, *Liberalism, Community and Culture* (Oxford: Oxford University Press, 1989), 1. See also his *Multicultural Citizenship: A Liberal Theory of Minority Rights* (Oxford: Oxford University Press, 1995) and *Multicultural Odysseys: Navigating the New International Politics of Diversity* (Oxford: Oxford University Press, 2007).

62. See chapter 25 for her extensive discussion on transnational identity; de los Angeles Torres, *In the Land of Mirrors*, 199.

63. Pamela M. Graham, "The Politics of Incorporation: Dominicans in New York City," *Latino Studies Journal 9*, no. 3 (Fall 1998), 59.

64. Grosfoguel, "The Divorce of Nationalist Discourses," 73.

65. Victor M. Valle and Rodolfo D. Torres, *Latino Metropolis* (Minneapolis: University of Minnesota Press, 2000), 189–90.

66. Kymlicka, "Multiculturalism and Minority Rights," 8

67. Kymlicka, "Multiculturalism and Minority Rights," 13

68. Kymlicka, "Multiculturalism and Minority Rights," 16.

69. The Washington Office on Latin America (www.wola.org) provides several recent publications on these topics see for example, Nielan Barnes, "Transnational Youth Gangs in Central America, Mexico and the United States," and Adriana Beltran, "The Captive State: Organized Crime and Human Rights in Latin America" (2007) and the impact of NAFTA and CAFTA and other policies on the well-being of the people. See also Tom J. Farer, *Transnational Crime in the Americas* (New York: Routledge, 1999).

70. Peter Hakim, "Latin America: The Next U.S. President's agenda," *Great Decisions 2008* (Washington, D.C.: Foreign Policy Association, 2008), 73.

71. Hakim, "Latin America," 67.

72. Marcelo I. Saguier, "The Hemispheric Social Alliance and the Free Trade Area of the Americas Process: The Challenges and Opportunities of Transnational Coalitions against Neo-liberalism," *Globalizations* 4, no. 2 (June 2007): 251–65.

73. Fran Ansley, "Local Contact Points at Global Divides; Labor Rights and Immigrant Rights as Sites for Cosmopolitan Legality," in Boaventura de Sousa Santos and César A. Rodríguez-Garavito, eds., *Law and Globalization from Below: Towards a Cosmopolitan Legality* (Cambridge: University Press, 2005), 158–79. On critical theory, see Richard Delgado, *Critical Race Theory: The Cutting Edge* (Philadelphia: Temple University Press, 1995) and Kimberlé Crenshaw and others, *Critical Race Theory: The Key Writings That Formed the Movement* (New York: The New Press, 1995).

74. Manuel Orozco and Andrew Wainer, "Latinos, Foreign Policy and Contemporary International Relations," (Claremont, CA: The Tomás Rivera Policy Institute, 2002).

75. Friedrich Nietzsche, *The Gay Science.* Quoted in Patricia Ewick and Susan S. Silby, eds., *The Common Place Of Law: Stories from Everyday Life* (Chicago: University of Chicago Press, 1998), 136.

*   *   *

Questions

1. How appropriate is it to apply mythological concepts like ethnos and polis, the Furies and Apollo, to present-day political experiences of Latinos/as in the United States and the status of democracy in the world?

2. Are there any conditions under which democracy should be restricted to certain people?

3. What are the pros and cons of the concept of the global market as one ethical system that uses the notion of "freedom" as a tool for dominations, as opposed to business decisions that are innocently done by thousands of business people?

4. How valid is the argument that Latinos/as are a canary in the miner of economic democracy? What if they continued to be ignored as integral members of U.S. society as long as the rest of the populations are doing well economically?
5. What might the United States (or the world) look like if it was based on the care of human bodies and ecology as opposed to the wedded notions of rationality and self-interest? Under what conditions might such a sociopolitical-economic system be built?

~

Appendix for the Instructor

First of all, if you have questions, suggestions or if you just want to share how you use this book in your class, I would appreciate hearing from you.

Francisco H. Vázquez, Ph.D.
Sonoma State University
Hutchins School of Liberal Studies
1801 E. Cotati Avenue
Rohnert Park, CA 94928
707-664-3185
francisco.vazquez@sonoma.edu

Exercises Based on "Introduction for Students"

(a) For first day of class, introduce yourself by sharing your name and two events of your political life (how your ancestors came to the United States and how your political ideas differ from your parents).

(b) As a foundation for essay and dialogue: List ten key events of your political life.

(c) Write a short essay describing the political beliefs, principles, or positions you "inherited" from your parents and ancestors. Include if or how these differ from your own politics or personal policies.

(d) Write a dialogue with one of your parents or ancestors about a political issue.

Assignments on Education

(a) List the ten key events, or stepping-stones, of your "educational life," then describe the image of where you are *now* in terms of your education. For example, have you been educated for domination or for liberation?

(b) Write a dialogue with society (specifically with your school principal or teacher).

(c) Write a short essay on your educational experiences using Paulo Freire's concepts of education.

Assignment on Political Involvement

Think about the ideas of politics, language, knowledge/power, and education as they affect your everyday life. What does your political world look like and what role do you play in it? In an essay or drawing (in a poster-sized paper) illustrate your political realities, that is, the many forces that affect you, and the ways you can affect them in return.

Seminar Discussions as the Practice of Democracy

Throughout this reader one reappearing notion is that most of the time, the voice of the people is not heard. This is especially true of the voices of the people who are marginalized on the basis of race, class, and gender. Also illustrated by the various texts are the misunderstandings, paradoxes, and contradictions that occur, even within the groups of people who are fighting for social justice. In effect, one of the pieces makes the claim that power is exercised primarily through the control of discourse, that is the control and manipulation of what is said by each one of us. Thus, an argument can be made that many of the crises that humans face today stem from the inability to communicate clearly. Although humans can do many things together, conversations often turn into disputes, divisions and even violence.

It is in this context that the value of the seminar as a practice of democracy becomes evident. In the Hutchins School of Liberal Studies at Sonoma State University, the seminar or group discussion has been the centerpiece of the learning process for almost forty years. What we have learned is that an ideal seminar discussion creates a safe environment where there is tolerance for ambiguity and diversity of ideas and political or philosophical positions. More than that, it is a forum for the hard work of analyzing, through close observation, how hidden values and intentions can control our behavior and how unconscious cultural differences clash without our realizing what is going on.

More specifically, a seminar contributes to the quest for democracy because it is designed to: (1) Encourage students to express their opinions and thus build self-validation; (2) Practice the ability to listen carefully to what others have to say (most of the time we do not listen to what others unless they represent some kind of authority, we tend to believe that only the experts have the truth); (3) Realize that one can learn from one's peers and from professors (is that not the idea behind the concept of a jury of your peers?).

As a pedagogical tool, when people interact in a respectful and caring manner the discussion of a written or visual text becomes a collective building of knowledge that benefits all the members of the seminar. Thus, this format is a good vehicle for critical pedagogy and the development of critical thinking. Because a dialogue seminar is a practice, fortunately or unfortunately, as the case may be, there is no one set of instructions on how to conduct one. In almost four decades, the Hutchins School has successfully resisted coming up with one "official" set of rules for directing a seminar. There are, however, many websites that provide basic rules for students to conduct a seminar or group discussion. One of them is www.hca.heacademy.ac.uk/resources/guides/perfsem.php#ten.

For an extensive discussion of the implications of dialogue for the creation of a better world see www.david-bohm.net/dialogue/.

Finally, a comment on a related topic on the journal section that is not included in this second edition. In addition to dialoguing with others it is important to dialogue with oneself and that can be done through a journal or a diary. As Antonio Gramsci stated:

> The starting-point of critical elaboration is the consciousness of what one really is, and is "knowing thyself" as a product of the historical process to date, which has deposited in you an infinity of traces, without leaving an inventory; therefore it is imperative at the outset to compile such an inventory.[1]

Thus, the keeping of a journal (what the Greeks called "a book of life") is a useful tool to encourage students to take themselves seriously as learners. For the Greeks, the objective of the book of life was to make the recollection of fragmentary experience (transmitted by teaching, listening, or reading) a means to establish as adequate and as perfect a relationship of oneself to oneself as possible: retiring into oneself, profiting by, and enjoying oneself. The notebook was used for the constitution of a sort of permanent political relationship to oneself: One must manage oneself as a governor manages the governed, as a head of an enterprise manages his enterprise, as a head of a household manages his household.[2] Surely, if most people do this, we may be able to manage an economic democracy.

Notes and Suggestions for Further Research

1. Antonio Gramsci, quoted in Edward W. Said, *Orientalism* (New York: Pantheon, 1978), 25. As Said notes, the English translation inexplicably leaves out the second part of the sentence. Gramsci, *The Prison Notebooks: Selections*, ed. Quintin Hoare and Geoffrey Nowell Smith (New York: International, 1971), 324.

2. Michel Foucault, afterword to Hubert L. Dreyfus and Paul Rabinow, *Michel Foucault: Beyond Structuralism and Hermeneutics* (Chicago: University of Chicago Press, 1983), 246–47 passim.

Glossary

center, centrists. See *political spectrum*.

citizenship. A citizen is a member of a legally constituted state who possesses certain rights and privileges, subject to corresponding duties. With certain restrictions, a citizen of the United States has the right to hold and transfer all types of property, to vote, to seek elective office, to hold governmental positions, to receive welfare and social security benefits, and to enjoy the protection of the Constitution and the laws. Some of these rights are denied to aliens, even though they may have been in the United States most of their lives. Both U.S. citizens and permanent resident aliens have the corresponding duties to pay taxes, obey the laws of the United States, and defend it against enemies. Citizens are also subject to jury duty. In most monarchies, including the United Kingdom, citizens are usually referred to as subjects, meaning that they owe their allegiance to the sovereign in return for protection, but not necessarily for rights of self-governance. The term *national* is used, particularly in international agreements, to mean all those who owe allegiance to a state. Nearly all nationals are now citizens, the main exceptions being inhabitants of some colonies who are nationals but not citizens.

commodity. Something useful that can be turned to commercial or other advantage. In some cases it is said that human bodies—people—are used also as commodities.

criollo. A Spaniard born in the Spanish Americas. Politically, she or he did not have the same status as the *peninsulares*, those born in Spain (on the

Iberian Peninsula). Not to be confused with "Creole," which is an inhabitant of southern Louisiana in the United States.

deductive. The process of reasoning in which a conclusion follows necessarily from the stated premises; inference by reasoning from the general to the specific. See also *inductive*.

dialectical. Simply put, the art or practice of arriving at the truth by the exchange of logical arguments. A method of argument or exposition that systematically weighs contradictory facts or ideas with a view to the resolution of their real or apparent contradictions. More popular is this word's meaning as the contradiction between two conflicting forces viewed as the determining factor in the continuing interaction of those forces. An example is the process of arriving at the truth by stating a thesis, developing a contradictory antithesis, and combining and resolving them into a coherent synthesis. This term is discussed in chapters 3 and 4.

diaspora. Once used to describe Jewish, Greek, and Armenian dispersion, now shares meanings with a larger semantic domain that includes words such as *immigrant, expatriate, refugee, guest worker, overseas community,* and *ethnic community*.

Enlightenment. Literally to shed light on the darkness of superstition and tyranny, this is a term for the rationalist, liberal, humanitarian, and scientific trend of eighteenth-century Western thought; the period also is sometimes known as the Age of Reason. The enormous scientific and intellectual advancements made in the seventeenth century by the empiricism of Francis Bacon and John Locke and by René Descartes, Baruch Spinoza, and others, fostered the belief in natural law and universal order, promoted a scientific approach to political and social issues, and gave rise to a sense of human progress and belief in the state as its rational instrument. Representative of the Enlightenment are such thinkers as Sor Juana Inéz de la Cruz and Carlos de Sigüenza y Góngora in México; Voltaire, Jean-Jacques Rousseau, Montesquieu, Adam Smith, Jonathan Swift, David Hume, Immanuel Kant, G. E. Lessing, Cesare Beccaria; and in the United States, Thomas Paine, Thomas Jefferson, and Benjamin Franklin. The social and political ideals such figures presented were enforced by "enlightened despots" such as the Holy Roman Emperor Joseph II, Catherine II of Russia, and Frederick II of Prussia. Diderot's *Encyclopédie* and the U.S. Constitution are representative documents of the Age of Reason.

Freemasonry. A tightly knit, all-male society, many of whose members hold influential positions, all of whom are bound by an oath of secrecy. It is claimed that all presidents of Mexico and the United States (with the exception of John F. Kennedy) have been masons.

Furies. In Greek mythology, the three Furies—Tisiphone, Megaera, and Alecto—were goddesses of vengeance. Their function was to punish crimes that had escaped detection or public justice. Although their usual abode was Hades, they also pursued the living, as in the story of Orestes. In appearance they were ugly, bat-winged, serpent-haired creatures born of the blood of Uranus when he was mutilated by the sickle of Cronus. In the afterlife, the Furies dispensed justice from the netherworld, where, armed with scourges, they meted out the torments of remorse and other punishments. The Furies, also known as Erinyes, were called the Eumenides in later Greek literature.

hegemony or **hegemonic.** A type of domination that implies the consent of those who are dominated. It is associated with the Italian thinker Antonio Gramsci who used it in the phrase *cultural hegemony* to mean that as citizens we allow the government to rule over us on the assumption that it has our best interest in mind. In this book this term is illustrated by the way the United States engaged in a cultural seduction of Northern Mexicans, Cubans, and Puerto Ricans before the military invasion.

inductive. The process of reasoning by which general principles are derived from particular facts or instances. See also *deductive*.

institutions. A set of behaviors that endure through time: Political institutions are for the distribution of power; economic institutions are for the production and distribution of goods and services; cultural institutions involve arts, religion, and traditions; kinship focuses on the family, marriage, and the raising of young. Other kinds of institutions include criminal gangs.

juridical. Of or relating to the law and its administration.

left, leftist. See *political spectrum*.

Maoist. Marxism-Leninism developed in China, chiefly by Mao Zedong.

mestizaje. The largest mixing of races in the world, which took place in what is now known as Latin America. Also used in a political sense.

nation-state. See *state*.

paradigm. A worldview that dominates how we perceive reality. It can be scientific, social, artistic, or other. For example, in terms of science, the Aristotelian paradigm dominated for over one thousand years; currently the Newtonian paradigm has been superseded by that of Einstein's theory of relativity. The *Enlightenment* and *postmodernism* are two other examples.

neoliberalism. Refers to a political movement that espouses economic liberalism as a means of promoting economic development and securing political liberty. The movement is sometimes described as an effort to revert to the economic policies of the eighteenth and nineteenth century's classical liberalism. And that is a doctrine stressing individual freedom. This includes the importance of human rationality, individual property rights, natural rights, the protection of civil liberties, constitutional limitations of government, free markets, and individual freedom from restraint as exemplified in the writings of Adam Smith, John Stuart Mill, Montesquieu, Voltaire, Thomas Paine, and others.

pigmentocracy. Relations of power based on skin color. I prefer the term *pigmentocracy* over the more general term of *racism* because the former specifically points to the universal practice of valuing light-skinned human bodies more than dark-skinned human bodies, a practice that occurs not only between blacks and whites but within all ethnic and cultural groups.

political spectrum. This concept includes *centrists* (middle ground, social democrat-liberal-moderate), *leftists* (anywhere from liberal to democratic socialist, socialist, communist, or anarchist), and the *right* wing (anywhere from conservative and neoconservative to reactionary, libertarian, or fascist) and comes from France. Before the French Revolution, there was an Estates General, a parliamentary body like a Congress, which was last called together in 1789. In that year, the King Louis XVI sat in the center with moderates, who favored compromise between the conservatives and liberals and the preservation of the monarchy based on concessions to the people. The conservative nobility and clergy, who advocated maintaining the status quo—retaining the monarchy and the privileges of nobility—sat on the King's right. On his left were the liberal and radical representatives of the common people, who advocated the abolishment of the monarchy and the nobility.

political technology. The techniques and tools that are available to govern a society, such as definitions (of who is entitled to rights, obligations, punishment); representation (one [hu]man, one vote, on the basis of the number of people or of geographical areas); division of power into legislature (makes the laws), executive (carries out the dictates of the law), and judiciary (interprets the law); contracts; and processes.

postmodern, postmodernism. A *paradigm* based on the realization that "Truth," once it is articulated, is subject to political interpretations and becomes part of a discourse, a *commodity* in a political economy. This leads to the questioning of everything that is, was, or ever has been considered "True" and the struggle to account for all the diverse, conflicting, invisible Truths that go into constructing what is claimed to be the one and only Truth. The purpose of postmodernism, however, was to question those categories that in the age of modernism (1700–2000) were considered as unchangeable *essences* and therefore obstacles to social justice.

Take, for example, categories such as the "Divine Right of Kings" or the "Natural Rights of Man": What about the rights of those who did not fit these categories, such as women, people of color, disabled, children, or gays? From a postmodern perspective, "man" is a social construction, an invention by society. The fact is that human experience is much too diverse and exuberant to be contained by a category. So the task is to "deconstruct" exclusive concepts, to open up a space for Others, in the arts, literature, painting, music, etc. Postmodernism means the tearing down of rigid, exclusive concepts about art and a free-for-all experimentation. Inclusive essences such as love, compassion, and respect, however, need not be deconstructed.

right. See *political spectrum*.

sovereignty. Sovereignty refers both to the powers exercised by an autonomous *state* in relation to other countries and to the supreme powers exercised by a state over its own members. In the context of international law, a sovereign state is independent and free from all external control; enjoys full legal equality with other states; governs its own territory; selects its own political, economic, and social systems; and has the power to enter into agreements with other nations, to exchange ambassadors, and to decide on war or peace. A *protectorate* (like Puerto Rico), because it has ceded some of its powers to another state, is not sovereign. Although a sovereign state theoretically enjoys absolute freedom, its freedom is in fact often abridged by the need to coexist with other countries and by treaties, international laws, and primarily by the strength of its military. Sovereign power, which is the power to make and enforce the law and to control the nation's finances and military establishment, may be vested in one person (e.g., a monarchy), in a small group of people (an oligarchy), or in all the people, either directly or through representatives (a democracy). It may be limited by natural or divine law, constitutions, or customs. See also *state*.

state. The state is frequently defined as the highest or most comprehensive political association having a recognized claim to primacy—first allegiance or ultimate authority. According to another common definition, statehood is the stable possession of preponderant power by a single authority within a delimited territory. There are two impediments, however, to any simple definition of the state. The first is that the term has been used quite loosely, to designate any sort of political rule at any period in history ("the Byzantine state," "the Papal states"), and at the same time quite restrictively, to designate the kind of political structure mainly characteristic of post-Renaissance Western societies. The second impediment is that notions about what the state is vary systematically with the various political philosophies: A Lockean liberal who advocates a minimalist state that merely enforces natural law and protects natural rights will never be able to agree with a Hegelian, who sees the state as the concrete actualization of rational freedom on earth, or with a Marxian, who sees the state as a mere committee for the management of the interests of the social class owning the means of economic production. Defining the state is not easy unless one is prepared to declare dogmatically that a particular theory of statehood is correct, to the exclusion of all others. The same difficulty afflicts any effort to say what the state's purpose is. A Benthamite utilitarian will urge that the end of the state is the greatest happiness of the greatest number, and that the pursuit of this end gives the state legitimate authority. A Kantian will suggest that the state exists to provide a legal context within which good will and respect for persons is more nearly possible.

Nor is the tracing of the origin of the state free of this same difficulty: Some have traced the foundation of the state to a desire for security and peace (Thomas Hobbes); some have insisted on natural sociability as creating states, believing that the stateless human is either a beast or a god (Aristotle); some have put forward economic motives, such as a desire for the division of labor and an economy of scale, which can be obtained only by centralizing power and authoritatively allocating work (Edmund Burke); still others have stressed human depravity in a fallen world creating the need for the state (Saint Augustine). In trying, then, to say what the state is, what its purposes are, and where its origin is, the problem always exists that the state itself is not simply a fact but a conceptual artifact. The most reasonable and candid way to treat the state, therefore, is to offer a history of theories about it.

Index

~

About the Author

Dr. Francisco Hernández Vázquez is professor of interdisciplinary studies in the Hutchins School of Liberal Studies and Director of the Hutchins Institute for Public Policy Studies and Community Action at Sonoma State University. He oversees the master's program, Action for a Viable Future, the Roseland Development Roundtable (addressing development issues in the barrio), and the Coalition for Latino Civic Engagement (voter registration in Sonoma County). He is a member of the board of directors of the Sonoma County Community Foundation and of the Advisory Board Roseland University Prep High School. Among his most recent publications are: *Ganas y Poder: Civic Engagement among Latino Youth: The Case of Sonoma County* (2003); *Civic Engagement of Latino High School Students in Sonoma County: Emerging Themes from Focus Groups* (2003); "The Furies and Apollo: Latino/as in the United States and Public Citizenship," in *Perspectivas Transatlánticas en la Literatura Chicana: Ensayos y creatividad* (2004). He is currently doing research for a book-length manuscript, "The Continental American."